THE PHILOSOPHY OF SYMBOLIC FORMS

Volume 3

By the same author

AN ESSAY ON MAN

THE LOGIC OF THE HUMANITIES

THE MYTH OF THE STATE

THE PROBLEM OF KNOWLEDGE

DETERMINISM AND INDETERMINISM IN
    MODERN PHYSICS

THE PHILOSOPHY OF SYMBOLIC FORMS
    VOLUME 1: LANGUAGE
    VOLUME 2: MYTHICAL THOUGHT

THE PHILOSOPHY

OF SYMBOLIC FORMS

VOLUME THREE: THE PHENOMENOLOGY OF KNOWLEDGE

BY ERNST CASSIRER

translated by Ralph Manheim

introductory note by Charles W. Hendel

NEW HAVEN AND LONDON

Yale University Press

Originally published with assistance from
the Louis Stern Memorial Fund
© 1957 by Yale University Press, Inc.
All rights reserved. This book may not be
reproduced, in whole or in part, in any form
(beyond that copying permitted by Sections
107 and 108 of the U.S. Copyright Law and
except by reviewers for the public press),
without written permission from the publishers.
Library of Congress catalog card number: 52–13969
ISBN 0–300–00039–1 (paper)

Printed in the United States of America by
BookCrafters, Inc.,
Fredericksburg, Virginia.

21 20 19 18 17 16 15 14 13

Contents

Introductory Note by Charles W. Hendel

THE PRESENT VOLUME completes the English translation of the series of three books entitled *The Philosophy of Symbolic Forms,* of which the first, *Language,* came out in 1953, and the second, *Mythical Thought,* in 1955. The translator, Ralph Manheim, has finished his difficult and challenging task of rendering this masterwork of Ernst Cassirer into another language and in such a well chosen "symbolic form" that it reveals and faithfully interprets the original to the English reader.

The Preface to the first of these volumes of translation aimed at making the reader acquainted with biographical facts and indicating the place and significance of *The Philosophy of Symbolic Forms* in the career of Cassirer. In addition to that Preface (pp. vii–xiv) there was a comprehensive Introduction (pp. 1–65), which undertook an interpretation through reference to both the "rich sources of inspiration," always handsomely acknowledged by Cassirer, and the subsequent studies and writings which he gave to the world in a succession of notable books. Since that Introduction and Preface were both meant to serve for all three volumes of the series, only an Introductory Note is here offered, as was previously done in Volume 2. Its function is simply to call attention to some special and interesting aspects of this third and concluding portion of the work, *The Phenomenology of Knowledge.*

It may be permissible for the editor to invite readers who have not seen the first translation to consult those portions of its Introduction which have a very particular bearing on the subject matter of the present book. The pertinent sections are "The Epochal Significance of Kant's Work and What Cassirer Made of the Developing Theory of Form" (21–35), and more especially under that same head, "Cassirer's Advance upon Kant" (27–8); "The Symbolic Function and the Forms" (47–54); and "Consequences for Philosophy" (54–65). Although the reading of those sections of the Introduction may be helpful, it is by no means essential in order to follow Cassirer's argument, which is relatively self-contained and self-explanatory.

It is worthy of note, however, that Cassirer himself deemed it appropriate in his own Preface to this book to refer back to certain of his previous works, and it is well to follow the hints given in the very opening sentence: "The third volume of the *Philosophy of Symbolic Forms* represents a return to the investigations with which I began my work in systematic philosophy two decades ago. Its central concern is again *the problem of knowledge,* the structure and articulation of a theoretical world view." He then names *Substance and Function,* which had been published in 1910, approximately two decades before the *Phenomenology of Knowledge,* 1929.[1] From that opening remark it appears that the "systematic philosophy" had taken its first form in 1920 and in a work whose subtitle announced "Investigations into the Basic Questions of a Critical Study of Knowledge." And Cassirer further discloses in the Preface now before us that during his systematic studies from that time onward his "central concern" had been "the problem of knowledge."

Here are clues and suggestions that merit some preliminary exploration. The present book, it is said, is a "return" to what was of central concern to Cassirer. This informs us that Part III brings the whole argument of the series of investigations on *Symbolic Forms* back to an original subject which had long been occupying Cassirer's mind. That subject was "the problem of knowledge." And thereby hangs a tale. Anyone who is the least familiar with the writings of Cassirer will recall that there was another series of three works sharing the common title: *Das Erkenntnisproblem, in der Philosophie und Wissenschaft der Neueren Zeit.* Volume *1,* published in 1906, dealt with the period from the Renaissance through the Cartesian philosophy; Volume 2, in 1907, with that from Empiricism through the Critical Philosophy of Kant; and Volume *3,* in 1920, with Kant and post-Kantian philosophy through Hegel and his contemporaries. These thoroughgoing treatises on the problem of knowledge had been preceded by several studies of some of the individual figures: *Descartes' Kritik der mathematischen und wissenschaftlichen Grundlagen,* which was Cassirer's inaugural dissertation at Marburg, 1899; *Leibniz's System in seinen wissenschaftlichen Grundlagen,* 1902; an edition and introduction to *Leibniz' Philosophische Werke,* 1906; and a short piece, "Der Kritische Idealismus und die Philosophie des Gesunden Menschenver-

1. Here, and below, in the text, works are referred to by English titles when English translations exist. See W. C. and M. C. Swabey, trans., *Substance and Function* (La Salle, Ill., Open Court Publishing Co., 1923). It was a historic coincidence that this work appeared in America the same year the original first volume of the *Philosophy of Symbolic Forms* was published in Berlin.

standes" in *Philosophische Arbeiten,* edited by Cohen and Natorp in 1906, also the year of the first volume of the *Erkenntnisproblem* series. Between the publication of the second (1907) and third (1920) books of the *Erkenntnisproblem,* there was an interval of thirteen years, and during this period Cassirer did work under the inspiration of and in conjunction with Hermann Cohen, producing several writings on Kant and mathematics, Kant's methodology, an edition, with others, of Kant's works, and a notable supplementary volume thereto, *Kant's Leben und Lehre* (1918). It was only after this extensive study of Kant that Cassirer was ready to produce the third volume of the *Erkenntnisproblem,* going beyond Kant and into the aftermath of the Kantian philosophy. By 1920, however, Cassirer had thoroughly reckoned with "the problem of knowledge" in its historic forms from the time of the Renaissance through that of Hegel.

Having achieved his historical interpretation of the problem, Cassirer was apparently prepared to resume the inquiries begun in the year 1910 into a systematic philosophy of knowledge. The emergence of the Einstein theory in physics, however, led to another special study, *Zur Einsteinsche Relativitätstheorie* in 1921, a work whose translation was appropriately included, later, in the *Substance and Function* volume in English. But Cassirer had a deep-lying general theory of his own to formulate which had to do not only with knowledge of the physical world but more comprehensively with "the structure and articulation of a theoretical world view," as he says in the Preface of the present book. He began, it will be recalled, with an investigation into language (1923) as a symbolic form and proceeded from there to the realm of mythical thought (1925), and at long last "returned" to the "problem of knowledge" with a solution, a philosophy taking the form of a "phenomenology."

It may perhaps be said with perfect propriety, in the light of the above considerations, that this book, *The Phenomenology of Knowledge,* is truly the central work of Cassirer's genius. It is the confluence of two streams of inquiry—the historical and the systematic. Indeed the conjunction of his vast historical knowledge with his constructive intention of interpreting the advances of contemporary science and relating its point of view to a general and comprehensive philosophical theory make this the consummate work of his career.

It was not by any means, of course, the end of Cassirer's achievement as a philosopher, but rather its apogee. He had obtained a vantage point from which to look ahead. He was no longer immersed in the problem of knowledge as defined by the great ones of the past. He was his own master and proceeded, after this book was done, to single out the problems in his own way and in the context of recent or contemporary science. The developments in physics had continued to be a constant challenge to him. Thus he produced in 1937 another special work like that on the Einstein theory sixteen years earlier, this time focused on a general problem that had emerged from the years of scientific discussions in the wake of those developments in physics: it was titled *Determinism and Indeterminism in Modern Physics*.[2] But his interest was not confined to physical knowledge. His study of symbolic forms had confirmed the theme that had lurked in *Substance and Function* that any theoretical construction of any durable character and history owed its existence to the functioning of a symbolic form. The symbolic forms were many and diverse. And besides physics there was the substantial and progressive science of biology, and alongside the development of these sciences through the nineteenth and twentieth century there had been notable advances in history and the historical sciences. Cassirer actually proceeded then to add one more volume to the previous three of *Das Erkenntnisproblem*. He wrote it in whole or part during the year 1940 amid the grave troubles and uncertainties of war in Europe and left it in manuscript form in Sweden when he departed in May 1941 to come to Yale University. The manuscript was retrieved in 1946, a year after his death, and it was translated into English and published in 1950 before it even appeared in the original German.[3] In this work, *The Problem of Knowledge: Philosophy, Science, and History since Hegel*, the author "briefly reviews the modern period and then describes the particular features of the last hundred years and how differently the problem of knowledge must be treated in reference to this changed situation. 'The relation of philosophy to the various sciences has altered fundamentally in this period of unceasing progress in specialization.'" What is required of the philosopher nowadays is a "patient steeping of oneself in the work of the separate sciences, which must not only be investigated in respect to principles but explained concretely, that is, in the way they conceive and handle their primary and fundamental problems. I do not conceal from myself

2. Trans. O. Theodore Benfey, with a preface by Henry Margenau (New Haven, Yale University Press, 1956).

3. Trans. William H. Woglom, M.D., and Charles W. Hendel (New Haven, Yale University Press, 1950).

for a moment the enormous difficulty involved in this conception of the task . . ." [4] It would be a mistake, however, to see in the different manner of treatment in this fourth volume of the *Erkenntnisproblem* merely the inevitable effect of the condition of specialization in the sciences. For the new mode was a proper consequence of the philosophy of symbolic forms as it had reached its fulfillment in this final volume on the Phenomenology of Knowledge.

The full "articulation of a theoretical world view," in the words of the Preface, called, however, for more than "phenomenology of knowledge" in its scientific form even if history were included under this rubric. The last words of *Determinism and Indeterminism in Modern Physics* may be recalled, where Cassirer speaks of seeking "the full concept of reality, which requires the cooperation of all functions of the spirit and can only be reached through all of them together." [5]

Other operations "of the spirit" were still to be explored. There was for instance the work *Zur Logik der Kulturwissenschaften* that came out in 1942. "Mythical thought," too, continued to interest Cassirer, and a particularly timely work appeared posthumously, *The Myth of the State,* 1946.[6] But the *Essay on Man: an Introduction to a Philosophy of Human Culture* [7] furnishes better than anything else the synoptic view of that "cooperation of all functions of the spirit" in the manifold forms of culture, in myth, religion, language, art, history, and science.

Central to all this panorama of human culture, however, was this third part of Cassirer's systematic philosophy formulated as a *Phenomenology of Knowledge.* The later developments seem to have radiated from it as a point of orientation. It is significant that the last chaper of *An Essay on Man* was that on science. Significant, too, that in the opening of that chapter Cassirer at once refers the reader to his *Phenomenology of Knowledge.*[8] And it is most appropriate that the meaning of the opening words in the Preface, quoted above, should be so felicitously clothed again in the English language by Cassirer himself when at the end of his chapter on science in the *Essay,* he wrote: "In language, in religion, in art, in science, man can do no more than to build up his own universe—a symbolic uni-

4. Preface, p. x.
5. Ibid., p. 213.
6. New Haven, Yale University Press.
7. New Haven, Yale University Press, 1944.
8. Page 207, n. 1.

verse that enables him to understand and interpret, to articulate and organize, to synthesize and universalize his human experience."

CHARLES W. HENDEL

New Haven, Connecticut
January 1957

Preface

THE THIRD VOLUME of *The Philosophy of Symbolic Forms* represents a return to the investigations with which I began my work in systematic philosophy two decades ago. Its central concern is again the problem of knowledge, the structure and articulation of a theoretical world view. But the question of the fundamental form of knowledge is now raised in a broader and more universal sense. In my book *Substanzbegriff und Funktionsbegriff* (1910) I started from the assumption that the basic and constitutive law of knowledge can most clearly be demonstrated where knowledge has reached its highest level of necessity and universality. This law was therefore sought in the field of mathematics and the exact sciences, in the foundations of mathematical-physical objectivity. Accordingly the form of knowledge as there defined coincided essentially with the form of exact *science*. Both in content and in method, the Philosophy of Symbolic Forms has gone beyond this initial formulation of the problem. It has broadened the concept of theory itself by striving to show that there are formative factors of a truly theoretical kind which govern the shaping not only of the scientific world view but also of the natural world view implicit in perception and intuition. And finally, the Philosophy of Symbolic Forms was driven even beyond the natural world view of experience and observation, when the mythical world disclosed relationships which, though not reducible to the laws of empirical thinking, are by no means without their laws, and reveal a structural form of specific and independent character. In the first and second volumes of this work I have attempted to set forth these relationships. In the present volume we shall seek to draw their consequences for systematic philosophy. We shall strive to bring out the newly acquired concept of "theory" in its full scope and entire range of formative potentialities. We shall show how the stratum of conceptual, discursive knowledge is grounded in those other strata of spiritual life which our analysis of language and myth has laid bare; and with constant reference to this substructure we shall attempt to determine the particularity, organization, and architectonics of the superstructure—that is, of science. Thus the

Philosophy of Symbolic Forms once more considers the world view of
exact knowledge, but now approaches it in a different way and accordingly sees it in a new perspective. Instead of considering this world view
solely in its factuality, the Philosophy of Symbolic Forms now seeks to
apprehend it in its necessary intellectual mediations. Starting from the
relative end which thought has here achieved, it inquires back into the
middle and the beginnings, with a view to understanding the end itself
for what it is and what it means.

The general perspectives in which the problem is considered are discussed in some detail in the Introduction: here I wish only to give a
brief explanation and justification of the title I have chosen for this
volume. In speaking of a phenomenology of knowledge I am using the
word "phenomenology" not in its modern sense but with its fundamental
signification as established and systematically grounded by Hegel. For
Hegel, phenomenology became the basis of all philosophical knowledge,
since he insisted that philosophical knowledge must encompass the totality
of cultural forms and since in his view this totality can be made visible
only in the transitions from one form to another. The truth is the whole
—yet this whole cannot be presented all at once but must be unfolded
progressively by thought in its own autonomous movement and rhythm.
It is this unfolding which constitutes the being and the essence of science.
The element of thought, in which science is and lives, is consequently
fulfilled and made intelligible only through the movement of its becoming.

Science for its part demands that self-consciousness raise itself into
this ether, in order that it may live with and for science. Conversely,
the individual has the right to demand that science shall at least provide him with a ladder by which to reach to this height, and show it
to him in himself. This right is based on the absolute independence
which he knows himself to possess in every form of his knowledge;
for in each form, whether it be recognized by science or not, and
regardless of what its content may be, it is absolute form—that is, it
is the immediate certainty of itself and, if this term is preferred, it is
therefore absolute being.[1]

1. G. W. F. Hegel, *Phänomenologie des Geistes,* in *Sämtliche Werke* (Leipzig, 1949), 2,
preface. Eng. trans. by J. B. Baillie, *The Phenomenology of Mind* (London and New York,
1949). Cf. above, Vol. 2 of the present work, pp. xv–xvi.

It would be impossible to state more sharply that the end, the *telos* of the human spirit, cannot be apprehended and expressed if it is taken as something existing in itself, as something detached and separate from its beginning and middle. Philosophical reflection does not set the end against the middle and the beginning but takes all three as integral factors in a unitary total movement. In this fundamental principle the Philosophy of Symbolic Forms agrees with Hegel's formulation, much as it must differ in both its foundations and its development. It, too, aspires to provide the individual with a ladder which will lead him from the primary configurations found in the world of the immediate consciousness to the world of pure knowledge. From the standpoint of philosophical inquiry every single rung of the ladder is indispensable; every single one must be considered, appreciated—in short "known"—if we wish to understand knowledge not so much in its result, in its mere product, as in its character of a process, in the mode and form of its *procedure* itself.

As for the actual treatment of the theme, the third section of this volume, which deals with the growth of the objective world of mathematics and physics, starts from the findings of earlier analyses. And I have adhered throughout to the principle which guided me in these analyses, the idea of the epistemological primacy of law over things: but now it becomes necessary to clarify and confirm this idea, to measure it by the vast development of mathematical and scientific thought in the last decades. I have aimed to show how, through all the radical transformations which exact science has undergone both in form and content, its purely methodological continuity has not been interrupted or sacrificed—but rather that these very transformations of content have reconfirmed and clarified its continuity. Here, as I have said, I was able to draw on earlier investigations.[2] But in the first two sections of this volume I was, from the outset, confronted with a more difficult task. The ground had not been previously defined and marked off, and I had to begin by trying to "acquire" and delimit my territory. It is true that these sections deal essentially with the basic forms of perception, the perception of expression and the perception of things, and that these are familiar problems which have been raised from time immemorial by psychology and epistemology, by phenomenology and metaphysics. But these questions take on a new form and meaning as soon as we consider them in relation to the basic systematic problem

2. Cf. my *Zur Einsteinschen Relativitätstheorie* (Berlin, 1921).

underlying the Philosophy of Symbolic Forms. For here they enter into a particular kind of over-all view which changes their whole intellectual orientation. In order to bring out this cultural synopsis I had to attempt to survey the material presented by the phenomenology, the psychology, and finally the pathology of perception, in all its diversity and concrete richness, and through this material to disclose a whole new set of problems. It was evident to me that this attempt could be no more than a beginning; if I undertook it, it was in the hope that my effort would be taken up and carried further by philosophers as well as students of the specialized sciences.

As in my earlier works, I have tried to avoid any cleavage between systematic and historical considerations and have striven for a close fusion between the two. Only through a reciprocal relation of this sort can the two promote and throw light on each other. But without exceeding the scope of this book, I could not aim at anything resembling completeness in the purely historical expositions; rather, I entered upon historical discussion only where it seemed necessary to the elucidation of specific systematic problems. I have proceeded in the same way with regard to modern philosophy. Although I have not avoided critical discussion of it where this seemed likely to add clarity and depth to our own problem, such discussion has not been allowed to become an end in itself. The original plan of this book provided for a final chapter defining and justifying the basic attitude of the Philosophy of Symbolic Forms toward present-day philosophy as a whole. When I abandoned that project, it was only to avoid making the present volume even longer than it is, and to avoid weighting it with discussions which, in the last analysis, lie outside the territory prescribed by its specific problem. However, I do not mean to renounce this discussion as such; the custom, which has once more become popular, of hurling one's ideas into empty space as it were, without inquiring into their relation to the general development of scientific philosophy, has never struck me as fruitful. Consequently the critical work with which I originally intended to conclude this volume will be reserved for a future publication which I hope soon to bring out under the title *Life and The Human Spirit—toward a Critique of Present-Day Philosophy.*[3]

---

3. Published as " 'Geist' und 'Leben' in der Philosophie der Gegenwart," *Die Neue Rundschau*, 41, No. 1 (1930), 244–64. Eng. trans. by Robert Waller Bretall and Paul Arthur Schilpp, " 'Spirit' and 'Life' in the Philosophy of the Present," *The Philosophy of Ernst Cassirer* (New York, 1949). *Ed.*

With regard to the philosophical and scientific literature to which this work refers, I should like to remark that the manuscript of the volume was completed at the end of 1927 and that publication was delayed only because at that time I still planned to include the final, critical chapter. Consequently, I have been able to take into account only a few of the works published in the last two years.

ERNST CASSIRER

Hamburg, July, 1929

Introduction

WHEN WE DESIGNATE language, myth, and art as "symbolic forms," the term seems to imply that they are all modes of spiritual formation, going back to an ultimate, primal stratum of reality which is perceived in them only as through a foreign medium. It would seem as though we could apprehend reality only in the particularity of these forms, whence it follows that in these forms reality is cloaked as well as revealed. The same basic functions which give the world of the spirit its determinacy, its imprint, its character, appear on the other side to be so many refractions which an intrinsically unitary and unique being undergoes as soon as it is perceived and assimilated by a "subject." Seen from this standpoint, the Philosophy of Symbolic Forms is nothing other than an attempt to assign to each of them, as it were, its own specific and peculiar index of refraction. The philosophy of Symbolic Forms aspires to know the special nature of the various refracting media, to understand each one according to its nature and the laws of its structure. But although it consciously enters this intermediary realm, this realm of mere mediacy, philosophy as a whole, as a doctrine of the totality of being, seems unable to remain in it. Again and again, the basic drive of knowledge makes itself felt: the drive to unveil the veiled image of Sais and behold the naked, unadorned truth. The philosopher desires to apprehend the world as an absolute unity; he hopes ultimately to break down all diversity, and particularly the diversity of symbols: to discern the ultimate reality, the reality of "being" itself.

The metaphysics of all times has faced this fundamental problem. It postulated a unitary and single being, because and insofar as truth could be thought of only as unitary and simple. In this sense the ἓν τὸ σοφόν of Heraclitus became the watchword of philosophy: it was an admonition to seek the one, unbroken light of pure knowledge behind the variegated colors of sensory experience, behind the multiplicity and diversity of the forms of thought. As Spinoza said, it is in the essence of light to illumine itself and the darkness—thus it was held that at some point there must be an immediate self-revelation of truth and reality. For thought and reality ought not merely to correspond to each other in some sense but must permeate each other. The function of thought should not be merely to "express" being, i.e. to apprehend and classify it under one of its own categories of meaning. Rather, thought held itself able to deal with reality on an equal footing, and was fully convinced that it could exhaust its meaning. There could be no final, unsurpassable barrier: for thought and the object toward which it is directed were one. Parmenides was first to state this proposition with classical succinctness and sharpness, and so became the founder of all philosophical rationalism. But the claim thus made did not remain limited to rationalism. The identity of subject and object, the adequation of the one to the other, was still regarded as the actual goal of knowledge, even after the conception of the means by which this goal is to be attained had changed completely. The perspective shifted, but there was no change in underlying principle when the task of laying a bridge from one to the other was entrusted to sensory experience instead of pure thought. The center of gravity now seemed to have shifted from one distinct theoretical view to another—from the aspect of the concept to that of perception; but for perception the same methodological presupposition and requirement remained in force. The concept as such—it now seemed—can never by its own power penetrate to reality: for it remains entangled in its own fictions and creations, its own denominations and significations. Sensation on the other hand is not merely significative or symbolic, it is no mere "sign" for being, but yields and contains reality in its immediate fullness. For at some point a direct contact must occur between knowledge and reality, if knowledge is not to be confined forever within its own sphere. Thus for Berkeley, Parmenides' theorem of the identity of thought and being is replaced by the epistemological and metaphysical equation: *esse = percipi*. The content of the proposition seems to have been reversed; but its pure form remained unchanged and unimpaired. For again we have a striving to lay bare a primal stratum of reality, in which reality itself may be apprehended free from all symbolic interpretation and signification. If we succeed in freeing ourselves from all these interpretations—if, above all, we succeed in removing the veil of words, which conceals the true essence of things, then at one stroke we shall find ourselves face to face with the original perceptions which contain the certainties of knowledge. Now there is no room for opposition between truth and error, reality and illusion. For the simple existence of sensory impressions remains free from all possibility of error. A sensory impression may exist or not exist, it may be given or not given, but it cannot be true or false. Such an opposition becomes possible only when another, mediated, relation is interpolated into the immediate presence of the impression, when a representative determination is added to the presentation, to the direct "having" of a sensation. Where a content of consciousness stands not only for itself but for another content, where it attempts to "represent" a content that is not immediately present, then and only then do we find that reciprocal relation between the parts of the context of consciousness which by its further mediated consequences can cause one part to be taken and mistaken for another. Therefore this phenomenon belongs not to the sphere of mere sensation but to that of judgment. And judgment, of course—even in its simplest form, where it seems to content itself with affirming and reinforcing a sensory datum—is distinguished from sensation precisely by the fact that it moves no longer in the realm of simple existence but in the realm of signs. Once we entrust ourselves to it, we enter into the sphere of that abstract thinking which operates with the signs that stand for things rather than with things themselves. Since the further the "science" of nature progresses, the more it loses itself in the tangle of these symbols, the basic task of all true philosophical reflection is, as Berkeley held, to dispel this illusion. Philosophy achieves what mere science, inseparably bound up as it is with the medium of language and the vehicle of linguistic concepts, can never achieve: it places before us the world of pure experience in its immediate existence and factuality, free from alien ingredients, unobscured by any admixture of arbitrary signification.

On this point, then, the whole history of philosophy, regardless of all controversies between schools and systems, seems unerringly to take the same course. For it is through this very act of self-affirmation—through this confidence in itself as the true organ for knowing reality—that philosophy as such is constituted. The assertion of the *adaequatio rei et intellectus* remains in this sense its natural point of departure. And yet, on the other hand, this fundamental act contains within it its own dialectical opposite. The more sharply philosophy seeks to determine its object, the more the object, through this very determination, becomes a problem for it. When philosophy sets up its own goal and consciously formulates it, there arises within philosophy itself through the immanent necessity of its own method the question of its attainability, of its inner possibility. Thus the positive answers of both rationalism and sensationalism to the question of whether reality can be known are followed by skepticism as by their shadow. The identity which they asserted between knowledge as such and its objective content is abandoned and is replaced by a difference which is exacerbated to the point of polar tension. Even the equation of knowledge—regardless of whether it is taken in a rationalist or sensationalist sense—fails to annul this difference: for equality—according to a definition introduced into the logic of mathematics by Bolzano—is nothing other than a special instance of difference. Thus the combination, the synthesis, asserted and expressed by the "equals" sign, does not dispel the difference of the terms standing on either side of it but rather intensifies this difference. In this respect the mere suggestion of an equation of knowledge contains within it a germ of destruction which skepticism needs only to develop and bring to fruition. The more self-consciousness there is about knowledge—the more clearly it is understood and the more clearly its form is known—the more this form seems a necessary limit which knowledge can never surpass. The absolute object which knowledge at first thought it could capture and gather into this form recedes more and more into the unattainable distance—until it seems given to knowledge not to apprehend the object but only to contemplate itself, as though in a mirror, with all its contingency and relativity.

It was the revolution in method effected in Kant's formulation of the problem which first promised a way out of this dilemma. Weary of the dogmatism that teaches us nothing and of the skepticism that does not even promise anything, Kant raised the fundamental critical question "Is any metaphysics possible?" [1] Now knowledge was saved from the peril of skeptical disintegration; but this salvation and liberation proved to be possible only through a shift in the aim of knowledge. Instead of a static relation between knowledge and object—as might be designated by the geometrical notion of a congruence between the two—a dynamic relation was sought and established. No longer does knowledge, whether as a whole or with a part of itself, "reach over" or "journey" into the transcendent world of objects. All these spatial images are now recognized as images. Knowledge is described neither as a part of being nor as

1. Cf. his *Prolegomena zu einer jeden künftigen Metaphysik,* 1st ed. Riga, 1783; 2d ed., in *Werke,* ed. Cassirer (Berlin, 1922), *4,* 22 ff.

its copy. However, its relation to being is by no means taken away from it but rather is grounded in a new point of view. For it is now the function of knowledge to build up and constitute the object, not as an absolute object but as a phenomenal object, conditioned by this very function. What we call objective being, what we call the object of experience, is itself only possible if we presuppose the understanding and its a priori functions of unity. We say then that we know the object when we have achieved synthetic unity in the manifold of intuition. To understand this operation as a whole and in its detailed conditions now becomes the central task of the analytic of the understanding. In it Kant strives to show how the various basic forms of knowledge, sensation, and pure intuition, the categories of the pure understanding and the ideas of pure reason, intermesh—and how by their reciprocal relation and mutual determination they define the theoretical form of reality. This definition is not taken over from the object but involves a "spontaneous" act of understanding. It is a specific mode and direction of formation that leads to the world view of theoretical knowledge. Consequently this view is not in some way forced upon us by the nature of things but is a result of free formation, which, however, is never arbitrary but always determined by law. How freedom can be compatible with necessity, how the purely immanent self-determination of thought can be compatible with objective validity: this is the central problem of Kant's entire critique of reason. From this comprehensive problem we now single out that factor which also lies at the core of the Philosophy of Symbolic Forms.

Where precritical metaphysics thought it had found an ultimate answer, Kant discovered the new and perhaps most difficult task of all philosophical knowledge. For him it was essential to follow through the theoretical intent of science and philosophy, and to grasp it for what it really is. As long as we consider this intention only in relation to its product, as long as we equate it with its result, it seems in a sense to keep vanishing with this result. Therefore, instead of concentrating on the product of theoretical knowledge, we should turn back to its function and specific law. It alone is the key that can open up the "truth of things." From then on, inquiry was to be directed not exclusively toward what has been discovered, but also toward the act, the mode and manner, of the discovering. The key which is destined to open the gates of knowledge must itself be understood; theoretical knowledge must be explored in its structure of meanings. There is now no road back to that relation of immediate congruence and correspondence which dogmatism assumed to exist between knowledge and its object. The critical justification and foundation of knowledge consists rather in its knowing itself to be a mediated and mediating spiritual organ, with its definite place and task within the world of the spirit as a whole.

It is true that such a turning back of knowledge upon itself seems possible only after it has surveyed its whole course and reached its highest point. Only transcendental philosophy is capable of such a conversion, for it alone is concerned not so much with objects as with our manner of knowing objects as such, insofar as such knowledge is held to be possible a priori. It alone strives to be not so much a definite knowledge of objects as a knowledge of knowledge. And this explains why Kant, while he raises his central problem to the heights of transcendental inquiry, strives constantly to stay within it. Where he investigates the form of theoretical knowledge, he believes that he can adequately apprehend it and set it before us in clear outline only by keeping in view the actual *telos* of knowledge, its end and fulfillment. Only in relation to this end can the logical structure of knowledge as such stand out in its necessity and purity, unmingled with contingent matters. Thus it could not but appear as a falling off from this arduously achieved level of philosophical inquiry, whenever the peculiar meaning of the theoretical *logos* is sought anywhere else than where it stands out in its true determinacy and exactness. And in Kant's opinion such exactness, such pure and complete self-realization of theoretical form, is the preserve of mathematics and the exact sciences. The question must therefore be directed primarily to them—and it must always remain oriented by reference to them. Thus no empirical datum partakes of the form of knowledge unless it has already passed through the medium of mathematical concept formation, unless it is determined by the pure intuitions of space and time, and by the concepts of number and of extensive or intensive magnitude: unless it has passed through this medium it remains formless matter. The question of whether this matter of sensation should perhaps not be designated only relatively as formless—of whether it does not reveal a certain formation in itself and conceal a "more concrete" formation of its own: this problem is not raised—at least not at the beginning of Kant's critical investigation. Here sensation appears as the "given," pure and simple—and the whole question is: how does this datum fit into the a priori forms of sensation and the understanding, whose significance and validity do not arise from it and are not based on it? But when we inquire into the origin of sensation itself, the first answer we obtain is merely a riddle. For there would seem to be no other way of understanding this origin than to thrust it back into the realm of the unknowable, to explain it as an affection of the mind by "things in themselves." The inextricable dialectical difficulties in which this explanation involves us have come to light in the history of Kantian philosophy—in the thinking of both Kant and his successors.[2] They become understandable when we recall that Kant was here concerned not so much with solving a problem as with sweeping a problem out of the way. From a purely historical point of view this seems understandable, even necessary, for only in this way could the road be cleared for Kant's most individual achievement. But once this road had been opened, it goes without saying that theoretical reflection had to go back to its starting point and turn its attention to the problem inherent in the dualistic opposition of "mere" matter and "pure" form.

It is not only in the post-Kantian systems that this development can be shown; to a considerable extent it determined the inner development of Kant's own thought. Long before the *Critique of Judgment* we discern this peculiar movement of Kantian thinking—we see how it keeps circling round the dualism of matter and form set forth in its beginnings, and how it gradually changes and deepens the meaning of this opposition. For the critical theory of knowledge, the matter of sensation seems at first to signify something that is simply present—a solid substrate which the formative powers of the spirit attack but which they cannot change and the essence of which they cannot penetrate. It remains the unpenetrated and impenetrable residue of knowledge. But the "analytic of the pure understanding" already goes one step farther. For it takes up not only the objective deduction of the categories but also the problem of subjective deduction—and the two orientations complement and further each other. The objective deduction is directed essentially toward the form of objective knowledge as we find it in the exact sciences, aiming at those principles through which the mere rhapsody of perceptions becomes a tightly enclosed unity, a system of empirical knowledge; subjective deduction, on the other hand, immerses itself in the conditions and particularity of the perceptive consciousness itself. It comes to the conclusion

2. Cf. my *Erkenntnisproblem in der Philosophie und Wissenschaft der neueren Zeit* (3d ed. 3 vols. Berlin, 1922–23), *3*, intro., esp. 5 ff.

that what we commonly call the world of perception, far from being a mere formless mass of impressions, already includes definite fundamental and original forms of synthesis. Without this, without the synthesis of apprehension, reproduction, and recognition, we should have neither a perceiving nor a thinking ego—there would be an object neither of pure thought nor of empirical perception. At the beginning of the *Critique of Pure Reason* sensation and understanding are differentiated as the two stems of human knowledge (which may, however, have sprung from a common root that is unknown to us). Here the opposition between the two, and their possible common factor, seemingly continued to be understood in a realistic sense: sensibility and understanding belong to different strata of existence, although both may have a common root in a primal stratum of being which precedes all empirical separations but which we cannot grasp or determine more closely. The analytic of the pure understanding, however, viewing the relationship from an entirely different standpoint, drastically shifts the point where sensation and understanding meet, as well as the point where they separate. For the unity between the two is no longer sought in an unknown foundation of things; rather, one might say, it is sought in the heart of knowledge itself. If this unity is at all discoverable, it must be grounded not so much in the essence of absolute being as in an original function of theoretical knowledge, and it is through this function that it must be intelligible. Kant designated this original function as the "synthetic unity of apperception"; it became the supreme point to which all uses of the understanding, even all logic and with it transcendental philosophy, must relate. And this supreme point, this focus of spiritual activity, is one and the same for all "faculties" of the spirit: hence it is the same for the understanding and for sensation. The "I think," the expression of pure apperception, must be able to accompany all my representations: "for otherwise something would be represented in me which could not be thought; in other words, the representation would either be impossible, or at least be, in relation to me, nothing." Here, then, a universal condition is established which applies equally to sensory and to purely intellectual representations. In transcendental apperception Kant finds a "radical faculty of all our knowledge," to which both can equally be related and in which they are indissolubly linked. This means that there cannot be any such thing as an isolated, "merely sensory" consciousness—that is, a consciousness remaining outside of any determination by the theoretical functions of signification and preceding them as an independent datum. The transcendental unity of apperception is by no means exclusively related to the logic of scientific thinking, or restricted to it. It is not only the condition for this thinking and for the postulation and determination of its object; it is also the condition "of every possible perception." If perception is to signify anything at all—if it is to be perception for an ego and perception of something—it must possess certain theoretical criteria of validity. And from now on it appears to be one of the specific tasks of the critique of knowledge to lay bare those criteria which constitute the form of the perceptive consciousness as such. The schematic opposition between "judgment of perception" and "judgment of experience," as retained in the *Prolegomena*—though more for reasons of exposition than of system— has thus in principle been overcome. For the union of sensory perceptions or representations in one consciousness and their reference to one object are never a matter of mere sensory receptivity but are always based on an "act of spontaneity." And now it becomes evident that just as there is a spontaneity of the pure understanding, of logical, scientific thought and construction, so there is also a spontaneity of the pure imagination. The imagination, too, is by no means solely reproductive, but is originally productive. Now an uninterrupted path leads from the mere "affection" of the senses, with which the critique of reason begins, to the forms of pure intuition—and from these in turn to the productive imagination and the unity of action expressed in the judgment of the pure understanding. Sensibility, intuition, understanding are not mere successive phases of knowledge to be apprehended in their simple succession, but are necessarily intertwined as its constitutive factors.

And only now is the relation between the matter and form of knowledge formulated in a manner corresponding to Kant's new fundamental insight, to his "Copernican revolution." For now the two are no longer absolute *potencies of being*, but serve rather to designate distinct *differences of signification* and *structures of signification*. The matter of sensation as Kant initially viewed it could still be interpreted as a kind of epistemological counterpart to the Aristotelian πρώτη ὕλη. Like this *prima materia* it was seen as the absolute indeterminate prior to all determination—like it, Kant's "matter" had to await all determination from the form that would be imprinted upon it from outside. But this changed entirely after Kant himself had fully developed the idea of his "transcendental topics" and after, within this general idea, he had fully defined the opposition between matter and form. For now both of them have ceased to be original determinations of being, ontological entities, and become *concepts of reflection,* which in the section on the "amphiboly of the concepts of reflection" are treated along the same line as agreement and opposition, identity and difference. They are no longer two poles of being which confront each other in a real and insurmountable opposition; they are, rather, members of a methodic opposition which is at the same time a methodic correlation. Now it is no longer contradictory but actually necessary that what from one point of view may be designated as the *matter* of cognition, is from another standpoint recognized as something *formed,* or at least form-containing. The consequence of the methodological relativization of this opposition is that the significance of the two terms changes according to our underlying system of reference. Applied to the problem of perception, this means that where we are concerned with distinguishing the world of prescientific consciousness from the constructive determinations of scientific cognition, we may look on perception itself as something relatively simple and immediate. In relation to these constructive determinations, it may appear as a simple datum, as something "given in advance." But this by no means deprives us of the possibility, or relieves us of the obligation, of recognizing it in another context as something thoroughly mediated and conditioned. This only makes it evident that the analysis of the theoretical "form" of knowledge cannot cling to a single stratum of knowledge and establish itself, as it were, in this stratum, but must always bear in mind the totality of the factors from which knowledge is built up. For not only the realm of scientific, abstract concepts, but even that of common experience is shot through with theoretical interpretations and meanings. And when the transcendental critique seeks to disclose the structure of objective knowledge, it may not limit itself to the intellectual "sublimation" of experience, to the superstructure of theoretical science, but must also learn to understand the substructure, the world of "sensory" perceptions, as a specifically determined and specifically organized context, as a spiritual cosmos *sui generis.*

In the *Critique of Pure Reason,* as we have seen, Kant by no means closed his eyes to this requirement; but in this work he did not explore in all directions the complex of problems which he had so clearly designated on the basis of his own presuppositions. For the methodic task of the *Critique* pointed from the start in another direction. The subjective deduction is here subordinated to the objective deduction: the analysis of the perceptive consciousness serves only as a preparation and at the same time as a counterpart and corollary to the central question: the question of the presuppositions and principles on which experience in the form of science is based. Such experience is made possible only by a necessary combination of perceptions. It is toward this necessary combination and its possibility that the inquiry must therefore be primarily directed. The structure of meaning, without which perception cannot be thought, is therefore conceived essentially as a structure of pure law: this structure implies that the particular perceptions may not remain isolated, that they may not form a mere aggregate, but must be gathered into an intellectual context, a "context of experience." "Whatever *coheres* with the material conditions of experience (sensation)"—so Kant formulates the second of the postulates of empirical thought—"is actual." This coherence, however, is created and its particularity and formal character determined by the general laws of the understanding, of which all particular laws of nature are merely specifications. Accordingly it is one and the same purely intellectual synthesis which according to Kant determines both the object of empirical intuition and the object of the exact sciences—and it is precisely this identity which for the first time provides a solution to the fundamental epistemological question of the applicability of pure mathematical concepts to sensory phenomena. The same action which imparts unity to the different representations in a logical judgment also gives to the mere synthesis of different representations in an intuition a unity which, expressed in general terms, is the pure concept of the understanding. The categories on which the system of mathematical and physical cognition is founded are accordingly the same as those on which our concept of the natural world rests. Here, it would seem, no difference, not to mention a cleavage in principle, may be recognized: for if we did recognize such a difference, the whole demonstration on which the transcendental deduction of the categories is based would appear to be eradicated—it would no longer be possible to answer the question of the *quid juris* of the categories, the question of their right to be applied to empirical-sensory phenomena. This right is grounded in the supposition that every synthesis—even the synthesis which makes objective perception, the perception of "something" possible—is subordinated to the pure concepts of the understanding.

When, then, for example, I make the empirical intuition of a house by apprehension of the manifold contained therein into a perception, the *necessary unity* of space and of my external sensuous intuition lies at the foundation of this act, and I, as it were, draw the form of the house conformably to this synthetical unity of the manifold in space. But this very synthetical unity remains, even when I abstract the form of space, and has its seat in the understanding, and is in fact the category of the synthesis of the homogeneous in an intuition; that is to say, the category of *quantity,* to which the aforesaid synthesis of apprehension, that is, the perception, must be completely conformable.[3]

And in the same sense, even the pure "whatness" of sensation, its simple quality, is determined by the understanding and hence can in certain respects be anticipated: for the principle of continuity, the principle of intensive quantity subjects the change in this quality to a definite condition and prescribes a determinate form for it. Thus it is proved "that the synthesis of apprehension, which is empirical, must necessarily be conformable to the synthesis of apperception, which is intellectual, and contained *a priori* in the category."[4] ". . . that the formative synthesis, by which we construct a triangle in imagination, is the very same as that we employ in the apprehension of a phenomenon for the purpose of making an empirical conception of it [is] what alone [connects] the notion of the possibility of such a thing with the conception of it."[5] Thus the idea of an original intellectual "form" underlying the world of perception is strictly carried through in every direction: but for Kant this form coincides essentially with the form of mathematical concepts. What distinguishes the two is at most their degree of distinctness, not their essence or structure. The conditions of the mathematical-physical concept of the object, the concepts of number and measure exhaust the whole theoretical content and meaning of perception. It must always pass through these universal mathematical determinations if it is to be fixated and formed for us in any way. The question of its "what" and its "how" can be answered with any cogency only if we can transpose it into a question of quantity, for ultimately what distinguishes one perception from another can be designated objectively and theoretically only if we can assign to it a place in a definite system of measurement or scale of magnitudes. Thus

3. Kant, *Kritik der reinen Vernunft,* 1st ed. Riga, 1787; 2d ed., in *Werke,* ed. Cassirer (Berlin, 1922), *3,* 162. Eng. trans. by J. M. D. Meiklejohn (Everyman ed., New York, E. P. Dutton, 1934), pp. 109–10.

4. Ibid., p. 162 n. Eng. trans., p. 110 n.

5. Ibid., p. 271. Eng. trans., p. 168.

the critical analysis of the perceptive consciousness and the analysis of the basic theoretical system of the exact sciences arrive at the same conclusion: both prove to be grounded in the same original stratum of the intellect, the same realm of a priori concepts.

And yet, necessary and consistent as this conclusion appears in the framework of Kant's general formulation of the problem, we must go beyond it, once the formulation of the problem is broadened, once we attempt to state the transcendental question itself in a more comprehensive sense. The Philosophy of Symbolic Forms is not concerned exclusively or even primarily with the purely scientific, exact conceiving of the world; it is concerned with all the forms assumed by man's understanding of the world. It seeks to apprehend these forms in their diversity, in their totality, and in the inner distinctiveness of their several expressions. And at every step it happens that the "understanding" of the world is no mere receiving, no repetition of a given structure of reality, but comprises a free activity of the spirit. There is no true understanding of the world which is not thus based on certain fundamental lines, not so much of reflection as of spiritual formation. In order to apprehend the laws of this formation, we had above all to distinguish their different dimensions. Certain concepts—such as those of number, time, and space—represent, as it were, original forms of synthesis, which are indispensable wherever a "multiplicity" is to be taken together into a "unity," wherever a manifold is to be broken down and articulated according to determinate forms. But as we have seen, this articulation is not effected in the same way in all fields: rather, its mode depends essentially on the specific structural principle which is operative and dominant in each particular sphere. Thus, in particular, language and myth each reveal a "modality," which is specific to it and in a sense lends a common tonality to all its individual structures.[6] If we hold fast to this insight into the "polydimensionality" of the cultural world, the question of the relation between concept and intuition immediately takes on a far greater complexity. As long as we remain within the sphere of pure epistemology and concern ourselves solely with the presuppositions and validity of the basic scientific concepts, the world of sensory intuition and perception is defined only with a view to precisely these concepts and is evaluated as a phase preliminary to them. Then sense perception is the germ from which the theoretical structures of science are expected to unfold—but into our description of

6. Cf. above, the general introduction to the present work, *1*, esp. pp. 78 ff., 95 ff.

this germ we unconsciously interpolate precisely those formations which will issue from it later. The structure of what is perceived and intuited is seen from the outset in the light of the one aim: scientific objectivization, the theoretical concept of the unity of nature. Thus, in the apparent receptivity of intuition, we again encounter the spontaneity of the understanding—of precisely that understanding which, by virtue of its own laws, is the condition for the pure knowledge of nature, for the laws of scientific experience and its object. But essential as this trend toward the systematization of experience—toward the universal system of natural science—may be for sensory intuition, it is not the only line of signification comprised in sensory intuition. For beside the logical forms into which conceptual scientific thinking fits the world of phenomena stand forms of a different character and meaning. We find such forms of spiritual vision at work in the concepts both of language and of myth. Measured by the concepts of exact science, those of language may appear to be mere preliminary concepts, provisional structures of thought, while mythical concepts may seem to be pseudoconcepts pure and simple. Yet this does not prevent them from possessing a very definite character and significance. They, too, are modes of spiritual "sight"; they, too, mark off, and give life to, the flowing, ever indifferent sequence of phenomena, and let them coalesce into definite forms. Language lives in a world of denominations, of phonetic symbols, with which it links definite meanings—it holds fast to the unity and determinacy of these denominations, and thereby the manifold sensory experiences which it strives to grasp and signalize take on a relative stability and come to a kind of standstill. It is the *name* which introduces the first factor of constancy and permanence into this manifold; the identity of the name is the preliminary step, an anticipation of the identity of the logical concept. The formation proceeds differently in the province of myth: for the objective world which is here built up, which is glimpsed as something enduring and constant behind the infinite variety of the phenomena of outward and inner perception, is a world of demonic and divine powers, a pantheon of animated and active beings. But in both cases we find the same relationship as in our analysis of theoretical-scientific knowledge. No more than scientific cognition could disclose a matter and a form as separable components, existing independently of each other and pieced together subsequently and from without, can we discern any such separation when we return to the primordial strata of language and myth. We never find naked sensation as a raw material to which some form is given: all that is tangible and accessible to us is rather the concrete determinacy, the living multiformity, of a world of perception, which is dominated and permeated through and through by definite modes of formation. The most careful and precise analyses of that "primitive thinking" on which myth rests have over and over again pointed with unmistakable clarity to this one conclusion: that a specific mode and trend of perception corresponds to the mode of this primitive thinking. The mythical structures do not resemble a multicolored veil that merely obscures the empirical perception of things, which behind it remain solid and immutable. On the contrary, what constitutes the power of these structures is that they provide an individual and peculiar mode of intuiting and perceiving reality—one subject to entirely different conditions from that mode of grasping reality which leads to the phenomenon of nature as a totality governed by wholly empirical laws. Mythical perception knows nothing of any such nature—although it is by no means lacking in combinations, in inner contexts, which make temporally and spatially separate elements appear as factors, as expressions of one and the same mythical meaning. The same is true of language: to examine its achievement solely from the standpoint of its influence on thought instead of considering as equally essential and original its influence on the growth and formation of the world of perception is one-sided and inadequate. It is not only in the organization and articulation of the conceptual world, but also in the phenomenal structure of perception itself—and here perhaps most strikingly—that the power of linguistic formation is revealed. Humboldt defines language genetically as the eternally repeated effort of the spirit to make the articulated sound capable of expressing thought. But on the other hand, he leaves no doubt that this effort of thought is intimately bound up with the work of building the world of intuition and perception. By the same spiritual act through which man spins language out of himself he spins himself into it: so that in the end he communicates and lives with intuitive objects in no other manner than that shown him by the medium of language.[7] Once we have become thoroughly imbued with this fundamental view, a whole world of formal problems arises which, though previously obscured, are in no way less significant for philosophy than the problems raised by the structure of scientific cogni-

7. Wilhelm Humboldt, *Einleitung zum Kawi-Werk*, in *Gesammelte Schriften*, ed. königliche preussische Akademie der Wissenschaften (Berlin, 1903–22), 7, 46, 60 ff.

tion. Only by surveying the totality of these problems can we gain an insight into that immanent dynamic of the human spirit which advances beyond all the fixed boundaries we customarily draw between its various faculties. In this dynamic, in the continuous mobility of the spirit, all sight, as Goethe put it, passes into contemplation, all contemplation into speculation, all speculation into combination, so that at every attentive glance into the world we are theorizing. In the following reflections and investigations we shall strive to take the concept of "theory" in the full breadth accorded it by these lines from the preface to his essay on color theory. Theory cannot and must not be restricted to the scientific knowledge of the world, and certainly not to a single, logically selected culminating point in it; rather, we must seek it wherever a specific mode of formation, of "sublimation" to a determinate unity of meaning is at work.

2

The peculiar character of philosophical concepts and the historical conditions of their . development make it quite understandable that philosophy should have been relatively late in taking up the totality of the problems of form involved in myth and language, that it should long have avoided and even rejected these problems. For the concept of philosophy attains its full power and purity only where the world view expressed in linguistic and mythical concepts is abandoned, where it is in principle overcome. The logic of philosophy first constitutes itself by this very act of transcendence. To achieve its own maturity, philosophy must above all come to grips with the linguistic and mythical worlds and place itself in dialectic opposition to them. Only in this way can it define and assert its concepts of essence and truth. Even where, as in Plato, philosophy continues to use myth as a form of expression, and even where it masters this form, it must stand outside and above this form: the philosopher must distinguish sharply and unambiguously between *logos* and myth. Myth remains attached to the world of change and hence of illusion, while the truth of being, the ἀλήθεια τῶν ὄντων, is alone apprehended in the pure concept. Philosophical knowledge must first free itself from the constraint of language and myth; it must, as it were, thrust out these witnesses of human inadequacy, before it can rise to the pure ether of thought.

And natural science arrives at the mastery of its specific task in very much the same way as pure philosophy. In order to find itself it, too, must first effect the great intellectual differentiation, the κρίσις, separating it from myth and language. This act of separation marks philosophy's hour of birth, and also the starting point of empirical research and the mathematical determination of nature. In the beginnings of Greek philosophy the two problems are still one and the same. Aristotle called the Ionian natural philosophers the first physiologists: it was they who disclosed the concept of *logos* through the concept of *physis*. And even where the *logos* became independent, even where, as among the Pythagoreans, it was taken as a pure numerical relationship and to this extent was detached from the matter of sense perception, it retained its relation to *physis*. Number was the foundation and source of all truth: but this truth *was* only through its embodiment, its manifestation in sensuous things themselves as their harmony, their measure and order. And this conceptual "essentiality," this οὐσία and ἀλήθεια of number, did not in turn spring forth unmediated but had to be slowly and gradually wrested from an alien world. The Pythagorean number, the number of mathematics and natural science, was wrested from the realm of mythical-magical number only after a steady intellectual advance. And natural science had to experience the same struggle with linguistic concepts as with mythical concepts. It could not simply take over the separations and differentiations, the combinations and groupings which occur in language, but had to replace them by distinctions and unities of an entirely different mode and intellectual character. Where language contents itself with denomination, science seeks definition; where language stops at the ambivalence of the name, science seeks the unambiguousness of the concept. But in raising this demand from its very beginnings, natural science made a still sharper break with the world view of common experience. This break separated from the world of the scientific object not only the world of words but also that of immediate perception. In order to penetrate to the sphere of these objects, in order to apprehend nature in its objective reality and objective determinacy, thought had to leave sensation and sensory intuition behind it, as well as names. Though the full significance of this fact is seldom appreciated, one of the most original and fruitful features of Greek thought is that it performed both tasks at once. This was possible only because, by an equation which at first sight seems extremely strange and paradoxical, sensuous reality itself was interpreted as a mere linguistic reality, a realm of names. Where the common world view saw the most secure and unquestionable reality, a reality beyond any possible doubt, the philosophical view recognized the unremitting change, the impermanence and arbitrariness of a mere nomenclature. "All things that mortals have established, believing in their truth," says Parmenides in his didactic poem, "are just a name: Becoming and Perishing, Being and Not-Being, change of position, and alternation of bright color." Here the pseudo-*logos* of language is combated from the standpoint of pure thought, from the standpoint of the true philosophical *logos,* and this battle represents the beginning of the scientific concept of nature. Here Democritus starts exactly where Parmenides left off: in the being of nature, of the *physis,* he discloses the same factor which Parmenides had demonstrated in the logical being of pure thought. The truth of nature, too, does not lie immediately before our eyes but is discovered only if we succeed in distinguishing the world of things from the world of words, the permanent and necessary from the accidental and conventional. And it is not only our linguistic designations that are accidental and conventional, but also our sense perceptions. Sweet and bitter tastes, as well as color and tone, exist only by convention: in reality there is nothing but atoms and empty space. And this equation of sensory qualities with linguistic signs, this degradation of their reality to a reality of names, is no merely isolated, historically conditioned feature in the genesis of the scientific concept of nature. It is no accident that we encounter exactly the same development when we examine the rediscovery of this concept in the philosophy and science of the Renaissance, where it is grounded in different methodic presuppositions. Again, Galileo separates objective from merely subjective determinations, primary qualities from secondary ones, by degrading the latter to the level of mere names. All the sensuous attributes which we customarily impute to a body, all the smells, tastes, and colors, are, in relation to the object in which we conceive of them as inhering, nothing but words, by which we designate not the nature of the object itself but only its action on us, on the sentient organism. Insofar as thought is directed toward a physical reality, it must endow this reality with determinate characteristics of quantity, shape, and number; it must conceive it as one or many, large or small, endowed with this or that spatial extension and figure. On the other hand, it has no bearing on this reality that it be apprehended as red or white, bitter or sweet, fragrant or malodorous; for all these denominations are merely signs that we use for changing states of being, states that are external and accidental to being itself.[8]

It would seem as though this methodological beginning of natural science, once achieved, must also signify its methodological end, as though science would never be able to advance beyond this aim, or raise questions that go beyond it. For if it did so, if it did surpass the concept of the object thus gained, it would appear to face a hopeless *regressus ad infinitum*. Behind all reality held to be true and objective, another reality would rise up; it would be impossible to call a halt to this progress and so secure an absolutely solid "foundation" of knowledge. For the physicist at least there was no need—indeed he did not seem to have the right—to yield to such a progression into the indeterminate. At some point he required something determinate and definitive—and this he found when he touched the solid ground of mathematics. Having reached this stratum from his starting point amid the mere signs and illusions of sensation, he felt that he had won the right to stay there and take a rest as it were. Even the modern physicist tends to dismiss any epistemological doubt as to the definitive character of his concept of reality. With Planck he finds a clear and conclusive definition of reality in the identification of the real with the measurable. This realm of the measurable is and subsists in itself: it sustains itself and is self-explanatory. The objectivity of mathematics, the firm foundation of quantity and number, must not itself be shaken, it must not be undermined as it were by reflection. It is this dread of being undermined that explains why natural science shuns the method of dialectical thinking; why the direction that is natural and appropriate to it consists of going back from observed phenomena to principles, and in progressing from principles to the inferences that can be deduced from them mathematically—and not in attempting to ground and legitimize these principles any more deeply. Where science gives itself over to this, its first tendency, it recognizes no sharp dividing line between principles and objects. Since the principles are regarded as objectively valid, they are held at the same time to represent reality strictly speaking. Science was at first unable to formulate its fundamental principle except as embodied in things. There prevailed a kind of methodological materialism, which was by no means limited to the concept of matter but which can also be demonstrated in the other funda-

8. Galileo, "Il Saggiatore," *Opera*, ed. Albéri (Florence, 1842–56), *4*, 333; cf. my *Erkenntnisproblem*, *1*, 390 ff.

mental physical concepts, particularly that of energy. Over and over in the history of scientific thinking we encounter this tendency—a striving to transpose function into substance, the relative into the absolute, quantitative concepts into concepts of things.

Yet the theoretical development of physics in the last decades shows the beginnings of a change of direction: it is indeed this change of direction which may be said to give all modern physics its methodological character. As long as the "classical" system of natural science, the system of Galilean-Newtonian dynamics, was uncontested, the principles on which it rested appeared to be the fundamental laws of nature itself. In the concepts of space and time, mass and force, action and reaction, as defined by Newton, the basic framework of physical reality seemed to have been established once and for all. Today, the immanent progress of the natural sciences has increasingly cut the ground from under this view. In the place of a single, seemingly rigid system of nature we now have a number of systems which may be said to be open and mobile. The profound transformations which particularly the concept of substance has thus undergone, the progress from the physics of material masses to field physics: all this has now shown critical self-reflection in physics a new road. It is noteworthy that the thinker whose discoveries provided the practical groundwork for the new electrodynamic world view was also the author of a revolution in method in the field of physical theory. Heinrich Hertz is the first modern scientist to have effected a decisive turn from the copy theory of physical knowledge to a purely symbolic theory. The basic concepts of natural science no longer appear as mere copies and reproductions of immediate material data; rather, they are represented as constructive projects of physical thinking—and the only condition of their theoretical validity and significance is that their logical consequences must always accord with the observable data.[9] In this sense, the whole world of physical concepts may now be defined as a world of pure signs, as was done by Helmholtz in his theory of knowledge. If we compare this formulation with the epistemological presuppositions of the "classical" theory of nature, a strange contrast becomes evident. In interpreting sensuous qualities as mere signs (*puri nomi*), Galileo severed them from the objective world view of natural science. They now bore

9. Heinrich Hertz, *Die Prinzipien der Mechanik*, in J. A. Barth, ed., *Gesammelte Werke* (3 vols. Leipzig, 1892–95), Vol. 3. Eng. trans. by D. E. Jones and J. T. Walley, *The Principles of Mechanics* (New York, 1956).

the character of the conventional, accidental, and arbitrary, in contradiction to the objective necessity of nature. Knowledge must overcome and cast off everything that is merely significative, in order to penetrate to authentic reality. But now the line dividing subjective appearance from objective reality is drawn in a new sense. For neither one nor the other, neither sensation nor the mathematical-physical concept, raises the pretension to direct coincidence with the reality of things in any absolute sense. Both have a purely indicative character; they are merely indices of reality—and the only difference between them is that their indications possess a different value, a different theoretical significance and mode of universality. Thus the concept of the symbol has become a center and focus of the whole epistemology of physics. It has been recognized and designated as such particularly in Duhem's investigations concerning the object and structure of physics. For Duhem it is this concept which forms the actual dividing line between mere empiricism and strict physical theory. Empiricism can apparently content itself with apprehending isolated facts as provided by sensory observation, and linking them in a purely descriptive manner. But no such description of concrete sensuous phenomena so much as approaches even the simplest form of a physical concept, not to mention the form of a physical law. For laws are never mere compendia of perceptible facts, in which the individual phenomena are merely placed end to end as on a string. Rather, every law, as compared to immediate perception, comprises a μετάβασις εἰς ἄλλο γένος—a transition to a new perspective. This can occur only when we replace the concrete data provided by experience with symbolic representations, which on the basis of certain theoretical presuppositions that the observer accepts as true and valid are thought to correspond to them. Every judgment concerning physics must necessarily move in this sphere: such a judgment by no means consists in merely establishing a multiplicity of separate observable facts; rather, it expresses a relation between abstract and symbolic concepts. The meaning of these concepts is not accessible to immediate sensation but can only be determined and ascertained by a highly complex intellectual process of interpretation: and precisely this process, this intellectual interpretation, is what constitutes the essence of physical theory. Thus there always remains a cleavage, a kind of hiatus, between the world of facts and the world of physical concepts. To speak of an identity or similarity between the contents of these two worlds has no intelligible meaning. Rather, there is always a disparity between the "practical" fact, which can actually be observed, and the theoretical fact, the formula in which the physicist expresses his observation. For between the two there stands the entire, highly complex intellectual effort, by virtue of which a record of concrete occurrences and events is replaced by a judgment, which as such has a purely abstract significance and cannot be formulated except by the use of certain symbolic signs.[10] Of course, this does not mean that the modern epistemology of physics, in contradiction to the classical theory, renounces all claims of reality for the physical concepts—it means only that it formulates this claim differently and must mediate it in a far more complex way. The knowledge of the symbolic character of these concepts does not conflict with their objective validity; rather, it constitutes a factor in this validity itself and in its theoretical foundation. This opens up a great number of new problems with whose solution we shall not for the moment attempt to deal.[11] For our introductory remarks it suffices to bear the question in mind and assign it a place within our investigation as a whole.

3

But now the objection rises that our inquiry was bound to miss its goal because this goal lies far from the road which up to now we have taken. When we ask whether there is any possibility that thought may pass through the stratum of mere symbol and signification to apprehend the immediate, unveiled reality behind it, it is self-evident that this aim, if it can be reached at all, cannot be attained by the road of "outward" experience. After all the progress made by epistemological analysis in the field of modern physics, it is scarcely open to serious doubt that the knowledge of the world of things is bound up with very definite theoretical presuppositions and conditions, and that consequently the objectivization progressively effected in the natural sciences is always at the same time a process of logical mediation. But it now seems all the more necessary to reverse the direction of inquiry. We should seek true immediacy not in the things outside us but in ourselves. Not nature, as the aggregate of objects in space and time, but our own ego—not the world of objects but only the world of our existence, of our existential reality—seems able to lead us to the threshold of this immediacy. Thus

10. Cf. Pierre Duhem, *La Théorie physique, son objet et sa structure* (Paris, 1906), pp. 245 ff., 269 ff.

11. Cf. below, esp. Chap. 6.

if we wish to see reality itself, free from all refracting media, we must submit to the guidance of inner instead of outward experience. We shall never find the truly simple and ultimate element of all reality in things; but no doubt it may be found in our own consciousness. Should not the analysis of consciousness lead us to something ultimate and original, neither requiring nor susceptible of any further dissection—something which may be clearly and unambiguously recognized as the original substance of all reality?

This question brings us to the point where metaphysics and psychology meet and seem to fuse indissolubly. In the history of philosophy this process of fusion is most evident in Berkeley, whose *Principles of Human Knowledge* begins with a critique of language which is amplified into a critique of all purely conceptual, abstract thought. Abstraction is rejected, because the more we rely on it, the more it threatens to confine us to the merely instrumental. For this very reason it can never become an organ of metaphysics: metaphysics aspires to be a doctrine of immediacy. We do not, Berkeley held, apprehend the immediate through the customary methods of natural science, by reducing its phenomena to laws and stating the laws in the formulas of mathematics. Rather, it discloses itself to us only if we reject this magic of conceptual formulas; if we take the world of inner perception as it discloses itself to us prior to all artificial, abstract transformation. Pure experience, which is the sole source and kernel of all our knowledge of reality, can never be sought elsewhere than in our simple, original perceptions, untouched by theoretical interpretations. The reality of perception is the only certain and utterly unproblematical—the only primary—datum of all knowledge. Here a thorough reversal and reevaluation have taken place, as compared with the theory of knowledge on which classical natural science was based. In order to affirm the reality of its objects, classical epistemology had to degrade sensation to subjective appearance, and ultimately set it down as a mere name. Now the opposite thesis is upheld: sensation has become the sole reality and matter a mere name. For Berkeley, precisely the scientific concept of matter is the prime example by which to demonstrate the weakness of abstract concept formation. Matter is given in no single perception; it is neither visible nor tangible; thus, if we go back to its basic signification, nothing remains of it but a general idea, which like all general ideas possesses no prototype in things but simply dissolves into the universality of a word. At best, the concept of matter yields a vague and elusive nom-

inal definition of reality, the real definition of which can be found only in
the sphere of sensation, in its individual facticity and individual differences. Thus the critique of language becomes a foundation for the
critique of knowledge. Berkeley distinguishes two forms of language, and
by them he shows the specific differences in the validity of our cognitions.
For him, perception itself, the whole aggregate of sensory phenomena, is
a form of language. But this is not the conventional language of words
and signs; rather it is the original language in which the metaphysical
primal being, God, speaks to men.[12] Scholastic logic, however, and the
science which followed it and became more and more subservient to it
had, in Berkeley's view, turned away more and more from this primal
stratum of all truth and reality: it had replaced the intuitive language of
the senses by the discursive language of universal concepts. Only if we
demolish the whole edifice that it has set up can we hope to apprehend
and understand being in its concrete and original character, in the primary elements from which it is built.

Thus Berkeley summons inner experience to battle against outward
experience, psychology against physics. This conflict runs through his
whole philosophy and is expressed most particularly in his continuous
polemic against the foundations of Newton's mathematics and theory of
motion. But nineteenth-century physics reveals a strange shift in the
battlefront. Berkeley's theory of knowledge, in which metaphysics declared war on mathematical physics, now enters into the field of physics
itself. A new foundation of physics and a revision of its principles were
sought precisely through this theory of knowledge. The logic of objective knowledge, which had developed hand in hand with the classical
system of physics and which culminated in the Kantian system of transcendental philosophy, seemed to have abdicated once and for all in favor
of psychology—and psychology now developed along strictly sensationalist lines, as a pure psychology of elements. This is the turn of thought
signalized in nineteenth-century epistemology, by Mach's analysis of sensation. Mach expressly states that the central methodological purpose of
his theory is to do away with the arbitrary distinctions which had hitherto
been made between inner and outward experience, between psychology
and physics. He called for a body of principles which would make it
possible to encompass the two in an immediate unity—which would re-
lieve us of the necessity of transposing our whole world of concepts

12. Regarding Berkeley's concept of a "visual language," cf. above, *1*, 100.

whenever we move from one field to the other. And he finds this common ground in the basic matter from which the physical and psychological worlds are woven, much as they may seem to differ in form. As soon as we go back to this matter, as soon as we carry analysis to its end, to the ultimate elements, all artificial partitions that we have set up between inner and outward worlds vanish. With our return to the primal stratum of sensation and its pure facticity, we have left behind us all that is mediate and that is significative—and with it all the equivocations, the ambiguities which the term "being" takes on in the abstract language of concepts. With regard to the primary experience of color and tone, taste and smell the question of whether they belong to an inner or an outward reality loses all justification or meaning: for the facticity in which all existence as such is grounded cannot be thought of as belonging to or reserved for a particular mode of existence. Thus the pure positivist view solves the riddles in which the metaphysical view involves us: the metaphysical claim to interpret and explain the world gives way to a pure description of the world.

For Mach, as a physicist, psychologist, and epistemologist, there remained no doubt that this description had achieved its aim once it had replaced physical or psychological "objects" by pure complexes, or more or less stable combinations, of elements. However, the subsequent development both of physics and of psychology was far from confirming his confidence. For physics, it suffices here to recall the resolute opposition of a thinker of Planck's stature to Mach's theory of knowledge. In it he saw not the grounding but rather the complete dissolution of the true physical concept of the object. And in psychology, the turn away from the basic assumptions of Mach's theory of elements has perhaps been still more marked. For the moment we shall not enter into this development; we shall merely raise one objection to Mach's theory, the very same objection which we have been compelled to make regarding every attempt to determine the mere matter of knowledge outside and independently of all formation. The most important thing, Goethe has said, is to recognize that all fact is in itself theory. If this applies to any fact at all, it is to the fact of simple sensation. Even the first rudiments of Mach's theory are valid only if we accept its underlying assumption: the assumption that the whole content and facticity of psychological structures are confined to the content of their simple elements and can be derived from it. If, however, we examine the source of this assumption and Mach's argument in its favor, we recognize to our surprise that it has its source not in immediate psychological experience but in Mach's view of the value and meaning of scientific *method*. It is incontestable that experience presents psychological structures, not as a sum of elementary sensations but as undissected totalities—whether these are taken in the sense of complex qualities or of psychological *Gestalten*. Mach himself did not wholly overlook this circumstance—not at least after the concept and problem of gestalt qualities made their appearance in modern psychology. But he still maintained that without going back to the elements, to the primary data of sensory experience, we can gain no knowledge of psychological processes. For knowledge consists not in the simple possession of a whole but in building it up from relatively simple facts; it is essentially constituted by the twofold process of analysis and synthesis, separation and recombination. If we look into the source of this conviction in Mach, it becomes clear that he is speaking less as an empirical psychologist than as a physicist, and we hear a distinct echo of Galileo's classical theory of the compositive and resolutive method as the two necessary and fundamental factors. in all knowledge. But in the field of psychology Mach did not practice the same sharp critique of this assumption as he demanded in the field of physics. He denied the elements of physics any right to pass as an expression of immediate reality. For him they were solely instrumental concepts, products of the economy of thought which we cannot dispense with in describing natural processes but which we may not regard as given contents of nature. With all his resulting skepticism regarding the reality of atoms, however, Mach never lost his credulity in respect to the reality of psychological elements. Here lies the evident limitation and paradoxical character of his epistemology, for we should expect the "simple" of sensation to be treated at least along the same lines as the "simple" of the atom —indeed we should expect him to exert even greater caution respecting a concept serving to describe the immediate reality of experience, than respecting one which serves to represent the world of physical things. Yet in Mach this relation is diametrically reversed. He never wearied of attacking the hypostatization of the concept of the atom—and he went so far in his philosophical attacks as often to underestimate the physical value of this concept and its importance for any objective science of nature. But nowhere does Mach seem to have objected seriously to the hypostasis of the concept of sensation. And yet it is evident that at least in the sphere of pure experience, in the psychological process itself, simple sensation is never encountered as an empirical fact. We need not deny the concept of simple sensation all theoretical value whatsoever—as many modern psychologists seem to do, but one thing is certain: it is the expression not of a fact but of a theoretical supposition. It is in no way immediately given but is postulated—and it is postulated on the basis of very definite preliminary concepts, which are themselves constructed. Modern psychology has subjected these preliminary concepts to an exacting critique which reduces the supposed facticity of sensory elements to a theoretical prejudgment. The immediate in the sense of mere matter has here again proved to be weighted down with an inner contradiction: the totality of psychological structures cannot be dissected in such a way as to demonstrate, side by side with the total form, an amorphous something, a substrate of this form. If any such substrate were laid bare and isolated, it would by this very act of isolation lose its significance, which it can have only as a factor within an articulated unity of meaning—and this loss of significance would at the same time include the loss of its specific psychological reality.

And from still another angle it may be seen how incapable the positivist theory of knowledge is of expressing and exhausting the truly positive aspect of psychology and its peculiar mode of postulation. Not only had Mach no doubt as to the bare facticity of simple sensation itself; he was also confident that the elementary contents of consciousness could be divided into distinct sensory spheres, and he made this division an integral part of the "natural world concept." Since the world is given to us by immediate sensation, it breaks down, in this very process of being given, into a diversity of sensory impressions. With the "what" of the world, its "how" is also unequivocally given, its dispersion into colors and tones, tastes and smells, sensations of temperature, and muscular sensations. But actually the phenomenon of perception, taken in its basic and primary form, in its purity and immediacy, shows no such division. It presents itself as an undivided whole, as a total experience, which is, to be sure, articulated in some way but whose articulation by no means comprises a breakdown into disparate sensory elements. This breakdown occurs only when the perception is no longer considered in its simple content but is viewed from a definite intellectual standpoint and judged accordingly. Only when it is no longer apprehended and determined according to its "what," only when the question of its "whence" is raised, does it become necessary to break it down into relatively independent sensory spheres. Thus this breakdown is not part of a simple "raw material" of the perceptive consciousness, but already comprises a factor of reflection, of causal analysis. When the perception is considered with regard to its origin, to the conditions of its genesis, it is dissected into different spheres, according to the different character of these conditions. With each special organ of perception, an independent world of perceptive contents is now correlated. To the eye there now corresponds the world of colors, to the ear the world of tones, to the sense of touch and temperature the world of the rough and smooth, the cold and warm, etc. The fact that this analysis does not begin with the development of science in the stricter sense but belongs also to the prescientific world view should not blind us to its specifically theoretical character. For not only the physical world of objects but the prescientific world of things is shot through with distinct factors of reflection, particularly with the causal interpretation of phenomena. And thus, even here, by a scarcely perceptible transformation, the genetic standpoint replaces the purely phenomenal standpoint: a real or supposed difference in origin is read directly into the structure of perception. The empirical differences in the genetic conditions of perceptions are looked upon as their natural, in fact as their only, principle of classification. Critical philosophy, on the other hand, which cannot simply accept the natural world view but must inquire into the conditions of its possibility, has every reason to question this principle and at least to doubt its exclusive and self-evident character. This doubt does not mean that the validity of the principle as such is negated but only that instead of being taken as absolute it is recognized as specific and relative—as a validity which is not given in the simple *content* of reality but partakes of a certain *interpretation* of reality. Here again positivism fails to recognize the pure energy, the activity and spontaneity of form; it regards a difference of formation as a difference in content, as a difference in the facticity of the empirical datum. But if we take a strict view of the positivists' own demand for pure description, we must insist on a clear distinction between description and explanation—we must insist that no factor pertaining to the causal understanding of the world, no factor whose validity and necessity can only be justified and deduced on the basis of this causal understanding, shall be injected into the description of data. The sharp separation between the "given" and the thought has been an accepted finding for empiricism ever since Hume and is also a basic demand of empiricism. Hume showed once and for all that the idea of causality in particular is not contained in the mere sensory impression and cannot be drawn from it by any kind of mediated inference. But in their theory of knowledge the positivists often forget that this conclusion applies also in the opposite direction—that no factor which is ultimately rooted in causal thinking and draws its nourishment from it may be injected into the exposition of the pure facts of perception. The confounding of descriptive and genetic elements constitutes an offense against the spirit of the empirical method itself, and precisely such a mixture occurs when in dealing with the pure phenomenology of perception one goes back to the facts of sensory physiology and makes them the actual basis of classification, the *fundamentum divisionis*. In setting forth his theory of elements, Mach did not escape this danger—and this gave it a very different methodological character from what he seems to have originally intended. Originally, it seems, Mach expected his theory to relax, as it were, the concepts of objectivizing science and particularly the concept of matter. Matter, he held, must no longer be regarded as a substantial something— it should be understood as a complex of simple sense impressions and defined as their mere juxtaposition. This was an attempt to correct the dogmatic materialism of the physicist with the help of psychology. Thus the physical simple was replaced by the psychological simple, the simple atom was replaced by simple sensation. And yet, on closer analysis, we find that the priority here given to psychological over physical reality, to consciousness over being, is a mere illusion. For the crucial question is not whether we designate as matter or as sensation the raw material from which reality as a whole is supposedly woven; the essential rather is the trend of our general interpretation of reality and its form, and what categories we take to be original and ultimate. And here it soon becomes evident that despite modifications in detail the categorial scaffolding on which Mach erected his theory of knowledge is none other than that of objective and objectivizing natural science. What Mach sought and demanded was a common basis for the object of psychology and the object of physics. The two should not be treated separately but should be derived from one and the same root. In this way he strove to promote a living interaction between inner and outward experience, to fructify physics through psychology. But actually even the beginnings of Mach's psychology show that he failed in this aim and show why he failed. In his very notion of the concept of simple sensation Mach remained a physiologist and a physicist. Here sensation is not taken in its pure actuality, it is not taken as a process, but is from the start interpreted as a substance, hypostatized as the universal matter of the world. The thing which Mach calls simple sensation is supposed to form the substrate of both physical and psychological reality; but if we take this postulation seriously, we find rather that the specific form of both modes of reality is misunderstood and basically negated.

This negation becomes still more evident if we follow the modern empiricist formulation of the problem back to its historical root. Hobbes declares that perception constitutes the essential problem of philosophy: prior to all phenomena is the φαίνεσθαι itself; prior to all manifestations is the fact that something is manifested: and this is the most wonderful and original fact of all.[13] But in interpreting this most original of phenomena, he at once goes back to physical categories and this quite consciously. He states as a principle that psychology can rise to the level of philosophical knowledge only if it imitates physics in its foundations and method. For all philosophical knowledge is a knowledge drawn from causes: and we can understand the cause of a thing only by making it come into being before our eyes, by building it up from its simple components. In arguing this thesis, Hobbes goes back explicitly to the form of Galilean natural science. However, he no longer restricts this form to any partial sphere of knowledge but demands its application to the entire field of the knowable—to psychology as well as physics, to jurisprudence and politics as well as logic and mathematics. Thus for him all thinking becomes arithmetic, addition and subtraction. Yet here a sharp distinction must be made between pure concepts, which as such are mere arithmetical signs, and the reality to which they ultimately refer—the content with which the arithmetic deals and which it seeks to apprehend and define. The concept as such has no other function than to indicate the real and it is so completely identified with that function that it can be distinguished in no way from the word of language, that it has no real meaning aside from its merely nominal signification. But behind this world of the mere sign stands the world of what is designated—and this can be nothing other than a world of bodies. Thus the seemingly phenomenological beginning with its emphasis on the pure fact or on "appearing" shifts at this point into its opposite: the thesis that matter is absolutely real and is the only knowable reality. Hobbes' empiricist successors combated this materialism on epistemological or metaphysical grounds; but in a methodo-

13. See Hobbes, *De Corpore* (London, 1655), Pt. IV, chap. 25, sec. 1.

logical sense they, too, failed to overcome it: *their* psychology, too, was thoroughly naturalistic; they, too, believed that before a phenomenon of perception could be described as such, it had to be broken up into parts, which were conceived as independently existing things. The question of whether such a concept of elements, such a concept of the psychological "atom" was itself adequate and admissible was not raised; the analogy of physics was taken as a guide to be followed unreservedly in all psychological inquiry.

The scientific psychology of the seventeenth and eighteenth centuries remained almost entirely in this sphere, holding that if it could establish the simple elements of consciousness and discover the rules according to which they composed themselves into associative groups, the essence of psychological reality would be revealed. Here only one thinker stood aside—so much so that his voice seems at first to have gone almost unheard. It was Herder who in his treatise on language and his *Vom Empfinden und Erkennen der menschlichen Seele* (*On the Feeling and Cognition of the Human Psyche*) first entered upon a new road. His purely philosophical argument was based on Leibniz' concept of the unity of consciousness as the unity of apperception. But he enriched this concept with all the concrete insights that had opened up to him in his own investigations. He came to psychology not from natural science—from physics or physiology—but from the philosophy of language. And he showed his originality and genius by not seeking to harness language to the traditional psychological categories. Instead, by living in it, by basing his interpretations on a concrete understanding of it, he for the first time really discovered the intellectual categories appropriate to it. Thus there entered into the phenomenology of perception a new stream of thought which immediately demonstrated its vitalizing and fructifying power. Now that the thread of orientation was sought no longer in the field of natural science but in the philosophy of language, the drift of the argument underwent a change. In natural science it may seem meaningful and even necessary to let knowledge of the parts precede knowledge of the whole, to ground the reality of the whole in that of the parts. But this road is closed to the investigation of language, for the specifically linguistic meaning is an indivisible unity and an indivisible totality. It cannot be built up piece by piece from its components, from separate words —rather, the particular word presupposes the whole of the sentence and can only be interpreted and understood through it. If we now apply this point of view to the problem of perception—if we take the unity of linguistic meaning as our guide and model—we gain an entirely new picture of sensibility. We then recognize that the isolated "sensation," like the isolated word, is a mere abstraction. Actual, living perception no more consists of colors or tones, tastes or smells than the sentence consists of words, the word of syllables, the syllable of letters. Starting from this insight, Herder, as a philosopher of language, proceeds to tear down the barrier which the analytical psychology of his time had erected between the diverse "spheres of sensation." How, he asked, could the linguistic sound designate and represent all these spheres, if there were really so fundamental a cleavage between its own contents—the world of tones— and the contents of the other senses? If this were so, would not all linguistic expression appear as an incomprehensible and unjustified transition, as the strangest sort of μετάβασις εἰς ἄλλο γένος? Herder removes this doubt by contesting its theoretical foundation, the traditional system of psychological classification. "How," he asks, "are sight and hearing, color and word, smell and tone connected?" And his first answer to this question is that we must seek in this connection not so much in the object, as in the opposite direction—not in the "things" of the outside world, but rather in the I, the subject of perception. Objectively considered, the data of the various senses may seem to lie ever so far apart: "but what then are these attributes of the *object?* They are mere sensations in *us* and as such do they not all flow into one? A thinking *sensorium commune,* that is merely acted upon from different sides: there lies the explanation." To designate this unity and totality of the sensory consciousness, which we must think of as preceding any division into different sensory spheres, into a world of the visible, the audible, the tangible, Herder goes back to the term "feeling." In feeling we encompass all those differences according to which we tend to divide sensation into classes, but here we apprehend them, as it were, *in statu nascendi.* Here, in place of the congealed difference, there still prevails the pure dynamic of consciousness, that original flowing and forming which contains in it the potentiality of all future configurations.

All the senses have feeling at their base, and this creates so intimate, powerful and ineffable a bond between the most diverse sensations that through it the strangest phenomena arise. I know of more than one example of persons who, naturally, perhaps in consequence of a childhood impression, could not help connecting this color with that sound, this obscure feeling with that totally different phenomenon, where comparison by lumbering reason showed no kinship whatsoever: for who can compare sound and color, phenomenon and feeling? We are full of such connections between the most diverse senses. . . . If it were possible for us to halt the chain of our thoughts and at every link seek its connections—what oddities we should find! By what strange analogies between the most divergent senses the psyche is forever prepared to operate! . . . Among creatures of sensibility, who gain sensation through many different senses at once, this grouping of ideas is inevitable; for what are all our senses other than mere modalities of one positive power of the psyche? . . . With great pains we learn to separate them for practical purposes, yet at a certain depth they always operate together. All the dissections of sensation undertaken by Buffon, Condillac, and Bonnet are abstractions: the philosopher must drop one thread of sensation and follow another—but in nature all the threads are one fabric.[14]

These lines of Herder may seem at first to be no more than an isolated *aperçu*, a mere parergon in relation to his basic theme: and yet they represent a turning point not only in psychology but also in the whole development of the cultural sciences. For they are the earliest indication of a struggle which extends down to our own time and which has given all modern psychology its specific methodological imprint. This is the struggle between a psychology which takes its essential orientation from natural science, whose methods of observation and analysis it seeks to imitate as faithfully as possible, and another form of psychological inquiry which aims above all at providing a foundation for the cultural sciences. Herder did not arrive at his conclusions by way of empirical psychology; he was guided by his great intuition of cultural life as a whole, which, with all its concrete richness and diversity, he sought to derive ultimately from one fundamental force, from a common root in humanity. He believed this unity to be threatened by the abstractions of psychological analysis, and thus there arose the psychology of the Storm and Stress period, which pressed for a living view of the psychological process as a whole, in opposition to that *encheiresis naturae* which takes

14. J. G. von Herder, "Abhandlung über den Ursprung der Sprache," in *Sämmtliche Werke*, ed. Bernhard Suphan (Berlin, 1877–1913), 5, 60 ff.

in hand nothing but its parts. What Herder sought was not the unity of the natural object, as constituted by the methods of objectivizing science, but the unity of all humanity. He followed Hamann, who, as Goethe tells us, believed fundamentally that everything which man undertakes to accomplish in word or deed must spring from a union of all his powers: "Everything isolated is bad." Thus it was the outlook on the world of objective spirit—on aesthetics, the philosophy of language, and the philosophy of religion—that gave a new and decisive impulse to the psychology and phenomenology of perception. Since then the central proposition which Herder took as his starting point has been increasingly confirmed, and confirmed by empirical psychology, too, which has shown that separation into distinct spheres of sensation is not inherent in the original datum of perception, but rather vanishes more and more as we go back to the primitive configurations of consciousness. In fact, it seems to be a distinguishing feature of these configurations that they never show the sharp dividing lines which we tend to draw between the sensations of the different senses. Perception forms a relatively undifferentiated whole, from which the various sensory spheres have not yet been singled out in any true sharpness. Modern developmental psychology has demonstrated this fact by innumerable examples from the psychology of animals, children and "primitive peoples." In all these worlds, the spheres of visual and auditory sensations, of smell and taste, show a far closer involvement than in our perception with its tendency to isolate the "qualities" of things. However, this interrelation is by no means limited to the primitive consciousness, but is retained far beyond it. Even in highly developed consciousness, phenomena of so-called synesthesia—for example of colored tones, numbers, smells, or words—are by no means mere anomalies but reveal a fundamental behavior and character of the perceptive consciousness. "Color and tone," Werner summarizes, "enter consciousness by an original experience akin to feeling, an experience in which the specifically optical 'matter' of color and the specifically acoustic 'matter' of color do not yet exist; this unity of tone and color is possible because the two have not yet become substantially differentiated—or at all events very little." [15] Thus it was empirical psychology itself which gradually shattered the psychological empiricist's dream of understanding the real by dissolving it into its ultimate sensory elements, the original data of sensation. These data have proved to be hypostases—so that the theory which seemed des-

15. Heinz Werner, *Einführung in die Entwicklungspsychologie* (Leipzig, 1926), p. 68.

tined to ensure the victory of pure experience over mere construction, of sensation over the abstract concept, actually contains an unmistakable and irreducible residue of conceptual realism. Thus once again the "matter" of reality seems to slip through our fingers as it were, just as we are about to seize it. Is there then no empirical necessity which governs the play of our inner and outward experience? Or instead of seeking forever new solutions to this question of matter, should we not radically reformulate the question itself?

4

There still remains one field into which we have not yet ventured and it is here if anywhere that we may hope for a definitive clarification and appeasement of our doubt. To anyone who has lost his naive confidence in empirical science, who has learned to see it with critical eyes, it must seem almost self-evident that scientific experience—the experience of empirical psychology or physics—cannot dispel this doubt. For obviously science can never jump over its own shadow. It is built up of definite theoretical presuppositions, within which it remains imprisoned. But is there not, *outside* of scientific methodology and in strict opposition to it, another possibility of bursting these walls? Is all reality accessible to us only through the medium of scientific concepts? or is it not evident, on the contrary, that a thinking which like scientific thinking moves only in derivations and in derivations from derivations can never lay bare the actual and ultimate roots of being? This does not cast any doubt on the existence of such roots. Everything that is relative must after all be rooted in an absolute. If this absolute persistently evades science, the evasion only shows that science lacks the specific organ for knowing reality. We do not apprehend the real by attempting to attain it step by step over the painful detours of discursive thinking; we must rather place ourselves immediately at its center. Such immediacy is denied to thought; it belongs only to pure vision. Pure intuition accomplishes what logical and discursive thought can never achieve, what indeed, once it recognizes its own nature, logical thought will never even attempt. When we seek to express the essence of logical schematism in general terms, we find that it goes back to a schematism of space. All understanding that is here at work follows the analogy of spatial grasping. Thought has its object in this sphere only by placing itself at a certain distance from it and by contemplating it from this distance. Thus every union with the object, however close, here signifies *eo ipso* a separation from it; all togetherness becomes separateness. If in place of this there is to be a true unity, in which being and knowledge no longer merely stand opposed but truly permeate each other, there must be a fundamental form of knowledge which has overcome this spatialization, this postulation of distance. Only that knowledge can be called metaphysical in the strict sense which has freed itself from the constraint of spatial symbolism, which no longer apprehends being in spatial metaphors and images but stands in the midst of being and there remains in an attitude of pure inner vision.

These sentences are a paraphrase of Bergson's basic conception. In one of his earliest works, which give the clearest insight into the genesis of his ideas, he formulated his problem in exactly this way. Metaphysics—he declared—is the science that aspires to dispense with symbols: "La métaphysique est la science qui prétend se passer des symboles." [16] It is only when we succeed in forgetting everything that is merely symbolic, when we tear ourselves away from the language of words and the language of spatial images and analogies, that true reality touches us. The dividing lines which the symbolism of language and the abstract concept introduces into reality may seem necessary and inevitable: however, they are necessary not from the standpoint of pure knowledge but only from the standpoint of action. Man can act upon the world only by breaking it into pieces—by dissecting it into separate spheres of action and objects of action. But where our relation to the world is not wholly taken up with such action but inwardness of contemplation is sought—where we seek not to change the world by our action but to understand it intuitively, we must break free from all abstract separations. In place of the discreteness in which all conceptual effort moves and in which it entangles us more and more as it progresses, it is now life itself that holds us in its unbroken unity and constancy; instead of remaining in the mere separation and juxtaposition essential to spatial representation, we have plunged into the flow of change, into pure duration.

Thus Bergson's doctrine is perhaps the most radical rejection of the value and justification of symbolic formation in the whole history of metaphysics. It is this act of formation which now appears as the actual

16. Henri Bergson, *Introduction à la métaphysique,* 1st pub. in *Revue de métaphysique et de morale,* 1900. Eng. trans. by J. W. Luce, *The Introduction to a New Philosophy* (Boston, 1912).

veil of Maya. But of course this verdict is based on a tacit assumption, without which it must at once become problematical. Bergson regards all symbolic formation not only as a process of mediation, but also as one of reification, and this is the basis of his critique of symbols. The thing-form seems to him the prototype of all mediated apprehension of reality. Thence it is only a necessary inference to remove the absolutes of the pure ego and pure time from this sphere—and seek to save the "unconditioned" from being distorted and rigidified by the category of conditionedness. How can the logical and conceptual instruments which were made for the description of physical being, the spatial being of things, and which are adequate for this description, apprehend the reality of the ego, which is never given to us otherwise than in the flowing movement of pure time? How can we hope to come closer to the essence of life by artificially interrupting its flow, by dividing it into classes and genera? This essence defies all our conceptual classifications: for instead of the homogeneity which must always be presupposed when different things are subordinated to the unity of a genus, we find here a thoroughgoing heterogeneity. And it is precisely this infinite heterogeneity that divides the authentic and original process of life from all its products. Thus the stream of life cannot be captured in the nets of our empirical-theoretical conceptual thinking but must always slip through them and overflow them. In this sense every imprinted form seems to Bergson an enemy of life; for form is essentially limitation, whereas life is essentially boundlessness; form is isolation and rest, while the movement of life as such has only relative stopping places.

But—we must now ask—does this *biological* view of reality exhaust the whole of its manifestations, or does it not rather represent only a partial aspect of it? Bergson's theory has one point in common with Schelling's natural philosophy, by which it was indirectly but decisively influenced: [17] it sets vitalism against mechanism, "nature in the subject" against "nature in the object." In his methodological proof that the subject cannot be apprehended through categories valid for the world of things, Bergson uses the very same arguments that Schelling formulated in his first book: *Vom Ich als Prinzip der Philosophie (On the Ego as a Principle of Philosophy)*. But for Bergson subjectivity itself, the world of that pure ego which we ascertain by intuition, is restricted to a much smaller area

17. In regard to this relationship cf. Margarete Adam, *Die Intellektuelle Anschauung bei Schelling in ihrem Verhältnis zur Methode der Intuition bei Bergson* (Patschkau, 1926).

than for Schelling. For Schelling nature, which like Bergson he interprets as "creative development," is nothing other than a development toward spirit. The formative activity of the spirit, as demonstrated in its supreme creations—in the creation of language and myth, religion, art, cognition— is a continuation and sublimation of the formative activity of nature: spiritual form does not conflict with organic form but is rather the fulfillment, the maturest fruit of the organic process itself. In Bergson, however, there is no longer any such superordination of the spiritual over the natural world. For him nature is entirely self-sufficient; it stands in pure substantiality on itself alone and should be understood through itself alone. Here, though Bergson never wearies of stressing the contrast between the way of metaphysical intuition and the way of scientific empiricism, he shows himself to be the son of a naturalistic era, with its orientations and limitations. For it is in keeping with this naturalistic trend when he imputes all true spontaneity, all productivity and originality to the *élan vital,* the pure life impulse, while he attributes a purely negative significance to the work of the spirit, which only builds as it were the rigid dikes and dams against which the stream of life forever breaks and which cause it in the end to dry up. But is not this image— like all the other images and metaphors which give Bergson's exposition its characteristic quality—not itself borrowed from the world of spatial existence and spatial motion, and hence inadequate as an expression for the dynamic of the spirit? In the intellectual sphere—and this precisely is one of the most significant factors determining that sphere—the concept of objectivity undergoes a transformation which no longer permits it to be equated in any sense with the "thing" concept of naive realism or even to be compared with it analogically. For here the central question refers not to the objectivity of existence but to the objectivity of meaning. And with this change in orientation the dualism on which Bergson's entire metaphysics is based shifts into a new light. For while that primary phenomenon of the ego, that experience of pure duration which for Bergson forms the starting point and key for all metaphysical knowledge, can be separated from all forms of the empirical reality of things and in principle set over against them—it cannot in the same sense be separated from the forms in which an objective signification is given to us. As opposed to the mere world of things, the pure ego may in a sense withdraw into its absolute solitude and inwardness in order to apprehend and affirm its own original vitality and mobility. It achieves its own form only by forgetting and persistently rejecting all schemata drawn from the world of things. But the world of the "objective spirit" nowhere shows this character of mere limitation. The entering of the ego as a spiritual "subject" into the medium of the objective spirit constitutes not an act of alienation but an act of finding and determining itself. The forms to which it here gives itself are no barrier to its movement; rather they are the vehicles of its spontaneous movement and self-unfolding. For they alone make possible that great process in which the I comes to grips with the world—that process which is the necessary condition for both the existence of the I and its knowledge of itself. Bergson's metaphysics starts from the pure phenomenon of life, which can only be apprehended through emancipation from all forms of knowledge; but it would not be metaphysics, it would not be philosophical knowledge if it did not at the same time promise a "knowledge of life." Yet on closer scrutiny his philosophy, which purports to be grounded in pure intuitive vision, is lacking in that very factor which might make such vision seem possible. Life cannot apprehend itself by *remaining* absolutely within itself. It must give itself form; for it is precisely by this "otherness" of form that it gains its "visibility," if not its reality. To detach the world of life absolutely from form and oppose the two means nothing other than to separate its "reality" from its visibility—but is not this separation itself one of those artificial abstractions which Bergson's metaphysics attacked from the very first? Must all form as such necessarily signify concealment rather than manifestation and revelation? To define the fundamental trend of metaphysical intuition and elucidate its nature Bergson often resorts to comparison with artistic intuition. Did not Ravaisson, his preceptor, go so far as to call art a "figurative metaphysic" and metaphysic a "reflection on art"?[18] But artistic activity, above all, shows how impossible it is to draw a line between inner vision and outward formation; it shows that here vision is already formation, just as formation *remains* pure vision. The "expression" is never something subsequent and relatively accidental that follows a finished and given inner prototype: rather, the inner image acquires its content only by composing itself into a work and so manifesting itself. The same is true of that universal creative process in which

18. "L'art est une métaphysique figurée, la métaphysique est une réflexion sur l'art et c'est la même intuition, diversement utilisée, qui fait le philosophe profond et le grand artiste." Bergson, *Notice sur la vie et les oeuvres de M. F. Ravaisson-Mollien* (Paris, 1904), quoted from Margarete Adam, p. 20.

the world of the spirit, a world of mediations, springs from the immediate unity of life. A metaphysic which from these necessary mediations stresses nothing but separation, falling off and alienation from true reality, is a prey to that delusion which Kant recognizes as one of the "sophistications" of human reason and which he designated by a famous comparison. This delusion consists in supposing that the *actus purus,* the energy of pure vital movement, must be manifested most fully where this movement is still left entirely to itself, where it encounters no resistance in a world of forms, and in forgetting that such resistance is a factor and a condition of this very movement. The forms in which life manifest itself and by means of which it acquires its "objective" form, signify both a resistance to life and an indispensable support. If they present obstacles to it, it is obstacles through which it becomes conscious of its power and learns to use this power. The apparent counterforce thus becomes the impulsion of the movement as a whole: the trend toward the outwardness not of things but of forms and symbols marks off the path by which pure subjectivity first finds itself.

But here let us break off and for the present refrain from entering into the problems which here assail us from all sides. This introduction was not intended to solve these problems, but rather to designate the difficulties and to point out the peculiar dialectic inherent in the mere question of immediacy, regardless of the direction from which it is raised. We have seen that neither epistemology nor metaphysics, neither speculation nor experience, whether taken as outward or as inner experience, can wholly master this dialectic. The contradiction can be moved further back, it can be shifted from one part of the spiritual cosmos to another, but it cannot in this way be resolved once and for all. Here philosophical thinking must not content itself with a premature solution; there is nothing it can do but resolutely take this very contradiction upon itself. The paradise of immediacy is closed to it: it must—to quote a phrase from Kleist's article "On the Marionette Theater"—"journey round the world and see whether it may not be open somewhere in back." But this "journey round the world" must really embrace the whole of the *globus intellectualis:* we must seek not to determine the nature of theoretical form through any one of its particular achievements, but rather to keep its total potentialities constantly in mind. And since any attempt simply to transcend the field of form is doomed to failure, this field should be not merely touched upon here and there but traveled from end to end. If thought cannot directly apprehend the infinite, it should at least explore the finite in all directions. The following investigations undertake to show that a coherent unity obtains, beginning with the ingenuous expressive value of perception and representative ideas—particularly those of space and time—and extending to the universal significations of language and theoretical cognition. The nature of this coherence can only be designated and made known by following its growth and through this growth discerning that, diverse and even contradictory as its separate phases are, it is nevertheless governed and guided by one and the same fundamental spiritual function.

PART I

The Expressive Function and the World of Expression

Chapter 1

Subjective and Objective Analysis

THE SIMPLEST and surest way to demonstrate the significance of the universal symbolic function for the formation of the theoretical consciousness would seem to be to turn to the highest and most abstract achievements of pure theory. For in them the connection stands out in full brightness and clarity. We find that all theoretical determination and all theoretical mastery of being require that thought, instead of turning directly to reality, must set up a system of signs and learn to make use of these signs as representatives of objects. Only to the degree to which this function of representation asserts itself, does being begin to become an ordered whole, a structure which can be clearly surveyed. The more fully we succeed in representing their content in this way, the more the particular reality and occurrence appear permeated by universal determinations. By following out these determinations and going on to represent each of them in turn symbolically, thought acquires an increasingly complete model of being and its general theoretical structure. Now there is no need, in order to be sure of this structure, to go back to the individual objects in their full concretion and sensuous reality. Instead of devoting itself to particular things and events, thought seeks and apprehends a totality of relations and connections; instead of material details, a world of laws opens up to it. Through the "form" of signs, through the possibility of operating with them in a definite way and combining them in accordance with fixed and constant rules, the character of theoretical self-certainty opens up to thought. The retreat into the world of signs forms the preparation for that decisive breakthrough, by which thought conquers its own world, the world of the idea.

It was Leibniz who first recognized this relationship in full sharpness, and in the structure of his logic, metaphysics, and mathematics he drew the conclusions from this insight. For him the problem of the logic of things is indissolubly bound up with the logic of signs. The *scientia generalis* requires the *characteristica generalis* as its instrument and vehicle. Leibniz' "characteristic" refers not directly to things themselves but to their representatives: it deals not so much with the *res* as with the *notae rerum*. But this in no way detracts from its thoroughly objective import. For the pre-established harmony which, according to the central thought of the Leibnizian philosophy, prevails between the world of the idea and the world of reality, also links the world of signs with the world of objective signification. The real never ceases to be governed by the ideal: "Le réel ne laisse pas de se gouverner par l'idéal et l'abstrait." But thought cannot manifest and assert this domination over the sensory world without, as it were, taking on the color of the sensory world, without being made sensible and corporeal. The analysis of reality leads back to the analysis of ideas, the analysis of ideas to that of signs. Thus at one stroke the concept of the symbol has become the actual focus of the intellectual world: here the guiding lines of metaphysics and of general epistemology run together; here the problems of general logic are linked with those of the special theoretical sciences. "Exact" science in particular is drawn wholly into its sphere: for the measure of its exactness lies precisely in the fact that it admits only such statements as may be transposed into signs, and moreover, into signs whose meaning can be strictly and unequivocally defined. Step by step, the development of the exact sciences in the nineteenth and twentieth centuries has brought this idea of knowledge closer to its fulfillment. From the basic ideas of the Leibnizian "characteristic" grew the ideas of modern symbolic logic; and from them in turn has grown a fundamentally new form of mathematics. Today mathematics stands at a point where it can nowhere dispense with the help of symbolic logic, and indeed the works on the principles of modern mathematics, particularly those of Russell, make it seem more and more questionable whether, aside from symbolic logic, mathematical theory can still lay claim to any special position or right of its own. Just as for Leibniz the concept of the symbol formed as it were the *vinculum substantiale* between his metaphysics and his logic, so in modern scientific theory it constitutes the *vinculum substantiale* between logic and mathematics—and further, between logic and exact science. Everywhere it proves to be the strict intellectual bond which cannot be severed without destroying the essential content along with the form of exact knowledge.

But if the symbolic concept is to be regarded as constitutive for the concept of exact knowledge, this would seem to imply that it must be restricted to this sphere. If it is the symbolic concept which actually opens up the realm of theoretical and exact science, it would seem to be confined to this realm and unable to pass beyond it. For the world of the abstract concept it may be possible and even necessary for abstract, conceptual thought to limit itself to signs. But highly as we may esteem the rational perfection which conceptual thinking achieves by its union with signs, it cannot be overlooked that cognition achieves this perfection only at its end. Having set out to survey the whole of knowledge, the totality of its forms, are we justified in restricting our attention to this end, in disregarding the beginning and the middle? All conceptual knowledge is necessarily based on intuitive knowledge, and all intuitive knowledge on perceptive knowledge. Should we also seek the achievement of the symbolic function in these preliminary stages of conceptual thinking, whose peculiarity seems to be that in place of mediated, discursive knowledge, they contain an immediate certainty? Would it not be an offense against this immediacy, a totally unjustified intellectualization of intuition and perception, if we sought to extend the hegemony of the symbol over them? Although we encounter the problem of the symbol at the very threshold of pure conceptual knowledge, must we not recognize on the other hand that it begins only on this threshold? What seems to distinguish conceptual knowledge once and for all from perception and intuition is precisely that it can content itself with mere representative signs, while perception and intuition have an entirely different and even opposite relation to their object. They are supposed at least to stand in direct contact with this object. To question or efface this dividing line between the immediacy of perception or intuition and the mediacy of logical-discursive thinking would be to disregard one of the securest insights of epistemology to abandon a truly classical distinction, growing out of a centuries-old tradition. In well known sentences which form the introduction to the Transcendental Aesthetic Kant, too, has fixated this distinction and made it a point of departure for all his further epistemological analyses. And yet, if we follow the guiding lines prescribed by our fundamental problem, a new question arises for us at this point. From the standpoint of our problem the dividing line between the different faculties on which theoretical knowledge is based and from which it is built up must be drawn in an essentially different way from that of traditional psychology or epistemology. The analysis of language and myth has granted us an insight into fundamental forms of symbolic apprehension and formation, which by no means coincide with the form of conceptual abstract thinking but possess and preserve an entirely different character. From this it follows that symbolism as such, understood in its entire breadth and universality, is by no means restricted to those systems of pure conceptual signs represented by exact science, and particularly by mathematics and mathematical natural science. At first sight the worlds of language and myth seem utterly incommensurate with the world of conceptual signs: and yet a common determination is manifested in all these worlds, insofar as they all belong to the sphere of representation. Thus the specific difference between them does not preclude membership in a common genus, but rather presupposes and requires it. The image world of myth, the phonetic structures of language, and the signs employed by exact knowledge—each determine a specific dimension of representation—and only taken in their totality do these dimensions constitute the whole of the spiritual horizon. We lose our eye for the whole if we restrict the symbolic function in advance to the plane of conceptual, abstract knowledge. We must recognize rather that this function does not belong to a particular stage of the theoretical world view, but conditions and sustains this view in its totality. Not only the realm of conceptual thinking, but those of intuition and perception are so conditioned. Intuition and perception also partake of spontaneity and not of mere receptivity; they show an ability not only to receive impressions from outside, but also to shape them in accordance with their own specific laws of formation. Thus those three original sources of knowledge which according to the *Critique of Pure Reason* make all experience possible—sensation, imagination, and understanding—prove, when viewed from the standpoint of the problem of symbolism, to be interrelated and linked to one another in a new way. This relationship by no means negates the difference between them: the boundaries between the different spheres are not effaced or blurred, but in spite of these boundaries a new order is now established, a fixed connection between the various phases through which the theoretical consciousness must pass before it arrives at its conclusive and definitive form.

But before we can follow this gradual progress in detail, we must first answer a preliminary question of a general methodological character. When we inquire into the form and structure of theoretical consciousness, the use of this term itself involves difficulties of all kinds. For the concept of consciousness seems to be the very Proteus of philosophy. It appears in most divergent spheres and never discloses the same shape, undergoing incessant changes of meaning. It is claimed by metaphysics and epistemology, by empirical psychology as well as pure phenomenology. This multiform inner relationship gives rise to continuous border warfare between the various regions of philosophical thought. For our own fundamental question the danger of becoming involved in these difficulties is particularly acute, since it is by no means established from the start to which of the conflicting fields our problem belongs. The question which the Philosophy of Symbolic Forms sets itself has strong ties with other questions which are traditionally assigned to epistemology or psychology, phenomenology or metaphysics. Although it may lay claim to a kind of methodological autonomy, although it must attempt to secure its own independent area of operation, it can nowhere dispense with a constant view of all these fields. And if the resulting connection is not to produce an amalgam, the sense in which it is to be sought and understood must be clear. Let us first of all consider psychology. Here the dividing line seems easy to draw as long as we see the task of psychology solely in the empirical-causal explanation of the phenomena of consciousness. For like pure epistemology in particular, the Philosophy of Symbolic Forms in general inquires not into the empirical source of consciousness but into its pure content. Instead of pursuing its temporal, generating causes, the Philosophy of Symbolic Forms is oriented solely toward what "is in it"— toward apprehending and describing its structural forms. Language, myth, and theoretical knowledge are all taken as fundamental forms of the objective spirit, whose being it must be possible to disclose and understand purely as such, independently of the question of its "becoming." We are in the realm of the universal transcendental question, that of the method which takes the *quid facti* of the particular forms of consciousness as its starting point only and goes on to inquire after their significance, their *quid juris*. On the other hand, Kant himself always stressed that this transcendental method contains within it two different directions of inquiry. "The one refers to the *objects* of the pure understanding and should represent and make comprehensible the objective validity of its a priori concepts—the other aims to view the pure understanding itself according to its own potentialities and the cognitive powers on which it rests, that is to say, to examine it in a subjective aspect." He could in this way connect the subjective with the objective deduction, without fear of a relapse into psychological idealism, because for him the meaning of subjectivity had undergone a corresponding transformation. For him pure subjectivity no longer pertained to the individual and empirically accidental; on the contrary, it had become the source and origin of all true universality. The subjectivity of space and time serves to ground and secure the objectivity of mathematics, of the principles of geometry and arithmetic. And similarly he goes back to the transcendental unity of apperception only in order to account for the unity of nature as an aggregate of universal and necessary laws. In this sense he eliminates the antithesis between subject and object by disclosing their necessary interrelation in building and constituting the object of experience: the conflict between the two gives way to a pure correlation. But this conflict threatens to break out anew when, instead of addressing the question only to scientific cognition, we direct it toward all the forms of "world understanding." Here again we take subjectivity as a totality of functions, out of which the phenomenon of a world and its determinate order of meaning is actually built up for us. But can this meaning—whatever significance and validity we may impute to it—lay claim to the same kind of universality that prevailed in the sphere of theoretical knowledge and its principles and axioms? Or is apriority not here in constant danger of slipping down to another plane, to the dimension of the merely subjective? That thinker who made the first attempt to adhere strictly to Kant's method, but at the same time to extend it beyond the sphere of the theoretical-scientific world view seems to lay himself open to this very danger. The leading thought of Wilhelm von Humboldt's analysis of language is that the spiritual meaning of speech can never be fully appreciated if we consider solely the objective factor in it—if we take it as a system of signs serving solely to represent objects and their relations. He stresses rather that

> the difference in the interpreting mood gives to the same sounds a different intensity of meaning; in all expression, something not absolutely determined by the words seem as it were to overflow from them. . . . Neither in concepts nor in language itself does anything ever stand isolated. But concepts actually become related only when the personality acts in inner unity, when full subjectivity radiates toward complete objectivity. When the soul actually awakens to the feeling that language is not merely a means of exchange for mutual understanding, but a real world, which the spirit must set between itself and objects by an inner exertion of its powers, the soul is on its way

to finding more and more in language and to putting more and more into it.[1]

Here unmistakably a different kind of subjectivity is invoked—subjectivity which cannot be formulated in principles and developed into a system of synthetic a priori principles—as was the case in theoretical knowledge. Language is not taken solely as an abstract form of thought, but must be understood as a concrete form of life; it must be explained not so much by objects as by the diversity of the interpreting mood. Is this shift possible unless we surrender ourselves to the guidance of psychology—does psychology not show us the only possible way which can lead us from the realm of abstract subjectivity to that of concrete subjectivity and thus effect the break through from thought form to life form?

In the present situation of philosophy, no clear and satisfying answer can be given to this question unless the concept of psychology itself is first examined and its method as well as its tasks clearly defined. It is the essential achievement of Natorp that, on the basis of Kant's general presuppositions, he did just this—that he built up a general psychology in accordance with critical method. Over against a psychology whose supreme ambition it was to vie with the natural sciences and imitate their method, the method of empirical observation and exact measurement, Natorp turned backward and inward. For him consciousness is not a part of reality, which can be treated and investigated by the methods valid for all objective knowledge; rather, it is the foundation and condition of reality. This position implies that psychology, insofar as it aspires to be purely a doctrine of "consciousness," does not stand as one among other members in the system of the critical philosophy, but that it represents as it were the polar opposite and methodological counterpart to all of them. For all the other links in the system—logic as well as ethics and aesthetics— are merely diverse factors in the one great task of objectivization. They build up a realm of objects or values, an aggregate of laws or of norms; and for these laws or norms they demand a definite measure and form of objective validity. Psychology, on the other hand, does not deal with a being which is already determined in this way, but inquires what must precede and underly every such determination. A psychology that is soundly understood cannot attempt to know consciousness by describing it as some sort of analogue of objective reality: it must rather see the fact

1. Humboldt, *Einleitung zum Kawi-Werk*, in *Gesammelte Schriften*, 7, 176.

of consciousness as something irreducible and ultimate, which can only be disclosed as such but which cannot be explained in accordance with the categorial forms of our knowledge of things, and in particular not in accordance with the categories of substantiality and causality. Thus the object of psychology, insofar as one may use the term, is in no way comparable to the objects of nature, to "things" in space and to processes and changes in time, nor does it in any way contest their rank. For the object of psychology is not itself a phenomenon, it is not something that exists in space and time, but is solely the pure fact of appearance itself. That such an "appearing" takes place, that there are phenomena which are related to a perceptive, intuitive or thinking ego and which are represented in this ego: this primary fact is here the sole problem.

But this makes it utterly impossible to articulate consciousness with nature in the manner of Aristotle, or like the overwhelming majority of modern psychologists, to consider it as juxtaposed to nature or even encompassing it, and yet to treat it with the same logical instruments, and thus actually to represent it as another nature. There is perhaps a second "world" over against that of theoretical knowledge ("nature" or "experience"), and it is the ethical world, as in Kant; a third world is that of art; and perhaps the world of religion represents a superworld over all the others. But the inner world of consciousness can no longer be logically subordinated in any way to these three or four, or set beside them or over them; to all of them, rather, to objectivizations of any kind and degree, it represents as it were a counteraction, a turning inward, the ultimate concentration of them all into the consciousness that experiences them. It is this ultimate concentration which the concepts of the psychical and of consciousness with its wholly concrete character must not merely ascertain as if it were something already given but which they must exhibit and in general develop.[2]

This view of the concept and task of psychology places us for the first time on ground where a fruitful exchange is possible between psychology and our own systematic problem, the problem of the Philosophy of Symbolic Forms. But here the question arises: how can we penetrate to this pure inner world of consciousness, this ultimate concentration of all spiritual life, if in exploring and describing it we must avoid all the con-

2. Paul G. Natorp, *Allgemeine Psychologie nach kritischer Methode* (Tübingen, 1912), pp. 19 f.

cepts and criteria which were created for the exposition of objective reality? Where shall we find a means of seizing the intangible—of expressing what has itself not yet entered into fixed form, whether of an intuitive spatial and temporal, or of a purely intellectual or ethical or aesthetic order? If consciousness is nothing but pure potentiality for all objective formations, the mere receptivity and readiness for them, as it were, it is impossible to see how this potentiality itself can be treated as a fact, indeed in a certain sense as the primary fact of all spiritual life. For facticity always implies more than mere determinability; it implies some mode of determination, the imprint of some form. Natorp would counter such misgivings by pointing out that actually "awareness," as he understands it, can never be immediately given or discovered. The inner world of which we are speaking is accessible neither to direct observation nor to any other instrument of empirical psychology; nor is it simply postulated by constructive thought as a hypothetical basis of explanation. For both facts and bases of explanation exist only within objectivizing thought itself, not outside it and before it. Here, however, our aim is not to remain within objectivizing thought and to establish the locus of consciousness from this standpoint; rather, we have undertaken a fundamental change in orientation. Instead of surrendering ourselves to the progress of knowledge toward its object, we are seeking a goal which, in a manner of speaking, is situated behind all objective knowledge. It is evident that if this paradoxical aim can be achieved at all, it is only indirectly. We can never lay bare the immediate life and being of consciousness as such. But it is a significant task to seek a new aspect and meaning for the unhalting process of objectivization by exploring it in a twofold direction: from *terminus a quo* to *terminus ad quem* and back again. In Natorp's opinion, it is only by a continuous back and forth, by this twofold direction of method that the object of psychology can be made visible as such. It comes to light only when a new reconstructive effort is opposed to the constructive effort of mathematics and natural science, and of ethics and aesthetics as well. True, this reconstruction will always be lacking in independence, since it must presuppose the constructive building as already completed. But even though it does not stop here, even though it looks behind this constructive edifice, it cannot on the other hand raise the question without taking the construction itself as a point of departure, without starting from what it has achieved and secured. This psychology, as Natorp sees it, seems engaged in a mere labor of Penelope, unraveling the intricate fabric woven by the various forms of objectivization. In this respect, it opposes a minus direction to the plus direction of pure theory, ethics, and aesthetics. Of course both terms should here be taken not in an absolute but in a purely relative sense.

> The relation of opposition becomes a relation of reciprocity, which at the same time signifies a necessary correlation. But in this correlation the minus direction no longer means a diminution, a regression to the nullity of consciousness. To the peripheral broadening there rather corresponds a deepening at the center. This to be sure is a referring back to the source, yet by it nothing of what has been gained by the objectivizing trend of knowledge is lost, but rather, what seemed lost, what was set aside as subjective in the pejorative sense, is taken up again and reinstated in its full rights, while all that is newly won is preserved and connected with the rest, so that the total content of consciousness is not reduced but increased, enriched, and intensified.[3]

Here strictly critical reflection has resulted in the drawing up of a truly universal program for a phenomenology of consciousness. The significance of this program is by no means diminished by the fact that it was not given to Natorp to realize it fully in the spirit in which it was projected. Down to the last years of his life and his very last works, he struggled unremittingly to carry through his plan. His General Psychology remained a fragment—and he himself later explicitly called its first and only completed volume a mere introduction to the statement of the problem, a "foundation of a foundation." What led him to strive beyond this beginning was above all the circumstance that the farther he advanced, the more clearly the polydimensionality of the spiritual world revealed itself to him. This polydimensionality forbids us to represent the course of objectivizing and subjectivizing thought, of constructive and reconstructive knowledge by the image of a straight line and of gauging this course by the twofold, plus-minus direction of the line. The difference between the spheres of spiritual meaning is specific and not quantitative—and precisely this specific difference is blurred as soon as we attempt to define it as a difference between a mere "more" or "less," between a plus or minus direction of objectivization. We cannot project the totality of the possible stages in the objectivization of the spirit upon a single straight line without obscuring essential traits. In the last period

3. Natorp, *Allgemeine Psychologie*, p. 71.

of his thinking, when he was attempting to build and develop a concrete system of philosophy, Natorp himself clearly recognized this and admitted it without reserve.[4] An obvious difficulty arises as soon as we attempt to fit the concrete whole of the Symbolic Forms into the general framework offered by Natorp's psychology. It is evident that the over-all plan of this psychology must allot an important role to the analysis of language, for determination by the word is an indispensable preparation for determination by the pure concept. And Natorp's psychology, in its program at least, expressly recognized this importance of language. It stresses that an objectivizing power and achievement is contained not only in the scientifically fixated concept or in the scientifically grounded judgment, but in every linguistic sentence.

> The immediacy of consciousness, one's own, not to mention that of others, cannot be grasped . . . immediately, in itself, but only in its "utterance," which as utterance [*Äusserung*] is indeed always alienation [*Entäusserung*], a stepping out of one's own sphere into the sphere of objectivity (at any stage). . . . It is certain that there is here a rich material for investigation, which should not be neglected by the psychologist; in their vocabulary, their syntactical relations, in each and every one of their components, the highly developed languages contain an inexhaustible treasure of primitive cognitions. . . . Cognitions, hence objectifications, which, within the limits of their own purpose, are scarcely inferior in sharpness and pregnancy to those of science.[5]

Even though science, from the heights of its own theoretical ideal of cognition, may look down on these objectifications as incomplete and preliminary, from the standpoint of psychology they represent independent and highly important stages, which must be investigated and fully recognized in their particularity.[6] But in its actual development Natorp's psychology does not do justice to this declaration of principles, for wherever the process of objectification is described, the description is oriented toward the ultimate and supreme phase that is manifested in scientific thinking and knowledge. The very definition of the subject-object relation is derived from this and this alone. The direction of objectivity coincides for

4. Cf. esp. the posthumous *Vorlesungen über praktische Philosophie* (Erlangen, 1925). For details see my "Paul Natorp," *Kant-Studien*, 30 (1925), 273–98.

5. Natorp, *Allgemeine Psychologie*, p. 99.

6. Ibid., p. 221.

Natorp with that of the necessary and universally valid—and this last in turn with that of law. Thus for him the concept of law includes all objectification—regardless of its form and stage. For him it is not only in natural science that every particular must be referred to the universal of law and taken and evaluated only as an instance of the law, but the same mode of determination applies also to ethics and aesthetics. Ethical and aesthetic knowledge also seek the law, even if they seek it only in and for the particular: and it is precisely in the degree that they attain it that they achieve the objective validity toward which they too are always striving.[7] Thus for Natorp not only logic but also ethics and even aesthetics and the philosophy of religion belong to the intellectual sciences—and all of them, accordingly, are objectifying in the same sense, in fact in a still more radical sense, than the sciences dealing with concrete objects. "While the latter . . . strive to draw from the phenomena of their field the laws of these phenomena, the former inquire after the laws which determine the entire procedure of this concrete knowledge of laws; they thus carry the work of reduction to laws, that is, the constructive process of scientific knowledge, one step farther back and one step higher into the abstract.[8]

But even if we were to grant that this applies without reservation to the disciplines of ethics, aesthetics, or philosophy of religion, does it therefore apply to the spiritual content toward which they are directed, to morality, art, and religion themselves? Do they, too, move in the sphere of laws, or does the objectification peculiar to them not follow a very different guide—do they not seek an objectivity of form rather than of law? Can the world of *praxis* and *poiesis*—to use the systematic concepts which Natorp later coined—be simply subsumed under the concept of law as the primary concept of theory? And even in the field of theoretical objectification, the role here assigned to the concept of law becomes problematic as soon as the inquiry—as Natorp's own basic principles demand—is directed not toward the concepts of scientific knowledge but toward the concepts of language. For these reveal throughout a form of determination which is by no means identical with determination in and through law. The universality of linguistic concepts does not stand on the same plane as the universality of scientific, and particularly of natural-scientific laws: the one is not merely an extension of the other; on the contrary, they move in different paths and express different trends of spiritual formation.

7. Ibid., p. 72.
8. Ibid., p. 94.

These trends must be kept sharply separate, each in its own peculiar determinacy, if the task of reconstruction is to succeed. And indeed it will be seen that the representative function which gives language its meaning and character is not identical with the significative function which governs the concepts of scientific knowledge, and that the latter is not a mere development—that is, a rectilinear continuation of the former, but that the two represent qualitatively different modes of signification. And a difference in the subject, in the specific attitude of consciousness, must correspond to this difference in objective formation. If we are to gain a concrete view of the full objectivity of the spirit on the one hand and of its full subjectivity on the other, we must seek to carry out the methodological correlation, which Natorp sets forth in principle, in every field of spiritual endeavor. It then becomes clear that the three principal trends of objectification which were put forward by Natorp in close adherence to the trichotomy of the Kantian Critiques and which provide as it were the fixed system of coordinates for his general orientation are not adequate. Our inquiry is driven beyond the three dimensions of the logical, ethical, and aesthetic: it must, in particular, draw the forms of language and myth into its sphere, if it aspires to find its way back to the primary subjective sources, the original attitudes and formative modes of consciousness. It is from this perspective that we now approach our question: the question of the structure of the perceptive, intuitive, and cognitive consciousness. We shall attempt to elucidate it without surrendering to the method either of scientific, causal-explicative psychology or of pure description. We start rather from the problems of the objective spirit, from the formations in which it consists and exists; however, we shall not stop with them as a mere fact; we shall attempt by means of reconstructive analysis to find our way back to their elementary presuppositions, the conditions of their possibility.

Chapter 2

The Phenomenon of Expression as the
Basic Factor in the Perceptive Consciousness

THE PROBLEM of perception presents itself to theoretical philosophy under a twofold aspect: it may be considered from a psychological and from
an epistemological standpoint. Throughout the history of philosophy the
two have been in constant conflict; but the more sharply the oppositions
develop, the more evident it seems that here precisely are the two focal
points around which the whole problem of perception must necessarily
move. The question is concerned either with the origin and development
of perception or with its objective significance and validity, either with
its genesis or with what it accomplishes for objective knowledge as a
whole. However the methodological rivalry between these questions may
have been decided, regardless of which one priority was accorded to, one
thing seemed certain: that they exhaustively define the interest of theoretical philosophy. For just as experience as a whole breaks down into two
sharply divided areas, an inside and an outside, so we seem to have
fully recognized the essence of perception as soon as we succeed in assigning it to its appropriate place in these two spheres, as soon as we have
apprehended it on the one hand as a psychological process subject to
definite rules, and on the other hand as the foundation, the first element, of
theoretical objectification.

In the first respect the task seems to be fulfilled if we can disclose the
development of perception and the causal laws governing this development. As *special* empirical laws, they can be found and defined only
within the framework of a general explanation of nature. Here the scientific picture of nature, particularly that of physics, must necessarily serve
as our starting point. The question is not directed toward the truth, the
objective validity of this picture itself, which must rather be postulated and

presupposed at the very outset. The concept of natural law and the general categories of our knowledge of nature are taken for granted; on this basis, the special explanation of perception is sought. Here, consequently, the psychology of perception will inevitably culminate in physiology and physics. Psychology becomes psychophysics, whose first task is to establish a dependency between the world of perceptions and that of objective stimuli. Whether this dependency is taken as a causal relation or as a functional correspondence, stimulus and sensation are in some way attuned to each other and must accordingly agree in certain fundamental structural relations. From this there spontaneously follows a parallelism of articulation between the world of stimuli and the world of perception and sensation. A certain sensation is always correlated with a certain stimulus in accordance with an assumption of a universal constancy. To this way of thinking there cannot be a recognition of any strictly original factors in perception: for the whole meaning and content of perception consist in the faithful reflection and reproduction of the relations of the outside world. Even the classification of perception will exactly follow the articulation of stimuli. The determinations of perception merely reflect differences in the physical causes of perception: the physical differentiation of the sensory organs necessarily leads to an analogous division in the sensuous phenomena.

The critical formulation of the question would seem to be the exact opposite of this. It moves not from things to phenomena but from phenomena to things. Accordingly, it must look on perception and its properties not as conditioned from outside, but as conditioning—that is, as a constitutive factor in our knowledge of things. But precisely because it envisages perception solely in this function it inevitably sees it from the very start in a definite light, in a definite theoretical perspective. Perception is no longer determined by the outside world as its cause: rather, it is determined by the aim appointed for it. And this aim is none other than to make possible the experience, that is, the science of nature. The significance of perception has changed completely; it is no longer the copy of an existing world, but in a sense the prototype of the natural object. It already contains this object in a kind of schematic sketch but cannot follow up the determination of the object except by the application of the functions of the pure understanding to that empirical material given in perception. This explains how here, too, perception is wont to be taken from the start as a kind of objective structure in every way analogous to the structure of nature, of the world of things. To the attributes of things correspond definite qualities of perception. Perception seems already articulated in itself and divided off according to certain basic forms and fundamental classes. But this means that the thing-quality category, which is a constitutive condition of the theoretical concept of nature, is injected into the pure description, the phenomenology of perception. It is described as a manifold—one into which order and cohesion may be brought only by the synthetic function of pure intuition and the synthetic unities of the pure understanding. And yet, on closer scrutiny, this entity, which ostensibly is merely determinable, itself contains highly characteristic features of theoretical determination. True, it is still by no means the real—the complete and definitive—object, but it nevertheless contains an intention toward it. And through this orientation toward the object it has imperceptibly become oriented according to the object. Thus, however far back pure critical epistemology may carry its description of immediate perception, this description is always subject to a universal norm which is itself derived from the concept and general task of epistemology itself. The essence of perception is defined according to its objective validity. But thereby a specific interest of cognition is injected into the exposition of perception. To understand it now means to apprehend it as one link in the structure of the knowledge of reality—to assign it to its appropriate place within the totality of the functions which form the basis for the relation of all our knowledge to the object.

But perception assumes an essentially different form for us as soon as we decide not to take it exclusively in this one aspect, in this prevision of the nature of theoretical science. True, any attempt to detach it from all intellectual reference, to cut it off from the totality of possible significatory intentions and represent it in its naked facticity—any such attempt seems from the start absurd and methodologically hopeless. Even sensation can never be conceived as preintellectual or nonintellectual; on the contrary, it "is" and exists only insofar as it is articulated according to determinate functions of meaning. But these functions are by no means limited to the world of theoretical meaning—in the restricted sense. To depart from the specific conditions of theoretical-scientific knowledge is not altogether to leave the realm of form. We do not thereby sink back into a mere chaos; rather, an ideal cosmos once more surrounds us. It was a cosmos of this kind that appeared to us with progressive clarity in the building up of language and the mythical world. And from this results a new and essentially broader aspect under which to investigate and evaluate perception itself. Now it reveals certain basic traits which are by no means directed from the outset toward the object of nature, or toward the knowledge of the outside world, but which disclose an entirely different direction. Myth, in particular, shows us a world which is far from being without structure, immanent articulation, yet does not know the organization of reality according to things and attributes. Here all configurations of being show a peculiar fluidity; they are differentiated without being separated from one another. Each of them is, as it were, ready at any moment to transform itself into another, seemingly antithetical configuration. Mythical metamorphosis is bound by no logical law of identity, nor does it find a limit in any fixed constancy of classes. For it there are no logical classes, no genera in the sense of things which are separated by definite and unalterable characteristics and which must remain forever in this separation. Here, on the contrary, all the boundary lines drawn by our empirical concepts of genera and species keep shifting and vanishing. Not only does one and the same being perpetually take new forms; at one and the same moment of its existence it also contains and combines within itself an abundance of different and even mutually opposed forms of being. This peculiar fluidity of the mythical world would not be comprehensible if immediate perception, purely as such and before any intellectual interpretation, contained within it, by a kind of necessity, a division of the world into fixed classes. If this were the case, myth would transgress at every step not only against the laws of logic but also against the elementary facts of perception. In truth, however, there is so little conflict between the content of perception and the form of myth that the two grow together and fuse into a thoroughly concrete unity. Where we do not reflect on myth but truly live in it, there is still no such cleft between the actual reality of perception and the world of the mythical fantasy. The mythical structures here bear the color of full, immediate perception—and on the other hand this perception itself is as though bathed in the light of mythical formation. Such an involvement becomes understandable only if perception itself discloses certain original traits in which, one might say, it approaches the mode and direction of myth. Developmental psychology has characterized primitive perception as diffuse and complex. But even this diffusion, this lack of differentiation and organization, is tenable only if we tacitly apply to primitive perception a definite intellectual standard, the standard of theoretical formation. In itself primitive perception is far from being inarticulate or blurred, but its differences lie on a totally different plane from that of the objective view, the view of reality as an aggregate of things and attributes. Consequently, if the philosophy of mythology is to meet the fundamental demand first made by Schelling, if it is to understand myth not only allegorically as a kind of primitive physics or history, but tautegorically as a symbol of independent significance and form,[1] it must do justice to that form of *perceptive experience* in which myth is originally rooted and from which it forever draws new nourishment. Without such a grounding in an original mode of perception, myth would hover in the void; instead of being a universal form of spiritual manifestation, it would be a kind of spiritual disease; however widely distributed, it would still be an accidental and pathological phenomenon.

But actually we cannot fail to perceive this correlate of the mythical world view, we cannot fail to perceive its foundation in a definite trend of perception, if we bear in mind that though the *theoretical* world view has in many ways modified this foundation and overlaid it, so to speak, with formations of different mode and origin, it has by no means dispelled it entirely. Even this theoretical world view does not know reality altogether as an aggregate of things and a complex of changes governed and linked together by strictly causal laws. It "has" the world in still another and more original sense, insofar as the world is revealed to it as a phenomenon of pure expression. We must go back to this stratum of expression in our reconstruction, for this is the ground from which myth grew, and an understanding of it is indispensable to us in explaining and deriving certain features of the empirical world view. For theoretical reality itself was not originally experienced as a totality of physical bodies, endowed with definite attributes and qualities. Rather, there is a kind of *experience* of reality which is situated wholly outside this form of scientific explanation and interpretation. It is present wherever the being that is apprehended in perception confronts us not as a reality of things, of mere objects, but as a kind of presence of living subjects. How such an experience of alien subjects, an experience of the "thou," is possible may present itself as a difficult metaphysical or epistemological question. But this question does not concern the pure phenomenology of perception—which is interested solely in the facticity, the *quid facti* of perception—and must not be allowed to mark off its road in advance. In any event, immersion in the phenomenon of perception shows us one thing—that the perception of life

1. Cf. above, 2, 4.

is not exhausted by the mere perception of things, that the experience of the "thou" can never be dissolved into an experience of the mere "it," or reduced to it even by the most complex conceptual mediations. Even from a purely genetic standpoint there seems to be no doubt to which of the two forms of perception we should accord priority. The farther back we trace perception, the greater becomes the preeminence of the "thou" form over the "it" form, and the more plainly the purely expressive character takes precedence over the matter or thing-character. The understanding of expression is essentially earlier than the knowledge of things.

And even psychological empiricism, where it strove not to fit the facts into a preconceived constructive schema but to follow them without bias, confirmed this relationship. Attempts to understand and describe the animal consciousness have shown that it would be an error to transfer with any immediacy to the world of animals the schema in which human perception can be applied. The dangers of such introjection are obvious—and it is understandable that a certain school of modern psychologists should believe that the only way to avert them is to ignore the whole problem. The behaviorist trend grew out of this negation, out of what we might call a methodological asceticism. It seemed safer in any case to deny the animal any kind of consciousness than to describe this consciousness anthropomorphically, in accordance with specifically human categories. Descartes with perfect consistency was only following the prescriptions of his own logic when in his psychology he denied animals any conscious life and made them into mere machines. For him consciousness is essentially the fundamental act by which the ego apprehends itself—the act by which the ego apprehends and constitutes itself as a thinking being. Without this fundamental act of pure reason there can be no act of sensation, perception, or representation. Insofar as there is any psychic reality, it can be conceived only in a definite rational formation and order: for the "clear and distinct idea" is the basic presupposition and the only valid criterion for all postulation of existence. It seems strange at first sight that the Cartesian thesis, which grew from such wholly rationalist foundations, should have been revived in modern psychology by those who like to think of themselves as radically empiricist. But it is no accident that the ways of rational deduction should meet with those of pure experience—insofar as by pure experience we mean the method of inductive observation and comparison. For precisely this induction, as a method of objectivizing natural science, is bound to very definite logical presuppositions, which show it to be a work of the intellect, of the thinking apprehension of reality. Thus its criteria of reality and truth are qualitatively no different from those of its apparent antithesis, the deductive method: rather, the two poles, by their very antagonism, establish a thoroughly unitary principle and ideal of knowledge. And from the standpoint of this ideal of knowledge, it is true, the world of animal consciousness remains problematic: it cannot be disclosed because it cannot be proved. But a different picture presents itself if we broaden our perspective and draw the line of demarcation differently. For although we may not inject the forms of our world of things and the intellectual categories at the base of its structure into the animal world, an entirely different relationship emerges as soon as we remember that for man, too, this intellectually conditioned world is far from being the only world in which he is and lives. If we were to reserve the concept of consciousness for the designation of the reflexive acts of knowing on the one hand and for objective intuition on the other, we should run the risk not only of doubting the possibility of animal consciousness but also of disregarding or disowning an entire province of human consciousness. If we seek to go back to the earliest stages of consciousness, the view that the world was here experienced as a chaos of unordered sensations, in each of which a definite objective quality such as light or dark, warm or cold was apprehended, proves to be absolutely untenable. "If this theory of original chaos were sound," remarks Koffka, for example,

we should expect that "simple" stimuli would first arouse the child's attention: for it is the simple which it will first be possible to separate out of the chaos and which will first enter into other combinations. This is contrary to all experience. The stimuli which most influence the behavior of the child are not those which seem particularly simple to the psychologist because simple sensations correspond to them. The first differentiated sound reactions respond to the human voice, hence to highly complex stimuli (and "sensations"). The infant is not interested in simple colors, but in human faces. . . . And as early as the middle of the first year of life the effect of the parents' facial expression on the child can be established. For the chaos theory, the phenomenon corresponding to a human face is merely a confusion of the most divergent sensations of light, dark, and color, which moreover are in constant flux, changing with every movement of the person in question or the child himself, and with the lighting. And yet by the second month the child knows his mother's face; by the middle of his first year he reacts to a friendly or an angry face, and so differently that there is no doubt that what was given to him phenomenally was the friendly or angry face and not any distribution of light and dark. To explain this by experience, to assume that these phenomena arose by combination of simple optical sensations with each other and with pleasant or unpleasant consequences from the original chaos of sensation, seems impossible. . . . We are left with the opinion that phenomena such as "friendliness" or "unfriendliness" are extremely primitive—even more primitive, for example, than that of a blue spot.[2]

It is only on the basis of this view, only if we recognize that experiences of pure expression are not of a mediated but of an original character, that we may conceivably strike a bridge to the phenomena of the animal consciousness. For this consciousness, particularly at its higher levels, seems to embrace an abundance of such experiences, and with astonishingly fine shadings. With regard to the chimpanzees, for example, W. Koehler writes:

There is a very great diversity of expressive movements, through which the animals "understand one another," although we cannot speak of any kind of language between them and cannot say that any particular movements or sounds possess a significative and representative function. We psychologists, who tend to reduce such understanding in man to analogies or reproductive completion from his own conscious experience, are here thrown into a theoretical perplexity which contrasts strangely with the self-evidence and certainty of the actual process of mutual understanding among the animals themselves.

This perplexity, this discrepancy between what a particular psychological methodology demands as an element of psychological life and the relatively first and original element that experiences seems to give us appears to be avoidable only through a fundamental change in our whole

2. Kurt Koffka, *Die Grundlagen der psychischen Entwicklung* (Osterwieck am Harz, 1921), pp. 94 ff. See analogous observations and conclusions in Karl Bühler, *Die geistige Entwicklung des Kindes* (Jena, 1929), pp. 83 ff. Also in W. Stern, *Die Psychologie der frühen Kindheit bis zum sechsten Lebensjahre* (Leipzig, 1923), p. 312; Eng. trans. by Anna Barwell, *Psychology of Early Childhood up to the Sixth Year of Age* (New York, 1924).

formulation of the question. "May it not be peculiar to certain formations," Koehler continues, "that they essentially bear the character of the terrible, the forbidding, etc., not because an innate ad hoc mechanism enabled them to do so but because, in a given state of the psyche, certain Gestalt conditions necessarily and in accordance with an empirical law produce the character of the terrible, while others call forth that of the charming, the awkward or the energetic and severe?"[3] Questions of this kind show how the modern psychology of perception is everywhere driven into a new territory which, to be sure, it sometimes seems to enter only hesitantly. This field can be truly opened up only if psychology frees itself once and for all from the sensationalist theory of perception which has dominated it for centuries. Sensationalism obstructs a free view of these problems in two ways. By positing the sensory "impression" as the basic element of all psychology it negates the actual life of perception in a twofold sense. In the "upper" sense, in respect to the problems of thought and knowledge, the entire significative content of perception, insofar as it is recognized at all, must now be transposed back into its sensuous "matter" and derived from it. Perception becomes an aggregate: it arises from the simple confluence and associative linking of impressions. Thus the peculiar theoretical laws governing the structure of the world of perception and the purely intellectual form of this world are misunderstood. And this misunderstanding is the starting point of a dialectic peculiar to sensationalist psychology. For in limiting the rights of the intellect as far as possible, it does not escape from its domination. Precisely this restriction of the legitimate claim of the intellect makes the intellect assert itself at another point, makes it attempt to break through "illegitimately." It now slips unnoticed into the determination of pure perception as such, which it "intellectualizes" where it seemingly threatened to "sensify." For to dissolve the world of perception into a sum of particular impressions is to underestimate the part played in it not only by the "higher," intellectual functions, but also by the strong, instinctive substrate on which it rests. The sensationalist theory of perception retains, as it were, only the bare trunk of the tree of knowledge—it sees neither its crown, which rises free into the air, into the ether of pure thought, nor its roots, which sink into the earth. These roots do not lie in the simple ideas of sensation and reflection, which empiricist psychology and epistemology regard as the ultimate

3. W. Koehler, "Zur Psychologie des Schimpansen," *Psychologische Forschung*, 1 (1922), 27 f., 39. Cf. Eng. trans. by Ella Winter, *The Mentality of Apes* (New York, 1925).

foundation of all knowledge of reality. They consist not in the "elements" of sensation but in original and immediate characters of expression. Concrete perception does not wholly detach itself from these characters even where it resolutely and consciously takes the road of pure objectivization. It never dissolves into a mere complex of sensuous qualities—such as light or dark, cold or warm—but is always attuned to a specific expressive tone; it is never directed exclusively toward the "what" of the object but encompasses the mode of its total manifestation—the character of the luring or menacing, the familiar or uncanny, the soothing or frightening, which lies in this phenomenon purely as such and independently of its objective interpretation.

But here we shall not continue along the path by which psychology is gradually finding its way back to this profound stratum of the pure experience of expression. Ludwig Klages in particular has proved to be a leader in this field, advancing from the appreciation and interpretation of these experiences to a general transformation of the method of the psychology of perception, thence to a revised formulation of its problem. But here again we see ourselves impelled to take another way than that of immediate observation and description. The course of our investigation leads us, as always, through the world of forms, through the region of the objective spirit, from where, by a process of reconstruction, we seek access to the realm of subjectivity. And in view of the findings of our earlier investigation there can be no doubt where we should apply our lever. In dealing with the problems and the phenomenology of the pure experience of expression, we can entrust ourselves to the leadership and orientation neither of conceptual knowledge nor of language. For both of these are primarily in the service of theoretical objectivization: they build up the world of the logos as a thought and spoken logos. Thus in respect to expression, they take a centrifugal rather than a centripetal direction. Myth, however, places us in the living center of this sphere, for its particularity consists precisely in showing us a mode of world formation which is independent of all modes of mere objectivization. It does not recognize the dividing line between real and unreal, between reality and appearance, which theoretical objectivization draws and must draw. All its structure moves on a single plane of being, which is wholly adequate to it. Here there is neither kernel nor shell; here there is no substance, no permanent and enduring something which underlies the changing, ephemeral appearances, the mere "accidents." The mythical consciousness does not deduce essence from appearance, it possesses—it has—the essence in the appearance. The essence does not recede behind the appearance but is manifested in it; it does not cloak itself in the appearance but in the appearance is given to itself. Here the phenomenon as it is given in any moment never has a character of mere representation, it is one of authentic presence: here a reality is not "actualized" through the mediation of the phenomenon but is present in full actuality in the phenomenon. When water is sprinkled in rain magic, it does not serve as a mere symbol or analogue of the "real" rain; it is attached to the real rain by the bond of an original sympathy. The demon of the rain is tangibly and corporeally alive and present in every drop of water.[4] Thus in the world of myth every phenomenon is always and essentially an incarnation. Here the essence is not distributed over a number of possible modes of representation, each of which contains a mere fragment of it, but is manifested as a whole, as an unbroken and indestructible unity in the phenomenon. We may express this relationship in subjective terms by saying that the world of mythical experience is grounded in experiences of pure expression rather than in representative or significative acts. Its reality is not an aggregate of things endowed with definite characteristics by which they can be known and distinguished from one another; it is a vast diversity of original physiognomic characters. As a whole and in its parts the world still has a distinctive face, which may be apprehended at any moment as a totality and can never be dissolved into mere universal configurations, into geometrical and objective lines and shapes. Here the given does not consist primarily in the merely sensuous, in a complex of sensory data, which are only animated and made meaningful by a subsequent act of mythical apperception. The expressive meaning attaches to the perception itself, in which it is apprehended and immediately experienced. It is only this fundamental experience that can fully account for certain traits of the mythical world. What perhaps divides it most sharply from the world of the purely theoretical consciousness is the peculiar indifference of the mythical consciousness toward the distinctions of signification and value to which the theoretical consciousness attaches the greatest importance. For myth the content of a dream is just as important as the content of any waking experience; for myth the image of a

4. Cf. above, 2, 42 ff., and my *Sprache und Mythos. Ein Beitrag zum Problem der Götternamen* (Leipzig and Berlin, 1925). Eng. trans. by Susanne K. Langer, *Language and Myth* (New York, 1946).

thing or its name is equivalent to the object itself.[5] This indifference becomes truly comprehensible only if we consider that in the mythical world there is no logical representative or significative meaning, but that pure expressive meaning still enjoys almost unrestricted sway. For in terms of pure expression, an area of being is not apprehended according to what it signifies for empirical reality as a totality of causal relations. Here being does not obtain its meaning, its weightiness, from any mediated consequences it produces; on the contrary, this meaning resides purely in itself. The decisive thing is not what it accomplishes but what it is and what it reveals itself to be in its simple existence. Phenomenon and effect—hence phenomenon and reality—can here not be detached from each other or reckoned against each other: all the power that a content exerts on the mythical consciousness is grounded and contained in the manner, the mode, of the appearance itself. From this point of view the relation between "image" and "thing" insofar as the two are differentiated must actually be reversed. The image must assert a peculiar primacy over the thing. For what "is" in the object in its expressive character is not taken up and destroyed in the image; on the contrary, it is set in high relief and intensified. The image frees this expressive reality from all merely accidental determinations and concentrates it in a single focus. In the empirical world view we determine and know the "object" by dissecting it backward into its conditions and following it forward into its effects. It is what it is only as a single link in a system of such effects, as part of a causal structure. Where, however, an occurrence is not thus viewed as a mere factor in a thoroughgoing and universal order of law but is experienced in its physiognomic individuality so to speak; where instead of the analysis and abstraction that are the precondition of all causal understanding, pure vision prevails—it is the *image* which opens up the true essentiality and makes it knowable. All "image magic" rests on the presupposition that in the image the magician is not dealing with a dead imitation of the object; rather, in the image he possesses the essence, the soul, of the object.[6] In his novel *Thais,* in which he gives a picture of primitive paganism

5. Cf. above, 2, 35 ff.
6. Cf. A. E. T. W. Budge, *Egyptian Magic* (London, Kegan Paul, Trench, Trübner, 1899), p. 65: "The Egyptians . . . believed that it was possible to transmit to the figure of any man or woman or animal or living creature the soul of the being which it represented and its qualities and attributes. The statue of a god in a temple contained the spirit of the god which it represented, and from time immemorial the people of Egypt believed that every statue and figure possessed an indwelling spirit."

and primitive Christianity, Anatole France relates how the Christian hermit Paphnuce, after converting the courtesan Thais and burning her clothing, her ornaments and house furnishings, is haunted both waking and sleeping by the images of the things he has destroyed. And now he understands that the destruction of the outward existence of all these things remains ineffectual, as long as one has not also exorcised and banished the images in which they live on. "Ne permets pas," he cries out to God, "que le fantôme accomplisse ce que n'a point accompli le corps. Quand j'ai triomphé de la chair, ne souffre pas que l'ombre me terrasse. Je connais que je suis exposé présentement à des dangers plus grands que je courus jamais. J'éprouve et je sais que le rêve a plus de puissance que la réalité. Et comment en pourrait-il être autrement, puisqu'il est lui-même une réalité supérieure? Il est l'âme des choses." The "soul" of things signifies here the pure expressive meaning with which they seize upon consciousness and draw it into their sphere, and this meaning is revealed with greater diversity, force, and purity in dreams and visions than in the waking world. For in waking, pure vision is replaced and inhibited by empirical efficacy: objects lose their original face and are taken only as colorless and formless nuclei for certain causal and teleological relations.

And in still another respect the mythical world of forms shows us a way to the understanding of the phenomena of pure expression. If we wish to describe this world of forms without theoretical preconception, we must dispense not only with a false concept of the thing, but also with a false— or at least inadequate—concept of the subject. Nothing is more usual and nothing seems more justified than the view that the fundamental act of the mythical consciousness is an act of "personification." One supposes that one has interpreted myth, that one has disclosed its psychological "mechanism," by explaining how consciousness succeeds in transforming empirical reality, the reality of things and their attributes, into a reality of another kind, a reality of animated and active subjects. Actually this it to misunderstand both the starting point and the end point of the mythical consciousness, both its *terminus a quo* and its *terminus ad quem*. For the mythical consciousness differs from the theoretical consciousness as much in its way of building the personal world as in its way of building the world of things. The mythical consciousness has its own category, its own specific view, of subjectivity as well as objectivity. Myth does not signify a mere transposition of the objective world view into a subjective view, for this would require both of these two aspects to be present and determined. But precisely this determination is the actual problem at which myth must work in its own way and according to its basic trend. It forms a kind of struggle between I and world—a struggle in which the two poles, by separating from each other and opposing each other, first gain their fixed form and shape. Thus we have seen that the representation of the I, of the living and active subject, is not the beginning but rather a determinate result of the mythical process of formation. Myth does not start from a finished representation of the I and the soul but is the vehicle which leads to such a representation; it is a spiritual medium through which subjective reality is first discovered and apprehended in its distinctiveness.[7] Thus in its most original, truly primitive configurations myth knows as little of a "soul" substance as of a "thing" substance in the metaphysical sense of the words. Reality—corporeal or psychic—has not yet become stabilized but preserves a peculiar "fluidity." Reality is not yet divided into definite classes of things with characteristics established once and for all; nor have any hard and fast dividing lines been drawn between the various spheres of life. Just as there are no permanent substrates for the world of outward perception, so there are no enduring subjects for the world of inner perception. For here, too, the fundamental motif of myth—the motif of "metamorphosis"—prevails. This mythical change of forms also draws the I into its sphere and absorbs its unity and simplicity. Like the boundary between natural forms, the boundary between "I" and "thou" is fluid throughout. Life is still a single unbroken stream of becoming, a dynamic flow which only very gradually divides into separate waves. Consequently, although the mythical consciousness imprints the form of life on everything it lays hold of, this giving of life to all things is not equivalent from the very start to pan-animation; at first, life itself shows a vague and flowing, thoroughly pre-animistic, character. It preserves a noteworthy indifference between personal and impersonal, between the "thou" form and the form of the mere "it." There is nowhere an "it" as a dead object, a mere thing; yet on the other hand, the "thou" likewise possesses no sharply determined, strictly individual face but is prepared at any moment to lose itself in the representation of a mere it, an impersonal general force.[8] Every single factor in intuitive reality has magical traits and connections; every occurrence, however ephemeral, has its magical-mythical

7. Cf. above, 2, 155 ff.
8. Cf. the discussion and documentation of the idea of mana in *Sprache und Mythos*, pp. 51 ff.; and in Vol. 2 of the present work, pp. 75–8; 158–9.

"meaning." A whispering or rustling in the woods, a shadow darting over
the ground, a light flickering on the water: all these are demonic in their
nature and origin; but only very gradually does this pandemonium divide
into separate and clearly distinguishable figures, into personal spirits and
gods. All intuitive reality is surrounded by a breath of magic, bathed in a
magical mist; but precisely this common atmosphere in which it is and
lives prevents its individual particularity from manifesting itself and fully
unfolding. Everything is connected with everything else by invisible
threads; and this connection, this universal sympathy, itself preserves a
hovering, strangely impersonal character. "There is a fitting in; there is
an omen; there is a warning"—but behind these there is not necessarily a
personal subject, the shape of any recognizable warner. It is the whole of
reality rather than any separate part of it that constitutes this subject.
Precisely because this perpetual pointing and warning forms the element
in which the mythical consciousness lives, it requires no special explanation; the pure act, the function of this showing and meaning, stands as it
were on itself, requiring no reduction to a personal substrate, to an agent.

But difficult as it may sometimes be to perceive this basic structure of the
mythical world from the standpoint of our highly developed theoretical
consciousness with its division of inner and outward, subjective and objective—the particularity of this world stands out clearly as soon as we
turn to a different field—the phenomena of expression. For here we at once
encounter that peculiar twofold character which myth shows us in its
primary formations. Where the "meaning" of the world is still taken as
that of pure expression, every phenomenon discloses a definite "character,"
which is not merely deduced or inferred from it but which belongs to it
immediately. It is in itself gloomy or joyful, agitating or soothing, pacify-
ing or terrifying. These determinations are expressive values and factors
adhering to the phenomena themselves; they are not merely derived from
them indirectly by way of the subjects which we regard as standing behind the phenomenon. It is a misunderstanding of the phenomena of
pure expression when a certain psychological theory makes them originate
in a secondary act of interpretation and declares them to be products of
"empathy." The main weakness in this theory, its $\pi\rho\tilde{\omega}\tau\text{o}\nu$ $\psi\epsilon\tilde{\upsilon}\delta\text{o}\varsigma$, is that
it reverses the order of the phenomenal data. It must first kill perception by
making it into a complex of mere sensory contents, before it can re-
animate this dead matter of sensation by the act of empathy. But the life it
acquires in this way is in the end a mere semblance of life—the product of

a psychological illusion. Perception is not "alive" by its own right but merely borrows this character from a foreign source. Here it is overlooked that perception is not immediately given as a totality of sensations, but that its pure "appearance" embraces definite modes of appearing, which lie on an entirely different plane. But no theory could conjure up these modes from the void if they were not in some absolutely original way given in the content of perception itself. Actually we arrive at the data of *mere* sensation—such as light or dark, warm or cold, rough or smooth—only by setting aside a fundamental and primary stratum of perception, by doing away with it, so to speak, for a definite theoretical purpose. But no abstraction, regardless of how far it is carried, can blot out this stratum as such; it remains what it is and asserts itself for what it is, even if, in pursuit of certain theoretical aims, we are compelled to look beyond it and finally to disregard it altogether. This disregard is perfectly justified from the point of view of the purely theoretical intention, the intention of building an objective order of nature and apprehending its laws; but it cannot do away with the world of expressive phenomena as such. And it is equally clear that we are no longer speaking the language of these phenomena themselves, that we are no longer understanding them from within, if we regard them as mere epiphenomena, additions to the sole original content of sensation. An expressive character is not a subjective appendage that is subsequently and as it were accidentally added to the objective content of sensation; on the contrary, it is a part of the essential fact of perception. This expressive character is not intrinsically subjective, since it is what gives to perception its original color of reality and makes it a perception of reality. For the reality we apprehend is in its original form not a reality of a determinate world of things, originating apart from us; rather it is the certainty of a living efficacy that we experience. Yet this access to reality is given us not by the datum of sensation but only in the original phenomenon of expression and expressive understanding. If an expressive meaning were not revealed to us in certain perceptive experiences, existence would remain silent for us. Reality could never be deduced from the mere experience of things if it were not in some way already contained and manifested in a very particular way, in expressive perception. And this manifestation does not automatically link the phenomenon of life with individual subjects, determinate and clearly differentiated I-worlds. What is primarily apprehended here is life as such far more than any individual spheres or centers of life; what originally appears in expressive perception is a universal character of reality, not the existence and facticity of distinct individuals. With all its diversity and vitality it preserves the character of the impersonal; it is always and everywhere manifestation, but for this very reason it stops within the phenomenon of manifestation as such and requires no determinate substrate for it. Precisely this throws a new light on the impersonal nature of certain primary mythical formations. Here again the thought form of myth proves to be closely bound up with its life form; it only reflects, and places before us in objective form, what is contained and grounded in a very concrete mode of perception.

This gives us one more penetrating insight into the methodological relation between phenomenological analysis and a purely objective philosophy of the human spirit. The two are so closely linked and necessarily interdependent that not only are their positive results closely related but, conversely, every false move in one direction makes itself felt forthwith in the other. An inadequate appreciation of the objective meaning of the particular symbolic forms always involves the danger that the phenomena in which this meaning is grounded will be misunderstood—and on the other hand, every theoretical prejudice that injects itself into the pure description of phenomena endangers our evaluation of the meaning of the forms that result from it. There is in particular one category the use of which has repeatedly obstructed an unprejudiced interpretation both of the phenomena of pure expression and of the fundamental structure of the mythical world. Both are often said to be rooted in an act of personification. At first glance this characterization may seem applicable and adequate if we consider only the negative aspect of the question, for unquestionably the pure phenomena of expression on the one hand and mythical configuration on the other do not yet show that form of objectivity which is sought and achieved in the building of theoretical knowledge. But this does not mean that because myth and expression possess no distinct thing-category in the empirical-theoretical sense of the word, they already possess a distinct category of personality on which they must necessarily lean. The development of the opposition itself, the tension that arises between the two poles, is achieved only at a certain spiritual level and may not simply be relegated to the beginnings, to the primary and primitive strata. As far as the mythical world is concerned, we have seen that this tension only sets in where man ceases merely to accept the reality that surrounds him, but actively opposes himself to it and begins actively to form it. As the different spheres of his action begin to diverge and to be apprehended in their particular meaning and value, the initial indeterminacy of mythical feeling recedes, and the intuition of an articulated mythical cosmos—the intuition of a world of the gods and a state of the gods—begins to arise.[9] In the same sense it is true that the world of expression does not from the start include a determinate, clearly developed consciousness of the I. For all experience and expression are at first a mere passivity, a being-acted-upon rather than an acting—and this receptivity stands in evident contrast to that kind of spontaneity in which all self-consciousness as such is grounded. If we fail to realize this, we are forced to conclude that the animal consciousness, insofar as it is filled and as it were permeated and satiated with expressive experiences, should for this very reason be described as a personally articulated and personally formed consciousness. This conclusion was drawn most sharply and radically by Vignoli in his *Mito e Scienza* (1879). Vignoli, whose ideas are based on a purely positivist theory of knowledge, seeks to understand and interpret myth by disclosing its biological roots. Myth seems to him a necessary and spontaneous function of consciousness, a function which is variable in its matter, constant in its form. We can account for its empirical universality only if we disclose a constant original disposition of the psyche, from which it arises and from which it perpetually draws new power. In line with this postulate, Vignoli sets out "to subject to careful examination the simplest elementary acts of the mind, in their physical and psychical complexity, in order to discover in their spontaneous action the transcendental fact which inevitably involves the genesis of the same myth, the primary source whence it is diffused by subsequent reflex efforts in various times and varying forms." But then it becomes evident that if we wish to lay bare this universal principle, this a priori, of myth, we cannot stop at an analysis of human sensation, perception, and representation: we must go back one step further. Even in the animal world there is an urge to give life in some way to every sensory influence that the animal receives from outside, to personify it. For the animal every sensation, in the form in which it comes to consciousness, is at once closely connected with the representation of a living something, corresponding to the animal's representation of its own inner life. The animal makes its life into a drama of actions, sensations, instincts, of hope and fear—though this

9. Cf. above, 2, 185 ff., 199 ff.

may come only dimly to consciousness. The keen sensation peculiar to the animal, which dominates its inner life, is transferred to all bodies and phenomena of nature which outwardly attract its attention. "Thus every form, every object, every external phenomenon becomes vivified and animated by the intrinsic consciousness and personal psychical faculty of the animal itself. Every object, fact, and phenomenon of nature will not merely appear to him as the real object which it is, but he will necessarily perceive it as a living and deliberating power, capable of affecting him agreeably or injuriously." [10]

Thus this psychic drama from which myth is born has its point of departure not in human consciousness but in the animal consciousness: there is a drive to interpret all existence of which the animal becomes aware in the form of personal existence. Man is not the first and only being whose world is governed by such a drive; he merely transforms the unformed, unconscious drive toward personification into a conscious, reflective act. In support of this thesis Vignoli adduces a large number of empirical data which he gathered in his observations of animals over a period of years. But if we examine these observations, they show only one thing with certainty: in how high degree characters of pure expression predominate in the world of animal perception, and how decidedly they outweigh any objective perception of things and attributes. [11] They do not, however, prove that for the animal these characters necessarily adhere to a definite subject, much less to a clearly apprehended person, and that they can only be experienced by way of this vehicle. In the postulation and presupposition of such a subject, a synthesis of a different kind and of a very different intellectual origin is obviously effected. One thing, however, must be admitted and stressed: this synthesis, too, cannot spring from pure nothingness, it cannot arise from a kind of *generatio aequivoca*. It is connected with a basic trend of sense perception, to which it remains

10. Tito Vignoli, *Mito e Scienza*, 1879. German trans., *Mythus und Wissenschaft* (Leipzig, 1880). Eng. trans., *Myth and Science* (New York, 1882), pp. 6 ff., 48 ff.

11. This "primacy of expressive experience" which seems to be determining and typical for the animal consciousness has been borne out by recent work in animal psychology, particularly by the observations and penetrating investigations of Pfungst. [Cf. Oscar Pfungst, *Der kluge Hans* (Leipzig, 1907).—Ed.] By abundant observations—which have so far not been published in their entirety—Pfungst has shown that a great number of the so-called "feats of intelligence" commonly attributed to the higher animals are in reality achievements of pure expression, that they are based not on inferences and intellectual processes but rather on the extremely fine feeling that animals possess for certain involuntary expressive movements of man.

attached and obligated even where it rises far above it. As for the idea which according to Vignoli determines the structure of the animal consciousness, the idea "that every cosmic reality is endowed with the same life and free will as the immediate utterances of the animal's own inner life seem to it to possess" [12]—of course we cannot impute any such idea to the animal, particularly in view of the fact that the total picture of *life* is far from appearing to man himself from the very beginning in this clearly delineated form, in the form of conscious and free *will*. When man, too, first seizes upon life, it appears far more as a totality than as an individually formed and limited life of particular subjects. At the beginning it contains the factor neither of I-constancy nor of thing-constancy: it breaks down neither into identical subjects, nor into permanent objects. If we seek the origin of this breakdown, of this differentiation and articulation, we find ourselves led beyond the sphere of expression to that of representation, beyond the spiritual region in which myth is preeminently at home, into the region of language. Only in the medium of language do the infinite diversity, the surging multiformity of expressive experiences begin to be fixated; only in language do they take on "name and shape." The proper name of the god becomes the origin of the personal figure of the god; and through its mediation, through the representation of the personal god, the representation of man's own I, of his "self," is first found and secured.[13]

But this comparison between the achievements of language and of myth seems to intensify a misgiving which must have arisen earlier in our investigation. Since our aim is purportedly an understanding of the structure of the theoretical world, what—it will be asked—justifies us in lingering amid the formations of the mythical consciousness? Must not every theoretical world view that can lay claim to the name begin by dismissing these forms and renouncing them once and for all without reservation? We can gain access to the realm of cognition only by freeing ourselves from the phantasm in which myth involves us, only by seeing through its image world as a world of mere illusion. And once this access has been gained, once the realm of truth has been opened up, what purpose is there in looking back from it to the realm of illusion? From the standpoint of this question, language is by no means equivalent to myth. It is

12. Cf. Vignoli (German trans.), p. 49.
13. Cf. my *Sprache und Mythos*, pp. 17 ff., 42 ff.

obvious that language participates in a particular and independent way
in the formation and articulation of the theoretical world. Even science
cannot dispense with its collaboration—it, too, must everywhere start
from the preliminary stage of linguistic concepts, from which it detaches
itself only gradually to attain the form of the pure logical concept. But
in relation to myth, the dividing line is sharper and more cogent. This
dividing line leads to an irrevocable separation, to an authentic and definitive crisis of consciousness. The world views of myth and of theoretical
knowledge cannot coexist in the same area of thought. They are mutually
exclusive: the beginning of one is equivalent to the end of the other. Once
the day has dawned, once the theoretical consciousness and theoretical
perception are born, no return seems possible to the world of mythical
shadows. For what can such a return be but a regression into a primitive
stage that has already been transcended?

Necessary as this conclusion may seem if we limit ourselves to purely
abstract considerations regarding the form of myth and science, it involves
great difficulties as soon as we consider both from the standpoint of a
universal phenomenology of the spirit. The world of the spirit forms a
very concrete unity, so much so that the most extreme oppositions in
which it moves appear as somehow mediated oppositions. In this world
there is no sudden breach or leap, no hiatus by which it breaks into disparate parts. Rather, every form through which consciousness passes
seems to belong in some way to its enduring heritage. The surpassing of
a particular form is made possible not by the vanishing, the total destruction, of this form but by its preservation within the continuity of
consciousness as a whole; for what constitutes the unity and totality of
the human spirit is precisely that it has no absolute past; it gathers up
into itself what has passed and preserves it as present. "The life of the
actual spirit," writes Hegel in this connection, "is a cycle of stages which
on the one hand still subsist side by side and only on the other hand appear as past. The features which the spirit seems to have left behind it
are also present in its depths." [14] If this view is sound, we shall not be
able to believe that even so strange and paradoxical a structure as mythical
perception is totally lost or superfluous within the general view of reality
which the theoretical consciousness projects. It is to be expected that the
basic tendency that plainly dominates this perception will not be abso-

14. Hegel, "Vorlesungen über die Philosophie der Geschichte," *Sämmtliche Werke* (Leipzig,
1949), 9, 98.

lutely extinguished, however much it is crowded out and modified by other modes of seeing. The submerging of the contents of the mythical consciousness does not signify the end of the spiritual function in which they originated. None of the mythical pictures need be salvaged in the reality of experience and in the realm of its objects—nevertheless it can be shown that the spiritual potency, whose first concrete manifestation was myth, asserts itself in a certain respect, and that within the new dimension of theoretical self-consciousness it survives and continues to act in new form, in a kind of metamorphosis.

At what point in our empirical world view this survival is most readily found becomes clear the moment we recall that we have taken not the perception of things but the perception of pure expression as the actual correlate of myth; for now the question reads: in the progress of the theoretical consciousness, is this expressive perception ever wholly eliminated by objective perception or does it claim an independent right side by side with objective perception and possess a territory of its own which cannot be built up and determined without it? As a matter of fact, this territory can be designated with perfect precision: it is that form of knowledge by which the reality not of natural objects but of other subjects is opened up to us. This knowledge of the other psyche seems to form a natural and self-evident part of our total knowledge of experience; yet from time immemorial it has formed the crux of epistemological and psychological reflection. New theories are forever being devised to explain it and justify it—but in every case it becomes evident that the degree of certainty to which these explanations can lay claim is far from approaching the certainty which is already present in the simple phenomenological fact. Instead of confirming or explaining this fact, theory has almost without exception been a denial of its existence. Despite the broad divergence in their points of departure and methods, these attempted explanations all agreed in one basic presupposition and in one methodological aim. They all started from the assumption that all knowledge which does not refer to, and is not limited to, one's own states of consciousness must be mediated by outward perception—and furthermore they all recognized outward perception as present and valid only in the form of thing perception. To reduce the perception of the "thou" to the general form of thing-perception thus appeared to be the true aim, and it was to this end that theory kept striving. But precisely this project constitutes a πρῶτον ψεῦδος, because to conceive of the whole of what can be experienced as a complex which either consists in things or must necessarily be composed of them as ingredients is an arbitrary theoretical narrowing of the horizon of experience. Within this horizon, actually, the expressive perception is not only psychologically earlier than the perception of things—it is not only the πρότερον πρὸς ἡμᾶς—but also the designation of an authentic πρότερον τῇ φύσει. It has its specific form, its own essentiality, which cannot be described, much less replaced, by categories valid for other regions of being and meaning. Far more clearly and convincingly than in the traditional psychology, which has almost always been guided in its descriptions by definite conceptual presuppositions to which it was bound, this expressive form stands out in the mirror of language. Here it is still immediately discernible how all perception of an object originally starts from the apprehension and differentiation of certain physiognomic characters, with which, in a manner of speaking, it remains saturated. The linguistic designation of movement, for example, almost always discloses this factor: instead of describing the form of the movement as such, as the form of an objective spatial and temporal process, language names and fixates the condition of which the movement in question is an expression. " 'Quick,' 'slow,' and if necessary even 'abrupt' "—writes Klages, who of all modern psychologists has most clearly recognized these relationships and who in many cases has been first to open them up to theoretical understanding—

> may be understood in terms of pure mathematics; but "violent," "hurried," "restrained," "circumspect," "exaggerated" are just as much names for conditions of life as for kinds of movement, and actually describe the latter by indicating their *characters*. Anyone who wishes to characterize forms of motion and spatial forms, finds himself unexpectedly entangled in a characterization of psychic attributes, because forms and movements have been *experienced* as psychic phenomena before they are judged by the understanding from the standpoint of objectivity, and because language can express objective concepts only through the mediation of the experience of impressions.[15]

Thus language shows us how the basic psychic-spiritual context from which mythical intuition arises survives long after consciousness has surpassed the narrow limits of this intuition and has advanced to other formations. The source does not suddenly cease to flow; it is merely conveyed

15. Ludwig Klages, *Ausdrucksbewegung und Gestaltungskraft* (Leipzig, 1923), p. 18.

into another and broader channel. For if we were to suppose that the original source of myth had gone totally dry, that pure experiences of expression were absolutely extinct, vast territories of experience would lie fallow. There is no doubt that not only the knowledge of things as physical objects but also the knowledge of "other subjects" is an original part of experience. No form of reflection, of mediated inference, can create this knowledge—for it is the concern of reflection not to produce the stratum of experience in which it is rooted but only to interpret it theoretically. It is a strange presumption on the part of theory, a kind of intellectual *hybris,* to suppose that it can not only disclose the peculiar mode of awareness that is here present but also create it. What is thus created remains in the end a phantom, a fiction which pretends to living reality but possesses no independent vital force. And indeed, almost all the well-known explanations of the knowledge of other subjects amount to sheer illusionism. What distinguishes these theories from one another is only the manner in which they describe the illusion and conceive its genesis. Sometimes it is viewed as a kind of logical illusion, sometimes as a kind of aesthetic illusion; it is described as a sophistication, sometimes of reason, sometimes of imagination. What these theories fail to take into account is that the meaning and content of the purely expressive function cannot be made intelligible by way of a single sphere of spiritual formation, because as a truly universal and as it were world-encompassing function it precedes differentiation into the various spheres of meaning, it precedes the divergence of myth and theory, of logical reflection and aesthetic intuition. Its certainty and its "truth" are, in a manner of speaking, premythical, pre-logical and pre-aesthetic; it forms the common ground from which all these formations have in some way sprung and to which they remain attached. And this of course is why this truth seems to slip through our fingers when we seek to fixate it—that is, confine it in advance within a single field and delineate and determine it solely by means of the categories pertaining to this one field. If we start from the standpoint of logic and theoretical cognition, it seems possible to secure the unity of knowledge only by taking all knowledge, regardless of what kind of objects it may refer to, as strictly homogeneous. The diversity in the content of what is known must imply no diversity in the principle of awareness, or in its method. Thus we seem justified in postulating that the knowledge of the "other ego" is subject to the same conditions as the knowledge of nature, the world of empirical objects. Since the natural object is truly constituted only in the idea of natural law, since object and law are correlative in the field of objectivizing knowledge, the same must apply to that form of experience through which the knowledge of other subjects is built up for us. This knowledge, too, must above all be secured by a universal principle; and where shall we find such a principle if not in the principle of causality, which is the actual a priori for all knowledge of reality and appears to be the only bridge by which we can pass beyond the narrowly circumscribed sphere of immanence, beyond the phenomena of our own consciousness? Even Dilthey—although his general view of the cultural sciences points in a different direction—was at first positivist enough to regard this reasoning as cogent and to make it the foundation of his epistemological reflections. According to Dilthey, the belief in the reality of the outside world—the world of bodies in space and the world of other subjects—is rooted in an analogy to which he essentially lends the form of a causal inference. The proposition that we never become *directly* aware of the reality of other subjects, but only *mediately*, through transference, is treated almost as an axiom [16]—though of course his own concrete view of the essence and structure of spiritual life contradicts it at almost every step. But even when we thus disregard the structure of concrete cultural reality and restrict ourselves to pure epistemology, the analogy theory itself contains a noteworthy paradox. For if this theory were sound, a theorem of truly universal importance for the whole of our view of the world and reality would be reduced to the narrowest conceivable epistemological basis. If our certainty of the "other ego" were based on nothing more than a chain of empirical observations and inductive inferences—if it were based on the supposition that the same expressive movements as we perceive in our body or similar ones appeared also in other physical bodies, and that the same cause must always correspond to the same effects—it would be hard to conceive of a conclusion with so little foundation. Both as a whole and in its details this inference proves on closer investigation to be thoroughly vulnerable. For one thing, it is a well known logical principle that although we can infer like effects from like causes, we cannot conversely infer like causes from like effects, since one and the same effect can be produced by very different causes. But even apart from this objection, an inference of this kind could at best provide the basis for a provisional assumption, a mere prob-

16. Cf. Wilhelm Dilthey, "Ideen zu einer beschreibenden und zergliedernden Psychologie," *Abhandlungen der königlichen Akademie der Wissenschaften zu Berlin*.

ability. Belief in the reality of the other ego would then, as far as its purely epistemological dignity is concerned, be justified in the same way as belief in the light-ether for example—though with the highly important and methodologically crucial difference that the latter hypothesis is based on incomparably more exact observations. Any brand of epistemological skepticism—down to the most radical solipsism—would need only to attack this analogy in order to be certain of success. The certainty that the reality of life is not limited to the sphere of one's own existence would itself be a purely discursive cognition and moreover one of highly questionable origin and value.

It was no doubt considerations of this sort which made it necessary to shift the center of inquiry from the sphere of the intellect and logic in general to another field. In place of a purely discursive foundation, an intuitive foundation was sought, one in the immediacy and originality of feeling rather than in the mediacy of reflection. The certainty of the other ego must—it was stressed—be grounded not in deductions and inferences, not in a sum of logical operations, but rather in an original mode of experience. As such a mode of experience Lipps puts forward the form of "coexperience or experience in accord with" (*Mit-oder Nach-Erleben*), which alone, he asserts, opens up to the ego the possibility of a "thou" and its reality. But this in turn implies that this reality can never be an original but only a borrowed reality. "The other psychological individual is . . . made by myself out of myself. His inner being is taken from mine. The other individual or ego is the product of a projection, a reflection, a radiation of myself (or of what I experience in myself, through the sense perception of an outside physical phenomenon) into this very sensory phenomenon, a peculiar kind of reduplication of myself." [17] Thus it is once again a process of mirroring, of reflecting, mediation to which the knowledge of the existence and nature of the "other individual" goes back. The process itself is the same; only the refracting medium has changed. But is the objective of this theory really achieved—has it moved closer to life—by shifting the center of gravity from logic to aesthetics? What assures us that this other ego which we gain from our own being and project outward is more than a phantasm, a kind of psychological *fata morgana?* If we follow the process of this theory, the other ego appears as a strange hybrid, composed of elements

17. Theodor Lipps, *Die ethischen Grundfragen* (2d ed. Hamburg and Leipzig, 1905), pp. 16 f.

of very diverse origin and epistemological dignity. The theory is based primarily on sensation: the starting point for the act of empathy is the perception of material attributes and changes, which we apprehend purely as such, as "merely physical" contents. It is not doubted that the world is originally given in this merely physical way; but it is stressed that only this primary phenomenon is not sufficient, that a new phenomenon, the phenomenon of life and animation, must be *produced* by a peculiar and fundamental act. Through acts of instinctive sympathy reality is redeemed from its initial mechanical rigidity and transformed into a spiritual and psychic reality. And yet, if this transformation is due solely to the empathy of our own ego into the "matter" of mere sensation, the phenomenon of life is degraded into an aesthetic illusion. According to this view, the world appears alive only as long as it is cloaked as it were in the twilight of aesthetic intuition: under the sharp beam of knowledge, this illusion must be dispelled. Now it must become evident that where we thought we grasped life itself, we grasped a mere idol of life. This conclusion can be avoided only if we expose the vicious circle in which both the analogy and the empathy theory move. They both presuppose as an empirical fact what is itself the product of a definite theoretical interpretation: they both accept the dualistic splitting of reality into an outside and an inside as given, without inquiring into the conditions under which this division is possible. But phenomenological analysis must here reverse the order and direction of inquiry. Instead of asking by what processes of logical inference or of aesthetic projection the psyche *becomes* psyche, it must follow perception back to the point where it is not a perception of things but is purely expressive, and where, accordingly, it is inside and outside in one. If there is any problem here at all, it is concerned not with internalization, but rather with the unremitting externalization by which the original expressive characters gradually become objective characteristics and determinations and attributes of things. This externalization increases as the world of expression passes into another form—as it moves toward the world of representation and finally of pure "meaning." But as long as it persists purely within itself, it remains self-centered in itself and uncontestable. Here there is no need to infer from the purely expressive characters a reality that is evinced in them; rather, it is they themselves which bear the immediate color of reality. For at this stage of development it is they alone which completely fill consciousness. There is still no other measure of reality or objective validity to contest this claim. Where life remains entirely within the phenomenon of expression, it contents itself with that phenomenon; it has not yet conceived the world otherwise than as a totality of possible expressive experiences, as their stage and arena as it were. It is true that over against this primary aspect of the world, the theoretical concepts of the thing and of causality create a new view and a new *definition* of "reality." To take this definition as exclusive, as the only possible definition, is to destroy all bridges to the world of pure expression. What was previously a phenomenon now becomes a problem—and a problem which no acuteness of knowledge, no theory however fine-spun, can fully solve. Once the phenomenon as such has concealed itself from view because the plane of vision in which it was originally seen has been replaced by another, no power of mediated inference can ever bring it back to us. We cannot find the way back by heaping up or refining the instruments of theoretical thought; we can find it only by penetrating more deeply into the general nature of theoretical thinking and by learning to understand its contingency as well as its uncontestable right and necessity. Once we have clearly understood the direction in which this thinking progresses, it becomes evident that we cannot find the world of expression in this direction. No reinforcement or refinement of the instruments of pure theory will bring us any farther unless we change our line of sight. The immediate ingenuous expressive sense must be distinguished from the meaning of theoretical knowledge; it must be restored as a whole, before the first step can be taken toward its explanation.

It is the achievement of Scheler to have clearly recognized this path, to have disclosed by his sharp critique the fundamental phenomenological weaknesses of the empathy theory no less than of the analogy theory. In his own theory he seeks to avoid both Scylla and Charybdis. He does not attempt to explain the awareness of the other ego by something else that precedes it, or to reduce it to something else. Instead, he takes the "evidence of the thou" as a certain and irreducible datum with which inquiry must *begin*. The basic weakness of both the analogy and the empathy theory, according to Scheler, is that in both of them the phenomenological standpoint is abandoned entirely and a realistic theory is covertly substituted for it. And, he declares, there is no graver pitfall for a philosopher than to orient himself not toward what is given but toward what, according to some presupposed realistic theory, "might be given." [18]

18. Cf. Max F. Scheler, *Wesen und Formen der Sympathiegefühle* (2d ed. Bonn, 1923), p. 282.

What is possible within the confines of such a theory must not be made into a measure of phenomenal reality. This reality, according to Scheler's theory of perception, consists of expressive units and expressive totalities rather than qualitatively determined and differentiated sensations. These totalities cannot be explained merely as a sum of color qualities combined with unities of sense and form, or as *Gestalten* of motion and change. Rather, they make up a primary and undivided whole, which attains distinct form only through being apprehended in two different directions of action. The perceptive experience can—in the act of so-called outward perception—assume the function of designating an individual's body as an object in nature, in the physical world; or it may assume the function of symbolizing an ego—either one's own or another—by an act of inner perception. At first this experience is an intuition neither of a corporeal world nor of a merely psychic reality. What is apprehended in it is rather a unitary life stream, so to speak, which is still wholly neutral toward the subsequent analysis into physical and psychic. Whether this original neutral foundation is later formed into the intuition of a corporeal object or of a living subject depends essentially on the direction of formation, the mode of vision: whether it is a separating vision (*Auseinanderschau*) or an identifying vision (*Ineinanderschau*).

Thus it is only through the different directions of perception (according as one or the other is the case) that the reactions take on one form of unity as an appearance in which the other individual's body comes to perception (or a phenomenon which is the intuitive consequence of impressions of our environment), and that there is another form of unity in which we perceive the other individual's ego (or a phenomenon that is the intuitive expressive consequence of the inner world). For this very reason it is fundamentally impossible to dissect the unity of an expressive phenomenon (e.g. a smile, a menacing or kindly or affectionate look) into a sum, however great, of phenomena whose parts would be identical with the parts of the phenomenon in which we perceive the body, or an impression from the physical environment. If I examine the phenomenal units given in outward perception, which might even become *views* of any small parts of the individual's body I will never in any possible combination of these units find the unitary reality of a smile or of an entreating or menacing gesture. And similarly, a quality of redness which lies before my eyes as the coating of a physical cheek will never be the phenomenon of blushing in whose redness a sympathetically felt shame seems to end.[19]

We shall go no further into the arguments with which Scheler supports his thesis but content ourselves with singling out the one motif which is exactly in line with our own investigation. It is characteristic that Scheler, in order to designate the actual phenomenological difference between inner and outward perception, must start not from a difference of material but from a difference in symbolic function. Here again we find confirmation of our fundamental view that what we call reality can never be determined from the standpoint of material alone but that into every mode of positing reality there enters a definite motif of symbolic formation which must be recognized as such and distinguished from other motifs. But in still another and more specific respect Scheler's conclusions are significant for us. His investigations once again show the expressive function to be a genuinely original phenomenon, which also asserts its originality and uniqueness in the building of theoretical consciousness and theoretical reality. If we did away with this function, all access to the world of inner experience would be closed to us—the bridge which alone can lead us into the realm of the "thou" would be cut. Any attempt to replace the *primary* function of expression by other higher functions, whether intellectual or aesthetic, leads only to inadequate substitutes, which can never achieve what is demanded of them. Such higher functions can only be effective insofar as they already presuppose the primary stratum of the experience of expression in its absolutely original form.[20] Certainly this stratum is very considerably modified and transformed as soon as we advance from the mythical to the aesthetic world and thence to the world of theoretical knowledge; but it is not totally eliminated. In the progress of theoretical, scientific knowledge, the purely expressive function loses ground, the pure "picture" of life is

19. Scheler, pp. 304 ff.

20. "It is impossible to say"—Scheler soundly remarks in opposition to the "empathy theory"—"on what datum the process of empathy into one's own ego should be based. Would, for example, any optical contents whatever suffice? Certainly not. For we do not 'feel into' any optical contents whatever. They say optical contents of 'expressive movements' or at least of the actions of some *animated* creature are necessary. But this answer does not advance matters. That optical images of certain movements are images of expressive movements is an insight which presupposes the knowledge of the existence of another *animated something*. To view it as an expression is not the basis but the consequence of this assumption" (p. 278).

transposed into an existence of things and the form of causal relations between things. But it can never wholly enter into this form and never be
submerged in it—for if it did so, not only would the mythical world of
demons and gods disappear, but the fundamental phenomenon of the
"livingness" as such would vanish. Thus we see that the basic motif of
consciousness which we have recognized as the actual organon of the
mythical world intervenes at a decisive point in the structure of empirical
reality. If we believe that we know and apprehend this reality as twofold, outward and inner, physical and psychic, it is not because we in
some way inject psychic being and psychic processes into the facticity of
the world of things. Rather, it is the one originally given sphere of life
which is differentiated and which by this differentiation becomes more
and more confined. Through this process the world of objects, of
nature and natural laws, becomes correlated with the phenomena of life;
yet in this correlation it can never entirely absorb these phenomena into
itself and so eliminate them.

The paths of subjective and objective analysis here lead to the same
goal. Scheler essentially took the first road: as a phenomenologist he
sought to explore the consciousness of the ego and the consciousness of the
other ego. In so doing, he took consciousness in its fully developed form:
he started from the world view of outward and inner *experience* and
only occasionally looked backward to draw more primitive formations of
consciousness into the sphere of inquiry. We, however—in line with our
general formulation of the problem—are compelled to take the opposite
direction. We begin with the characterization of the mythical world as a
formation of the objective spirit and seek by reconstruction to arrive at
the stratum of consciousness corresponding to this formation. It is only
when the results of the two methods of inquiry illuminate and confirm
each other that we can gain the double perspective in which the purely
expressive experience will reveal its dimension of depth. From the
purely psychological standpoint it remains a kind of paradox when
Scheler declares that the consciousness of the other ego is earlier than
the consciousness of the ego, that perception of the thou precedes that
of the I. For as soon as we rely exclusively on introspection, the method of
psychological self-observation, everything that is apprehended in it and
through it seems to be placed within the sphere of one's own self. Here
it would seem that the ego must in some way be pre-given before a
world—either of outward objects or of other subjects—can open up to it.

But a very different state of affairs prevails if we start from a study of the symbolic forms and particularly of myth, for perhaps nothing is so characteristic of the mythical world view as the circumstance that within it the knowledge of the I, of a strictly individual self insofar as such a knowledge is present, stands not at the beginning but at the end. The presupposition that the epistemology of psychological idealism has so often set forth as self-evident—the assumption that only our own states of consciousness can be given, and that it is only through them, by inference, that the reality of other worlds of experience and of a physical nature can be acquired—is shown to be thoroughly problematic as soon as we glance at the structure of mythical phenomena. Here the I is in itself only insofar as it is at the same time in its counterpart, and only insofar is it related to this counterpart, to a "thou." Insofar as it knows itself, it does so only as a point of reference in this fundamental and primary relation. Except for this mode of being directed toward, of intention toward other centers of life, the I is nowhere in possession of itself. It is no thinglike substance, which can be thought of as existing in total isolation, separate from all other things in space, but acquires its content, its being-for-itself, only by knowing itself to be with others in *one* world and by distinguishing itself from others within this unity: "It is not," Scheler stresses,

> as though from a primarily given material of our own experiences we had to build up pictures of other people's experiences, in order then . . . to inject these experiences into the bodily phenomena of others; rather, there is first of all a stream of experiences, which is indifferent in respect to the I-thou and which contains factual contents of the ego and of the other ego in undifferentiated mixture; and in this stream there gradually form the clearly defined eddies which slowly draw new elements of the stream into their circles and in this process are correlated with successive and very gradually differentiated individuals.[21]

Our study of the form of the mythical I-consciousness has everywhere given us the most striking examples of this process. In myth we can still look directly into the growth of the more stable eddies which gradually detach themselves from the continuum of the life stream. We can see how, from life as a whole, from its undifferentiated totality, which along with

21. *Wesen und Formen*, p. 285.

the human world also contains the world of animals and plants, one's own being and also a form of what is human rises up and separates out only very slowly—and how within this being the reality of the genus and the species always precedes that of the individual. From such formations of the cultural consciousness and the law of sequence visible in them we gain a clearer view of the basic traits of the individual consciousness. Much that is difficult to recognize and interpret in the study of the individual psyche appears here, as Plato said, as though "written in large letters." It is only in the great creations of the cultural consciousness that the becoming of the I can truly be discerned, for man matures to the consciousness of his ego only in his spiritual deeds; he possesses his self only when instead of remaining within the ever identical flow of events he divides the stream and gives form to it. And only in this picture of a formed reality of experience does he find himself as subject, as a monadic center of multiform existence. In myth this act of turning inward (*Innen-Wendung*) and becoming aware (*Inne-Werdung*) can be followed step for step. The primary mythical fact is a man divided and torn to and fro by manifold outward impressions, each bearing a definite magical-mythical character, each laying claim to the whole of human consciousness and drawing it into its sphere, each imprinting its own color and mood. At first the ego has nothing to oppose to this impression and is unable to change it but can only accept it and in the act of acceptance become its prisoner. It is tossed this way and that by the expressive factors of the various phenomena, which assault it suddenly and irresistibly. These factors follow one another without fixed order and without transition; unpredictably, the various formations change their mythical "face." Without transition, an impression of the homelike, familiar, sheltering, and protective can shift into its opposite, the inaccessible, terrifying, monstrous, and gruesome.[22] As Usener showed by his notion of "gods of the moment" and "special gods," reality is demonic in this wholly indeterminate sense, long before it becomes a realm of determinate demons, delimited from one another and endowed with personal attributes and

22. As an illustration I should like to cite a single example taken from Jakob Spieth's book *Die Religion der Eweer in Süd-Togo* (Leipzig, 1911), pp. 7 f.: "When the first settlers arrived in Anvo, it is related that a man saw a giant baobab tree in the bush. At the sight of the tree he took fright. He therefore went to a priest for an interpretation of this occurrence. He was told that the baobab tree was a *trō* who wished to live with him and be worshiped by him. Thus fear was the sign by which the man recognized that a *trō* had been revealed to him.

characteristics.[23] This occurs when the confusion of diverse, swiftly changing impressions gradually condenses into separate figures with a determinate being. From the elementary mythical experiences which rise up out of nothing and dissolve into nothing, there now emerges something resembling the unity of a *character*. The pure phenomena of expression still preserve their old force; but they enter into a new and closer relation with one another; they fuse into formations of a higher order. The expression is not only experienced but is, as it were, characterologically evaluated. It is by determinate, relatively constant traits that the demon or god is recognized and distinguished from others. And what myth begins in this direction is completed by language and art: the god acquires full individuality only through his name and image. Thus the intuition of himself as a determinate, clearly delimited individual is not the starting point from which man progressively builds his general view of reality: rather, this intuition is only the end, it is only the mature fruit, of a creative process in which all the diverse energies of the spirit are at work and acting reciprocally on one another.

23. Cf. my *Sprache und Mythos*, pp. 18 ff.; and Vol. 2 of the present work, pp. 199 ff.

Chapter 3

The Expressive Function and the
Problem of Body and Soul

It is the pure fact of expression—the fact that a certain phenomenon in its simple "givenness" and visibility makes itself known to be inwardly animated—which first and most immediately tells us how consciousness, while remaining purely within itself, can at the same time apprehend another reality. Here we can no longer inquire into the origin of this fact itself and seek to explain it, for any attempted solution is bound to move in a circle. How can the sheer phenomenon of expression be understood by and *derived* from something else which transcends it when expression is itself the vehicle which *leads* us to every kind of transcendence, to all consciousness of reality? A skeptical denial of this original symbolic character of perception would cut off all our knowledge of reality at the root, but on the other hand any dogmatic attempt to explain this symbolic character itself is doomed to failure. Here we stand at a point where, as Goethe said, the most indigenous and necessary of concepts, the concept of cause and effect, threatens to lead us astray,[1] for the application of the category of causality to the pure expressive function cannot explain it but can only obscure it by robbing it of its character as an authentically original phenomenon.

But are we not running the same risk of obscuring this character if instead of considering the phenomenon of expression purely for itself and letting it subsist in itself, we link it with others—if we conceive of it as a species in a genus? Can we look on expression as a particular species and trend of symbolism without losing sight of its particularity, its irreplaceable uniqueness? Does such classification not weight it down

1. Cf. Goethe, "Über Naturwissenschaft im Allgemeinen," *Naturwissenschaftliche Schriften* (Weimar ed.), *11*, 103.

with a problem from which expression in itself is totally and happily exempt? Its peculiar privilege is precisely that it does not admit of a difference between image and thing, the sign and what it designates. In expression there is no cleavage between the mere sensuous existence of a phenomenon and a spiritual-psychic meaning which it mediately divulges. It is essentially an utterance—yet an utterance which remains entirely within itself. Here there is neither kernel nor shell; there is no first and second, no one and other. Consequently if we define the concept of symbolism in such a way as to limit it to those cases in which precisely this differentiation between mere image and the thing itself stands out clearly and in which this differentiation is emphasized and elaborated, we shall find ourselves beyond any doubt in a region to which this concept can have no application.

We on the other hand have given the concept of the symbol another and broader meaning from the very start. In it we have attempted to encompass the totality of those phenomena in which the sensuous is in any way filled with meaning, in which a sensuous content, while preserving the mode of its existence and facticity, represents a particularization and embodiment, a manifestation and incarnation of a meaning. Here it is not necessary for the two factors to have moved sharply apart, for them to be *known* in their otherness and opposition. This form of knowledge marks not the beginning but the end of the development. The duality of these factors is, to be sure, embedded in every phenomenon of consciousness, however primitive; but this potency is not from the very beginning unfolded into actuality. However deeply we may penetrate into the formations of the sensuous-spiritual consciousness, we never find this consciousness absolutely objectless, as something absolutely simple, prior to all separations and distinctions. It always appears as a living unity divided within itself, as a ἓν διαφερόμενον ἑαντῷ. But although the difference exists, it is not yet *posited* as such; this occurs only when consciousness passes from the immediacy of life to the form of the spirit and of spontaneous spiritual creation. It is only in this transition that all those tensions which are implicit in the sheer facticity of consciousness unfold: what previously was a concrete unity despite all its inner antitheses now begins to separate (*auseinandertreten*) and in this analytical differentiation to interpret (*auslegen*) itself. The pure phenomenon of expression has as yet no such form of dichotomy. In it a mode of understanding is given which is not attached to the condition of conceptual interpretation: the simple baring of the phenomenon is at the same time its interpretation, the only one of which it is susceptible and needful.

But this unity and simplicity, this self-evidence, vanish at once, giving way to highly complex problems, as soon as the purely theoretical view of the world, i.e. philosophy, turns to the phenomenon of expression and draws it into its jurisdiction. For now the divergence of the factors contained in expression is intensified by being seen as a diversity of origins. The phenomenological question is transformed into an ontological question; acceptance of what expression proclaims as its meaning is replaced by the question of its underlying reality. This reality cannot be conceived as simple; it is represented rather as a combination of two heterogeneous components. In it the physical and the psychic, body and soul, are combined and interrelated. But how is such a combination of two poles possible when each of them originates in and belongs to a different world? How can two entities coexist in experience which in their metaphysical essence seem absolutely antithetical? Thus the bond which links psychic and corporeal existence in the phenomenon of expression breaks as soon as we pass from the plane of the phenomenon to that of true being, to the plane of metaphysical knowledge. Between what the body is and what the soul is as metaphysical substance no mediation is possible. It is everywhere the striving of ontology—a striving rooted in its original question—to transpose problems of meaning into problems of pure being. Being is the foundation in which all meaning must ultimately be in some way grounded. No purely symbolic relation is looked upon as known and certain unless its *fundamentum in re* can be found—that is to say, unless what it signifies in itself is reduced to some *real* determination. And here it is above all two determinations which dominate the whole problem of metaphysics: the concept of the thing and the concept of causality. All other relations culminate in these two categories, which literally absorb them. What is not directly given as a relation of things and attributes, causes and effects, or what cannot be converted into such a relation by a logical process remains ultimately unintelligible—and this impossibility of understanding throws suspicion on its very existence and threatens to dissolve it into a figment without being, a delusion of the senses or imagination.

Nowhere is this general context more clearly revealed than in the fate which the problem of the body and the soul undergoes as soon as it is definitively removed from the sphere of experience and passes into the sphere of metaphysical thinking. What is demanded above all in this transition is that we should unlearn the language we already have. The language of the purely expressive function is treated as meaningful and comprehensible only if it can be translated into the language of the substantial metaphysical world view, into the language of substantial and causal concepts. But every effort spent on this translation proves in the end inadequate. There is always an obscure remainder which seems to defy all metaphysical thought. The entire labor of metaphysics since Aristotle has been unable to dispose of this remainder completely, to eliminate in principle the irrationality of this body-soul relationship. Despite all the exertions of the great classical systems of modern times, despite all the attempts undertaken by the rationalism of Descartes and Malebranche, Leibniz and Spinoza, to subject this problem to its domination, it still seems to persist in its own place, to preserve a strange and paradoxical meaning of its own. Here the modern metaphysician, insofar as he means to be at the same time a phenomenologist, finds himself in a dilemma. Even he does not succeed in drawing the problem wholly into the sphere of the metaphysical knowledge of being and essences and in throwing any penetrating light upon it. But on the other hand he is forced to recognize that this impenetrability cannot be absolutely imputed to an original obscurity in the problem itself. It is only the change of illumination, the change from the aspect of experience to the metaphysical aspect, which creates that strange twilight in which the problem of the body and soul has stood throughout the history of metaphysics. It is an essential merit of Nicolai Hartmann to have grasped this situation with his characteristic acuteness and rigor and to have stated it without reserve.[2] In his metaphysics of knowledge Hartmann no longer undertakes, like the older metaphysical systems, to dispel this twilight: he attempts solely to disclose it. He no longer seeks to solve the riddles of metaphysics at any price but contents himself with stating them clearly and fully. Thus for him "aporetics" becomes an essential component of metaphysics. As far as the body-soul question is concerned, there would, it is true, seem at first sight to be no room for such skepticism if we consider only the purely phenomenological "fact." Hartmann himself starts from the assumption that the unity of body and soul is present in the nature of man and therefore does

2. In connection with the following remarks on Nicolai Hartmann's metaphysics, cf. the more detailed treatment in my article "Erkenntnistheorie nebst den Grenzfragen der Logik und Denkpsychologie," *Jahrbücher der Philosophie*, 3 (1927), 79 ff.

not require to be made accessible. This unity is and subsists as long as it is not artificially torn apart. But all traditional metaphysical theories which claim to give an explanation of the relation between body and soul have been guilty of precisely such an artificial separation. Neither the theory of interaction nor that of psycho-physical parallelism does justice to its task: instead of describing or at least circumscribing what is phenomenally given, they replace it by a context of a wholly different kind. But even for Hartmann himself the unity, which from the standpoint of the phenomena stands unquestionable and secure, collapses as soon as we attempt to clarify and explain it by thought. From the standpoint of pure experience, from the standpoint of consciousness, it is certain that we know neither a soul without body, nor a body without soul. On the other hand, this *known* unity is by no means a *cognitive* unity. Although immediate knowledge shows us physical and psychic factors, not only in combination but indissolubly linked, we cannot succeed in translating this actual bond into a conceptual bond having necessity in the sense of a concept.

How a process can begin as a bodily process and end as a psychic process is absolutely incomprehensible. We can well understand *in abstracto* that this can be so, but not *in concreto*. Here there is an absolute limit of the knowable, where all categorial concepts, both physiological and psychological, fail. To assume a psycho-physical causality, which is meant to act both ways across this dividing line, was naturalistic naiveté. Indeed, it is even highly questionable whether the two fields, physiology and psychology, are adjacent, whether they actually touch at a common, so to speak, linear borderline, or whether they do not rather gape far apart, with a whole territory—a third, irrational territory—between them . . . For since the unity cannot be denied ontologically but can be apprehended neither physiologically nor psychologically, it ought probably to be taken as a purely ontic unity, independent of all apprehension, as a unity which is at once metaphysical and metapsychical, in short as an *irrational stratum underlying psychophysical being* . . . The unitary being of the psychophysical process lies then in this profound ontological stratum; it is an ontically real, irrational process, which is in itself neither physical nor psychic but has in these two only its surface areas that are exposed to consciousness.[3]

3. Nicolai Hartmann, *Grundzüge einer Metaphysik der Erkenntnis* (Berlin and Leipzig, 1925), pp. 322 f.

These sentences of Hartmann disclose with exemplary pregnancy and clarity the kind of reasoning which in general characterizes the relation of metaphysics to the body-soul problem. When it becomes apparent that the unity of body and soul, though undeniable as a *phenomenon,* cannot be represented in metaphysical concepts without grave contradictions, the metaphysicians infer not a deficiency in the *concepts* but an irrationality in *being.* They do not find fault with metaphysical thinking for shattering the unity of the phenomenon and dissolving it into disparate elements; instead they shift the incomprehensibility and contradiction into the core of reality itself. In being itself there is a yawning *hiatus irrationalis* which can be closed by no effort of thought, and there seems to remain only one way of bridging this gulf between psychic and physical reality. Although the two must remain heterogeneous, as long as they are viewed from the standpoint of empirically known and empirically accessible existence, there is still a possibility of establishing a close relation between them insofar as they originate in a common source. This common source, to be sure, cannot be found in the realm of experience but must be sought in a transcendent realm—and this implies that it can no longer be *known* in the strict sense but can only be surmised or at best posited as a hypothesis. "The parallelism of psychic and physical phenomena," Hartmann accordingly infers, "would then be a necessary consequence of their common root. The unitary, ontically real processes which must . . . ultimately be at work, begin or end neither in the physical nor the psychic sphere, but in a real third realm of which there is no immediate consciousness: it is only different parts or links in these real processes that are manifested as a physical or a psychic process." [4] From this we see that the answer of modern metaphysics to the question of the relation between body and soul differs in content, but not in general conceptual type from that of the older systems. The primal source in which a resolution of oppositions is sought is no longer, as in occasionalism, as in the Spinozist philosophy of identity, or in Leibniz' system of preestablished harmony, defined as divine; but its appointed function of uniting what cannot be united empirically, of effecting a *coincidentia oppositorum* in the sphere of absolute being—this function has remained unchanged. It does not solve the problem, however, but merely postpones it. For the question of the nature of the relationship between body and soul is raised for us by the *phenomenon,* which shows us the two never separate but always in their mutual rela-

4. Ibid., p. 324.

tion. This question is not answered if, instead of explaining the unity of the phenomenon, we have recourse to the unity of an unknowable, transcendent source. What is experienced in every simple phenomenon of expression is an indissoluble correlation, a thoroughly concrete synthesis of the physical and the psychic—but we cannot explain this concrete experience and cannot understand it by going back to that *"caput mortuum* of abstraction,"* as Hegel called it, to the thing in itself as the ultimate common root of all empirically different and separated entities. It is experience itself which set the task; the problem grew up within experience, and accordingly we must expect and insist that it be solved by its own means. A leap into the world of metaphysics can no longer help us here, for the problem of the body and soul belongs—if any problem does —to the natural world view and is bound to arise within its limits, within its theoretical horizon.

But in order to discern our problem in its original and genuine form, we must of course consider this horizon itself in all its breadth and in the full diversity of its possible aspects. This horizon is arbitrarily narrowed and the diversity curtailed when we take the category of causality as the only category, or as the truly constitutive category for all empirical existence and events. From the standpoint of theoretical natural science, to be sure, this assumption seems justified; since for natural science nature ultimately signifies nothing other than "the existence of things insofar as it is determined according to universal laws." And yet this order and determination according to laws, through which the object of natural science is first constituted, is by no means the only form of empirical determination. Not every empirical nexus can be mediately or immediately dissolved into a causal nexus; rather, there are certain basic forms of combination, which can only be understood if we resist the temptation to dissolve them into causal relations, if we leave them as they are and consider them as structures *sui generis*. And the body-soul relationship originally appears as the very prototype of such a nexus. As for metaphysics, it has been forced to recognize more and more clearly in the course of its history that this relationship cannot simply be fitted into the schema of causal thinking, and indeed that it is precisely the application of the causal schema to such a situation that gives rise to all manner of aporias and antinomies. But from this, most metaphysicians have merely concluded that empirical causality must at this point be replaced by a causality of a different form and dignity, by a transcendent causality. The relation is taken not fundamentally as a noncausal one but rather as a transcausal relation, resting on a causality of a higher order. "The type of determination," Hartmann stresses,

> which prevails in the ontological field, in the all-embracing sphere of being, and which links formations of being which are merely connected by their ontic character but are often heterogeneous in other respects, can of course only be a bond of a far more universal order than the causal nexus. Its relation to the causal nexus, as the nexus of objectivized nature, must be that of the transobjective to the objective. But it may not be sought on this side of causality, but only beyond it; it can be neither causal nor ciscausal, but only transcausal: a transobjective type of determination, insofar as it belongs to the same ontic sphere as the subject and the transsubjective entity that stands behind it.[5]

Thus instead of the empirical determination that prevails in the world of spatial-temporal events, another, an "intelligible" determination is assumed, which to be sure can only be posited on condition that we admit its irreducible irrationality, its fundamental unknowability. But actually should we not seek the deeper source of this irrationality in the false scale that is here applied from the very first to the phenomenon which we wish to elucidate? The history of metaphysics shows us clearly that every attempt to describe the body-soul relationship by transforming it into a relation of the conditioning and the conditioned, cause and effect, has culminated in inextricable difficulties. The body-soul relationship proves ever and again elusive, regardless of whether thought seeks to catch it in the meshes of an empirical causality or of a purely intelligible determination. For every kind of determination makes body and soul appear as two independent, self-subsistent entities, one of which is conditioned and determined by the other: and the peculiar mode of "in-volvement," of mutual interwovenness disclosed by the body-soul relationship, never ceases to resist this form of determination.

It is not an advance into the world of metaphysics—a world which is essentially built and governed by the concepts of substantiality and causality—but only a return to the primary phenomenon of expression that can here lead us toward a solution. For every metaphysics which does not set out to be an ontology but which recognizes the phenomenon of expression

5. Ibid., pp. 260 f.

in its peculiar structure, the problem indeed assumes a totally new form. In modern metaphysics it was Klages who first took this road. He looks on pure expressive experience as a kind of Archimedean point, from which he seeks to lift the world of ontology off its hinges. Thus for him the division of being into a physical and a psychic half fades away. "The soul," he stresses,

> is the meaning of the body and the body is the manifestation of the soul. Neither acts upon the other, for neither one belongs to the world of things. Since "acting upon" is inseparable from the interaction of things, the relation of cause and effect is merely a designation of separated parts of a relationship already thus analyzed; meaning and appearance, however, are themselves a relationship, or rather they are the prototype of all relationships. Anyone who finds it difficult to visualize a relation which is incomparably different from that of cause and effect, and of an infinitely closer kind, need only consider the analogous relation of the sign to what it designates . . . As the concept inheres in the linguistic sound, so does the soul inhere in the body: the former is the meaning of the word, the latter the meaning of the body; the word is the cloak of the thought, the body is the manifestation of the soul. No more than there are wordless concepts are there souls without manifest form.[6]

We take up this pregnant formulation because it brings us back to the center of our own systematic problem. The relation between body and soul represents the prototype and model for a purely symbolic relation, which cannot be converted either into a relation between things or into a causal relation. Here there is originally neither an inside and outside nor a before and after, neither an agent nor an effect; here we have a combination which does not have to be composed of separate elements but which is in a primary sense a meaningful whole which interprets itself, which separates into a duality of factors in order to interpret itself in them. A genuine access to the body-soul problem is possible only if we recognize as a general principle that all substantial and causal connections are ultimately based on such relations of meaning. The latter do not form a special class *within* the substantial causal relations: rather they are the constitutive presupposition, the *conditio sine qua non,* on which the substantial and causal relations themselves are based. In the course of our

6. Ludwig Klages, *Vom Wesen des Bewusstseins* (Leipzig, 1921), pp. 26 f.

investigation it will become increasingly clear that it is the symbolic functions of representation and meaning which first give access to that objective reality in which we are justified in speaking of substantial relations and causal relations. And thus it is the spiritual triad—the functions of pure expression, representation, and meaning—which first makes possible the intuition of an articulated reality. Precisely for this reason any explanation which seeks to bring the import of these functions closer to us by comparisons drawn from the world of things, is an ὕστερον πρότερον. The relation of the appearance to the psychic meaning that is expressed in it; of the word to the meaning presented through it, and finally of any abstract sign to the meaning content to which it points—all this has no analogy in the manner in which things stand side by side in space, in which events follow one another in time, or in which empirical changes are produced by one another; its specific meaning can only be taken from itself but not explained through analogies from the world that is made possible only by this meaning.

What makes it difficult to know of this relation is that all these acts of expressing, representing and signifying are not immediately present as such and can never become visible except in their achievement as a whole. They *are* only insofar as they are active and manifest themselves in their action. They do not originally look back at themselves but look toward the work that they accomplish, toward the being whose spiritual form they have to build up. And this implies that by and large the only possible description of their reality and efficacy is one which is drawn from their work, their accomplishment, and which in a sense speaks its language. This relationship does not first appear in the strictly speculative interpretation of metaphysics. Particularly where the body-soul relationship is concerned, the naive, unbroken unity represented by every experience of simple expression has become questionable long before the beginning of any formal metaphysics. The mythical world view has already effected the breech; for here begins the dualism which separates the twofold factors into substantially different entities. In its beginnings, to be sure, myth does not seem to have decided clearly between the two attitudes—it seems to stand halfway between the attitude resulting from the purely expressive phenomenon and that which follows from a theoretical, metaphysical interpretation. Here we have the beginning of a division between body and soul, but it is far from having the radical sharpness it will later disclose. Barely separated, body and soul seem prepared at any time to flow back into one another. The world is governed by a magical power which may be regarded equally well as corporeal or spiritual and which is totally indifferent toward this distinction. It inheres in things as well as persons, in the material as well as the immaterial, the living as well as the lifeless. One might say that what is here apprehended and mythically objectivized is the mystery of efficacy as such—and within this mystery no dividing line is drawn between the species of psychic and corporeal efficacy.[7] This delimitation does not occur until consciousness ceases to have and experience the world merely as a totality of expressive characters and begins to grasp reality by providing it with fixed substrates. This substantialization—at the level of concrete thinking on which we still stand— is possible only if it passes directly into the form of a *spatial* determination and a spatial intuition. The kind of community which subsists between body and soul seems now to be a mere coexistence—and in principle this coexistence implies at the same time a separation. The duality of factors has become a duality of zones: reality has definitively broken down into an inner world and an outward world. The corporeal no longer appears as the plain expression, the immediate manifestation of the psychic. The body does not reveal the soul but rather is a shell that conceals it. Only when it breaks through this shell in death does the soul come into its own essence and value and meaning. But this original mythical-religious conception still maintains the bond between body and soul, insofar as the two, although different in essence and origin, remain intimately linked by their destiny. Here the unity of mythical destiny replaces the ontic unity of essence. By a primordial decree of fate, the soul is confined to the cycle of corporeal becoming, fastened to the "wheel of births." This ineluctable mythical bond does not negate the separation that has been effected between the spheres of corporeal and psychic being; but it prevents the mythical mind from drawing all the logical consequences implicit in this separation. It is metaphysical thinking which first takes the final and decisive step. It makes the "coexistence" of body and soul a merely empirical and therefore accidental affair. This accidental link cannot resolve

7. Cf. above, 2, 158 ff., and my *Sprache und Mythos*, pp. 53 ff. It becomes evident that this indifference reflects a basic trait of the primary experience of expression, when we consider the parallels which other primitive formations of consciousness show to this mythical-magical view. It has often been pointed out that the same indifference prevails in the psychology of the child—that "the child experiences spiritual-personal contents as concrete and corporeal." Cf. Werner, *Einführung in die Entwicklungspsychologie*, Sec. 43; and Stern, *Die Psychologie der frühen Kindheit*, pp. 417 ff.

the opposition which necessarily results from the essence of both. No *vinculum substantiale* is strong enough to forge these originally heterogeneous entities into a true unity. In the course of its history metaphysics has been increasingly impelled to take this road. In Aristotle the soul is still the entelechy of the body and thus its most proper "reality," but modern metaphysics, by stripping the body of everything that belongs to the sphere of pure expression, makes it a mere physical body—and moreover defines the matter of this body as a purely geometrical matter. For Descartes, the only necessary characteristic that remains of the concept of matter is: extension in length, breadth, and depth. On the other hand, all psychic being, the whole reality of consciousness, is exhausted in the act of *cogitatio*. But between the spatial world built up by geometry and mechanics and that fundamentally aspatial being that we apprehend in the act of pure thought there is no possible logical or empirical mediation; the only medium in which the two can find each other and in which their opposition is resolved is the transcendence of the divine primal source. But it goes without saying that this absorption which they experience in the absolute does not allay the empirical-phenomenal contradictions; it only makes them stand out all the more sharply as such. Ultimately, we can avoid these contradictions only by returning to their actual source; by putting ourselves back at the center of that symbolic relation in which the psychic appears related to the bodily and the bodily to the psychic—in the purely expressive phenomenon. But of course the peculiarity of this relation can only be made clear if we take the expressive function not as an isolated factor but as a member within a comprehensive spiritual whole, and seek to determine its position and particular achievement within this whole.

PART II

The Problem of Representation and the Building of the Intuitive World

Chapter 1

The Concept and Problem of Representation

IF WE WISH to go forward from the primary form of consciousness contained in the pure experience of expression to richer and higher forms of experience, we can find the clue once again only in the objective configurations of cultural life. If we here discern products which lie beyond the realm of naive expressive experience, it must be our task to go back from them to the functions in which they are grounded. We have found that the meaning and basic trend of the pure expressive function could be apprehended most clearly and surely if we took the world of myth as our point of departure. It is still wholly dominated by this meaning, which as it were permeates and animates it. And yet as the mythical world unfolds more richly, a new motif asserts itself. The very fact that for myth reality is a self-contained cosmos—that it sees reality not as a mere sum of particular traits and characters but as a totality of *forms*—points toward this motif. In the earliest forms of mythical consciousness to which we can make our way back the face of the world seems to change unremittingly. This mobility and instability, this abrupt, unmediated shifting from one form into another, would seem to lie in the very essence of the mythical world view. The world nowhere stands fast as one contemplates it but in every moment appears in a different, strangely hovering, and ephemeral light. Even when more fixed formations gradually rise out of its surge and flow—when the individual phenomena not only show a fluid and indeterminate demonic "character" but are apprehended and experienced as the manifestation of demonic or divine beings, these very beings still have no true constancy and universality. "The particular phenomenon is deified in full immediacy, and no generic concept, however limited, plays a part in the process; the *one* thing that you see before you, that thing itself and nothing more is the god." But myth is driven further and further beyond this first intuition of mere "momentary gods" as it enters into relation with a new and fundamental power of the spirit and becomes permeated with that power. It is the power of language that lends stability and permanence to the formations of myth. In his book on the names of gods Usener has striven to follow this process in detail and to clarify and interpret it with the help of the history of language. Though many of his interpretations may be uncertain or questionable, he has clearly grasped a universal tendency of the mythical consciousness.[1] Language first provides that possibility of "finding-again" and of recognition by virtue of which totally different, spatially and temporally separate, phenomena can be understood as manifestations of one and the same subject, as revelations of a determinate and self-identical divine being. Even at this elementary stage language thus accomplishes in principle what it will achieve in its highest logical development: it becomes the vehicle of "recognition in the concept," without which myth could not attain to permanent, stable configurations. But this common achievement of language and myth brings us to the threshold of a new spiritual world. Myth already reveals the striving and the power, not simply to glide along in the stream of feeling and affective agitation, but to fetter this movement and bring it into a kind of spiritual focus, into the unity of an "image." But as its images rise directly from its flowing inner movement, they are always in danger of being swept back into it. A factor of rest and inner permanence is achieved only when the image grows, as it were, beyond itself—when, in a transition which is at first almost imperceptible, it becomes *representation*. For the representation of a god comprises two different spiritual elements and dissolves them into each other. It grasps the god in his wholly immediate living presence, for representation is not intended to be taken as a mere copy; rather, it is the god himself who is embodied and active in it. On the other hand, this momentary action does not exhaust the whole of his being. The representation, as presence, is at the same time actualization: what stands before us as here and now, what is given as this particular and determinate thing, announces itself also as the emanation and manifestation of a power which is not wholly exhausted in any such particularity. Through the concrete uniqueness of the image we now perceive this total power. Though it may hide itself in a thousand forms, it remains its identical self in them all: it possesses a fixed nature and es-

1. Cf. above, p. 90; and 2, 22, 200–5.

sence which in all these forms is captured mediately—that is, "represented" in them.

But although this kind of representation can be fully understood and appreciated only from the standpoint of language, all modes of linguistic utterance are not bound up with it in the same way. There seems rather to be an elementary stratum of linguistic utterance in which the tendency toward representation is present only in its germinal beginnings, if at all. Here language moves almost exclusively in purely expressive elements and characters. The linguistic sound seems at first to be wholly confined to the phase of mere phonetization. It does not designate any particular factor in objective reality, but is a mere outpouring of the speaker's inner states and an immediate discharge of dynamic tension. All that is customarily designated as animal language seems to be confined permanently to this phase. Diverse as the animal cries and calls may be—cries of fear or pleasure, mating calls, and calls of warning—they do not go beyond the sphere of mere sounds expressing sensation. They are not "significant" in the sense of being correlated as signs with definite things and happenings in the outside world. According to the observations of W. Koehler, even the language of the most highly developed anthropoid apes, rich as it is in direct expressions for the most diverse subjective states and desires, remains confined to this sphere: it never produces a sign or designation for an object.[2] Likewise in the child the function of designation stands only at the end of linguistic development; here, too, the words of the objective language which he acquires by learning have for a long time not the specific, objectivizing meaning which highly developed language connects with them. Rather, all meaning is rooted in the stratum of effectivity and sensory stimulation and is referred back to it over and over again. Thus the first attributives used by the child do not so much designate attributes and characteristics of things as express inner states; and similarly, as late as the second year of life the affirmation and negation, the "yes" and "no," are used not as a statement in the logical sense but rather as an expression of an affective attitude, a desire or rejection.[3] Only in the course of gradual development does the purely representative

2. Cf. Koehler, "Zur Psychologie des Schimpansen," p. 27; Eng. ed., appendix, p. 317. Cf. Vol. *1* of the present work, pp. 190 ff.

3. Cf. Clara and William Stern, *Monographien über die seelische Entwicklung der Kindes* (2 vols. Leipzig, 1907–09), Vol. *1*, *Die Kindersprache*, pp. 35, 39, 224 ff.

function assert itself, growing stronger and stronger and finally dominating the whole of language.[4] But even now it must unmistakably share this domination with other factors and tendencies. Far as language may progress in the direction of representation and purely logical signification, it never loses its connection with the primary expressive experience. Very definite "expressive characters" remain interwoven with its supreme intellectual achievements. All the phenomena that we call onomatopoeia belong to this sphere, for in the genuine onomatopoeic formations of language we are dealing far less with the direct limitation of objectively given phenomena than with a phonetic and linguistic formation which still remains wholly within the purely physiognomic world view. Here the sound attempts, as it were, to capture the immediate face of things and with it their true essence. Even where living language has long since learned to use the word as a pure vehicle of thought it never wholly relinquishes this connection. And it is above all the poetic language which persistently strives back toward this original physiognomic expression, in which it seeks to plunge as in a primordial source and eternal fountain of youth. But even where language is solely concerned with working out a logical meaning, which it simply seeks to set forth as such in its objectivity and universality, it cannot dispense with the possibilities of melodic and rhythmic expression, which prove to be not superfluous embellishments but genuine vehicles and constituents of signification itself. The factors which we subsume under the concept of linguistic melody play a part in determining the logical structure and understanding of the sentence. "Formed out of a unitary meaning, the linguistic melody makes a decisive contribution to the precise determination of signification; thus it is the sensuous expression, the representation of the over-all meaning as a unity."[5] Clinical observation in the pathology of language shows

4. I use the term "representative function" (*Darstellungsfunktion*) in the same sense as Karl Bühler, whose works were not known to me when I treated the problem from the standpoint of the philosophy of language in the first volume of the present work (see esp. pp. 94, 186 ff.). This is all the more reason to mention here the fundamental agreement between the findings of a general analysis from the standpoint of the philosophy and history of language and of Bühler's investigations, which are essentially oriented toward psychology and biology. See Bühler, "Kritische Musterung der neueren Theorien des Satzes," *Indogermanisches Jahrbuch*, 6 (1919); "Vom Wesen der Syntax," *Festschrift für Karl Vossler* (Heidelberg, 1922). And cf. his recent article "Über den Begriff der sprachlichen Darstellung," *Psychologische Forschung*, 3 (1923), 282–94.

5. Julius Stenzel, "Sinn, Bedeutung, Begriff, Definition. Ein Beitrag zur Frage der Sprachmelodie," *Jahrbuch fur Philologie, 1* (1925), 182.

that in cases of so-called "amusia," where the musical components of language are not correctly apprehended, the perception of grammatical and syntactic meaning also tends to be altered and impaired in some way. Certain modal orientations of linguistic meaning which are indispensable to its understanding and interpretation, such as the interrogative or imperative character of certain sentences, are in many cases expressed almost exclusively by musical elements.[6] Here again it is confirmed that the spiritual factor of signification is closely bound up with the sensuous factor of expression; it is both factors together in their close interdetermination that first constitute the actual life of language. This life can never be merely sensuous any more than it can be purely spiritual; it can only be apprehended as body and soul at once, as an embodiment of the logos.

But although the sensuous character of expression and the logical factor of signification cannot be separated in the actual reality of language, the purely *functional* difference between them remains unmistakable. Any attempt to dissolve expression in signification or to derive one from the other genetically remains in vain. Similarly, as seen by developmental psychology, the function of representation does not always grow out of formations belonging to the sphere of mere expression but always represents something specifically new, a decisive turning point in relation to them. The world of animal sensation seems to be situated wholly on the other side of this great dividing line. Just as the animal lacks representation in the word, he lacks the genuine "indicative" gesture; the "reaching into the distance," which is a part of all interpretive movement, remains closed to it. Here nature acts wholly as an outward stimulus which must be sensuously present in order to arouse the sensation corresponding to it; it does not enter into the relationship of the mere image, which is projected in the imagination, and which in a sense anticipates the existence of the object.[7] "Because man responds no less to images than to physical impressions," writes Ludwig Klages in his *Ausdrucksbewegung und Gestaltungskraft* [*Expressive Movement and Formative Power*],

his expressive movement is often connected with the representative content of his spatial intuition . . . admiration, because oriented toward elevation, is aimed upward; envy, because oriented toward abase-

6. Cf. Arnold Pick, *Die agrammatischen Sprachstörungen* (Berlin, 1913), *1*, 162 f.
7. Cf. above, *1*, 180 ff.

ment, is aimed downward. Such feelings and expressive factors are alien to the animal, just as on the other hand the animal is without intuition of space, and consequently, for example, totally disregards all painted or sculptured reproductions of life . . . For the animal a man drawn or painted in perspective is never anything more than a piece of colored paper or canvas.[8]

But even for man it is evident that long after he has learned to live in images, long after he has completely implicated himself in his self-made image worlds of language, myth, and art, he must pass through a long development before he acquires the specific *consciousness* of the image. In the beginning he nowhere distinguishes between the pure image plane and the causal plane; over and over again, he imputes to the sign not a representative function but a definite causal function, a character not of signification but of efficacy.[9] And here again ontogeny has faithfully reproduced phylogeny. The ontogenetic development shows that wherever the function of representation stands out *as such,* where, instead of giving himself wholly to the actuality, the simple presence of a sensuous content, man succeeds in taking it as a representative of another, he has achieved an entirely new level of consciousness. The moment in which any particular sensory impression is used symbolically and understood as a symbol is always the dawn of a new era, so to speak. Anne Mansfield Sullivan, the teacher of the deaf and blind Helen Keller, has given us an account of this first break-through of linguistic understanding; it is one of the most important records of this relationship, whose actual significance goes far beyond the sphere of individual psychological problems.[10] Here we

8. Klages, pp. 95, 198. The fact that animals often "react" strongly to pictures, i.e. shrink back from them with violent expressions of fear, does not refute this view, but rather confirms it. Pfungst tells us that a young ape which he had brought up took a violent fright one day at the sight of a human portrait, a drawing of Frederick the Great by Fidus, with strongly accentuated eyes. The animal could only be quieted after the picture was removed. But obviously the drawing had not been taken as a picture of a man; the ape had merely grasped certain expressive factors in it. What affected the animal was the physiognomic experience of the "eyelike" as such, which by no means presupposes recognition of a human face and of the eye as part of this face. With regard to this difference see Werner's remarks in *Einführung in die Entwicklungspsychologie,* p. 53.

9. Cf. above, 2, 38 ff., 237 ff.

10. Well known as this report is, I should like to quote it here because of its characteristic details. "We went out to the pump-house, and I made Helen hold her mug under the spout while I pumped. As the cold water gushed forth, filling the mug, I spelled 'w-a-t-e-r' in Helen's free hand. The word coming so close upon the sensation of cold water rushing

have striking evidence that the pure *function* of representation is not attached to any concrete sensuous *material,* optical or acoustical, that this function, even where the material at its disposal is restricted in the extreme—reduced to the purely tactile sphere—can nevertheless assert itself successfully and without impairment. When the representative function of names has thus dawned on a child, his whole inner attitude toward reality has changed—a fundamentally new relation between subject and object has come into being.[11] Only now do the objects which hitherto acted directly on the emotions and will begin in a sense to recede into the distance: into a distance where they can be "looked at," "intuited," in which they can be actualized in their spatial outlines and independent qualitative determinations.

For this power of intuition Herder chose the term "reflection." We have seen that for him the concept of reflection had a different meaning from that given it by the linguistic philosophy of the eighteenth century, particularly that of the French Encyclopedists. For him it no longer designates the mere power of the human intellect to shift sensuous-intuitive contents about at will, to dissect them into their elementary components and create new structures from them by free combination. Reflection, as Herder understood it, is no mere thinking about given intuitive contents; rather it helps to determine and to constitute the form of these very contents. "Man demonstrates reflection when, emerging from the nebulous dream of images flitting past his senses, he can concentrate upon a point of wakefulness, dwell voluntarily on one image, observe it calmly and lucidly, and distinguish characteristics proving that this and no other is the object."[12] But how do we come to this *positing* of characteristics, which must necessarily precede any comparison between them and everything that we

---

over her hand seemed to startle her. She dropped the mug and stood as one transfixed. A new light came into her face. She spelled 'water' several times. Then she dropped on the ground and asked for its name and pointed to the pump and the trellis, and suddenly turning round she asked for my name. I spelled 'Teacher.' Just then the nurse brought Helen's little sister into the pump-house, and Helen spelled 'baby' and pointed to the nurse. All the way back to the house she was highly excited, and learned the name of every object she touched, so that in a few hours she had added thirty new words to her vocabulary." Helen Keller, *The Story of My Life* (New York, Doubleday, 1903), p. 316. Cf. Clara and William Stern, *Die Kindersprache,* pp. 176 ff.

11. Good examples for the decisive importance of the appellative function may be found in Karl Bühler, *Die geistige Entwicklung des Kindes* (2d ed. Jena, 1921), pp. 207 ff., 374 ff.

12. Herder, "Abhandlung über den Ursprung der Sprache" (1772), *Werke, 5,* 34 ff. Cf. Vol. *1* of the present work, pp. 152–3.

customarily call "abstraction" in the logical sense of the word? Here it does not suffice to single out from the given, still undifferentiated totality of a phenomenon certain elements toward each of which consciousness turns in a separate act of "attention." The crucial factor is rather that from this totality a factor is not only detached by abstraction but at the same time taken as a representative of the whole. For it is thus that the content first gains the imprint of a new universal form without losing its material "particularity." Only then does it function as a characteristic in the true sense: it has become a sign which enables us to *recognize* it again when it reappears. This act of recognition is necessarily bound up with the function of representation and presupposes it. Only where we succeed, as it were, in compressing a total phenomenon into one of its factors, in concentrating it symbolically, in "having" it in a state of "pregnance" in the particular factor [13]—only then do we raise it out of the stream of temporal change; only then does its existence, which had hitherto seemed confined to a single moment in time, gain a kind of permanence: for only then does it become possible to find again in the simple, as it were, punctual "here" and "now" of present experience a "not-here" and a "not-now." Everything that we call the identity of concepts and significations, or the constancy of things and attributes, is rooted in this fundamental act of finding-again. Thus it is a common function which makes possible on the one hand language and on the other hand the specific articulation of the intuitive world. The question of whether the articulation of the intuitive world must be conceived as preceding or following the genesis of articulated language—the question of whether the first is the cause or the effect of the second—must here be regarded as falsely formulated. What can be demonstrated is no "earlier" or "later" but only the inner relationship subsisting between the two fundamental forms and trends of spiritual articulation. Neither of them, in a purely temporal sense, "arises" from the other: rather they are like two stems springing from the same spiritual root. We cannot lay bare this root as such, we cannot disclose it as a datum of consciousness immediately accessible to observation: we can only find it indirectly by devoting ourselves without preconception to the investigation of the two offshoots, both of which stand before us in a clear bright light, and then seek to follow them back to their common source. Here again the indissoluble unity of the psycho-physical relationship is disclosed. In each one of its acts the power of re-

13. On the concepts of "pregnance" and "pregnant having" see below, Chap. 5.

flection operates at once inward and outward: it appears on the one hand in the articulation of the sound—in the articulation and rhythmization of the linguistic movement—and on the other hand, in the sharper differentiation and relief of the perceptual world. The processes always go hand in hand: it is from this living, dynamic interrelation that a new equilibrium of consciousness gradually arises and a stable world view is produced.

The investigation of language has shown us the general direction in which this positing of characteristics moves. From the passing dream of images, language first singles out certain factors, certain stable particularities and attributes. Such attributes may be viewed in a purely material sense; they may be of an entirely sensuous nature; but to posit them as attributes nevertheless signifies a pure act of abstraction, or rather of determination. Such an act of determination is alien to the purely expressive experience which lives in the moment and spends itself in the moment. But here there is a demand that consciousness—contrary to its fundamental character, contrary to the Heraclitean flux in which alone it seems to subsist—shall step twice, in fact many times, into the same river. Transcending objective time and experienced time, it must seize upon a permanent and stable content and posit it as identical with its self. Identifications of this kind—even if they do no more than establish and postulate purely sensuous qualities—contain the germ and beginning of every form of concept formation. For the identity or similarity which we apprehend in two different and temporally separate impressions is itself no mere impression that is added to the others and simply embeds itself in the same plane with them. If something that is given here and now is taken and recognized as a "this,"—if for example it is recognized as a certain shade of red or as a tone of a certain pitch—we already have to do with a genuinely "reflective" factor. But the qualifying concept formation that develops in language does not stop here. It does not content itself with positing different things as identical because of some similarity or identity that stands out in them; it also composes the individual positings thus gained into comprehensive totalities, into distinct groups and series. Thus, for example, not only can the most diverse color phenomena with all the variety of tonality, brightness, etc. that they disclose be taken as instances of red, green, etc., but "red" and "green" themselves appear in turn as special instances, as representatives, of "color pure and simple." Here we have come to the phenomena which Lotze subsumed under the term "first universal." Lotze stressed that the generic concepts of "color" or "tone" were not formed by suppressing and effacing the individual and specific differences of color and tone phenomena, by subsuming the totality of these phenomena in some way under a general idea. The decisive act is rather that within the sequence of these particulars we create definite intervals which provide a characteristic division and articulation. In its unremitting, constant flow certain favored points are gradually singled out, and around them the other members group themselves; certain formations arise which are held fast as clearly essential factors and as such endowed with a kind of special accent. Our analysis of linguistic concept formation has shown how language plays a decisive part in this accentuation and articulation. The "first universal" is only guaranteed by the fact that it finds a hold and a firm precipitate in language.[14] Here consciousness, under the guidance of language, rises, one might say, to a new dimension of reflection. The manifold and dispersed is not only gathered together but composed into independent and characteristic structures of a higher order, and these structures form the actual centers of crystallization, to which all that is newly arising clings. Thus far we have sought to follow this process in language; through its formations we have sought to disclose the analysis of reality, its breakdown into substances and qualities, things and attributes, spatial determinations and temporal relations. Now we shall have to examine the same question once again, but from a different point of view. The inner bond that exists between the form of language and the form in which we apprehend intuitive reality will be disclosed in full clarity only if we find that the building of the two leads through essentially the same stages. As soon as we find that the classification of the world, the *divisio naturae,* into objects and states, genera and species is by no means "given" from the very beginning, the question arises: to what extent is the rich and varied fabric of our intuitive world itself wrought and governed by definite spiritual energies? We can answer this question only by unraveling the fabric, so to speak, and following its various threads separately. But in this methodologically necessary division we must never lose sight of our task as a whole. Here analysis can and must be taken as no more than a preparation for a future synthesis. The more closely we follow the special paths taken by the universal function of representation and recognition, the more clearly their nature and specific unity will be revealed to us—and it

14. Cf. above, *1*, 278 ff.

will be increasingly evident that it is ultimately one and the same fundamental achievement by which the spirit rises to the creation of language and the intuitive world view, to the discursive understanding and objective *intuition* of reality.

Chapter 2

Thing and Attribute

THE QUESTION of the relation between language and thought is as old as philosophy and probably older: it is among the earliest problems that forced themselves on the human spirit. The problems of language seemed to have stirred the human mind earlier than the problems of nature. Like a primordial miracle, language kindled the philosophical emotion of wonder. When man first turns his attention to it, it confronts him not as something that has become but as something that always is and has been: not as his own work but as a foreign power to which he feels subject and before which he bows down. The magical world view is thoroughly imbued with this belief in the omnipotence of the word and the name. Philosophical reflection dissolves this magical bond; but in its beginnings it, too, is wholly dominated by that "archaic logic" for which the forms of thought and language form an indissoluble unity.[1] And although philosophical logic gradually sought to relax this bond—although it sought more and more to arrive by reflection at the independent and autonomous laws of "pure" thought—the philosophy of language stubbornly adhered to them for a much longer time. Here the thesis of the identity of speech and thought recurs in ever new forms, supported by ever new arguments. "Language created reason; before language man was without reason"—this is the thesis succinctly formulated by so late a thinker as Lazarus Geiger. Thus language seems assured of the highest rank in the realm of spirit; an absolutely universal value seems accorded to its achievement. But if we examine more closely this supposed identity of language and reason, we find of course that it remains imperfect in two different ways—it gives language both too much and too little. Those who advocate this view overlook that there are forms in

1. Cf. Ernst Hoffmann, "Die Sprache und die archaische Logik," *Heidelberger Abhandlungen zur Philosophie und ihrer Geschichte, 3* (Tübingen, 1925).

which conceptual thought frees itself from the guidance of language and builds an independent realm of theoretical signification; they also fail to see that the spiritual function of language cannot be narrowed to the sphere of strictly logical problems, the sphere of concepts, judgment, and inferences. The power of the linguistic form is not exhausted in what it accomplishes as a vehicle and medium for logical-discursive thought. It already permeates the intuitive view and formation of the world; it plays no less a part in building the realm of perception and intuition than that of concepts. This building of perception and intuition is possible only if consciousness as a whole effects the general turn which we have designated as the transition to "representation." Already the world of intuition is essentially determined by the fact that its particular elements possess no merely "presentative" but rather "representative" character: they do not simply "stand there"—they stand for one another; they can refer to one another and in a sense represent one another. Even where it is strongly emphasized that the sound is no mere outward cloak for the thought but "the indication and cause of a determinate formation of thought," it is not always made clear that in principle the same inference must also be drawn for the sphere of intuition, and even more so for that of perception. Lazarus writes, for example: "Outside of language and before it, there is to be sure an intuition of particular things, or rather phenomena, but there can be a grasping and knowing only through language." [2] But is it actually possible to separate intuitive recognition

2. Moritz Lazarus, *Das Leben der Seele in Monographien über ihre Erscheinungen und Gesetze* (Berlin, 1857), 2, 193. The modern psychology of thought—in the form represented by Hoenigswald, for example—also seems at first to seek the achievement of language exclusively in the field of discursive thinking and to limit it expressly to this sphere. But if we examine it more closely, it becomes plain that the doctrine of the "verbality of thought" (*die Worthaftigkeit des Gedankens*), as developed by Hoenigswald, has a far more inclusive meaning. According to Hoenigswald, there is no idea without primary verbal reference, no experience of thought whose possibility is not contingent on a possible correlation with the word. For anyone who thinks "something" reaches out in the very postulation of this something into a sphere of objective being and objective validity: he presumes that what he thinks is the same for all, or ought to be. Accordingly, to think "something" and the possible communication of what has been thought are interchangeable concepts: anyone who thinks "something" necessarily seeks a linguistic expression, because and insofar as he presumes such an objective meaning for his thought. The "verbality of thought" is accordingly "the decisive condition for any linguistic-constructive unfolding of ideas in sentences and discourse" and, "taken psychologically, it also explains the unerring striving of thought for the linguistic-constructive unfolding of its ideas." If we examine this argumentation more closely, we recognize that it is by no means restricted to the sphere of logical-discursive thinking but refers to all acts of the theoretical consciousness, insofar as they lay any claim to objectivity,

in this way from grasping and knowing, and to make it their presupposition as a purely material substance? Is there an immediate intuition of things; or is the knowledge of things, the articulation of reality according to things and attributes, not itself the result of a mediation which we do not ordinarily discern simply because we are always effecting it and always in the midst of it?

Actually a glance at certain findings of developmental psychology will show us that the articulation of the world according to things and attributes is by no means self-evident and does not necessarily pertain to every form in which reality can be experienced. Thus, for example, it would seem that animal perception does not yet yield stable things with determinate attributes which may change in the thing itself but also possess an intrinsic property of permanence. From the complex whole of a perceptive experience the animal does not detach particular characteristics by which it recognizes a content and which identify it as the same content regardless of how often and under what different conditions it appears. This sameness is not at all a factor that is contained in the immediate experience—on the plane of sensory experience itself there is no "recurrence of the same." Every sense impression, taken purely as such, possesses a peculiar, never recurring tonality or coloration. Where the purely expressive character of this tonality or coloration predominates, the world is not yet homogeneous and constant in our sense. Particularly since Hans Volkelt's painstaking observations, there seems to be no doubt that for the animal there are in general no stable things, but that its perceptive

---

insofar as they refer to and are oriented toward an object in any way. This intention toward the objective is by no means limited to thought as logical judgment and inference, but belongs properly to perception and intuition: in them, too, *something* is to be perceived, *something* intuited. If the postulation of a something is bound up with verbality, verbality must appear in these primary strata and participate decisively in their structure. Actually, it is a striking feature of Hoenigswald's psychology that, compared with the traditional view and the traditional psychological terminology, it considerably broadens the concept of thinking. For here, "thinking" no longer signifies a single class of psychological phenomena, over against other classes (such as sensation or intuition, feeling or volition), but is the fundamentally psychological phenomenon as such: it is what *makes* every psychic content psychic. "Thinking" here becomes the universal term for meaningfulness of experiences and precisely this meaningfulness—which, as Hoenigswald stresses, belongs to even the most elementary psychological fact, whether we call it sensation, representation, perceptual element, etc.—is truly constituted only by the "verbality of meaning." Cf. Richard Hoenigswald, *Die Grundlagen der Denkpsychologie* (2d ed. Leipzig, 1925), pp. 28 ff., 128 ff., 157 ff.

reality is built up of still inarticulated "complex qualities."[3] "Things it reacts to," writes Thorndike, ". . . are not the hard-and-fast, well-defined 'things' of human life," but lie as though embedded and fused in certain concrete general situations, and these must be wholly identical in order to move the animal to an identical behavior.[4] Thus it is clear also from this angle that the "thing" is by no means grounded in the sensory character of perception, in the mere impression, but is of a reflective character —in the sense of Herder's concept of reflection. Likewise in the development of the child there is no doubt that the intuition of the world of things does not exist from the beginning but must in a sense be wrested from the world of language. The first "names" which the child masters and uses with understanding seem to designate no fixed and permanent objects but only more or less fluid and vague general impressions. Any change in these general impressions, however slight from our standpoint, suffices to prevent the use of the same name. "His mother need only have on another hat or dress; a thing need only occupy a different position in the room to produce an impression of strangeness on the child and no longer release the word which otherwise occurs regularly."[5] Only as the word is freed from this initial restriction, only when it is apprehended in its universal signification and applicability, does the new horizon of the "thing" arises in the child's consciousness. Here again it is the awakening of the symbolic consciousness as such which seems to open this new horizon. All observers agree in describing the almost insatiable hunger for names which seizes the child at this point; he wants to know the name of every new impression. For a time, some writers have pointed out, this desire to name things becomes a kind of mania.[6] But the mania becomes understandable once we realize that it is no empty mental game but an original urge toward objective intuition. The hunger for names is ultimately a hunger for forms, an urge for essential apprehension. Thus characteristically the child at first asks not what a thing is called but what it is. For him the being and the name of an object fuse wholly into one:

3. Cf. Hans Volkelt's observations on the spider; for details see his *Über die Vorstellungen der Tiere* (Leipzig, 1912), pp. 15 ff., 46 ff.

4. Edward L. Thorndike, *Animal Intelligence*, 1898; (New York and London, 1911), pp. 119 ff.

5. Bühler, *Die geistige Entwicklung des Kindes*, p. 128.

6. Cf. David R. Major, *First Steps in Mental Growth* (London, 1906), p. 321, quoted from Clara and William Stern, *Die Kindersprache*, p. 176.

in and through the name, he *has* the object. Even before he uses the name for the conscious purpose of communication, it becomes crucially significant for the building of his perceptual world.[7] The knowledge of the identical signification of the name develops hand in hand with the knowledge of thing identities and attribute identities: both are only different aspects of the transformation undergone by consciousness in coming under the domination of the pure "representative function." Only now that the *meaning* of the name is gained does reality stand fast under our gaze; now our attention can dwell on it. And only in this standing-fast is the object gained and secured. The mythical-magic view of the world knows as yet nothing of such truly enduring objectivity. It also lacks the "thing" in the characteristic, specific signification it assumes in the sphere of theoretical intuition. Here all reality is still interchangeable —all attributes are transferable from one object to another.[8] Only as the pure symbolic consciousness develops with language does the category of the thing gain significance and stability, until in the end it comes to permeate all intuition, setting its stamp upon it more clearly and more sharply, and in a sense we may say more and more inflexibly and one-sidedly.

But precisely because of the almost unlimited domination that this category exerts in the realm of theoretical being and knowledge, it seems difficult if not impossible to disclose its origin within this sphere itself. If everything that is theoretically known to us gives itself to us only as imprinted form, how can we hope to gain a theoretical understanding, as it were, of the act of imprinting as such; how can we hope to derive it? We can never gain any immediate grasp of the function as it works here, because it gives itself to us only in its product and always vanishes with this product. And yet there is a way of making it at least indirectly visible, for all the structures of the theoretical world do not show one and the same mode and stability of articulation. In the structures of consciousness the phenomena are always charged, so to speak, with definite purely representative characters; but the dynamic tension that here prevails is not everywhere the same. And precisely this inequality, this variability, shows us a way of differentiating the two factors which we know only in their interrelation—of differentiating them precisely in this interrelation. In making this distinction we must, to be sure, resist the temptation

7. For documentation cf. *Die Kindersprache*, pp. 175 ff.
8. Cf. above, 2, 55 ff.

of seeking to make the differences of meaning and significance intelligible by tracing them back to ontically real differences—of explaining them through realistic assumptions concerning the nature and structure of the world of things or the world of simple sensations. We have shown the vicious circle in which such explanations move in our appraisal of the attempts to stamp the pure expressive phenomenon as a mediated phenomenon grounded in certain acts of judgment and inference.[9] The same form of reasoning occurs over and over again in attempted explanations of the representative function. There is always a striving to replace the indication contained in every true phenomenon of representation by another, purely mediated form of disclosing or demonstrating. The act of intention, of objective meaning in general, is somehow transformed into a discursive act, a series of logical steps. But no more than the simple expressive experience can the phenomenon of representation be broken down into a chain of analogies, insofar as we take this phenomenon in its fundamental form and original determinate character. To say that the "perception" represents an object for us, that this object "gives itself to be recognized" in and through the perception, is radically different from saying that one content is dependent on another and is attached to it either by an empirical or a transcendent causality. The form of reasoning by which this mode of causality is known, the inductive inference or deductive derivation, cannot grasp the phenomenon and problem of representation. For this problem in no way pertains to the sphere of abstract thinking; here we are situated in the very midst of the intuitive apprehension of reality. Of course the mode of this apprehension is entirely different from that of the purely expressive experience. In place of the mode of "thou-perception," such as prevailed in the expressive experience, a new mode, that of "it-perception" begins to stand out. But in the one case as in the other we do not deduce the "thou" or the "it," but have it in a specific and original manner of vision. It is futile to ask whence this vision comes—we can only ascertain what it veritably is in itself. For our task is not to subsume it under some already existing and accepted theory but rather to understand how the pure "theory" as such, the postulation and apprehension of objective determinations and relations, are made possible by this vision. In genuine representation the mere material of sensation is not subsequently *made* into the representation of an object and interpreted as such, by having certain acts performed

9. See above, pp. 72–4.

upon it. Rather, a formed total intuition stands before us as an objectively significant whole, filled with objective meaning. Here we need only recognize this fundamental symbolic relationship, like that of pure expression, as an authentic primary phenomenon, which can be shown to be a constitutive factor in all knowledge of an object. The phenomena of consciousness do not flit by as mere momentary images; what is given *here* points to a *not-here,* and what is given *now* points backward or forward to a *not-now;* without this, the phenomenon of an intuitive world could not be understood or even described. It is only in and through this function of showing, that we have any knowledge of objective reality and a special articulation, a classification according to "thing" and "attribute." But the representative function itself cannot conversely be explained on the basis of objective determinations and presuppositions.

In looking into this relationship more closely let us take a limited sphere of sensuous-intuitive phenomena as our starting point. Sensationalist psychology generally regards colors as a group of sensations which may be classified according to definite differences—that is to say, graduated according to brightness and color tone. But in his epoch-making optical investigations Hering protested, for good reason, against this designation. To call colors "sensations," he points out, "is to represent them primarily as subjective determinations." But though this designation of subjectivity may be warranted on physical grounds, phenomenologically it is not. For from the standpoint of pure existence, color is not at all given to us as a state or modification of our own ego; rather, what is disclosed to us in it is always some objective determinations, relations pertaining to objective reality. In this sense therefore color—as long as we do not pass from a phenomenological to a physiological or physical point of view—is to be designated far more as an attribute than as a sensation. In it neither a state of the ego, nor any property of light is directly and genuinely perceived, but through it we look at objective structures. "In vision we do not see rays as such, but outside things mediated by rays: the eye is expected to inform us, not concerning the intensity or quality of the light that comes from these outside things, but concerning the things themselves." [10] Thus even from the standpoint of physiological optics it proves necessary to draw a sharp dividing line between the mode of sight, which consists of a mere receptivity to im-

10. Ewald Hering, *Grundzüge der Lehre vom Lichtsinn* (Leipzig, 1920), p. 13 (first appeared in *Handbuch der gesamten Augenheilkunde,* ed. A. K. Graefe, Pt. I, chap. 12).

pressions of light and their differences, and the mode of vision, in which our intuitive world is built up. The so-called color constancy of the objects of vision makes it particularly evident that mere similarity of stimuli, for example in the quantity of light entering the eye, does not suffice to determine the content of an intuition. According to the special conditions to which the perception is subject, the same light stimulus can be used in very different ways for the building of reality—and apparently the same sensation of light can have a very different objective signification. A closer phenomenological analysis—such as that carried out in exemplary fashion by Schapp in his *Contributions to the Phenomenology of Perception*—shows first of all that in the phenomenon which we call "color," certain orders can be differentiated and that the phenomenon itself possesses a very different significance for us according to whether it belongs to one or the other of these orders. In the one order, color is taken as a light image which is apprehended and determined as such, and it does not have the function of making an object visible and representing it. In the other order, on the contrary, the attention is directed purely toward objective determinations; color serves only as a medium for perceiving the object that appears in it and is not considered in its own mode of manifestation. "There is a difference," writes Schapp,

between the naive man's and the artist's ways of seeing things, even if we disregard all aesthetic considerations. The naive man . . . sees things only in the color they apparently preserve in all changes of light, which one may also call their real, inherent color; he does not see the reflections, the lights, the colored shadows, except where they force themselves on the attention. True, he sees the shadow which his form makes on the ground when the sun is shining, he also sees the reflection cast on the wall by a moving hand mirror, the glittering of a helmet in the sunlight, the flickering of light on the walls when a fire is burning in the fireplace—but when the sky is overcast, it does not occur to him that a cherry or an eye always has this spot of light regardless of the illumination . . . Thus although the object cannot be perceived without such light images, it is certain on the other hand that the light images themselves need not be perceived if the object is to be represented . . . One can contemplate them, as they group themselves in the object, as they lie on it in shadows, as they infuse it with light, as they cast a radiant sunshine over it . . . In this case, to be sure, the things seem to be somewhat neglected. It seems to me that one can be so much taken up with the light images that the object almost vanishes. The perception of things does not seem to be compatible with that of light images; rather, the perception of a thing requires that the light images recede modestly into the background, where they are indispensable. When they are situated in the appropriate place, there is perception of the thing. Where they stand out so vividly that one cannot overlook them, perception is disturbed. They should "guide" the eye to the thing; the eye must not become caught in them.

And Schapp goes on to show that when we interchange the two factors here differentiated—when a color which we had hitherto taken as a mere light effect becomes for us an inherent color, the "color of the thing"—or conversely—then, at this moment, the total perception takes on another character and meaning. There is a very definite dependency between the order in which color enters into relation with our consciousness and the object represented by this order of color: "the immediate consequence of a change in the color order is a change in the object represented." [11] What Schapp calls the order of color is precisely that very determinate "vision" which results in every case from the special representative function of color. Color as such—Schapp also stresses—is what represents things to us.

> But the mere presence of color does not suffice to represent things; the color must be articulated and ordered, it must enter into forms . . . It is by means of this order of color that space and form are represented for us. In relation to color, space then is something represented. Color itself is not represented, it is directly given, but it represents forms in space . . . Form for its part represents the thing with its attributes. It does not yet belong to the thing, nor is it an immediate form of the thing; it is something represented, which in turn represents.[12]

From this it follows that color is not itself a content which is present as such in an objective space and variously articulated in this space but that taken in the diversity of its potential modes of manifestation it provides the substrate out of which the representation of objective reality, the idea

11. Wilhelm A. J. Schapp, *Beiträge zur Phänomenologie der Wahrnehmung* (Göttingen, 1910), *1*, D, 78 ff., 106 f.

12. Ibid., p. 114.

of things in space, is gained and built up. What the naive man thinks he has present, what he thinks he can grasp so to speak, as a thing, owes this very corporeal presence to the forms and orders of representation.

Yet we should not let this insight obscure the originality of these forms themselves and mislead us into assigning them to a stratum of mere mediacy, from which they are essentially removed by their significance and achievement. Both the rationalist and the empiricist theories of knowledge have committed the same error in this respect. For much as they may differ in their answers to the question of how our representations are related to the object, they agree, far more than their proponents seem to realize, in their formulation of the problem and their methodological approach to it. Both theories seek a way by which mere representation, through definite mediating acts which are applied to it, can be transformed into objective intuition; they seek to explain the metamorphosis by which the phenomenon develops from a mere datum of consciousness into a content of reality, of the "outside world." Empiricism reduces this metamorphosis to associations and reproductions; rationalism reduces it to logical operations, judgments, and inferences. But what both overlook in equal degree is the circumstance that all the psychological or logical processes, here invoked, come in a manner of speaking too late; they all refer to a combination of elements which are viewed as in some way existing, as established before the combination. But the question involved here does not begin with the possibility and basis of combination; it is concerned with the possibility of positing the ability to combine. No associative connection of mere impressions and no logical interweaving of them, however close, can explain the original mode of postulation inherent in the fact that a phenomenon points to an objective reality, that it is given as a factor in an objective intuition. The rationalists suppose they can explain this mode of postulation by stamping it as an achievement of the concept, an act of pure intelligence. This basic tendency is already apparent in the founder of modern rationalist philosophy. What Descartes primarily sets out to show in his *Meditations* is precisely this: the idea of the identity and constancy of the thing is not contained as such in the mere sensory data of perception, in the qualities of color and tone, touch, smell, and taste, but is brought to them only secondarily through logical reflection. Only by applying the innate idea of substance to the manifold and in themselves totally disparate phenomena of sensation do we gain the intuition of an identical and constant object, to which these phenomena refer and whose determinations and attributes they represent. The piece of wax which I have before me in sense perception and which shows itself to me as white and round, hard and fragrant, may change in every single respect; it may, in melting, suffer a change in all its accidents: nevertheless it remains for me the same wax, because it does not have this sameness from the senses but derives it from the pure understanding. "Ma perception n'est point une vision, ni un attouchement, ni une imagination et ne l'a jamais été, mais seulement une inspection de l'esprit." Thus at one stroke the act of perception is transformed into an act of pure thought by virtue of the objective relation that inheres in it. It is the "vision of the spirit," the *inspectio mentis,* which first makes mere impressions into modes of objective manifestation. The ability of the sensuous phenomenon to make objective reality "visible" and to represent it is reduced to a faculty of the understanding, to its power of unconscious inference—and here of course Descartes forsakes his original ground and prepares the way for a transition from the phenomenology of perception to the metaphysics of perception. Having combated the realism of the absolute object by starting out from the "Cogito," he succumbs in the end to the realism of innate ideas. Just as the clear idea of God must bring him back to that scholastic ontology which he had overcome in its basic form and method, so his pure analysis of the theoretical consciousness must bring him back to metaphysical assumptions regarding its origin.[13]

To avoid this step, which amounts to an outright μετάβασις εἰς ἄλλο γένος, there remains only one way: instead of seeking to explain the phenomena by deriving them from their transcendent sources we must apprehend them solely in their interrelation and so let them elucidate one another. Such elucidation is made possible by the circumstance that the character of representation, which belongs as such to the very essence of consciousness, does not stand out with equal fullness and distinctness in all the structures of consciousness—and this enables us to break it down into diverse phases and to observe the transition from one to the other. This kind of examination clearly brings out the differences in dynamic tension between the content and representative function of a phenomenon, to which we have already referred in general terms. Every sensuous content, however elementary, is charged, as it were, with such

13. Cf. the introduction to my *Leibniz' System in seinen wissenschaftlichen Grundlagen* (Marburg, 1902).

a tension. It is never simply "there" as an isolated and detached content, for in this very existence it points beyond itself, forming a concrete unity of presence and representation. As consciousness advances to richer and higher formations, this unity also gains a sharper and more determinate imprint. Its factors are set off more and more clearly from one another— yet the inner relation between the factors is not impaired but is brought out increasingly by this differentiation. By comparing the various sensory spheres in respect to this progress, we can establish a kind of hierarchical structure in them, a certain order of sequence, leading from the relatively indeterminate to higher and higher degrees of determinacy, of intuitive distinctness. The primitive senses show the bare beginnings of such a determinacy. They move essentially in an area of expressive values, which though often extremely intensive cannot be delimited from one another with any true sharpness. The data of the sense of smell, for example, seem to be differentiated primarily by such expressive characters: by the character of the attractive or repellent, the pungent or mild, the pleasant or unpleasant, the soothing or exciting. But these affective differences do not as yet lead to a truly objective distinction of qualities. Here a grada-tion and order such as we find in other sensuous manifolds, particularly in the spheres of tone and color, proves impracticable. On the one hand a clear spatial determination is still lacking: the smells do not adhere to definite places; in respect to localization, they are characterized by a thoroughgoing vagueness, a "rubberlike flexibility."[14] This vagueness is shown by the difficulty language has in expressing itself in this field and permeating it with its power. Where language seeks to designate deter-minate qualities of smell, it is usually compelled to proceed indirectly, through substances which it has coined on the basis of other sensory-intuitive data. A classification, such as that of color, into "universal" names—red, blue, yellow, and green, etc.—is not possible. "Either our words for smell convey it adjectivally (flowery, camphory) or they merely involve a comparison with the 'actual' bearer of smell (raspberry-like, jasmine-like). Nowhere is an abstraction of smell possible: from jasmine, lily-of-the-valley, camphor, and milk we can easily abstract out the common color, namely 'white,' but no one can analogously abstract out a common smell by regarding the common factor and disregarding the distinguishing factors."[15] Here then we stand outside the sphere of that

14. Cf. Hans Henning, *Der Geruch* (2d ed. Leipzig, 1924), pp. 275, 278.
15. Ibid., p. 66.

first universal which is the starting point for language formation and all true concept formation. We take an important step toward raising impressions to representations as soon as we pass from the realm of smell to that of tactile sensations. The tactile sense has sometimes even been called the true sense of reality—the sense whose phenomena have the most efficient sense of reality—and an epistemological primacy over all other senses is often imputed to it.[16] But even though it has this peculiar tendency to objectivization, it stops, as it were, half way. For it makes no sharp dividing line between merely circumstantial and purely objective determinations but gives us the latter clothed in the former. Here we can apprehend objects only through our perception of our own body and cannot detach them from this foundation. The phenomena of touch thus remain bipolar in the sense that here a subjective component, relating to our body, inevitably goes hand in hand with another component, oriented toward things and their attributes. "There are tactile phenomena which, particularly where the inner attitude is suitable, seem to be exclusively an indication of an objective reality, but a change in this attitude can . . . make the factor of sensation in them—that is to say, a circumstance of our body—stand out as an intuitively given and not as a merely disclosed attribute. . . . Though in an actual sense either the subjective or the objective aspect of tactile perception may be almost unnoticeable, its bipolarity remains . . . intuitively realizable."[17] Thus the trend toward representation is unmistakable here, but it does not yet achieve actual fulfillment: the "objective" content stops, as it were, at the limits of our own body, instead of becoming a true "other," instead of moving into an ideal distance. Such distance is achieved only in the highest, objective senses, in hearing and vision. And even here a kind of gradation of the representative function can be shown, since all phenomena in the two fields do not disclose this function with equal determinacy and emphasis. As to colors, the basic investigations of Hering, which were continued and amplified by Katz, disclose a threefold mode of manifestation. We may take them as simple optical conditions, as light images or determinate brightness and tonality, which we apprehend purely as such. Or else we may take them as objective colors, which do not hover in the void but adhere to definite things and come to our consciousness as the attri-

16. David Katz, *Der Aufbau der Tastwelt* (Leipzig, 1925), p. 255.
17. Ibid., p. 19.

butes of these things. In the first case we have before us the phenomenon of plain colors, which are given to us as a simple, flat *quale,* linked to no objective substrate: in the latter case, color appears to us as a surface color, an inherent property of a definite object. From both these modes a third is differentiated: spatial colors, i.e. colors which seem to fill a definite three-dimensional space. Here we need not go into the numerous specialized questions resulting from this threefold view of the world of colors.[18] For us the crucial point, the factor of universal significance, is that with the change of viewpoint under which the phenomenon of color is considered, the phenomenon as a whole, as an intuitive datum, undergoes at once a characteristic shift. If by a change of inner attitude we take a phenomenon which we have hitherto taken as a surface color and as such related to a definite objective vehicle and transfer it into a phenomenon of mere plain color, the total picture is transferred—it stands before us in a different intuitive determinacy. Helmholtz pointed out that the colors of a landscape stand out much more brilliantly and distinctly if one slants one's head or holds it upside down. "In the usual mode of observation," he interprets this phenomenon,

> we seek only to judge the objects correctly as such. We know that at a certain distance green surfaces appear in a somewhat modified color tone; we accustom ourselves to disregard this change and learn to identify the altered green of distant meadows and trees with the corresponding color of nearby objects. In the case of very distant objects, such as mountains, little of the object's color can be recognized, for it is largely covered over by the color of the illuminated air. This indefinite blue-green color, on which border the light-blue field of the sky or the reddish-yellow sunset above and bright-green of the meadows and woods below, is very much subject to changes by contrast. For us it is the indefinite and changing color of the distance; we know the change it undergoes at different times of day and in varying illuminations, but we do not define its true character, since we have no definite object to transfer it to: what we know is precisely its shifting character. But as soon as we place ourselves in unusual circumstances, for example looking under our arm or between our legs, the landscape appears as a flat picture. . . . And thereby the

18. For detailed treatment cf. Katz' penetrating analysis in *Die Erscheinungsweise der Farben und ihre Beeinflussung durch die individuelle Erfahrung* (Leipzig, 1911).

colors also lose their relation to near or distant objects and confront us purely in their intrinsic differences.[19]

By and large, psychologists have found two ways of explaining this peculiar change in the total sense impression brought about by a change of "inner attitude." One was that of Helmholtz: to regard the phenomenon as the outcome of an intellectual activity, of a process of judgment and inference—though this process of course had to be taken as a fabric of unconscious inferences and so transferred from the realm of pure phenomenology to that of metaphysics. In this shift, even the empiricist Helmholtz showed that he was still heir to the rationalist theory of perception formulated by Descartes. The psychologists of perception on the other hand sought to remain with the pure phenomenon, as Hering persistently did in his arguments against Helmholtz. They insisted that what was involved in these phenomena is "an essentially different manner of seeing, and not merely our knowledge of a difference in outward circumstances." [20] Nevertheless, in order to make this "different manner of seeing" intelligible, they traced it back almost exclusively to the reproductive factors which accompany and modify the act of vision. A logical function was now replaced by the function of the memory and reproductive imagination. "What we see in a given moment," Hering stresses,

is not conditioned only by the type and intensity of the radiations entering our eye and the state of the retina as a whole; rather, these are only, so to speak, the primary genetic factors of the colors caused by the radiations. With them are associated the reproductions of former experience, induced by all sorts of subsidiary circumstances, and these secondary and as it were accidental factors also play a part in determining vision at any particular time. . . . The color in which we have most often seen a thing is imprinted ineffaceably on our memory and becomes a fixed attribute of the remembered image. . . . All

19. H. L. F. von Helmholtz, *Handbuch der physiologischen Optik*, 1867; (2d ed. Hamburg and Leipzig, 1896), p. 607. Eng. trans. of 3d ed. (1909–11) by James P. C. Southall, *Helmholtz's Treatise on Physiological Optics* (Rochester, N.Y., 1924–25).

20. Hering, *Grundzüge der Lehre vom Lichtsinn*, p. 8. On the basis of the fundamental consideration that "Gestalt impressions and true data of judgment are thoroughly different from one another," Karl Bühler also sharply criticized Helmholtz' "judgment theory"; cf. *Die Struktur der Wahrnehmungen*, Pt. I of Bühler, ed., *Handbuch der Psychologie* (Jena, 1922), secs. 15 ff.

things that are already known to us from experience or that we regard as known to us in respect to color, we see through the glass of remembered colors and hence often differently than we should otherwise see them. In view of the usually fleeting nature of vision, the remembered color of a visible thing can even take the place of an entirely different color which we should have seen if all occasion to reproduce a remembered color had been excluded, on the assumption, to be sure, that we do not give special attention to the color. We possess a great aptitude for distinguishing the so-called real color of a thing from its accidental colors. Thus we distinguish those finely graduated shadows on the surface of a body—which help us to perceive its form, its relief, its distance as something accidental—from the color of the surface that bears the shadow, and we suppose that outside of the darkness of the shadow and through it we see the "real" color of the surface. The reflected colors that appear on smooth surfaces are in a sense separated in perception from the "real" color of the surface.[21]

The phenomena which Helmholtz interprets as logical and intellectual, products of judgments and inferences, are thus defined by Hering as essentially "mnemic" phenomena, and for him memory is in general an essential factor in all organized matter.[22] But in the long run, psychological empiricism could not content itself with this explanation either. Katz expressly pointed out that remembered colors did not suffice to interpret his experiments which supplemented those of Hering; that even where the colored papers which were to be judged were neither individually defined nor known to the observers from former experience, the characteristic phenomena of "light perspective," i.e. the differentiation of an object's "real" color from a quality of illumination "accidentally" attaching to it, still occurred.[23] From this he concludes that the remembered colors, to which he himself had at first attributed a central position in color vision, would have to be relegated to a subordinate role.[24] Here empirical psychology itself stands at the threshold of our general philosophical problem. For again it turns out that in the structure, order,

21. Hering, pp. 6 ff.

22. Cf. Hering, *Über das Gedächtnis als eine allgemeine Function der organisierten Materie* (Vienna, 1876).

23. Cf. Katz, *Die Erscheinungsweise der Farben*, esp. pp. 214 ff.; on the concept and problem of "light perspective" cf. esp. pp. 90 ff.

24. Ibid., p. vii.

articulation of the world of color, and also in the role which this world of color plays in the representation of spatial and objective relations, we have to do not so much with an achievement of the discursive understanding, or of the merely reproductive imagination, as with that productive imagination which Kant designated "a necessary ingredient of perception itself." [25] An "ingredient of perception" in the strict sense can never be a factor which is simply added to the given sensation—whether to reinterpret it by judgment or to complement it by reproductive elements of the memory. Here we have no such subsequent completion but an act of original formation which applies to the intuition as a whole and first makes it possible as a whole. On the basis of our earlier investigations we have designated this act one of "symbolic ideation," and it should be realized that this mode of ideation is no secondary and as it were accidental factor, by which vision is for the time being partly determined, but that, from a psychological point of view, the symbolic ideation first constitutes vision. For there is no seeing and nothing visible which does not stand in some mode of spiritual vision, of ideation. A seeing and a thing-seen outside of this "sight," a "bare" sensation preceding all formation, is an empty abstraction. The "given" must always be taken in a definite aspect and so apprehended, for it is this aspect that first lends it meaning. This meaning is to be understood neither as secondary and conceptual nor as an associative addition: rather, it is the simple meaning of the original intuition itself. The moment we pass from one form of vision to another, it is not only a single factor in the intuition, but the intuition itself in its totality, its unbroken unity, that undergoes a characteristic metamorphosis. There is creation in the very act of seeing, said Goethe, "and though scientists may do their utmost to exorcise it, they are driven before they know it, to invoke the help of the productive imagination." [26] And this applies not only to the scientifically determined or the artistically formed intuition, but to simple empirical intuition as well. For Goethe himself this relation to the "productive imagination" led to that "difference between seeing and seeing," on which he insists over and over again, concluding that all "sensuous" seeing is already a "seeing with the eyes of the spirit." When the physiologist or physiological opticist seeks to cut off the sensory from the spiritual factor; when he tends to regard the former as primary and the latter as

25. See below, pp. 247–8.
26. Goethe, *Naturwissenschaftliche Schriften* (Weimar ed.), 6, 302.

secondary and accidental, this tendency may be relatively justified from the standpoint of the vision in which he himself stands and which prescribes his direction of intuition—that is, from the standpoint of the causal analysis, the genetic "explanation" of the process of perception; but such a relative justification must not be absolutized. From the phenomenological point of view, if he speaks of any "earlier" or "later" in this connection, one should rather be disposed to reverse the relation and stress that ideation, the mode of vision, is the true πρότερον τῇ φύσει, because it is only in it and through it that the signification of the thing seen is determined.

If we now consider color and its diverse "modes of manifestation" from this standpoint, we find thoroughgoing confirmation of our general conclusion. However far we may carry the "reduction" of colors—however far we may go in divesting color of its representative character, its value in representing the spatial and objective world—we never succeed in tracing it back to a point where it becomes mere "sensation" without any intuitive articulation. The so-called plain colors appear to be the original mode in which color is manifested—and both biologically and psychologically the proposition may be put forward that "the center of the retina presents to consciousness the plain colors as the first reaction to light, or that this is a condition which must be passed through as a condition of the perception of surface colors." [27] Even where there is a fully developed consciousness of color, space, and objects, all spatial, objective colors, under artificially selected experimental conditions, can be transposed into mere plain colors—that is, a "complete reduction of color impressions" can be brought about. [28] Then color no longer makes space visible for any determinate thing, but in a sense discloses only itself: it appears as a member within a diversity of graduated "experiences of light." But these experiences of light still show a distinct formation insofar as they stand out sharply from one another and assume an order. Not only do they possess different degrees of "coherence," so that one color seems separated from another by a greater or lesser interval which produces a very definite principle of sequence, but in this sequence itself certain points are distinguished around which the various elements gather. Even taken as a mere light impression, a color tint is not simply

27. Katz, *Die Erscheinungsweise*, pp. 306 ff.

28. On the concept and method of this "complete reduction" of color impressions, cf. ibid., pp. 36 ff.

"present" but is at the same time "representative": what is given here and now, for example a momentary and individual red, not only gives *itself* to our consciousness but is known to us also as a red, a member of a species which is represented through it. It is so embedded in a total sequence of shades of red that it appears to belong to and be ordered within that sequence, and through this order it can represent the totality or the sequence. Without this relation, not even the impression would be determined as "precisely this one," as τόδε τι in the Aristotelian sense. And we arrive at a still further dimension of representation when an individual color impression not only represents the color species to which it belongs, but also functions as a means of representation for something quite heterogeneous—for determinations of things and space. The color quality as such now becomes a mere "accident" which points to its vehicle, its enduring substrate. As soon as consciousness follows this indication, this mode of ideation, color itself as a pure intuitive experience may be said to appear in another light: the new form of vision makes something else visible in it. As long as we stop at plain color, we can speak neither of a change of color by illumination, nor of varying degrees of distinctness in one and the same color.[29] For both these statements presuppose an act of identification which is still totally lacking in our view of plain color as such, as a simple, flat *quale*. Here every color phenomenon is valid only for a single moment, though it completely fills this moment, which is *its* present. It relates only to itself and is centered in itself: so that any change in its properties immediately and necessarily comprises a change in its essence. But it is just this peculiar self-sufficiency, this autarchy of color that falls away as soon as we cease to take it merely in itself, but use it as a means of representation, a "sign." Now it becomes as ambiguous as every sign by its very nature is and must be. Just as a particular word can be interpreted only in the sentence as a whole and in the light of the whole meaning which is linguistically forged in the sentence, so the particular color phenomenon can tell very different things according to the context in which we take it. And the varied relevancies and the fullness of signification remain entirely within the sphere of the intuitive experience itself. In a purely intuitive sense, a color seems different, it looks different as soon as, taken representatively, it is moved out of its position—as soon as it is seen not as a surface color but as a plain color, or conversely. If, for example, two colors *a* and *b* are

29. Cf. ibid., pp. 264 ff.

compared as plain colors, *a* clearly appears as the brighter and *b* as the darker—but this relation can change at once as soon as we pass to a different order of vision—that is, as soon as we take *a* and *b* as colors of things or spatial colors. The investigations of Hering and Katz are full of striking examples of this characteristic shift of color phenomena that accompanies a passage from one order of color to another.

Stand at the window [one of these examples runs] and take in one hand a piece of white paper, in the other a piece of grey paper. Hold them at first horizontally at a slight distance from one another. If you incline the grey paper toward the window and the white paper away from it, the retinal image of the grey paper will soon have a greater light intensity than that of the white paper, but although you notice the changes in brightness, you will still, despite its greater light intensity, see the paper that is "really" grey, as grey, and the "really" white one, despite its weaker light intensity, as white. But if you look at the paper with only one eye through some sort of fixed tube, it will be easy to see their colors on one and the same plane, provided the two images are immediately adjacent and neither is shaded, and only a segment of each paper is visible. Now you will see the grey paper as lighter and the white one as darker, in accordance with the difference in their light intensities. . . . If we incline a grey or white paper alternately toward the window or away from it, we take the visible increase in whiteness (brightness) or blackness (darkness) of the surface as a mere accident to its "real" color: the white as well as the grey paper retains the color which it really has, even if it accidentally looks lighter or darker. Here we do not see the real color of the surface change, as is the case when for some reason a spot arises on the surface; rather, the color belonging to the surface seems to persist, although we actually observe its change. In many cases an accidental increase in the whiteness or blackness of a surface is seen as something totally separate from its real color: thus for example, when a shadow passes across a surface or when a moved mirror casts a moving spot of light on the surface.[30]

As we see, the phenomenon here goes back to a change in the point of reference. If the thing that bears a certain color is taken as this point of reference, the recognition and representation may be said to follow the

30. Hering, *Grundzüge einer Lehre vom Lichtsinn*, p. 9.

guidance of the thing. A constant color is imputed as a permanent attribute to the constant object—and all color phenomena have only the one meaning and the one function of representing this attribute for us, of serving as a sign for it. Accordingly we disregard the change in lighting effects and regard only the permanent color of the object. But as soon as this purpose and point of view are changed, the total face of the color phenomenon changes with them. It takes on a different appearance according to whether it is seen in the aspect of the substantiality of the thing, or whether it is seen as an effect based on a passing combination of circumstances. To cite another of Hering's examples, "I am walking along a path beneath a covering of dense foliage; for a brief space direct sunlight falls through a gap in the leaves: at the first moment I think I see a spot colored white by spilled lime, but when I look more closely, I see no more white, but only light on the grey-brown earth." Thus the direction of ideation drives the purely optical phenomenon into very definite channels. In one case the optical phenomenon is used as a representation of a thing-attribute context, in the other as a representation of a causal context: in the one case it symbolizes a substantial reality (the reality of the spot), in another a light reflection as a momentary effect. But in both cases it would be misleading to say that the category of substantiality or causality was only subsequently added to an intrinsically identical sensation and that it pressed this sensation into a ready-made formal schema. For this would be to overlook the crucial factor, namely that the identity of the point of reference, which prescribes the path of recognition and representation, does not simply exist in the sense of being given in advance but results only from the direction of vision and from the ideal goal toward which the vision aims. If the intention is toward the unity of the object in the sense of objective experience, the color of the illumination appears as an accident that we disregard in order not to lose sight of the continuity of the object. But if, on the contrary—though in general this occurs only in a very particular scientific attitude—we are investigating phenomena of light and color as such, if we do not look through them toward the objects they represent, but immerse ourselves in their own make up, the identity moves from the sphere of the thing to that of the phenomenon. This last in all its transience and variability, in its momentary facticity, is what we now wish to hold fast and know: what represents has become what is to be represented. Yet we have not departed from the mutual relation of the representing and the represented as such, for if we did, we should be leaving the sphere of concrete intuition. Only the poles of the basic relationship, only the points of reference have shifted; the relationship itself subsists in its universal function.[31]

31. It is characteristic that Katz, who at first seems bent on fitting his observations and experiments into the framework of a general theory of association, that is, of explaining them by mere laws of the "reproductive imagination," was increasingly forced away from this basis of explanation by the facts themselves. He points out expressly that the phenomenon of so-called "light perspective," the differentiation of the "true" colors of objects from the colors they take on only in a definite "abnormal" illumination, cannot be adequately explained "by central reproductions of optical residues." "To operate simply with reproduced perceptions," he writes, "is not permissible [in the present case] because the processes in question . . . are not in every respect identical with those which we ordinarily have in mind in connection with the association of impressions and perceptions." For in association in the usual sense of the word, he writes, a full independence is imputed to the elements that associate with one another; each of them is susceptible of entering into any other association as well as the present one. Furthermore, there need be no "inner" relationship between the elements combined in association: they only come together "externally" and are not necessarily interrelated in any way. Finally, the two links in the association must be either coexistent or successive. But none of these three presuppositions applies to the process which leads to the differentiation between the illumination and what is illumined. "According to the prevailing view, the impression that occurs where the lighting is not normal reproduces the color impression that would occur in normal illumination. Thus the surface colors themselves are taken as the elements. But this view is false; for I can never experience the surface colors for themselves without a definite illumination; a definite illumination is not associated with a definite surface color; rather, the elements that enter into relation with one another are themselves products of surface color and illumination." Furthermore, the elements here combined have an inner relationship: they are color experiences which can always pass over into one another by a continuous process of change. And finally these color experiences are never given simultaneously, nor, in order to combine with one another, do they have to follow one another with a certain rapidity, as is the case with syllables, for example, if they are to enter into association with one another. By way of fixating these differences, Katz substitutes the term "chain association" for the usual concept of association. What distinguishes the "chain association" from associations in the common sense of the word is "that the associated elements are products of two quantities (illumination and the illumined), whose nature as products of a variable (illumination) and a constant quantity (the illumined) must first be drawn from the experience of a chain of elements" (pp. 376 ff.). This concept of chain association, however, does not broaden the framework of the classical theory of association, but destroys it. For here we have an entirely different form of relation from that which is present in any so-called association of similarity or contiguity. Here we have that relation of "symbolic co-givenness" (*Mitgegebenheit*) through which a particular phenomenon, given here and now, represents not only itself but a total complex (the phenomenon of the same object in different illumination). Thus what holds the members of the series together is not their similarity or the frequency with which they were given in empirical succession or coexistence, but the common function of indication which they fulfill: the fact that with all their sensuous heterogeneity, they relate to a common reference point (namely the X of the identical "object"). *This* relation is not explained by association; rather, it is what makes possible the association, the combination

At the same time, it becomes evident that the sensuous phenomena can achieve a representative character, can become vehicles of representative functions only by progressively articulating themselves—and that conversely each sharper articulation of an intuitive whole gives rise to richer and broader possibilities of representation. Only within an articulated manifold can a factor stand for the whole—and on the other hand, consciousness, wherever a formed whole is present, need only select one of its factors in order to apprehend and have the whole in it and through it. Thus in general each change in point of reference, each re-centering of an intuitively given structure, brings with it a corresponding shift in what is represented in it and through it. In mere plain color such a change in perspective is possible only to a limited degree, for as long as it is taken as such, as long as it is taken as a mere flat *quale,* it still has within it no functional difference of signification, no foreground and background so to speak. But this difference appears at once as soon as the color becomes surface color, as soon as it is taken as an attribute, as the lasting property of a thing. In the sensuous experience which in the mere here and now is given as a single undivided complex, certain basic factors now stand out clearly and are sharply delimited from one another. The unitary intuition breaks down into a constant and variable factor: the invariable color of the object is seen through all changes in illumination; it is set off from all the modifications that these changes bring with them. If this setting off, this inner articulation, occurs in a different way, the object of

_____

of the manifold and diverse. "The consciousness of the one object in which the color changes take place," says Katz himself, "supplies the bond which links the color experiences yielded by this object in different lights" (p. 379). But precisely the specific form of *this* consciousness, as we have seen, can never be adequately designated, let alone explained, by the "association of ideas" (cf. above, *1,* 102 ff.). Katz' investigations show very instructively how the pure color phenomena enter into a totally different relation with one another and gain an entirely new ordering as soon as we pass from the order of "plain colors" to that of "surface colors"—that is, as soon as we relate them, and fasten them, to the objective unity of the object. While before this they were relatively isolated and each phenomenon in a sense represented only itself, now—thanks to this common reference— they form an unbroken series, a closed chain in which every link represents the whole and stands for the whole. The particular sensuous phenomena are not externally connected with one another by mere empirical similarity or by relations of empirical succession and coexistence, but are gathered together and made into one by the common medium of the unitary object which each of them symbolically represents. This gathering together, which first gives them their "spiritual bond," is an act of signification: because and insofar as the manifold and particular color phenomena all "mean" and "represent" the same object, they themselves enter into the unity of an intuition.

the seeing is thereby changed. The isolated bright spot which breaks the darkness of the forest path—to resume Hering's example—can be referred to either this or that thing: it can be taken as the dark ground in the sunlight or as the whitish color of spilled lime. In the first case the factor of illumination is taken as variable and the difference revealed to us at a certain point in our optical field is explained by its variation; in the second case this factor is regarded as constant, and the difference is explained by the supposition that two different visual things (the ground and the lime lying on it) are given. In each case the color phenomenon takes on a different character and a different purely intuitive meaning according as one or the other thing is attached to it. It is something different as soon as it moves into a different series of objects and represents this series in its totality and coherence. For the reality of the phenomenon cannot be separated from its representative function; it ceases to be the same as soon as it signifies something different, as soon as it points to another total complex as its background. It is mere abstraction to attempt to detach the phenomenon from this involvement, to apprehend it as an independent something outside of and preceding any function of indication. For the naked core of mere sensation, which merely *is* (without representing anything), never exists in the actual consciousness; if it exists at all, it is the prime example of that illusion which William James called "the psychologist's fallacy." Once we have fundamentally freed ourselves from this illusion, once we have recognized that not sensations but intuitions, not elements but formed totalities, comprise the data of consciousness, we can only ask: what is the relationship between the form of these intuitions and the representative function they have to fulfill? Then it becomes evident that a genuine relation of reciprocity is present: the formation of intuition is the actual vehicle required by representation, and on the other hand the use of intuition as a means of representation unceasingly brings out new aspects and factors in intuition and forms it into an increasingly richer and more differentiated whole.

Chapter 3

Space

THE BUILDING of intuitive reality begins, as we have seen, when the continuous flow of sensuous phenomena begins to divide. In the midst of the unremitting stream of phenomena, determinate unities are held fast, which now form the fixed center of orientation. The particular phenomenon takes on its characteristic meaning only by being referred·to these centers. And all further progress of objective knowledge, all clarification and determination of intuitive existence as a whole, go hand in hand with a broadening of this process to include ever new spheres. With the dissection of phenomenal reality into presentative and representative factors, into the representing and the represented, a new motif is acquired which operates with increasing force and henceforth determines the entire movement of theoretical consciousness. The original impulse propagates itself, as it were, in the form of waves; it does not, to be sure, put a halt to the flowing mobility in which phenomena as a whole are at first given to us but gradually causes definite individual vortices to separate òut of it with increasing distinctness. The articulation of the phenomenal world under the aspect of thing and "attribute," which we have alone considered up to now, forms of course only a single factor in this process. It is itself only made possible by its link with other factors, by operating along with them. In positing fixed thing-unities, to which, as it were, the changing phenomena are fastened, we determine them at the same time as spatial unities. The "permanence" of the thing is bound up with the stability of such spatial unities. We judge that a thing is precisely this one and continues to be so, chiefly by designating its place in intuitive space as a whole. At every moment we impute a determinate place to it—and then recompose the aggregate of these places into an intuitive totality which represents the movement of the object as a continuous, lawfully determined change. And just as the thing thus appears linked to a fixed point in space, and its position relative to the position of all other objects seems determined in "real" space, so we also ascribe spatial magnitude and form to it as objective determinations. Thus there results the union of the thing motif and space motif that has found its most pregnant scientific expression in the concept of the atom. But this concept is only the continuation of an impulse which, before operating in the construction of the theoretical-physical world view, was already at work in the building of the world of empirical perception. Perception, too, succeeds in positing things and in differentiating them from their variable states and properties only by "settling" them, so to speak, in an objective space. Each single, real thing bears witness to its reality above all by occupying a segment of space from which it excludes everything else. The individuality of the thing rests ultimately on the fact that it is in this sense a spatial individual—it possesses a sphere of its own, in which it is and in which it asserts itself against every other reality. Thus our inquiry is led directly from the thing-attribute problem to the problem of space, the very statement and formulation of the former include certain basic determinations of the latter.

But here, of course, we confront an almost inextricable complex of problems; for there is no field of philosophy or theoretical knowledge in general into which the problem of space does not in some way enter and with which it is not interwoven in one way or another. Metaphysics and epistemology, physics and psychology are all equally interested in the problem and its solution. Here we cannot think of following the problem into all these ramifications; from its rich and intricate fabric we shall only single out the one thread by which it proves to be linked to our own central question. How, then, is the problem of space related to the general problem of symbolism? Is the space in which things are represented to us a simple intuitive datum, or does it follow from a process of symbolic formation?

With this formulation of the problem we find ourselves on new ground, far from the beaten paths of psychological and epistemological inquiry. For now, though it may seem strange and paradoxical at first sight, the center of gravity is shifted from the philosophy of nature to the philosophy of culture. The question of what space signifies for the constitution of the world of things is transformed into another profounder question: what does it signify and accomplish for the building and attainment of specifically spiritual reality? We cannot fully understand its origin or its value or its peculiar "dignity" until we have determined its position within a universal phenomenology of the spirit. What connection, we must now ask, is there between the objectivizing achievement of the pure intuition of space and those other spiritual energies which play a decisive part in the progress of objectivization? What part, in particular, does language play in gaining and ascertaining the world of spatial intuition? Traditional psychology and epistemology give no adequate answer to all these questions; indeed, they do not seem to have propounded the question with any real precision. But by neglecting to do so they have closed off an important approach to the problem of space. They may be said to have dropped the thread which connects this problem not only with the universal problem of being but also with the problem of meaning. And yet, on the other hand, precisely the most familiar theories of space disclose a point at which their proponents, though for the most part unconsciously and as it were involuntarily, were compelled to consider the question along precisely this line. From the moment when the problem of space was first seen with truly systematic clarity, one fundamental concept began to occupy a central position in it. This concept may be followed through the whole history of the theories of space. Whether rationalist or sensationalist or nativist in orientation, all these theories are led back to the concept of the sign. We find this trait in the spatial theory of Kepler and Descartes, who in the seventeenth century laid the first foundation for an exact, mathematical treatment of the problem; we find it, far more sharply expressed, in Berkeley's new theory of vision which became the starting point of physiological optics; and it can be followed equally through the modern theories on the origin of the idea of space, down to Helmholtz and Hering, Lotze and Wundt. Here it seems worth while to consider this context in a brief historical survey; for such a survey will lead us almost automatically to the methodological question that is latent in all theorizing about space.

Descartes' analysis of the concept of space is very closely bound up with his analysis of the concept of substance. Here there is a methodological unity and correlation which exactly reflect the ontological-metaphysical relationship between the problems. For according to the basic presuppositions of the Cartesian metaphysics, the thing, the empirical object, can be clearly and distinctly defined only through its purely spatial determinations. Extension in length, breadth, and depth is the only objective predicate by which we can determine the object of experience. Whatever else we customarily regard as an attribute of physical reality, if we wish to gain a strict understanding of it, must be reduced to relations of pure extension. But another reason for the indissoluble bond between the concept of the thing and the mathematical concept of space is that both are rooted in one and the same fundamental logical function. For as Descartes shows, the identity of the thing, like the continuity and homogeneity of geometrical extension, is not an immediate datum of sensation or perception. "Sight gives us nothing but images, hearing gives us nothing but sounds or tones: thus it is clear that that something which, outside of these images or tones, we conceive as what is *designated* by them, is given to us not by sense perceptions coming from outside, but rather by innate ideas, having their seat and origin in our own power of intellection." [1] Thus, on closer scrutiny, all those determinations which we customarily attribute to intuitive space are nothing other than purely logical characters. It is by such characters, by characteristics such as constancy, infinity, uniformity, that we define the space of pure geometry; but the intuition of the space of things, of physical space, arises in the same way: our understanding assembles the particular data provided by the senses, compares them, and in a sense attunes them to one another. In this attuning, this correlation, space comes into being, a constructive schema of thought, a creation of that "universal mathematics" which for Descartes is the universal science of order and measure. Even where we suppose that we have an immediate perception of space, we stand in the domain of this universal mathematics. For what we call the magnitude, the distance, the reciprocal position of things is nothing that can be seen or touched; it can only be estimated and calculated. Every act of spatial perception comprises an act of measurement and thus of mathematical inference. Thus ratio, in its twofold signification of reason and calculation, here invades the realms of intuition and perception, subjecting them to its fundamental law. All intuition is bound up with theoretical thinking, which in turn consists of logical judgment and inference, so that it is a fundamental act of pure thought that first opens up reality to us as an independent world of things and also as an intuitive world of space.

In its structure and epistemological presuppositions Berkeley's theory of vision seems the exact reverse of this Cartesian doctrine; yet it has the same starting point. For Berkeley, the sensationalist, who held that all

1. Descartes, *Notae in programma quoddam*, ed. C. Adam and P. Tannery (Paris, 1897–1909), *8*, 360; cf. my *Erkenntnisproblem*, *1*, 489 f.

original reality was contained in simple sensation, also recognized that sense perception did not in itself suffice to explain space and the spatial order in which empirical objects are given to us. In his view, sensory data do not immediately contain spatial determinations, which are produced rather by a complex process of interpretation which the mind applies to these data. Our picture of spaces does not come into being through the addition of a qualitatively new perception to the perceptions mediated by our senses, particularly those of sight and touch; it requires rather that a determinate relation establish itself between the data of the various senses, enabling us to pass from one group to another and correlate them according to fixed rules. But while Descartes, to explain this correlation, had recourse to an original function of the intellect and its innate ideas, Berkeley takes the opposite course. For him the pure space of the geometer Descartes as well as the absolute space of the physicist Newton are not so much ideas as idols. They do not stand up to the psychological critique which seeks to disclose the simple facts of consciousness. Observation and unbiased phenomenological analysis fail to disclose the abstract space with which the mathematician and the mathematical physicist operate; they reveal no absolutely homogeneous, unlimited extension, free from all sensuous qualities. But they also reveal no special class of sensations which inform us regarding the magnitude, position, and distances of objects. Here, rather, a different psychological faculty makes itself felt. This faculty can be reduced neither to simple perception nor to the logical-discursive activity of the understanding; it can be designated neither as merely sensory nor yet as rational. In it we have an authentic activity, a synthesis of the spirit, but one which is grounded not so much in the rules of abstract logic and formal mathematics, as in those of the imagination. What distinguishes these rules from those of mathematics and logic is above all the circumstance that they can never produce universal and necessary combinations but only empirical and accidental ones. It is not any objective, any actual inner necessity, but habit and custom that combine the particular sensory spheres and finally make them grow together into such a concrete whole that they can mutually represent one another. According to Berkeley, the development of the intuition of space is bound up with this capacity for representation: it presupposes that the sense impressions, over and above their initial merely presentative content, gradually take on a representative function. But according to him this representation is effected through nothing more than reproduction.

To make possible the building of our spatial experience, the no less significant power of suggestion must be joined with the power of perception.[2] As this power increases, as the particular sense impression gains the ability to suggest others totally different from it, and in a certain sense to make them physically present to consciousness, the chain closes for us by which the elements of reality fit themselves into a whole, into a world of space and of things in space.

Descartes' rationalist theory of space and Berkeley's empiricist theory are only the beginning of a vast number of speculative, psychological, and epistemological theories which appeared in the thinking of the nineteenth century. But much as all these theories differ from the standpoint of pure content, they may be said to have undergone little essential change in type since Descartes and Berkeley. The inquiry is still confined within the general methodological alternative which they first made clear and precise. All subsequent theories of space seem in a sense bound to this alternative—they must go the way either of reflection or of association. Of course, there is not always an unequivocal, definitive decision between the two; we often encounter theories which hover between the two poles. Thus Helmholtz as a mathematician and physicist is governed by Cartesian intellectualism, while as a physiologist and empiricist philosopher he approaches Berkeley. His theory of unconscious inferences shows a clear historical and methodological continuity with Descartes' "dioptrics"; but the character of these inferences is changed by the fact that their analogue and model is sought no longer in the syllogisms of logic and mathematics but in the forms of inductive inference. Here too the associative combination and reproductive completion of sense impressions ultimately suffices to explain their articulation in a spatial order. If we look into the basis for this methodological duality in Helmholtz' theory of space, we find that it rests on an analogous cleavage in Helmholtz' general theory of signs. His whole theory of knowledge is anchored in the concept of the sign; for him the world of phenomena is nothing other than an aggregate of signs, which are in no wise similar to their causes, real things, but which are lawfully correlated with them in such a way that they can express all differences and relations of things. But though Helmholtz seems to recognize the primacy of the symbolic concept, he does not ad-

2. George Berkeley, *A New Theory of Vision* (New York, 1934), and *The Theory of Vision Vindicated and Explained* (London, 1860); on the concept of "suggestion" and its position in Berkeley's system cf. my *Erkenntnisproblem*, 2, 283 ff.

here to it with truly systematic rigor. For instead of subordinating the problem of causality to the general problem of signification, he takes the opposite course, interpreting the function of the sign itself as a special form of causal relation and seeking to explain it as such. The category of causality, which according to Helmholtz is the condition for the "intelligibility of nature," thus forces its way into the pure description of phenomena and diverts it from its proper course.[3]

But for us this raises the question of what form this description must take if the problem and phenomenon of representation are left in their place, if we seek to elucidate and understand them on their own terms. Analysis has already shown us that the thing-attribute relation could not be grasped in its core and crucial significance as long as we sought to explain it by discursive judgments or mere reproductive processes. But nearly all sign theories which have appeared in connection with the theory of space, from Berkeley down to Lotze's theory of local signs, are dominated by this very dilemma. In order to explain the form of space on the basis of its own premises, empiricist philosophy was compelled to come to closer grips with its own fundamental concept of sensation. It had to separate what simple sensation "is," in its own immediacy, from other factors which are added to it only in the course of experience and which in many ways modify its initial facticity. It was only through such transformations that the intuition and idea of space could be developed from the data of mere sensation. Yet no such "psychic chemistry"—despite the increasing refinements that have been brought to it—has been able to solve this problem in a satisfactory way, has really succeeded in surprising the secret of spatialization. Hering's nativism disposes of all these derivations by stressing that a spatial element can never originate in a co-existence or succession of aspatial elements, that, on the contrary, extension and spatiality must in a sense be recognized as irreducible characters of our sense perception. Thus modern psychology has more and more given up the hope of surprising consciousness at the point where it effects its crucial transition from intrinsically aspatial sensation to spatial perception. It seeks no longer to disclose the origin of spatiality, but rather to differentiate phases, accentuations, articulations within spatiality. We cannot show how something that was previously aspatial achieves the quality of spatiality—but we can and must inquire through what mediations mere spatiality passes over into space, how pragmatic space becomes

3. For further detail see below, Pt. III, Chaps. 1, 2.

systematic space. For it is a long way from the primary mode of spatial experience to formed space as the condition for our intuition of objects, and from this intuitive-objective space to the mathematical space of measure and order.[4] At the present stage in our investigation we entirely disregard this last phase of space, the structure of mathematically "defined" and "constructed" space;[5] for the present we take space solely as the form of empirical intuition and of the empirical object world. But even so, it becomes at once apparent that this form is shot through with symbolic elements. What we call "space" is not an independent object that is mediately represented to us, that presents itself and is to be recognized by certain signs; rather, it is a particular mode, a peculiar schematism of representation itself. And through this schematism, consciousness gains the possibility of a new orientation—it gains a specific direction of spiritual sight which transforms all the configurations of objective, objectivized reality. This transformation signifies no objective transition from mere quality to quantity, from pure intensivity to extensivity, from intrinsically aspatial sensation to a somehow spatial perception. It does not relate to the genesis—whether metaphysical or psychological—of the spatial consciousness; rather, it is a change in the signification which spatial consciousness experiences, by which the totality of the meaning contained and implicit in it is brought to light.

In seeking to elucidate this metamorphosis we shall not begin with psychological observations and considerations but once again, in line with

4. Martin Heidegger, in "Sein und Zeit," *Jahrbuch für Philosophie und phänomenologische Forschung*, 7 (1925), 102 ff., devoted a sharp analysis to the primary experience of space —that is, to purely pragmatic space. According to Heidegger, any characterization of what is primarily at hand, of what is present as a "thing," comes up against the factor of spatiality. "The place and the place-manifold may not be interpreted as the where of any random presence of things. The place is the determinate 'there' and 'here' where a thing belongs. . . . This regional orientation of the place-manifold of things at-hand [*zuhanden*] makes up the aroundness, the around-us, of what is in our closest environment. Never is a three-dimensional manifold of possible positions filled with existing [*vorhanden*] things given to begin with. This dimensionality of space is still cloaked in the spatiality of the at-hand. . . . All 'wheres' are disclosed and exhibited round about us through the comings and goings of everyday life, not ascertained and specified by reflective spatial measurement." What distinguishes our own undertaking from that of Heidegger is above all that it does not stop at this stage of the at-hand and its mode of spatiality, but without challenging Heidegger's position goes beyond it; for we wish to follow the road leading from spatiality as a factor in the at-hand to space as the form of existence, and furthermore to show how this road leads right through the domain of symbolic formation— in the twofold sense of "representation" and of "signification" (cf. below, Pt. III).

5. In regard to the structure of this "mathematical" space see below, Pt. III, Chaps. 3–5.

our general methodological presuppositions, attack the problem from its purely objective side, from the standpoint of the objective spirit. There is no achievement or creation of the spirit which is not in some way related to the world of space and which does not in a sense seek to make itself at home in it. For the turning toward this world signifies the first necessary step toward objectivization, toward the apprehension and determination of being. Space forms as it were the universal medium in which spiritual productivity can first establish itself, in which it can produce its first structures and formations. How language and myth immerse themselves in this medium, how they draw their images from it, we have already seen. The two do not proceed uniformly in the process but take different basic directions. Throughout its spatial orientation myth clings to the primary and primitive modes of mythical world-feeling. The spatial intuition that myth achieves does not conceal or destroy this world-feeling but is rather the decisive instrument for its expression. Myth arrives at spatial determinations and differentiations only by lending a peculiar mythical accent to each "region" in space, to the "here" and "there," the rising and setting of the sun, the "above" and "below." Space is now divided into definitive zones and directions; but each of these has not only a purely intuitive meaning but also an expressive character of its own. Space is not yet a homogeneous whole, within which the particular determinations are equivalent and interchangeable. The near and far, the high and low, the right and left—all have their uniqueness, their special mode of magical significance. Not only is the basic opposition of sacred and profane interwoven with all these spatial oppositions; it actually constitutes and produces them. What makes a province spatially distinct is not some abstract, geometrical determination, but the unique mythical atmosphere in which it stands—the magical aura that surrounds it. Accordingly, the different directions in mythical space are not conceptual or intuitive relations—they are independent entities, endowed with demonic powers. One must immerse oneself in the artistic representations of the gods and demons of the directions—as we find them for example in the ancient Mexican culture—in order wholly to feel this expressive meaning, this physiognomic character which all spatial determinations possess for the mythical consciousness.[6] Even the systematic order of space (for this is by no means lacking in mythical thinking) does not go

6. Cf., for example, the illustrations of T. W. Danzel, *Grundzüge der altmexikanischen Geisteskultur* (Hagen and Darmstadt, 1922).

beyond this sphere. The augur who marks off a *templum,* a sacred precinct in which he differentiates various zones, thus creates the basic precondition, the first beginning and impulse toward "contemplation." He divides the universe according to a definite point of view—he sets up a spiritual frame of reference, toward which all being and all change are oriented. This orientation is designed to insure a vision of the world as a whole, and with it a prevision of the future. But of course this vision does not move within a free, ideal, linear structure, as in the realm of pure "theory"; the zones of space are inhabited by real, fateful powers, powers of blessing or of doom.[7] The magical circle that embraces the whole existence of nature and of man is not burst asunder but only reinforced; the distances conquered by mythical intuition do not break its power but serve only to confirm it anew.

In comparison with this fundamental attitude of myth, language seems from the start to take a new and basically different road. For what characterizes the very first spatial terms that we find in language is their embracing of a definite "deictic" function. We have seen that a fundamental form of all speech goes back to the form of showing—that language can only come into being and thrive where consciousness has developed this form. The indicative gesture is already a milestone in this development—a crucial stage on the way to objective intuition and objective formation.[8] But what is embedded in this gesture comes to clear and complete unfolding only when language takes up this tendency and guides it into its own channels. With its deictic particles language creates the first means of expression for near and far and for certain fundamental differences of direction. These, too, are seen at first entirely in terms of the speaking subject and from his special standpoint—the difference in direction from the speaker to the person addressed and conversely from the person addressed to the speaker seems to constitute one of the earliest distinctions ever to have been noticed and fixated in language. But with this difference, with this distinction of the I from the "thou" and from objective being which it confronts, man has broken through to a new phase of his world view. Between the I and the world a bond is now formed which, while binding them closer together, at the same time keeps them

7. Cf. above, *2*, 83 ff., 99 ff.
8. Cf. above, *1*, 171 ff., 180 ff. Hans Freyer in *Die Theorie des objektiven Geistes* (Leipzig, 1923) agrees in stressing the decisive importance of the "indicative" gesture and the fundamental difference between it and any mere "expressive movement" (cf. esp. pp. 16 ff.).

separate. The intuition of space that is elaborated in language is the plainest indication of this peculiar twofold relationship. Here distance is posited, but by this very positing it is in a sense surpassed. In the intuitive space acquired with the help of language the factors of separateness and juxtaposition, of absolute discreteness and absolute combination, may be said to counterbalance one another, to stand in a kind of ideal equilibrium.

But even in its highest and most universal forms, myth can apprehend spatial differences only by injecting a difference of another type and origin into them. For myth all difference of spatial aspect involuntarily changes into a difference of expressive features, of physiognomic characters. Thus its spatial view, in spite of its tendencies toward objective formation, remains bathed in the color of feeling and subjective sensation. Language, too, is still thoroughly rooted in this sphere, but it manifestly effects a new turn: from expressive space to representative space. The particular localities are no longer distinguished only by certain qualitative and perceptible characters; now they disclose determinate relations of "the between," the spatial order. Even those very primitive spatial terms in which for example a nuance in vowel coloration is used to express varying degrees of distance indicate this basic trend of language. They distinguish the "here" from the "there," the "present" from the "absent"; but at the same time they link the two by creating the first rudimentary beginning of a measurement relation between them. Thus the progress from merely pragmatic space to objective space, from the space of action to the space of intuition, while not completed, is at least anticipated in general principle. The mere space of action, which we must impute also to the world of the animal, still comprises no free survey of spatial determinations and relations—no "synopsis" which makes it possible to compose locally separate factors into the unity of a simultaneous view. Instead of such a συνορᾶν εἰς ἕν, as Plato calls it, there prevails a mere relation of correspondence, in which certain movements are accorded with one another. Such a correspondence need not necessarily be accompanied or guided by a synopsis.[9] Certain movements may be fixed by long practice, they may

9. This "space of action" to which the animal world seems in general to be limited is typified in Hans Volkelt's account of the spatial orientation of the spider in his *Über die Vorstellungen der Tiere:* "When an object had fallen into the web, the spider, if it reacted at all, hastened to it only when the object moved; but if the object hung quietly, the spider did not run directly from its home to the object, but made a stop in the center of the net in order—to speak in human terms—to determine the direction of the object caught in the net by feeling the radial threads. . . . When a house fly flew into the

always be performed identically with the help of certain mechanisms, but this does not necessarily lead to a representative consciousness, to any representation and actualization of the separateness and succession of their different stages.

There is no doubt that this transition to the pure representation of spatial relations is also a relatively late step in the development of human consciousness. Reports on primitive peoples show that their spatial orientation, though very much keener and more precise than that of civilized man, moves wholly in the channels of a concrete spatial feeling. Though every point in their surroundings, every bend in a river for example, may be exactly known to them, they will still be unable to draw a map of the river, to hold it fast in a spatial schema. The transition from mere action to the schema, to the symbol, to representation, signifies in every case a genuine "crisis" of the spatial consciousness; moreover it is not limited to the spatial consciousness but goes hand in hand with a general spiritual transformation, an authentic revolution in the mode of thinking.[10]

In order to clarify the general character of this transformation, let us glance back at the result of our analysis of the thing-attribute relationship.

net, the victim sometimes escaped the spider in this way; for sometimes the fly would freeze in some desperate posture the moment it touched the net. Attracted to the center by the first jerk, the spider would feel the radial threads one by one; sometimes it detected the direction in which the fly lay motionless, sometimes it did not; in the latter case it returned home empty-handed. . . . From all this it follows unquestionably that even in the center of the web the spider does not obtain adequate information of what is going on in the periphery through optical qualities (whether through an image or a mere seeing of motion), but that touch plays an essential part in conditioning its behavior . . . even when the object hangs in the net at a very slight distance (2–3 cm.) from the spider, the insect sometimes fails to find it" (pp. 51 f.).

10. Certain experiments dealing with pathological modifications in the spatial consciousness also throw light on this difference between "active space" and "symbolic space." They show that many persons whose ability to recognize spatial forms and to interpret them objectively is gravely impaired can perform highly complex spatial tasks if these can be approached in another way, through certain movements and "kinesthetic" perceptions. Cf. Adhémar Gelb and Kurt Goldstein, "Über den Einfluss des vollständigen Verlustes des optischen Vorstellungsvermögens auf das taktile Erkennen," in *Psychologische Analysen hirnpathologischer Fälle, 1* (Leipzig, 1920), 157–250. (For further detail, see below, Chaps. 4, 6.) It would seem—as can be gathered from the penetrating self-analyses of blind persons —that we must conceive the "space" of the blind not as a representative image-space but primarily as a dynamic "behavior space," a definite field of action and movement. Cf. Wilhelm Ahlmann, "Zur Analyse des optischen Vorstellungslebens, ein Beitrag zur Blindenpsychologie," *Archiv für die gesamte Psychologie, 46* (1924), 193 ff.; and J. Wittmann, "Über Raum, Zeit und Wirklichkeit," ibid., *47* (1924), 428 ff.

Here we already found that we can arrive at the "constancy" of the thing only through the mediation of space—that "objective" space is the medium of all empirical objectivity. Both the intuition of space and the intuition of the thing are made possible only when the stream of successive experiences is in a sense halted—when the mere "one-thing-after-another" is transformed into an "at-one-time." This transformation occurs when a different signification, a different "valence" is attributed to the factors of the flowing change. Insofar as we conceive each phenomenon as belonging solely to the sphere of change it is, strictly speaking, "given" only in a single point of time: the moment creates it and snatches it away. Definite halting places, relative points of rest, can be gained in this unceasing change only because the particular contents, though variable and ephemeral in their facticity, point beyond themselves to something permanent—something of which all these changing images are only diverse aspects. Once the variable has thus been taken as the representation of a constant, it takes on an entirely new face. For now the eye no longer rests on it but sees through it and beyond it. Just as in the linguistic sign—where it is not the tone or sound or its sensuous modifications that we notice, but the meaning it communicates—so the particular phenomenon loses its independence and self-sufficiency, its individual concretion, as soon as it functions as a sign for a "thing," for something objectively intended and objectively formed. The fact of color transformation has already called our attention to this state of affairs. A color that we see in an unusual light is oriented and transposed with respect to the normal illumination; it is, in a sense, restored to its normal color tone and taken as a merely accidental deviation from it. This differentiation of the constant and the variable, the necessary and the accidental, the universal and the individual contains the germ of all objectivization. "In every perception of abnormal lighting," writes E. Kaila in describing this phenomenon,

> there is a more or less pronounced phenomenal split of the color sensations into illumination and what is illumined. . . . The material of sensation produced by the optical stimulation is split by the inner eye in such a way that the components of the color process corresponding to the objective colors are used for the building of the objective images, while that component which is distributed more or less intensely over the whole somatic field of vision, and which corre-

sponds to the color of the illumination, appears as abnormal illumination.[11]

As Katz stresses, the illumination is also "taken into consideration" in this way, where the eye is presented with very unusual variegated illuminations which accordingly could not have been previously experienced.[12] From this it follows that as soon as the optical phenomenon of color is seen from the standpoint of the thing, as soon as color is taken as a means of representing things, the optical experience itself is articulated in a very characteristic way and so transformed.

This breakdown of an intrinsically unitary phenomenon into components of different signification is also indispensable for the building of spatial intuition. Here again there is a split by which the permanent is divided from the variable, the typical from the transitory. Space as objective space is posited and achieved only when a representative value is attributed to definite perceptions, when they are selected and distinguished as fixed points of reference. Certain fundamental configurations are set up as norms by which we measure others. Since William James, the psychological theory of spatial intuition has taken this state of affairs into account by stressing the motif of selection as an essential condition for the development of the idea of space. James espoused nativist theories of space; he started from the assumption that "We *have* native and fixed optical space-sensations; *but experience leads us to select certain ones from among them to be the exclusive bearers of reality: the rest become mere signs and suggesters of* these." [13] In all our perceptions such a selection takes place: in all of them we pick out certain formations which, we say, represent the real form of the object, while we regard others as only peripheral or more or less accidental manifestations of this object. The shifts and distortions of perspective which the image of an object undergoes under certain conditions of vision are in this way corrected. The seeing of an image thus always comprises a definite evaluation of it: we do not see it as it immediately gives itself to us but place it in the context of the total spatial experience and thus give it its characteristic

11. E. Kaila, "Gegenstandsfarbe und Beleuchtung," *Psychologische Forschung, 3* (1923), 32 f.

12. Katz, *Die Erscheinungsweise der Farben*, pp. 275 f.

13. William James, *The Principles of Psychology*, 1890; (2 vols. New York, Henry Holt, 1910), 2, 237.

meaning.[14] It is assuredly no accident, but symptomatically and methodologically significant that in elucidating this relation, James has recourse to a comparison with language:

> The signs of each probable real thing being multiple and the thing itself one and fixed, we gain the same mental relief by abandoning the former for the latter that we do when we abandon mental images, with all their fluctuating characters, for the definite and unchangeable *names* which they suggest. The selection of the several "normal" appearances from out of the jungle of our optical experiences, to serve as the real sights of which we shall think, is psychologically a parallel phenomenon to the habit of thinking in words, and has a like use. Both are substitutions of terms few and fixed for terms manifold and vague.[15]

By means of this process the particular spatial values gain a peculiar transparence for us. Just as we look through the accidental illumination-color in which an object is set to its "permanent" color, so, with all their particularity and change, the manifold optical images that arise for example in the movement of an object, point the way to its enduring form. They are not mere impressions but function as representations; they are no longer "affections" but symbols.[16]

14. If, for example, a square figure is seen on a surface placed obliquely to the eye, it should, according to the image it casts on the retina, appear as a quadrangle with two acute and two obtuse angles, while in reality it retains its square character. Similarly an optical impression which in itself would correspond to an ellipse is transformed into a circle, i.e. to the figure that we should see if it were represented on a frontal-parallel surface. Here it is noteworthy and characteristic that this phenomenon seems to be entirely lacking or very much impaired in pathological cases of so-called "mental blindness." In the report of Gelb and Goldstein, when a circle or square was first presented in a frontal-parallel position and the optical images of the two figures were then changed by rotation on a vertical axis, the patient distinctly saw an ellipse or an upended rectangle when the turn amounted to 25 or 30 degrees. In binocular vision, the phenomenon of "apparent shape" was regained, but in limited degree, since the patient now saw the image more according to the "real" formal nature of the object than according to the reproductive conditions on the retina. Cf. Gelb and Goldstein, in *Psychologische Analysen*, pp. 36 ff.

15. *Principles of Psychology, 2,* 240.

16. From the purely genetic standpoint, it seems established, here again, that this characteristic "symbolic consciousness" developed only late. We have seen that it must be acquired in the growth of language, and the psychology of visual perception also indicates the first reaction to light which the retina presents to consciousness consists in plain colors, while the consciousness of surface colors is a later development. Cf. Katz, *Die Erscheinungsweise der Farben*, pp. 306 ff., 397 ff.

Here again we find that the symbolic function reaches back to a far deeper stratum of consciousness than is usually supposed. It gives its imprint not only to the world view of theoretical knowledge or science, but also to the primary formations of consciousness. We can best perceive the connection as well as the difference between the two spheres by comparing the structures of perceptive space and abstract geometrical space. Obviously the two structures cannot be viewed as identical; to perceptive space we cannot attribute uniformity, constancy, or infinity in the mathematical sense of these predicates. But despite this difference, the two disclose a common factor, insofar as a definite mode and direction of constant-formation is at work in them. Felix Klein has shown that the form of every geometry depends on which spatial determinations and relations it selects to posit as invariable. The usual metric geometry starts from the assumption that the essential factors in a spatial structure are those attributes and relations which are unaffected by certain clearly defined changes—by a shift of the structure in absolute space, by a proportionate growth or diminution of its determining parts, and finally, by certain reversals in the arrangement of its parts. A figure may pass through any number of such transformations—for metric geometry, it remains the same; it still represents an identical geometric concept. But in establishing such concepts we are not restricted once and for all to any fixed choice of transformations. Metric geometry becomes projective geometry as soon as we include all possible projective transformations in whose presence a spatial form should remain unchanged. Thus according to Klein, every special geometry is a theory of invariants which is valid in reference to definite groups of transformations.[17] But precisely in this respect we find that the conception of the various "geometries" and the formation of the concept of space underlying each one of them merely extends a process that is already embedded and forecast in the formation of our empirical space, the space of our sensory experience. For this space, too, comes into being only when a multiplicity of phenomena, of particular optical images, are composed into groups and these groups are taken as representations of one and the same object. From this moment on the changing phenomena only form a periphery; and every part of this periphery sends out points, as it were, which guide our sight in a definite direction, which lead it back over and over again to the same thing as a center. And here too—though not to the same extent as in the building of purely geometrical, symbolic space—it is possible to situate these centers differently. The point of reference itself can be shifted; the mode of relation can change; and whenever such a change takes place, the phenomenon takes on not only a different abstract signification but also a different concrete-intuitive meaning. A striking example of this transformation in the intuitive meaning of spatial forms is provided by the well known phenomena usually subsumed under the name of "optical inversion." One and the same optical complex can be transformed now into this, now into that spatial object, can be "seen" as this or as another object. Such inversions are neither errors of judgment nor mere ideas, but genuine perceptive experiences.[18] And here again it is confirmed that a change in sight changes the perceptive content, that every shift in viewpoint transforms the pure phenomenal facticity of the thing seen. And as consciousness progresses in its formation and articulation, as its separate contents become more "significant," i.e. as they acquire greater power to "indicate" other contents, one form can more freely change into another through a change of sight.[19]

We have already seen that this act of concentration, this formation and creation of centers, goes back to a basic productive function of the spirit, and that accordingly it can never be fully explained by mere reproductive processes.[20] In his theories of the concept and of the origin of the idea of space, Berkeley falls into a vicious circle by invoking the function of representation but then seeking to reduce this function to mere habit and custom.[21] In the *Critique of Pure Reason* Kant exposes this vicious circle and at the same time attacks the problem at its root, by inquiring into the conditions under which association itself is possible.

18. See Erich M. von Hornbostel's excellent treatment of the phenomenon in his "Über optische Inversion," *Psychologische Forschung, 1* (1922), 130–56.

19. In his intelligence tests of anthropoid apes Koehler also stressed how closely all the intelligent actions of the anthropoids are connected with the faculty of optical-spatial articulation and a relatively free optical-spatial "synopsis." A large share of the difficulties created for the animal by certain intelligence tests arose precisely from this transformation of optical structures. Cf. W. Koehler, "Intelligenzprüfung an Anthropoiden, I," *Abhandlungen der königlichen preussischen Akademie der Wissenschaften, physikalisch-mathematische Klasse* (Berlin, 1917), esp. pp. 90 ff., 105 ff. This faculty of regrouping and recentering within purely visual space seems, from a psychological view, to be the beginning and precondition for the acquisition of that schematic space which, as Leibniz said, is no real thing but rather "an order of possible coexistences" (*un ordre des coexistences possibles*).

20. Cf. above, esp. pp. 132–5.

21. Cf. my *Erkenntnisproblem, 2,* 297 ff.

. . . upon what, I ask, does this rule, as a law of nature, rest? How is this association itself possible? The ground of the possibility of the association of the manifold, so far as it lies in the object, is named the *affinity* of the manifold. . . . There must, therefore, be an objective ground (that is, one that can be comprehended *a priori*, antecedently to all empirical laws of the imagination) upon which rests the possibility, nay, the necessity, of a law that extends to all appearances— a ground, namely, which constrains us to regard all appearances as data of the senses that must be associable in themselves and subject to universal rules of a thoroughgoing connection in their reproduction. This objective ground of all association of appearances I entitle their *affinity*. . . . That the affinity of appearances, and with it their association, and through this, in turn, their reproduction according to laws, and so [as involving these various factors] experience itself, should only be possible by means of this transcendental function of imagination, is indeed strange, but is none the less an obvious consequence of the preceding argument. For without this transcendental function no concepts of objects would together make up a unitary experience.[22]

Yet this transcendental function of the imagination is not grasped in its core even where an attempt is made to reduce it to apperceptive rather than mere reproductive processes. True, this seems to constitute a decisive step beyond any sensationalist foundations, for apperception not only signifies the apprehension and subsequent synthesis of given impressions but also represents a pure spontaneity, a creative act of the spirit. But most psychological theories—and this has been eminently true of Wundt's —tend to obscure this independence by identifying apperception with the phenomenon of attention. Jaensch in particular has taken this phenomenon as a basis for explaining the perception of space. Here, attitudes of attention are the decisive factor which determines all localization in space. "Where other factors of localization are absent," so Jaensch formulates the general principle governing this localization, "visual impressions are localized at the distance of the locus of attention."[23] But even if we accept all the detailed conclusions that Jaensch draws from his experi-

22. *Kritik der reinen Vernunft*, 1st ed., pp. 113 f., 122 f. Eng. trans. by Norman Kemp Smith, *Immanuel Kant's Critique of Pure Reason* (London, Macmillan, 1950), pp. 139, 145 f.
23. E. R. Jaensch, *Über die Wahrnehmung des Raumes*, Supplementary Vol. 6 of *Zeitschrift für Psychologie* (Leipzig, 1911), esp. chap. 5, on localization of attention.

ments, a general methodological question forces itself upon us: has this principle of attention been sufficiently clarified, has it been sharply enough defined to serve as a foundation for a theory of space? Attempts have also been made to base a general theory of the concept on this principle. The "abstraction" which supposedly gives rise to the concept has also been looked upon as an achievement of attention. When our consciousness runs through a series of sense perceptions, we do not, according to this theory, consider all their attributes uniformly, but always detach a definite factor, on which we dwell more than on the others. In this way the disregarded components are repressed and only those others which stand at the center of attention are retained; and it is thus that the concept came into being as an aggregate of those factors that are taken into account. But if we examine this theory of the concept more closely, we soon find that it, too, involves us in a vicious circle; that what is sought is confused with what is given, what is to be proved with its premise. For attention can become a concept-creating act only by taking a determinate direction from the very outset and retaining this direction throughout its movement—by apprehending the multiplicity of perceptions from a unitary point of view and so comparing them. And this unity of "sight" does not first create but already implies the concept and is its logical meaning and function. Attention as such does not suffice to form a concept, for attention can also accompany any act of mere sensation, representation or fantasy. The crucial circumstance is rather to be sought in that to which attention is directed, in the goal which thought has in view when it passes over a series of particular contents, and to which it refers these contents as a whole.

The acquisition of characteristically determined spatial forms requires the same fundamental act as is necessary to concept formation. The various geometrical "spaces" make this particularly evident: according as the eye is directed toward one or another goal, as it posits one or another factor as "invariant," one or another mode of space originates: the concept of "metric" or "projective" space, etc. is constituted. But, as we have seen, our empirical intuitive space also goes back to a persistent act of selection—and this selection always requires a definite principle, a determining viewpoint. Here, too, certain fixed points are posited, cardinal points around which the phenomena revolve. Since both the center and the direction of rotation may change, a particular perception may assume very different meanings and values for the total structure of spatial reality. But beyond all these differences, the unity of the basic theoretical function that governs the totality of these relations asserts itself. By not merely grasping a particular that is given here and now, by taking on the character of "representation," perception gathers the variegated multiplicity of phenomena into a context of experience. The division between the two fundamental factors of representation—the representing and the represented—bears in itself the germ from which the world of space unfolds as a world of pure intuition.

Chapter 4

The Intuition of Time

HIGHLY DEVELOPED theoretical thinking tends to consider time as an all-embracing form for all change; as a universal order in which every content of reality "is" and in which an unequivocal place is assigned to it. Time does not stand beside things as a physical being or force: it has no independent character of existence or action. But all combinations of things, all relations prevailing among them, go back ultimately to determinations of the temporal process, to divisions of the earlier and later, the "now" and the "not now." Only when thought succeeds in composing the multiplicity of events into a system within which the particular events are determined in respect to their "before" and "after," do phenomena unite into the form of a totality of intuitive reality. The particularity of temporal schematism first makes possible the form of objective experience. Thus time, as Kant says, forms "the correlative of the determination of an object in general." The transcendental schemata, which, according to Kant, guarantee the relationship between understanding and sensibility, are "nothing but *a priori determinations of time* according to rules," and these relate to the series in time, the content in time, the order in time, and finally to the complex or totality in time in regard to all possible objects. But there is a sharp and basic difference between schema and image, for the "image is a product of the empirical faculty of the productive imagination—the schema of sensuous conceptions (of figures in space, for example) is a product and, as it were, a monogram of the pure imagination a priori, whereby and according to which images first become possible." [1]

In thus formulating the problem of time, Kant adds, to be sure, that this "schematism of our understanding in regard to phenomena and their mere form is an art in the depths of the human soul, whose true modes

1. *Kritik der reinen Vernunft*, 2d ed., pp. 181 f. Eng. ed., pp. 119, 121.

of action we shall only with difficulty discover and unveil." Indeed, regardless of whether we approach this problem from the standpoint of metaphysics, psychology or epistemology, we seem here to encounter an unsurpassable "limit of human comprehension." Augustine's dictum still seems to retain its full force; time, which to the immediate consciousness is the most certain and most familiar of facts, shrouds itself in darkness the moment we seek to pass beyond this immediate givenness and draw it into the sphere of reflective inquiry.[2] Any attempt at a definition or even of an objective characteristic of time threatens to involve us in inextricable antinomies, though, to be sure, a common source of all these antinomies and aporias seems to reside in the fact that neither metaphysics nor epistemology observed Kant's strict division between image and schema. Instead of relating sensuous images to the "monogram of the pure imagination," they have repeatedly succumbed to the temptation of "explaining" the imagination by purely sensuous determinations. What makes this temptation all the more dangerous is that it never ceases to be renewed and fostered by a positive and fundamental power of the human spirit, the power of language. In designating temporal determinations and relations, language is at first wholly dependent on the mediation of space; and from this involvement with the spatial world there results also a bond with the world of things, which are conceived as existing in space. Thus the form of time is here expressed only insofar as it can in some way be based on spatial and objective determinations.[3]

So great is the power of this dependency that it makes itself felt beyond

2. The following chapter was written before the appearance of Heidegger's recent analysis of "time" and "temporality" ("Sein und Zeit," *Jahrbuch für Philosophie und phänomenologische Forschung*, 1927), which in many respects points to entirely new roads. Here I shall not attempt a detailed critical discussion of this analysis. Such a discussion will be possible and fruitful only when Heidegger's work is available as a whole. For the basic problem of the Philosophy of Symbolic Forms lies precisely in that territory which Heidegger expressly and intentionally excluded from the first volume of his book. It does not deal with that mode of temporality which Heidegger elaborates as the original *Seinssinn des Daseins*. The Philosophy of Symbolic Forms does not question this temporality which Heidegger discloses as the ultimate foundation of existentiality and attempts to explain in its diverse factors. But our inquiry begins *beyond* this sphere, at precisely the point where a transition is effected from this existential temporality to the *form* of time. It aspires to show the conditions under which this form is possible, the conditions for the postulation of a "being" which goes beyond the existentiality of "being-there." In regard to time as to space, this μετάβασις from the meaning of existence to the objective meaning of the "logos" constitutes its proper theme and problem (cf. above, p. 149 n.).

3. Cf. above, *1*, 215 ff.

the world of language in the concept formation of exact science. Exact science also seems able to give an objective description of time only by representing it in spatial images. It, too, takes the image of the endless straight line as a figurative representation of time. But does any such figurative character catch the actual form of time? Does it not rather inject a specifically different, essentially alien factor into it? All linguistic determination is necessarily a fixation—but does not the mere attempt at any such fixation deny time its true meaning, which is precisely pure change? Here myth seems to penetrate more deeply than language into time; it seems able to dwell in the original form of time, for it takes the world not as rigid being but as constant change; not as a finished form but as an ever renewed metamorphosis. And from this fundamental view it rises to a wholly universal intuition of time. For in myth the intuitions of what is in process of becoming and what has become are separate from that of becoming itself. All particulars and individuals are subject to the power of change, which is here the universal and irrefragable power of destiny. This is the power that metes out their life and existence. The gods themselves are not masters over time and destiny but subject to their primal law, the law of μοῖρα. Thus time is here experienced as destiny—long before it was conceived as a cosmic order of change in the purely theoretical sense.[4] It is no mere ideal network for the order of the "earlier" and "later"; rather, it is itself the spinner of the net. With all the universality that is already imputed to it, it remains alive and concrete: it is the original actuality of all being—earthly and celestial, human and divine.

But a new relationship appears as soon as the question of origins is asked by philosophy, by theoretical reflection in place of myth. The mythical concept of the beginning is now transformed into the concept of the principle. At first, to be sure, a concrete temporal intuition enters into the purely conceptual determination of this principle. The enduring "ground" of being is at the same time the first and earliest form of being that we must find if we follow the chain of becoming back to its beginning. But these interwoven motifs break apart once thought ceases to inquire solely into the foundation of things and turns to the foundations of its own being and its own validity. Where philosophy first raises this question—where, instead of seeking the foundation of reality, it asks after the meaning and foundation of truth—the bond between being and time seems to be severed at one stroke. The true being that is now discovered is timeless.

4. Cf. above, 2, 104 ff., 112 ff., 116.

What we call time is henceforth no more than a name—a fiction of language and human opinion. Being itself knows no earlier or later: "It never Was, nor Will Be, because it is without end." [5] With this concept of timeless being as the correlate of timeless truth, "logos" has torn itself away from myth—pure thought has declared its independence from the mythical powers of fate. Over and over again in the course of its history, philosophy returns to its origin. Spinoza like Parmenides sets up the idea of a timeless knowledge, a knowledge *sub specie aeterni*. For him, too, time becomes a structure of the *imaginatio,* the empirical imagination, which falsely injects its form into substantial, absolute being. But by thus dismissing time from its threshold, by "driving away" becoming and destruction, as Parmenides put it,[6] metaphysics did not of course dispose of the riddle. For while being, having been made absolute, seems freed from the burden of contradiction, a still graver contradiction now weighs upon the world of phenomena. From now on the phenomenal world is subject to the dialectic of change. The history of philosophy shows how this dialectic, which Eleatic thought discovered in the abstract concepts of multiplicity and motion, gradually penetrates empirical knowledge, physics, and its theoretical foundation. Newton completed this development by postulating as the keystone of his system an "absolute time," flowing along in itself, without regard to any outward object. But on closer scrutiny it becomes increasingly evident that this absolute time, as Kant put it, is an "existing non-entity." In making flux the basic factor of time, we situate its being and essence in its passing away. Time itself, to be sure, is not supposed to participate in this passing away; for the change applies not to time itself but only to the content of the process, to the successive phenomena. But then we would seem to have posited a reality, a substantial whole which is composed of nonexistent parts. For the past is "no more" and the future is "not yet." Thus the only existence that remains of time seems to be the present as a medium between the "no-longer" and the "not-yet." If we give to this medium a finite extension, if we regard it as a length of time, the same problem appears anew; the medium becomes a multiplicity of which only a single factor subsists at any time, while all others are prior to being or have left it behind them.

5. Parmenides, Fragment 8, in Hermann Diels, ed., *Die Fragmente der Vorsokratiker* (6th ed. 3 vols. Berlin, 1951–52). Eng. trans. of 5th ed. by Kathleen Freeman, *Ancilla to the Pre-Socratic Philosophers* (Cambridge, Mass., 1948), p. 43.

6. Ibid., verse 22. Eng. trans., p. 43. Cf. above, 2, 129 ff.

If on the other hand we understand the now in a strictly punctual sense, it ceases because of this isolation to be a member in a temporal series. Against such a "now" Zeno's paradox applies: the flying arrow is at rest because at any point in its course it occupies a single position and therefore is not in a state of becoming, of transition. The problem of time measurement, which as much as any problem would seem to be purely empirical, a problem propounded by experience itself and fully soluble by means of experience, involves philosophy over and over again in a labyrinth of dialectical considerations. In the correspondence between Leibniz and Clarke, Clarke as Newton's advocate deduces the absolute and real character of time from its measurability, for how can something that does not exist possess the attribute of objective magnitude and number? But Leibniz at once reverses this argument and seeks to show that a quantitative determination of time is conceivable without contradiction only if we think of it not as a substance but as a purely ideal relation, an "order of the possible." [7] Thus all progress in our knowledge of time, whether from the standpoint of metaphysics or of physics, seems only to disclose its intrinsically antinomic character the more clearly and inexorably; by whatever means we seek to grasp it, the "being" of time threatens to slip forever through our fingers.

This dialectic that arises whenever thought seeks to master the concept of time by subordinating it to a universal concept of being has been most pregnantly and clearly expressed in that classical chapter of St. Augustine's *Confessions,* which for the first time in the history of Western philosophy sets forth the problem of time and surveys it in its full scope. If, Augustine argues, the present becomes a determination of time, a temporal present, only by flowing into the past, how can we speak of a being that subsists only by destroying itself? Or how can we attribute magnitude to time and measure this magnitude, since we can effect such a measurement only by linking past and present and drawing them together into a single spiritual view—while actually the two factors are essentially contradictory? Here there is only one way out; a mediation must be found which, while not resolving this contradiction, at least relativizes it—which makes it appear not as an absolute contradiction but as a merely contingent opposition. And

7. Cf. my edition of G. W. Leibniz, *Hauptschriften zur Grundlegung der Philosophie,* in *Philosophische Werke,* ed. A. Buchenau and E. Cassirer (Leipzig, 1874–1906), *1,* 142, 159, 189 ff., 225 ff.

for Augustine this mediation is effected in every genuine act of the consciousness of time. We find the Ariadne's thread that can lead us out of the
labyrinth of time only when we express the problem in a fundamentally
different form—only when we remove it from the realm of realistic-
dogmatic ontology and place it within the framework of a pure analysis
of the phenomena of consciousness.[8] Now the division of time into present,
past, and future is no longer a substantial division attempting to determine
three heterogeneous modes of being in their essence and to differentiate
them from one another; now it applies solely to our knowledge of phenomenal reality. Strictly speaking, we cannot say that three times "are";
rather, we should say that the present time comprises three different relations and through them three different aspects and determinations. There
is a present of past things, a present of present things and a present of
future things. The present of past things is called memory, the present of
present things is called intuition, that of future things is called expectation.
Thus we may not think of time as an absolute thing, divided into three
absolute parts: rather, the unitary consciousness of the "now" encompasses three different basic directions and is first constituted in this triality.
The conscious present is not confined, as it were, within a single moment,
but necessarily passes beyond it, both forward and backward.[9] To comprehend time is therefore not to compose it out of three separate but ontically related substances—it is rather to understand how three clearly
separate intentions—the intentions toward the now, toward the earlier, and
toward the later—are composed into the unity of meaning. True, the
possibility of such a synthesis cannot be derived from something else or
proved by something else—rather, we stand here before a genuine original
phenomenon which as such can only be accredited and explained out of

8. In the structure of St. Augustine's thinking the time motif reveals its power in the
very fact that it leads to a fundamental reorientation, a transformation of the question of
being itself. Here it fulfills the same essential function as later in the development of
modern "ontology," which also sees its task above all as the disclosure and authentic
apprehension of time as the "horizon for all understanding and interpretation of being,"
and finds "the central problem of all ontology rooted" in the right view and explanation
of the phenomenon of time (cf. Heidegger, "Sein und Zeit," esp. sec. 5).

9. "Nec proprie dicitur Tempora sunt tria: praeteritum, praesens et futurum; sed fortasse
proprie diceretur: Tempora sunt tria, praesens de praeteritis, praesens de praesentibus, praesens
de futuris. Sunt enim haec in anima tria quaedam et alibi ea non video: praesens de praeteritis memoria, praesens de praesentibus contuitus, praesens de futuris exspectatio" (Augustine,
Confessiones, XI, 26).

itself. "Quid est ergo tempus? Si nemo ex me quaerat, scio, si quaerenti explicare velim, nescio." [10]

Consider the example of a bodily voice. It begins to sound, it sounds and goes on sounding, then it ceases: and now there is silence, the sound has passed, the sound no longer is. It was future before it began to sound, and so could not be measured, for as yet it did not exist; and now it cannot be measured because now it exists no longer. Only while sounding could it be measured for then it was, and so was measurable. But even then it was not standing still; it was moving, and moving out of existence. . . .

Deus creator omnium: This line is composed of eight syllables, short and long alternatively. . . . Each long syllable has double the time of each short syllable. I pronounce them and I say that it is so, and so it is, as is quite obvious to the ear. As my ear distinguishes I measure a long syllable by a short and I perceive that it contains it twice. But since I hear a syllable only when the one before it has ceased . . . how am I to keep hold of the short syllable, and how shall I set it against the long one to measure it and find that the long one is twice its length— given that the long syllable does not begin to sound until the short one has ceased? And again can I measure the long one while it is present, since I cannot measure it until it is completed? And its completion is its passing out of existence.

What then is it that I measure? Where is the short syllable by which I measure? Where is the long syllable which I measure? Both have sounded, have fled away, have gone into the past, are now no more: yet I do measure, and I affirm with confidence . . . that one is single, the other double, in the length of time it occupies. . . . Thus it is not the syllables themselves that I measure, for they are now no more, but something which remains engraved in my memory.

It is in you, O my mind, that I measure time. . . . What I measure is the impress produced in you by things as they pass and abiding in you when they have passed: and it is present. I do not measure the things themselves whose passage produced the impress; it is the impress that I measure when I measure time. . . .

. . . in the mind . . . there are three acts. For the mind expects, attends and remembers: what it expects passes, by way of what it attends to, into what it remembers. Would anyone deny that the future is as yet not existent? But in the mind there is already an expectation of the future. Would anyone deny that the past no longer exists? Yet still there is in the mind a memory of the past. Would anyone deny that the present time lacks extension, since it is but a point that passes on? Yet the attention endures, and by it that which is to be passes on its way to being no more. Thus it is not the future that is long, for the future does not exist: a long future is merely a long expectation of the future; nor is the past long since the past does not exist: a long past is merely a long memory of the past.[11]

From now on a sharp dividing line is drawn between the time of things and the time of pure experience—between the time which we conceive as the riverbed of the objective process and the time of consciousness, which by its very essence can be given to us only as present. Once it has been thus clearly apprehended, the problem here disclosed never abates but moves through the whole history of metaphysics and epistemology; it has taken on a new sharpness in recent attempts to establish a modern psychology of thought.[12] And here we, too, find ourselves referred back to the very center of our inquiry. For it is evident that the phenomenon of the *representation* of time must not be confused with the problems of ontically real, metaphysical time. We cannot begin with the latter and thence advance to experienced time, the time of the ego, but can take only the opposite path. The question is: how can we be guided from the pure phenomenon of the "now," which includes future and past as constitutive factors, to that mode of time in which these three stages are distinct from one another, in which they are posited as objectively "separate" and successive? The direction of inquiry can only be from the ideal to the real, from the intention to its object. And on the other hand there is ultimately no road that leads back from the metaphysical category of substantiality to

11. Ibid., XI, 27. Eng. trans. by F. J. Sheed, *The Confessions of St. Augustine* (New York, Sheed and Ward, 1943), pp. 281-4. "Non igitur longum tempus futurum, quod non est, sed longum futurum longa expectatio futuri est; neque longum praeteritum tempus, quod non est, sed longum praeteritum, longa memoria praeteriti est." The "longa expectatio" and the "longa memoria" should here of course not be taken as the real duration of expectation and memory as psychic acts, but mean that the expectation or memory determines the content toward which it is directed as "short" or "long": the temporal determination applies not to acts but to their "intentional object."

12. Cf. Hoenigswald, *Die Grundlagen der Denkpsychologie:* on the difference between "present time" and "objective time," "formed time" and "transient time," see esp. pp. 67 ff., 87 ff., 307 ff.

the pure intuition of time. Here the only logical conclusion is precisely to reject this intuition itself, to call it with Parmenides nonexistent, or with Spinoza a fiction of the imagination. But since pure phenomena cannot simply be done away with by metaphysical decree, the only possibility of solving the problem consists in fundamentally reversing it. What must be sought is the transition from the original time structure of the ego to that temporal order in which empirical things and events stand for us, in which the object of experience is given to us. And here it becomes apparent that what this object means and signifies not only stands in a mediated relation to the temporal order but can only be posited through this order. In modern philosophy this view of the matter begins not with Kant but with Leibniz. Leibniz shows—and this is a central point in his polemic against Newton's theory of time—that "monadological" time is the πρότερον τῇ φύσει, and that we can only thence arrive at mathematical-physical time. According to the system of monadology, the "presence" of the I, which includes past and future within it, is the starting point, the *terminus a quo,* whose being and meaning can be explained by no *influxus physicus,* by no causality from without. It forms the medium for all other objective being and for all objective knowledge. For Leibniz, who reverses the realistic concept of substance, the monad *is* only through its power of representation: but it can represent only by envisaging and expressing the past and the future in the present. This expression of the many in the one (*multorum in uno expressio*) belongs to the essence of every phenomenon of consciousness; but perhaps it is more clearly disclosed in the character of temporal phenomena than anywhere else. In every other sphere, it may seem as though the representation were simply an act of mind additional to the mere content of consciousness which is somehow immediately given; as though it did not originally belong to the stuff of consciousness but were only superimposed on it. In space, it is true, every content necessarily refers to the others, so that every "here" is linked with a "there" by causal determinations, by dynamic actions; but the pure meaning of the "here" seems at first sight capable of standing alone; it seems possible to conceive and define it independently of the "there." For time, however, such a separation is not even abstractly possible. Every moment immediately comprises the triad of temporal relations and temporal intentions. The present, the now, obtains its character as present only through the act of representation, through the reference to past and future comprised in it. Here, accordingly, "representation" is not merely added to "presentation"; rather, it constitutes the very meaning and core of the present. Any attempt to separate content and representation, existence and symbol, would, if successful, destroy the vital nerve of temporality.

And with this specific form of temporal consciousness the form of the ego-consciousness would also be destroyed. For the two condition each other: the ego finds and knows itself only in the threefold form of the temporal consciousness, while on the other hand the three phases of time compose themselves into a unity only in and through the ego. Time determinations, when taken in the abstract, seem to be at odds; but they actually go together in time, and this is something that can only be made comprehensible from the standpoint of the I and not from that of things. For on the one hand, as Kant put it, the "standing and enduring ego forms the correlate of all our representations, insofar as we can become conscious of them"—but on the other hand the ego can only assure itself of its identity and permanence through its own unbroken flow. It is constancy and change, permanence and transition in one.

> When I feel myself to be standing in this *now*, I not only find myself unceasingly in transition with respect to the past but I also never find myself sharply cut off in the forward direction, stopping at one moment and then after a pause beginning again. Also in the forward direction I am ever-flowing. While in this now I feel myself passing from the now that has just become past, I am at the same time certain that this now in which I stand vanishes forthwith and flows into another now. My experience of the now has these two aspects: it feels itself to be coming from a before and moving into an after. Every now is for me a vanishing just-having-been-present and at the same time a transition into another now, that is, into a not-yet-having-been-present-a-moment-before.[13]

Of course this form of the self-experience cannot be shown otherwise than in pure description—it cannot be explained by being reduced to something else, to something deeper. Regardless of what direction this explanation takes, regardless of whether it follows metaphysical or psychological trends, the attempted derivation reduces to an annulling of the experience. In assigning time to the realm of the imagination, Spinoza must also assign the ego to the same realm. True, for Spinoza too, con-

13. Johannes Volkelt, *Phänomenologie und Metaphysik der Zeit* (Munich, 1925), pp. 23 f.

sciousness, *cogitatio,* appears as an attribute of the infinite substance and thus seems to be defined as eternal and necessary. But he leaves no doubt that this consciousness has no more than the name in common with the human ego-consciousness. When we attribute the predicate of self-consciousness to substance, when we speak of divine understanding and divine will, we are, in Spinoza's view, letting ourselves be governed by a mere linguistic metaphor: actually there is no greater kinship between the two "consciousnesses" than between the dog as dog-star and the dog as a barking animal. The primordial and independent character of both the ego-consciousness and the time consciousness are attacked from an opposite side by the criticism of psychological empiricism and sensationalism.

Here again we are under the ban of a substantial view: except that now it is not the "simple" of being but the "simple" of sensation to which all formations of consciousness are reduced and dissolved. This elementary substance as such contains in its pure "in itself" neither the form of the ego nor the form of consciousness. Both appear rather as secondary products—accidental determinations requiring a genetic derivation from the simple. Thus the ego becomes a "bundle of perceptions," while time becomes a mere multiplicity of sensory impressions. Anyone who seeks time among the fundamental facts of consciousness, among the simple perceptions, will find nothing corresponding to it: there is no single perception of time or duration as there is of a tone or a color. Five tones played on a flute—Hume insists—produce the impression of time in us; but this is not a new impression which is added to the purely acoustical impressions and of the same sort as they are. Nor does the mind, under the stimulus of mere auditory sensations, create a new idea, an idea of "reflection," which it draws from itself. For though it may dissect all its representations a thousand times, it will never gain the original perception of time from them. What it actually becomes aware of in the hearing of the tones is, then, in addition to the tones themselves, nothing other than a modal character that adheres to them, the particular "manner" in which they appear. Later we may reflect that this mode of appearance is in itself not confined to the material of the tones but can manifest itself in any other sensuous matter. In this case, however, time becomes separable from every particularity of sensuous material, but not from sensuous material as such. For Hume, accordingly, the representation of time is not an independent content; rather, it arises from a certain form of noticing or considering sensuous impressions and objects. Yet this derivation, which Mach essentially takes over unchanged from Hume, obviously moves in the same vicious circle as all attempts to reduce specific modes and directions of intention to mere acts of attention.[14] In order to become aware of time, we take notice of the sequence, and of it alone, and not of the particular contents that appear in this sequence.[15]

But it is clear that precisely this *direction* of attention already comprises the whole of time with its general structure and characteristic order. Here psychological empiricism succumbs to the same fallacy as realistic ontology. It, too, seeks to derive phenomenal time from some sort of objective determinations and relations, the only difference being that its objects are no longer absolute substances but sense impressions which are posited as no less absolute. Yet neither things in themselves nor sensations in themselves explain the fundamental relation that confronts us in the temporal consciousness. The succession of ideas is by no means synonymous with the representation of succession—nor is there any way of seeing how the latter might simply result from the former. For as long as the flow of representations is taken purely as an actual change, an objectively real process, it contains no consciousness *of* change as such—of that mode in which time is posited *as* sequence and yet as unremitting present, of the manner in which it is posited as representation in the ego and given to the ego.[16]

It is precisely this stumbling block that has frustrated all other attempts to understand the symbolic inclusion of the past in the now, as well as the anticipation of the future from the now by deriving both from causal laws of objective being and objective change. Here again an attempt is made to make a purely cognitive context intelligible by substituting a purely cognitive text for it. But closely as the two may be linked, the substantial context remains generically different from what it is supposed to explain. Even though the past may in some sense subsist in the present, no bridge

14. Cf. above, pp. 24 ff.

15. Cf. David Hume, *A Treatise of Human Nature* (Oxford, 1951), Bk. I, Pt. II, sec. 3: "But here it only takes notice of the manner in which the different sounds make their appearance; and that it may afterwards consider without considering these particular sounds."

16. On the difference between phenomenological time and objective, "cosmic" time cf. Edmund Husserl, *Ideen zu einer reinen Phänomenologie und phänomenologischen Philosophie* (Halle, 1928), secs. 81 ff. I have unfortunately been unable to take into account the penetrating analysis of the temporal consciousness given by Martin Heidegger, "Edmund Husserls Vorlesungen zur Phänomenologie des inneren Zeitbewusstseins," *Jahrbuch für Philosophie und phänomenologische Forschung,* 9 (1928), 367–498, on the basis of Husserl's lectures.

can be built from this supposed subsistence to the phenomenon of representation. For "representation" differs from mere "retention" not in degree
but in kind.[17] That the past somehow exists substantially in the present,
or that the two are linked by unbreakable threads, does not suffice to
explain the specific "mnemic consciousness," to explain the knowledge of
the past *as* past. For precisely when the past "is" in the present, when it
is thought as nonexistent in the present, it remains obscure how consciousness can nevertheless view it as non-present, how the being of the past can
recede into a temporal distance. Any real coincidence that may be asserted
here does not include this distance, but rather threatens to exclude it and
make it impossible. How can the present point of time which, according to
Parmenides, is in regard to being "altogether present only in the now,"
and which "remaining the same in the same place, rests by itself and thus
remains there fixed"—how can this point of time nevertheless divide in
two and set up a distinction? How can it, as present, separate and differentiate the past and future from itself? In his polemic against the sensationalist epistemology of Protagoras, Plato referred to the specific form of
remembered certainty, μνήμη, which in itself alone sufficed to refute the
equation of "knowledge" and sense perception.[18] This argument by no
means loses its force when the phenomenon of memory is made into the
starting point of a naturalistic psychology of knowledge. Such a physiological theory of "mneme" has been developed particularly by Richard
Semon—and recently Bertrand Russell has taken it up as a basis for his
analysis of consciousness. According to Semon, what we call memory does
not belong merely to the sphere of consciousness; rather, it should be
regarded as a basic attribute of all organic matter and organic life. What
distinguishes the living from the dead is precisely that all living things
have a history; that is to say, that the way in which they react to certain
present actions depends not only on the nature of the momentary stimulus
but also on earlier stimuli that have affected the organism. The impres-

17. This is sometimes admitted even by thinkers of a strictly positivist and psychologist
orientation; cf., for example, Theodor Ziehen, *Erkenntnistheorie auf psychophysiologischer
und physikalischer Grundlage* (Jena, 1913), pp. 287 ff. Eng. trans. by C. C. van Lieu and
Otto W. Beyer, *Introduction to Physiological Psychology* (London and New York, 1895).
I have attempted to show that in his own logic and epistemology Ziehen does not draw the
systematically necessary consequence from this, and fails to take into account this fundamental difference which he himself has disclosed. See "Erkenntnistheorie nebst den Grenzfragen . . ." *Jahrbücher der Philosophie, 3* (1927), 39 ff.
18. Cf. Plato, *Theaetetus,* 163D ff.

sion produced on an organic structure is in a sense retained even after its cause has ceased to exist. For every stimulus leaves behind it a certain physiological trace, an "engram": and each of these engrams plays a part in determining the manner in which the organism will respond in future to the same or similar stimuli. Thus what we call conscious perception never depends solely on the present state of the body, and particularly of the brain and nervous system, but on the totality of the effects that have been exerted on them.[19] Russell invokes these considerations and seeks to show that they and they alone can yield an exact differentiation between matter and mind. Matter and mind differ not in their essence or "substance," but rather in the form of causality that prevails in them. In the one case we can arrive at an adequate description of the process and its law by going back to merely physical causes—that is, to causes whose effect does not in general endure more than a single moment. In the other sphere, however, we find ourselves carried further; if we would fully comprehend an event that is given here and now, we must, as it were, go back to temporally remote forces. According to Russell, this difference between physical and mnemic causality suffices to explain the phenomenological difference between perception and memory—which indeed signifies nothing other than precisely this twofold form of causality. It is never possible, in this view, to differentiate perceptions and representations, sensations and ideas, by purely inner criteria, such as their greater or lesser intensity or any other psychic "character" inhering in them. What separates the one from the other, what designates and constitutes the sphere of images as such, is rather the circumstance that in it different laws of connection prevail:

> the distinction between images and sensations can only be made by taking account of their causation. Sensations come through sense-organs, while images do not. . . . An image . . . has a mnemic cause —which does not prevent it from also having a physical cause. And I think it will be found that the causation of an image always proceeds according to mnemic laws, i.e. that it is governed by habit and past experience. . . . And I think that if we could obtain an exact definition of the difference between physical and mnemic causation, we could

19. Cf. Richard W. Semon, *Die Mneme als erhaltendes Prinzip in Wechsel des organischen Geschehens* (Leipzig, 1904; 3d ed. 1911). Semon, *Die Mnemischen in ihren Beziehungen zu den Empfindungen* (Leipzig, 1909). Eng. trans. by Bella Duffy, *Mnemic Psychology* (New York, 1923).

distinguish images from sensations as having mnemic causes, though they may also have physical causes. Sensations, on the other hand, will only have physical causes.[20]

But even in this theory, in itself so consistent, Russell forgets that the phenomenological differences in signification cannot be elucidated or leveled by being transposed to the plane of empirical existence and causality.[21] He fails to recognize that a difference of causality as such is given only for a foreign observer who in a manner of speaking regards consciousness from outside. This observer, who already operates with an objective time, by which he seeks to articulate and arrange the flow of consciousness, may in so doing distinguish two modes of causal connection: the one subject to purely physical, the other to both physiological and psychological laws. But every such differentiation within the natural causes of the mental process obviously presupposes the idea of a natural order as such and with it the idea of an objective order of time. Only a consciousness that knows how to distinguish between present, past, and future and to recognize the past in the present can link the present with the past, can see in the present a continuance of the past. This differentiating remains in every instance the radical act, the primordial phenomenon that cannot be explained by any causal derivation because it must be presupposed in every causal explanation. Even if we take the naturalistic theory of mneme in its full scope, even if we start from the supposition that no impression can be made on the living organic substance without being oriented toward and modified by previous impressions—still, this modification itself remains only a factual process that replaces one occurrence by another. But how—we must go on to ask—can this change as such be recognized; how can the present not only be objectively determined by the past, but *know* itself to be so determined and relate itself to the past as the ground of its own determination? Even though engrams and traces of the "earlier" may be left behind, these factual vestiges do not in themselves explain the characteristic form of relation to the past. For this relation presupposes that a multiplicity of temporal determinations occur within the indivisible moment of time, that the total content of consciousness given in the simple now is distributed over present, past, and future. This form of phenomenal differentiation constitutes the true

20. Bertrand Russell, *The Analysis of Mind* (London, Macmillan, 1921), pp. 149–51; cf. pp. 287 ff.

21. Cf. my critical comment on Russell's work in *Jahrbücher der Philosophie*, 3, 49 ff.

problem. And the mneme theory can at best explain only how the early though nonexistent is nonetheless real, but it cannot make comprehensible how in the content given here and now an articulation is effected, through which particular determinations are selected and distributed over a temporal dimension of depth. Thus this theory, like Hume's, puts the question aside in the belief that one can derive the "representation of succession" from the "succession of representations."

In naturalistic psychology memory becomes, as it were, a mere duplication of perception, a perception of the second power. Memory, said Hobbes, is the perception of a past perception: *sentire se sensisse meminisse est.* But in this very formula a double problem is implicit. Hobbes defines sensation as nothing more than the reaction of the organic body to an outward stimulus. But how under these circumstances can the phenomenon of memory arise—how can the reaction that follows a present stimulus be interpreted as the cause of an absent stimulus? How is it possible to "perceive that one has perceived"? The whole difficulty is evident in Hobbes' formulation of his proposition: *Sentire se sensisse* implies that two different sensations belonging to different times are linked to the same subject, that it is the same "ego" which feels and has felt. And it also implies that precisely this ego differentiates its states and modifications, that it gives them different temporal positions and orders these positions into a continuous series. Thus Hobbes actually reverses the relation that was initially posited: though according to the principles of his system he must conceive of sensation as the precondition of memory, memory becomes for him at the same time an ingredient of sensation. Even this consistent materialist writes:

I know there have been philosophers, and those learned men, who have maintained that all bodies are endued with sense. Nor do I see how they can be refuted, if the nature of sense be placed in reaction only. And, though by the reaction of bodies inanimate a phantasm might be made, it would nevertheless cease, as soon as ever the object were removed. For unless those bodies had organs, as living creatures have, fit for the retaining of such motion as is made in them, their sense would be such, as that they should never remember the same. And therefore this hath nothing to do with that sense which is the subject of my discourse. For by sense, we commonly understand the judgment we make of objects by their phantasms; namely, by comparing and distinguishing those phantasms; which we could never do, if that motion in the organ, by which the phantasm is made, did not remain there for some time, and make the same phantasm return. Wherefore sense, as I here understand it, and which is commonly so called, hath necessarily some memory adhering to it, by which former and later phantasms may be compared together, and distinguished from one another.[22]

According to Hobbes, this state of affairs becomes particularly evident in the treatment and analysis of tactile phenomena, since tactile qualities are perceived not by sense alone, but also by the memory. "For although some things are touched in a point, they cannot be felt without the flowing of a point, that is to say, without time; but to feel time requires memory." Actually, as the most recent investigations in the field have clearly shown, motion, and hence time, are among the formative factors of the tactile phenomena themselves. The study of these phenomena is therefore eminently suited to confuting that "temporal atomism" which for a long time held almost undisputed sway in the psychology of perception. It shows that precisely the basic qualities of the tactile sense—qualities such as hard and soft, rough and smooth—arise only through motion, so that if we limit tactile sensations to a single moment, they can no longer be discerned as data. It is not a temporally detached stimulus filling only a definite moment, it is not the corresponding sensation or a sum of such momentary sensory experiences that lead to tactile qualities; rather, if we view them from the standpoint of their objective causes, they are processes of stimuli which do not call forth separate "sensations" but constitute a total impression having no temporal components. Here, then, we have exactly the reverse of the relation described by Hume: the representation of the flow of time does not arise from a succession of sensory experiences; rather, a peculiar sensory experience results from the conception and articulation of a definite temporal process. Strange as it may seem at first sight, the idea of time is not abstracted from the sequence of impressions—rather, the passage through a sequence which can be apprehended only in succession, leads ultimately to a product that has cast off all succession and seems to stand before us as unitary

22. Hobbes, De Corpore, Pt. IV, chap. 25, sec. 5. Eng. trans. in The English Works of Thomas Hobbes, ed. Sir William Molesworth (London, 1839), 1, 393. On Hobbes' Psychology, cf. Richard Hoenigswald, Hobbes und die Staatsphilosophie (Munich, 1924), pp. 109 ff.

and simultaneous. Thus from a new angle it is shown that the function of memory is by no means limited to the mere reproduction of past impressions but performs a genuinely creative task in the building of our perceptive world—that memory not only repeats perceptions that were previously given but constitutes new phenomena and new data.[23]

This creative trait of the pure time consciousness is more clearly apparent, and more characteristically as well, when we consider the prospective view of the future rather than the retrospect of the past. For this prospective future, too, is of the essence of time consciousness, which is only complete in a unity of present intuition, memory, and expectation. St. Augustine stressed that expectation is as necessary a part of the

23. It is of historical as well as philosophical interest to observe how the psychological and epistemological problems presented by the 'mnemic consciousness" have repeatedly led to a crisis in strict sensationalism and positivism and forced them at a certain point to reverse their position. In the philosophy of the nineteenth century this transformation is perhaps most conspicuous in Hans Cornelius. On precisely this point Cornelius, who had originally advocated a strict empiricism in the manner of Mach and Avenarius, effected a reversal which ultimately brought him very close to Kant's transcendental formulation of the problem. He starts from the supposition that the form of the temporal experience can in no way be explained—that is, reduced to other facts—because any attempt at such an explanation must presuppose that which is to be explained. That a diversity of experiences and every particular experience are given as part of a temporal totality and an ego-totality is "one of the facts which must be recognized as valid for every period in our lives—that is to say, it is a transcendental law." Further, Cornelius seeks to show that the traditional view of memory (put forward by sensationalism and association psychology) by no means suffices to account for the fact that in the moment when a definite content *a* appears in consciousness, not only itself but also another content *b* which preceded it is given. The memory of an experience *a* cannot be explained by saying that some sort of after-effect, a "remembered image" *a*, remains behind. "For the existence of such an after-effect would only be a content belonging to the *new* moment—that is, this after-effect would be given as a present content appearing simultaneously with *b*. Rather, in order that a knowledge of the past should be given in the present, it is requisite that this after-effect should also have the attribute of communicating this knowledge to us, that it contain as it were a reference to this past content. The fact that a knowledge of a past experience is contained in the present experience of memory, that the first thus represents the latter for our knowledge—this fact I designate as the *symbolic function* of the experience of memory." "It may readily be seen that here again we have to do with a transcendental law. For if memory were not universally and primarily a memory of complexes of experiences, the knowledge of the passage of time would not come into being." From this investigation, in which he expressly refers to Kant's corresponding exposition of the "'synthesis of reproduction" and the "synthesis of recognition in the concept," Cornelius arrives at a new epistemological orientation which leads him from his original positivist position to a transcendental system. Cf. Hans Cornelius, *Transzendentale Systematik. Untersuchungen zur Begründung der Erkenntnistheorie* (Munich, 1916), pp. 53 ff., 73 ff.

temporal consciousness as memory, and wherever "monadological"—not objective-physical—time is under consideration, the phenomenon of expectation occupies a central position. The "expression of the manifold in the one," which characterizes the monad according to Leibniz, holds just as fundamentally for the future as for the past. The ego, which sees itself as standing "in time," views itself not as a sum of static events but as a being extending forward into time, striving from the present toward the future. Without this form of striving, what we call the "representation," the actualization of a content can never be given to us. The authentic ego is never a mere bundle of perceptions but is the living source and foundation from which new contents are produced: *fons et fundus idearum praescripta lege nasciturarum.*[24] Its meaning escapes us if we think of it as purely static, if we define it through the concept of mere being, rather than of force. Leibniz described this relationship by a bold neologism: *percepturitio,* to which he accords equal rank with perception, *perceptio.*[25] The two are inseparably linked, for what distinguishes consciousness as such is that it does not remain within itself, but always reaches out beyond itself, beyond the given present to the not-given.

Modern psychology, too, has extended its analysis of memory in this direction: it, too, stresses that one of the most essential achievements of memory is to be found in expectation, in the direction toward the future.[26] From a genetic point of view, expectation actually seems to precede memory: a specific orientation toward the future seems to be manifested in the very earliest behavior of the child.[27] Only as it reinstated the Leibnizian concept of the "tendency" and came to recognize its fundamental significance did the psychology of the nineteenth century free itself from the rigid view which pieced together particular impressions as present fixed entities, like the stones of a mosaic. Here it was William James above all who plainly stated that on such presuppositions one could not possibly gain a true insight into the dynamic process, into the stream of con-

24. G. W. Leibniz to de Volder, in *Philosophische Schriften,* ed. C. J. Gerhardt (7 vols. Berlin, 1875–90), 2, 172.

25. "Quaecunque in anima universim concipere licet, ad duo possunt revocari: expressionem praesentis externorum status, animae convenientem secundum corpus suum, et tendentiam ad novam expressionem, quae tendentiam corporum (seu rerum externarum) ad statum futurum representat, verbo: perceptionem et percepturitionem." *Briefwechsel zwischen Leibniz und Christian Wolff,* ed. Gerhardt (Halle, 1860), p. 56.

26. Cf., for example, Koffka, *Die Grundlagen der psychischen Entwicklung,* p. 171.

27. Cf. Stern, *Die Psychologie der frühen Kindheit,* p. 66.

sciousness. Characteristically, it was the study of language which led James to this conclusion:

> The truth is that large tracts of human speech are nothing but *signs of direction* in thought, of which direction we nevertheless have an acutely discriminative sense, though no definite sensorial image plays any part in it whatsoever. Sensorial images are stable psychic facts; we can hold them still and look at them as long as we like. These bare images of logical movement, on the contrary, are psychic transitions, always on the wing, so to speak, and not to be glimpsed except in flight. . . . If we try to hold fast the feeling of direction, the full presence comes and the feeling of direction is lost. . . . One may admit that a good third of our psychic life consists in these rapid premonitory perspective views of schemes of thought not yet articulate.[28]

But how can these "premonitory perspective views" be explained, if all psychological life is held to be contained and ultimately grounded in simple sensations; if we cling to the dogma that all our percepts and ideas are nothing other than copies of previous impressions? Memory might in a certain sense be fitted into this schema: an attempt might be made to reduce consciousness of the past to a kind of factual continuance, an effect extending from the past into the immediate present. But with consciousness of the future any such reduction is out of the question. A thing or an occurrence may act upon us even after it has vanished—but can there be any such action on the part of things *before* they exist? And if not, what actual "stimulus," what objective "cause" may we adduce for the expectation of what is to come, for the characteristic "intention" toward the future? From the standpoint of any naturalistic, objectivistic theory of consciousness the only possibility is to reverse this relationship: what *appears* to us in an immediate and purely phenomenological sense as expectation must be dissolved into mere memory, so that it may be explained by laws of association and reproduction. With this, to be sure, the direction of consciousness toward the future is not so much understood as denied and destroyed. Our anticipation of the future becomes a mere illusion, a phantasmagoria in contrast to our real consciousness as a combination of what now exists and what has been.

But even if we were able to grasp the form of objective time underlying

28. James, *Principles of Psychology*, *1*, 252 f.

exact science and to explain it adequately from this point of view, historical time, the time of culture and history, would still be set aside and divested of its true meaning. For the meaning of historical time is built not solely from recollection of the past, but no less from anticipation of the future. It depends as much on the striving as on the act, as much on the tendency toward the future as on the contemplation and actualization of the past. Only a being who wills and acts, who reaches into the future and determines the future by his will, can have a "history"; only such a being can *know* of history because and insofar as he continuously produces it. Thus true historical time is never a mere time of events; rather, its specific consciousness radiates as much from will and accomplishment as from contemplation. Here the contemplative factor is inseparably interwoven with the active factor: one draws nourishment from the other. For the historical will is not possible without an act of the productive imagination —while on the other hand the imagination can be truly creative only where it is determined and inspired by a living impulse of the will. Thus the historical consciousness rests on an interraction of active force and imaginative force: on the clarity and certainty with which the ego is able to set before itself an image of a future being and direct all particular action toward this image. Here again the mode of symbolic representation is manifested in its full power and depth, for in a manner of speaking the symbol hastens ahead of reality, showing it the way and clearing its path. Symbolic representation is no mere looking back on this reality as something finished, but becomes a factor and motif in its unfolding. It is this form of symbolic vision that specifically distinguishes the cultural, historical will from the mere will to live, mere vital instinct. Although it seems to drive impetuously forward, instinct is always determined and directed from behind. The powers that direct it lie behind, not before it: they arise from sense impression and immediate sensory need. But will breaks loose from this bond. It reaches forward into the future and outward into the realm of mere possibility, by placing them before itself in a purely symbolic act. Every phase of action now occurs in view of an ideal plan, which anticipates the action as a whole and which assures its unity, cohesion, and continuity. The greater the force of this pre-vision and free synopsis, the richer will be the dynamic, the purer the spiritual form of the action itself. Its significance now lies not solely in its product but in the process of action and formation itself, which also contains within it the condition for a new basic direction of our understanding of the world.

Here it is once again confirmed that historical reality exists for us and obtains its characteristic form only through a determinate and distinctive mode of vision. The determinations resulting from our analysis of the spatial consciousness now find their counterpart in the formation of time. We were impelled to differentiate mere active space from symbolic space; and in the temporal sphere we encounter a similar distinction. Every action that occurs in time is in some way articulated in time; it discloses a definite sequence, an order in succession, without which it could not subsist as a coherent totality. But it is a long way from the ordered sequence of events as such to the pure intuition of time and its particular relations. Even animal life moves in active processes which are highly complex and subtly articulated in respect to time. The animal organism can assert itself in its environment only by "responding" in the correct way to the stimuli which strike it from outside—and this response comprises a very definite sequence, a temporal combination of the particular factors of action. Everything that we are accustomed to subsume under the name of animal "instinct," seems ultimately to go back to the fact that certain situations in which the animal is placed repeatedly release the same chains of action, each one of which discloses a very definite direction. But the unity of direction which appears in the performance of the action is not given *to* the animal, it is not in any way "represented" in its consciousness. In order that the particular stages and phases may be intermeshed, it is in no way necessary that they be subjectively comprehended by an ego. The animal that moves in such a sequence of actions is, as it were, a captive within it. It cannot voluntarily depart from that chain of actions, or interrupt the sequence by representing its factors singly. Nor is an anticipation of the future in an image or ideal plan possible or requisite for the animal. Only in man does a new form of action arise, which is rooted in a new form of temporal vision. He distinguishes, chooses, and judges—and this "judging" always comprises an extension of himself into the future. What was previously a rigid chain of reactions now shapes itself into a flowing and mobile, yet self-centered and self-contained, sequence in which every link is determined by reference to the whole. In this power of "looking before and after" lies the essential property and basic function of human "reason." [29] It is in one and the same act discursive and intuitive: It must differentiate the particular stages

---

29.   Sure he that made us with such large discourse,
        Looking before and after, gave us not
        That capability and godlike reason
        To fust in us unus'd (*Hamlet*, IV.4.36–9).

of time and set them off clearly against one another, and then reunite them in a new synopsis. It is this temporal differentiation and integration which first gives to action its spiritual imprint, which demands free movement and at the same time requires that this movement be unswervingly directed toward the unity of a goal.

From this we see why it is not permissible to dissect the unitary consciousness of time by singling out one or another of the basic determinations it comprises and attaching a particular and exclusive value to it in its isolation. Once a single phase of time is thus distinguished from others and made into a norm for all others, we have before us no longer a total spiritual picture of time but only a particular perspective, however significant it may be. We have seen how such perspectivist differences of temporal "vision" are disclosed in the mythical world view. According as the accent of thought and feeling is laid on the past, the present, or the future, divergent mythicoreligious intuitions and interpretations of the world process arise.[30] But the same difference is preserved in the sphere of purely conceptual, metaphysical interpretation. There are forms of metaphysics which belong to a very definite type of temporal intuition within which they seem in a sense confined. While Parmenides and Spinoza embody the pure "present type" of metaphysical thinking, Fichte's metaphysics is wholly determined by a looking into the future. But such one-sided orientations always seem in some way to do violence to the pure phenomenon of time, to dismember it and so destroy it. No thinker has argued more strenuously against such abstract dismemberment than Bergson—and it may be said that the whole structure and development of his thought from the *Essai sur les données immédiates de la conscience* to the *Evolution créatrice* become intelligible only if we bear this point in mind. It is the lasting achievement of the Bergsonian metaphysic that it reversed the ontological relation assumed between being and time. Our view of time should not be formed and modeled in accordance with a dogmatically fixed concept of being; rather, the content of reality and metaphysical truth should be determined according to the pure intuition of time.

But did Bergson's own doctrine wholly fulfill this demand which it states so sharply? Does it remain wholly and exclusively within the intuition of time, of "pure duration" as an original datum—or do certain premises, certain "pre-data" and "pre-judices" once again obtrude themselves into the description of this original datum? In order to attain clarity

30. Cf. above, 2, 119 ff.

on this point, we must go back to Bergson's theory of memory. Matter and memory are the two cornerstones and poles of Bergson's metaphysics. Whereas the older metaphysics drew a sharp dividing line between extensive substance and thinking substance, body and soul, Bergson's system makes a fundamental division between memory and matter. Neither factor is in any way reducible to the other, and. any attempt to explain memory as a "function of organic matter" is a basic contradiction. Bergson held that attempts of this kind could be undertaken only as long as no clear and certain distinction was made between the two fundamental forms of what is customarily called "memory." There is a purely motor memory that consists merely in a sequence of movements acquired by practice—which is thus solely a form of habit. But truly spiritual memory is strictly and fundamentally separate from this type of motor memory, of mechanism and automatism. For with spiritual memory we have left the realm of necessity for the realm of freedom: we are no longer under the constraint of things but in the center of the ego, of the pure self-consciousness. The true self is not the self that reaches and acts outward; it is the ego that is capable of looking back into time in pure recollection and of finding itself again in its depth. This view into the depth of time is opened up to us only when action is replaced by pure vision—when our present becomes permeated with the past, and the two are experienced as an immediate unity. But this mode and direction of vision are continuously obstructed and diverted by the other trend, which is directed toward action and its future goal.

Now our earlier life is no longer preserved in pure images of memory; rather, every perception has validity only insofar as it contains within it the germ of an incipient activity. But this gives rise to an experience of a wholly different kind. A number of functionally ready mechanisms, offering more and more numerous and diverse reactions to outward stimuli, presenting ready responses to a steadily increasing number of questions that may come to it from the outside world, are now deposited and as it were stored up in the body. The sum of these mechanisms, constantly reinforced by practice, may be called a kind of memory; however, this memory no longer represents our past but only enacts it: it does not retain images of it but only extends useful previous activities up to the present moment.[31] But according to Bergson, only the memory of

31. Henri Bergson, Matière et mémoire (2d ed. Paris, 1900). German trans. (Jena, 1908), pp. 74 f. Eng. trans. by Nancy Margaret Paul and W. Scott Palmer, Matter and Memory (London, 1929).

recollection, the image memory turned back toward the past, possesses a truly spiritual significance; the motor memory has no speculative, cognitive value but only a pragmatic value. It serves to preserve life, but it pays for this achievement by renouncing all apprehension of the source, by losing access to the knowledge of life. Once we enter the realm of action and utility, we must leave pure contemplation behind us. We no longer stand in the intuition of pure time; rather, another image, the image of space and of bodies in space, is injected into it. "Things" in space are set side by side and treated as rigid, mutually exclusive unities: through such unities alone does our action gain definite centers that it can take hold of. And every step toward this "reality," this aggregate of possible activities, removes us farther and farther from true reality, from immersion in the original form and life of the self. If we wish to regain this life, we must free ourselves by a kind of violent decision from the dominance of perception, for this power drives us forward, while we wish to go back into the past. Thus feeling and memory can never take the same road. The one involves us more and more in the constraint of mere accomplishment, the other frees us from it; the one places us in a world of "objects," the other enables us to discern the essence of the self, prior to all objectivization and free from the fetters of spatial-objective schematism.

A system such as Bergson's, which represents the unfolding of a unitary, self-contained intuition, may claim that it should not be viewed and judged from outside but should be measured by its own standards. Accordingly we ask only this one question: has it remained faithful to its own task and norm—has it apprehended time in its totality, as it presents itself to pure intuition, and described it as a whole? And here we are immediately assailed by misgivings. For in the intuition of time the three stages, past, present, and future, are given to us as an immediate unity in which no stage is differently evaluated from the others. No phase is singled out as the genuine, true, and original stage—for all three are equally given in the simple meaning of time. In St. Augustine's dictum there are not three times but only the one present, which is, however, a present of past things, a present of present things, and a present of future things (*praesens de praeteritis, praesens de praesentibus, praesens de futuris*). And similarly the ego, in its intuition of itself, is neither split into three entirely different directions of temporal consciousness nor confined within a single one, to which it is exclusively or preeminently subject. If we take time not as a substantial but rather as a functional unity, as a function of representation comprising a threefold direction, none of its factors may be detached from the whole without causing it to disintegrate as a whole. But it is precisely such a detachment of one factor that gives Bergson's metaphysics its characteristic imprint. Fundamentally he recognizes only the past as originally temporal, whereas the consciousness of the future does not belong to pure temporal intuition. Where we do not see the past but act, where we wish to produce and give form to future things, the picture of pure time is blurred and beclouded, and in its stead we see a structure of different type and origin. What now stands before us is no longer genuine, original temporality but the abstract schema of homogeneous space. "In order to awaken the past in the form of an image, it is necessary to abstract from present activity; we must know how to esteem the useless, we must wish to dream. Perhaps only man is capable of an effort of this sort. And even then the past, to which we rise in this way, is continuously on the point of slipping away from us, as though this backward-moving memory stood in contradiction to that more natural memory, whose forward-striving movement drives us to action and life." [32]

Here, despite all Bergson's emphasis on the *élan vital,* a strange Romantic quietism enters into his thinking. The recollection of the past is philosophically transfigured: it alone leads us to the ultimate source of the self and into the depths of speculative knowledge. Any such idealization is denied the direction toward the future: it has only a pragmatic and no theoretical value. But is the future given to us only as the aim of immediate action, of practical activity in the most restricted sense, or must not a purely spiritual intention, an ideal factor, underlie all action that is to rise to true power and freedom? Plato did not discover the meaning of the "idea" solely in knowledge and pure cognition—he found it in all formative action, in ethical action no less than in productive, demiurgic activity. Thus the artisan who produces a certain implement does not act on the basis of mere habit and the "routine" of his craft. Rather, it is an original form of spiritual vision that determines his action and shows him the way. The carpenter who fashions a loom does not imitate an already existing thing that stands before him as a sensuous model, but looks toward the form and purpose, the *eidos* of the loom itself. [33] Even the divine demiurge, according to Plato, proceeds no differently. His creation is determined and guided by the form of his vision, by his view of the idea of the good as prototype and model.

This ideality of action is contested by Bergson. For him all action is ultimately grounded in sensory need and breaks down into definite motor mechanisms and automatisms. Thus the pure intuition that leads us back to the past comes into the sharpest opposition with any kind of intention that points and strives toward the future. But a purely phenomenal analysis of the temporal consciousness offers no support for such an evaluation. It shows us no brusque opposition between the consciousness of memory and the consciousness of expectation; rather, it shows that in both a common and characteristic power of the spirit is at work. The power of the spirit to set future contents before itself in an image is not inferior to its power to transform past contents into an image and renew them in an image: in both it evinces the same original function of "making present," of "representation." The spirit's knowledge of itself can only be gained and secured in this twofold way: such knowledge arises only if the spirit preserves its history in its pure presence, if it preserves its past and anticipates its future. Bergson himself takes development as "creative evolution," but his concept of creativeness is essentially derived from the intuition of nature, not of the spirit; it is oriented toward biological, not historical time. In historical time we cannot draw the sharp dividing line between the functions of memory and action which is determining and decisive for Bergson's whole metaphysics. Here the two are perpetually intertwined. Action is determined and guided by the historical consciousness, through recollection of the past, but on the other hand truly historical memory first grows from forces that reach forward into the future and help to give it form. Only to the degree in which the spirit itself "becomes," to the degree in which it unfolds toward the future, can it see itself in the image of the past. The form of this "reflection" is inseparable from that of its striving and its will.[34]

34. Cf. above, pp. 184 ff. The same fundamental view of the nature of historical time is eloquently expressed by Theodor Litt, *Individuum und Gemeinschaft* (3d ed. Leipzig and Berlin, 1926), p. 307: "I see what has been and what has become moving toward me as the center of the process, because this center also designates the only place at which I can apply the lever to complete what has been begun, to correct what has been done amiss, to realize what is required. And it is no outward coexistence of two forms and directions of formation that this center like all vital centers unites in itself; it is no series of acts of contemplation and acts of doing that are connected solely by the formal principle of free configuration—rather, the two are connected in their content down to the last and smallest particle. Every line of becoming that I see running toward me from

Thus for the ego its own history changes and undergoes a progressive intensification and sublimation, as it reaches out more freely, more boldly and comprehensively into the future, and unfolds toward the future. Accordingly, from the standpoint of historical life and the historical consciousness, the direction toward the past and the direction toward the future can be viewed not as a real opposition but only as factors in an ideal correlation. When nevertheless the former view prevails with Bergson, it seems almost as though he had succumbed to the very illusion which he himself had so clearly exposed. For him, too, a spatial intuition and schema seem to have slipped unnoticed into the analysis of time and the different stages of time. In space, if we wish to effect any movement at all, we must decide on a single direction for it. We must move forward or backward, right or left, up or down. But in regard to temporal directions such a rigid separation is only apparent. Here, on the contrary, there is a multiplicity whose elements permeate one another even in their mutual differentiation; here, to use Bergson's own, characteristic words, there prevails *une multiplicité de fusion ou de pénétration mutuelle.* Only in their immediate concrescence do the two beams of vision—the one leading back from present to past and the other leading out into the future— yield the one concrete total intuition of time. True, this concrescence must never be conceived according to the analogy of spatial relations. Rather, there is always an opposition of motifs, which are perpetually at grips with one another. But this battle may not end with the victory of the one and the defeat of the other, for the two are destined to act perpetually against each other, and only through this opposition, to weave the living mesh of

the past signifies for me not only a motif of articulation and interpretation for the present, which besieges me and claims me as a realm of history still in becoming, but also a call to a decision with which I, the active one, play my part in determining the future of this reality. . . . Thus in what we with half truth call the image of the past, there also lives a will that is turned toward the future—and a knowledge of the past is embedded in the guiding image to which this will devotes itself." Starting from essentially different presuppositions, Heidegger arrived at the same result, the intuition of the motif of futurity in historical time, and this is one of the most fruitful and important features of his analysis of being and time. In summing up this analysis he writes: "Only a reality that is essentially *future* in its being, so that it is free to shatter against it and let itself be thrown back upon its facticity in death—that is to say, only a reality which with equal originality is future and having-been—can . . . be actual for its time." Only genuine temporality which is at the same time finite makes possible anything like destiny—that is, authentic historicity ("Sein and Zeit," Pt. I, sec. 74). These lines are perhaps the sharpest expression of the fundamental opposition between Bergson's and Heidegger's "metaphysics of time."

time and historical consciousness. In this sense the historian, as Friedrich Schlegel said, is a prophet turned backward. The true intuition of time cannot be gained in mere recollective memory, but is at the same time knowledge and act: the process in which life itself takes on form, life in the spiritual not merely the biological sense, and that process in which life comes to conceive and know itself—these two must eventually constitute a unity, and hence this conceiving is not the merely external apprehension of a finished and ready form into which life has been squeezed but is the very way life gives itself form in order that in this act of form giving, this formative activity, it may understand itself.

Chapter 5

Symbolic Pregnance

OUR INVESTIGATIONS up to now have shown us how the perceptive world is build up as the particular contents that present themselves to consciousness are filled with increasingly richer and more diverse functions of meaning. The farther this process progresses, the broader becomes the sphere that consciousness can encompass and survey in a single moment. Each of its elements is now saturated as it were with such functions. It stands in manifold meaning-groups which in turn are systematically related to one another and which by virtue of this relationship constitute the totality that we call the world of our experience. Whatever complex we may single out from this totality of experience—whether we consider the coexistence of phenomena in space or their succession in time, the order of things and attributes or the order of causes and effects—always these orders disclose a determinate structure and a common formal character. They are so articulated that from each of their factors a transition is possible to the whole, because the organization of this whole is representable and represented in the whole. Through the reciprocal involvement of these representative functions consciousness acquires the power to spell out phenomena, to read them as experiences. Each particular phenomenon is now no more than a letter which is not apprehended for its own sake or viewed according to its own sensuous components or its sensuous aspect as a whole; rather, our vision passes through the letter and beyond it to ascertain the signification of the word to which the letter belongs and the meaning of the sentence in which this word stands. Now the content is not simply *in* consciousness, filling it by its mere existence—rather, it speaks to consciousness and tells it something. Its whole existence has in a sense transformed itself into pure form; henceforth it serves only to communicate a definite meaning and to compose it with others into structures of signification, complexes of meaning.

Even sensationalist psychology, despite its basic tendency to disengage the elements of consciousness from their meaning-groups and lay them bare in their pure facticity, has been unable wholly to overlook the difference between what the individual sense perception is as such and the function it performs in the systematic building of the unity and totality of consciousness. But it blurs this difference by attempting to reduce the function itself to some sort of empirical existence. How, ask the sensationalists, can the single impression mediate a meaning, unless this meaning is inherent in it? Must the meaning not be contained, then, as component in the total impression? The discernment sharpened by psychological analysis must be able to discover and to isolate this component. Thus the sensationalists do not mean to deny the factor of signification in the particular perception, but, true to their basic trend, they attempt to explain this factor by composing it from particular sensory elements. They strive to make the spiritual form intelligible by transforming it back into sensuous matter; by showing how the mere coexistence and empirical concrescence of sense impressions suffices to produce this form or at least an image of it. So seen, it is true, this image remains a fiction: the image itself has no form of truth; truth and reality are imputed only to the substantial elements from which it is pieced together like a mosaic. But this insight gained by the psychological critic need not hamper or restrict the use that we make of this image in actual physical life. Even though the image may be recognized and, as it were, epistemologically exposed as a fiction, it has reality as a fiction—that is, it arises according to definite and necessary laws of the imagination—and that suffices. A necessary and uniform mechanism of consciousness produces it from the sensory experiences and their associative combination. Thus the image acquires no logical independence and no specific meaning different from mere sensation.

Still, a practical, biologically significant role is imputed to it and therein consists its character. In the sensationalist view, what we have designated above as the symbolic value of perception is nothing other than a purely utilitarian value. Consciousness cannot devote itself in every moment with equal intensity to all the various sense impressions that fill it; it cannot represent them all with equal sharpness, concretion, and individuality. Thus it creates schemata, total images into which enter a number of particular contents, and in which they flow together without distinction. But these schemata can be no more than mere abbreviations, compendious condensations of the impressions. Where we wish to see sharply and exactly, these abbreviations must be thrust aside; the symbolic values must be replaced by "real" values—that is, by actual sensations. Accordingly, all symbolic thinking and all symbolic perception amount to a mere negative act growing out of omission and the need for omission. A consciousness possessing sufficient scope and power to live in the particulars themselves and to apprehend them all immediately would not require these symbolic unities; it would be wholly presentative, instead of remaining representative in the whole or in particular parts.

As long as this view prevailed, the first presuppositions for any true phenomenology of perception were lacking. By restricting themselves in principle to the data of sensation, sensationalism and positivism had blinded themselves, as it were, not only to the symbol, but also to perception itself. For they had eliminated precisely the characteristic factor by which perception differs from mere sensation and grows beyond it. From two different sides a transformation and fundamental methodological correction of this attitude was achieved, and the ground so prepared for a deeper epistemological and phenomenological understanding of perception. The *Critique of Pure Reason* took the lead by recognizing "transcendental apperception" as a "condition for the possibility of perception" itself. The first thing that is given to us—writes Kant—is the appearance which, when it is connected with consciousness, is called perception; for without a relation to an at least possible consciousness, the appearance would never become an object of knowledge. "But because every appearance contains a manifold, so that different perceptions are encountered dispersed and singly in the mind, a connection between them is necessary, which they cannot have in sensation itself." This corrects the fundamental fallacy of sensationalism, which according to Kant lay in the erroneous assumption that "the senses not only provided us with impressions but also composed them and produced images of objects, for which beyond a doubt something more is needed than the receptivity to impressions, namely a function of their synthesis." [1] Thus, images and sensations no longer belong in the same class epistemologically and phenomenologically, nor can the former be derived from the latter; for every genuine image contains within it a spontaneity of combination, a rule of formation. *The Critique of Pure Reason* subsumes the totality of these possible rules, on which the structure and articulation of the world of perception

1. *Kritik de reinen Vernunft*, 1st ed., pp. 120 ff.; 2d ed., pp. 129 ff. Cf. above, pp. 7–10.

are based, under the concept of the "understanding." The understanding is the simple transcendental term for the basic phenomenon that all perception as conscious perception must always and necessarily be *formed* perception. Perception could be conceived neither as belonging to an ego, nor as relating to a "something," a perceived object, if both modes of relationship were not subject to universal and necessary laws. It is these laws which first lend perception its subjective as well as its objective significance, which free it from its particularity and give it a position in the totality of consciousness and objective experience. Thus the pure concepts of the understanding, which express nothing other than precisely this correlation of the particular with the whole and the various directions of this correlation, are not subsequently added to perception but are the constituents of perception itself. Perception "is" only insofar as it takes determinate forms. The analysis by which sensationalist psychology determines the elements of consciousness actually presupposes the structure of consciousness as such—that is, it presupposes synthesis: "for where the understanding has previously conjoined nothing, it cannot make any analysis, because nothing can be given to the imagination other than what is conjoined through the understanding." The analytical unity of apperception, the dissection of perception as a whole into particular elements, is only possible if we presuppose some sort of synthetic unity.[2] The fact that they stand in those characteristic sense-relationships, expressible through the several categories—that is what makes the perception into a definite perception, into the expression of an "I" and into the appearance of an object, an object of experience.

But here there still remains a difficulty and ambiguity which the *Critique of Pure Reason* did not fully elucidate and eliminate. For the new idea it outlined did not at first find its adequate expression, insofar as Kant, precisely where he most decisively attacked the methodological presuppositions of the old psychology, nevertheless continued to speak its language. The new transcendental insight which he was striving ·to establish is expressed in the concepts of eighteenth century faculty psychology. Thus here again "receptivity" and "spontaneity," "sensation" and "understanding" might seem to be conceived as "psychic faculties," each of which exists as an independent reality but which, then—in their empirical cooperation, their causal concatenation—bring forth experience as

2. Ibid., 2d ed., pp. 130, 133.

their product. It is evident that this would negate the meaning of the transcendental idea; for had Kant himself not defined this meaning by saying that the transcendental question was concerned "not so much with objects as with our mode of knowing objects," insofar as it is possible a priori? And had he not repeatedly stressed that he was concerned not with explaining the genesis of experience, but with analyzing its pure content? Yet all these explanations did not suffice to prevent Kant's analytic of the understanding from being interpreted as a new type of psychological "manufacture of the forms" of thought. If this interpretation were justified, Kant's formulation of the problem would of course have no advantage over sensationalism, except that it shifts the relation of forces within consciousness and adds one more to the number of psychic faculties. As much as one may esteem this new faculty, the Kantian deduction would still occupy the same methodological plane as the attempted sensationalist explanations. For in this case it would represent only a new attempt to solve pure problems of meaning by transposing them into problems of reality, by tracing them back to a real process and the causal forces determining this process; a new attempt to justify the objective validity of the pure concepts of the understanding—which originally were Kant's sole concern and which he sought to apprehend in the "conditions of their possibility"—by deriving them from a self-subsistent transcendental subject as their author. But with this, of course, an ontic problem would be substituted for the critical-phenomenological problem, a substantial for a purely functional view. The understanding would become a magician and necromancer animating dead sensation, awakening it to the life of consciousness. But—we should then be compelled to ask—is this mysterious process, this magic of the understanding, needed once we have recognized that this purportedly dead sensation is itself no reality but a mere fiction of psychological thinking? Can we continue to ask how signification, a meaning, issues from the mere raw material of sensation, considered as something fundamentally alien to meaning, once we have seen that this "unmeaningness" is itself a mere fiction? If it is true, as Kant emphatically declares, that "an appearance would be nothing for us without a relation to an at least possible consciousness; and because it has in itself no objective reality and only exists in knowledge, there would nowhere be anything" [3] —if this is true, by what right does critical philosophy inquire how this

3. Ibid., 1st ed., p. 120.

nothing becomes something, how it is taken into the forms of consciousness, and as it were recast—in view of the fact that it exists only *in* these forms and not *before* them?

We are led to a similar methodological question by another school of thought, which not only differs from Kantian thinking in its historical point of departure but seems to be diametrically opposed to it. In its definition and analysis of perception, modern phenomenology starts much less from Kant than from Brentano's concepts of consciousness. Brentano's *Psychologie vom empirischen Standpunkt* finds the distinctive factor of consciousness and of all psychic life in the character of "intentionality." A content is a psychic content insofar as it embraces a distinctive direction, a determination of meaning. "Every psychic phenomenon is characterized by what the medieval scholastics called the intentional (or mental) inexistence of an object and what we, though in not entirely unambiguous terms, would call the relation to a content, the direction toward an object (which is not to be understood as reality), or immanent objectivity. . . . This intentional inexistence is peculiar to psychic phenomena. . . . And thus we may define psychic phenomena as phenomena which intentionally contain an object in themselves." [4] Here again it is stressed that psychic contents do not first subsist in themselves and only subsequently enter into relations, but that the relation belongs to the very determinateness of their being. They *are* only because by their very being they go beyond themselves, toward something else. Yet there is still something unclear in the expression of this relationship, for in designating this fundamental relational direction, Brentano, too, speaks of a difference of existence, distinguishing between the real existence of the thing and intentional or mental "inexistence." Once again the function of meaning seems to be explained by a substantial existence—as though the representation were directed toward the object only because it inheres in it in some form, because it enters into it and is contained in it. But with this, of course, the distinctive character of the intentional which was to be emphasized would again be effaced. In this point full clarity was achieved only by Husserl's continuation and development of Brentano's basic idea in his *Logische Untersuchungen* and *Ideen zu einer reinen Phänomenologie*. For when Husserl speaks of significative and meaning-giving acts, by which an object is represented to consciousness, he makes it very clear that this relation of the representing to the represented can be explained by no

4. Franz C. Brentano, *Psychologie vom empirischen Standpunkt* (Leipzig, 1874), *1*, 115.

analogies taken from the world of things. He frees himself entirely from the "mythology of activities," which looks upon acts as the activities of a real psychic subject; and likewise he explicitly states the relation of the act to its object in such a way that one can no longer be said to "be" or "dwell" in the other. Now a sharp distinction is made between the factual component contained in an act and what it ideally represents, the goal of its intention. Where this distinction is not made or not strictly carried out, we end, as Husserl emphasizes, in a vicious circle; for if the representation can only relate to the object by containing a fragment of it, so to speak, an *eidolon* of it as a factual component, this interpolation must be repeated indefinitely.

> The image as a factual part of an empirical psychological perception would again be a fact—a fact functioning as an image for something else. But it could do this only by virtue of an image-consciousness, in which something appears—whereby we should have a first intentionality, and in which this something in turn functions consciously as an "image-object" for something else—wherefor a second intention grounded in the first would be necessary. But it is no less evident that each single one of these modes of consciousness already requires a differentiation between immanent and real object, and thus contains the same problem which was to have been solved by the construction.[5]

We always arrive at antinomies of this sort when we forget that the fundamental relationship of representation or intention is the condition of the possibility of all objective knowledge, and that consequently no objective fact or occurrence belonging to the world of things which is first made possible by this relationship may be drawn into the description of it. Now the lines are sharply drawn against sensationalism. Husserl went so far as to call it a mark of the backward state of descriptive analysis, that it had hitherto disregarded the specificity of significative acts, supposing that what these acts accomplish must consist always and necessarily in arousing certain fantasy-images, which are constantly correlated to expression.[6] In order to characterize the relationship here prevailing, Husserl now divided the stream of phenomenological reality into a "material" and a

---

5. Husserl, *Ideen zu einer reinen Phänomenologie*, p. 186. Cf. his *Logische Untersuchungen* (2 vols. Halle, 1913–21), 2, 372 ff.

6. Cf. Husserl, *Logische Untersuchungen*, 2, 61.

"noetic stratum." To the latter belong all purely functional problems, that is to say, all the genuine problems of consciousness and meaning. For "to have meaning," or "to mean something" is the basic character of all consciousness, which for this reason is not just experience in general but a meaningful "noetic" experience.[7] "Consciousness is precisely a consciousness 'of something,' its character is to contain 'meaning,' the quintessence so to speak of 'soul,' 'spirit,' 'reason.' Consciousness is not a title for 'psychological complexes,' for fused 'contents,' for 'bundles' or streams of 'sensations' which, meaningless in themselves, cannot in any quantity whatever yield a 'meaning.' . . . Consciousness is . . . a world apart from what sensationalism wishes alone to see, from actually meaningless, irrational matter—which however is accessible to rationalization." [8]

Thus two different movements and directions of thought, the concept of synthesis and the concept of intention, lead us back to our problem. But from the standpoint of this problem there still remains a doubt and a misgiving. If we equate the spheres of consciousness and meaning—as Husserl does with such radical sharpness—can we still, *within* consciousness, retain an absolute opposition between matter and form? Do we still have here two strata, one of which can be designated as merely material? Do we not, rather, in speaking of the animating acts that give life to the matter of sensation, which first fill it with determinate meaning, still retain a vestige of that dualism which sees a cleavage between the physical and the psychic, which instead of regarding body and soul as correlative sees them as different in respect to substance? The necessity of this correlation has already become apparent in our investigation of the phenomena of pure expression,[9] and with every step we have taken toward the problems of representation it has been confirmed anew. Thus it becomes fundamentally untenable to set off existence and consciousness, matter and form from one another as different strata. Husserl dissects the whole of experience into two halves: primary contents, which still contain no meaning, and experiences or factors of experience, which are grounded in a specific intentionality. Above the sensory experiences, the data of sensation, color, touch, tone, etc., lies as it were, an animating, significative stratum: "a stratum through which the concrete intentional experience is generated out of the sensory experience which in itself has

7. Husserl, *Ideen,* pp. 175, 185.
8. Ibid., p. 176.
9. Cf. above, pp. 101–2.

no intentionality." [10] But—it must here be asked—is this "generation" itself phenomenologically demonstrable? Since phenomenology as such necessarily remains within the sphere of meaning and intentionality, can it even attempt to designate that which is alien to meaning? The "remarkable duality and unity of sensuous μορφή and intentional ὕλη" may indeed obtrude itself over and over again; but does it justify us in speaking of "formless matter" and "matterless form"? This separation may in a sense be an indispensable instrument of our analysis of consciousness. But may we impose this analytical division, this *distinctio rationis* upon phenomena, upon the pure data of consciousness itself? Can we here speak of an identical matter which enters into different forms—since we know only the concrete totality of the phenomena of consciousness—since, to speak in Aristotelian terms, we know only the σύνολον of matter and form? From the standpoint of phenomenological inquiry there is no more a "matter in itself" than a "form in itself"; there are only total experiences which can be compared from the standpoint of matter and form and determined and ordered according to this standpoint. We may say, for example, that it is "the same" melody to which we hearken, now in immediate perception and now in mere memory; but this means not that the two experiences, that of perception and that of memory, coincide in any substantial component, but solely that they are functionally correlated. Here it is not the same sensuous content that recurs in different forms; what happens is rather that certain experience-totalities, which are numerically and qualitatively different, are nevertheless directed toward the same thing; they represent the same object. And this at the same time produces the relativization which, as we have seen throughout, flows out of the concept of representation itself. For no content of consciousness is in itself merely present, or in itself merely representative; rather, every actual experience indissolubly embraces both factors. Every present content functions in the sense of representing, just as all representation demands a link with something present in consciousness. It is this mutual relationship, and not the form, the noetic factor alone, that constitutes the foundation of all animation and spiritualization.

What nevertheless gives rise over and over again to an abstract separation between the "hyletic" and "noetic" factors, and what seems to justify this separation, is the circumstance that the two, though never separable in an absolute sense, are to a great extent independent variables in respect to

10. Husserl, *Ideen*, p. 172.

each other. Matter must of course always stand in *some* form; however, it is confined to no mode of signification but can in a sense shift from one to another. This appears most clearly in examples where the shift changes the modality of meaning. Let us, for example, consider an experience from the optical sphere. Such an experience is never composed of mere sensory data, of the optical qualities of brightness and color. Its pure visibility is never conceivable outside and independently of a determinate form of vision; as sensory experience it is always the vehicle of a meaning and stands as it were in the service of that meaning. But precisely therein it is able to perform very different functions and through them to represent very different worlds of meaning. We can consider an optical structure, a simple line, for example, according to its purely expressive meaning. As we immerse ourselves in the design and construct it for ourselves, we become aware of a distinct physiognomic character in it. A peculiar mood is expressed in the purely spatial determination: the up and down of the lines in space embraces an inner mobility, a dynamic rise and fall, a psychic life and being. And here we do not merely read our own inner states subjectively and arbitrarily into the spatial form; rather, the form gives itself to us as an animated totality, an independent manifestation of life. It may glide quietly along or break off suddenly; it may be rounded and self-contained or jagged and jerky; it may be hard or soft: all this lies in the line itself as a determination of its own reality, its objective nature. But these qualities recede and vanish as soon as we take the line in another sense—as soon as we understand it as a mathematical structure, a geometrical figure. Now it becomes a mere schema, a means of representing a universal geometrical law. Whatever does not serve to represent this law, what merely appears as an individual factor in the line, now becomes utterly insignificant; it has departed, one might say, from our field of vision. Not only the qualities of brightness and color but also the absolute magnitudes that appear in the design are included in this negation: for the line as a geometrical structure they are absolutely irrelevant. Its geometrical significance depends not on these magnitudes as such but only on their relations and proportions. Where we previously encountered the rise and fall of a wavy line and in it the rhythm of an inner mood, we now perceive a graphic representation of a trigonometric function; we have before us a curve whose total meaning for us is ultimately exhausted in its analytical formula. The spatial form is nothing but a paradigm for the formula; it remains the mere outward cloak of an essentially unintuitive mathematical idea. And this idea does not stand for itself alone: in it a more comprehensive law, the law of all space, is represented. On the basis of this law every single geometrical structure is linked with the totality of possible geometrical forms. It belongs to a definite system, to a set of truths and theorems, of grounds and consequences—and this system designates the universal form of meaning, through which every particular geometrical form first becomes possible, through which it is constituted and made understandable. And once again we stand in an entirely different sphere of vision when we take the line as a mythical symbol or as an aesthetic ornament. The mythical symbol as such embraces the fundamental mythical opposition between the sacred and the profane. It is set up in order to make a separation between the two provinces, and to warn and frighten, to bar the uninitiated from approaching or touching the sacred. Yet here it does not act merely as a sign, a mark by which the sacred is recognized, but possesses also a factually inherent, magically compelling and repelling power. Of such a power the aesthetic world knows nothing. Viewed as an ornament, the drawing seems remote both from signification in the logical-conceptual sense and from the magical-mythical warning symbol. Its meaning lies in itself and discloses itself only to pure artistic vision, to the aesthetic eye. Here again the experience of spatial form is completed only through its relation to a total horizon which it reveals to us—through a certain atmosphere in which it not merely "is," but in which, as it were, it lives and breathes.[11]

We find the same relation within a more restricted area if, instead of comparing the different modalities of signification, we confine ourselves to a single one of them. Here again we can follow the same characteristic process of differentiation, by which a content may assume very different shades of signification and pass from one to another. We have seen, for example, how color only seemingly represents an absolutely uniform optical quality. Depending on whether it is taken as a simple and independent determination or as the color of an object, it obtains a different valence. Seen in the one aspect, the world of colors, as Goethe said, represents to us nothing other than the "acts and sufferings of light"—while in the other it appears related and in a sense confined to the world of things. In the one case, colors may be said to be free-floating light structures; in the

11. Cf. my lecture at the Congress on Esthetics in Halle (1927): "Das Symbolproblem und seine Stellung im System der Philosophie," *Zeitschrift für Ästhetik und allgemeine Kunstwissenschaft,* 21 (1927), 191 ff.

other they make visible not themselves but through themselves something else. And, once again we cannot discern an indifferent substrate of all color, which later enters into different forms and is thereby modified in diverse ways. Rather, we have seen that the color phenomena themselves, in their purely phenomenal character, are already dependent on the order in which they stand—that their pure mode of manifestation is determined by precisely this order. It is with a view to expressing this mutual determination that we introduce the concept and the term "symbolic pregnance." By symbolic pregnance we mean the way in which a perception as a sensory experience contains at the same time a certain nonintuitive meaning which it immediately and concretely represents. Here we are not dealing with bare perceptive data, on which some sort of apperceptive acts are later grafted, through which they are interpreted, judged, transformed. Rather, it is the perception itself which by virtue of its own immanent organization, takes on a kind of spiritual articulation—which, being ordered in itself, also belongs to a determinate order of meaning. In its full actuality, its living totality, it is at the same time a life "in" meaning. It is not only subsequently received into this sphere but is, one might say, born into it. It is this ideal interwovenness, this relatedness of the single perceptive phenomenon, given here and now, to a characteristic total meaning that the term "pregnance" is meant to designate. If, for example, we turn in one of the basic directions of our temporal consciousness—if we advance, as it were, into the future—this advance does not signify that a new impression, a fantasm of the future, is joined to the sum of present perceptions, as given to us in the now. Rather, the future presents itself as a wholly distinctive mode of vision: it is anticipated from the standpoint of the present. The now is filled and saturated with the future: *praegnans futuri*, as Leibniz called it. We have everywhere seen that this kind of pregnance is distinguished by unmistakable characteristics from any purely quantitative accumulation or associative combination of perceptive images, and that it cannot be explained by reduction to purely discursive acts of judgment and inference. The symbolic process is like a single stream of life and thought which flows through consciousness, and which by this flowing movement produces the diversity and cohesion, the richness, the continuity, and constancy, of consciousness.

Thus this process shows from a new angle how the analysis of consciousness can never lead back to absolute elements: it is precisely the pure relation which governs the building of consciousness and which stands out in it as a genuine a priori, an essentially first factor.[12] It is only in the reciprocal movement between the "representing" and the "represented" that a knowledge of the ego and of objects, ideal as well as real, can arise. Here we feel the true pulse of consciousness, whose secret is precisely that every beat strikes a thousand connections. No conscious perception is merely given, a mere datum, which need only be mirrored; rather, every perception embraces a definite "character of direction" by which it points beyond its here and now. As a mere perceptive *differential*, it nevertheless contains within itself the *integral* of experience.[13] This integration, this apprehension of the totality of experience starting from a single factor, is only made possible by definite laws which govern the transition from one to the other. The single factor of momentary perception must—to preserve the mathematical metaphor—be apprehended as one which stands in a universal functional equation and can be determined on the strength of it. This determination itself is no mere accumulation and additive combination of particular values but is attainable solely through the order that they assume within certain basic categorial forms. We determine the single existing thing in respect to its objective meaning, by articulating it with the spatial-temporal order, the causal order, and the order of thing and property. Through this ordering it takes on a specific directional meaning—a vector as it were, pointing to a determinate goal. Just as, mathematically speaking, directed and nondirected quantities cannot simply be added together, we cannot, in our phenomenology and critical theory of knowledge, speak of "matters" and "forms," "phenomena" and categorial "orders" being "combined" with one another. On the other hand, we not only can but must determine every particular in respect to such orders, if experience is to come into being as a theoretical

12. On this basic idea of the primacy of the relation, I agree with Natorp, who sees in it the very foundation and presupposition for all critical psychology. "Relatioh," he writes, "seems to be so essential to consciousness that all genuine consciousness is relation, and that is to say that not presentation but representation is the original factor, that presentation is merely represented by the representative consciousness, as a factor contained in it. . . . Actually, what is present to consciousness seems to detach itself by abstraction only as a basis for representation; only for theoretical reconstruction does it precede, while actually, in the real life of consciousness, the relation is the first and immediate factor, to which the other point of reference always belongs and is equally essential" (*Allgemeine Psychologie*, p. 56).

13. For this concept of integration see above, *1,* 104 ff.

structure. It is participation in this structure that gives to the phenomenon its objective reality and determinacy. The symbolic pregnance that it gains detracts in no way from its concrete abundance; but it does provide a guarantee that this abundance will not simply dissipate itself, but will round itself into a stable, self-contained form.

Chapter 6

Toward a Pathology of the Symbolic Consciousness

1. The Symbolic Problem in the History of the Theory of Aphasia

EVER SINCE the birth of logic and of the philosophy of language there has been incessant concern with the relation between thought and speech. From the first conscious beginnings of philosophical reflection this problem has been the center of inquiry. The Greek language is a living witness to this fact, since it designates the two fundamental questions of thought and speech by one and the same term. The unity of concept and word, of the thought and the spoken *logos*, forms in a sense the starting point, the *terminus a quo* of all Greek speculation—while on the other hand, the separation and methodological differentiation of the two was a basic task which had to be clearly apprehended before logic could become possible as a science.[1] But only very gradually was this difference recognized and given a clear-cut systematic expression. Over and over again the original view returned to the fore; over and over again, attempts were made to elucidate the complex relationship between thought and language by transforming it back into a simple relation of identity. Medieval nominalism found no other way to solve the riddle of the logical concept. All that the concept is and all that it means is not derived in and through itself; it borrows its universality and significance exclusively from language. In the centuries-long struggle of medieval logicians over the nature of universals, it was ultimately the modernists, the nominalists and terminists of the school of William of Occam, who emerged victorious. And in modern philosophy, the victory has seemed final and decisive. Not only did Hobbes proclaim that *veritas non in re, sed in dicto consistit;* even Leibniz, in his very first work, *De principio individui*, took the side

1. Cf. Hoffman, "Die Sprache und die archaische Logik."

of the nominalist logicians: the whole structure of his logical theory of forms is based on the proposition that the knowledge of things is dependent on the proper use of signs, so that the establishment of a universal characteristic becomes the precondition for a universal scientific doctrine, a *scientia generalis.*

Only much later than this problem of the inner relation between speech and thought did the closely related problem of the significance of language for the building of the perceptual world force itself upon philosophical reflection. This is quite understandable: from time immemorial it has passed as the characteristic difference between thought and perception that all thought moves in the sphere of mere mediacy, while perception possesses an immediate certainty and reality. If we were to sacrifice this certainty and reality to the domination of the word—of signs and symbols—we should be in danger of losing all solid ground beneath our feet. Somewhere, so it seems, the signification of symbols must rest on something that is absolutely given and meaningful in itself. For mere signs seem from the outset to be fraught with the curse of ambiguity; all representation in symbols involves the danger of equivocation. Only a return to the foundations of knowledge, which are given to us in perception, can save us from this ambiguity; this alone will enable us to gain a foothold on a "well-grounded earth." Thus the aim and goal of the struggle against conceptual realism seemed to be to open a path to true and original reality and usher in a realism of perception. Hobbes, who saw all truth in the word, excepted one field from this radical nominalism. Though by nature arbitrary and conventional, thought and speech encounter an ultimate limit in immediate sensory appearance, which they must simply accept and recognize as such. If the whole edifice erected by language and thought over this original stratum were taken away, the sensory appearances would still remain intact in their unassailable certainty. It is this dogma of the autarchy and autonomy, the self-sufficiency and self-evidence of perceptual knowledge, that formed the foundation of sensationalist psychology. Only here and there did a psychologist venture an explicit attack upon it—and only gradually and relatively late was it driven from that dominant position by a change in psychological method. But much earlier a breech had been made in this dogma from an entirely different angle. It was not empirical psychology but the critical philosophy of language which made the first decisive attack. Perhaps nothing is so remarkable about Wilhelm von Humboldt's contribution to the philosophy of language as the circumstance that from the start he directed his inquiry not solely toward the world of concepts but also toward the world of perception and intuition. And here again he found no confirmation of the view that language merely provides a phonetic designation of already perceived objects. Where this belief prevails—said Humboldt—the full, profound meaning of language can never be grasped. Man not only thinks the world and understands it through the medium of language; his whole intuition of it and the way in which he lives in this intuition are conditioned by this very medium. His grasp of an objective reality—the way in which he sets it before himself as a whole and forms, divides, and articulates it in particular—none of this would be possible without the living energy of language. These programmatic principles of Humboldt's philosophy of language raised a significant problem for psychology, but it was a long time before psychologists recognized its full import. True, the school of Herbart—Lazarus and Steinthal—held that without a profounder insight into the nature of linguistic processes, psychology could have no solid foundation. In one and the same work Steinthal attempted to provide an introduction both to psychology and to a general science of language.[2] And this bond seemed to become even closer when Wundt began the edifice of his *Ethnic Psychology* with a comprehensive theory of language. Yet it is clear that although Wundt recognized language as one of the most important objects of psychological inquiry, he credited it with no decisive influence over the method of this inquiry. For him, the analysis of language did not essentially modify the fundamental schema of psychology, but merely extended it to one more object. This analysis of language would add an important new chapter to psychology; but this chapter simply takes its place beside those already written. It brings about no fundamental change in the inner organization of psychology, in its view of the basic structure of psychic life. When Wundt began his inquiry into language, his psychological principles had long been established. The concepts of sensation and perception, idea and intuition, association and apperception had been firmly defined in his work on physiological psychology. Far from attempting to remould these concepts, Wundt's *Völkerpsychologie* merely sought to confirm and reinforce them on the strength of the new material derived from language, myth, religion, art, etc. It was only after a long and arduous effort that modern psychology

2. Chajim Steinthal, *Einleitung in die Psychologie und Sprachwissenschaft* (Berlin, 1871). Lazarus, *Das Leben der Seele.*

succeeded in freeing the investigation into language from this ready-made schematism and came to regard it not only as a new field of application but as a genuine essential of the method of psychology.[3]

But while psychology in the more restricted sense embarked only slowly and hesitantly on the new road, a powerful impulsion in this direction came from a different quarter. The question of the relation between the formation of language and the structure of the world of perception was asked only relatively late in the *psychology* of language; but from the very first it inevitably forced itself upon the study of speech *pathology*. The first step was to describe and analyze the disturbances which certain pathological speech disorders bring about in the pure intellectual processes. But the greater the advance in this direction, the more evident it became that the frame was too narrow. The purely clinical picture of the various clinical disorders could not be sharply drawn as long as they were regarded as mere disturbances of the intelligence. Not the intelligence alone, but the total behavior and mental state of the affected person proved to be modified by the change in language consciousness and in the use of language. It seems that the true inner connection between the language world on the one hand and the world of perception and intuition on the other can only be apprehended clearly when, because of special conditions, the bond between the two begins to slacken. Only then does the affected function stand out in its full and positive meaning; only then does it become evident how much the world of perception, which one tends at first sight to interpret as a datum of the senses, owes to the spiritual medium of language, and how every impediment of the process of spiritual communication effected in language also affects the immediate nature and character of perception. In this respect, the observation and exact description of pathological cases proved directly of value to phenomenological analysis. Here, as it were, a natural analytic comes to the help of our intellectual analytic; for in pathological states the factors that in normal consciousness are given only in close combination, in a kind of concrescence, begin to separate, so to speak, and their different significations begin to be set off from one another. And now it becomes fully apparent to

3. The significance which the problem of language has acquired in contemporary psychology and most particularly for its methodology may be most clearly followed in the writings of Karl Bühler; cf. his summary in *Die Krise der Psychologie* (Jena, 1929). On the position of the problem of language in Hoenigswald's "psychology of thought," see above, pp. 119–20.

how great an extent not only our thinking of the world but even the intuitive form in which reality is present for us is subject to the law of *symbolic* formation. Here the old scholastic dictum *forma dat esse rei* acquires a new validity. The content of truth and the relative justification of this saying become fully evident only when we transpose it from the field of ontological metaphysics in which it was originally coined to the phenomenal sphere—when we take "form" not in a substantial but in a purely functional sense.

Here, then, the pathology of speech touches upon a problem whose significance goes far beyond its own confines and actually exceeds the limits of any special science, and of this students of speech disorders have themselves become increasingly aware. In his recent systematic summary of the theory of aphasia, Henry Head explicitly accords central emphasis to the symbolic concept.[4] The disturbances of consciousness in aphasia are designated by Head as disorders of "symbolic formulation and expression." With this he has established a general concept with the help of which he seeks to arrange and group the various symptoms of the disease.

It now becomes impossible for the general philosophy of language to disregard the observations made in this field and the questions they raise.[5] For it is always a matter of methodological significance when the Heraclitean saying that the way up is the same as the way down is confirmed in the field of science. Jackson—whose investigations carried on from 1860 to 1890 formed the starting point for Head's studies—had treated the problem of the pathology of speech in a general frame, linking them with certain questions in the phenomenology of sense perception. He found a close connection between speech disorders and certain disturbances of optical and tactile recognition, which he described under the common title "imperception." With this the significance of language not

4. Henry Head, *Aphasia and Kindred Disorders of Speech* (2 vols. Cambridge, Cambridge University Press, 1926). Large sections of this book were previously published by Head in the periodical *Brain, 43* (1920), 87–165; *46* (1923), 355–528. All the quotations in the text refer to the book publications.

5. I myself became acquainted with Head's investigations only after the phenomenological analyses of perception contained in the two first volumes of this book were largely completed. This made me attach all the greater importance to the indirect confirmation of my conclusions by Head's observations and the general theoretical view which he developed solely on the basis of clinical experience. The purely philosophical significance of these observations was first stated by Henri Delacroix in his work *Le Langage et la pensée* (Paris, 1924), cf. Bk. IV, pp. 477 ff.

only for logical thought but also for the formation of the perceptive world was recognized in principle.[6] Today such outstanding authorities in the field as Goldstein and Gelb take the position that the true aphasic disturbances never merely affect speech as an isolated act, but rather that every change in a patient's language world always brings about a characteristic change in his behavior as a whole—in his perception as well as in his practical, active attitude toward reality. Thus, from an entirely new angle, we find confirmation of the words with which Humboldt headed his philosophy of language.[7] If we wish to obtain a clear idea of the complex of problems that here lies before us, we must not shun the labor of dividing it into its various threads and following each one separately. Let us begin with a glance at the historical development by which the symbolic concept gradually attained to the central position it occupies today in the theory of aphasia.

As early as 1870 Finkelburg introduced the term *asymbolia* in attempting to find a common denominator for aphasic disorders.[8] But he took the concept of the symbol itself in a restricted sense, interpreting it in the main as an artificial or conventional sign. He held that the ability to form and understand such artificial signs was a special psychic faculty, a faculty *sui generis,* and for this view invoked the authority of Kant, who treats the *facultas signatrix* in a special section of his *Anthropology* and distinguishes it from sensuous knowledge as well as purely intellectual knowledge. "Insofar as the forms of things (intuitions) serve only as means of representation by concepts," Kant had written, "they are symbols, and knowledge obtained through them is known as symbolic or figurative." In this connection, Kant speaks of mimetic signs (gestures),

6. Concerning Jackson's work, see the penetrating work by Head, who also re-edited the most important of these works: "Hughlings Jackson on Aphasia and Kindred Affections of Speech," *Brain, 38* (1915), 1–190. See also Head's *Aphasia and Kindred Disorders of Speech, 1,* 30–53.

7. It was only after completion of the first and second volumes of this work that study of the work of Gelb and Goldstein drew my attention to this connection between the findings of the modern pathology of speech and the basic view on which Humboldt builds his theory of language. But I should scarcely have had the courage to go into it more deeply if aside from the literary stimulation of these works I had not also received the personal encouragement of the two authors. Here I must particularly thank Goldstein for demonstrating to me a large number of the pathological cases to which his publications refer and so enabling me to gain a true understanding of them.

8. Finkelburg's lecture at the Niederrheinische Gesellschaft der Ärtze in Bonn; cf. *Berliner Klinische Wochenschrift,* 7 (1870), 449 f., 460 ff.

written signs, musical signs (notes), numbers, the signs of caste or service (coats-of-arms and liveries), and signs of honor or disgrace (decorations and brand marks.[9] Finkelburg saw the core of aphasic disturbances in inability to grasp the meaning of such symbols and cited cases in which aphasiacs were unable to recognize musical notes or coins or to make the sign of the cross. But with progress in the study of aphasia the concept and term of asymbolia quickly grew beyond this narrow meaning. It was soon taken to cover not only a total or partial failure to understand artificial signs, but also the inability to identify visible and tangible objects and make appropriate use of them, even where the sensory function was unimpaired. A distinction was made between "sensory" and "motor" asymbolia: in the former the main factor was "inability to recognize things," and the inability to make proper use of them was held to be secondary and derived; the latter manifested itself chiefly in certain disturbances of the motor functions which made it difficult or impossible to plan and properly carry out certain simple movement or complexes of movements. In his book on the aphasic symptom complex (1874), Wernicke uses the term asymbolia to designate the clinical picture which Freud termed (optical or tactile) agnosia. And in his *Klinische Vorlesungen über Psychiatrie,* Meinert spoke of a "motor asymbolia of the upper extremities" to designate those phenomena which Liepmann later grouped under the head of "apraxia." [10]

But another parallel development began with Jackson. In his effort to understand the aphasic disorders and to find a feature common to all of them, Jackson started from the use not of the word but of the sentence. Although it is certain that he had no detailed knowledge of Humboldt, he proceeded on the basis of his fundamental insight that speech cannot be

9. *Anthropologie,* in *Werke,* ed. Cassirer, *8,* 78 ff.

10. Theodor Meinert, *Klinische Vorlesungen über Psychiatrie* (Vienna, 1890), p. 272. For the use of the word "asymbolia" in the older literature, cf. Karl Heilbronner, "Über Asymbolie," *Psychiatrische Abhandlungen, 3,* No. 3 (1897), esp. pp. 41 ff. The term "agnosia" was first used by Freud, whereas the concept of "apraxia" was used by Steinthal as early as his *Einleitung in die Psychologie und Sprachwissenschaft* (1871), though it was first brought into general use by Hugo Liepmann in *Das Krankheitsbild der Apraxie* (Berlin, 1900) and *Über Störungen des Handelns bei Gehirnkranken* (Berlin, 1905). Cf. also Arnold Pick, "Asymbolie, Apraxie, Aphasie," *Proceedings of the First International Congress on Psychiatry* (Amsterdam, 1908); and Karl Heilbronner, "Die aphasischen, apraktischen and agnostischen Störungen," in Max Lewandowsky, *Handbuch der Nervenkrankheiten, 2* (1911), 1037.

pieced together from words which preceded it, but that on the contrary words follow from speech as a whole.[11] For him the analysis of the sentence and its function accordingly became the key to the study of aphasia. If in the clinical observation of aphasiacs we start from a mere inventory of their vocabulary, if we seek to determine what words they lack and what words they have use of, this method, Jackson stresses, will lead to highly fluctuating and unreliable results. For clinical experience shows that performances in this field vary exceedingly. A patient who has the use of a particular word today may be unable to use it tomorrow; or he may be able to use it without difficulty in one context and not at all in another. Consequently, if we wish to investigate the special nature of aphasic disorders, the essential is to examine these contexts more closely, to consider not so much the use of the word as such as the specific meaning in which words are used, the function which they fulfill in the whole. And now Jackson makes a first basic distinction: he divides the phenomena of speech into two groups, the one consisting of emotional utterances, the other of statements and expositions. In aphasic disorders the former tend to be affected far more rarely than the latter, or are damaged in much less degree. Thus the observation of these disorders makes it clear that there are two very different and relatively independent strata of speech: the one in which only inner states are disclosed, the other in which objective relations are "intended" and designated. Jackson compares these two strata, which he designates as "inferior" and "superior" speech. It is only to the utterances of superior speech that we may attribute "propositional value." Our entire "intellectual" language moves among such propositional values which dominate and permeate it; it does not serve to express feelings and emotions, but is directed toward objects and relations between objects. It is precisely this ability to form and understand propositional values, and not the mere use of words, that is considerably impaired or entirely eliminated in aphasic disturbances.

Single words are meaningless, and so is any unrelated succession of words. The unit of speech is a proposition. A single word is, or is in effect, a proposition, if other words in relation are implied. The English tourist at a French *table d'hôte* was understood by the waiter to be asking for water when his neighbours thought he was crying "oh" from distress. It is from the use of a word that we judge of its

11. Humboldt, *Einleitung zum Kawi-Werk*, p. 72.

propositional value. The words "yes" and "no" are propositions, but only when used for assent and dissent; they are used by healthy people interjectionally as well as propositionally. A speechless patient may retain the word "no," and yet have only the interjectional or emotional, not the propositional use of it; he utters it in various tones as signs of feeling only.[12]

According to Jackson, all the truly intellectual power of language, everything that it accomplishes for thought, is contained in this power of "statement," of predication.

> Loss of speech is, therefore, the loss of the power to propositionize. It is not only loss of power to propositionize aloud (to talk), but to propositionize either internally or externally, and it may exist when the patient remains able to utter some few words. We do not mean by using the popular term "power" that the speechless man has lost any "faculty" of speech or propositionizing; he has lost those words which serve in speech, the nervous arrangements for them being destroyed. There is no "faculty" or "power" of speech apart from words revived or revivable in propositions, any more than there is a "faculty" of co-ordination of movements apart from movements represented in particular ways. We must here say, too, that besides the use of words in speech there is a service of words which is not speech; hence we do not use the expression that the speechless man has lost words, but that he has lost those words which serve in speech. In brief, speechlessness does not mean entire wordlessness.

Head starts from Jackson's conceptions. What Jackson had designated as the faculty of "statement," the "propositional" use of words, Head terms the faculty of symbolic expression and symbolic formulation. But he takes a significant step beyond Jackson in that he does not limit this symbolic function to language alone. To be sure, language is and remains the most evident exponent of this function, but language does not exhaust the entire range of its activities. Rather, according to Head, symbolic behavior occurs in human achievements and activities which are not directly connected with speech. A close analysis of action in particular shows it to be shot through with the same contrast as may be found in the sphere of language.

12. Jackson, in *Brain*, *38* (1915), 113 f.; on the distinction between "emotional" and "propositional," "inferior" and "superior" language in Jackson, cf. Head, *1*, 34 ff.

There is a form of action which consists in direct motor activity, which is, as it were, mechanically released by a given outward stimulus, and there are others which are possible only if the idea of a definite goal is formed, only if the goal toward which the action aims is anticipated in thought. And in this latter variety of action a part is always played by a trend of thought which is closely related to linguistic thought and which we may group with it under the common head of symbolic thought. According to Head, most of our "voluntary" movements and activities embrace such a symbolic element, which must be clearly recognized and defined if we wish to understand their special character. In action as in speech there is a mediated and an immediate, a superior and an inferior stratum. And again it is the aphasic disorders which clearly show us the limit between the two. An aphasiac will be able to perform certain actions, if they are caused and necessitated by a certain concrete situation; but he will not be able to perform the same actions of his own free will, without such concrete stimuli. For this, Jackson had cited numerous examples: he had shown, for example, that certain patients were not able to show their tongue when asked to do so, but readily executed the same movement in order to moisten their lips. Head amplified these observations according to a systematic plan: in a series of carefully prepared tests he had the patients progress from easier, more direct operations to those that were more difficult and indirect, and in every single case exactly noted their behavior. From his observations he concluded that a common deficiency, an incapacity for "symbolic" behavior and formulation, lay at the root of the disorders of speech as well as action. "By symbolic formulation and expression," Head sums up his fundamental view,

I understand a mode of behavior, in which some verbal or other symbol plays a part between the initiation and execution of the act. This comprises many procedures, not usually included under the heading of the use of language, and the functions to be placed within their category must be determined empirically; no definition can be framed to cover all forms of action which may be disturbed at one time or another according to the nature and severity of the case. . . . But anv act of mental expression, which demands symbolic formulation, tends to be defective and the higher its propositional value the greater difficulty will it present. . . . Any modification of the task, which lessens the necessity for symbolic representation, will render its performance easier.[13]

Thus at a very early date the theory of aphasia took a definite direction, leading toward the universal problem of the symbol—though to be sure the basic trend was not adhered to or unambiguously recognized at every phase of the development. The reason for this may be found in the form of psychology which for a long time was accepted both by medical theorists and clinical observers. Aside from Jackson, nearly all the leading students of aphasia can be said to have worked largely with the notion of the intellectual process that came to them from the sensationalist psychology of elements. They believed that they had understood and explained an intellectual act if they could break it down into its simple components— and they held it to be evident and dogmatically certain that these components themselves could consist in nothing other than simple sense impressions or a sum of such impressions. But it was precisely this fundamental view which inevitably removed them in theory from the peculiar principle and problem of the symbolic, however close they came to it in their observations. For there is no road leading from sensationalism to the center of the symbolic problem; sensationalism is the typically symbol-blind attitude.[14] Consequently, as long as the students of aphasia followed the lead of sensationalist psychology, their only means of grasping and defining the significance of the function of speech lay in an attempt to break it down into an aggregate of sensuous images. Speech was "explained" as a combination of such images, an aggregate of optical, acoustic, and kinesthetic sensations. And this psychology had its counterpart in physiology: it was held that every class of sense impressions must have as its physical substrate a special center in the brain. In his work on the aphasic symptom complex (1874) and in his *Manual of Brain Disorders* Wernicke identified a special center for sound images localized in the first temporal convolution; another, localized in the third frontal convolution, for motor images, which he believed to be crucial for the articulation of speech; and finally a concept center, which he believed communicated and mediated between the first two. Later these schemata were considerably amplified and differentiated: every step forward in

13. Head, *I,* 211 f.
14. See above, pp. 192–4.

clinical experience and observation brought a new, more or less complicated "diagram." [15] Here the psychological concept of the impression as defined by Berkeley and Hume was in all seriousness elaborated anatomically and physiologically. Every cell or group of cells in the brain was held to be endowed with a special ability acquired by experience, to receive and preserve certain impressions and then to compare these stored-up visual, auditory, and tactile images with new sensory contents. The old metaphor of the *tabula rasa* reappears: Henschen, for example, in explaining how we learn how to read, declares that certain letters or engrams are stamped on our brain cells, very much "as the form of the seal ring is imprinted on the wax." [16] If we consider this whole development only in its methodological aspect, it presents a strange and highly instructive anomaly. For all psychologists who adhered to this method were beyond a doubt convinced empirical scientists; they believed that they were working only with facts and that all their inferences were prescribed entirely by direct observation. But once again the difference between empirical inquiry and "empiricism" becomes apparent. For what these researchers produced was by no mean a pure description of phenomena; rather, the phenomena were subjected in advance to definite theoretical presuppositions and prejudices and interpreted accordingly. Head particularly attacked the school of the Diagram Makers, as he calls them, for building on a purely speculative foundation; instead of giving an unbiased description of the facts, he wrote, they let themselves be guided by certain general and a priori considerations. [17] And he points back to Jackson, who had first broken with this method, who had demanded and put into practice a strictly phenomenological approach to aphasia. [18] A phenomenological attitude can never favor a theory which holds that the faculty of speech is rooted in the possession of certain verbal and phonetic images, while that of writing and reading is grounded in the possession of certain literal images, and which attributes "agraphia" and

15. Highly characteristic for this general tendency are the diagrams provided by Lichtheim in his *Aphasia* (1885).

16. Henschen, "Klinische und anatomische Beiträge zur Pathologie des Gehirns," quoted from Head, *1*, 83 f.

17. Head, *1*, 135.

18. "Every worker on the affections of speech has claimed to deal with the 'facts' of each case; but no one except Jackson recognised that all the phenomena are primarily psychical and only in the second place susceptible of physiological or anatomical explanation" (Head, *1*, 32).

"alexia" to the loss of such images. Such a theory never does justice to the variability and fluid character of clinical phenomena: it attempts to reduce to purely static elements a process that can only be grasped and described dynamically. If, as clinical experience teaches, a patient in a particular situation can have the use of a certain word which he lacks in another situation, this difference cannot be explained by the destruction of the verbal image in question; for once destroyed, this image could not under certain circumstances be recovered.[19] It was observations of this sort which little by little drove medical researchers away from "brain mythology"—as these attempts to establish definite anatomical centers for various psychic "faculties" have been called. In Germany it was particularly Goldstein who in his works on the theory of aphasia stressed from the very outset that phenomenological inquiry must be paramount in the interpretation of aphasic and agnostic disorders—that it is only after careful individual observation has revealed the specific form of a patient's experiences that one can hope to discover what material processes in the central nervous system correspond to a particular pathological change. An attempt at localization, he declared, can be based only on a psychological and phenomenological analysis uninfluenced by any preconceived localizing theories.[20] Pierre Marie also started from a sharp methodological critique of the image theory when in the year 1906 he called for a revision of the aphasia question, thus opening up a new path of research:

> We should like them to tell us how the fixation of those famous verbal images takes place. Is every word separately inscribed in this center for auditory images? But what an immense development of this center would then be needed, particularly in one who speaks many languages!

19. One of Goldstein's patients whom I had the opportunity to observe in the Frankfurt Neurological Institute could not find the "name" for the watch [German, *Uhr*] that I showed him; but in answer to my question of what time it was, he replied at once "one o'clock" [German, *ein Uhr*]. Thus he had lost the word *Uhr* in its function as a "name for a thing," while in other functions he used it freely. Similarly Head tells of a patient who could use the words "yes" and "no" in answer to questions, but not when asked to repeat them. In one of the experiments, the patient shook his head when asked to repeat the word "no," and then added: "No, I don't know how to do it" (Head, 2, 322).

20. Kurt Goldstein, "Einige prinzipielle Bemerkungen zur Frage der Lokalisation psychischer Vorgänge im Gehirn," *Medizinische Klinik* (1910); Gelb and Goldstein, *Psychologische Analysen hirnpathologischer Fälle, 1*, 5 ff. Cf. their article in *Psychologische Forschung, 6* (1925), 127–214.

Or is it perhaps the individual syllables of which the words consist that are fixated in this center? Then we should have a simpler operation and one for which a smaller number of images would be requisite; but then an intellectual effort would immediately be required to piece together these scattered syllables and reform them into words. . . . But why should we suppose that there is a special phonetic image center for words, when nothing whatsoever proves its existence? [21]

Philosophically speaking, Marie's essential step forward was that he abandoned any attempt to explain the spiritual function of speech by building it up from purely material, "hyletic" factors. Speech was apprehended as a unitary whole, which according to Marie can originate nowhere else than in the unitary totality of the intelligence. Accordingly, every disturbance in speech points back to a disturbance of the intelligence, which is its actual base. From the clinical standpoint Marie distinguished between two basic forms of disorder. One form is Wernicke's sensory aphasia, the essential symptom of which is that the patient's understanding of speech is destroyed or gravely impaired. But this symptom never stands alone; it always goes hand in hand with a general intellectual defect. In the other form which Marie distinguishes, the understanding of speech is retained, the faculty for written expression is also undiminished, but the use of the word is seriously impaired. Here in his opinion we do not have a disturbance of the intelligence, but a purely articulatory disturbance on a central foundation, an "anarthria," which must be carefully distinguished from true "aphasia" (Wernicke's aphasia). What had hitherto impeded the distinction, Marie held, was the existence of a complex disorder in which the symptoms of true (Wernicke's) aphasia and of anarthria are mixed. A mixture, a syndrome, of this sort occurred in the disorder which was commonly diagnosed as Broca's aphasia or subcortical motor aphasia: Broca's aphasia was Wernicke's aphasia plus a fundamentally different disorder, an anarthria.[22] But Marie's theory encountered a twofold objection and difficulty. On the one hand it turned out that a pure anarthria in Marie's sense was not demonstrable as a clinical fact. Even where the patient's understanding of speech seemed to

21. Pierre Marie, *Revision de la question d'aphasie,* from *La Semaine médicale,* October 17, 1906 (Paris, 1906), pp. 7 f.

22. See Marie, pp. 33 ff. Cf. the penetrating exposition of Marie's theory by his student François Moutier, *L'Aphasie de Broca* (Paris, 1908), esp. pp. 244 ff.

be fully preserved, there proved to be no such thing as an isolated motor aphasia; the articulatory defects of speech were always accompanied by certain changes in the patient's general behavior. "The motor disturbance of the anarthriac," Marie had stressed, "has nothing to do with true aphasia. The anarthriac understands, reads, writes. His thinking is not impaired, and it is possible for him to express his thoughts in every other way than by the word, since his inner speech is not affected." But this theory did not hold up under sharp observation: even those patients who could be called pure anarthriacs according to Marie's criteria revealed certain deficiencies in the understanding of speech as soon as the tests were made more difficult. Although their understanding of speech and capacity for written expression seemed intact at first glance, nevertheless in both these respects they lived on a different plane from the normal individual. On the one hand, their written expression was restricted and included only a relatively small selection of words: the abstract terms of speech had been replaced by more concrete terms, closer to the purely sensuous sphere.[23] On the other hand, the diminution in intelligence which Marie regarded as the actual basis of true aphasia required a closer definition. Marie himself endeavored to provide such a definition—that is, to clarify and complement the mere generic concept of intelligence by the addition of a specific difference: he repeatedly stressed that the "spiritual" disorder which he took aphasia to be must not be confused with a dementia. He expressly conceded, in his controversy with Déjerine, that if the actions of everyday life are taken into account, aphasiacs can scarcely be distinguished from normal persons. Intellectual degeneration, he declared, became apparent only in another sphere, and then only under sharp, methodical examination. "The demented and the paralytics are no aphasiacs, even though in dementia and in paralysis there is a considerable diminution of the intellectual faculties; on the other hand, the aphasiacs are not psychopaths in spite of the intellectual deficiencies they present." For in aphasiacs not the intelligence as a whole, but only a certain side, a certain partial aspect of it, is impaired.[24] But if we ask for a closer characterization of this partial aspect, Marie and his disciple Moutier merely speak of a deficiency in the "special linguistic intelligence" (un déficit intellectuel spécialisé pour le langage). "L'aphasie n'est pas une démence; elle peut présenter comme celle-ci un déficit intellectuel général, mais

23. For documentation, see Head, *1*, 200 ff.; 2, 252 ff.
24. Marie, pp. 11 f.

elle présente en plus, et c'est ce qui la distinguera toujours des démences banales, un déficit particulier du langage." [25] But this explanation amounts of course to a mere tautology. What—it now became necessary to ask— is the nature of this linguistic thinking which is said to be disturbed or diminished in aphasiacs, and by what characteristics is it distinguished from other forms and trends of "thought as a whole"? Is there a stratum of everyday, practical thinking which does not yet require the symbolic thinking that governs language, and which proves to be relatively independent of it? And how are the two strata to be marked off from each other? Such students of speech pathology as Jackson,[26] Head, Goldstein, and Gelb asked these questions more and more insistently. And they could not answer them by starting from general speculative considerations on the relation between speaking and thinking but were bound to seek their answer in the opposite way, by developing more and more precise means of clinical observation and phenomenological analysis of individual cases. But precisely this empirical method led them to the threshold of universal and basic problems which could not be solved merely by a further accumulation of observed facts but called for a renewal and a kind of reversal of the psychological point of view.

2. The Change of the Perceptual World in Aphasia

If we wish to appraise correctly the significance of pathology for our knowledge of the symbolic function, we must not restrict ourselves to the pure speech disorders. Clinical observation has long pointed to a close relationship between aphasia in the restricted sense and disorders of a different kind which are usually termed "agnostic" or "apractic." Here we need not concern ourselves with the precise distinction between these two groups, which can only be a matter for specialized research. Despite all the divergencies that still obtain in basic theory and interpretation, one thing seems to have been universally recognized by the students of these disorders, namely that the pathological pictures commonly designated by the terms aphasia, agnosia, and apraxia are intimately related. Heilbronner stresses in a comprehensive survey of aphasic, apractic, and agnostic disorders that it is not possible to draw a fundamental distinction between

25. Moutier, L'Aphasie de Broca, p. 228; cf. esp. p. 205.

26. Jackson had already pointed out that the question raised by aphasia research must not be "How is the general mind damaged?" but "What aspect of mind is damaged?" Cf. Head, 1, 49.

them: the aphasic symptoms do not form a separate group over against those of apraxia and agnosia, but represent only a variety of the general picture.[27] According to Heilbronner, the singling out of aphasia as an independent pathological grouping may be explained and justified more by practical requirements than by any purely theoretical considerations.[28] Even in the case of the patient of Goldstein and Gelb, who seemed at first to be afflicted with a purely optical blindness to form while his understanding of speech and spontaneous speech appeared to be wholly intact, a more penetrating analysis revealed highly characteristic deviations from the speech of the normal individual: for example, this patient could neither understand nor make use of metaphoric expressions. Thus it would seem justified that an inquiry such as ours, definitely concerned with purely theoretical considerations, should not start with any sharp line between the different pathological groups but seek rather to bring out a common fundamental factor. Of course as we progress, this factor itself will require and be susceptible of a more precise definition and differentiation; but perhaps the general conclusions that can be gained from an analysis of the symbolic function as a whole will help to prepare the ground for a differentiation of this sort, by enabling us to survey more clearly the diversity and gradation of the various symbolic operations which may be assumed to be the conditions of speech, perceptual knowledge, and action.

The building of the world of perception requires an articulation of the sensory phenomena—that is to say, certain centers must be created, to which these phenomena as a whole are referred and toward which they are oriented and directed. The formation of such centers may be prosecuted along three main lines: the ordering of phenomena according to the point of view of "thing" and "attribute" is as necessary and constitutive as their ordering in spatial coexistence and temporal succession. The formation of these orders always requires that the even flow of appearances be interrupted in some way and that certain favored points be singled out. What was previously an unremitting flow of events now coalesces, as it were, about these favored points: in the very midst of the stream there form separate vortices, whose parts seem to be linked in a common movement. It is the creation of such dynamic rather than static totalities, this formation of functional rather than substantial unities, that gives rise to the inner relationships between phenomena. For now there is no longer

27. Heilbronner, in Lewandowsky's *Handbuch der Nervenkrankheiten*, 2, 1037.
28. Heilbronner, "Über Asymbolie," p. 47.

any absolutely isolated thing; every element that is engaged with others in such a common movement bears in itself the general law and form of that movement and is able to represent it for consciousness. And now, wherever we penetrate the stream of consciousness, we find definite living centers, toward which the individual movements strive. Every single perception is a *directed* perception; aside from its mere content, it possesses a vector which makes it significant for a definite direction or meaning.[29] The experience of speech pathology may serve to confirm this general structural law of the perceptual world and to test it from the negative side. For the spiritual powers on which the structure of the world of perception is based stand out more clearly where their operation is in some way altered or impeded than where it is without friction or obstruction. To carry on with our metaphor, the pathological cases may be regarded as a kind of disintegration of those "vortices," those dynamic unities through which normal perception functions. This disintegration can never mean total destruction, for that would mean the extinction of the sensory consciousness itself. But it is conceivable that this consciousness moves within narrower limits, in smaller and more restricted circles than in the case of normal perception. In this case a movement beginning at the periphery of the vortex would no longer be communicated to its center but would in a manner of speaking remain within the original zone of stimulation or its immediate vicinity. Now comprehensive unities of meaning would no longer be formed within the perceptual world; though within the more restricted spheres assigned to it the perceptual consciousness might still operate with a certain sureness. For the vibration of this consciousness itself would not be obstructed, but only its amplitude diminished. Each sense impression would still be provided with a vector of meaning, though these vectors would no longer possess a common direction toward very definite main centers but would diverge in far higher degree than is the case in normal perception. Particularly, a pathological disturbance of the function of speech can be adequately explained only by an approach of this sort, and not by any such notion as the disappearance of certain "phonetic images." Humboldt pointed out that men do not understand one another by relying on definite phonetic signs which produce the same sense impression or identical or similar images in all the members of a linguistic community: rather, the same key of an identical instrument is struck in every single subject when the phonetic sign is

29. For a more detailed argument, see above, esp. Pt. II, Chaps. 2–4.

heard, whereupon corresponding but not identical concepts arise. "When
. . . the link in the chain, the key of the instrument is touched in this
way, the whole organism vibrates, and the concept that springs from the
soul stands in harmony with everything surrounding the individual link,
even at the greatest distance from it." [30]

In disturbances of the process here described by Humboldt, the older
school of speech pathologists assumed that particular keys of the spiritual
instrument which we call speech must be destroyed: whereas the modern
view contents itself with establishing that they are no longer correspondent
in the same way, that they can no longer release the movement of the
whole as they did before. But now, in order to grasp the problem more
sharply and describe it with greater precision, we must pass beyond
general considerations and turn to the pathological phenomena themselves.

Gelb and Goldstein have described and analyzed in detail the case of a
patient who suffered from amnesia with respect to the universal color
names. He could neither spontaneously use these terms—such as "blue"
and "yellow," "red" and "green,"—nor relate them to a fixed meaning
when they were presented to him by others. If for example he was asked to
pick a red or yellow or green sample from a series of colored strips of
wool or paper, he was utterly baffled: the problem had no meaning for
him. However, there was no doubt that he saw the various shades of
color correctly and that he distinguished them in the normal way. All the
tests to which he was subjected showed that his faculty for distinguishing
colors was perfectly intact, that he was in no way color blind. It was only
when he attempted to classify different colors, to sort them in some way,
that his characteristic disturbance was manifested. For it appeared that he
had at his command no fixed principle of classification. Whereas a normal
person regards all colors which in any way belong to the base tone of a
pattern as related, the patient established a connection only between colors
which disclosed a close sensuous similarity, which were in exact agreement
in respect to color tone, brightness or some similar factor. And here again
he might suddenly slip from one form of classification into another—
first grouping colors which resembled the model before him in tonality
and then choosing the colors which resembled it in brightness. On the
other hand, he did strikingly well when the general color names did not
occur in the tests and he was asked to select from a group of samples a
shade corresponding to the color of a definite object. Then he always

30. Humboldt, *Einleitung zum Kawi-Werk*, p. 169. Cf. above, *1*, 159 ff.

chose with great certainty and precision: the color of a ripe strawberry, a mail box, a billiard table, chalk, violets, forget-me-nots, etc., provided these objects were present. The patient always responded perfectly to this form of test: he never pointed to a color which did not correspond to that of the named object. And this very ability made it possible for him under certain conditions to act differently from usual in respect to general color names. When, for example, he was asked to choose a "blue," he was at first, in line with his basic disturbance, unable to connect a definite meaning with it; but sometimes he solved the problem by translating it, so to speak, into another problem that he could understand. Since he knew the current verse: "Blue is the little flower called forget-me-not," by reciting it he provided himself with a means of passing from the realm of general color names to that of concrete thing names. And so similarly with other rhymes which he knew purely by rote. Then he could point out a forget-me-not blue, provided it was among the samples, but he never selected any other shade of blue, however close to it, for no other shade exactly corresponded to the remembered color of the forget-me-not that determined his choice. Not infrequently the patient succeeded by the same detour in using a word such as "red" or "green" to designate a color that had been shown him. He seemed to use the term correctly, but only in connection with colors for which he had some ready-made expression such as sky-blue, grass-green, white as snow, red as blood, etc. These phrases were used like set formulas; a color shade released the thought of blood and then, by an automatic linguistic act, he pronounced the word "red." But it still remained an empty word for him and did not correspond to the intuition which a normal individual associates with the term "red."

In what respect and in what specific characteristic did the patient's intuitive world differ from that of a normal individual? The real difference, Gelb and Goldstein concluded, is that this patient had ceased to command the principle of systematic articulation through which the normal individual dominates the world of color. The process by which the patient classifies colors seems more primitive and irrational than that of normal persons, for his choice is determined solely by degree of sensuous similarity in disregard of all other criteria. In order to recognize colors as related to one another in any way, he must have a very definite and concrete experience of coherence; they must be given him in their immediate manifestation as alike or identical.

Every strip of yarn aroused a characteristic color experience in the patient: according to the objective character of the sample, the determining factor in the experience might be color tone or brightness or delicacy etc. If two colors—the model and a strip from the pile, for example—had objectively the same tone color but different degrees of brightness, they did not necessarily seem related to the patient because brightness or warmth was the prevalent factor. . . . He could establish a relation only on the basis of a concrete experience of coherence. And such an experience actually occurred only where the colors were identical.

To see a relation between colors, the normal individual requires no such identity: for him color impressions very different and very remote from each other may still belong to the same color category. In countless shades of red he perceives the identical species "red" and regards each particular shade merely as an example, a member of this species. It is this view of the particular as a *representative* of a definite color species that is denied our patient. "In sorting the colors," Gelb and Goldstein sum up this distinction:

the normal individual is impelled in a certain direction by the instructions given him. In accordance with the instructions, he considers only the basic color of the model, regardless of its intensity or purity. The concrete color is not taken in its purely singular facticity, but more as a representative for a certain color category, redness, yellowness, blueness, etc. Let us designate this "conceptual" . . . attitude as a "categorial" attitude. The patient is more or less lacking any principle of classification because for him this categorial attitude is impossible or impeded.[31]

For us this case is particularly significant because it confirms from a new angle one of our most universal conclusions. In the course of this investigation we have repeatedly seen that in the analysis and characterization of pure perception a sharp distinction must already be made between the immediate and the mediated, the presentative and the representative content of perceptive experiences—between the direct "data" of these experiences and the representative *function* they fulfill. In the case here described what distinguishes the color phenomena of the patient from

31. "Psychologische Analysen," *Psychologische Forschung*, 6 (1925), 152 f.

those of the normal individual seems indeed not to be any purely substantial property we can find in them; the actual difference is, rather,
that they no longer function in the same way as means of representation.
They have ceased to be vectorial values and become mere static values:
they lack the direction toward particular favored points in the color
series, through which normal color perception first acquires its characteristic form. Here every optical experience remains, one might say, in itself
or can at most be related to experiences in its immediate vicinity. The representative function is confined within the narrowest limits: only factors
that are closely similar can represent and stand for one another. We can
indeed, with Gelb and Goldstein, designate this whole attitude as more
concrete, "closer to life," but it pays for this closeness to life by a total
loss of its freedom of survey. For perception gains this freedom only by
progressively filling itself with symbolic meaning—by interposing definite
forms of spiritual vision and spontaneously passing from one to another.
This is possible only when the attention does not fasten upon any single
sense impression but merely uses the particular as a kind of road sign,
pointing the way to the universal, to definite theoretical centers of meaning. By a highly characteristic and fortunate turn, the German language
sums up this twofold process in the one word *absehen.*[32] When we take
a color of a certain brightness and tonality, not only as this particular color
experience that is given here and now but even more as a specimen of
the species red or green, we orient ourselves toward that species by means
of it—our consciousness is focused not so much on the particular color as
on the species it serves to represent. And insofar as we aim in this way at
the species red and green, we must learn to disregard an abundance of
particular circumstances that are present in the sensuous and actual impression.

The patient can perform neither of these operations as fully as a normal
individual. He lacks the fixed centers in regard to which he can survey
the color world as a unity—and at the same time he lacks the possibility
of singling out one factor from the concrete totality of the color experience
while he disregards other factors that are immediately fused with it. To
be sure, he, too, can change the direction of his regard: in classifying
colors, he can start now from an agreement in basic tone and now from an
agreement in brightness. But in this change he himself is not free: he slips
into this or the other "direction of regard" and cannot spontaneously

32. This word may mean either "to aim at" or "to disregard." *Trans.*

adhere to one and exclude the other. Even if we attempt from outside to force the patient into a certain direction of regard, he cannot grasp its characteristic meaning—he cannot look steadily toward the point of fixation that has been shown him, but keeps losing sight of it.[33] Thus he lives within the momentary impression, in which he remains confined and entangled.[34] The normal perceptual consciousness—and this is one of its basic traits—not only is filled and permeated by definite vectors of meaning but can in general vary them freely. For example, we can consider an optical figure from this or that point of view; we can apprehend and determine it in regard to one factor or another. And whenever the form of determination changes, something different stands out as essential; thanks to our new vision, something different always becomes "visible." [35]

Here it seems pertinent to ask once again whether the new degree of freedom which perception gains in its purely representative achievement is *due to language,* or whether it does not first *make language possible.* Which here is the prior and which the posterior—which the original and which the derived—factor? Goldstein and Gelb also asked themselves these questions, and decided that this was no relation of one-sided dependency but rather a relation of pure reciprocity. True, they did not doubt "that language is one of the most effective means for turning away . . . from the primitive closer-to-life attitude, toward the categorial attitude."

33. Cf. Gelb and Goldstein, in *Psychologische Forschung,* 6, 150 f.

34. I should like to cite another striking example of this. Heinrich Embden—to whom I wish to express my warmest thanks—gave me an opportunity to observe a number of aphasia cases in the Barmbecker Hospital in Hamburg. One of the patients as a test for his understanding of written signs was shown a slip of paper on which was written the name of the firm by which he had formerly been employed. The physician had written the firm name as "X and Y," though the exact title was "X, Y, and Co." The patient, who could hardly speak spontaneously, shook his head after reading the paper and indicated with gestures that something was missing at the end. But even after the missing words were added, he showed that he was not fully satisfied and indicated that something was still missing between the names X and Y. It took some time before the physicians observing him discovered what was wrong and were able to satisfy the patient by correcting it: the comma between the two names had been omitted. Here it became clear that for the patient a circumstance which for a normal individual would have been totally irrelevant was just as important as any other feature in the total experience: instead of turning toward the meaning of the letters, he clung to the image as such. It seems to me that this case excellently elucidates the difference between what Gelb and Goldstein designate as a "mere experience of coherence" and what they call a "categorial attitude": the sensuous experience of coherence is not complete without the comma, whereas the "categorial attitude," for which the letters are mere means of representation, can and must disregard it.

35. Cf. above, pp. 158–9.

But they declined to regard language as the actual foundation of this attitude. "The facts of pathology," they emphasize,

> teach us only that name-amnesia and the absence of the categorial attitude go hand in hand, but they do not tell us which of the two is primary and which one secondary. . . . The categorial attitude and the possessions of language in its significatory function are expressions of one and the same basic attitude. Presumably neither of the two is cause or effect. It seems to us that the disturbance which gives rise to all the symptoms we find in our patients consists in an impairment of this fundamental attitude and a corresponding lapse into a more primitive attitude.[36]

And indeed, when we investigate and seek to understand the thoroughgoing connection between the structure of language and that of perception, we can discover no causalities, no relations of cause and effect. The essential is not a temporal relation of "earlier" and "later," but an objective relation of "grounding." It is in this sense that in our analysis of language we have striven to differentiate three strata, which we termed the phases of sensuous, intuitive, and purely conceptual expression.[37] This classification was not meant historically—as though we supposed that in the development of language we could single out successive stages, one embodying the purely sensuous type, the others the purely intuitive or conceptual type. That would be an absurdity, if only because the total phenomenon of language is first constituted by the whole of its structural elements, so that this whole must be regarded as present in the most primitive as well as the most highly developed language. There was no question of isolating the different factors in any substantial sense, but only of considering the changing dynamic relationship into which they entered with one another. And now we must ask to what extent this point of view by which we oriented ourselves in the world of language is applicable to the world of perception. Are we justified in speaking of an ideal stratification, such as may be demonstrated in the structure of language? Where, as is normally the case, the totality of perception is given to us in a purely static, crystallized form, already differentiated according to distinct linguistic concepts and categories, it is difficult to recognize any such stratification. But it stands out far more clearly where the linguistic schematism is

36. Gelb and Goldstein, in *Psychologische Forschung, 6,* 155 ff.
37. Cf. above, *1,* 186 ff.

relaxed and perception confronts us not in a static condition but rather in a kind of fluid equilibrium. Speech pathology is of methodological value for us, because it presents such cases of unstable balance. Speech pathologists themselves became aware at an early date that the degeneration of functions in aphasic disorders does not occur arbitrarily but seems to follow a definite plan. Jackson pointed out that the changes affect the "higher" far more than the "lower" language—that they relate less to the emotional side of speech than to its purely "intellectual" aspect.[38] It has been generally observed that aphasiacs who no longer know how to use certain words and sentences with a purely objective representative intent can employ them correctly as soon as they take on a different meaning within speech as a whole, as soon as they become an expression of affectivity and emotion.[39] And at the same time a kind of shift occurs in the sphere of representation as well: abstract terms are replaced by concrete ones; universal terms give way to particular and individual ones; and thereby speech as a whole, compared to that of the normal individual, takes on a predominantly sensuous coloration. Linguistic concepts expressing a purely intellectual relation and determination give way to others which bear a kind of "sensitive" stamp; picturesque terms become prevalent; while all purely significatory expression is more or less inhibited.[40] In the world of perception this stands out particularly in connection with terms for color. Like the amnesic aphasiac of Goldstein and Gelb, many of Head's patients had lost all command of the universal color names—the names for red and yellow, blue and green—although their sense of color was quite intact. These universal terms were replaced by the names for certain object colors: the patients indicated the color of a model set before them by saying that it looked "like grass," "like blood," etc. And frequently even these object colors gave way to others referring to the use of the color. One of Head's patients, for example, replaced the word "black," which he could not find, by the word "dead," because black is the color of mourning for the dead.[41] Here we discern a definite direction of the perceptual con-

38. Cf. above, pp. 212–3.

39. A wide variety of examples are given in Head. Cf., for example, his Vol. *1*, pp. 38 f., 348 f.

40. Examples for this prevalence of the "picturesque" term are frequent in Head's case histories: cf. case history No. 17, in *2*, 252; see also *1*, 200.

41. See Head's case history No. 2, in *2*, esp. 25, 28; another of Head's patients (No. 22), who had been a house painter before his illness, could not name the color samples set before him but described exactly from what materials and by what method each color could be produced; Cf. Head, *1*, 527; *2*, 337.

sciousness, running parallel to a basic trend in the linguistic consciousness. For language did not arrive immediately at the fixation of universal color terms but began with concrete, sensuous designations. The languages of primitive peoples seem for the most part to have no other means of distinguishing color qualities than to name the objects in which they are to be found.[42] We can appreciate phenomena of this sort only if we constantly bear in mind that the process by which the different factors of perception obtain a purely representative character, by which they are filled with a definite representative meaning, is inconclusive—that we can never establish its beginning or end but can only pick out diverse stages from it and order them in accordance with a certain ideal gradation. When we attempt to do this, we find that the articulation of perception and that of language are similar in all their principal features. The study of linguistic concept formation shows us again and again that language begins with concrete designations and thence gradually opens a path to purely relational and abstract, significatory expression. All primitive linguistic concept formation differs from the higher stages chiefly in its diversity, in the extraordinarily rich particularization of concepts which do not as yet crystallize around fixed points of unity. One and the same natural species or one and the same process—such as sitting or walking, eating or drinking, striking or breaking—is designated by a separate word, according to the special accompanying and modifying circumstances. In attempting to characterize this process, we wrote:

If we conceive of the whole intuitive world as a uniform plane, from which certain figures are singled out and differentiated from their surroundings by the act of appellation, this process of specification at first affects only a particular, narrowly limited portion of the plane. . . . each word has only its own relatively limited radius of action, beyond which its force does not extend. Language still lacks the means of combining several different spheres of signification into a new linguistic whole designated by a unitary form. The power of configuration and differentiation inherent in each single word begins to operate, but soon exhausts itself, and then a new sphere of intuition must be opened up by a new and independent impulse. The summa-

42. In the Ewe language, as Diedrich Westerman points out in his *Wörterbuch der Ewe-Sprache* (Berlin, 1903), p. 78, the word "unripe lemon" designates green, while the word "ripe lemon" designates yellow: this presents an exact analogy to the above-cited usage of Head's aphasiac.

tion of all these different impulses, each of which operates alone and independently, can form collective, but not truly generic unities. The totality of linguistic expression here attained is only an aggregate but not an articulated system; the power of articulation has exhausted itself in the individual appellation and is not adequate to the formation of comprehensive units.[43]

The facts of speech pathology confirm this relationship from an unexpected angle. The color world of a sufferer from color-name amnesia differs from that of the normal individual precisely in its lack of the latter's comprehensive unities. In comparison to the normal color world, there prevails throughout it a character of diversity and shifting variegation. As Goldstein and Gelb stress, a normal individual can also gain such an impression of variegated color if he simply moves over the pile of color samples with the model and takes the most passive possible attitude.

> Then we do not have the experience of a very determinate focusing on a particular color tone for example, but feel ourselves to be at the mercy of the experiences of coherence that force themselves upon us. . . . At one stroke the whole phenomenological picture changes when we begin to sort in accordance with the instructions. The pile itself, which previously struck us as a multicolored hodge-podge, now undergoes a specific differentiation: the colors belonging to the category of the model's base tone stand out against the others; those which do not belong to it become irrelevant and are simply disregarded.[44]

Thus it is through differences of significance, of relevance, that the world of perception as well as language first gains its systematic articulation. The question of whether the new form of perception comes first and that of language merely follows it—or whether conversely it is language that creates this form—need not trouble us. What is important for us is to recognize that a real separation is not possible, that the language of the senses and the pure phonetic language develop hand in hand. There is no doubt that if configurations of the perceptive or intuitive world are to be designated in language, they must first be comprehended in a determinate vision—but on the other hand this kind of vision acquires stability and permanence only by being fixated in the linguistic sound. The unities so created would at all times be exposed to destruction and dis-

43. Above, *1*, 291 f.
44. Gelb and Goldstein, in *Psychologische Forschung*, 6, 151 f.

integration if the bond of language did not hold them together. What was intended and begun by sense perception is concluded by linguistic meaning.

These considerations for the first time controvert one of the chief arguments that have been raised by the skeptics of ancient as well as modern times against language and its specific cognitive value. Over and over again it has been asserted that true reality, the reality of immediate experience, must remain closed to it, because it is not adequate to the abundance and individuality of this reality. How could a limited number of universal signs encompass and reproduce this multiplicity? What is overlooked in this argument is that the tendency toward the universal which it ascribes to language is not proper to language alone but is already grounded and contained in the form of perception. If perception did not embrace an originally symbolic element, it would offer no support and no starting point for the symbolism of language. The πρῶτον ψεῦδος of the skeptical critique of language consists precisely in making the universal begin only in the concept and word of language, whereas perception is taken as something utterly particular, individual, and punctual. When this is done, there remains of course an unbridgeable gap between the world of language, which is a world of meanings, and the world of perception, which is regarded as an aggregate of simple sensations. But the question takes on a different form once we realize that the dividing line that is here drawn between the worlds of perception and language should actually be drawn between the worlds of sensation and perception. Every conscious, articulated perception presupposes the great spiritual crisis which, according to the skeptics, begins with language. Perception is no longer purely passive, but active, no longer receptive, but selective; it is not isolated or isolating, but oriented toward a universal. Thus perception as such signifies, intends, and "says" something—and language merely takes up this first significatory function to carry it in all directions, toward realization and completion. The word of language makes explicit the representative values and meanings that are embedded in perception itself. And, on the other hand, the thoroughly individual, singular perception which sensationalism and with it the skeptical critique of language sets up as a supreme norm, an ideal of knowledge, is essentially nothing more than a pathological phenomenon—a phenomenon which occurs when perception begins to lose its anchor in language, and when its most important access to the realm of the intellectual is thereby closed.

3. The Pathology of Thing Perception

The concept of optical or tactile agnosia comprises a number of disturbances whose common characteristic is a grave impairment of the perceptual knowledge of objects. In cases of this sort the sensory discernment seems to have remained intact or in any event not to have been seriously affected. When tested for his ability to apprehend and distinguish optical and tactile qualities, the patient does not seem to differ greatly from the normal individual. He distinguishes rough and smooth, hard and soft, bright and dark, colored and colorless, but cannot make use of these data in the same way as the normal individual for the recognition of objects. If a sufferer from tactile agnosia is given an object familiar to him in daily life, he can indicate that it feels cold and smooth and heavy, but not that it is a coin, that it feels soft, warm, and light, but not that it is a piece of absorbent cotton, and so on. The disturbance, it is interesting to note, is usually limited to a particular sector of perceptual recognition, outside of which the cognitive process operates normally. Tactile agnosia, for example, usually affects only one hand: an object which the patient can designate only as hard, cold, and smooth when he holds it in his left hand is recognized and named as a watch as soon as it is put in his right hand. In general we may say that in disorders of this type the data of certain sensory spheres are still supplied to the patient, though perhaps in a modified way, but that they no longer carry an index of objectivity as they do for a normal individual.[45] The character of this disturbance is especially clear in the optical sphere, in cases of so-called "psychic blindness." For the sufferer from psychic blindness "sees": he apprehends differences of brightness and color with normal sharpness and, at least in the lighter cases, also interprets simple differences of magnitude and geometrical form correctly. Yet where he is dependent on optical data alone, he gains no knowledge of objects and of what they objectively are and signify. He consistently makes the crudest blunders: a patient on whom Lissauer reports at length once mistook an umbrella for a leafy plant and on another occasion for a pencil, and thought a bright-colored apple was

45. As far as I can see, writers disagree as to whether tactile agnosia can occur without any impairment of the sensibility of the hand. Heilbronner, in Lewandowsky, *Handbuch*, 2, 1046, sums up the findings of the most recent research by saying that in the typical cases of "tactile paralysis" a certain impairment of the sensibility can be observed, but that it is by no means proportionate to the impairment of tactile recognition. Hence the latter cannot be reduced to and adequately explained by a disorder of the sensibility.

the portrait of a lady. Often this patient seemed to recognize an object, but it soon developed that he had guessed its meaning only by some individual characteristic, some diagnostic sign, and possessed no general optical picture of it as an articulated whole. In some cases a picture was correctly identified as a representation of a certain animal, but the patient could not say which end was the head and which the tail.[46] Here we discern a common factor which links these pathological cases with those considered above, much as the individual traits and general clinical pictures may seem to differ. For here again we have a characteristic disturbance in the experience of meaning. Thus pathology leads us to a question which extends far beyond its own confines, which can be clarified and answered only by a more universal form of knowledge.

The analysis of the objective consciousness is one of the fundamental preoccupations of modern philosophy. No less a thinker than Kant regarded it as the most important task of all theoretical philosophy. In his famous letter of 1772 to Markus Herz that contains in germ the whole "critique of reason," he formulates the question of how the "representation" is related to the "object as the key to the whole mystery of the metaphysics that has hitherto been concealed from itself." But Kant's predecessors, too, had been by no means unaware of this problem; they all regarded it as radical and unremittingly brought new means to bear on its solution. Much as these attempted solutions varied, there is still an inner coherence among them; it became more and more apparent that the distinction between them was basically one of method. Two different solutions were possible in principle, two sorts of answer to which all these attempts harked back. On the one hand, it is reason from which an elucidation of the problem is expected and demanded; on the other hand, it is experience. On the one side it is a rationalistic, on the other an empiricist, theory that is expected to close up the gap separating mere representation from the object to which it points. In the first case a purely logical function is held to strike a bridge between the two factors; in the second the desired link is assigned to the faculty of the imagination. The representation takes its objective value and meaning either from a purely intellectual process that attaches to it or from an associative process connecting it with others of its kind. Either a deduction—most particularly a deduction of the cause from the effect—is expected to lead across to the realm of objectivity and

46. H. Lissauer, "Ein Fall von Seelenblindheit nebst einem Beitrage zur Theorie derselben," *Archiv für Psychiatrie und Nervenkrankheiten*, 21 (1890), 239.

in a sense to conquer it; or the object itself seems ultimately to be nothing other than an aggregate of sensuous particulars linked together according to definite rules.

The basic fault of both these persistent contentions in the history of epistemology as well as psychology is this: in the endeavor to arrive at an explanation of the objective consciousness one is always compelled to transpose and arbitrarily modify the pure content of this consciousness in some way. In the end, neither theory captures the pure phenomenon itself; in both cases it is forced into compliance with the theoretical presuppositions. The fact that in a particular perceptual experience an object is "represented"; that in this experience as given here and now, a thing which is neither given nor present is "made visible": this fact is not brought closer to our understanding by any number of sense impressions amalgamated with each other, or by the methods of discursive thought, of theoretical inference and deduction and going beyond what is immediately given. Far from providing an explanation, both attempted solutions merely neglect the matter of fact. Neither the bond of mere association nor the seemingly tighter and stricter bond of the syllogism proves strong enough to constitute the absolutely unique form of combination that is the relation of the representation to its object. Here, rather, there lies another fundamental and original relation, namely a symbolic relation which as such belongs to an entirely different plane from all those relations between empirical objects, between real things. Instead of reducing this symbolic relation to thinglike determinations, we must rather recognize in it the condition which makes it possible to posit such determinations. The representation is not related to the object as effect to cause, or as the image to its prototype; rather, its relation to the object is analogous to that of the means of representation to the represented content, of the sign to the meaning expressed in it. We have designated as symbolic pregnance the relation in consequence of which a sensuous thing embraces a meaning and represents it for consciousness: this pregnance can be reduced neither to merely reproductive processes nor to mediated intellectual processes—it must ultimately be recognized as an independent and autonomous determination, without which neither an object nor a subject, neither a unity of the thing nor a unity of the self would be given to us.[47]

In pathological cases this close-knit unity is loosened or may threaten

47. Cf. above, pp. 122–4, 158–61.

to disintegrate entirely. The contents of certain sensory spheres seem somehow to lose their power of functioning as pure means of representation: their existence and facticity no longer bear any representative character or objective pregnance. This is made clear by a few characteristic examples. Lissauer's case of psychic blindness has already been mentioned. Lissauer himself, in accordance with the prevailing psychological attitude of the time—the work appeared in 1890—interpreted the case as a "pathological disturbance of the capacity for association": the patient had command of the individual sense impressions corresponding to definite physical stimuli, but an inhibition of association prevented him from combining these impressions in the correct way. Lissauer further distinguished two different forms of psychic blindness, which he termed "apperceptive" and "associative." In the apperceptive form—in philosophical usage we should call it "perceptual"—sense perception itself is affected; in the associative form, perception is intact, the quality of the optical impressions is unchanged, but the association between the optical perceptual content and the other components of the corresponding concept is broken off. In this latter case the patients perceive but do not understand what they have perceived: they possess the various optical qualities but cannot effect the transition from them to other groups of qualities, which first makes it possible to fit any given perception into the organization of a determinate thing. Here, then, theoretically speaking, we have an attempt to explain the act of "understanding" by breaking it down into a mere sum of impressions, a regulated sequence of sensuous images. And this view was amplified by the physiological notion of a lesion of the optical "mnemonic field" or of the associative fibers connecting this field with the optical center of perception.[48] In a monograph entitled *Über Seelenblindheit,* appearing in 1914, Von Stauffenberg distinguished two basic forms of the disorder, which in their combinations, he believed, covered the known clinical cases: the one was "a disturbance in the central elaboration of crude optical impressions, as a result of which the finer forms can no longer be produced, or at most inadequately; in the other, there is a general impairment of the imaginative faculty which eliminates or impedes the ecphorization of old stimuli complexes, with the consequence that the more or less incomplete optic-formal elements no longer set up a companion vibration in these old complexes."[49]

48. Cf. Lissauer, pp. 249 ff.
49. Wilhelm von Stauffenberg, *Über Seelenblindheit* (Wiesbaden, 1914).

This explanation once again subjects the clinical observations to a very definite interpretation that is essentially in keeping with certain fundamental physiological views on brain processes and the channels of communication between the various centers. Over against efforts of this sort the work of Goldstein and Gelb which first appeared in 1918 meant above all a new methodological approach—quite aside from the fact that it was based on hitherto unobserved clinical phenomena. For the two authors started from the assumption that before one can venture a physiological explanation of a pathological picture, a phenomenological analysis must be carried out in every detail; the observer must ask himself: what is the actual nature of the change that has come over the patient, of his pathological experience? This question must be answered first, independently of all hypotheses regarding the seat of the ailment or its causes.

This demand, which had already been raised in principle by Jackson, was now carried through in connection with a case whose facts presented considerable difficulties. The patient's optical recognition had been gravely impaired, so that by purely optical means he was unable to recognize even the simplest forms. He could grasp the meaning neither of geometrical plane figures nor of forms composed of discontinuous elements, such as a square indicated by its four corners. "What the patient sees optically," write Goldstein and Gelb in summing up the results of their investigation, "lacks a specific and characteristic structure. His impressions are not firmly formed like those of a normal person; they lack, for example, the characteristic stamp of the square, triangle, straight line, curve, etc. He has 'spots' in which he can only apprehend optically such crude qualities as height and breadth and their relation to one another." [50]

The patient's optical recognition of objects was, as we have said, gravely impaired. But the remarkable circumstance was this: the patient performed certain operations which at first sight were scarcely to be expected in a disturbance of this sort. He adjusted himself extremely well to his environment and his behavior in practical life did not deviate materially from the norm. Before the shot in the head which was the cause of his ailment, he had been a miner. After his wound had healed and his general condition had improved, he was able to learn a new trade, which he soon

<hr>

50. Gelb and Goldstein, "Zur Psychologie des optischen Wahrnehmungs- und Erkennungsvorgangs," first pub. in *Zeitschrift für die gesamte Neurologie und Psychiatrie, 41* (1918); rep. in *Psychologische Analysen hirnpathologischer Fälle, 1.* In the following the quotations are from the book publication.

mastered without difficulty. He could describe the content of colored pictures quite accurately, and when solid objects were shown him he had little trouble in naming them; as a rule he recognized familiar, everyday objects at once. What was even more striking, he could draw these objects with considerable precision, and he could also read, though somewhat more slowly than is normal. The explanation for this anomaly was found only when detailed observation, into the particulars of which we cannot enter here, showed that the patient did not perform these operations on the basis of his optical experience but in an entirely different way. He succeeded in recognizing flat pictures and solid objects, in reading written and printed letters, only when it was possible for him to accompany what was presented to his optical perception with certain movements. He had, as it were, to participate in writing what he read, that is to say, he would form the letters by following their outlines, which appeared to him only as colored spots, with peculiar movements of his head. It was through the kinesthetic impressions thus gained that he differentiated the letters and finally the word pictures as a whole. But if he were prevented from making such movements, if for example his head were held still, he was no longer able to recognize a letter or a simple geometrical figure such as a circle or rectangle. Nevertheless, his sensations of light and color were intact or so little modified that their impairment could be regarded as irrelevant to optical recognition. "The patient sees colored and colorless spots distributed in a certain way through his field of vision. He also, it may be presumed, sees whether a certain spot is higher or lower, to the right or left of another, whether it is thin or thick, large or small, short or long, nearer or farther than another, but no more: all together, the spots arouse a chaotic impression and not, as in the normal individual, the impression of a specifically formed whole." [51] Thus the patient's optical experiences offered only isolated fragments of meaning, which could no longer combine to form a meaningful whole, a unity of significatory pregnance. In normal perception every particular aspect is always related to a comprehensive context, an ordered and articulated totality of aspects, and draws its interpretation and meaning from this relation. The cases of optical and tactile agnosia show us a kind of breakdown in this continuity. Whereas normally all particular perceptions stand in a kind of ideal unity of meaning, through which they are held together, very much as the meaning of a sentence embraces the particular interpretations of its

51. Ibid., pp. 128 f.

separate words and contains them as factors in itself—in these cases of agnosia they seem to break apart. More and more the continuum of signification dissolves into a series of mere points. It is not the particular sensory phenomenon as such but the syntactical organization of these phenomena that seems to be dislocated; we seem to have before us a kind of "agrammatism" of perception analogous to what we can observe in so-called agrammatical speech disturbances.[52]

Thus considered, this case of psychic blindness—greatly as the general clinical picture differs from that of the case of color-name amnesia also described by Gelb and Goldstein—falls into the same theoretical line and can be embraced in a common perspective. In the case of color-name amnesia, the particular color experiences subsisted in themselves but were no longer oriented toward certain favored points in the color series and could no longer represent these points. In the agnostic phenomena we also have such disturbances of the representative function of perception. The perception remains flat, as it were; it is no longer determined and directed toward a dimension of depth, an object.[53] And an unbiased study of the clinical facts shows unmistakably that what takes place here is more than a mere inhibition of association. Gelb and Goldstein state emphatically that the facts cannot without violence be squeezed into the schema of association psychology, and actually run counter to any such explanation. The notion of a disturbance of discursive thinking, of the power of judgment and inference, is no more helpful. If Gelb and Goldstein's sufferer from psychic blindness showed certain disturbances of the intelligence, they lay in an entirely different sphere: he was deficient not only in optical space but also in numerical space: he was unable to arrange numbers according to their pure positional value, their "greater" and "smaller," and consequently could not reckon with them meaningfully.[54] On the other hand, most of his processes of purely formal judgment and inference operated correctly. In my own frequent conversations with him, I was always surprised at the clarity and sharpness of his thinking, the aptness and formal soundness of his inferences. And it was precisely this highly developed activity of discursive "reasoning" that enabled him in many cases to compensate almost entirely for his gravely impaired power of optical representation and memory, so that for practical purposes it scarcely

52. Cf. Pick, *Die agrammatischen Sprachstörungen*, *1*.
53. Cf. above, pp. 225–7.
54. Cf. below, Sec. 4 of this Chap.

made itself felt. For though he could not immediately recognize any object on the strength of its optical phenomenon, he used what sparse and indefinite optical data remained to him as pointers from which he indirectly derived the meaning of this. Of course these pointers did not have the power of immediate actualization—that is, inherent in any true, symbolically pregnant perception: they served, one might say, as signals but not as symbols. From the relatively few spatial forms he was able to apprehend—determinations such as "wide below and narrow on top," or "evenly broad and narrow"—he could gain certain pointers on which he based an assumption as to the nature of the object or picture before him. But closer investigation always showed that these cases did not present a true perceptual recognition, but only a guess as to the nature of the object. It can have been no more than guesswork of this sort when Lissauer's patient once recognized a portrait of Bismarck but was then unable to say where the eyes, ears, and cap were. And in the case of Gelb and Goldstein's sufferer from psychic blindness, the meticulous records that were kept with regard to his manner of recognizing objects clearly show the specific difference between true perceptual pregnance and any merely discursive knowledge of objects, based on "pointers." Pregnant perception "has" the object in the sense that the object is physically present to it in one of its aspects; knowledge makes an inference "toward" the object from a definite characteristic. In symbolic perception we have a "unity of view" by virtue of which the diverse aspects appear as different perspectives of an object which in them is intuitively intended as such; in knowledge, perception must grope its way slowly and cautiously from one manifestation to another in order to arrive ultimately at the meaning of what has been perceived. This is also expressed characteristically in the modality of perceptive judgment: for pregnant perception always leads to an assertive statement, while discursive perception usually stops at a problematic one. The former contains in itself an intuition of the whole—the latter leads, under the most favorable circumstances, to a correct combination of distinguishing features: the former is symbolically meaningful, the latter is only symptomatically indicative.[55] This difference is well illus-

55. The difference between the "representative pregnance" that characterizes the normal recognition of objects and the groping "discursively combining" method employed by the patient struck me forcefully every time I had occasion to see and speak with him. For a full understanding of the specific factor here at work one must read the records kept by Gelb and Goldstein. A brief, characteristic sample from these records gives one a good idea of the patient's general approach to his environment and his manner of "recognizing"

trated by the difference between reading letters and merely spelling them out. Goldstein and Gelb wrote of their patient: "He could correctly indicate the form of cardboard figures, such as a rectangle, disc, oval, and rhombus, by feeling them. He arrived at the correct conclusions by recognizing the details (angles, straight lines, edges, bends, etc.) in the manner described above and from them inferring the whole; he had no simultaneous picture of the objects." This fragmentary nature of experience seems to be common to agnostic disturbances and certain aphasic disorders. Certain aphasiacs seem actually to have a feeling of this fragmentation: they complain that in listening to spoken words or reading a book they understood the particulars, but that these particulars did not join together quickly enough or correctly. "With me it's all in bits," said one of Head's patients. "I have to jump like a man who jumps from one thing to the next; I can see them, but I can't express." [56] It could scarcely be stated more clearly that every impairment of the representative character of perception or of the significatory character of the word affects the continuity of experience in some way, that the patient's world threatens to go to pieces. We cannot help being reminded of Plato, who replies to Protagoras' sensationalist theory of perception, which breaks down perception into punctual particulars, by saying that it would be a sad state of affairs if diverse perceptions stood side by side in us like wooden horses, instead of all being composed into one idea (εἰς μίαν τινὰ ἰδέαν). For Plato it is this unity of the idea as a unity of vision that first constitutes the unity of the soul. [57] The optical-

---

familiar objects. In the course of a walk in the park, various objects and happenings are pointed out to the patient.

(1) (Man sweeping at a distance of about 50 paces.) The patient says spontaneously: "That man is sweeping, I know it, I see him every day." (What do you see?) "A long line, then something down below, sometimes here, sometimes there." On this occasion he relates spontaneously how he distinguishes people from cars on the street. People are all alike: narrow and long, cars are wide; you notice that at once, much thicker.

(6) (Lamp post with a large rock beside it.) Patient reflects at length, then says: "Lamp post." According to his account, he had seen a long black line with something wide on top; afterward he also said: "The thing on top is transparent and has four bars." He identified the rock as an "elevation"; "or it might be earth" (Gelb and Goldstein, *Psychologische Analysen*, p. 108).

56. Statement made by Head's Patient No. 2, a very intelligent young officer. See Head, 2, 32. Another patient (No. 8) reports: "I tried working out jigsaw puzzles, but I was very bad at them. I could see the bits, but I could not see any relation between them. I could not get the general idea" (Head, 2, 113).

57. Plato, *Theaetetus*, 184D.

agnostic disorders are disturbances not so much of sight as of this kind of vision.[58] In them consequently—as the sharpest observers in this field have repeatedly stressed—it is not only individual traits of the world picture that are distorted or obscured, but rather the picture itself that is changed as a whole: it takes on a different general form, because its structure and the spiritual principle according to which it is built up have been modified.

4. Space, Time, and Number

The disorders grouped under the head of optical agnosia, as clinical observation shows, seem almost always to involve serious pathological changes in the sense of space and in spatial perception. The ability to localize sensory stimuli is usually very much reduced; the patient's idea of his own body and of the relative position of its parts becomes extremely defective. One psychic blindness patient could not, with his eyes shut, orient himself in regard to the position of his head or any other part of his body. If one of his limbs was placed in a certain position, if, for example, his right arm was raised sideways into a horizontal position, he could not *immediately* make any statement regarding the posture of the arm, although by an arduous detour, by executing certain pendulum-like movements of his whole body, he could ultimately come to certain conclusions about the arm's position. Here again the general conclusion had to be drawn from particular operations by a kind of spelling-out process. Nor did the patient have any immediate feeling in regard to the general position of his body in space; for example, he could not state with certainty whether he was standing or was stretched out on a sofa horizontally, or was at an angle of 45°. As to passive movements of his limbs—that is, movements effected by others—he could say nothing about

58. One of the patients of Gelb and Goldstein—unlike the sufferer from psychic blindness—could call up good visual images but they were decidedly fragmentary. "He could . . . only actualize separate pieces, parts of an object, but these were sometimes very clear. It mattered little whether the object was large or small; the essential was whether the object was poor or rich in detail. If the latter were the case, he could only inwardly imagine the object in fragments, successively, part for part, and, as he himself spontaneously said, the moment he had one part clear, the others fell away." When asked, for example, how a lion looked, this patient answered: "Brown, the head is large and has a mane. . . . But when I'm at the head I've lost the legs" (p. 122). An analogous case is reported by Head. One of his patients is quoted as saying: "I can get the meaning of a sentence if it's an isolated sentence, but I can't get all the words. I can't get the middle of the paragraph, I have to go back and start from the proceeding full-stop again" (*Brain*, 43, 114).

their direction or extent except by the indirect method we have mentioned. And as long as the patient had his eyes shut, all voluntary movements were very difficult for him: when asked to move a particular part of his body, he was at first completely at a loss. However, he succeeded relatively well in performing certain movements of daily life, which he executed more or less automatically: for example, he could take a match from a box and light a candle with it relatively quickly. From all this it is evident that the patient could still, chiefly by means of certain kinesthetic movements, more or less find his way in space, that in certain definite situations his behavior in regard to space was appropriate but that his representation of space as a whole was gravely impaired. Gelb and Goldstein believed that when his eyes were shut, the patient possessed no spatial representations at all.[59]

Here again the pathology of perception confirms one of the most important conclusions of the pure phenomenology of space. For over and over again the difference between the space of mere activity and purely representative space has compelled the attention of the phenomenologist.[60] In the one, space signifies a mere field of action; in the other, it means an ideal structure of lines. And the mode of orientation is specifically different in the two cases: in the one, it results from certain practiced motor mechanisms, in the other, from a free survey which embraces the totality of possible directions in space and places them in a determinate relation to one another. "Above" and "below," "right" and "left," etc. are not designated solely by certain bodily feelings which provide them with a qualitative index, a certain sensuous token; rather, they represent a form of spatial *relation* which is connected with other relations in a systematic total plan. Within this total system the starting point and zero point can be freely chosen and shifted at will. The various fundamental directions can have no absolute, but only a relative value: they are not fixated once and for all, but can vary according to the point of view. Hence this space is no longer a rigid vessel which embraces things and events like a hard substantial shell but is rather an ideal sum of possibilities, as Leibniz calls it. Orientation in this space presupposes an ability of consciousness to actualize these possibilities freely and to reckon with them in advance, in an intuitive and intellectual anticipation. When Goldstein, in an article on the dependence of move-

59. Gelb and Goldstein, *Psychologische Analysen,* pp. 206 ff., 226 ff.
60. Cf. above, pp. 237–9.

ments in optical processes,[61] stresses the predominantly optical nature of this space, this is doubtless true insofar as optical data provide the most important material for building it up, so that where they are seriously curtailed as in cases of optical agnosia, this building cannot be so successful as in the normal individual. But this statement is incomplete, for the characteristic form of symbolic space cannot be derived from optical impressions, which are only a single factor in its formation—of which they are indeed a necessary, but not a sufficient condition.

Clinical observation seems to confirm this conclusion, since it shows that even in cases where the patient's optical perception is not seriously affected, there may be highly characteristic changes in his spatial intuition. Some asphasiacs who orient themselves quite well by purely optical means without the help of movements, and who can distinguish the position of the objects around them on the basis of their sense of sight, are baffled when asked to perform an operation requiring a kind of transposition into schematic space. They cannot hold fast and represent what they have recognized in a drawing. They cannot make a simple sketch of their room, marking in it the situation of the objects. When they attempt to do so, they do not take the spatial relations alone into account, but add and even emphasize some detail which is irrelevant or disturbing to the pure order of space. The particular things—the table, the chairs, the windows—are concretely drawn, but the patient seeks to render all their details instead of merely marking their situation in space. This incapacity for schematism and "marking" seems to be one of the basic symptoms of aphasic as well as agnostic and apractic disorders. We shall have more to say of it in another connection.[62] Here we consider this deficiency only insofar as it throws light on the decisive difference between the space of intuition and the space of mere action and behavior. The space of intuition is not based only on the presence of certain sensory and particularly optical data, but presupposes a basic function of representation. Its localities, its "here" and "there," must be clearly differentiated, but precisely in this differentiation they must be united in a total view, a synopsis, which first provides us with the representation of space as a whole.

This process of differentiation contains within it a process of integration, and it is precisely this integration that the aphasiac is often unable to effect, even where his spatial orientation, provided it is pieced together point for point and one might say step for step, is not seriously impaired. Head reports that many of his patients could follow a route that was familiar to them, for example, the way home from the hospital, but that they could not name the streets they had to pass through or give any coherent description of the route as a whole.[63] This reminds us very much of the more elementary form of spatial intuition, not yet saturated with symbolic elements, which we find for example among primitive peoples who know every bend in a river but cannot draw a map of its course. And at the same time the aphasic disorders give us a new insight into the underlying cause of these difficulties. Many patients who are not able to draw a sketch of their room can orient themselves relatively well on such a sketch if the basic schema is already laid down. If for example the doctor prepares a sketch in which the situation of the table where the patient usually sits is indicated by a point, the patient often has no trouble indicating the position of the stove, the window, or the door on this sketch. Thus the truly difficult operation consists in knowing how to proceed in the spontaneous choice of a plane as well as the center of the coordinates. For precisely this choice unmistakably involves a constructive act. One of Head's patients expressly stated that he could not effect this operation because he could not correctly establish the "starting point, but that once it was given him everything was much easier." [64] We perceive the true nature of the difficulty when we consider how long it took science or theoretical knowledge to perform this same operation with clarity and determinacy. Theoretical physics also began with "thing space" and only gradually progressed to "systematic space"— it, too, had to conquer the concept of a system and center of coordinates by persistent intellectual effort.[65] Obviously it is one thing to apprehend the togetherness and apartness of perceptible objects, and another to con-

63. Cf. Head's case history, No. 2, in Vol. 2, p. 31: on the above, see 1, 264, 339, 393, 415 f.

64. Cf. Head's case history No. 10, in Vol. 2, p. 170: "When you asked me to do this first," said the patient who could not by himself draw a plan of his room, "I couldn't do it. I couldn't get the starting point. I knew where all the things were in the room, but I had difficulty in getting a starting point when it came to setting them down on a plan. You made me point out on the plan, and it was quite easy because you had done it."

65. Cf. my Individuum und Kosmos in der Philosophie der Renaissance, Studien der Bibliothek Warburg, 10 (Leipzig, 1927), 183 ff.

ceive of an ideal aggregate of surfaces, lines, and points embodying a schematic representation of pure positional relations. Thus patients who can execute certain movements quite correctly are often baffled when they are expected to describe these same movements—that is, to differentiate them in universal, linguistically fixated concepts. In certain aphasiacs the correct linguistic use of "above" and "below," "right" and "left" is very much impaired. Often the patient can show by means of gestures that he has a feeling for the distinction expressed in these universal spatial terms; but he cannot sufficiently understand their meaning to be able, at the doctor's request, to make a certain movement first with his right and then with the left hand.[66] In general the pathological disturbances of the spatial sense in aphasiacs point clearly to the dividing line between concrete space, which is adequate for the performance of certain actions relating to a single concrete purpose, and abstract, purely schematic, space. In grave cases of aphasia, it is true, especially in the clinical form that Head designated as "semantic aphasia," there seems also to be a disturbance of concrete orientation. The patients are no longer able to find their own way: they mistake their room in the hospital or the situation of their bed.[67] But over against these cases there are others in which one cannot speak of an actual spatial disorientation, in which the patients' behavior clearly shows that they can find their way in space, whereas closer investigation reveals that they have lost the use of certain spatial concepts and cannot properly grasp certain fundamental spatial distinctions that are familiar to normal individuals. One of these patients, whom I had occasion to see in the Neurological Institute at Frankfort,[68] had lost all understanding for direction and the size of angles. If an object was set on his table, he was unable to lay another object parallel to it. Only if the two objects were permitted to touch, could he solve the problem: he could stick the objects together, so to speak, but he could not recognize and retain directions in space. He had also lost the

66. One of Head's patients (case history No. 2) had lost the abstract use of the concepts "right" and "left" but in the course of a conversation with the doctor he was able to indicate by gestures that the way in which cars passed one another in England was different from abroad—that in England they passed one another "from left to right" and abroad "from right to left" (Head, 2, 23 f.).

67. Head's case history No. 10, in Vol. 2, pp. 170, 178. Cf. Vol. 1, pp. 264 f., 528.

68. The case has not yet been treated in the literature; in the following I must therefore draw on Goldstein's oral account of it.

characteristic sense for the size of angles: when asked which of two angles was larger or smaller, he was baffled at first but then usually said that the angle with the longer sides was the larger. Similar disorders were observed in an aphasiac on whom Van Woerkom reported at length. Here again the essential deficiency in the patient's spatial sense seems to have been that he could not conceive a fixed axis in space and use it as a starting point for spatial distinctions. When, for example, the doctor sat across the table from him and placed a ruler between himself and the patient, the patient could not put down a coin on the doctor's side or his own side of the ruler: he did not grasp the difference between the two sides. Or, when the ruler was placed in a certain position, he was not able to lay down a second ruler in the same direction; instead of placing his ruler at some distance from the other and parallel to it, he moved the two together and in spite of all efforts to explain the aim of the problem finally placed one on top of the other. Van Woerkom sums up the nature of his disorder by saying that all the purely perceptive functions were unimpaired, since by means of his senses of sight and touch the patient was able to recognize the shapes and outlines of things and handle them correctly; that the feeling of direction as such had not suffered, since when the patient was blindfolded and his name was called, he always moved in the direction of the call; but that he had lost all power of spatial projection.

The patient who can execute movements in their simplest form (as reactive movements in response to certain outward stimuli) is not able to evoke the principle of motion in the higher intellectual forms, that is, in projective acts. He cannot draw the main lines of orientation (to the right, to the left, upward, downward), nor place one stick parallel to another. This disturbance also affects his body: he has lost the schema (the imaginative notion) of his body and though he can localize his sense perceptions, he cannot project them.[69]

Here, as we see, pathology is forced to make a distinction which empirical psychology long misunderstood and denied, but to which we have been led over and over again in establishing our general theoretical foundations: in Kantian terms, pathologists have found it necessary to dis-

69. W. van Woerkom, "Sur la notion de l'espace (le sens géométrique), sur la notion du temps et du nombre," *Revue neurologique, 35* (1919), 113–19.

tinguish between the image as "a product of the empirical faculty of the productive imagination" and the schema of sensuous concepts as a "monogram of the pure imagination a priori." [70]

Yet as early a thinker as Kant did not limit this "faculty" of schematism to spatial intuition but related it above all to the concepts of number and of time. And again pathological cases show very strikingly that there is indeed a close connection between the three. Van Woerkom's patient showed the same characteristic disturbance in the form of his temporal intuition and in his understanding of certain numerical problems as he did in his grasp of spatial relations. For example, he could recite the days of the week and the months of the year, but when given the name of a day or month, he could not correctly designate the day or month preceding or following it. He was also unable to count a concrete quantity of things, although he knew the correct order of the numerals. Instead of progressing from one thing to another, he frequently went back to one that had already been counted; and when in his counting he had arrived at a certain number, let us say "three," he had no notion that in this word he possessed a designation for the magnitude of the quantity, for its cardinal number. If two rows of sticks, one of four, the other of five, were placed before him and he was asked which of the two contained more sticks, the patient pointed to each stick in the second row and counted correctly to five, but then became confused, pointed again to the last stick counted and said "six." Often he would go back to another, already counted member of the first row, or slip over into the second row, still counting in a loud voice. Every attempt to teach him the purpose of the problem remained as fruitless as the efforts to make him lay down one stick parallel to another.[71] And even where the aphasiac seems more or less capable of mere counting the most elementary arithmetical operations, whether written or oral, create insuperable difficulties.[72] Head reports that most of his patients could count properly up to ten and often beyond, but that many were no longer able to solve the simplest arithmetical problems. When, for example, two numbers of three digits were written one under the other and the patient was asked to add them, he did not take the numbers in their total value but added the digits singly.

70. See above, p. 134.

71. Van Woerkom, p. 115. The above-mentioned patient of Goldstein showed exactly the same disturbance of his understanding of numbers: he could count in series, but he could not compare two given numbers as to their magnitude.

72. Cf. the material compiled by Moutier, *L'Aphasie de Broca*, pp. 214 ff.

If he was supposed to add 864 and 256, he would successively perform the operations $4+6$, $6+5$, $8+2$, merely setting the results side by side, and even in this he often made mistakes.[73] Mistakes were especially frequent when the sum of two numbers amounted to more than ten, so that the patient could not simply write down the net result but had to carry in his head a determinate number of units before adding them in the next column. And often in written addition and subtraction the patients went from left to right instead of right to left; or in subtraction they would subtract the upper from the lower number.

For a better understanding of the feature by which all these clinical observations are related, it will be profitable to look back at the universal conditions of the process of enumeration and calculation and seek to differentiate the particular phases of this process according to their involvement and their degree of basic difficulty. The counting of a concrete quantity requires on the one hand an act of discretion and on the other hand an act of ordering. The individual elements of the quantity must be kept sharply apart and at the same time unequivocally correlated with the members of the natural number series. This form of discretion in itself involves an act of reflection, which is first completed in and through language and which is necessarily affected in every serious impairment of the function of speech. According to the Pythagoreans, the essence of number is defined by the fact that it introduces the first intellectual limitation into the limitlessness of perception. The same may be said of language. The two are allies, as it were, in this intellectual operation and only together can they effect it with true sharpness and clarity.

Despite its shaky foundations and the weighty arguments raised against it by such outstanding mathematicians as Frege, the mathematical nominalism which regards numbers as mere signs nevertheless embodies the sound idea that for any adequate representation of the meaning of pure numerical concepts the support of language is indispensable. Only when specified in the word can the apartness of elements that is posited and demanded in the concept of number be fixated. When the power of language fails, when numerical terms can still be recited by rote as a motor sequence of sounds but can no longer be understood as meaningful signs, the sharp distinctions in the apprehension of quantity itself are effaced; its individual members are no longer set off sharply against one another and begin to run together. And to this

73. Cf. Head's case histories Nos. 7, 15, 19.

lack of distinction is linked an analogous deficiency in the seemingly contrary but actually correlative act of unity formation. Where the quantity no longer stands before us as a sharply articulated multiplicity, it cannot be strictly apprehended as a unity, as a whole built up of parts. Even though thought may succeed in running through it in successive synthesis and in actualizing its elements singly, nevertheless, after the process is concluded, all these particulars are not composed into one proposition. What remains is a simple succession and there is no synopsis of this succession into one concept, the concept of the magnitude of a quantity. But even if this formation of the many and the one, the parts and the whole, succeeds relatively well where it is a question of enumerating concrete quantities, the simplest act of arithmetical reckoning still calls for new and difficult intellectual operations. For every such act requires not only that the number be posited as this or that one, as a determination within a series, but at the same time that this positing of unities can be freely varied. It not only requires correlation with the numerical series as a fixed schema; this schema despite its fixity must be regarded as mobile.

The nature of the union of the two seemingly contrary requirements and the way in which it is achieved, are shown by every elementary example in addition or subtraction. Essentially, to find the sum 7 and 5, or the difference between them, means nothing more than to count five steps forward from 7 or five steps backward. Thus the decisive factor is that the number 7, although retaining its position in the original series, is taken in a new meaning, as the starting point of a new series where it assumes the role of zero. Every number in the original series can thus be made into the starting point of a new series. Now the beginning is no longer an absolute beginning, but a relative one: it is not given but must be posited in each case according to the conditions of the problem.[74] Thus the difficulty presents a perfect analogy to the difficulty we have seen in the perception of space: it consists in the free positing and free removal of a center of coordinates, and also in the transition between systems based on different centers. The fundamental unities must not only be fixated, but precisely in this fixation must be kept mobile, so that it remains possible to change from one to the other. In our example, the number seven must retain its meaning as seven and at the same time

74. In regard to the "relativization of zero" as the foundation of the elementary arithmetical operations of addition and subtraction, cf. Paul G. Natorp, *Die logischen Grundlagen der exakten Wissenschaften* (Leipzig and Berlin, 1910), pp. 131 ff.

assume the meaning of zero: it must be able to function as zero. As we see, all this requires a complex involvement of genuinely symbolic operations; and accordingly we need not be surprised at the aphasiac's failures in this sphere. For even where he has at his command the numerical series as a rigid series, he can never use it except in this rigid order. To grasp the significance of a given number, its position within the general system, he must start from one and grope his way to it. When asked which of two numbers, let us say 13 or 25, is the larger, many aphasiacs, in so far as they can answer the question at all, can only do so by counting through the whole series from 1 to 25 aloud, and then determining that in this process the word 25 comes after the word 13. But by this method a true understanding for the relative magnitude of the two numbers is not achieved. For such an understanding presupposes something more: it presupposes the possibility of considering the two numbers in themselves and of referring them to zero as the common starting point of enumeration.

And it is no less characteristic that aphasiacs should become confused when, as in the written addition and subtraction examples, they are expected not only to use different figures as numerical signs, but also to distinguish the positional value of the figures. For here again we have the same difficult change of viewpoint. The same sensuous sign, let us say the sign for 2, may stand for 20 or for 200. A similar difficulty arises when the aphasiac is asked to perform any other operation requiring him to move within a numerical system composed of several unities standing in a fixed relation to one another. This is the case in regard to time when for example he is asked to indicate a certain hour of the day by setting a clock; in respect to number, when within a certain system of values, a monetary system for example, he is asked to compare coins of different denominations. For both operations Head devised testing methods which he systematically applied to all his patients. The clock test showed that even patients who could read the time correctly from a clock were unable to set a clock at a given time. Often they confused the meanings of the big and little hand and were unable to distinguish between "to" and "after" in indications such as twenty minutes to, or ten minutes after, five.[75]

75. Head's patient No. 8, when asked to set a clock at twenty minutes to six, set it at six twenty. When the mistake was pointed out to him he declared: "I can't make out the difference between *past* and *to* six." When asked to mark "a quarter to nine," he

Similarly in the use of coins, many patients were found to have retained the ability to use them correctly in daily life, but to have lost all understanding for their abstract value. In general they made no mistake as to the type and value of the coins given them as change for a larger coin when they made a purchase; but this was not because of any definite reckoning or estimation of the relative value of the coins, for frequently they were able to indicate these relative values (for example, how many pennies to a shilling) only inaccurately if at all. Thus all these disturbances of the temporal and numerical consciousness point in the same direction as we have observed in disturbances of the spatial consciousness: they seem to be essentially grounded in an inability to create fixed systems of reference for the apprehension of spatial, temporal, and numerical relations and to move freely from one to another. In regard to space, the aphasiac is unable to posit planes of coordinates and to pass from one to another: the transformation of coordinates is impossible for him.

This again points back to our earlier reflections. For if we recall the case of color-name amnesia treated above, the actual basis of the disorder seemed to be that the patient was too closely involved with his individual, momentary optical experiences to look at them from outside and refer them to certain favored points in the color series as centers. He clung, one might say, to his sensuous experiences of coherence: he could progress from one member of the color series to the next, but he could not relate two far removed color shades to one another indirectly, through the medium of definite universal color concepts. Moreover, he shifted between different "directions of attention" (between the correlation of colors according to their basic tone and according to their brightness) and could not keep the two sharply and securely apart: he did not pass consciously from one to the other, but slipped from one into the other unawares. This slipping, this inability to adhere to a definite mode of vision and, on the other hand, to make a free choice between different modes of vision, seems also to be the fundamental deficiency underlying the pathological deviations of the aphasiac's intuition of space, time and number; and it seems to provide a homogeneous basis for our understanding of them.

---

set the clock at nine o'clock and said: "I don't know from which side to approach" (2, 114).

We gain new confirmation of this view when we look back from the point we have now reached to the problems of "optical agnosia."

At first sight, to be sure, we seem to have here an entirely different state of affairs, for the "psychic blindness" case of Gelb and Goldstein showed none of the more obvious aphasic disorders. The patient expressed himself fluently and often with striking clarity—and his understanding of language seemed normal. And yet, a more thorough examination revealed certain "disturbances of the intelligence," which corresponded exactly to the observations made by Head and others in their studies of aphasiacs. He, too, had lost all true understanding of the concept of number, although he was able to reckon in a certain mechanical sense, i.e. to perform certain elementary operations in arithmetic. But he solved all these problems by reducing them to a simple counting process. He had relearned the multiplication table, which he had forgotten immediately after his injury; but when asked such questions as "How much is 5×7?" he could answer only by beginning with $1 \times 7 = 7$, $2 \times 7 = 14$, and going on until he reached 5×7. The same was true of addition. If, for example, he was asked to find the sum of $4 + 4$, he counted on the fingers of his left hand from the little finger to the pointer, and continued from the thumb of his left hand to the middle finger of his right hand. Then he folded in the ring finger and little finger and ran through the whole series of fingers again (from the little finger of his left hand to the midle finger of the right hand), until at length he arrived at the number 8. But the patient had no form of insight into the relations of number and magnitudes; he was unable to answer such a question as "Which is larger, 3 or 7?" except by the roundabout method of reciting the whole numerical series beginning with 1, and so establishing that 7 comes "after" 3. Nor had he the slightest insight into the relation between different arithmetical operations. Although in multiplying both 2×6 and 3×4, he arrived at the result 12, he could recognize no connection between the two operations but declared that they were "absolutely different." By means of his counting method, he could solve a problem such as $5 + 4 - 4$, but it was impossible to make him understand that the result could be arrived at without all this counting, since the two operations of counting four steps forward and four steps backward canceled each other out. The patient himself reported that whereas he connected a definite intuitive meaning with other words, for example, with the word "house," numerals possessed no such significance: for him they had become meaningless signs.[76]

Aside from this impediment in reckoning, careful observation revealed another, rather obscure disturbance in the patient's thinking and speech. Although at first sight they disclosed no noteworthy deviation from the norm, he was utterly unable to understand any analogy or linguistic metaphor. Here, for the most part, he showed total disorientation—he made no use of analogies and metaphors in his own thinking and speaking, and it was impossible to explain their meaning to him: he simply rejected them entirely. In every case he lacked understanding for the true *tertium comparationis*.[77] And perhaps still more remarkable was a peculiarity that could be observed in the patient's speech. Even in repeating what was said to him, he could express only "realities"—that is, he could only make statements which corresponded exactly to his own concrete sensuous experiences. Once, on a bright sunny day, I asked him to repeat after me: "It is bad, rainy weather today"; he was unable to do so. He said the first words easily and surely, but then he faltered and stopped. Nothing could induce him to complete the sentence in the form given him; each time he slipped into another wording that was in keeping with the real facts. Another psychic blindness patient whom I saw in the Frankfurt Neurological Institute had suffered a serious hemiplegia and was unable to move his right arm. He could not repeat the sentence: "I can write well with my right hand." He always replaced the wrong word "right" with the correct word "left."

At first sight there seems to be no relation between these two disorders, between the impediment in reckoning and the disturbance in the use of language, analogy, and metaphor; they seem to belong to entirely separate spheres. And yet when we look back at the results of our previous investigation, do we not find a common factor? Have we not

76. This "concrete" counting, in which the finger being counted always had to be looked at, recalls counting methods which are still in use among primitive peoples, and which have also left their deposit in their language; cf. in particular the excellent exposition of the counting methods of primitive peoples in Lucien Lévy-Bruhl, *Les Fonctions mentales dans les sociétés inférieures* (Paris, 1910). German trans. by V. Wilhelm, *Das Denken der Naturvölker* (Leipzig and Vienna, 1921), Pt. II, chap. 5. Eng. trans. by Lilian A. Clare, *How Natives Think* (New York, 1926).

77. For particulars the reader is referred to the detailed records in W. Benary, "Studien zur Untersuchung der Intelligenz bei einem Fall von Seelenblindheit," *Psychologische Forschung,* 2 (1922), 209–97.

in both cases the same impairment of symbolic behavior? We have seen the importance of symbolic behavior for arithmetical reckoning, for the meaningful handling of numbers and numerical magnitudes. In order to solve such a simple problem as $7 + 3$ or $7 - 3$ not mechanically but with understanding, one must consider the natural number series in two ways. It is used at the same time as an enumerating series and as an enumerated series. In every such calculation, the numerical series repeatedly undergoes a kind of reflection in itself. The process of counting begins first with one, whence it unfolds the series of natural numbers in a fixed and determinate order. But it does not stop here, for at every point in this series the same operation can and must begin again. When I construct the sum of $7 + 3$, this means that the beginning of the natural number series is moved seven points and that a new enumeration begins at the new starting point thus gained. Now zero corresponds to the former 7, 1 to the former 8, etc.—and the solution of the problem consists simply in the insight that the 10, or in subtraction the 4, of the first series corresponds to the 3 of the second series. To express it schematically, we have here beside the base series (*a*) two derived series (*b* and *c*) which are correlated with it in a definite and unequivocal way:

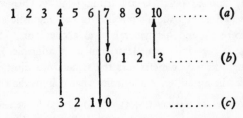

In any operation of addition or subtraction, a transition must be effected from the base series to one of these derived series and back again (as indicated by the arrows of our diagram). But it is precisely this placing of the same numerical value in different series that seems impossible for the patient. In order to perform the operation not mechanically but meaningfully, he would have to begin a new counting, either forward or backward from 7, in other words to regard 7 as zero, 8 or 6 as 1, etc. This regarding of 7 as zero (while at the same time keeping it in mind as 7) is a difficult task, a task of pure representation. The 7 must remain what it is, its relation to the original zero must be retained; but in the course of the addition the 7 must also represent and stand for the original zero (and in the course of other operations for any other desired number). While continuing to be 7, it can nevertheless function as zero, 1, or 2.[78]

It is these diverse functions of one and the same number that the patient could not understand: it was impossible for him to orient himself simultaneously toward different points and in different directions. This we have already seen in the case of color-name amnesia, where the patient was unable to regard a particular, concretely given color phenomenon as this particular phenomenon while at the same time considering it in respect to its base tone or brightness, and to differentiate these directions of regard clearly and sharply from one another. Similarly the psychic blindness patient cannot understand that one may start a new numerical series with the number seven, thus treating this number as zero. "If the patient was given the problem of counting on from 7 and prevented from actually counting softly beginning with 1, he could not do so. He admitted that he became confused, because he had no point of support."[79]

As we see, this corresponds exactly—even the wording is very similar —to the situation of Head's patient who declared that he could not make a plan of his room because it was difficult or impossible for him to take an arbitrarily selected point as a starting point.[80] This shows us the connection between the patient's inability to use linguistic analogies and metaphors correctly and his general psychic condition. The operation required here is the same, or at least similar in principle. For a correct understanding and use of metaphors the same word must, precisely, be taken in different meanings. Aside from what it immediately and sensu-

78. Let us represent the problems $(7 + 3)$ $(6 + 3)$ $(5 + 3)$ in the form of the above diagram

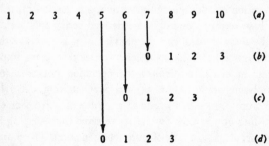

The number 7 of series (a) functions as zero in series (b), as 1 in series (c), as 2 in series (d), etc.

79. Benary, p. 217.

80. See above, p. 245, n. 64.

ously actualizes it has another mediated and transferred meaning: the understanding of the metaphor depends on one's ability to place oneself now in one, now in another meaning. And again it is this spontaneous change of viewpoint that has become difficult or impossible for the patient. He clings to what is present and sensuously demonstrable and cannot replace it at will with something else that is not present. His language follows the same fundamental tendency: he can form a sentence when he has solid support in something given, immediately experienced; without this support he is rudderless—he cannot venture out on the high seas of thought, which is a thought not only of realities but also of possibilities. Hence he can express only what is actual and present, not what is merely imagined or possible.[81] For this requires precisely that a present content be treated as though it were not present, that one disregard it and look toward another purely ideal goal.

Such articulation of one and the same element of experience with different, equally possible relations, and simultaneous orientation in and by these relations, is a basic operation essential to thinking in analogies as well as intelligent operation with numbers and numerical signs. The Greek language, it is interesting to recall, uses the word "analogy" in precisely this twofold sense, to designate certain linguistic as well as arithmetical relations. Here analogy is still the general term for the concept of the relation, of proportion in general: a linguistic usage which has been preserved down to Kant and his treatment of the "analogies of experience" in the *Critique of Pure Reason*. It expresses a basic trend of relational thinking, which is equally indispensable for apprehending the meaning of number and the meaning of relational thought formulated in language, of a linguistic metaphor. In his book *Was sind und was sollen die Zahlen?* Dedekind, a modern mathematician, reduces the whole system of natural numbers to a single basic logical function: he considers this system to be grounded in the "ability of the mind to relate things to things, to make a thing correspond to a thing, or to image a thing in a thing." [82] Such an imaging—not in an imitative but in a purely symbolic sense—is equally requisite for the appropriate and meaningful execution

81. A similar situation occurs among "primitive" peoples. In his book on the Bakairi language, Karl von den Steinen reports how difficult it was to make his native interpreter translate sentences whose content for any reason seemed senseless or impossible to him: he would shake his head and decline to render such sentences (*Die Bakaïri-Sprache*, Leipzig, 1892).

82. Richard Dedekind, *Was sind und was sollen die Zahlen?* (2d ed. Braunschweig, 1893), p. viii.

of an arithmetical operation and for the proper understanding of a linguistic analogy. In both cases a statement which had previously been understood in an absolute sense, must be transposed into a relative statement. It was in effecting such a transposition that the sufferer from psychic blindness repeatedly encountered difficulties: just as he always took the number seven as seven and never at the same time as zero, so he could understand language only when he could take everything that was said to him literally.[83]

Light is thrown on the relationship between the aphasic and agnostic disorders from still another and very different side. So far we have sought to find a common denominator in disorders of counting and reckoning, and in those which affect the understanding and use of linguistic analogies; now we shall consider other disturbances which go hand in hand with these but which, theoretically speaking, seem unrelated to them at first sight. Head devised a series of tests in which the patient was asked to repeat movements made by the doctor who sat facing him. The doctor pointed with his right hand to his right eye, with his left hand to his left eye—or in more difficult tests with his right hand to his left eye, etc.—and asked the patients to make the identical movement. In most cases mistakes and misunderstandings resulted: instead of making the symmetrically corresponding movements, the patient very often made movements that were merely congruous. If for example the doctor touched his left eye with his left hand, the movement as such was repeated but the patient used his right hand, which was directly opposite the doctor's right hand. But except where a deficient understanding of language prevented the patient from grasping the nature of the problem, the error vanished almost entirely as soon as the doctor, instead of sitting opposite the patient, sat beside him and had him observe in a mirror the movements he was to reproduce. Head's explanation for this was that in the latter case the patient performed a mere act of imitation; a perceived act was merely imitated, while in the former case such an imitation did not suffice, and before it could be correctly reproduced the movement had to be transposed into a linguistic formula. He could perform the action as long as it called for nothing

83. For particulars see the detailed records in Benary, pp. 259 ff. In one of these records it is shown very strikingly how by logical detours—in his discursive, groping way—the patient was gradually able to master the relational comparisons which he expressly termed difficult (p. 271).

more than a direct reproduction of a sense impression; he failed where an act of "inner speech," of "symbolic formulation" was required.[84]

We do not contradict this explanation, but we believe on the basis of our preceding theoretical investigation that we can now take a more universal view of this symbolic formulation and at the same time define it more sharply. For if we look back at these investigations, we see that the core of the difficulty lies not so much in the transposition of sense perception into words as, one might say, in transposition as such. If the patient is to repeat correctly the movements of the doctor facing him, it will not suffice to copy them mechanically; he must previously transpose their meaning so to speak. What is "right" from the doctor's point of view is "left" from his point of view, and conversely: the correct movement can be made only when this difference has been clearly apprehended and in every single case taken into account, when the action is transposed from the doctor's system of reference into that of the patient. In the present case, as in connection with arithmetical reckoning or the understanding of a metaphor, the transposition or transformation is unsuccessful.[85] Here we are not imposing an artificial interpretation on

84. Cf. Head, *1*, 157 ff., 356 ff. See, in particular, *1*, 208: "Most patients with aphasia imitated my actions extremely badly when we sat face to face, or if the order was given in the form of a picture; when, however, these movements or their pictorial representations were reflected in a mirror, they were usually performed without fail. For in the first case the words 'right' or 'left,' 'eye' or 'ear,' or some similar verbal symbol, must be silently interposed between the reception and execution of the command; but, when reflected in the glass, the movements are in many instances purely imitative and no verbalisation is necessary. It is an act of simple matching and such immediate recognition presents no greater difficulty than the choice from amongst those on the table of a familiar object laid before his sight or placed in his hand."

85. The difficulty of passing freely from one form of "orientation" to another is stressed also by Goldstein as an essential factor in aphasic disorders (*Neurologische und psychiatrische Abhandlungen aus dem Schweizer Archiv für Neurologie und Psychiatrie*, ed. C. von Monakow, Zürich, 1927): "Many of the perseverations that we so often find in aphasiacs," he writes, "and which observers so often attempt to explain or rather to explain away by an abnormal tendency to perseveration, become understandable—even as to content—once we take into account the factor of deficient orientation and particularly the impairment of the power to change orientation quickly. This accounts above all for the fact that the so-called perseveration does not appear equally in all operations and in some may not appear at all" (pp. 44 f.). I also believe that I have found confirmation of this fundamental view in an article by L. Bouman and A. A. Grünbaum which became known to me only after the above was written: "Experimentell-psychologische Untersuchungen zur Aphasie und Paraphasie," *Zeitschrift für die gesamte Neurologie und Psychiatrie*, 96 (1925), 481 ff. The patient observed by Bouman and Grünbaum was a former clerk. He could still master certain elementary rules of calculation, on the basis of which he could correctly

the clinical phenomena to make them fit into a self-contained system: the phenomena themselves point entirely in the direction of this explanation. Not infrequently the patients themselves stress this character of the disorder with surprising sharpness and aptness by comparing the difficulty of the problem before them with that of translating a text from a foreign language into their mother tongue.[86] Here it might be recalled that language itself was formed only gradually into an organ of purely relational thinking, and that this precisely was one of its highest and most difficult achievements. It, too, starts with the representation of particular concrete-intuitive determinations and develops steadily, through numerous intermediate stages, into a logical expression of relation.[87]

But the problem which concerns us here does not belong solely to the sphere of language and linguistic concept formation, nor can it be fully elucidated within this sphere. The pathology of the symbolic consciousness compels us to take a broader view of the problem, for it is mani-

---

perform certain arithmetical operations. But from the fact that he could not clearly separate the various unities employed in a calculation and keep them apart in the course of the process it was evident that he was not operating meaningfully with numbers and numerical concepts. When asked, for example, to figure out how much five pounds of apples cost if one pound costs 30 cents, the patient after some exertion arrived at the amount 150, but the "denomination" was lacking; he believed the answer to be "150 apples." Again, when asked how long he could live for 100 gulden if he spent 5 gulden a day, the patient found the strictly arithmetical result but was totally at a loss to say whether this figure referred to days, weeks, years, or, for that matter, gulden (*op. cit.*, pp. 506 f.). No less characteristic was his behavior in the presence of certain geometrical problems. A number of figures were set before him, e.g. triangles, squares, and circles, some of them inside one another or overlapping, so that various points in the enclosed surfaces belonged to several figures, while others belonged only to one. The patient could always indicate a point that belonged only to one figure; but when asked to indicate a point that was common to the triangle and square, to the triangle and circle, or to the triangle, square, and circle, he could do so only after much pondering and exertion, and remained very doubtful about the correctness of his solution (p. 485). Thus here again the main difficulty seems to lie in the need for placing one and the same "element" simultaneously in different relational contexts, in conceiving of it as "belonging" and referring to different geometrical totalities: for this presupposes precisely the free change of vision that is inhibited in the aphasic-agnostic disorders.

86. One of Head's patients, a young officer, responded very poorly at first to the hand, eye, and ear tests. Much later, after his condition had considerably improved, he was able to perform these tests relatively well. In explaining his method he said: "I look at you and then I say 'he's got his hand on my left, therefore it's on the right.' I have to translate it, to transfer it in my mind" (case history No. 8, in Vol. 2, p. 123). Another patient explained: "I've always said it is like translating a foreign language which I know, but not very well; it's like translating from French into English" (case history No. 17, in Vol. 2, p. 257).

87. Cf. above, *1*, 206 ff., 219 ff., 229 ff., 309 ff.

fested in certain disturbances of action no less than in disorders of speech and perceptual knowledge. Side by side with aphasia and optical and tactile agnosia stands apraxia, which we shall now attempt to draw into the framework of our general problem. This we shall do by asking whether and to what extent the apractic disorders also give us a deeper insight into the structural laws of action, in much the same way as the agnostic and aphasic disorders helped us to grasp more sharply the theoretical structure and peculiar articulation of the perceptual world.

5. The Pathological Disturbances of Action

It was early observed that the speech disorders subsumed under the head of aphasia and the disturbances of perceptual knowledge which have been designated as optical or tactile agnosia are linked to definite disturbances of action. And these observations repeatedly brought forth the opinion that in the symptom complex of aphasia and agnosia it could not be any strictly defined particular functions that were damaged or destroyed, but that the intelligence in general must be in some way impaired. If with Pierre Marie one should take this intellectual deterioration as the cause of aphasia, it would seem understandable and even necessary that this deterioration should make itself felt not only in the patient's understanding and use of language but also in the field of action, of practical behavior. And indeed, observation often showed grave disturbances in this sphere. When asked to do so, the patients might perform a certain simple action correctly; but they were not able to perform correctly a complex act composed of such partial actions. At the doctor's bidding a patient could, for example, show his tongue, close his eyes, or hold out his hand—but his performance became uncertain and he made mistakes as soon as he was asked to perform several such acts at once.[88] Disturbances of this sort stand out even more clearly when the patient is confronted with a choice, when in a concrete situation he must choose between "yes" or "no." For example, he may be able to give a proper answer to questions such as "Do you wish to go out?" or "Do you wish to stay home?" if the questions are presented singly, but he does not understand the question when asked whether he wishes one *or* the other.

One of Head's tests consisted in setting on the table before the patient a number of objects of daily use—a knife, a pair of scissors, a key, which he was asked to compare with others that were shown him or placed in his

88. Cf. Head's case history No. 9, in Vol. 2, p. 139.

hand. Many patients could do this without error as long as it was merely a question of indicating the duplicate on the table of an object presented to their sight or touch; but they became confused when two or more objects were held out to them at once. The act of comparison between the model and the duplicate was then performed hesitantly or faultily if at all.[89] In other cases a patient could perform a certain action automatically but not produce it voluntarily; for example, he could stick out his tongue to moisten his lips when the doctor asked him to, but he could not do so without such a cause.[90] In all this it seems unmistakable that the aphasiac's disorder alters the form not only of his thinking and perception but also of his will and voluntary action. We are encouraged to ask whether this transformation does not also point in a very definite direction which may be observed in detail, and whether to do so may not help us toward further insights into the theoretical problem that is central to our investigation.

But before putting the question in this general form, we must define the clinical picture of apraxia more closely and examine its subdivisions. It was Hugo Liepmann who in the course of his fundamental researches in this field first attempted a sharp theoretical definition which would cover the diversity of clinical symptoms. Liepmann takes the general concept of apraxia to include every disturbance in voluntary movements pursuing a definite purpose, provided this disturbance is conditioned neither by lack of mobility in the pertinent part of the body nor by deficient perception of the objects toward which the action is directed. In apraxia the mobility of the limbs is retained, the impairment is due neither to paralysis nor paresis, and the patient's mistakes in action are not brought about by a failure to recognize objects. In cases of faulty recognition such as we find in optical or tactile agnosia, we should not speak of an apraxia in the strict sense. "When a man uses an object wrongly because he mistakes it, his action, his πράττειν, is obviously quite correct in itself but only turned about because of faulty presuppositions. The action itself is entirely in keeping with the presuppositions. A man who mistakes a toothbrush for a cigar acts quite correctly in attempting to smoke it.[91]

89. Cf. case history No. 1, in Head, Vol. 2, p. 6.
90. Cases of this sort are mentioned by Jackson in *Brain*, *38*, 37, 104.
91. Liepmann, *Über Störungen des Handelns bei Gehirnkranken*, p. 10; on the following cf. his *Das Krankheitsbild der Apraxia*. For purposes of orientation we have also drawn on the comprehensive reports of Karl von Kleist, "Der Gang und der gegenwärtige Stand

Starting from this general definition of apraxia, Liepmann goes on to differentiate two basic forms of the disorder. The performance of an action may be impeded by an error of will, faulty planning, an insufficient "idea"; or else the plan may be adequate but when the will attempts to carry out the plan, some part of the body may fail to obey its command. Liepmann distinguishes the two varieties as ideational and motor apraxia. In ideational apraxia the intention of the total action and the ability to break down this intention into separate steps have been affected in some way. In order that the parts of the action may intermesh, in order that they may join to form a whole action, they must be intended and performed in a certain order: it is this process that seems to be disturbed in ideational apraxia. The components of a complex action are confused or misplaced in point of time. If, for example, a cigar and a match box are put into the patient's hand, he opens the box and presses it as though it were a cigar cutter; then, instead of taking out a match, he rubs the cigar on the side of the match box.[92] In this case the movements that are made do actually belong to the desired action complex, but are performed neither with the requisite completeness nor in the proper order.

In motor apraxia, on the other hand, there is no pathological change in the plan of action; in general the plan is correctly conceived, yet it cannot be translated properly into action. The part of the body affected by the ailment refuses, as it were, to obey the will: it no longer takes the direction that the will prescribes. This is most strikingly evident where a single member is excluded from the general organization of will and performance, while the other members of the body have preserved their ability to carry out purposive movements. In the famous case of Liepmann's cabinet minister (*Regierungsrat*), which has become a kind of classic in the literature on aphasia, the simplest movements went wrong when the patient attempted to perform them with his right hand, but he could, in general, perform the same actions faultlessly with his left hand. Here it cannot be said that the patient's ego—he himself as a unitary subject—lacked the proper understanding of the problem or was deficient in any other psychological or intellectual requirements for its

der Apraxieforschung," *Ergebnisse der Neurologie und Psychiatrie, 1* (1911), sec. 2; and K. Goldstein, "Über Apraxie," *Medizinische Klinik* (1911).

92. K. Bonhoeffer, in *Archiv für Psychiatrie, 37* (1903), quoted from Liepmann, *Über Störungen des Handelns*, pp. 22 f.

solution. With his left hand, for example, the patient could remove the stopper from a bottle and pour himself a glass of water, so demonstrating that intellectually he mastered all the movements which enter into this action sequence and knew how to arrange them in the proper order. Hence his ideational process was entirely normal; his inability to perform the same operation with his right hand proves that the trouble was not in the ideational process but in its transference to the motor mechanism of the right hand. Here we have a localized, rather than a general psychic disturbance. Such a case shows that the sensomotor apparatus of a single member can split off from the total psychological process.[93] The patients themselves seem to sense this peculiar splitting off. One left-side apractic observed by Heilbronner declared that he could not trust his left hand: his right hand would stay where he put it, but he could never prevent his left hand from occasionally performing certain movements that he had not intended. The patient never referred to the actions of this hand as his own; he felt that they did not belong to him in any way, and spoke of them in the third person.[94]

There can be little doubt that pathological disorders of this kind are of crucial significance for the entire psychology of action, that they open up a deeper insight into the central problems of the "will" and of voluntary motion. But in connection with our own fundamental inquiry, we must for the present disregard these phenomena of moter or kinetic apraxia and turn toward what Liepmann subsumes under the head of "ideational" apraxia. For here theory and practice are close together: here we find that the form of action is inseparably bound up with the form of thought and consciousness.

Now the general question arises: what is the mode, the tendency and direction, of consciousness that characterizes our voluntary acts and specifically distinguishes them from actions of other kinds? Can we demonstrate here the difference that has been confirmed in the previous investigation: the difference between an immediate and a mediated form of action, between a presentative and a representative attitude of mind, between a clinging to the sense impression and to sensuous objects, and an attitude which detaches itself from this bond and passes into a symbolic, ideal sphere?

93. Liepmann, *Über Störungen des Handelns*, pp. 36 ff.
94. Heilbronner, in Lewandowsky, *Handbuch*, 2, 1044.

It has been widely observed that the clinical picture of apractic as of related disorders is extremely variable if the observer contents himself with listing the individual operations of which the patient is capable. It soon becomes evident that here as in the description of aphasic disorders no sharp and unequivocal result can be achieved in this way. We have seen that the nature of speech disorders cannot be derived from the patient's mere use of words and that under certain conditions a patient may have command of a word that is denied him under other conditions. The same is true of action and the performance of definite movements. In some situations these movements are executed with difficulty and in others they cannot be executed at all. One patient cannot ordinarily make a threatening gesture, but the moment he becomes angry, he can do so perfectly. Another patient cannot, when merely asked to, raise his hand in oath, but he places it in the correct position as soon as the words of the oath are recited to him.

To express differences of this kind a distinction has been made between concrete and abstract movements. By abstract movements are meant isolated, voluntary movements made on demand; by concrete movements, those movements of everyday life which are made more or less automatically in certain situations. One of Goldstein's patients, whose power to perform any abstract movements whatsoever was gravely impaired, was not seriously hampered by this in his everyday operations: he washed himself alone, he shaved himself, he arranged all his belongings, he could open a faucet, turn on the light, etc. But he could execute these movements successfully only when he had the real object at hand. If he was asked to knock on the door, he could do so as long as the door was within reach; but the movement, though begun, was broken off at once if he was withdrawn one step from the door and so prevented from actually touching it with his finger. Similarly, the patient could hammer in a nail if, hammer in hand, he stood directly by the wall; but as soon as the nail was taken away from him and he was asked merely to *indicate* the motion of hammering, he stopped still, or at best made an indefinite movement that differed unmistakably from the one he had previously executed. If a scrap of paper was laid on the table, he could blow it away when asked to, but once the paper was taken away, he could not make the same motion of blowing. The same was true of the purely expressive movements: the patient was not able to laugh on request, but he laughed perfectly well when a comical remark was made in the course of the conversation.[95] Even where the desired movement is performed for patients of this kind, they are seldom able to imitate it, or else in the imitation the patient does not repeat the movement as a whole but merely attempts to build it up piece by piece from the separate parts he has grasped. Even where the imitation seems to be relatively successful in its outward effect, the general *type* of the action is changed.

If one drew a circle for the patient, he kept looking back and forth between the doctor who made the movements and his own hand. It could be seen plainly that he imitated the movement part for part. What he drew was really no circle, but only short lines which he joined together and which produced an effect somewhat similar to a circle, but actually represented a many-sided polygon. How far he was from drawing a circle was plainly shown by the fact that a sudden change in the movements he was watching would make him abruptly transform the circular shape he had begun into an ellipse or any other figure.[96]

Here we have attempted to give only a few main characteristic features of the pathological picture of apraxia. Let us pause at this point to ask how these features may be evaluated from the theoretical standpoint. Here again, as in connection with aphasic disorders, the loss of certain mnemonic images was formerly regarded as the actual cause of the altered behavior. Just as disturbances in the understanding of words or the use of writing were attributed to the loss of phonetic images or graphic images, these changes in action were ascribed in the main to impairment of memory, of the ability to reawaken previous impressions, particularly impressions in the kinesthetic sphere. Under the influence of Wernicke, who sought to apply this explanation to the whole field of asymbolic disorders, Liepmann at first found the basic condition for the pathological changes in such an impairment of memory: "The memory for certain acquired forms of motion is extinguished or is at least difficult to awaken, so that, in the handling of objects, for example, it emerges only with the help of the optical-tactile-kinesthetic impressions flowing from the objects in question." This inability to execute movements from memory

95. Cf. Goldstein's article, "Über die Abhängigkeit der Bewegungen von optischen Vorgängen," pp. 147 ff.

96. Ibid., p. 166.

—an inability that is by no means limited to expressive movements but is manifested in familiar manipulations of objects—appeared to Liepmann as the core of the apractic disorders.[97] It seems, however, that in the long run this theory, which essentially reduced apraxia to an impairment of the purely reproductive processes, did not satisfy Liepmann: he sought to refine and modify it.[98] The first objection to it is to be found in a fact which he himself recognized and stressed:[99] deficiencies very similar to those found in "free" movement occur also in the mere imitation of movements. If the patient is unable to perform a certain movement merely because he cannot arouse its mnemonic image, should he not at least be able to repeat it when someone else performs it for him and so recalls it directly to his memory? And in other respects as well, this type of explanation seems inadequate to the subtler features of apraxia observed by Liepmann himself; it does not seem to account precisely for the specific character of the apractic anomalies. When Goldstein, in the Frankfurt Neurological Institute, demonstrated to me the case of his patient "Sch.," of whom we have spoken above, what struck me particularly was that after performing a movement perfectly correctly, the patient would interrupt it at once if his objective substrate was taken away from him. Standing by the door, he had just correctly executed the movement of knocking with his left hand; but he stopped as soon as he was removed even one step from the door: the upraised arm remained in midair as though spellbound, and nothing the doctor could say could impel him to continue the movement. Are we really to suppose that in this case the mnemonic image of the knocking movement which he had performed only a few seconds before had vanished from the patient's memory? Or was the deficient kinesthetic memory of blowing to blame if the patient who had blown the scrap of paper from the table a moment before could not repeat his movement when asked to do so without the object to blow, as it were, into the void? So peculiar a phenomenon obviously requires another and deeper explanation than can be provided

97. Cf. Hugo K. Liepmann, *Die linke Hemisphäre und das Handeln* (1905); rep. in *Drei Aufsätze aus dem Apraxiegebiet* (Berlin, 1908), pp. 26 ff., 33.

98. In a lecture which Liepmann delivered in January, 1908, to the annual congress of alienists in Frankfort on the Main, it seems to me that he breaks once and for all with the theory attributing apraxia to mere disturbances of "reproduction": here he himself stresses that apraxia cannot *in general* be defined as a loss of memories or as the consequence of a disturbance of the intelligence in line with Pierre Marie's theory (*Über die Funktion des Balkens beim Handeln*, rep. in *Drei Aufsätze aus dem Apraxiegebiet*, p. 66).

99. Cf. Liepmann, *Drei Aufsätze*, pp. 27 ff.

by a mere return to mechanisms of association. Goldstein attempted to give such an explanation by pointing out the fundamental dependency of all movements and especially of all abstract, voluntary actions on optical processes. By the example of his two psychic blindness cases, he was able to show how every impairment of optical recognition and optical representation tends to be linked with grave impairment of the ability to move and act. The ultimate reason for this, he believed, was that every voluntary movement we perform occurs through a definite medium and against a certain background. "We do not effect our movements in an 'empty' space, unrelated to them, but in a space that stands in a very definite relation to them; actually movement and background are factors in a unitary whole, that can be separated only artificially." Because the psychic blindness patient whose optical-spatial experience is severely damaged can no longer create for himself an optically grounded medium for his movements, these movements as a whole are bound to be gravely hampered, or at least to show a form very different from those of the normal individual. Even when the general effect seems relatively normal, they are actually built on an entirely different foundation, for their background has shifted from the optical to the kinesthetic sphere.

And for Goldstein the important difference between the optical and the kinesthetic spheres is that the latter is much less susceptible of free variation. The optical background is independent of my body and its movements; optically represented space does not move with the changes in the position of my body; it is outside, fixed; in it we can execute our movements in different ways. But kinesthetic space is much more intimately bound up with our body. A kinesthetically grounded surface always stands in a definite relation to my body; the kinesthetic image of writing contains from the outset a writing surface in a very definite relation to my body, whereas I adjust my body to the optically grounded writing surface. Experiments with one of Goldstein's pychic blindness patients showed that his space was always oriented toward the actual position of his body. "Above" always meant to him the direction toward his head, "below" the direction toward his feet; if he was lying on a sofa, he could not correctly indicate the upper and lower parts of the room. All the movements he made in writing or drawing were in approximately the same plane, which was not quite vertical but tilted a little backwards. He had learned this position as the most comfortable one in which to write when standing up; but he could not simply transpose this plane, i.e. write on another plane. If asked to do so, he had to exert a great effort and create a new plane. . . . When asked, for example, to draw a circle on a horizontal plane, he pressed the upper part of both arms tight against his body, held his forearms at right angles, and made pendulum-like movements of his trunk; in this way his forearms moved in an approximately horizontal position. Then on the basis of his kinesthetic sensations he identified the plane on which his forearms were moving as the horizontal, and performed the writing movement in it as described. Since the kinesthetic plane is firmly anchored, a change in the position of the body as a whole inevitably changed the plane that was most comfortable for him. This we could demonstrate very simply by letting him write first in a standing and then in a recumbent position. The plane in which he wrote always took the same position relative to his body; the two planes were then of course at right angles to each other, and the two body positions as well.[100]

Here again we have a very characteristic relationship that is extremely significant for our purposes; for it is precisely this total or partial inability to transpose, to vary freely the system of reference, that we have encountered in the most diverse operations of aphasiacs or agnostics, that seemed in fact to be a nodal point of their intellectual disorder. Time and time again we find this same inability in their arithmetical operations, in the form of their orientation in space, in their linguistic utterances. But—we must ask for this very reason—can so general a change in the patients' behavior really be adequately explained by the altered form of their optical experience? Or must we not rather seek a general cause in keeping with the general character of the disorder? To begin with, Goldstein's detailed clinical observation of his patient "Sch." shows that in performing certain movements, this patient required the help of tactile as much as optical experience. Even if he continued to look at the door, he could no longer carry out the same knocking movement once he was prevented from reaching the door, from actually touching it. The plan of action broke down not only if its optical, but also if its tactile support was taken away—if the door was hidden from his view, or if it was removed from his immediate, tangible vicinity.

100. Goldstein, "Über die Abhängigkeit der Bewegungen von optischen Vorgängen," pp. 162 ff., 169 f.

On the other hand, we have seen that the fundamental impediment in "transposition" is not found only in those patients whose optical recognition and representation are seriously impaired. We have found this difficulty in aphasiacs whose optical representation is virtually intact. In Head's hand, eye, and ear tests the cause of the faulty solutions was not any deficiency in the patients' optical experience, for as soon as the doctor stood behind them and let them watch his movements in the mirror, they could, as a rule, repeat the movements without mistake.[101] This, I believe, suggests the direction in which action is modified in aphasia as well as optical agnosia. The same Goldstein patient whose apractic disorder we have just considered also showed what seemed at first sight to be a highly remarkable speech impediment. He had some difficulty in repeating sentences said by others, but the degree of difficulty depended on the *content* of what was said. He repeated correctly: "I can write well with my left hand"; but he could not utter the same sentence if the word "right" were substituted for "left." For then he would have been saying something "unreal," since his one-sided paralysis prevented him from moving his right hand.[102]

Is it not the same limitation, the same attachment to the object and to the concrete, objective position of things that is disclosed in the patient's whole behavior? In every case he could act only toward a real, sensuously given and present object and not toward a merely represented object. As long as he had this support in the real object, he performed operations which differed hardly at all from those of the normal individual. He possessed an adequate orientation in space: in his usual environment he oriented himself perfectly well; he could move around the hospital by himself, find the door to his room without difficulty, etc. But all these capabilities forsook him when, instead of moving in a fixed thing-space, he was expected to move in a space of free fantasy. He hammered the nail into the wall properly, but this movement just performed was suddenly inhibited as soon as its sensuous, concrete foundation was removed. He could not repeat the gesture by hammering into the void. Heilbronner reports that many of his patients, when asked to perform movements without object—the gesture of counting money, opening a door, etc.—first paused to reflect and then went through the strangest probing motions with their fingers and contortions of the joints, making all sorts

101. See above, p. 259, n. 84.
102. Cf. above, p. 254.

of "grimaces of the extremities," accompanied by evident anger and dissatisfaction. One of these patients, a pharmacist, who was asked to perform the movement of rolling pills with his apractic left hand, called the test a regular teaser.[103] Another patient was able to handle all the objects of everyday life correctly as long as they were given him in the customary way and under the usual circumstances but failed as soon as they were given him under unaccustomed circumstances. At mealtime in the dining room he handled spoon, glass, etc. like any normal individual, while at other times he made perfectly senseless motions with these same objects.[104]

Here the various actions have preserved their meaning within very definite concrete situations but at the same time have become fused, as it were, with those situations; they cannot be freed and performed independently. What impedes this free use seems to be not so much the patient's inability to create a sensuous, optical space as the medium and background for his movements, as lack of any free play for them. For this latter is a product of the "productive imagination": it demands an ability to interchange present and nonpresent, the real and the possible. A normal individual can perform the movement of hammering a nail just as well into a merely imagined wall as into a real wall, because in free activity he can vary the elements of the sensuously given; by thought he can exchange something present here and now with something else that is not present, and substitute the latter for the former. But as we have seen, it is precisely this form of variation, of substitution, that is seriously impeded in apractics. Their movements and actions have something stereotyped: they can only be made in fixed and customary channels and in rigid combinations. The space in which they move relatively well and securely is the restricted space in which solid things meet; it is no longer the free and broad symbolic space of representation. The patient can wind a watch if it is put into his hand, even though this requires a highly complicated movement, but he is not able to represent this movement and perform it out of this pure imagination, once its sensuous substrate is removed; once the watch is taken from his hand.[105] For this representation presupposes more than a mere thing-space: it requires a schematic space.

103. Heilbronner, in Lewandowsky, *Handbuch,* 2, 1039 f.
104. Heilbronner, "Über Asymbolie," p. 16.
105. Cf. the case of patient "Sch." in Goldstein, "Über die Abhängigkeit," p. 153.

This incapacity for schematization, for moving within an intellectual as well as a spatial schema, was also manifested repeatedly in the linguistic behavior of the patients, even when their ordinary understanding for words and sentences and their use of language in everyday life were virtually unimpaired. Here again the disturbance is scarcely perceptible as long as the patient can hold fast to the object and can progress from the designation of one concrete object to another; but it becomes apparent as soon as he is expected to substitute one object for another, to understand or make use of a linguistic analogy or metaphor.[106] This also gives a peculiar rigidity to his manner of speaking—it lacks the free play that first gives language its scope and mobility and makes it come to life. In both cases—in his speech as well as his action—it is precisely his power of representation that quickly fails, though he continues to be relatively successful in all operations that can be accomplished by mere presentation.[107]

Accordingly, to use the terms that we have introduced above, it is not so much the mode of seeing as the form of vision that seems to be impaired in these cases, and which, once damaged, affects the whole of the plan of movement. For every free plan of movement demands a definite kind of vision—an intellectual anticipation, a pre-view into the future, into the merely possible. Sometimes an apractic seems to apprehend a certain goal correctly: but every new sensory stimulus offered him from outside can at once deflect him from his course and guide the action into a wrong direction. The idea of the goal—as Liepmann put it—is thrust

106. See above, pp. 254–7.

107. This patient's peculiar stereotype of action could be observed in his general behavior as well as in his particular actions. If, for example, he was asked to perform the motion of a military salute, he first softly repeated the request, using it as a kind of fixed formula, in response to which his right hand, as by an automatic impulse, went up to his right temple. But if his right arm was held fast and he was asked to salute with his left hand, he could after some hesitation perform the desired movement: but instead of rising to the *corresponding* place, this hand moved to the *same* place, to the right, not the left, temple. This place was fixated as the "goal" of the military salute and could not be voluntarily exchanged for another. This attachment to a fixed formula in the linguistic and motor sense appears also in cases where the patient can execute the movement of taking an oath, but can only raise his right hand when the words of the oath are actually recited. "Dans les épreuves ordinaires," writes Van Woerkom concerning the patient disclosing the characteristic disturbance in spatial understanding (see above, p. 247), "l'apraxie ne se manifeste pas: il allume une bougie, plante un clou dans une planche, fait un serment, le geste menaçant, etc. Cependant au début d'une action, il y a toujours une période latente; pour le faire marquer le geste menaçant, la réaction ne vient qu'après que je lui ai dit: Comment ferais-tu, si on t'avait volé quelque chose? Le geste du serment n'est exécuté qu'après que j'ai prononcé la formule réglementaire" (*Revue neurologique, 26,* 114).

aside by another "esthesiogenous" idea.[108] In other cases a more or less indefinite idea of a goal seems to run through a certain sequence of acts, but it is no longer apprehended sharply and clearly enough to place the whole action under one perspective and articulate it accordingly. The various phases of the action form a mere aggregate; they are still executed more or less together, but they are not interlocked in the appropriate order. A teleological structure is replaced by a mere happening; the formation by a purpose, which to each phase of action assigns its unequivocal place in the whole, its unique temporal and spatial determination, is replaced here by a mere mosaic of partial acts, which slide together now this way and now that. The result is the form of "loosened" action which Liepmann has described as "ideational apraxia." "In the voluntary operation," so early a writer as Jackson pointed out, "there is preconception; the operation is nascently done before it is actually done, there is a 'dream' of an operation as formerly doing before the operation." [109] The patient who in most cases can still perform certain actions out of the immediate requirement of the moment, cannot "dream" in this way, cannot reach forward into the future with a plan. Some patients who cannot pour themselves a glass of water when asked are able to do so when impelled by thirst.[110] In general the more directly the operation is aimed at a definite goal, the more successful it will be, whereas it deteriorates in proportion as beginning and end are separated by intermediary links which must be taken into account as such and evaluated in their significance for the action as a whole. This is strikingly shown by those of Head's patients who were unable to effect indirect shots in billiards: they could hit a ball when they aimed at it directly but could not play off the cushion or from one ball to another through the intermediary of a third.[111] For such mediated operations are always symbolic: one must tear oneself away from the presence of the real object and freely

108. Cf. Liepmann, *Über Störungen des Handelns*, pp. 27 ff.; and the examples cited there from Arnold Pick, *Studien über motorische Apraxie und ihr nahestehende Erscheinungen* (Vienna, 1905).

109. Hughlings Jackson, in *Brain*, 38 (1915), 168.

110. Liepmann, *Drei Aufsätze*, p. 15. In general Liepmann stresses (pp. 28, 34) that only in a small fraction of the cases treated by him and under very special conditions could a deficiency in the manipulation of objects be observed, that such actions were performed without important disturbances. "In at most one quarter of the cases does the disorder extend to an impairment of the ability to manipulate objects."

111. Head's case history No. 8 (Vol. 2, pp. 113, 122); No. 10 (2, 171). "A straight shot with two balls was not so bad," says the patient in this latter case, "but the third ball confused me. I seemed to think of the three functions at the same time and got muddled."

actualize an ideal aim that exists only in thought. Here lies the same reflective attitude that characterizes language and is indispensable for its development. An impairment of this attitude impedes and inhibits the use not only of language but also of every other activity which—like reading or writing—deals with the "signs" for objects and their meaning rather than with objects themselves.

And here we may observe a similar gradation: in most cases it is not reading and writing as such that appear to be affected, but certain operations within them which most particularly disclose a deviation from the norm. The more the operation requires a kind of transposition, a transition from one system to another, the more evident becomes the deviation. A text may be successfully copied if every letter can simply be reproduced, stroke for stroke; but a shift from one kind of writing to another, the change for example from printing to handwriting, is difficult or impossible.[112] Spontaneous writing may be gravely impeded, although the patient may still write relatively well from dictation. And here again there may be remarkable differences, according as the performance consists in the use of a stereotype formula or in a free act of written expression. One of Head's patients could write his own name and address correctly, but he was unable to write his mother's address, though she lived in the same house.[113] Here again the essential was not so much the content of the operation as its form; here again the criterion lies not so much in the mere performance as in what this performance means when all the attendant circumstances and conditions are taken into consideration.

But at this point we shall pause. The philosophical reader has no doubt been thinking that we have dwelled too long on our pathological cases and gone into excessive detail. And yet this method could not be avoided if we wished these cases to throw any real light on our general problem. The foremost authorities in this field, whose guidance we have followed, are agreed that in evaluating these disorders no general symptomology, no simple list of performances and deficiencies, can help us. Each case presents a new picture and demands to be understood out of its own particular center. For what is impaired is never any general "faculty"—the faculty of speech, of purposive action in reading or writing. As Head drastically formulated it, there are no such general faculties of this kind, any more than there is a general faculty of eating

112. Documented in Head, *I*, 317 ff.
113. Ibid., pp. 38, 198.

or walking.[114] Such a view in terms of substance must everywhere be replaced by a view in terms of function; it is not the loss of a faculty that we have here, but the transformation of a highly complex psychic and intellectual process. According as the change affects this or that characteristic phase of the total process, very different pathological pictures may arise, none of which need resemble the next in its concrete traits and symptoms but all of which are nevertheless linked together insofar as the change or deviation in all of them points in the same direction. We have sought to establish this general direction while laboring with the detail of particular cases as presented in the descriptions of the most thorough and precise observers; we have sought, in a manner of speaking, to reduce the aphasic, agnostic, and apractic disorders to a common denominator.

But this, in turn, does not mean that we may regard the various representative-symbolic operations that are the indispensable condition for speech, perceptual knowledge, and action as manifestations of a fundamental power or diverse activities of the symbolic faculty as such. The philosophy of symbolic forms requires no such hypostases, nor, in view of its methodological presuppositions, can it countenance them. For what it is seeking is not so much common factors in *being* as common factors in meaning. Hence we must strive to bring the teachings of pathology, which cannot be ignored, into the more universal context of the philosophy of culture. Can the pathological changes in speech and in the related symbolic achievements provide an indication of what these achievements mean for the structure and general form of culture? By way of distinguishing the behavior of persons affected by these disorders from normal categorial behavior, Gelb and Goldstein have characterized it as more primitive and closer to life. And this term "close to life" does actually apply if by "life" we mean the totality of the organic, vital functions as distinguished from the specifically spiritual functions. For what stands between these two spheres and what marks the sharp dividing line between them is precisely those spiritual configurations which may be summed up in the concept of symbolic forms.

Long before it passes into these forms, life is purposively formed in itself; it is oriented toward determinate goals. But the knowledge of these goals always implies a breach with this immediacy and immanence of life. All knowledge of the world, and all strictly spiritual action upon the

114. Ibid., pp. 143 f.

world require that the I thrust the world back from itself, that in contemplation as in action it gain a certain distance from it. Animals do not know this distance: the animal *lives* in his environment; he does not place himself over against it and so represent it. This acquisition of the world as idea is, rather, the aim and product of the symbolic forms—the result of language, myth, religion, art, and theoretical knowledge. Each of these builds up its own intelligible realm of intrinsic meaning, which stands out sharply and clearly from any merely purposive behavior within the biological sphere. But where this dividing line begins once again to be blurred—where, above all, consciousness lacks the secure guidance of language, or no longer obtains it with the same definiteness as before, perceptual knowledge and action also take on a different character. A surprising light is thrown on many of the symptoms of aphasia, agnosia, and apraxia, when instead of measuring them by the standard of normal behavior we choose a norm drawn from a relatively simpler biological stratum. An apractic uses his spoon or cup properly if it is given him during a meal but fails to recognize them or use them appropriately at other times. The behavior of animals often provides striking analogies to this phenomenon. We recall the spider which immediately attacks a gnat or fly that flies into its net in the usual way but runs away from it if the encounter takes place under unusual circumstances. The sand wasp does not carry its prey directly into its hole but first drops it to inspect the hole, and repeats the visit as many as thirty or forty times if this customary action sequence is interrupted by outside intervention.[115]

Here again we have an analogy to the rigid, stereotype action sequences that may be observed in apractics. In both cases the representation as well as the action is forced into fixed channels from which both the insect and the apractic are unable to break loose in order to represent independently either the individual characteristics of an object or the separate phases of an action. Action is subject to an impulse from behind that drives it into the future; it is not determined by the ideal anticipation of this future. When we follow the course of *objective* culture, this determination, this progress into the ideal makes itself felt in two ways. The form of linguistic thinking and the form of instrument thinking seem here to be closely linked and interdependent. In language as in the instrument, man gains a new fundamental trend of mediated behavior that is specific

115. Cf. Volkelt, *Über die Vorstellungen der Tiere*, pp. 19, 29 (see above, pp. 152–4).

and pecular to him. In his representation of the world and in his action upon it he now becomes free from the compulsion of the sensory drive and the immediate need. The direct grasp gives way to new and different types of acquisition, of theoretical and practical domination: man has entered the path from physical to conceptual "grasping" [from *Greifen* to *Begreifen*].[116]

The aphasiac or apractic seems to have been thrust one step backward along this path which mankind had to open up by slow, steady endeavor. Everything that is purely mediated has in some way become. unintelligible to him; everything that is not tangible, not directly present, evades both his thinking and his will. Even though he can still apprehend and in general correctly handle what is "real," concretely present, and momentarily necessary, he lacks the spiritual view into the distance, the vision of what is not before his eyes, of the merely possible. Pathological behavior has in a sense lost the power of the intellectual impulse which forever drives the human spirit beyond the sphere of what is immediately perceived and desired.[117] But precisely in this step backward it throws a new light on the general movement of the spirit and the inner law of its structure. The process of spiritualization, the process of the world's "symbolization," discloses its value and meaning where it no longer operates free and unhindered, but must struggle and make its way against obstacles. In this sense the pathology of speech and action gives us a standard by which to measure the distance separating the organic world and the world of human culture, the sphere of life and the sphere of the objective spirit.

116. See above, *1*, 180 ff.

117. How difficult it is for even the highest animals to break through this circle is shown most instructively by Koehler's observations of anthropoid apes. Among these animals we find a certain primitive "use of tools." Here again the use of the tool becomes most difficult where its manipulation requires some sort of "detour"—where, for example, the animal, instead of drawing a fruit directly toward himself, must first move it away and then bring it toward him around an obstacle. Such an operation represents a kind of reversal of "natural," biological behavior, and this precisely is what seems to create the greatest difficulties for apractics, agnostics, etc. A patient of Gelb and Goldstein, who was supposed to group a number of objects according to their relation to one another, declined to place a corkscrew with a bottle in which the cork was loose, on the ground that the bottle was "already open." In such a case the "possible" purpose of the corkscrew is not regarded as a principle of correlation—the decision is based only on the real, concrete, particular case and its special requirements. Cf. W. Koehler, "Komplextheorie und Gestalttheorie," *Psychologische Forschung*, 6 (1925), 380 ff.

PART III

The Function of Signification and the Building Up of Scientific Knowledge

Chapter 1

Toward a Theory of the Concept

1

IF WE WISH to apply a single, over-all name to the field in which our investigation has moved so far, we may call it the realm of the "natural world concept." This realm disclosed throughout a very definite theoretical structure, an intellectual formation and articulation—but on the other hand the universal rules of this formation seemed so deeply and inextricably shot through with sensuous particulars that they could only be described in conjunction with them. At this stage of our investigation what theoretical form itself is and wherein consist its specific significance and validity could only be shown through its product. Its principles remained, one might say, fused with this product—they were not determined *in abstracto,* detached and in themselves, but could be demonstrated only through a certain order of objects, of objective structures of intuition. Here, accordingly, reflection and reconstructive analysis were not yet directed toward the function of form as such, but were directed toward one of its particular achievements. In forming a determinate image of objectivity, in producing it, so to speak, out of itself, thought nevertheless remains confined within this very image which originates from its own depths—knowledge of itself can come to it only through this medium, through the mediation of an objective knowledge. Its regard is directed forward toward the reality of things, not backward toward itself and its own achievement. In this way it conquers the world of the "thou" and the world of the "it"—and both appear to it at first as unquestionable, utterly unproblematic certainties. In the form of the simple expressive experience or of the perceptual experience, the I apprehends the existence of subjects and objects outside us—and lives in the concrete intuition of this existence. How this intuition itself is possible is not

281

asked here and need not be asked; it stands for itself and bears witness to itself, requiring no support or confirmation in anything else.

But this absolute trust in the reality of things begins to be shaken as soon as the problem of truth enters upon the scene. The moment man ceases merely to live in and with reality and demands a knowledge of this reality, he moves into a new and fundamentally different relation to it. At first, to be sure, the question of truth seems to apply only to particular parts and not to the whole of reality. Within this whole, different strata of validity begin to be marked off, reality seems to separate sharply from appearance. But it lies in the very nature of the problem of truth that once it arises it never comes to rest. The concept of truth conceals an immanent dialectic that drives it inexorably forward, forever extending its limits—it does not content itself with questioning particular contents of the natural world concept, but assails its substance, its general form. All those witnesses to reality that have hitherto been taken as absolutely sure and reliable—sensation, representation, intuition—are now haled before a new forum. This forum of the concept and pure thought is not established merely with the emergence of strictly philosophical reflection; it belongs to the beginnings of every scientific view of the world. For even here, thought no longer contents itself with simply translating into its own language what is given in perception or intuition, but subjects it to a characteristic change of form, a spiritual recasting. The primary task of the scientific concept seems in fact to be simply this, to set up a rule of determination which must be confirmed in the intuitive sphere. But precisely because and insofar as this rule is to have validity for the world of intuition, it is no longer a mere part or element of this world. Over against this world it signifies something peculiar and independent, even though this independent meaning can be manifested at first only through the matter of the intuitive world. The farther the scientific consciousness develops, the clearer this difference becomes. Now the rule of determination is no longer simply posited, but in this very positing is apprehended and understood as a universal achievement of thought. And it is this understanding that now creates a new form of insight, of spiritual perspective. With it we stand for the first time on the threshold of the actual theoretical world view. We have a classical example of this process in the genesis of Greek mathematics. For here the decisive factor is not that the basic significance of number is recognized, not that the cosmos is subjected to the law of number. This step had been taken long before the beginnings of strictly theoretical, scientific thinking. Myth had already elevated number to a universal, truly world-embracing significance; myth already knew and spoke of its dominion over the whole of being, of its demonic omnipotence.[1] The first scientific discoverers of number, the Pythagoreans, were still wholly dominated by this magical-mythical view of number. And aside from this mythical fetter, their concept of number discloses another, purely intuitive tie. Number is not conceived as an independent entity but must always be considered as the enumeration of a concrete quantity. It is bound up most particularly with spatial determinations and spatial configurations; it is originally of a geometrical as well as arithmetical nature. But as this bond loosens, as the purely logical nature of number becomes recognized, the groundwork is laid for a pure science of number. Even then, to be sure, number is not separated from intuitive reality, for it aspires to demonstrate nothing less than the fundamental law governing this reality, governing the physical cosmos. But number itself ceases to resemble a physical thing in any way or to be definable by the analogy of any empirical objects. Although it has physical existence solely through concrete things that are ordered according to it, nevertheless one must attribute to it a form of knowledge that is clearly separate from sense perception or intuition. Solely by virtue of this separation was the number of the Pythagoreans able to become a genuine expression of the truth of the sensuous world.[2]

And this relationship that emerges in the beginnings of pure theory remains a determining factor in its further development. Time and time again it becomes apparent that theory can achieve the desired closeness to reality only by placing a certain distance between itself and reality, by learning more and more to look away from it. It is through this characteristic relegation to a distance that the *configurations* within which the natural world view dwells and through which it gains its formation are transformed into strict theoretical *concepts*. What lay like undiscovered treasure within the intuitive forms is now gradually brought to light by conscious intellectual effort. The prime achievement of the concept is precisely to apprehend as such the factors on which rests the

---

1. Cf. above, 2, 140 ff.

2. Concerning this twofold position of the Pythagorean number, see my "Die Geschichte der antiken Philosophie," in Max Dessoir, ed., *Lehrbuch der Philosophie* (Berlin, 1925), *1*, 29 ff.

articulation and order of intuitive reality and to recognize their specific significance. It develops the relations which in intuitive existence are only posited implicitly, as merely concomitant; it detaches these relations and sets them forth in their pure "as suchness"—in Plato's words as an αὐτο καθ' αὐτό.

But with this transition to the realm of pure meaning, thought is confronted with an abundance of new problems and difficulties. For only now is the final break made with mere existence and its immediacy. Expression, and to an even greater extent representation, already reached out beyond this immediacy—for they did not remain within the sphere of mere presence but sprang from the basic function of signification. Yet it is within the sphere of pure meaning that this function not only increases in scope but first clearly discloses its specific direction. Now there develops a kind of detachment, of abstraction that was unknown to perception and intuition. Knowledge releases the pure relations from their involvement with the concrete and individually determined reality of things, in order to represent them purely as such in the universality of their form, in their relational character. It is not sufficient to construe being itself in the various directions of relational thinking, for knowledge also demands and creates a universal system of measurement for this procedure itself. As theoretical thinking progresses, this system is more and more firmly grounded and is made more and more inclusive. The naive relation between concept and intuition that characterizes the natural world concept is replaced by a new critical relation. For the theoretical concept in the strict sense of the word does not content itself with surveying the world of objects and simply reflecting its order. Here the comprehension, the "synopsis" of the manifold is not simply imposed upon thought by objects, but must be created by independent activities of thought, in accordance with its own norms and criteria. And whereas within the sphere of the natural world concept the activity of thought still shows a more or less sporadic character; whereas it begins now at this, now at that point from which it unfolds in different directions; here it takes on an increasingly full comprehensiveness and a strict and conscious concentration. All concept formation, regardless of the special problem with which it may start, is ultimately oriented toward one fundamental goal, toward determination of the "absolute truth." Ultimately thought seeks to fit all particular propositions, all particular conceptual structures into a unitary and all-inclusive intellectual context.

This task would not be possible if thought, in undertaking it, did not at the same time create a new organ for it. It can no longer content itself with the ready-made configurations that come to it from the world of intuition but must begin to build up a realm of symbols in full freedom, in pure spontaneous activity. It constructively draws up the schemata by which and toward which it orients the whole of *its* world. Of course these schemata cannot remain in the vacuum of sheer abstract thinking. They require a foundation and support—but this is no longer taken simply from the empirical world of things; it is created by thought. The system of relations and of conceptual significations is now provided with an aggregate of signs which is so constituted that the relationship prevailing between the various elements of the system can be surveyed and read from it. The farther thought advances, the closer this bond is drawn. And now it would actually seem to be one of the ideal goals of thought to provide every combination among the contents toward which it is directed with a corresponding combination or operation with signs. The *scientia generalis* now calls for a *characteristica generalis*. In this characteristic the work of language continues; but at the same time it enters into a new logical dimension. For the signs of the characteristic have cast off everything that is merely expressive or for that matter intuitive: they have become pure signs of signification. With this we have a new mode of objective relation that differs specifically from every kind of relation to the object that occurs in perception or empirical intuition. To apprehend the factors in this difference must be the first task of any analysis of the function of the concept. In every concept, whatever its particular character, there may be said to live and prevail a unitary will to knowledge, whose direction and trend as such must be determined and understood. Only when the nature of this universal form of the concept has been clarified, only when it has been sharply set off from the special character of perceptual and intuitive knowledge, can we progress to special investigations, advance from the function of the concept as a whole to its particular manifestations and workings.

2

The analysis of intuitive knowledge has shown us that the form of intuitive reality rests esentially on the fact that the particular factors from which it is built up do not stand by themselves, but that a peculiar relation obtains between them, a relation of being "com-posited." Nowhere in the intuitive world do we find anything isolated and detached. Even what seems to belong to a definite and particular point in space, or to a single moment in time, does not remain confined to a mere here and now. It reaches out beyond itself—it points toward the totality of the content of experience and joins with them into definite totalities of meaning. In the construction of every spatial intuition, of every apprehension of spatial forms, of every judgment as to the position, magnitude, distance of objects, the individual experiences "weave themselves into the whole." In order to be spatially determined in relation to the whole, every spatial content must be referred to and interpreted according to certain typical spatial configurations. These interpretations, as effected in the sign language of sense perception, may be regarded as primary achievements of the concept. For indeed they contain one factor that tends wholly in the direction of the concept and its truly fundamental achievement. They articulate the individual and particular into a determinate totality, and in the particular they see a representation of this totality itself. As intuitive knowledge progresses along this path, each of its particular contents gains greater power to represent the totality of the others and to make it indirectly "visible." If we take this representation as a characteristic determinant of the function of the concept as such, there can be no doubt that the worlds of perception and spatial-temporal intuition can nowhere dispense with this function. In the modern theory of perception this view was upheld primarily by Helmholtz, who made it the basis for the whole structure of his physiological optics. "If 'to understand' means to form concepts," he writes,

and if in the concept of a class of objects we sum up the like characteristics they disclose, it follows analogously that the concept of a number of phenomena which changes in time must seek to embrace what remains the same in all their stages. What remains the same without dependency on anything else through all the changes of time, we call *substance;* the unchanging relation between variable magnitudes we call *law.* It is only the latter that we perceive directly. . . . The first product of the intellectual understanding of phenomena is the *lawful.* . . . What lies within our reach is knowledge of the lawful order in the realm of the real, and this to be sure only as represented in the sign system of our sense impressions.

In this view the logical concept accomplishes nothing other than to fixate the lawful order that already lies in the phenomena themselves: to establish consciously the rule which perception follows unconsciously. In this sense Helmholtz holds, for example, that our mere intuitive idea of the stereometric form of a physical object entirely fills the role of a concept condensed from a large number of sensuous intuitive images. This concept however is not necessarily held together by determinations expressible in words such as a geometrician might construct, but only by the living idea of the law in accordance with which the manifold perspective-images of this particular physical thing follow one another. Hence the representation of an individual object must already be designated as a concept, because this representation "embraces all the possible aggregates of sensation which this object can call forth when regarded, touched, or otherwise examined from different sides."[3]

Helmholtz himself saw and stressed that this view, which places the function of the concept in the midst of the perceptual process itself, accords neither with the usual linguistic usage nor with traditional logic. The logical tradition finds the true and salient characteristic of the concept in its universality, and it regards the universal as that which is common to many. But how can such a community prevail where we are not comparing one object with others but, rather, constituting, acquiring the idea of an individual object? Yet Helmholtz would have been justified in rejecting this argument, for on closer scrutiny it contains within it a *petitio principii*. Precisely that universality which is here regarded as the necessary condition of the concept signifies not so much a secure result of logical analysis as a latent postulate to which logic as formal logic has been subordinated since its beginnings. The modern development of logic has increasingly shown the questionable nature of this very postulate. The notion that the concept must necessarily embrace the idea of a "class" and that all relations that can obtain among concepts must ultimately be reducible to a single fundamental relation of subsumption, of subordination of genera and species, has been combated from the most diverse angles by modern logicians.[4] If we abandon this view and with Kant interpret the concept as nothing other than the unity of rule by which a

3. Helmholtz, *Handbuch der physiologischen Optik*, pp. 599 ff., 948.

4. Cf. Wilhelm M. Wundt, *Logik. Eine Untersuchung der Prinzipien und der Methoden Wissenschaftlicher Forschung* (2d ed. Stuttgart, 1893–95), *1*, 99 ff. Christoph Sigwart, *Logik* (2d ed. 2 vols. Freiburg, 1889–93), *1*, 319 ff.

manifold of contents are held together and connected with one another—then it is clear that the structure of our perceptual or intuitive world cannot dispense with such a unity. For only through this unity do determinate configurations stand out within intuition itself; only through it are stable affinities created by virtue of which manifold and qualitatively different phenomena are taken as properties of one and the same object.

What is decisive here is obviously not that a common factor is detached from the phenomena and that they are subsumed under a universal idea, but that they fulfill a common function—that precisely in their thoroughgoing diversity they are oriented toward and indicate a definite goal. But the form of this indication is of course different in the sensory-intuitive world and in the world of the logical concept in the restricted sense. For the indication that is merely *employed* in perception or intuition becomes *conscious* in the concept. It is this new mode of awareness that first truly constitutes the concept as a form of pure thought. Even the contents of perception and pure intuition themselves cannot be thought as *determinate* contents without a characteristic form of determination—without a viewpoint, under which they are placed and in regard to which they are looked upon as belonging to one another. But the regard of perception or intuition rests on the elements which are compared or in some way correlated, not on the manner, the mode, of the correlation. It is with the logical concept that this mode of correlation first emerges. It first effects that reversal by which the I turns from the objects apprehended in vision, toward the manner of the seeing, the character of the vision itself. Only where this specific mode of reflection is practiced do we stand in the true realm of thought, and in its center and focus. And this is the source of the rich significance that the concept assumes within the problem of symbolic formation. For now this problem appears in a different aspect and enters into a new logical dimension.

The dividing line between intuition and concept is usually drawn so as to distinguish intuition as an immediate relation to the object from the mediated discursive relation of the concept. But intuition itself is discursive in the sense that it never stops at the particular but strives toward a totality it never achieves in any other way than by running through a manifold of elements and finally gathering them into one regard. Yet over against this form of intuitive synthesis the concept establishes a higher potency of the discursive. It does not simply follow the fixed directives provided by the similarity of phenomena or by any other intuitive relation between them—it is no ready-made path but a function of pathfinding itself. Intuition follows set paths of combination, and herein consists its pure form and schematism. The concept, however, reaches out beyond these paths in the sense that it not only knows them but also points them out; it not only travels a road that is opened and known in advance but also helps to open it.

It is of course this fundamental power of the concept that from the standpoint of a strict empiricism makes it seem to be tainted once and for all with subjectivity. This suspicion and reproach run through the whole positivist and empiricist theory of knowledge. It was the essence of Bacon's critique of conceptual thinking that it does not content itself with the reality of experience as something purely given—that, instead of solely receiving this reality, it transforms it in one way or another and so falsifies it. Thus the freedom and spontaneity of the concept are looked upon as sheerly arbitrary. But the profounder reason for this reproach is that empiricism fails to take this freedom itself in its full significance and scope but interprets it as a mere freedom of combination. In the empiricist view the concept can posit and produce no new content of knowledge; it can only transpose in various ways the simple ideas presented by sensation, and join them and separate them at will. Thus from the original data of knowledge it fashions derived phenomena which are mere products of mixture and accordingly have all the instability of such products. "Mixed modes"—so Locke formulates this fundamental view—arise wherever the understanding does not content itself with apprehending what is present in inward or outward perception but from it forms new connections which belong solely to itself. For these modes there are no prototypes, no originals either in sensation or in the world of real objects:

> But if we attentively consider these ideas I call mixed modes, we are now speaking of, we shall find their original quite different. The mind often exercises an active power in making these several combinations: for it being once furnished with simple ideas, it can put them together in several compositions, and so make variety of complex ideas, without examining whether they exist so together in nature. And hence I think it is that these ideas are called notions, as if they had their original and constant existence more in the thoughts of men than in

the reality of things . . . Every mixed mode consisting of many distinct simple ideas, it seems reasonable to inquire, "whence it has its unity, and how such a precise multitude comes to make but one idea, since that combination does not always exist together in nature?" To which I answer, it is plain it has its unity from an act of the mind combining those several simple ideas together, and considering them as one complex one, consisting of those parts; and the mark of this union, or that which is looked on generally to complete it, is one name given to that combination.[5]

This meager recognition of the concept in Locke's system of empiricism places it of course on so narrow and insecure a foundation that the very first attack will suffice to shatter its whole substance and validity. Here Berkeley proceeds more acutely and consistently when he takes back even this limited concession—when he declares the concept to be not so much an independent source of knowledge as the source of all illusion and error. If the foundation of all truth lies in simple sensory data, only mere fictions can arise as soon as this foundation is left behind. In this verdict which Berkeley pronounces upon the concept as such, concepts of every kind and of every logical rank are included—in fact it is primarily directed against the very concepts that would seem to be "most exact," those of mathematics and mathematical physics. In this view concepts taken all together are not roads to reality, to the truth and essence of things, but roads away from it; they do not sharpen the mind but blunt it to the single true reality that is given us in immediate perceptions.

Yet in this most radical rejection of the concept, we may say that from both the historical and the methodological point of view a peculiar reversal of thought is in preparation. Berkeley supposed that by his critique he had struck the concept in its root; but if we carry his critique to its conclusion, a positive factor results that is highly fruitful for the understanding and appreciation of the concept. For it is not the concept as such that Berkeley destroys; what he destroys at one stroke is rather the connection between the concept and the general idea which had hitherto been upheld by a centuries-old logical and psychological tradition. It is this that Berkeley resolutely set aside and recognized as an inner contradiction. The general idea, the image of a triangle that is not right-angled, acute-angled, or obtuse-angled but is all these at once, is an empty fiction. Yet in combating this fiction Berkeley, contrary to his own basic

5. John Locke, *An Essay Concerning Human Understanding*, Bk. II, chap. 22, secs. 2–4.

purpose, prepared the way for another and deeper view of the concept. For he, too, with all his opposition to the general idea, leaves the universality in the form of the representative function intact. A single concrete, intuitive image, a triangle with a definite magnitude of sides and angles, can despite its concrete character stand for all other triangles, can represent them for the geometrician. Thus from the intuitive idea of a triangle there arises its concept—and this does not mean that we simply obliterate certain determinations that are contained in it but that we posit them as variable. What holds together the various structures which we regard as examples of one and the same concept is not the unity of a generic image but the unity of a rule of change, on the basis of which one example can be derived from another and so on up to the totality of all possible examples. In rejecting the unity of the generic image, Berkeley does not contest the "unity of the rule." [6]

But now one must ask whether and to what extent this admitted unity can be grounded in a pure psychology of ideas. The rule remains valid, although the manner of its validity cannot be made visible in any concrete image, in any direct perception. Consequently, when Berkeley seeks some sort of intuitive substrate for it, he must have recourse to the word, the name. Yet this nominalism does not solve the problem of the concept but only moves it one step backward. For the name becomes a name only through its power to designate and signify something. To take away this function is to take away its whole character as a name and reduce it to a mere sensuous sound; but if this function is recognized, the riddle of nominal signification merely revives the whole riddle of the concept. Instead of approaching the problem of signification indirectly through the name, we must move it into the center and focus of our investigation; we must inquire into the meaning of precisely that power of representation, of "standing for," which even empiricism and the empiricist critique could not help acknowledging in the concept.

Here the most obvious method would seem to be to explore this basic relation by reducing it to a quantitative relation. The definition of the concept as the "one in the many" seems in itself to call for a quantification of this sort. This definition goes back to the very beginnings of concept thinking, to the discovery of the concept in Socratic induction and the Platonic dialectic. Ever since then it has been a classical tenet of logic and of philosophy in general. Kant, too, in distinguishing the con-

6. In regard to this positive core of Berkeley's theory of the concept, see the account of this theory in my *Erkenntnisproblem* (3d ed.), 2, 297 ff.

cept from intuition, defines it as a representation which is contained in an infinite number of different possible representations as their common characteristic, and which therefore encompasses these representations in subordination to itself.[7] And the surest if not the only way to define this characteristic, to ascertain its significance, would seem to be to effect the *discursus*, actually to run through the quantity from which the common factor is expected to stand out. We simply set the elements of this quantity side by side and by merely counting through them we shall immediately find the form of their unity; in them and through them we shall apprehend the logical bond that holds them together. A sensationalist psychology of the concept cannot but adopt this method, since for this sensationalism the unity of the concept, like the unity of the ego, breaks down into a mere bundle of ideas.

But the same reduction is demanded and favored by still another camp from what would seem to be a diametrically opposite point of view. The more logic tended toward mathematics, the more it strove to grasp the content of a concept through its extension, and ultimately to replace content by extension. For only insofar as this could be done did the aim of mathematical logic—a quantitative analysis of the qualitative factors of the concept—seem attainable. The concept seemed to be accessible to exact quantitative inquiry only if it were defined as an aggregate in the strict sense—only, that is to say, if it were taken as a class of elements forming none other than a purely collective unity. Only in this way, it was supposed, could logic take the step which natural science had taken long before, and through which it had first been raised to the rank of strict cognition. The homogenization of logic was achieved: the mutual relation and determination of concepts had been reduced to the basic rules of a calculus of classes. In this sense Schröder in particular, in his "Algebra der Logik" [below, note 9], sought to build up a pure logic of classes. Such a logic asks only whether or not classes fall within one another and considers the class as an aggregate of the elements it includes. What links these elements together is a mere *and*-relation: a relation which, according to Russell, may equally well connect a teaspoon with the number three and a chimera with four-dimensional space.[8] Yet even among mathematical logicians grave critical objections

7. Cf. *Kritik der reinen Vernunft*, 2d ed., p. 40.

8. Cf. Bertrand Russell, *Principles of Mathematics*, Cambridge, 1903; (2d ed. New York, W. W. Norton, 1938), p. 71.

were soon raised against this view of the concept. No less a logician than Frege argued in opposition to Schröder that the calculus of classes, whose fundamental relation is that of the part to the whole, must be regarded as wholly distinct from logic. "Indeed," he wrote, "I hold that the concept logically precedes its extension and regard as a fallacy any attempt to base the extension of the concept as a class not on the concept but on particular things. In this way one may arrive at a calculus of classes but not at a logic." Here the relation between mathematics and logic is seen and grounded in a fundamentally different direction than in Schröder: the connection between the two is sought not in the concept of classes but in the concept of the function, and the concept itself is essentially understood and defined as a function.[9]

The modern logic of mathematics has taken this view into account: even where it has adhered to the basic concept of the class and to the presuppositions of the calculus of classes, it has recognized, side by side with the calculus of classes, a wholly independent brand, a calculus of relations. In Russell's treatment of the principles of mathematics the concept of relation gradually achieves logical primacy over the concept of class. In the *Principles*, appearing in 1903, he wrote:

A careful analysis of mathematical reasoning shows . . . that types of relations are the true subject-matter discussed, however a bad phraseology may disguise this fact; hence the logic of relations has a more immediate bearing on mathematics than that of classes or propositions, and any theoretically correct and adequate expression of mathematical truths is only possible by its means. . . . it has always been customary to suppose relational propositions less ultimate than class-propositions (or subject-predicate propositions, with which class-propositions are habitually confounded), and this has led to a desire to treat relations as a kind of classes.[10]

Once relation has thus been recognized as the basic and essential factor in mathematical concepts and concepts in general, the attempt to explain

9. That Frege himself did not adhere strictly and consistently to his own basic view, but replaced it by a purely quantitative view of the concept, has been aptly shown by Wilhelm Burkamp in his *Begriff und Beziehung, Studien zur Grundlegung der Logik* (Leipzig, 1927), cf. esp. the fourth study, "Klasse und Zahl in der Begriffslogik." The quotation from Gottlob Frege [Friedrich Ludwig Gottlob] is to be found in his "Kritische Beleuchtung einiger Punkte in E. Schröder's Vorlesungen über die Algebra der Logik," *Archiv für systematische Philosophie*, new ser. *1* (1895), 433–56. Cf. Burkamp, p. 198.

10. Russell, *Principles*, chap. 2, sec. 27.

the content of a concept by its extension becomes untenable. Russell himself, it is true, goes on to define the concept purely as a class of elements; but in so doing he is compelled to distinguish between two definitions of classes. There are, he stresses, two ways to determine classes: one by pointing out their members one by one and connecting them as a mere aggregate, by a simple "and"—the other by stating a universal characteristic, a condition which all members of the class must fulfill. Russell sets this latter generation of the class, the "intensional," over against the former, which is explained by means of "extension." And they do not remain in such juxtaposition, for it becomes gradually clearer that the definition by intension has precedence over the definition by extension. First of all it has the advantage of greater logical universality, for it alone makes it possible to include classes embracing an infinite quantity of elements. Russell, it is true, seems at first to minimize this difference as "purely psychological." "Classes," he declares,

> may be defined either extensionally or intensionally. That is to say, we may define the kind of object which is a class, or the kind of concept which denotes a class: this is the precise meaning of the opposition of extension and intension in this connection. But although the general notion can be defined in this two-fold manner, particular classes, except when they happen to be finite, can only be defined intensionally, *i.e.* as the objects denoted by such and such concepts. I believe this distinction to be purely psychological: logically, the extensional definition appears to be equally applicable to infinite classes, but practically, if we were to attempt it, Death would cut short our laudable endeavour before it had attained its goal.[11]

But, as far as I can see, Russell's logic was not able, in its development, to sustain this equivalence. More and more, the definition by intension assumes, in this logic, not only a subjective but also an objective priority—and comes to represent not only a πρότερον πρὸς ἡμᾶς but also a genuine πρότερον τῇ φύσει. For it is evident that before one can proceed to group the elements of class and indicate them extensively by enumeration, a decision must be made as to which elements are to be regarded as belonging to the class: and this question can be answered only on the basis of a class concept in the "intensional" sense of the word. What seems to hold together the members united in the class is that they

11. Ibid., chap. 6, sec. 71.

all meet a certain condition which can be formulated in general terms. And now the aggregate itself no longer appears as a mere sum of individuals, but is defined by this very condition, whose meaning we can grasp and state by itself, without having to ask in how many individuals it is realized, or even whether it is realized in any individual at all. "When I pronounce a sentence with the grammatical subject 'all men,'" Frege had argued against Schröder, "I do not by this mean to say anything about an unknown chief in Central Africa. Thus it is absolutely false to say that in using the word 'man' I am in any way designating this chief." It is in line with the same fundamental view when Russell himself, in his *Principia Mathematica,* expressly declares that an extension is an *incomplete symbol, the use of which* takes on meaning only through its relation to an intension.[12] What holds the class together, according to the theory developed here, is the circumstance that all the members united in it are thought of as variables of a determinate propositional function: it is therefore this propositional function and not the mere idea of a quantity as a pure collective that becomes the core of the concept.

Here the propositional function as such must be strictly distinguished from any particular proposition, from a judgment in the usual logical sense. For what it primarily gives us is only a pattern for judgments but in itself is no judgment: it lacks the decisive characteristic of a judgment, since it is neither true nor false. Truth or falsity attach only to the individual judgment in which a definite predicate is related to a definite subject; whereas the propositional function contains no such definiteness but only sets up a general schema which must be filled with definite values before it can achieve the character of a particular statement. "A propositional function," Russell defines, "in fact, is an expression containing one or more undetermined constituents, such that, when values are assigned to these constituents, the expression becomes a proposition. In other words, it is a function whose values are propositions." In this sense every mathematical equation is an example of such a propositional function. Let us take the equation $x^2 - 2x - 8 = 0$. This statement is true if for the wholly indefinite value of x we substitute the two roots of the equation; for all other values it is false.[13] On the basis

12. Alfred North Whitehead and Bertrand Russell, *Principia Mathematica,* Cambridge, 1910; (2d ed. 1925), 2, 75. Cf., for greater detail, Burkamp, pp. 186 f.

13. Cf. Bertrand Russell, *Introduction to Mathematical Philosophy,* 1919; (2d ed. London and New York, Macmillan, 1920), pp. 155 f.

of these determinations we may give a general purely "intensional" definition of class. If we consider all x's so constituted that they belong to the type of a certain propositional function $\phi(x)$ and group together the values of x which prove to be "true" values for this function, we have defined a determinate class by means of the function $\phi(x)$. In this sense every propositional function yields a class, namely the class of x's constituted so that they are $\phi(x)$—and precisely this "so that" cannot be broken down into other determinations, but must be recognized as a meaning *sui generis,* a "logical indefinable." Each class becomes definable only through the statement of a propositional function which is true for the members of that class and false for all other things.[14] But with this, what logic calls a concept has by no means been broken down into a collective quantity; on the contrary, the quantity is once again grounded in the concept. Here, accordingly, pure logical calculus has led us no further: it becomes apparent that it cannot replace the pure analysis of meaning—can never do any more than state it in the strictest and simplest formula.

Here, then, mathematics may be expected to furnish an analytical clarification but no truly genetic definition of the concept; yet in another respect it seems able to help logic toward such a definition. For although, as Kant argued in his methodology of pure reason, philosophy can expect no salvation from an "imitation of the methods" of mathematics, nevertheless mathematics provides it with those contents through which the specific meaning of the pure function of the concept can most clearly be discerned and most adequately apprehended. The concept seems to stand out with full clarity only in its exact mathematical formulation: here and only here do we seem to find, written in bold letters, what it is, signifies, and achieves. I myself took this path in an earlier investigation: by the example of mathematical and mathematical-physical concepts I attempted to arrive at a universal definition of the function of the concept. Of course it can be argued that such an approach takes the part for the whole; that a truly logical and phenomenological analysis of the concept must attempt to apprehend it in the totality of its meaning, in all its achievements and phases of achievement, whereas mathematics and exact science disclose it to be sure in perfection but by that very token only at the end of its development. Must not this end, the argument runs, be-

14. Cf. Russell, *Principles,* chap. 7, secs. 80, 84; *Introduction to Mathematical Philosophy,* chap. 17, pp. 181 ff.

linked with the beginning, and must we not survey and pass through all mediate and intermediate stages if we are to arrive at an exhaustive definition of the concept?

Actually some logicians have gone so far as not only to distinguish what they called the "logical concept" from the "scientific concept" but actually to regard them in a sense as polar opposites. According to Wundt, the logical and the scientific concept form the opposite ends in the development of thought, since it begins with the logical concept and concludes every determinate line of activity with the scientific concept. The logical concept is bound by only two fundamental conditions: its content must be determined and it must stand in a logical connection with other concepts; the scientific concept presents an additional requirement: in it knowledge must have arrived at a certain, at least relative, conclusion, and it must have justified its validity on all sides and so raised itself to the level of universality.[15] Consequently, any attempt to derive the structure of the logical concept as such from that of the scientific concept seems to amount to a confusion of genus and species. And what makes it harder to escape the force of this objection is that one of the most important findings of our present inquiry is precisely that it is necessary to recognize certain types of spiritual formation which, though differing sharply in character from the form of the scientific concept, cannot dispense with intellectual determinateness.[16]

Must this insight not react on our conception of logic itself—must we not expect to find here, too, a complex and differentiated totality of forms of thought and knowledge, instead of a single unitary type of "concept as such"? Indeed, our inquiry up to now has repeatedly shown us that what we called the symbolic formation of the perceptual and intuitive world does not begin with the abstract concept, and certainly not with one of its highest expressions, the concept of exact science. In order to understand this mode of formation and its fundamental direction, we had to begin our inquiry at a much lower level—with the natural world concept. But this step backward led us to a further truth which, far from altering our previous analysis of the exact concept, confirmed it from a new angle. For we found that the extended scope we were compelled

15. Wundt, *Logik*, 2d ed., *1*, 95 ff. A similar conception has recently been put forward by Gerard Heymans, "Zur Cassirerschen Reform der Begriffslehre," and my counterremarks, both in *Kant-Studien*, *33* (1928), 109–28, 129–36.

16. Cf. my *Die Begriffsform im mythischen Denken, Studien der Bibliothek Warburg, 1* (Leipzig, 1922).

to give our problem made no change in the pure meaning which we had sought to clarify by the example of mathematics with its relational concepts. Wherever we attacked this problem, whether at the highest or lowest levels of knowledge, whether we inquired into intuition or pure thought, into linguistic or logical-mathematical concept formation—in every case we found that logical "one in many" which appeared with identical meaning in the most diverse stages of concretion. And in all these cases this "over-arching" One is not so much a unity of the genus under which the species and individuals are subsumed as a unity of the relation by which a manifold is determined as inwardly belonging together.

Outstanding mathematicians have designated this fundamental form of relation as the core of the numerical concept and hence of mathematical thinking,[17] but it is by no means limited to this realm. It is at work both in the smallest and the largest phenomena: it dominates the whole of knowledge from the simplest sensuous "remarking" and recognition up to those supreme intellectual conceptions in which thought transcends everything that is given, in which, surpassing the mere actuality of things, it establishes its free realm of the "possible." It is here, consequently, that the "concept" must be grounded and anchored. For a close logical and epistemological analysis, "to conceive" and "to relate" always prove to be correlates, genuine reciprocal concepts.[18] This correlation as such remains in force, regardless of which world concept we move in; regardless of whether we are dealing with the empirical "things" of our perceptive and intuitive world, with the hypotheses of natural science, or with the constructions of pure mathematics. Here the content of what is thought does not affect or alter the pure form of thought any more than, in Descartes' well-known metaphor, the light of the sun is changed by the various objects it illumines. For the building of a "world"—whether it is

17. Cf. Dedekind, *Was sind und was sollen die Zahlen?* (see above, p. 257).

18. This thesis I put forward and justified in detail in *Substanzbegriff und Funktionsbegriff* (Berlin, 1910). Eng. trans. by William C. and M. C. Swabey, *Substance and Function* (Chicago, 1923). It is confirmed in all essential points by the most recent investigations of the problem of the concept, contained in Burkamp's *Begriff und Beziehung*. In a penetrating critique of the theories of Schröder, Frege, and Russell, Burkamp definitely takes the step from a mere logic of classes to a pure logic of relation. For him, too, the intellectual functions of positing, identity, difference, and relation that form the basic presupposition for the form of number are the presupposition for all pure form in general: "They are the deeper foundation on which form of any kind can first be built up" (Burkamp, fourth study, sec. 86; fifth study, secs. 95 ff.).

taken as an aggregate of sensuous or logical, of real or ideal objects—is possible only in accordance with definite principles of articulation and formation. And the concept does nothing other than to separate out these formative factors and fixate them for thought. It sets up a definite direction and norm of *discursus:* it indicates the point of view under which a manifold of contents, whether belonging to the field of perception, intuition or pure thought, are apprehended and "seen together." The ultimate reason for all the logical and epistemological disputes over the nature of the concept is that it was taken not thus, as a pure viewpoint, but as a visible thing, a something that was supposed to have its home in the sensory world, side by side with it or above it.

The two parties that confronted each other in this battle of the giants have erred in the same sense: the one by striving to seize the concept as though in their hands, the other by assigning it to a suprasensory abode while still regarding it as something substantial that exists precisely in this place. It is characteristic that where Plato comes closest to a knowledge of the pure relational nature of the concept, where he deepens the original form of his theory of ideas by insistence on a κοινωνία τῶν γενῶν, he rejects both conceptions—that here, in the *Sophist,* he is driven to attack both the concept blindness of the sensationalists and materialists and the conceptual realism of the "friends of ideas."[19] But even the counter movement against this conceptual realism, the "nominalism" of the Middle Ages and modern times, is itself by no means free from the fetters it scoffs at. For where it attempts to determine the nature of the concept, it, too, is fundamentally grappling with shadows. Failing to find the concept as a thing, it makes it into a mere sound, a *flatus vocis.* But it also treats this sound, this word of language, like a kind of existence, though of a secondary nature, instead of setting off the pure function of signification in it and grounding its objective meaning precisely therein. Time and time again, materialists and spiritualists, realists and nominalists reach back into some sphere of being when they attempt to ascertain and hold fast the meaning of the concept. But right there they lose the deeper insight into the symbolic content either of language or of knowledge, for this insight is that no being is tangible or accessible except through meaning. Hence if we wish to conceive of the concept itself, we must not attempt to clutch it like an object.

At this point the inner contradiction in the sensationalist theory of

19. Cf. Plato, *Sophist,* 245E ff.

knowledge is most clearly revealed. Some idealist logicians have supposed that they could leave the world of appearance, the world of the senses, to the sensationalist view, in order the more securely to defend the intellectual world from all admixture with the sensuous and confirm it as an independent sphere subject to its own laws. Our fundamental problem, however, has led us along the opposite path from the very first: it has shown us more and more plainly that sensationalism is unable to gain a unitary and uncontradictory view even of the sensuous world. We were impelled to meet the sensationalists in a field which from time immemorial they have claimed as their own inalienable domain—to discredit their theory from the standpoint not of the idea but of the sensory phenomenon itself. For the analysis of sensory appearance showed that its very *appearing,* its presentation is impossible without an ordered and articulated system of purely representative functions. Before the aggregate of the visible could be constituted as a whole, as the totality of an intuitive cosmos, it required certain basic forms of vision which, though they may be disclosed through visible objects, cannot be confounded with them, and cannot themselves be taken as visible objects. Without the relations of unity and otherness, of similarity and dissimilarity, of identity and difference, the world of intuition can acquire no fixed form; but these relations themselves belong to the makeup of this world only to the extent that they are *conditions* for it, and not parts of it.

This relationship that disclosed itself to us in the basic and primal stratum of intuitive knowledge finds its confirmation when we go on to other and "higher" levels of thinking and understanding. Here the world of pure meaning adds nothing new in principle to the world of representation, but only unfolds what is already potentially contained in this world. On the other hand, to be sure, this progress from potency to act is the most difficult achievement of knowledge. For now knowledge must free the functions of "indication," contained in the forms of intuitive reality, from this containment and apprehend them purely as modes of functional validity. A theory of this validity is demanded: a theory of forms which on the one hand isolates the various kinds of relation that already prevail in the intuitive world and are here demonstrable *in concreto;* and on the other hand apprehends them in their mutual determinacy, their interdependence. Thus we have seen, for example, that definite theoretical norms prevail in the structure of the spatial world and that this structure is made possible only because the various spatial perceptions continuously orient themselves by certain basic forms.[20] But it is geometrical knowledge that first apprehends the law to which these forms are subject and expresses it as such with objective determinacy. Here again the theory of the concept must avoid confusing the form of determination with the contents which through it are first made determinable: it must avoid confusing the law with what is subject to it. Though brought into a thoroughgoing relation with each other, the two must remain sharply separate in their meaning. Here the symbolic language of logical calculus can come to the help of an analysis of meaning, for in a sense such a logical calculus places the intellectual distinction here involved immediately before our eyes. If we conceive of the concept as defined, not by a listing of what falls under it, but purely intensionally by the indication of a definite propositional function, this propositional function $\phi(x)$ contains two factors which are obviously dissimilar. The universal form of the function as designated by the letter ϕ stands out sharply against the values of the variable x which may enter into this function as true variables. The function determines the relation between these values, but it is not itself one of them: the ϕ of x is not homogeneous with the x series, x_1, x_2, x_3 etc. "It is to be observed," Russell stresses in his theory of the propositional function,

> that according to the theory of propositional functions here advocated, the ϕ in ϕx is not a separate and distinguishable entity: it lives in the propositions of the form ϕx, and cannot survive analysis. I am highly doubtful whether such a view does not lead to a contradiction, but it appears to be forced upon us, and it has the merit of enabling us to avoid a contradiction arising from the opposite view. If ϕ were a distinguishable entity, there would be a proposition asserting ϕ of itself, which we may denote by $\phi(\phi)$; there would also be a proposition not-$\phi(\phi)$, denying ϕ (ϕ). In this proposition we may regard ϕ as variable; we thus obtain a propositional function. The question arises: Can the assertion in this propositional function be asserted of itself? The assertion is non-assertibility of self, hence if it can be asserted of itself, it cannot, and if it cannot, it can. This contradiction is avoided by the recognition that the functional part of a propositional function is not an independent entity.[21]

20. Cf. above, pp. 155–8.
21. Russell, *Principles of Mathematics*, chap. 7, sec. 85.

In this familiar logical paradox, we once again run into a difficulty that has troubled logic from time immemorial and deeply affected the whole development of metaphysics, none other than the old problem of universals, which now confronts us in a new form. Regardless of how this problem has been solved—whether the universals were conceived as preceding or following particular things, or as contained in them—all these supposed solutions disclose the same fundamental fallacy. For a pure relation of meaning they substitute a relation such as exists between empirical things or events. For it is only between empirical things and events that a statement of "before" or "after," "inner" or "outer" can be made. Nearly all the parties in this struggle over universals were destined to take these metaphors of before and after, inner and outer, for valid logical if not metaphysical determinations. But such metaphors can no longer deceive us once we have noted that the "universal" and the "particular" are distinguished from each other not in being but in meaning, and that a difference in dimensions of meaning can never be reduced to such differences as prevail between spatial and temporal dimensions, or be adequately expressed in terms of them. Of all the solutions here attempted the most relatively satisfactory still seems to be the one which sought the being of the universals in particular things: *universalia non sunt res subsistentes, sed habent esse solum in singularibus.*[22] For here at least the outward division is avoided; here, though the image be borrowed from space, the strict correlation, the reciprocal relation between the universal and the particular, is rightly maintained.

But this same correlation immediately involves new difficulties; for it is in danger of being confounded with the homogeneity of the factors that are related to each other. The conceptual universal then becomes a mere common factor, a something which though itself not an independent, new thing, expresses a similarity that is present in things. The significance of the universal now seems reducible to this category of similarity, of *similitudo.* But with this the significance of the concept as a purely relational concept suffers an unwarranted restriction: in the system of relations, similarity is only a special case which cannot be magnified into the type of the conceptual relation as such. It is not solely in respect to similarity that a manifold can be compared and grouped together: to this form of grouping we must juxtapose others, equal in rank, which are determined according to totally different criteria, through other modes of

22. Thomas Aquinas, *Contra gentiles,* 1, 65.

"respect." And every such mode of respect, every relation R_1, R_2, R_3 etc. may raise the same claim; each of them defines a fully legitimate concept.[23] In regard to the universal factor of meaning which the concept sets up and outlines, all the things that fall under it are not only similar but identical: in order to be thought of as special instances of a concept the particular examples must satisfy the whole concept, i.e. the totality of the conditions it embraces.

But this identity of the respect in which it is to be considered does not require the elements of a multiplicity that are to be grouped together by the concept to disclose any common content: the respect itself is not any kind of thing which can be wholly or partly contained in these elements, which by some sort of spatial analogy may be said to "lie" in them. Does the functional equation, for example, in any way lie in the various values of the variables that we can insert in it as "true values"? The equation of a plane curve may be designated as the concept of this same curve, for in it we have a propositional function that is true for all values of the coordinates of the points in the curve but false for other values.[24] Through this condition the different points in the curve are composed into a unity, which, however, designates no common factor in them except for that which consists in this form of correlation. Once the law of such a correlation is established, the totality of possible points in space immediately breaks down into two distinct classes in respect to it: the points which fulfill the relation stated in this law and those which do not fulfill it. What intuition apprehends as a particular form with certain spatial characteristics and attributes now seems to be reduced by intellectual analysis to a universal rule of correlation. And this not only is true for mathematical concepts but represents an essential feature of all true conceptual structures. For it is always the basic function of the concept to gather together—συνάγειν εἰς ἕν as Plato called it—what is dispersed in intuition, even things that are totally disparate from the standpoint of intuition, by establishing a new, ideal reference point for them. Particulars which had previously tended apart, order themselves according to this point of reference, and through this unity of direction a unity of essence is stamped upon them—though this essence is not to be taken ontically but logically, as a pure determination of meaning. The convergence by which

23. Cf. my more detailed remarks in *Substanzbegriff und Funktionsbegriff*, chap. 1, esp. pp. 18 ff.

24. Cf. Russell, *Introduction to Mathematical Philosophy*, p. 156.

their sensuous or intuitive heterogeneity is overcome does not signify that a substantial sameness or accord is disclosed in the elements of the manifold but that, however different they may be from one another, they are taken as factors of a context of meaning, that each in its own place and role constitutes the totality and function of this meaning.

If we take this view of the unity of the concept, we perceive of course that—to employ a term which Kant coined in a different context—it can never be anything other than a "projected unity." For the concept only establishes a standpoint of comparison and correlation, but makes no statement of whether anything exists which meets the determination it provides. For this reason alone it is obvious that an adequate explanation can never be gained from a consideration of its mere extension, from a consideration of the particular or the particulars. For it is by no means certain that any particular corresponds to the unity it establishes, that any particular falls under it. In the way of handling mathematical logic that sought to reduce the concept to the class, the introduction and insertion of the zero class always raised special difficulties. The zero class was indispensable to any complete logical theory of the concept as well as of number; but on the other hand it was loaded down with paradoxes and contradictions for every purely extensional view. It was precisely these paradoxes that ushered in a change of attitude, that led Russell, for example, to regard a purely extensional view as inadequate and to round it out and deepen it with an intensional approach. Obviously a class that has no elements cannot be defined by indication of its elements—it can only be designated intensionally by virtue of a definite propositional function.[25] One of the limitations of the usual abstraction theory of the concept is that it must presuppose as given the elements from which the concept is supposedly built up, from which it is supposedly abstracted. If the concept is to bring out the common factor in a series of particulars, it must have them as distinct sensuous or intuitive realities, before it can stamp them with its own form. According to this theory, it can designate only what is— not what is not. And it is this postulate that stands at the beginning of all logic; it constitutes the fundamental idea of the Eleatic logic. But Parmenides is followed by Democritus and Plato, both of whom give to nonbeing a new justification and meaning, the former in the realm of physics, the latter in the field of dialectics. The system of knowledge, the

25. In Russell's logic the zero class is defined as the class of all x's which satisfy any function ϕx, but which is false for all values of x: see *Principles*, chap. 2, sec. 25.

community of interlocking concepts—Plato's *Sophist* teaches—is not achieved until we resolve to recognize being and nonbeing as equally justified and equally necessary factors. Every single concept embraces, side by side with a statement about being, an abundance of statements about non-being; every "is" in a predicative sentence can be fully understood only if we conceive of an "is not" as correlative with it.[26] Indeed the concept cannot effect an ideal determination of the real as long as it remains exclusively within the confines of this reality. Its peculiar and supreme achievement requires that it progress from the contemplation of the real to that of the possible—and this it cannot do if it shrinks back from its opposite, the "impossible." The whole history of science teaches us how eminently important the conception of the "not-possible" can be and how in many cases it is precisely this conception that opens up a free survey of the realm of the possible and of its systematic formation and structuring. If the concept is a mere criterion of relation and correlation, it must be free also to link contradictories: precisely in order that through this link it may learn to recognize the contradiction and penetrate its foundation. Thus it is wholly fruitful and meaningful to form such a concept as that of the "regular decahedron"—for precisely the non-being that it contains within it opens up to thought a new insight into the being of the geometric world, the structure of space. We have said that the concept is not so much a ready-made path along which thought progresses as a method, a process of pathfinding. In this process thought can operate wholly on its own initiative; it does not bind itself to fixed goals that are already finished and given but sets up new goals and asks whether there is a path leading to them, and if so what path. In the language of symbolic logic this means that neither truth nor falsity is imputed to the propositional function in which the concept is grounded, that it remains open for the time being whether there are definite values of the variable x's for which this function holds. Such a propositional function *intends* a definite meaning but does not yet *fulfill* it: it gives no fixed and ready answer but only establishes the direction of inquiry. But all knowledge must be preceded precisely by such a fixing of the question if a clear and secure answer is to be found. Until certain lines of aim are set up for knowledge—as is done in the concept—inquiry cannot begin, the valid relations in the realm of empirical as well as ideal being cannot be determined. Here it is characteristic that in the history of philosophy

26. Cf. Plato, *Sophist*, esp. 248E ff.

the concept itself first emerges in the form of a question. Aristotle designates Socrates as the "discoverer" of the universal concept. But this discovery in Socrates takes the form not of a new kind of knowledge, but
of a kind of nonknowledge. The Socratic question concerning "what
is" contains within it the method of Socratic induction of the λόγοι
ἐπακτικοί. And so it remains true, even in highly developed knowledge,
that each newly acquired concept is an attempt, a beginning, a problem;
its value lies not in its copying of definite objects, but in its opening up
of new logical perspectives, so permitting a new penetration and survey
of an entire problem complex. Thus while among the basic logical functions the judgment closes and concludes, the concept, by contrast, has
essentially the function of opening up. It throws out questions, the final decision of which falls to the judgment; it merely sets up an equation, the solution of which is expected from analysis of a definite ideal realm of objects or
from advancing experience. In this sense a concept can be effective and
fruitful for knowledge, long before it is itself exactly "defined," i.e.
carried to a complete and definitive determination. For one of its essential
tasks is not to let the problems of knowledge come prematurely to rest,
but to keep them in a steady flux, by guiding them toward new goals
which it must first anticipate hypothetically. Here again we find that the
concept is far less abstractive than prospective; it not only fixes what
is already known, establishing its general outlines, but also maintains a
persistent outlook for new and unknown connections. It not only takes
up the similarities or connections which experience offers it, but also
strikes new connections; it is a free line stroke that must always be attempted anew if the inner organization of the realms both of empirical
intuition and of the logical-ideal object is to be brought out clearly.

This makes it evident why every theory of the concept that seeks to explain it by purely reproductive tendencies and to reduce it to such tendencies must necessarily fail. In the field of intuition and the pure "representative function" this limitation has already proved impossible; even at
these levels it was not possible to devise a theory of perception and
empirical knowledge in general without invoking the aid of the "productive imagination" at every step. In the concept, the work of the productive imagination stands before us in an intensified form. Hence we
fall into a misunderstanding of its sheer "whatness" as soon as we attempt
to transform it into a sum of reproductions, a mere aggregate of remembered images. For simple phenomenological reflection tells us that

if we take the "concept" as it is immediately given, it appears as something totally different from the mnemonic image, as something very individual that is by no means interchangeable with it. We must go behind the sphere of consciousness, we must pass from pure logic and phenomenology to physiology if we wish to maintain an equivalence between concept and remembered image. The concept then becomes a product of unconscious traces and residues that have been left behind in the brain by earlier sense perceptions. But aside from the fact that this notion distorts the simple meaning of the logical question, transforming logic into a brain metaphysics, the concept would be very inadequate to its task if this *were* its actual task. Here, we should have a true application of Bacon's quip that anyone who supposed he could grasp reality through conceptual thought seemed to him like a man who, to gain better knowledge of a distant object, climbed a high tower and looked out from it even though he was perfectly free to approach the object itself and observe it close at hand. Here one thing is seen correctly: that the concept, in accordance with its characteristic attitude must, unlike direct perception, move its object off into a kind of ideal distance, in order to bring it within its horizon. The concept must annul "presence" in order to arrive at "representation." But for us this transformation no longer has the purely negative significance that it must have for strict positivism. The analysis of both perception and intuitive knowledge has shown us that even here this transition is required and within certain limits effected. The function of the concept does not create a break in the totality of knowledge—it continues a basic trend which already proved to be at work in the first stages of sensory, perceptual knowledge. And it is precisely in this continuation that the trend is truly authenticated and justified.

It has been argued that my critique of the theory of abstraction applies if one starts from the most highly developed concepts, those of mathematics and mathematical physics, but that it falls down as soon as we consider the prior stages of scientific knowledge, as soon as we take as our basis those concept formations which are already found—far from the aims of science—in our natural world view that is not yet modified by theories. Here, it is maintained, the theory of abstraction remains in full force, for the "intuitive concept" is actually developed from the "general mnemonic image" that has been deposited in us by a series of concrete sense perceptions. This attempt to rescue the abstraction theory was undertaken by Max Brod and Felix Weltsch in their book *An-*

schauung und Begriff. But it seems to me that precisely through the sharpness and pregnance with which it elaborates the essential features of the "abstractive" view of the concept, this work only reveals all the more clearly the dialectic in which the view must always ultimately become entangled. For according to this view, the true and essential achievement of the concept is to transform the sharp, individually determined images provided by sensation and perception into unclear and blurred ideas. This vagueness is regarded as the necessary condition for the concept—the element in which it alone can live and breathe. By detailed psychological analyses Brod and Weltsch seek to show how the perception and the intuitive image gradually enter into this element. Memory functions as a medium, for here begins that blurring of boundaries between the particular sense impressions that is taken up and continued by the concept.

Actually self-observation shows how rare separate remembered images are, i.e. images in which the memory of a unique, truly punctual experience has remained securely free from the influence of similar ensuing experiences. Almost always a remembered image represents a whole series of impressions. The memory of a friend represents him to me in many connections at once. If I think of a landscape, it stands before me as I have seen it time and time again, in varying extension, illumination, mood. But these images, which represent so much deviation, do not for that reason cease to be intuitive. Thus the general remembered image actually meets our . . . condition: to save the world from its infinitely progressing pulverization; ideas thus arise which bring back to a higher unity what is crumbling into disparate, detailed images. This mission is accomplished by the general memory image: as a blurred idea, which because it can be interpreted into many sharp, deviating images, embraces these images in itself. . . . In the alternately sharp and blurred parts of this general memory image there is a kind of copy of all the images we have experienced; they are all represented through the special stratification of the vagueness in the memory image.

By way of characterizing this relationship, Brod and Weltsch introduce a special symbol: $A + x$. A signifies what was common to the various experienced images—that is, for example, to the landscape in different illuminations and moods, whereas the divergent blurs into x. "In the blur we have thus found the instrument by which two seemingly opposed attributes, hitherto regarded as crass contradictions, are brought into one: the intuitive and the abstract. For some intuitive images are at the same time abstract; these are the blurred images of the form $(A + x)$." And here, it is claimed, we have for the first time a foundation for a true psychology of thought—insofar as we do not arbitrarily restrict thought to the realm of scientific knowledge but seek to apprehend it in the totality of its living manifestations. It consists then in nothing other than "the living play of the $(A + x)$ formations": "It seems certain that we think in blurred general intuitions." [27]

With this, however, the Gordian knot of the problem of the concept is not untied but hacked to pieces. For are we really saved from the infinite diversity and fragmentation of individual impressions by fleeing from them into a blurred general idea? Can we, and do we, wish to renounce this multiplicity? Does not the meaning of concept formation consist precisely in the fact that it gives us an Ariadne's thread *within* the labyrinth of the many and the particular? The genuine concept turns away from the world of intuition only in order to lead back to it with all the greater certainty: it serves to determine the particular itself. Here it cannot be argued that this function resides only in strictly scientific concepts. For although it is in the scientific concepts that this function of the concept first stands out with full pregnance, although it is here most clearly apprehended and immediately accessible to logical analysis, still it is not limited to the scientific concepts. It already belongs to those preliminary stages, those germ cells of the theoretical-scientific concept which Brod and Weltsch designate as "intuitive concepts." For these too are not so much generic concepts as concepts of combination. They do not present blurred general images of things but strike bridges between the things that are given in perception as merely singular and relatively isolated. Thus for example the intuitive image of color is no generic image in which red and blue, yellow and green fade into each other in some vague way; through the image of color, rather, a characteristic field is marked off from sensory experience as a whole and "defined" by a definite factor of relation, the relation to light and to the eye. How would such an insight into the order, the articulation, the concrete differences of a multiplicity be possible if the concept consisted essentially in a turning

27. Max Brod and Felix Weltsch, *Anschauung und Begriff. Grundzüge eines Systems der Begriffsbildung* (Leipzig, 1913), pp. 72 ff., 144.

away from them, a leveling of these differences? [28] And is it not a leveling when, understanding the differences through the concept and deriving them from it, we suppose them rather to be blurred in it?

But if instead of merely examining these conflicting views of the concept, of the concept as such, we inquire into the underlying reasons for them, we find ourselves once again carried back to our central problem, the problem of representation. For it is the view of representation and the "conditions of its possibility" that dominates and determines the view of the concept. If Brod and Weltsch have recourse to the "blurred image," it is explicitly because in their eyes only such an image, only an image that is not thoroughly determined but is in a sense opalescent, possesses the power of representing a multiplicity of contents. This relative indeterminacy of an image seems to be the sole basis for its having meaning, seems alone to give it the possibility of being taken now in this and now in that sense. "The property which blurredness has of meaning something," it is thus concluded,

> gives the $(A + x)$ in germ that primary characteristic of the concept, which has created so much difficulty for theoreticians, namely its extension side by side with its content. . . . How must a single image be constituted in order to serve as a denominator for many objects? On the basis of all the foregoing we may answer as follows: An $(A + x)$ with its ability, within the limits which its A imposes on its x, to transform itself into different images and thus link itself without difficulty with these recent, disparate images through a judgment of identity, can name the objects corresponding to these images. The

28. Cf. my *Substanzbegriff und Funktionsbegriff*, pp. 23 ff. In agreement with the view there put forward, Burkamp has recently written: "From individual things we rise to concepts such as 'chair' and 'dog,' and then to still higher concepts such as 'living creature,' 'body,' 'mass.' From individual states we rise to concepts of 'quantity of electricity,' 'strength of current,' 'energy.' From the individual numbers we rise to the concepts of the prime number and of 'number' in general. Between these concepts we set the connecting law. . . . But this lawgiving acquires meaning only through the fact that we can return downward to the basic stages. The law that applies to body and mass will now, on the strength of the law of the logical concept, also be valid for 'chair' and 'carpet,' and finally also for the individual chair that may lie in my path. This individual chair is now enriched in its being for me by the interweaving of all the concepts under which it stands. . . . In all this the enrichment of the individual is grounded in the knowledge of the general, of the laws that apply to the general concept. This enrichment in the knowledge of the particular and especially of the individual is the purpose of the whole hierarchy of concepts. . . . It is for the sake of the lower levels that we work in the higher levels" (*Begriff und Beziehung*, first study, pp. 2 f.).

power of the $(A + x)$ to be the subject of different identity judgments makes possible the concept's function of denomination. Thus two distinctly disparate individual images, the image of the dog lying (L) and that of the dog standing (S), may be given to me. But if from L and S and the other positions of a certain dog which are known to me now I form its $(A + x)$, i.e. if I detach from them a blurred general image of "the" dog, the image of lying (x_1) or that of standing (x_2) may be added to this image, and accordingly the $(A + x)$ can designate for me now an $(A + x_1)$ and now an $(A + x_2)$.[29]

But if we look back over our previous reflections, it is this context that best clarifies the contrast between our view of representation and the view that is here expressed. For at every step we have had to combat this very assumption that the symbolic meaning of an image, what lends it a definite significance, may be disclosed as something in itself, as a real, distinguishable part of it. "Meaning" and "existence" are not homogeneous in the sense that they may be disclosed as components of an image which they "compose." The very formula that is here chosen as the expression of the concept must appear questionable insofar as it joins the A and the x, the expressions of the universal and the particular, by a simple plus sign. Can the universal and the particular, the content and extension of a concept, what is "meant" in the concept and what is "given" by perception or sensory intuition, really be added in this way? Such an addition transforms the organic unity that characterizes and distinguishes the concept into an aggregative juxtaposition. In the propositional function $\phi(x)$ that designates a certain concept, the expression for the function itself and the expression of the particular values that are grouped together by it do not stand on the same line: the "factors" that are here brought into relation with each other cannot be conceived as elements of a sum. There in an inherent contradiction in attempting to make the term $\phi(x)$ intelligible by dissecting it into separately existing ingredients, by making the $\phi(x)$ into a $\phi + x$. For the function sign ϕ is not an expression for a single numerical quantity that might be combined with other quantities of the variable by elementary arithmetical operations. We have above compared the "concept" with the "universal member" of a series, which designates the rule of the succession of its individual mem-

29. Brod and Weltsch, pp. 77 ff.

bers. This law of the series restricts the individual elements belonging to it to definite conditions; but it does not itself constitute a member of the series. If an arithmetical series of the form ½ ⅔ ¾ ⅘ etc. is designated by the formula $\frac{n}{n+1}$, this $\frac{u}{n+1}$ no longer designates an individual magnitude; it stands rather for the whole of the series, insofar as this series is taken not as a mere sum of parts but as a characteristic relational structure. Similarly, to choose a geometrical example—the universal concept of the conic section is not gained through images of individual circles, ellipses, parabolas and hyperbolas flowing together and forming a blurred general image; what happens rather is that circle and ellipse, hyperbola and parabola are retained as thoroughly determined geometrical forms, but at the same time are moved into a new relational context; they all obtain the trend and characteristic vision toward the right cone, from which they may arise as results of the various sections that may be made in it. And the same is true in principle of the simplest intuitive concepts. They never form a mere conglomerate of sense impressions and remembered images but contain a peculiar articulation of these impressions and images, a form of organization. In them the separate is "seen together"—not in the sense that its components are mingled but in the sense that their connection in regard to some linking factor is retained. When the Greek language designates the moon as the "measurer" ($\mu\acute{\eta}\nu$), and the Latin language as the "glittering" (*luna*), different intuitive concepts underlie these different designations—but these concepts act in both cases only as a factor of comparison and correlation, as a point of view, which is not itself given as either a distinct or a blurred visible thing. And here it is largely immaterial whether this point of view asserts itself in the further objective progress of knowledge or is superseded by another mode of vision. Such changes mark the content and scientific validity of the concept, but not its sheer form. If, for example, certain languages designate the butterfly as a bird, the connection thus expressed must of course be severed as soon as thought progresses to describing the zoological orders systematically in accordance with definite scientific, morphological, or physiological criteria—but the original viewpoint of classification which focuses not on such criteria but solely on the intuitive factor of "flying" is not thereby declared to be absolutely meaningless, but merely to represent a standard of meaning which from the standpoint of scientific synopsis must be replaced by another, more complete one. The circumstance that such a change of standard proves to be necessary in the transition from intuitive to scientific concepts does not prove that the operation of measurement as such is not already practiced in the prescientific concepts—that they, too, do not already follow determined rules of relational thinking. In the theory of Brod and Weltsch, however, at least the prescientific concept—for in connection with the scientific concept they restrict their thesis in very important and even crucial respects[30]—is produced by a mere flowing together of representations and remembered images. In this theory, consciousness resembles a photographic plate, on which in the course of time various images are produced which overlap and mix with one another, until they finally become a single unclear general image.[31] But even if we accept this metaphor as an expression for the genetic process of concept formation, it remains impossible to see how it can elucidate the logical function of the concept, its ability to "name" and designate various particular intuitions. For its origin in the particular impressions can never in itself enable the concept to *represent* exactly that from which it sprang. Admitted that a general image of this sort is formed on the photographic plate; still, the plate will never be able to know it as such, to refer it back to the particular elements from which it grew. Such a relation would require the process in which the concept was acquired to be in a sense annulled, and the elements from which it is composed to be freed from the mixture into which they have entered. If we attribute to the photographic plate the faculty of mixing all the particular impressions that are made on it, shall we also impute to it the power of separating them? Yet precisely this is presupposed and required in "representation" in the strict sense. Every function of representation embraces within it an act of differentiation—and both must be conceived not as a mere succession but as a genuine involvement—the positing of identity must be performed in the differentiation and vice versa. For this kind of systole and diastole, or syncrisis and diacrisis, of concepts, all analogies drawn from the world of things and from its processes are inadequate. Here only the opposite formulation of the problem carries us farther; here we must begin with what the concept *means,* and proceed to what it proves to be in objective knowledge and what it performs for the building of this

30. Cf. esp. the critical argument against my *Substanzbegriff und Funktionsbegriff* in Brod and Weltsch, pp. 234 ff.

31. Brod and Weltsch, pp. 74 f.

knowledge. Conversely, we can never understand the basic spiritual act of "representation," of intending a "universal" in the particular, by dissecting it and in a sense smashing it into bits. When we do this, we do not retain the fragments, the parts of representation; rather, we pass altogether from the area of their meaning to an empty existence, whence no road leads back to the sphere of meaning.[32]

32. For a more complete treatment of this context I refer the reader to my article "Erkenntnistheorie nebst den Grenzfragen der Logik und Denkpsychologie," *Jahrbücher der Philosophie, 3* (1927), 55 ff.

Chapter 2

Concept and Object

ONE OF THE most important achievements of the *Critique of Pure Reason* is to have given the problem of the relation between concept and object an entirely new formulation and a fundamentally different methodological meaning. What made this development possible was that at just this point Kant took the decisive step from universal logic to transcendental logic. The doctrine of the concept was thereby freed from the deadly futility into which it had fallen as a consequence of the traditional treatment. The function of the concept now no longer appears as merely formal and analytical; it is a productive constructive function —no longer a more or less remote and pale copy of some absolute, self-subsisting reality, but a presupposition of experience and hence a condition of the possibility of its objects. The question of the object has become for Kant a question of validity, of the *quid juris;* but the *quid juris* of the object cannot be decided before the other question, the *quid juris* of the concept, has been answered. For the concept is the last and highest stage to which knowledge rises in the progress of the objective consciousness. In the building up of objective knowledge the synthesis of "apprehension in intuition" and of "reproduction in the imagination" must be completed by the synthesis of "recognition in the concept." To recognize an object means nothing other than to subject the manifold of intuition to a rule which determines it in respect to its order. And the concept is nothing other than the consciousness of such a rule and of the unity that is posited through it. "Thus a transcendental ground for the unity of consciousness must be found in the synthesis of the manifold of all our intuitions, hence also of our concepts of objects in general, and consequently of all objects of experience, without which it would be impossible to think any object for our intuitions: for an object is nothing

315

more than that something of which the concept expresses such a necessity of synthesis.[1]

This common referral of the problems of the concept and of the object to the problem of synthetic unity immediately places the concept on a basis other than in universal logic. Now it no longer suffices to take it as a mere generic concept, a *conceptus communis*. For such a concept is lacking in precisely the characteristic and decisive factor; it is a mere expression of the analytical, but not of the synthetic unity of consciousness. But it is only the previous thought of a synthetic unity that makes an analytical unity thinkable. "A representation which is cogitated as common to *different* representations, is regarded as belonging to such as, besides this common representation, contain something *different;* consequently it must be previously thought in synthetical unity with other although only possible representations, before I can think in it the analytical unity of consciousness which makes it a *conceptus communis.*"[2] And from this there follows directly a far-reaching and fruitful insight respecting the character of the thing-concept. The older metaphysics and ontology take the unity of the thing as a "substantial" unity: The thing is what remains identical amid the change of states. Thus it confronts these states, the "accidents," as something independent and self-subsistent; it is the solid core to which the accidents come only from without. But here again the transcendental logic transforms the analytical unity of the thing into a synthetic unity. Now the thing is no longer a kind of substantial thread along which the variable determinations are arranged; in it, rather, the process, the form of the arrangement itself, is expressed. "When we inquire what new character the relation to an object gives our representations and what dignity they obtain thereby, we find that it does nothing other than to make the combination of representations necessary in a certain way, and to subject it to a rule; that conversely, it is only because a certain order is necessary in the temporal relation of our representations that objective significance is conferred on them."[3] Thus it is not the object as an absolute object, but the objective *meaning* that constitutes the central problem; the question is no longer directed toward the nature of the object as a thing in itself, but toward the possibility of a relation to an object. This relation arises only because knowledge does not stop at the particular phenomenon as given in an

1. *Kritik der reinen Vernunft,* 1st ed., p. 106.
2. Ibid., 2d ed., p. 133 n.; Eng. ed., p. 95 n.
3. Ibid., pp. 242 f.

individual here and now, but weaves it into the context of experience. And it is the concept that is unremittingly at work on this mesh, that strikes the thousands of connections on which rests the possibility of experience. Its first activity is to overcome the discreteness of the individual empirical data, to unite them in a continuum, the continuum of space and time. But it can do this only by creating fixed and universally valid rules of correlation between them, by subjecting the juxtaposition in space and the succession in time to definite laws. The union which the particular perceptions achieve in and through the concept constitutes for us the idea of nature: this idea means nothing other than the existence of things, insofar as it is determined according to universal laws.

With this the object is removed from "transcendence" in the metaphysical sense of the word; but at the same time—and this is what characterizes the critical theory of knowledge—it is determined as something absolutely and fundamentally unintuitive. For just as, according to the opening sentences of the *Transcendental Aesthetic,* "that in which our sensations are merely arranged, cannot be itself a sensation," similarly the rule which links manifold intuitions cannot itself be an intuition. Over against the constant values of intuition what we call the "object" thus becomes a mere x, a purely cogitated point of unity. "What then do we understand when we speak of an object that corresponds to knowledge and is therefore also differentiated from it? It is easy to see that this object must be thought only as a something $= x$, because outside of our knowledge we have nothing that we can set over against this knowledge as corresponding to it." [4] This formulation of the idea of the object was needed to promote a strict and exact correlation between concept and object. No longer is an object concept possible in which the object is actually seized, grasped, embraced by our thinking. Such figurative descriptions of the basic relation of knowledge are now replaced by a purely ideal relation, a relation of the condition to the conditioned. The concept relates to the object because and insofar as it is the necessary and indispensable presupposition of objectivization itself, because it represents that function for which alone there can be objects, for which there can be constant and fundamental unities amid the flow of experience.

Once this insight is achieved, all views of knowledge that seek to transpose the logical, conditional relation, here disclosed, back into a relation to a particular thing—and to explain it in this light—lose their validity and meaning. Knowledge and object no longer confront each other as spatial objects, a "here" and a "there," an "inside" and an "outside." All such designations, which for centuries have dominated the formulation of the problem of knowledge, are recognized to be absolutely inadequate—mere metaphors. The object is neither outside nor inside, neither on that side nor this; for our relation to it is not ontic and real, but symbolic. Among modern psychologists and epistemologists it is above all Theodor Lipps who, by roads far removed from those taken by Kant, arrived once again at a sharp and pregnant formulation of this basic problem. He, too, to be sure, began by representing as separate spheres the relation between consciousness and object in the language of spatial imagery. In order to confront an object and place itself in relation to it, consciousness must reach out beyond itself; and this progress and transition, this reaching into the transcendent, is its peculiar function. The very essence of consciousness is to be sought in this jumping over its own shadow. But Lipps soon corrected his initial description by expressly admitting its purely metaphorical character. For the fact that the content of consciousness is directed toward something objective, which it represents, must not, as he now stresses, be mistaken for a relation between cause and effect. "Designation" can never be interpreted as a special case of causation, or derived from the universal form of causation.

The relation between the phenomenon in the strict sense of the word (e.g. between the sensory content of sound) and the reality underlying it (the sound wave in the physical sense) is no causal relation but is a relation of an entirely different kind, a relation of the symbol to what is symbolized in it. And this symbolic relation consists not in the fact, susceptible of no further description, that in or through the sensory content called sound I think an object similar to it and regard it as real, and then in accordance with the law of causality transform this real object mentally into sound waves. In this transformation the peculiar symbolic relation, the thinking of a real object in a content, the relation of representation . . . remains in force. This is not surprising, since in the mental transformation the sound waves have replaced what was at first regarded as objectively real, or precisely because this latter was mentally transformed into them.[5]

5. Theodor Lipps, "Inhalt und Gegenstand; Psychologie und Logik," *Sitzungsbericht der Münchener Akademie, philosophisch-philologische Klasse* (1903), p. 594. Cf. Lipps' *Das Denken und die Gegenstände im Leitfaden der Psychologie* (3d ed. Leipzig, 1909), p. 12.

We quote these lines because they indicate with particular clarity and emphasis the cardinal point in both the history of philosophy and the philosophical systems around which the problem of the concept as well as that of the object revolve. The two have frequently been treated as mere parallel problems: the order of "ideas" was held to move along side by side with the order of "things" and to correspond to it point for point. Yet these supposed parallels determine one common point: they focus on the basic phenomenon of representation. But there is a still sharper distinction to be made within this general phenomenon. It has already been seen that even before undergoing its explicit, properly logical formation the concept does its work within the sphere of intuition. It assembles the fundamental factors of intuition, it links them and relates them to one another—but all the relations that arise in this way are realized over and over again in separate concrete structures and stand out in them as determinations of them. They are no merely abstract relations that are apprehended in pure knowledge; rather, they condense into forms of intuitive reality and stand before us as such. We have seen that Helmholtz, in his theory of perception, stressed the part played by the concept in precisely this primary creation of forms, and actually regarded this as one of its essential achievements.[6] But the concept in its stricter and more restricted form, in its specifically logical character, must of course be distinguished from the intuitive concepts, which are nothing other than the living representation of the law governing a concrete succession of intuitive images. Here the meaning of the concept no longer adheres to any intuitive substrate, to any *datum* or *dabile*—rather it is thought as such in a definite relational structure, within a system of judgments and truths. And precisely to this twofold meaning, this gradation that can be disclosed in the concept, there now corresponds a twofold formation of the object consciousness. The first phase of object formation takes objective being as purely intuitive—as a being that belongs to and is articulated into the fundamental orders of intuition, the orders of space and time. It "stands" in these orders—it possesses a definite spatial outline and a fixed temporal duration. But as scientific knowledge progresses and creates its own methodological implements, the immediate bond between the concept and intuition is loosened. The concept no longer remains attached to the reality of things but rises to the free construction of the possible. It draws precisely what has nowhere and never happened

6. Cf. above, pp. 286–8.

into the sphere of thought and sets it up as a norm and intellectual standard. And this is what separates "theory" in the strict sense of the word from mere intuition. Theory fulfills itself as pure theory only when it breaks through the barriers of intuition. No theory, and particularly no exact one, no mathematical theory of the natural process, is possible unless pure thought detaches itself from the matrix of intuition, unless it progresses to structures which are fundamentally unintuitive in nature. And now the last decisive step is taken—now these very structures become the actual vehicles of "objective" being. Because it is only through them that the lawfulness of being can be expressed, they constitute a new kind of object which may be designated as objects of a higher order over against those of the first phase. As soon as science arrived at a critical insight into its own method, as soon as it not only practiced its method but also understood it, it had to ward off any attempt to create an identity or similarity between its objects and those of "immediate" perception or intuition. It recognizes that though its objects are thoroughly related to the objects of intuition, they may never be reduced to them. For any such reduction would negate the specific achievement of scientific thinking, would transform the understanding of the world and its contexts into a mere reduplication of the given.

But the recognition of this difference also involves a logical dilemma. For—one might ask—does not the inner multiformity that has thus been disclosed in the object consciousness run counter to its actual task? Must not the object if it is to be thought at all be thought as absolutely unambiguous? The diversity, the movement, the transition from one stage to another—all these seem to enter into consciousness itself, but not to apply to the being toward which it is oriented and which it seeks to express. Being, at least, can only be understood as the counterpole and opposite of movement, its fixed, unchanging and immovable goal. Thus being would seem to be susceptible of no further differentiations and gradations, and only the simple alternative of Parmenides would seem to apply: Is it or is it not? Mere thoughts may readily live side by side, graduated according to the varying degrees of their universality—but in the realm of the "things" that clash in space no such compatibility prevails. Here, where one takes up a space, another must give way, and a clear decision must be made between the claimants to reality. But every such decision involves a sacrifice. We must choose between the immanent

contents of consciousness—between reality as it presents itself to immediate sensation, to perception and intuition—and that other transcendent
reality that reaches out beyond it, namely the being to which theory, the
scientific concept, leads us. If we hold to this reality as the true and
genuine being, the world of perception is in danger of dissolving into a
mere phantasmagoria. In the real world of scientific objects nothing is
left of the subjective qualities of color, tone, etc. But if the weight of reality
is laid in the other pan of the scales, the objects of theory, the atoms and
electrons, become mere abstractions: the matter of natural science cannot
justify itself in the presence of pure perception and in a manner of speaking shatters against it.

Yet this either-or which we encounter over and over again in the history
of epistemology holds within it a hidden dogmatic presupposition, for it
simply postulates what was to be proved; it contains a *petitio principii.*
The substantial view of the world, it is true, seeks in "being" something
absolutely permanent; it takes being as an attribute, a predicate, which
is to be imputed to certain subjects and not to others. But for a critical
view of knowledge this alternative no longer applies; here being has
altogether ceased to designate a real predicate. What is here called the
"object" of knowledge acquires determinate meaning only by being
referred to a certain form or function of knowledge. And these functions
themselves are not engaged in a mere contest or conflict but stand to one
another in a relation of correlative and complementary correspondence.
One does not simply negate or destroy the other, but takes it up and sets
it in another systematic context, where it will be shaped and determined
anew. And it is solely in this kind of comprehension that the object of
knowledge can be grounded and explained. If, as Kant put it, this object
is nothing other than "the something of which the concept expresses such
a necessity of synthesis," the question of its being cannot be answered
independently of the question of what this necessity of synthesis means
and on what conditions it rests. Within this view, there is no contradiction in the fact that this meaning as such does not suddenly spring into
existence but must be constituted through a hierarchy of operations—
that it passes through a series of different phases of meaning before it
achieves its true and adequate determination. Thus in the realm of meaning the various factors and possibilities of signification are implicated and
interwoven in far higher degree than would be conceivable on the plane

of mere being. The "object" is thought as one, but this does not prevent this unity itself, as a functional unity, from being built up progressively. It must run through a series of determinations, and it is exhausted in no member of the series, not even in the final, concluding member, for the object is the all-embracing principle of the series, according to which the progression from member to member is determined.

We have accordingly seen that even the mere object of perception is not immediately given, but can only be represented in and through perception. It is from the standpoint of such representation that one may first speak of the unity of a "thing." In its continuous flow, actual perception as a process knows nothing of such a unity. Every content that emerges in it is immediately replaced by another content, every form that it seems to mold is caught up in the vortex of the process and carried away with it. If the always variable and fragmentary data of perception nevertheless join to form the totality of an object, this is possible only because, instead of being taken as mere fragments, they are seen as belonging together, as different expressions of a determinate totality of meaning. This vision transcends the directly given in two ways: it subjects the contents of perception to the two viewpoints of continuity and of coherence. This fact even strict sensationalism could not fail to recognize; even Hume wrote that the "thing" is not merely a bundle of individual perceptions, but that the idea of an object identical with itself first arises through the concepts of constancy and coherence. Only, in accordance with his fundamental view, he was bound to set this concept itself down as a mere fiction —a delusion of the imagination to which it must succumb in accordance with universal psychological laws but to which we may attribute no objective-logical value.[7] But this is to misunderstand the dignity and power of pure synthesis, as is shown by the *Critique of Pure Reason,* particularly in the section where reality is said to be a "postulate of empirical thinking." It is a postulate of this kind when, in a manner of speaking, we bid the transient and fleeting sense impressions to stand still—when we attribute to them a duration that goes beyond the time span of their immediate existence and facticity. In a purely qualitative sense this duration does not extend beyond the realm of the perception as such; it is the content of the perception itself, that is repeated as such and endowed, so to speak, with a certain index of duration. But thought does not stop at this temporal completion and integration. It does not simply extend the

7. Cf. Hume, *A Treatise of Human Nature,* Pt. IV, sec. 2.

content beyond itself and beyond the time span in which it is actually given but also considers its changes and inquires after their law. Where such changes occur, it is not arbitrarily; they are thought as subject to definite rules. But this requirement now compels thought to take a further step. For it becomes evident that exact rules of change cannot be established as long as we limit ourselves to defining the elements to which these rules are to apply, by the very same determinations as appear in mere perception. The definition must be amplified and deepened; the particular quality, the facticity of the perception must not form a barrier to the determination of its object's being. If phenomena are to be interpretable and form an intelligible whole, knowledge must undertake a further transformation that is fraught with grave consequences. It must not only establish new links between the contents of perception themselves but in order to give these links a strictly conceptual expression must change the character of the perceptual contents. The sensory world is now provided with a foundation in an ideal world, a world of meaning and pure theory, because it is only for the structures of such an ideal world that we can formulate those laws of combination that are necessary if the separate phenomena are to be read as experiences. Only now has knowledge gained "objects" in the strict sense—contents that really stand firm and fit into an unequivocal order.

Thus if we are to penetrate the sphere of pure knowledge, the meaning of perception must be fundamentally transformed, it must be "transcended" in the strict sense. But this significatory transcendence must not be confused with an ontic transcendence, for it is subject to an entirely different principle. This transition is a transition in meaning, not in being —and as such it cannot be apprehended or adequately explained on the basis of the fundamental relation which governs and regulates relations within being. The symbolic relation of intention, the way in which the "phenomenon" relates to the "object" and expresses it in this relation, is lost if we attempt to think it as a special case of a causal relation, if we seek to subordinate it to the principle of sufficient reason. What obstructs an insight into this specific difference, what has again and again beguiled thinkers into reducing pure relations of meaning to causal relations and explaining the former by the latter, is, above all, an equivocation that resides in the concept of the sign itself and in its use. Husserl has stressed that a fundamental distinction must be made between genuinely symbolic, truly significative signs and merely "indicative" signs. All signs do not embody signification in the same sense, for example, as we think of a word as a vehicle of signification. In the sphere of natural existence or processes a thing or an event can also become a sign for something other, as soon as it is connected with this other by some constant empirical relation, particularly the relation of cause and effect. In this way, for example, smoke can designate fire, thunder can designate lightning. But such signs, as Husserl stresses, express nothing, unless, side by side with their function of indication, they also fulfill a function of signification. "Meaning is not a mode of the sign in the sense of indication." [8] But this basic difference is always in danger of being blurred and leveled as soon as the function of the sign, instead of being understood as a primary and universal function, is regarded from some special point of view, and particularly when it is regarded exclusively in terms of scientific concept formation. Because this last is subject to the norm and domination of causal thinking, it tends involuntarily to transpose all the problems it touches into the language of causality, and to regard such transposition as indispensable to their treatment. This process of transposition stands out with particular clarity in Helmholtz's theory of knowledge. Of all modern physicists it is perhaps Helmholtz who has most sharply stressed that the concepts of mathematical physics may lay no claim to resemble real objects but can function only as signs for these objects. "Our sensations," he writes in support of this view,

> are . . . effects that have been produced in our organs by outward causes, and how such an effect is manifested depends of course essentially on the type of apparatus that is affected. Insofar as the quality of our sensation informs us regarding the peculiarity of the outward stimulus by which it is aroused, it can pass as a sign for it, but not as a reproduction of it. For of a reproduction we demand some kind of similarity with the reproduced object, from a statue similarity of form, from a drawing similarity of perspective projection upon the field of vision, from a painting, also, similarity of color. A sign, however, need have no manner of similarity with that for which it is a sign. The relation between the two is limited to the fact that the same object, acting under the same circumstances, will produce the same sign, and that dissimilar signs always correspond to dissimilar actions.[9]

8. Husserl, *Logische Untersuchungen,* 2, 23 ff.
9. Helmholtz, *Handbuch der physiologischen Optik,* 2d ed., p. 586.

But in this use of the sign concept two different views and attitudes imperceptibly merge. On the one hand we have the sign in its purely "deictic" function: as a something that points to an object, that intends and means it. But on the other hand this something is transformed into a determination that is *caused* by this same object. The intensional object to which the perception relates and which it represents, has thus become a real thing which is somehow hidden behind it and which knowledge can only apprehend indirectly, by means of an inference from the effect to the cause.

With this we leave the sphere of pure signification for that of mediated inference—and at the same time of course we find ourselves a prey to all the uncertainty which inheres in such merely mediated processes. On closer scrutiny, it becomes evident that in Helmholtz' theory of perception and in his epistemology the causal function has to fulfill a twofold and fundamentally contradictory function. It is the "condition of nature's intelligibility," because it first makes it possible to knit together the manifold of empirical observations into a strictly unitary order; so enabling us to arrive at concepts of empirical objects. But then the form of causal thinking impels us to take an entirely different road; instead of apprehending the pure context of phenomena as such, we are now expected to infer from them as effects their unknown and intrinsically forever unknowable causes. And for these two utterly different notions Helmholtz uses the concept of the sign. Sensation serves as a sign: first in the sense that what it indicates is nothing other than the context of experience itself. "Thus to call a phenomenon a real thing before perception and independently of it," Kant had formulated this relationship in the *Critique of Pure Reason,* "either means that in the progress of experience we must encounter such a perception, or else it has no meaning at all. If we do not start from experience, or if we do not proceed according to laws of the empirical context of phenomena, we shall seek in vain to guess or to discover the existence of anything whatever." [10] We may say that Helmholtz, in the whole groundwork of his *Physiologische Optik,* took these Kantian sentences as a methodological prototype and in a sense as his motto. For Helmholtz, too, the only certain statement of reality that we can make concerning phenomena lies in the proof of their connection according to thoroughgoing empirical laws. But directly beside this stands the other view, which throws Helmholtz back into all the difficulties of the pro-

10. *Kritik der reinen Vernunft,* 2d ed., p. 274.

jection theory. Now the signs which signify an object to us are themselves held to be caused by the object, and the work of knowledge now
seems to consist simply in reversing this same process of causality. The
chain of causality runs from the outside in. And knowledge must turn
the inward back into something outward; from the given sensation it
must infer something that is not given and not giveable, something beyond sensation. But the very first step in this inference is problematic. For
the causal dependency in which the sensation supposedly stands to the
thing would not in itself enable the sensation to act as a sign for the
thing. The real relation here supposed contains as such no adequate
foundation for the representative relation it is held to explain. In order
to indicate, to represent, an object, sensation would not only have to *be*
an effect of it but would also have to *know* that it is an effect of it—and
the very possibility of such knowledge remains incomprehensible until we
have left the sphere of merely "indicative" signs and entered into the
realm of genuine truly and originally significative signs.

But the deeper reason for the difficulties that arise here lies in the
attempt to explain a fundamentally unintuitive relationship through
analogies taken from the world of intuitive objects and the relations prevailing between them. We cannot explain the particularity and specific
nature of the pure category of meaning, through which the relation of
the perception to its objects is constituted, on the basis of any sort of ontic
determinations—whether of causality, of identity or similarity between
things, or on the basis of relations of the whole to the part.[11] Here we must
go back not to any attributes of given things, not to the image of an
already existing reality, but to the pure conditions under which a reality
can be posited. Because and insofar as the pure concept belongs to these
conditions, thought can relate itself to reality, can claim objective significance in it and through it. This stands out most clearly when we take the
concept in the purely logical sense as a propositional function and define
it as such. The formula for such a propositional function $\phi(x)$ serves
both to disclose the nature of all those theoretical conflicts over the problem of the concept and of the object, and to give them precise and pregnant expression. The sensationalists, on the one hand, suppose that they
can apprehend the functions of the concept and of the object by considering those values of the variable which enter into this function and
simply coordinating them. They take the ϕ as though it were itself an x,

11. Cf. above, pp. 99–101. 312–14.

or as though it were at most the mere sum of the x's, an $x_1 + x_2 + x_3$ etc. The other view starts from the distinction of the factors linked in the propositional function; it imputes an independent logical validity to the concept, just as it attributes an independent transcendent reality to the object, thus sharply distinguishing it from the immanent data of consciousness. But in the last analysis the adherents of this view believe that they can secure both concept and object only by cutting the function $\phi(x)$, straight through the middle. They not only impute a peculiar "dignity" to the relation ϕ, but even raise it to the level of an absolute, detached and unconditional being. Yet what gives this relation its whole meaning and character is that it singles out the factor in respect to which the different values of the variable are regarded as determinable and determined. To be sure, the function ϕ and the values of the variable still belong to very different logical types, hence can never be reduced to one another, but this irreducibility does not mean that they are strictly separable. Thus, for example, the unity of the "thing" never dissolves into a single one of its appearances—a particular spatial view, for example—but can be determined only through the totality of the possible views and the rule of their combination. Each individual appearance represents the thing but as a particular can never truly coincide with it. In this, critical idealism also holds that the mere appearance necessarily points beyond itself, that it is an "appearance of something." But this something does not signify a new absolute, a new ontic-metaphysical reality. For even though the representing and the represented are far from identical, the one can never produce an intelligible meaning without the other. The function holds for the individual values precisely because it "is" no individual value—and on the other hand the individual values "are" only insofar as they stand to one another in the connection expressed by the function. The particular, the discreet value itself subsists only in reference to the part it plays in some form of universal, whether by this we mean a universality of the concept or of the object—and similarly, the universal can be manifested only through the particular, and can then be certified only as the order and rule for the particular. Thus if we wish to understand the specific validity of the concept and the character of empirical objectivity, we find ourselves ultimately referred back to the function of meaning—which though it shows no cleavage is built up of fundamentally different elements of meaning. For no true meaning is perfectly simple; it is both one and twofold; and this inherent polarity does not divide and destroy it but rather represents its actual fulfillment.

Chapter 3

Language and Science. Thing Signs and Ordinal Signs

THUS FAR OUR INVESTIGATIONS of the connection between the problems of the concept and the object have led us back to general logical and epistemological principles, but we may seem to have almost deviated from our path and lost sight of our main goal. For our central concern was not with the logical problem of meaning or with the epistemological problem as such; supposedly we were considering these two only in their relation to a third problem, that of the sign and of designation. But the deeper we go into the structure of the concept and of objective knowledge, the farther this last problem seems to recede into the distance. For however far we may carry the idea of nominalism, it always proves impossible to dissolve the problem of meaning in the problem of designation and to derive the one entirely from the other. The meaning remains a logical essential, a true πρότερον τῇ φύσει. It proves to be the core and center, while beside it, the designation is forced more and more into a peripheral position. The more resolutely the character of the concept as a pure relational texture is worked out in modern logic, the more sharply the inference tends to be drawn that over against the ideal meaning of this structure the name remains something secondary and external. "A concept," writes Burkamp, for example,

is a relational structure that can be related to an indeterminate manifold. For our thinking this concept becomes a unity and in important cases is designated by a name. The name, the word, however, is no more the concept than my name is myself. The name is something external to the concept and has nothing to do with its essence. . . . If I understand a new mechanical contrivance, it is a concept for me, even if I do not give it a name. The functional relation, transferable to an indeterminate manifold, is the concept. The name is a convenient appendage. It serves primarily as a badge and means of expression for the concept.[1]

An "abbreviation" of this kind can—it would appear—claim no independent value, no autonomy. Its function is solely one of substitution, and all knowledge must at some time learn to dispense with such representation and confront things themselves in their pure being. It becomes knowledge in the strict sense only insofar as it succeeds in doing this—insofar as it casts off the covering in which language and the word threaten to obscure it.

But here the relation between linguistic and scientific concept formation presents the same dialectic we have encountered in a wholly different cultural sphere—in the advance from the mythical to the religious consciousness. The religious consciousness, too, as we have seen, could not dispense with the mythical image world from which it struggled free and to which it opposed itself. It had to make its way through the very midst of this image world; it could not triumph over the mythical forms by negating them and rejecting them, but only by holding them fast and thereby permeating them with a new meaning.[2] In the relation of science with its pure logic to language, the same opposition can again be discerned. All strict science demands that thought free itself from the constraint of the word, that it become independent of it. But once again this act of liberation cannot be performed by a mere turning-away from the world of language. The road begun in language cannot be abandoned but must be followed to its end and continued beyond this end. Thought presses beyond the sphere of language; but precisely in so doing it takes up a tendency which is originally contained in language and which from the very outset was active as a living factor in its own development. This tendency is now worked out in full force and purity, it is freed as it were from mere potentiality and translated into its full efficacy. But it is implicit in this process that the new intellectual reality which now arises, the supreme energy of the pure scientific concept, will retain its secret bond with language. However high the pure concept may rise above the world of the senses into the realm of the ideal and intelligible, in the end it always returns in some way to that "worldly, earthly organ" that it possesses in

1. Burkamp, *Begriff und Beziehung*, first study, p. 7.
2. Cf. the last part of Vol. 2, above: "The Dialectic of the Mythical Consciousness."

language. The indispensable act of detachment from language proves to be conditioned and mediated by language.

For the progress from the linguistic concept to the scientific concept consists not in a negation, a simple reversal of the intellectual process on which the formation of language rests, but in a continuation and ideal heightening of that process. The same fundamental spiritual force which brought forth linguistic concepts from intuitive concepts ultimately refashions these into scientific concepts. We have seen how the function of representation prevails even in the sphere of the natural world view. Only through representation could the world of the senses be molded into a world of intuition and perception. But this process of formation still proved to be wholly confined within the matter of the sensuous world. Even where it was used as a pure means of representation, the perception, seen in a purely substantial sense, seemed to consist of the same matter as the world of the senses. And over and over again this contradictory relation carried with it the danger of a leveling regression; no sooner had a separation between content and function been achieved than it was in danger of being lost. For as long as representation requires a definite intuitive image as its vehicle it cannot detach itself sharply and fundamentally from its intuitive substrate. The mind's eye is only too easily caught in the details of this same image, instead of taking it only as a starting point and transition, as a medium of meaning. Here it is language that first brings about a new and crucial turn. The word of language differs from the sensuous, intuitive image precisely in that it is no longer weighted down, so to speak, with a sensuous matter of its own. Considered in its mere sensuous content, it appears volatile and indeterminate, a mere breath of air. But from the standpoint of the pure representative function precisely this intangible, ephemeral quality is also the basis of its superiority over the immediate, sensuous contents. For the word, one might say, no longer possesses any independent, self-subsistent mass which might offer resistance to the energy of relational thinking. The word is open to every form which thought wishes to imprint upon it, for it is itself no independent being, no concrete, substantial thing, but first takes its meaning from the predicative sentence and from the context of speech.[3]

---

3. Strictly speaking, to be sure, this becomes true only at a stage in which the word is clearly and sharply apprehended in its purely representative and symbolic character—and at which consequently the name is no longer taken, as in mythical thinking, as a real part of the thing it designates. As long as this last is the case, the name retains its fixed,

It is only in the living dynamic of speech that the word takes on its peculiar meaning, that it first becomes what it is. Herein language shows itself again and again to be the mighty and indispensable vehicle of thought—a kind of flywheel that carries thought along with its own unceasing momentum. This free mobility is denied to the particular sensory intuition, because of its concrete abundance and static concreteness. Though there is undeniably a thinking without words, such thinking always remains far more confined within the particular, within what is given here and now, than is true of linguistic thinking. It is in linguistic thinking that the concept first rises clearly above the sphere of perception and intuition. To use Platonic terms, the pure appellative function of the word draws the first sharp dividing line between the realm of the λόγοι and the realm of the πράγματα.[4] Thus though the word does not create the concept, it is by no means a mere appendage to it. It constitutes, rather, one of the most important instruments for its actualization, its liberation from immediate perception and intuition. This liberation may seem like a kind of fall from grace, whereby knowledge is driven from the paradise of the concrete and the individual; still, by this very token, it is also the beginning of that boundless endeavor of the spirit by which it conquers and gives form to its world.

When we seek to clarify the type and direction of this process from a genetic standpoint, we find that the facts of developmental psychology accord fully with the results of our purely theoretical analysis. It seems that in the development of the individual we can still discern the point where the two worlds part, where the shift from merely intuitive general percepts to linguistic concepts takes place. Psychologically the former may be described as schematized percepts, "which are indeed still 'percepts,' that is to say, they still have intuitive definiteness, but their mode of manifestation is no longer so detailed and individualized as individual memories. They are, one might say, sensuous abstractions, simplifications, which, however, still remain within the sphere of sensory intuition." But now the development goes farther. "The schema still has a certain, though ever so vague, resemblance to the intuition, which it still *recalls*. Gradually the need of representing what is meant by something similar vanishes, and an intuitive vestige of this sort suffices to designate the relation

---

substantial character and bondage; the mythical "hypothesis" even fashions it into a demonic entity (cf. 2, 40 ff.).

4. Plato, *Phaedo*, 99D ff.

to the object—that is, the intention: the schema becomes a mere sign." It is this shift that carries us into the sphere of language and of actual conceptual thinking.[5] And we come to a similar conclusion when we seek to delimit the particularity of human speech from those forms and types of semantics that we find more or less clearly developed in the animal kingdom. In the life of animal communities we can also see how the individual communicates with his fellows by means of distinct signs. A bee for example returns from the feeding place it has discovered to the hive, and here enlists companions for a new flight with the help of set movements, a kind of "rallying dance." In so doing it gives to each companion a sample of the specific nectar it has gathered, and this serves the swarm as a means of orientation, as a recognition by which its members are led to the source of the smell. When we compare this mode of signification and communication by signs with the representative function of human speech, we find two essential differences. "Let us concentrate our critical thinking," writes Bühler,

> on the significative function of this nectar that they are given to carry along with them. When the bees go out searching in accordance with their instincts, it may operate very much like a mark of recognition impressed on the human memory. But on close scrutiny this arrangement lacks two factors which are essential to the incomparable freedom and the almost unlimited scope of human linguistic designations. First, the dematerialization of the signs. For it is and remains the real scent of the flowers that provides the communication of the bees, whereas the distinguishing marks provided by human nomenclature make possible a communication without material samples. . . . Only if (the receiver of the material sample) were able to communicate its mnemonic impression to other bees without recourse to the actual material sample, only such independence . . . would provide a basis of comparison with human speech.

The second factor is that of detachability. The "names" of which human speech makes use are no longer a part of the thing to which they point: they no longer attach to it as real attributes, as "accidents," but belong to an independent, purely ideal province. It is these two factors taken together—the step from the material sample to the genuine sign and the essential detachability of the sign from the things for which it functions

5. Cf. William Stern, *Die Psychologie der frühen Kindheit,* pp. 301 ff.

as a sign—which constitute the particularity and the characteristic meaning and value of human speech.[6] And it is on these same two factors that the further progress, the progress from the "verbal signs" of language to the pure "conceptual signs" of theoretical science, is essentially based. In science the process that was devised and initiated in language is completed. For although the word is clearly distinguished from the particular contents of intuition, and confronts them as something independent, endowed with a definite, logical character—it never ceases to cling to the intuitive world as a whole. This attachment appears even where the word functions as an expression of pure relation, where it no longer serves to indicate any sort of datum, where it fulfills no deictic but only a purely predicative function. In studying the growth of language we have repeatedly seen how the predicative function gradually develops from the deictic function. All logical determinations of relation derive at least their means of linguistic expression from intuitive and particularly from spatial relations. Even the copula of judgment, even the "is" of the purely predicative sentence, was seen to be thus permeated by intuitive content; logical "being" and "being-so" could only be expressed through transposition into some kind of intuitive existence. And language, as though by an inner pressure, is impelled over and over again to efface the boundary between essence and existence, conceptual being and intuitive reality.[7] The development of distinct linguistic suffixes has shown us clearly how the kernel of their formal meaning must gradually be freed from the husk of sensuous matter, how the formal relation can only be apprehended through material terms.[8] Here scientific concept formation and scientific terminology go one step further, freeing the sign from all its restrictive sensuous conditions. The processes of dematerialization and detachment continue; the sign tears itself free from the sphere of things, in order to become a purely relational and ordinal sign. Now it is no longer directed toward any single thing which it aims to "represent" directly, to set before the mind's eye in its intuitive contours. It aims rather to mark out a universal, a determination of form and structure which is manifested in the individual example but can never be exhausted in it. In order to apprehend this universal, it does not suffice to take up particular contents as presented by immediate perception or intuition, and provide them with a linguistic

6. Bühler, *Die Krise der Psychologie*, pp. 51 ff.
7. Cf. above, *1*, 315 ff.
8. Ibid., pp. 306 ff.

badge, a "name"; nor in the sense of linguistic class formation does it suffice to gather larger groups of phenomena into unities. Rather, the grouping must follow a definite systematic plan: it must progress methodically from the simple to the complex. This requirement drives the semantics of science out beyond the sphere of "natural" language. Science can no longer take its terms from this sphere but must begin to fashion them for itself, giving them the required completeness and unambiguousness. The original activity of the sign, which gave the word its peculiar spiritual imprint,[9] now stands out for the first time in full force and purity: it no longer works with the random and accidental material given from outside but gives itself the material it requires, the material upon which it can set the stamp of its own character.

Here then the difference between linguistic and scientific concept formation is clearly revealed—but on the other hand, this difference does not interrupt the continuity between them. For far as the scientific concept may rise above the linguistic concept, the transition from one to the other signifies no actual $\mu\epsilon\tau\acute{a}\beta\alpha\sigma\iota\varsigma$ $\epsilon\acute{\iota}\varsigma$ $\ddot{a}\lambda\lambda o$ $\gamma\acute{\epsilon}\nu o\varsigma$. It is the same "logos" that was effective in language formation from the very first, which in the progress to scientific knowledge frees itself from its initial restrictions— which passes from its implicit to its explicit form. This relation, to be sure, appears in a different light if we look upon language not as a logical but as a purely aesthetic form, if we hold that it not only originates in the sphere of pure "intuition" but is permanently and essentially confined within this sphere. A philosophy of language which thus stresses not the logical but the aesthetic factor cannot but regard the difference between linguistic and logical thinking as a positive chasm. "From linguistic to logical thinking," Vossler writes,

> there are no comfortable, gentle, imperceptible transitions; in fact there
> is no progress at all, no ascending or descending gradation; there is
> only reversal. . . . What is to come alive in logical thinking must die
> away and become inert in linguistic thinking. The thought cannot be-
> come a concept without slipping out of the larva of its linguistic past
> and casting off the dead cocoon. These . . . remnants or shells are
> no longer directly meaningful linguistic forms, but only a kind of
> trace or footprint that the logos has left behind in its leap. By their
> formula-like, pallid, and rigid look, by their grammatical schematism,

9. Ibid., pp. 86 ff.

we may still study and recognize the work which logical thought had to perform in order to free itself from linguistic thought.[10]

But apt as this picture is, a different systematic conclusion lies inherent in it from the one which Vossler drew. For admitted that a true transformation is effected in the progress from language to the logical concept, is not this transformation itself still an evolution? Even though in language the logos may appear as a larva, has it not at work within it the forces that will one day enable it to burst through the shell in which it lies confined? It seems to me that in pursuing his own thought Vossler himself is led to a view of this sort. For sharply as he stresses the contrast and the tension between language and science, he shows how precisely at the stage where the two are most remote from one another, a reversal sets in, a "speculative or reflective turning point." At this point the abstract concept becomes dialectical, whereupon logical thinking first discovers its own essence—and at the same time its unity with linguistic thought. But how could thought discover this unity if it were not somehow, if only latently, fundamental to it? Vossler himself speaks here of a "return of thought to itself—that is, the linguistic trend of thought which was at first free from doubt, and external, is aroused from its dream and critically illumined by the logical concept. The logical concept does not destroy and negate it but merely stops it in its somnambulistic course, in order to show it the way." [11] On the basis of our own findings we have no need to contest this formulation of Vossler's thesis. We must only stress this one point: that though the "reflective turning point" of which Vossler speaks is indeed achieved only beyond the confines of language, it is already recognizable and in a certain sense prepared and anticipated in language. For the spoken word itself should never be thought of as a mere product of intuition, but contains within it an act of reflection. The first sign of reflection, as Herder points out, was the "word of the soul," an awakening from the "hovering dream of images," of mere sensuous experiences.[12] It is implicit in the very nature of the spirit that its return to itself does not occur in a single isolated climax of its development but dominates and determines the whole of this development. Over and over again, the same characteristic process begins at different levels—and it is this process which brings about

10. Karl Vossler, "Sprache und Wissenschaft," in Vol. *8* of *Geist und Kultur in der Sprache* (Heidelberg, 1925), pp. 220 ff.

11. Ibid., pp. 227 ff.

12. Herder, *Über den Ursprung der Sprache*. Cf. above, *1*, 152 ff.

the separation of linguistic concepts from the world of immediate intuition, as well as the detachment of logical, scientific concepts from the concepts of language.

For the process of finding distinguishing marks, of qualifying concept formation, starts in language, though it is only in science that it is guided into set, systematic channels. What seems to begin haphazardly in language is directed methodically toward a fixed goal in science. Even the linguistic concept, even the primary function of appellation, is not possible unless a "one in many" is apprehended and fixed in the mind's eye. A manifold of perceived or intuited contents is moved into a definite perspective, through which it is seen as a unity. Every single linguistic concept thus establishes a definite center and focus in which the rays from the various spheres of intuitive being come together and permeate one another. But all these centers are still separate; they do not form a unitary and homogeneous whole. The space of speech and thought presents itself at first more as an aggregate than as a system; it consists of particular points and places, which as yet stand in no thoroughgoing, enduring combination. Still, as language progresses in its development, this deficiency is more and more made good. For the process of speech does not consist solely in coining more and more new names, in gaining new particular significations; these significations must also enter into mutually determining relationships with each other. Every predicative sentence is the beginning of such a determination. Here the subject is related to a predicate and vice versa, and one is determined by the other. Each individual concept first obtains its full meaning by this unremitting work of determination. The infinitely diverse interconnections into which it enters in the whole range of speech first give it its content and its form. This means of course that the linguistic concept may never be thought of as absolutely fixed and definitive. It subsists only by reestablishing and asserting itself in the surge and flow of speech. Language does not flow along tranquilly in a ready-made bed; at every turn it must dig out its channel anew—and it is this living flow which at every step produces new and more highly developed forms. Herein lies its true and fundamental strength, but from the standpoint of the concept and of conceptual thought also its weakness. For the concept in the strict sense tends to set a goal for this surge and flow; it demands stability and unambiguousness. In its *being* it seeks to transcend and negate everything that language must tolerate in its becoming. Hence, although the concept requires and demands representation in its symbolic sign, it does not content itself with any sign at all but sets up very definite requirements which must be met by the world of signs into which it immerses itself. The first of these is the postulate of identity; the same sign must always be chosen for the same content. The free play of signification that is essential for language and that makes possible its movement, the power of a word to be taken sometimes in one and sometimes in another sense, must now be deliberately abolished. The concept strives for a strict, unambiguous correlation between sign and signification. And this basic postulate implies another. Every new concept that is set up in scientific thought is related from the outset to the totality of this thought, to the totality of possible concept formations. What it signifies and is depends on its meaning in this totality. All truth that can be attributed to it is bound to this continual and thoroughgoing verification with respect to the whole range of the contents and propositions of thought. From this it follows that concept signs must form a self-contained system. It does not suffice that certain signs be correlated with certain thought contents; in addition, all must stand in a fixed order, so that the totality of the signs is articulated in accordance with a set rule. Just as one thought content is conditioned by and grounded in another, so one sign must also be grounded in another—that is to say, it must be possible to derive one sign from another in accordance with a definite structural law. This requirement, to be sure, can only be fulfilled with true strictness where the concept itself meets all the needs of precision, where it is susceptible of a definition which bounds it and determines it on all sides. But the tendency toward such a determination is at work in the concept even where the nature of the objects toward which it is directed sets barriers to its complete fulfillment. Even where the concept still clings to the concrete individual intuition and seeks to exhaust it, it is never oriented toward this intuition as a particular but seeks to gather it into the continuum of its forms and to understand it through this continuum. The particular concept strives toward a community of concepts—the particular *eidos* or *genos* aims, to speak in Platonic terms, toward the κοινωνία τῶν γενῶν. This striving cannot content itself with a mere manifold of signs such as the words of language but requires a determinate structure in the signs; they must not only stand side by side—they must unfold from one another; and it must be possible to survey them in accordance with a definite principle.

If the sign is to fulfill this new task, it must of course disengage itself from intuitive existence far more energetically than was the case in the sphere of language. The word of language also had to rise above this existence, yet kept returning to it over and over again. It developed its power in the pure function of indication, but even so continued to actualize the object of the indication in some immediate fashion. We have seen that in the formation of its deictic particles that were the source of certain basic grammatical forms, language again and again proceeded in this way. Where these particles—designating the "here" and the "there," spatial proximity to or distance from the speaker, the direction from the speaker to the person addressed or vice versa—first appear, a wholly sensuous tonality still clings to them. They are intimately fused with the direct gesture of showing, whereby a particular object is singled out from the sphere of immediate perception. The first formation of the spatial words of language, the formation of the demonstrative pronouns, the article, etc. everywhere reveals this primary unity of language and gesture. Originally all these words are nothing other than phonetic metaphors, which first draw their meaning from the whole of the intuitive situation in which they are uttered.[13]

And even where language has long since broken free from this bond with what is sensuously present, even where it has raised itself to the relation of purely intellectual and abstract concepts, it retains this metaphoric trait. Here too it strives to give the concept a body, to grasp it through definite corporeal features. The sensationalists cite this metaphoric character of all speech in order to conclude that basically all thought is determined by sensuous factors.[14] Yet this conclusion would only be valid if the symbolism which thought makes use of, and which even "pure" thought cannot dispense with, depended solely on language. But the development of thought shows quite the contrary; it shows not only that thought uses the signs which language offers it ready-made, but that whenever thought enters into a new form, it provides itself with the appropriate signs. And what distinguishes these pure "concept signs" from the word of language is precisely that no intuitive secondary meaning adheres to them, that they no longer bear any sensuous individual coloration. From means of expression and means of intuitive representation they have become pure vehicles of meaning. What is "meant" and intended in them stands out-

13. Cf. above, *1*, 186 ff., 190 ff., 200 ff., 211 ff.
14. Cf. ibid., pp. 133 ff.

side the sphere of real or even of possible perception. Language can never definitively leave and break through this sphere; for even where as discourse, as objective logos, it is directed toward something absolutely nonsensuous, it can only designate this nonsensuous something from the standpoint of the speaker. It is never pure statement, for it always contains a mode, an individual form of saying, in which the speaking subject expresses himself. All living speech contains within it this dichotomy, this polarity of subject and object. It not only embraces a reference to certain relationships, but also expresses the position of the subject toward them. This inward participation of the ego in the content of what is said is expressed in innumerable subtle shadings, in changes of dynamic accents, in changes of tempo, rhythm, and melody. To divest speech of this "feeling tone" would be to destroy its heartbeat and breath. And yet there is a stage in the development of the human spirit, at which this very sacrifice is demanded of it. The spirit must progress to a pure apprehension of the world, in which all particularities resulting from consideration of the apprehending subject are effaced. As soon as this demand arises, as soon as its necessity is consciously recognized, the intellect must pass beyond the pillars of Hercules erected by language. And it is this transition that opens up the realm of genuine, strict "science." In its symbolic signs and concepts everything which possessed any sort of mere expressive value is extinguished. Here it is no longer any individual subject, but only the thing itself that speaks. On the one hand this seems to signify a monstrous impoverishment: for the movement of language now seems to have been stopped, its inner form seems to have frozen into a mere formula. But what this formula lacks in closeness to life and individual fullness it makes up for by its universal scope and validity. In this universality national as well as individual differences are annulled. The plural concept "languages" loses its justification: it is thrust aside and replaced by the idea of a *characteristica universalis,* which enters the scene in the form of a *lingua universalis.*

Here we stand at the birthplace of mathematical and scientific knowledge. From the viewpoint of our general problem we may say that this knowledge begins exactly at the point where the idea breaks through the cloak of language—yet not in order to appear absolutely unclothed, bereft of all symbolic dress, but in order to enter into a fundamentally different symbolic form. The word of language, with its variability, its variegated ambiguity, must now make way for the pure sign with its determinacy and constancy of meaning. "In the presence of mathematical and scientific concepts," writes Vossler,

> all languages are outwardly equal; these concepts are capable of making themselves at home in every language, since they not only lodge in the outward form of the language but consume and hollow out the inward form. The mathematical concepts of the circle, the triangle, the sphere, of number etc., or the scientific concepts of power, matter, the atom etc., only become fully and strictly scientific when all intuitive, imaginative, mythical, and linguistic thinking that may still haunt them is eradicated.[15]

And yet this eradication signifies no break in the life of the spirit; rather, it manifests the unity of the law which it follows in its development. For the very same process of de-materialization and detachment we have seen to be at work in the beginnings of language now returns at a new stage, where it undergoes a dialectical intensification and sharpening. True, there seems to be a yawning gulf between the scientific concept and the linguistic concept, but on closer scrutiny it is seen to be the same gulf which thought had to bridge before it could become linguistic thought. If we look back at the examples of animal semantics discussed above, their essential limitation seems to lie in their confinement to a particular moment and to a single perceptive situation. This attachment to the here and now is characteristic of all forms of "communication" in the sphere of animal life. When the individual bee informs its fellows of the nectar it has discovered, it does so through a literal sharing of the stuff itself. The scent must be moved from the place where it is into the perceptual field of the bees who are to be enlisted for flight; it must literally be transposed there, in order to serve as a signal and spur for the swarm. Even though more complicated mechanisms may gradually be added to this simple form, even though a "contact of a higher order" may be created by the interpolation of middle links, still it is the sensuous, intuitive presence of the object which first creates this contact, which makes the sign understandable.[16] It is human language which first overcomes this confinement to the immediately given and present sensory situation, which first reaches into the spatial and temporal distance. This reaching into the distance be-

15. Vossler, "Sprache und Wissenschaft," p. 225.
16. Cf. the remarks of Bühler, *Die Krise*, pp. 40 ff.

comes the beginning of all conceptual thought.[17] But thought ultimately comes to a point where this striving into the spatial and temporal distance no longer suffices, where a progress of a fundamentally different and more difficult order is required of it. Now it must not only tear itself away from the here and now, from the present place and moment, but must reach out beyond the whole of space and time, beyond the limits of intuitive representation and of all representability. And it must detach itself from the native soil not only of intuition but also of language. And yet it could not accomplish this last supreme feat if it had not previously gone through the school of language. For here it gathered and concentrated the power which ultimately raised it over language itself. It was language which taught it to survey the whole sphere of intuitive existence, which raised it from the sensuous particular to the whole, the totality of intuition. And now thought no longer contents itself with this totality, but goes beyond it to put forward the claim of necessity and of universality. This claim language can no longer satisfy; for despite the large part played by the basic powers of reason in its structure, every particular language represents its own "subjective world view," from which it cannot and will not detach itself. This very diversity is the medium that enables them to unfold; it is like the air in which alone they can breathe. If on the other hand, we progress from the words of language to the signs of pure science, particularly to the symbols of logic and mathematics, a kind of vacuum seems to enfold us. But at the same time it becomes evident that the movement of the spirit is not obstructed and destroyed thereby, but rather that the spirit for the first time truly discovers itself as that which contains within itself the principle, the beginning of movement. The "vehicle" of word language on which it had so long relied can carry it no farther—but now the spirit feels strong enough to risk the flight that will carry it to a new goal.

In attempting to follow the separate stages in this way we must begin with a process which at first sight seems to belong wholly to the field of language formation and which is at all events deeply rooted in it. All exact concept formation starts from the realm of number, from the determination and designation of the "natural number series." The sequence of numerical signs is the first example and enduring prototype of all pure ordinal signs. But although the pure form of science thus begins with the form of the number, on the other hand, number itself begins in a dif-

17. Cf. above, *1*, 180 ff.

ferent and far earlier stratum than that of strict scientific concept formation. For there is no phase of language formation in which some impulse
toward number formation cannot be disclosed, in which, though with
ever so primitive means, the difference between unity and multiplicity is
not apprehended and fixated through definite linguistic instruments. Consequently, the form of the number and of enumeration is the connecting
link in which we can best discern the relationship between linguistic and
scientific thinking, and also mark the characteristic contrast between
them. The origins of number carry us back to a realm in which language
does not yet seem to have attained its independence, its autonomy. Phonetic language and gesture have not yet separated, but are still closely
intertwined. The meaning of the enumerative act can only be grasped
with an appropriate bodily movement, a specific gesture of counting.
Consequently, the sphere of numbers and the enumerable does not extend
beyond the sphere of these movements. At this stage, the number appears
far more as a manual concept than as an intellectual concept. We have
everywhere disclosed this relationship in the way in which primitive
languages form their numerical terms. We have seen that precisely these
words are weakest in objective, representative meaning: they do not
designate an objective state of affairs but serve, rather, as directives or
one might say imperatives for certain motor processes. The word for
"five," for example, may mean that the hand used in counting should be
closed—the word for "six" that a "jump" should be made from one hand
to the other.[18] No greater confinement to the subject would seem possible:
for here the subject must be present and perceptible not only as an individual ego but even as a definite material body, before the stages of the
enumerative act can be differentiated. Yet even in the most primitive mode
of counting, closer analysis reveals a motif which points in a new direction. For however sensuous and material the original numerical terms
may seem, this does not detract from the function they have to fulfill. They
are closely dependent on words for things: the names for the hand, for
the fingers and toes, etc. serve at the same time as terms for particular
numbers. Yet it is not the hand or the finger itself which is meant when
the numeral in question is spoken and toward which the linguistic intention is directed. Rather, the thing-names must in each instance be repeated
in a definite sequence which must be firmly fixed in the mind, so that
they always recur in the same order. Once this condition is met, each

18. For details see above, *1*, 229 ff. Cf. Lévy-Bruhl, *Das Denken der Naturvölker*, pp. 155 ff.

element belonging to the sequence grows beyond its initial significance: having started out as a mere thing-sign, it has now become a sign of position. When the natives of New Guinea count, they first name the fingers of the left hand, then the wrist, the elbow, the shoulder, the neck, the breast. This naming of the parts of the body does not serve to point them out as sensuous objects, but rather to distinguish the stages in the act of enumeration itself. The thing-name functions as an index of enumeration: it indicates an "earlier" or "later" step within the total series. The extent to which such a differentiation is possible may be extremely limited; for example, an independent name may be given only to the first and second, or at most to the third and fourth, member of the series, while beyond this limit there is only a vague expression for "indefinitely many." But even in this extreme limitation a new venture of thought is discernible. For the word of language has now become the expression of an intellectual operation, however simple. It still leans, almost anxiously as it were, on the intuition of sensuous objects for support; but in them, though at first unclearly and uncertainly, it apprehends a factor of their form—a factor that refers not to the simple "whatness" of these objects but to the manner in which they are ordered and in which they may be correlated.

The scientific concept of number arises when this first beginning is freed from all accidental restrictions and raised to the level of the universal. It requires a universal system of ordinal signs, posited on the basis of a universal principle. No outward limits may be set to the progression of the system. The quantity of "things" that we can distinguish in sense perception or intuition, may no longer serve as a measure for our formation of ordinal signs. Rather, these signs now possess a purely ideal character: to speak with Leibniz, they designate orders of the possible, not of the real. The investigation of language has taught us, to be sure, what difficulties stand in the way of this turn toward the idea—what obstacles and setbacks thought must face on this road to itself. Here the transitions and intermediaries may be disclosed step for step. Number has at first no independent, no abstract, meaning but can only be manifested through the enumerated things and is still tainted with all their particularity. It does not refer to objects in general without distinction, but in each instance only to a particular class of objects, so that different numerical terms must be employed for different types of object. Persons and things, animated and inanimate things, flat or long or round objects—each class requires a special group of numerical terms to designate it. The numerical concept of mathematics, however, differs from the numerical word of language precisely in the fact that it has freed itself from all these involvements. It has overcome the heterogeneity which seems to be forced upon thought by the diversity of objects and has attained to homogeneity, to the *genus* and *eidos* of number.[19] Now, diverse numbers have no being that can be detached from their positional value, no individuality in the sense of a concrete datum. Once thought thus differentiates the pure form of the numerical relation from everything that can enter into it, it can make unlimited use of this form. The outcome is what we may call a qualitative and quantitative infinity of number: quantitative, because the operation from which the individual numbers arise may be applied over and over again to its result; qualitative, because the principle by which the order and series are established is independent of the particular nature of the content in which the serial relation is disclosed. "It is an old saying," writes Leibniz in a fragment on the Universal Characteristic, "that God created all things according to measure, weight, and number. But there are things that cannot be weighed, namely those that possess no potency or energy; there are things that are without parts and thus admit of no measurement. But there is nothing that evades number. Hence number in a manner of speaking is a metaphysical figure and arithmetic is a kind of statics of the universe, in which the energies of things are investigated."[20] The root of this ontological universality of number is that it provides an absolutely universal and ideal standard. This standard is applicable wherever any multiplicity of contents, however constituted in other respects, meets one condition, namely that it fixates elements which may be ordered and articulated according to a determinate viewpoint. In his natural philosophy, Plato designated space as the original form of all material being, because it provides the "receptive principle," the πρῶτον δεκτικόν for all material things—because all material forms are only special determinations of the universal form of space. Similarly the realm of numbers provides a kind of receptacle for all apprehension of concrete orders. It is through the universal system of signs provided by number that thought is first enabled to apprehend all being toward which it turns as a thoroughly determinate being, and to understand it under the category of the universal and necessary.

One of the most striking features of modern mathematics is that it

19. Cf. above, *1*, 233 ff.
20. Leibniz, *Philosophische Schriften*, ed. Gerhardt, *7*, 184.

recognizes this logical universality of the pure concept of number and has built up a system of analysis upon it. Even today, to be sure, the attempts to explain the concept of number differ greatly on particulars. But in the work of Cantor and Dedekind, of Frege and Russell, of Peano and Hilbert, the characteristic methodological direction in which this explanation is sought stands out clearly. Only a few decades ago a thinker of the stature of Helmholtz could attempt a derivation of the numerical concept along essentially empiricist lines, but since then strict empiricism has steadily lost ground in this field. Frege's classical argument against Mill's "arithmetic of cookies and pebbles" seems to have cleared the air once and for all. As Frege defines and derives "number," it can no longer be termed an attribute of any "thing" whatsoever, and surely not of a sensuous, perceptible object, but may only be defined as an attribute of a concept. "When I say: the Emperor's carriage is drawn by four horses," writes Frege, "I attribute the number four to the concept of the 'horse that draws the Emperor's carriage.'"[21] But here Dedekind goes a different way; though for him too it is settled that the numerical concept is to be regarded as an "immediate emanation of the pure laws of thought."[22] And Russell's whole theory of the principles of mathematics aims to prove that in order to determine and establish the meaning of the numerical concept, we need presuppose nothing other than purely "logical constants." Even mathematical "intuitionism" presents no opposition to this basic trend. For sharply as it differs from the formalistic and logistic tendency in its view of the relation between mathematics and logic, the "original intuition" which it sets up as the source of number is anything but an intuition of empirical objects. Even Brouwer, in his attempt to establish a purely intuitionistic mathematics, starts not with the notion of things but with the positing of a basic relation, from which he derives the concept of order and with it the concept of number. "A species P," he writes, "is said to be virtually ordered if an asymmetrical relation which we shall designate as an ordering relation is defined for the element pairs (a, b) of P within it. This relation—which we express by $a < b$, or a before b, or a to the left of b, or a lower than b, or $b > a$, or b after a, or b to the right of a, or b higher than a—possesses very definite 'ordering attributes,' which must be designated universally and exactly."[23]

21. *Grundlagen der Arithmetik* (Breslau, 1884), p. 59.

22. See above, *1*, 227.

23. L. E. J. Brouwer, "Zur Begründung der intuitionistischen Mathematik, II," *Mathematische Annalen*, 96 (1927), 453.

But compared to this development of number in pure mathematics, the picture is very different in epistemology, where the basic contradictions stand out much more clearly. Even within the sphere of "critical philosophy," the conflicting views seem irreconcilable. According to the *Critique of Pure Reason* the theory of numbers belongs neither to the transcendental aesthetic nor to the transcendental logic but forms, rather, an intermediary link that connects the two. Kant calls number "the pure schema of quantity as a concept of the understanding," because it "encompasses" the successive addition of one to one (homogeneous quantities). Thus it is nothing other than the "unity of the synthesis of the manifold in a homogeneous intuition," in that consciousness generates time itself in the apprehension of the intuition.[24] This fundamental view developed in two different directions, according as the stress was laid on the factor of understanding or on the sensuous—on synthesis or on intuition. In the first case, number was regarded not merely as a product of pure thought, but as its very prototype and source. It not only grew out of the pure regularities of thinking, but designated the primary and original act to which they ultimately go back. Accordingly, an exponent of logical idealism writes: "For thought there can be nothing more primary than itself, thought—that is, the positing of relation. Anything else that one might claim as the basis of number would include this positing of relation, and it can appear as the foundation of number only because it contains the true foundation, the positing of relation, as a presupposition."[25] A radically different view is stated by Rickert in *Das Eine, die Einheit und die Eins*. For according to Rickert, number cannot be dissolved into logical elements but actually forms the prototype by which the epistemologist may most clearly apprehend and demonstrate the essence of the "alogical." Thus any attempt to derive even the most elementary arithmetical truth from purely logical premises remains hopeless. "Even a proposition such as $1 = 1$ presupposes a factor of experience or at least of intuition, a factor which is barely encompassed in the logical form of unity but is, moreover, alogical."[26] This thesis seems to cut the ground from under any attempt to penetrate the essence of number through the presuppositions of pure logic. And yet the problem takes on a different

24. *Kritik der reinen Vernunft*, 2d ed., p. 182. Eng. ed., p. 120.

25. Natorp, *Die logischen Grundlagen der exakten Wissenschaft*, p. 99.

26. Heinrich Rickert, *Das Eine, die Einheit und die Eins*, Heidelberger Abhandlungen Zur Philosophie und ihrer Geschichte, *1*, ed. Ernst Hoffmann and Heinrich Rickert (2d ed. Tübingen, 1924), p. 87.

aspect if we consider not simply the conclusion but also the methodological foundations of Rickert's theory. For then we find that the root of Rickert's difference with "logical idealism" lies not so much in his view of number as in his view of the nature of the logos. As far as number is concerned, Rickert resolutely rejects any attempt at an empiricist derivation of it, any attempt to ground its meaning and essence in the "things" of empirical reality. Its independence of experience, its apriority and ideality remain intact. If he nevertheless designates it as an alogical product, this in his language means only that over against the logical object that is constituted by unity and otherness—identity and difference— the object of "number" represents a content *sui generis*. Identity and difference represent the logical minimum without which no sort of objectivity can be conceived of; but this minimum does not suffice to build up the concept of the numerical "one," the concept of "quantity" and of the numerical series as an ordered sequence of elements. "The insights of mathematics, like all purely theoretical insights," Rickert writes, "are certainly logical in the broader sense of the word. But still they must contain something which is added to the pure logos and makes it into a specifically mathematical logos. Or does mathematical ratio . . . coincide with the purely logical ratio? Is the mathematical method not, rather, 'rational' only in a very special sense?"[27] Thus formulated, Rickert's view is doubtless justified, but of course it is no clear and adequate expression of the relationship here prevailing to say that number is alogical because it is not exhausted by logic. For this would inevitably make it appear as though something other, something transcending purely logical identity and difference were posited in the essence of number, and moreover as though this "other" were in some way alien to thought, opposed to logic. But mere differentiation does not include any such opposition; the species does not depart from the genus or negate the genus but contains rather a closer determination of it. Logical idealism itself is far from asserting a simple coincidence of number with the logical: rather, it regards number as a determination of the logical.[28] If we take the logical in

27. Ibid., p. 4.
28. Here, to be sure, it must be admitted that in Natorp, against whom Rickert's demonstration in the revised version of his article on the logos is chiefly directed, the two viewpoints are not sharply differentiated. When Natorp attempts to derive the concept of number purely from the "synthesis of the manifold," i.e. to show that the mere containment of different "species" in a "genus" is a numerical difference, the objections raised by Rickert strike me as wholly justified (cf. *Das Eine*, pp. 27 ff.). The "numerical"

Rickert's sense, if we regard identity and difference as the only strictly logical categories, there can be no doubt that these categories in themselves are insufficient to produce the realm of number and of mathematics in general. Insofar as it aimed merely to substantiate this proposition, Rickert's demonstration would have been greatly simplified and sharpened if he had made use of the instruments provided by modern logical calculus, and particularly by relational calculus. For, expressed in the language of this calculus, identity and difference are symmetrical relations, whereas for the building of the realm of number and for the concept of ordered sequence in general, an asymmetrical relation is indispensable.[29] But if on the other hand, we take the concept of logical form

---

difference indubitably means something more and something other than the "generic" difference. But on the other hand, it cannot be inferred from the non-coincidence of "quantity" and "concept" that quantity brings into the concept an alogical element that is alien to it. Rather, the synthesis of number like that of concept rests on the same basic act of "positing relation"—a positing that is at the same time a differentiating—except that this logical act "specifies" itself differently in the number than in the concept, i.e. it proceeds from a different determining viewpoint, the viewpoint of the series and of serial order. For further detail cf. my remarks, below.

29. It has been shown, particularly by Russell, that the concept of an "order among elements" can be reduced analytically to the existence of an asymmetrical, transitive relation among them and necessarily presupposes a relation of this form; cf. esp. chaps. 24 and 25 of the *Principles of Mathematics*, and chap. 4 of the *Introduction to Mathematical Philosophy*. Even Aloys Müller testifies to this in his *Der Gegenstand der Mathematik mit besonderer Beziehung auf die Relativitätstheorie* (Braunschweig, 1922). Working with Rickert's terminology and basic assumption, namely that "identity and difference exhaust the characteristic of the specifically logical—of the original logical phenomenon" (p. 31), he comes to the conclusion that in the logical sphere there is and can be no series, and that it consequently lacks the important and absolutely indispensable factor for the building of number (p. 34). It is not this inference as such but the premises from which it flows that are questioned in logical idealism, where the concept of "logic" is different and considerably richer than that of Rickert and Müller. It might, indeed, appear that with this insight the whole controversy had been reduced to a terminological difference and thus rendered sterile: for must not every thinker be free to use the term "logical" in any sense he pleases? Actually this right is not questioned: but one thing should be borne in mind, that if Rickert's terminology is accepted, logic itself, in its classical form as well as the modern form given it by Peirce and Boole, Frege and Peano, Schröder and Russell —can no longer be designated as the theory of the "logical object." For, from a historical point of view, there has never been a science of logic limited to what Rickert calls the "purely logical object." Such a limitation is found at most in the beginning of logic, in Parmenides, for whom in fact the whole problem of logic is exhausted in identity and difference, in "being" or "non-being." But even Plato in his *Sophist* goes far beyond this "basic phenomenon" of the One and Other. For here it is the notion of the "community" of ideas, the κοινωνία τῶν γένων, which is central and which first makes possible a science of logic. This community is based on the relation of systematic dependency of concepts

in its full universality—if we take it as an expression of relatedness in general, under which all particular varieties of relation, the transitive and the intransitive, the symmetrical as well as the nonsymmetrical and asymmetrical, are subsumed as special cases—then number cannot be denied admittance into this universal system. Number neither exhausts the system nor is an exception to it, but constitutes, rather, a foundation stone which cannot be removed without disrupting the whole edifice.

For precisely because number represents the schema of order and series in general, thought is always thrown back upon it, as soon as it seeks to apprehend the content of being as an ordered content. Here thought possesses its essential means of orientation, the ideal axis around which its world rotates. Wherever it is confronted by a manifold of "given" contents, thought attempts this transposition into its own ideal norm. In their first enthusiasm over the philosophical and scientific discovery of number, the Pythagoreans expressed this basic relationship by saying that number is being. For being cannot be thought except in the form of determinacy, of harmonious order: but determinacy and harmony are present only where number prevails. But side by side with their basic tenet of the metaphysical identity between being and number, the Pythagoreans had another that is both methodologically sharper and more cautious. Here number is designated no longer as being pure and simple, but as the "truth of being." Truth and number are essentially related: the one can be known only in and through the other. The subsequent development of theoretical knowledge shows of course that logical form as such is not restricted to the sphere of number and the enumerable but obtains wherever there is necessary and lawful combination. The realm of numbers provides the clearest example of a manifold that is built up in accordance with strict law, and that follows unequivocally and completely from a first funda-

---

and judgments, on the relation of "ground" and "consequence" that exists between them. But this logical "consequence" can no more be derived from sheer identity and difference than can that of the numerical series. Like the numerical relation, the basic relation of "implication" is itself something new and distinct over against mere unity and otherness. The disparity becomes still more evident if we start from the new form of logic, which historically goes back to Leibniz. For this logic aspires to comprehend the totality of "pure forms," of connections possessing a priori validity, to establish the specific laws governing each of them, and fixate these laws by means of a symbolic calculus. For this the logical minimum which Rickert finds in the "purely logical object" can never suffice. And one can gain a lively impression of how far one must go beyond it by studying the modern form of this logic as epitomized, for example, in the systematic work of Russell and Whitehead.

mental position and from a principle which regulates the advance from it to a second position and thence to a third, etc. From now on, wherever thought is confronted by a construction of the same conceptual type, it possesses an analogy to number. In his earliest philosophical conceptions, Leibniz started with a plan for a universal arithmetic; but this he soon extended to a plan for a universal "combinatorics." Such a system, he held, need not be limited to numbers but can equally well extend to formations of a different type—for example, to points—and for this Leibniz provided an example in his *analysis situs,* which is a pure calculus of points. Wherever there is an original generative relation, and where it is such that the whole of a field is completely determined, we have the essential presupposition for the dominance of logical form. The condition for this dominance is that by repeated application of the fundamental relation, every element of the manifold may be reached in a regulated sequence of steps of thought, and defined by means of this sequence. Thus logical form, taken in this most universal sense, is never exhausted in the positing and differentiation of the "one" and the "other" but requires that the one be determinable by the other. Wherever this determinability is not only empirically given but also follows from a necessary law that is valid for all elements, a strictly deductive progress from member to member and a synopsis, a single synthetic survey of all the members, becomes possible; and it is this specific mode of vision, not any special content that might be expressed in a particular factor and characteristic, that determines the object as a logical-mathematical object.

Step by step modern logic and modern mathematics have approached the fulfillment of this ideal—but the ideal was set forth by systematic philosophy long before it was concretely realized. The fundamental conception was expressed by Descartes with surprising universality and a positively prophetic clarity.[30] At the age of twenty-two he wrote in his diary: "Larvatae nunc scientiae sunt, quae larvis sublatis pulcherrimae apparerent; catenam scientiarum pervidenti non difficilius videbitur eas animo retinere quam seriem numerorum" ("Today the sciences are masked, but if the masks were removed they would stand forth most beautiful; to him who perceives the chain uniting them they will be no more difficult to keep in one's mind than a series of numbers").[31] The sciences,

30. On the following cf. my *Das Erkenntnisproblem,* 3d ed., *1,* 445 ff.
31. *Oeuvres inédites de Descartes* (Paris, Foucher de Careil, 1859), p. 4.

which had hitherto existed side by side as a mere aggregate, should now be forged into a chain, each single link of which reaches over into the next and is connected with it in accordance with a strict rule. From this concept of the chain, which in Descartes contains the germ of an entirely new scientific theory, Dedekind was to derive his new fundamental theory of arithmetic. The immediate consequence, in Descartes' own case, was the development, on the basis of the methodological perspective here attained, of a newer and deeper insight into the object of science. Arithmetic and geometry, statics and mechanics, astronomy and music seem to deal with very different objects; yet on closer scrutiny they are all merely diverse aspects and manifestations of one and the same cognitive form. It is with this cognitive form that the universal scientific theory, the *mathesis universalis* treats. It does not relate to number, to spatial form, to motion as such, but extends to everything that is determined according to order and measure.

As early as Descartes the concept of order appears as the more universal, the concept of measure as the more specialized, factor in this determination. All measurement that we undertake in a manifold is ultimately grounded in a definite function of order, but without special new assumptions everything ordered is not measurable. Thus the decisive characteristic of the mathematical object is increasingly concentrated in the one fundamental concept of order. In Leibniz this logical process is completed, and at the same time a new demand is clearly formulated, namely that an exactly determined order of signs must correspond to the order of what is thought. It is through this order of signs that thought first achieves a truly systematic survey of the totality of its ideal objects. Every single operation of thought must be expressible by an analogous operation in the signs and must be verifiable through the universal rules that have been established for the combination of the signs. With this postulate the standpoint of the modern *mathesis universalis* is achieved. Though this *mathesis universalis* demands a thoroughgoing formalization of the entire process of mathematical thought, it by no means annuls the relation to the object: the objects themselves, however, have ceased to be concrete things and have become purely relational forms. It is not the "what" that is combined but the "how" of the combination that decides whether a certain manifold belongs to the sphere of mathematical objects. "If we have a certain class of relations," writes a modern mathematician in summing up this view, "and if the only question we ask is whether or not certain ordered groups of objects fulfill these relations: then the results of these investigations are called 'mathematical.' " [32]

In this formulation, the mathematical is extended beyond its initial, classical territory, beyond the realm of quantity and magnitude. Leibniz himself defined combinatorics as the "scientia de qualitate in genere," and equated quality in the most universal sense with form. And it is perfectly true that modern mathematics discloses a number of disciplines in which there can no longer be any question of investigating or comparing extensive magnitudes. Side by side with metric geometry we have an independent and autonomous projective geometry, whose structure has no need of the specific relation of magnitude, of the standpoint of the larger or smaller. The same is true of *analysis situs* and of the geometrical characteristic that was founded by Leibniz and developed by Hermann Grassman, who directly enlarged on Leibniz' basic ideas. Even in the sphere of arithmetic, determination by the concept of magnitude proves to be too narrow. The theory of substitutions takes its place side by side with the theories of number developed by elementary arithmetic, and moreover it develops that the basic theorems of elementary arithmetic can be strictly deduced only on the basis of this theory.[33] And from here the road leads to what has been said to be "perhaps the most characteristic concept in nineteenth-century mathematics." [34] For investigations of groups of letter substitutions give rise to the general concept of a group of operations and the new discipline of a theory of groups. Not only was the group theory an important addition to the system of mathematics, but it soon became increasingly plain that this was a new, far-reaching component of mathematical thought itself. Felix Klein's famous "Erlanger Programm" shows how it changes the inner form of geometry. Geometry now becomes subordinated to the theory of invariants as a special case. What links the various geometries is that each of them considers certain

32. M. Bôcher, "The Fundamental Conceptions and Methods of Mathematics," *Bulletin of the American Mathematical Society, 11* (1905), 115–35. Cf. also Gregor Itelson's definition of mathematics as the "science of ordered objects," in *Revue de métaphysique et de morale, 12* (1904), 1037 ff. For further detail see Aurel E. Voss, *Über das Wesen der Mathematik* (3d ed. Leipzig, 1922), pp. 26 f.

33. Cf. the descriptions of arithmetic by Otto Stolz and Alfredo Capelli; cf. Otto Hölder, *Die mathematische Methode* (Berlin, 1924), pp. 173 ff.

34. Cf. Hermann Weyl, "Philosophie der Mathematik und Naturwissenschaft," *Handbuch der Philosophie*, ed. A. Baeumler and Manfred Schröter (Munich and Berlin, 1927), Pt. II A, p. 23.

basic properties of spatial forms, which prove invariant in relation to certain transformations; what distinguishes them is the fact that each one of these geometries is characterized by a particular transformation group.[35] To convince ourselves that the group theory has thus influenced the general conception of geometry and the development of other basic mathematical disciplines, we need only recall the importance of Lie's theory of transformation groups for the theory of differential equations. All this suggests that a primary epistemological significance should be imputed to it. And indeed we find an inner methodological relationship between the concepts of number and of the group. From an epistemological point of view, the latter seems to continue on a higher plane the same relationship from which the concept of number started. The natural numerical series begins by fixating a first "element" and indicating a rule, through whose repeated application more and more new elements can be produced. They are all joined in a unitary whole by the fact that every combination we effect with elements of the numerical series defines in turn a new "number." When we form the sum of the two numbers a and b or their difference, their product, etc., the values $a + b$, $a - b$, $a \cdot b$ do not fall out of the basic series but belong to it as determinate positions, or at least can be indirectly related to the positions of the basic series in accordance with fixed rules. Thus, however far we progress in ever renewed syntheses, we are still certain that the logical framework in which we move, much as it may be extended, will never be totally broken. The idea of the self-contained, unitary realm of numbers means precisely this: the combination of ever so many arithmetical operations always leads back ultimately to arithmetical elements. In the group theory this same conception is now raised to true and strict universality. For here, in a manner of speaking, the dualism of "element" and "operation" is annulled: the operation itself has become an element. A totality of operations forms a group when any two successive transformations lead to a definite result, which may also be arrived at through a single operation belonging to the totality. The group, accordingly, is nothing other than an exact expression for what we mean by a "self-contained" sphere, or system, of operations. The theory of transformation groups—whether we think of it in reference to finite discrete groups or to continuous transformation groups—can thus, logically speaking, be designated

35. Cf. Felix Klein, "Vergleichende Betrachtungen über neuere geometrische Forschungen," *Mathematische Annalen, 43* (1893), 63–100.

as a new dimension of arithmetic: it is an arithmetic that refers no longer to numbers, but to forms, to relations and operations. Here again each new penetration into the world of forms and its inner law proves to be a step toward the real, an advance in our knowledge of the empirical world. Once again we find confirmation of Leibniz' dictum, "le réel ne laisse pas de se gouverner par l'idéal et l'abstrait." Kepler called number the "eye of the mind," through which reality becomes visible to us; and the group theory, which has been termed the most striking example of purely intellectual mathematics,[36] may also be said to have made certain physical relationships discernible for the first time. Through the concept of the group Minkowski was able to translate the special theory of relativity into purely mathematical form and so elucidate it from an entirely new angle. And again, the group theory of "space-metrics" led to important insights in modern physics by divesting certain observed facts of their merely accidental character and making it possible to consider them from a universal systematic standpoint.[37]

If on the basis of these general theoretical considerations, we now attempt to define the position of number in the general system of mathematics, we find that to this end it is necessary to differentiate clearly two factors that have often crossed and intertwined in the course of the historical development. As early as the Pythagorean doctrine, we find a characteristic vacillation in the expression of the central idea. Side by side with the fundamental formula, according to which all being is essentially number, stand other formulations to the effect that all being imitates number and participates in it through this imitation. In the fragments of Philolaus it is said not only that things *are* numbers but also that everything knowable, whatever its nature, *has* its number.[38] At first sight this "having" of number strikes one as a strangely contradictory and baffling relationship. For it embraces unity and otherness, identity and difference—it maintains the separation between being and number, but at the same time measures one by the other and links them indissolubly together. Time and time again this original tension has threatened to break out into dialectical conflict. Only modern mathematics has created the means by which to maintain the tension and at the same

36. Cf. Weyl, *Philosophie der Mathematik*, p. 23.

37. For detailed treatment see Hermann Weyl, *Raum, Zeit, Materie; Vorlesungen über allegemeine Relativitätstheorie* (4th ed. Berlin, 1921), pp. 124 ff. Eng. trans. by Henry L. Brose, *Space—Time—Matter* (London, 1922; New York, 1950).

38. Cf. Philolaus, Fragment 4 (Diels, 32B).

time to gain intellectual command over it. Modern mathematics has apprehended the polarity but at the same time developed it into a pure correlation. Now it becomes evident that the realm of objects with which mathematics deals cannot be reduced to mere quantity, to number or magnitude; but at the same time the continuous relation of all mathematical objects to number and its fundamental order is preserved. Thus the road that leads beyond number always leads back to it. One must take both tendencies together in order to gain an insight into the intellectual structure of modern mathematics. However far its object may go beyond the realm of numbers, it still remains attached to number in its method. "The modern development of our science," writes Hermann Weyl, "has shown the old explanation of mathematics as the theory of number and space to be too narrow; yet there is no doubt that even in such disciplines as pure geometry, *analysis situs,* group theory, etc., the natural numbers are brought from the very start into relation with the objects treated." [39] Thus precisely in the amplified form of modern mathematics the tendency toward "arithmetization" is preserved and actually stands out with particular sharpness. All the great thinkers who have given the mathematics of the nineteenth century its intellectual imprint have contributed to this progressive development. Gauss, who called mathematics the queen of the sciences, termed arithmetic the queen of mathematics. [40] In the same sense Felix Klein called for a thoroughgoing arithmetization of mathematics. [41] And it appeared that mathematical knowledge could only be ultimately secured if this method was followed. Hilbert, for example, proved that geometry was free from contradiction by devising a means of reducing the elements and theorems of geometry to purely arithmetical terms. If it is shown that such an arithmetical expression is free from contradiction, and why, then the coherence of the geometrical statement seems assured. Thus Hilbert regards the numerical order as the ultimate and fundamental stratum of the axiomatic thinking that is characteristic of mathematics as such. In general the axiomatic method consists in continuously sinking the foundations of the various spheres of knowledge to a deeper level—but a truly radical foundation is achieved only if we succeed

39. Hermann Weyl, *Das Kontinuum. Kritische Untersuchungen über die Grundlagen der Analysis* (Leipzig, 1918), p. 17.

40. Hermann W. K. Sartorius von Waltershausen, *Gauss zum Gedächtnis*, p. 79; quoted from Voss, *Über das Wesen der Mathematik*, p. 113.

41. Felix Klein, "Über die Arithmetisirung der Mathematik," *Nachrichten von der königlichen Gesellschaft der Wissenschaften zu Göttingen* (1895), 82–91.

in anchoring the axioms of a scientific sphere in number. "Everything that can be the object of scientific thinking," Hilbert concludes, "falls to the axiomatic method and thus indirectly to mathematics, as soon as it is ripe for the formation of a theory. By penetrating to deeper and deeper strata of axioms we also gain ever deeper insights into the essence of scientific thinking itself and become increasingly aware of the unity of our knowledge. Under the sign of the axiomatic method, mathematics seems called upon to play a leading role in all science." [42]

In all this we perceive that it is number not as an intellectual content but as a type of thought which determines the specific character of modern mathematics. But if "pure mathematics" is thus defined as the science of numbers and numbers as "signs manufactured by us for the ordering faculties of our understanding," [43] the question of the truth content of these signs becomes all the more urgent. Are they mere signs to which we should impute no objective significance, or have they a *fundamentum in re?* And if the latter is true, where shall we seek this foundation? Is it provided ready made by intuition—or must it, aside from and independently from all the data of intuition, be acquired and secured in independent acts of reason, in a pure spontaneity of thought? With these questions we stand at the center and focus of the methodological struggle that is now being waged again over the meaning and content of the fundamental concepts of mathematics. Here we cannot go into the details of this controversy or into its origins: we shall merely ask what significance it has for our own basic problem, the problem of symbolic thinking.

42. D. Hilbert, "Axiomatisches Denken," *Mathematische Annalen, 78* (1918), 405–15.
43. Cf. Voss, *Über das Wesen der Mathematik,* 29 ff., 106 ff.

Chapter 4

The Object of Mathematics

1. The Formalistic and Intuitionistic Theories of Mathematics

BEFORE WE CONSIDER the conflict between "formalism" and "intuition-ism" in its present acute form, let us look back at its presuppositions and the historical events leading up to it. Such a retrospect is of philosophical as well as historical interest. For it appears that much misunderstanding between the contending factions might have been avoided, that the essence of the conflict might have been made to stand out more plainly, if both camps had been aware of the long preliminary history of the problem in both logic and philosophy. As early as Aristotle we find a remark sug-gesting that he found the essence of geometrical definition not in a mere conceptual explanation but only in an explanation embracing a theorem and proof of existence. The geometer assumes the *meaning* of the word "triangle," but he must prove that there *is* a triangle.[1] Elsewhere as well the concept of geometrical construction as seen by the philosophical and mathematical theory of the ancients is closely bound up with the problem of the proof of existence.[2] And the renaissance of mathematical thinking that occurred in the sixteenth and seventeenth century starts from this very point. Here Spinoza and Hobbes, Tschirnhaus and Leibniz worked in the same direction: for them all the problem of genetic, or as they call it "causal," definition takes on a philosophical significance extending far beyond the sphere of mathematics.[3] It was Leibniz with his supreme methodological clarity who gathered all these tendencies into one and determined their place in the general structure of logic. The controversy between nominalism and realism which had dominated all medieval logic

1. τί μὲν γὰρ σημαίνει τὸ τρίγωνον ἔλαβεν ὁ γεωμέτρης, ὅτι δ' ἔστιν δείκνυσιν (Analyt., II, 7, 92b, 15).

2. See Hieronymus G. Zeuthen, "Die geometrische Construction als 'Existenzbeweis' in der antiken Geometrie," *Mathematische Annalen,* 47 (1896), 222 ff.

3. Cf. my *Erkenntnisproblem,* 3d ed., 2, 49 ff., 86 ff., 127 ff., 191 f.

now took on a new form: redeemed from sterile speculation it entered into the very heart of concrete work in the exact sciences. Hobbes had endeavored to demonstrate that the truth and universality of mathematical concepts were of a purely verbal character. According to him, they were grounded not in reality but in the word; they rested solely on a convention regarding linguistic signs. To this view Leibniz opposed the idea that the sign itself, insofar as it is to be a meaningful sign, is subject to certain objective conditions. The symbols and characters of mathematics cannot be formed at random or combined arbitrarily but are subservient to definite norms of combinability, which are imposed by the necessity of the object. Yet this object by which they must always orient themselves and whose inner truth they strive to express is to be conceived not as an empirical thing but as the existence of certain relations that obtain among pure ideas. It is here that all mathematical concept formation and all mathematical signification find their support and inner measure. The combinations of characters must correspond to the objective relations of ideas.[4] "The art of characteristics is the art of forming and ordering characters in such a way that they relate to thoughts, or, in other words, have to each other that relation which the thoughts have to each other. An 'expression' is the aggregate of the characters representing the thing which is expressed. The law of expressions is this: The expression of a thing is composed from the characters of things in the same way that the idea of the thing to be expressed is composed from the ideas of these things."[5] With this the relation between the mathematical formula and the reality to which it refers is unambiguously established. The formula first acquires its significative function through its intention toward the reality—and on the other hand, it should be so constituted as to embrace all the essential features of the latter and give them a pregnant and exact expression.

Thus for Leibniz the building of the world of mathematical signs, the creation and combination of the various characters, are bound up from

4. Cf. Leibniz, "Meditationes de veritate cognitione et ideis," *Philosophische Werke*, ed. Cassirer and Buchenau, *1*, 22 ff.

5. "Ars characteristica est ars ita formandi atque ordinandi characteres, ut referant cogitationes, seu ut eam inter se habeant relationem, quam cogitationes inter se habeant. Expressio est aggregatum characterum rem quae exprimitur repraesentantium. Lex expressionum haec est: ut ex quarum rerum ideis componitur rei exprimendae idea, ex illarum rerum characteribus componatur rei expressio." *Die Leibnizhandschriften der königlichen öffentlichen Bibliothek zu Hannover*, ed. Edward Bodemann (Hanover and Leipzig, 1895), pp. 80 f.

the very outset with a definite restrictive condition: the "possibility" of the object of combination must be assured. For not every combination of elements of thought and the correlated signs yields a possible object of thought. Among the contents of thought there are some which, when one seeks to unite them synthetically, do not determine one another more closely in this synthesis, but instead negate one another. Consequently, an "intrinsically" possible, logically determined and logically grounded structure does not correspond to every possible combination of signs. The "ground," the *fundamentum in re* must, rather, be established and demonstrated for each concept formation. Thus definition may not be taken as a finished, ready-made structure, which designates the object toward which it is directed by merely indicating a particular property or a sum of properties. For there is always a danger that this sum will be made up of components which negate one another, and the danger becomes particularly acute for an infinite manifold. Here methods of concept formation which are perfectly reliable and unobjectionable in the realm of the finite may well result in determinations that embrace a contradiction to the structural principle of the manifold. Thus, for example, we can always indicate the largest of a finite series of numbers; but transferred to the infinite totality of numbers, the concept "largest" contains a contradiction. The situation is analogous for concept formations such as the "smallest fraction" or the "smallest velocity." But Leibniz does not stop at such examples of concepts whose elements are incompatible; he uses them as a basis for the universal inference that every concept which attempts to designate and determine a mathematical object merely by naming a single one of its attributes stands on uncertain ground. The mere indication of such characterizing attributes provides no guarantee that something corresponds to them in the sphere of logical contents. If, for example, we define a circle as a plane curve so constituted that a given length of line will enclose a maximum area, the question always remains open whether, under the presuppositions of our geometry, such a curve "exists," and if so, whether the condition indicated can be fulfilled only by one kind of curve. In the first case our explanation determines no geometrical form at all; in the second case, the form is not fully and unequivocally determined. Here we can dispel our doubts only by indicating a *modus generandi,* a definite manner of producing the curved line and proving by strict deduction that the desired property is necessarily contained and postulated in this mode of production. Only now does the definition, which formerly had a purely nominal character, become a real definition—that is, one which builds up the object from its constitutive elements. But according to Leibniz, we can assure ourselves of the coherence and inner consistency of this structure only if we accompany every intellectual step with an analogous operation in the signs. If with each simple idea we correlate a simple sign, and if we set up certain universal rules of combination, we acquire a symbolic language that has its own laws. An infringement of these laws, such as results in the formation of impossible object concepts, would then inevitably be manifested in the form of the signs themselves, and we should be able to discern and disclose the latent logical contradiction through the direct, sensuously tangible symptom. A relationship belonging to the world of pure concepts thus becomes discernible in an image; in a manner of speaking, we have compelled thought to come forth from its inner workshop and manifest itself in its involvements and complexities.[6]

This theory of mathematical definition and of the mathematical object establishes a sharply determined, precise relation between the sensuous world and reason. The two spheres are clearly separated; they cannot mix or merge at any point. No mathematical content as such arises from the sensuous world, for the sensuous world lacks the characteristic feature, the constitutive principle of the mathematical. In order to pass as a mathematical content, a content must be apprehended distinctly—that is, it must be built up from simple, intrinsically certain elements of knowledge, in the same way that every number can be represented unequivocally as a product of prime numbers. Sensuous experiences are not susceptible of such thoroughgoing analysis; here we must ultimately stop at some totalities which can no longer be further subdivided into their constitutive factors, their determining grounds, but which we can only apprehend confusedly. The direct consequence of this differentiation of "distinct" and "confused" knowledge is that, for Leibniz, no single, truly mathematical object is grounded in sense perception. This applies not only to number but also no less strictly to geometrical extension. It, too, is no datum of perception but an idea of the pure understanding ("une idée de l'entendement pur").[7] But even though the understanding is thus declared to be

6. See my *Leibniz' System in seinen wissenschaftlichen Grundlagen*, chap. 1. On the position and importance of the symbolic concept in Leibniz cf. Dietrich Mahnke, "Leibniz als Begründer der symbolischen Mathematik," *Isis*, 9 (1927), 279 ff.

7. Cf. *Nouveaux essais sur l'entendement* (Paris, 1842), Bk. II, chaps. 13 ff.

the source of all mathematics, it is a certainty for Leibniz that human knowledge can gain a firm foothold in the region of intelligible mathematical objects only with the help of sensuous signs. All human knowledge is based on original insights of pure reason, but it can only master and retain these original intuitions of reason by making them tangible in images, in symbols. Thus the intuitive always remains the "first by nature," the πρότερον τῇ φύσει; but on the other hand, the symbolic proves indispensable, since it represents the "first for us," the πρότερον πρὸς ἡμᾶς. Our finite understanding is forever in need of images and would unquestionably lose itself in the labyrinth of the thinkable without the Ariadne's thread of a universal characteristic. Thus in the purely logical order, the order of objects, it is always the intuitive that forms the actual foundation; but by nature we can penetrate back to this foundation only through the medium of sense perception, through the intermediary of symbolism.[8]

Yet this essentially so clear and simple relation between mathematical reason on the one hand and the sensuous world on the other becomes more difficult and complex as soon as we take the step from Leibniz to Kant. In one point, to be sure, the Kantian theory of mathematics seems to be a direct continuation of Leibniz: it, too, makes the constructibility of mathematical concepts the necessary condition of their truth and validity. Even in the precritical period this view was central to Kant's mathematical methodology. No mathematical concept, he held, can be gained through mere abstraction from the given; a mathematical concept always comprises a free act of combination, an act of synthesis. Proof of the possibility of this synthesis is the necessary, but also the adequate, condition for the truth of the mathematical object. "Elsewhere a cone may mean what it will; in mathematics it arises from the voluntary representation of a right-angle triangle rotating around one of its sides. Here, as in all other cases, the explanation obviously arises through synthesis."[9] Thus all mathematical demonstration is ultimately grounded in construction. Philosophical knowledge is rational knowledge through concepts—mathemati-

8. Cf. the following passage from a MS dated 1675, quoted by Mahnke, p. 286: "Habemus ideas simplicium, habemus tantum characteres compositorum. . . . Non possumus facile judicare de rei possibilitate ex cogitabilitate ejus requisitorum quando singula ejus requisita cogitavimus atque in unum conjunximus . . . etsi ope characterum unire possimus . . . quod non potest fieri nisi sentiendo sive imaginando simul characteres omnium."

9. "Untersuchung über die Deutlichkeit der Grundsätze der natürlichen Theologie und der Moral," Werke, ed. Cassirer (2d ed. 1922), 2, 176.

cal knowledge is rational knowledge through the construction of concepts.

But although Kant thus looks on the factor of constructive production as a basic and original characteristic of all concept formation, for him the ordering of knowledge brought about by this factor takes on a different form than for Leibniz. The dividing line is now made at a different point in the total system. Leibniz was concerned with making a sharp separation between pure rational knowledge and sensuous knowledge according to their justification, but he strove to bind them closely together in application through the middle link of the "universal characteristic." Here mathematical and logical thinking stand on the same side; both belong to the realm of the pure understanding, of the *intellectus ipse*. Over against both of them stands the world of perception, the world of mere factual truths; but at no point can this difference become an opposition, a true conflict. For the basic metaphysical principle of Leibniz' philosophy, the principle of "preestablished harmony," applies also to the relation between reason and experience. No pure rational truth can be gained from experience, from the contemplation of sensuous examples; but every such truth applies without restriction to experience. Thus a conflict can never arise between logic and mathematics on the one hand and empirical-physical knowledge on the other. Hence the problem of the applicability of mathematics has no place in the structure of Leibniz' system.

But it is precisely this problem which Kant puts forward more sharply than ever before, and out of which grew the final form of his "critical" philosophy. Rejecting the dogmatic notion of pre-established harmony, he inquires into the ground of the possibility of agreement between a priori concepts and empirical facts. And he gains the answer to this question from the insight that even the empirical object as an object is not simply given but contains within it a factor of mathematical construction. Empirical objectivity comes into being only on the basis of an order in the empirical world; but this order itself is possible only by virtue of our purely sensuous intuition of space and time. This concept of pure intuition is equally far removed from Locke's "sensification" of knowledge and its "intellectualization" by Leibniz. Now the mathematical no longer possesses an absolutely autonomous logical dignity; its significance, its *quid juris*, now stands out fully in what it accomplishes for the building up of empirical knowledge. Without this continuous relationship and function the doctrine of "pure space" and "pure time" would be nothing more than preoccupation with a mere phantasm. Now Kant goes so far as to declare that pure mathematical concepts in themselves represent no knowledge at all, except insofar as we assume that there are things that can be represented to us only in accordance with the form of pure sensory intuition.[10] Hence the truth of mathematical ideas is closely bound up with their empirical fulfillment. Thus the methodology of intellectual construction has conquered a new territory, having been introduced, as it were, into the realm of empirical knowledge. But a consequence of this is that logical and mathematical knowledge have grown much farther apart than they were in the Leibnizian epistemology. Where thinking does not relate to the pure intuitive forms of space and time, it becomes an aggregate of mere analytical propositions which, though they contain no contradiction, can lay no claim to meaning, to positive fruitfulness for knowledge as a whole.

But this makes it apparent that the postulate of "constructibility" in the Kantian system embodies a twofold meaning. On the one hand, it asserts nothing more than the very same principle which we found at work in the Leibnizian theory of the "genetic definition," namely that the given must always be understood and derived through a productive rule. But for Kant, on the other hand, to define a concept means to represent it immediately in intuition—that is, to apprehend it in a spatial or temporal schema. The meaning of mathematical concepts is now bound to this form of schematization. Here, then, "pure sensibility" has acquired a position in the total structure of mathematics very different from that which it occupied for Leibniz. Sensibility has ceased to be a mere means of representation, as in Leibniz, and has become an independent ground of knowledge: intuition has now achieved a grounding, legitimizing value. For Leibniz the sphere of intuitive knowledge, referring to the objective combination of ideas, is separate from the sphere of symbolic knowledge, in which we have to do not with the ideas themselves but with the signs that represent them: but the intuition to which he goes back does not stand in opposition to the logical; rather it comprises both the logical and mathematical as special forms. For Kant, however, the dividing line does not pass between intuitive and symbolic thinking, but rather between the discursive concept and "pure intuition," and the meaning of mathematics can only be provided by, and grounded in, the latter.

In this methodological divergence it seems clear that modern mathe-

10. *Kritik der reinen Vernunft,* 2d ed., p. 147.

matics has followed the road indicated by Leibniz rather than that suggested by Kant. This has followed particularly from the discovery of non-Euclidean geometry. The new problems growing out of this discovery have turned mathematics more and more into a hypothetical-deductive system, whose truth value is grounded purely in its inner logical coherence and consistency, and not in any material, intuitive statements. Mathematicians no longer invoke intuition as a positive means of proof but use it only to give a concrete representation to the universal system of relations that they build up in pure thought. And, it develops, there is not only one such representation but infinitely many of them; a particular system of "axioms" is not realized only in a single sphere of intuitive data, but is susceptible of very different kinds of realization. The diversity of these representations is not contested, but it has ceased to be a mathematically significant fact. For from a mathematical point of view, all the diverse intuitive spheres designate only one object and one form: they are all "isomorphous," insofar as the same relations R', R'', etc. apply equally in them all, and insofar as this validity of pure relations—according to the new view which has gained universal acceptance in the nineteenth and twentieth centuries [11]—is the only one that constitutes a mathematical form as such. George Boole, one of the founders of modern symbolic logic, defined the concept of formal science in a sense that was later fully confirmed by the development of abstract mathematics. He stressed that the validity of analytical processes is dependent not on the interpretation of the symbols that occur in them but on the laws of their combination. Thus it must appear all the more surprising at first sight that all the difficulties involved in the concept and problem of intuition should have reappeared in mathematics itself in the course of the last few decades, and that they have increased steadily in importance. Today the controversy is once more critical, and with it the relationship between mathematics and logic seems again to have become ambiguous and questionable. On the one side stand those who not only ground pure mathematics in logic but wish to take it back into logic—who in principle deny the possibility of drawing a dividing line between them.[12] Opposed to this view, we find those who

11. Concerning this historical development, cf. the examples and proofs in Federigo Enriques, *Zur Geschichte der Logik*, pp. 159 ff., 165 ff. Eng. trans. by Jerome Rosenthal, *The Historic Development of Logic* (New York, Holt, 1929), pp. 110 ff.

12. Cf., for example, the characteristic remark of Russell, *Introduction to Mathematical Philosophy*, p. 194: "Mathematics and logic, historically speaking, have been entirely distinct studies. Mathematics has been connected with science, logic with Greek. But both

stress the autonomy and independent meaning of mathematics so strenuously that the "object" of mathematics becomes independent of logic, and the basic principles of classical logic, such as the principle of the excluded third, are attacked from the standpoint of mathematics.

From this standpoint, logic in its usual form ceases to be the foundation of all thinking, since there are fully autonomous operations of thought that cannot be derived from it. In this view logic, far from laying the actual foundation of truth, ultimately borrows what significance and truth it possesses from another source, from the certainty of a primal mathematical intuition. For Brouwer, who represents this view in its sharpest form, numerical thinking stands at the beginning of all thought: the elementary rules of logic have been abstracted from the theory of number, from arithmetic. Here, however, both mathematics and logic refer originally to nothing other than finite quantities. They set up rules for such quantities and admit of no processes other than those which can be brought to a definite conclusion, a final decision. As soon as this barrier is surpassed and thought proceeds to conceptions which contain within them the concept of the infinite, it faces an entirely new problem, for which its old instruments are inadequate. According to Brouwer, modern analysis has attempted in vain to solve this problem; the farther it advanced, the more involved it became in paradoxes and contradictions. A remedy for these contradictions cannot be expected from the development of new instruments of thought, but only from a critical limitation of the possible objects of thought. The theory of sets will only take on a form free from contradiction when it abandons the attempt to drive thought artificially beyond its natural limits and restricts itself consciously and explicitly to finite processes.[13] Here, then, modern mathematics faces a true methodological dilemma. However it decides, something must be sacrificed. If

have developed in modern times: logic has become more mathematical and mathematics has become more logical. The consequence is that it has now become wholly impossible to draw a line between the two; in fact, the two are one. They differ as boy and man: logic is the youth of mathematics and mathematics is the manhood of logic. This view is resented by logicians who, having spent their time in the study of classical texts, are incapable of following a piece of symbolic reasoning, and by mathematicians who have learnt a technique without troubling to inquire into its meaning or justification. Both types are now fortunately growing rarer."

13. Cf. L. E. J. Brouwer, "Intuitionism and Formalism," *Bulletin of the American Mathematical Society*, 20 (1913). On the significance of the principle of the excluded third in mathematics see *Crelles Journal für die reine und angewandte Mathematik, 154* (1925), 1 ff.

mathematics intends to uphold its old claim to evidence, it would seem to be compelled to return to the primal source of this evidence, to the fundamental intuition of the whole number. But such a return, on the other hand, would seem to call for a heavy intellectual sacrifice which would close up wide and fruitful fields that classical analysis has conquered step by step. The final solution of this conflict among mathematicians is not in sight.[14] But however it should fall out, the mere fact of such a conflict represents an important and fertile problem from the standpoint of pure epistemology; for in the shifting balance between these two views the epistemologist can clearly discern the diverse intellectual forces which have contributed to the building up of modern mathematics and which have determined its present form.

2. The Growth of the Theory of Sets and the Fundamental Crisis of Mathematics

The paradoxes of the theory of sets which gave the first impetus to a revision of the basic principles of modern analysis have presented themselves to mathematical thinking in various forms, but from a purely methodological standpoint they may be reduced to a unitary conceptual formula. Each of these paradoxes contains this question: whether and to what extent is it permissible to mark off a sphere of objects by mere indication of a conceptual "characteristic" and declare that the cogitated totality of these objects will represent an unequivocally determined and valid mathematical object? When it first considered the theory of sets, mathematical thinking placed unsuspecting trust in this mode of object formation: a set seemed to be determined as a unitary and inherently clear object if any criterion was given on the basis of which one could decide whether any thing whatsoever was an element belonging to this set. This one requirement seemed to define the set and secure its existence as a legitimate mathematical object. As for whether the element belonged to the set, it was sufficient if this could be decided in principle; an actual decision was not demanded in each particular instance: the set of transcendent numbers, for example, "exists" in the above-mentioned sense, even if, in the present state of mathematical knowledge, we cannot say

14. Here we cannot go into the details of the struggle between "intuitionism" and "formalism"; for particulars, cf. H. Weyl, "Die heutige Erkenntnislage in der Mathematik," *Symposion, 1* (1925), 1 ff.

whether the number π belongs to it or not.[15] According to this view, a set is "given" in a purely factual sense if, through any defining determination from the sphere of the thinkable, a certain field is marked off and all its elements conceived as united in one aggregate. The nature of this union is subject to no limiting conditions. Equality in relation to the defining attribute is the only connection demanded of the members of the set. If it is present, no other inner bond between the members is required. The set is characterized from the outset by the form of mere aggregation, not by that of a specific system: fundamentally this means that regardless of any consideration of qualitative affinity of meaning, anything can be united with anything into a conceptual totality.

If we consider the theory of sets from this point of departure, it cannot surprise us that its application was ultimately bound to encounter certain difficulties which might be designated as problems of specific meaning. If we assume that the realm of the thinkable is governed by any specific laws of meaning whatsoever, these laws must sooner or later set a limit to the arbitrary combination of "everything with anything." Certain fundamental laws of combination will manifest themselves, on the strength of which certain unity formations will be recognized as empirically valid, while in others this validity will be contested. It is in formations of this latter kind that nineteenth-century mathematicians found the antinomies of the theory of sets. At first there was a wide divergence of opinion as to whether these antinomies were susceptible of solution, and the direction in which a solution was to be sought. But one thing was certain: the old "free" definition of sets had to be abandoned. In line with axiomatic thinking, the restriction which was now recognized as indispensable, was at first understood in a purely formal sense. The definition of sets and statements regarding their elements were now held to be limited by certain axioms. Thus it was believed that contradictions in the theory of sets could be avoided, while, despite the restrictions, the scope and application of the theory remained unimpaired.[16]

By such logical safeguards it seemed possible to satisfy all technical requirements of mathematics. Zermelo took this road in his investigations on the foundations of the theory of sets and Russell in his theory of

15. On this and the following cf. Adolf Fraenkel, *Zehn Vorlesungen über die Grundlegung der Mengenlehre* (Leipzig and Berlin, 1927), Lectures 1, 2.

16. Ernst F. F. Zermelo, "Untersuchungen über die Grundlagen der Mengenlehre, I," *Mathematische Annalen*, 65 (1908) 261–81. Cf. Hilbert, "Axiomatisches Denken," *Mathematische Annalen*, 78 (1918), 411 ff.

types. In the latter, for example, a certain method of set formation—the so-called "nonpredicative" method, in which a concept belonging to a certain totality is so characterized that the totality enters as a whole into its definition—is denied admittance into legitimate mathematics.[17] It is established that no totality may contain members that are definable only by means of the totality itself. But even if contradictions can be avoided through such prohibitions, a fundamental question still remains to be dealt with. For axiomatics merely sets up a pragmatic prohibition—it tells us nothing about its methodological ground. An axiom—for example, of the proposition introduced by Russell as the "axiom of reducibility"— proves its validity by its favorable consequences, by its exclusion of paradoxical set formations, but it is not understood in its own inner necessity. We know that it applies, but we do not know why. Thus axiomatics merely helps us to avoid the manifestation of a certain symptom, but a doubt remains as to whether the disease behind the symptom has been truly diagnosed and cured. And as long as we have no certainty of this, we may expect it to break out in another place. Fraenkel has characterized this state of affairs in a drastic metaphor:

The fence of axiomatics, to speak with Poincaré, preserves the legitimate sheep of an unexceptionable theory of sets from an incursion of the paradox-tainted wolves. As to the enduring quality of the fence no doubt is possible. But who can be certain that some wolves have not been left inadvertently inside the fence, and that, though today they still pass unnoticed, they will not one day burst in upon the flock and devastate the fenced-in field as they did at the beginning of the century? In other words, how shall we safeguard ourselves against the possibility that the axioms bear within themselves germs which, once set in motion by inferences, will produce still unknown contradictions? [18]

The endeavor to achieve such a permanent assurance has inevitably led modern mathematics back into the center and core of the controversy, to the problem of mathematical definition and mathematical existence. With this the difference between nominal and real definitions, as clearly estab-

17. Russell, "Mathematical Logic as Based on Theory of Type," *American Journal of Mathematics*, 30 (1908), 222–62; *Introduction to Mathematical Philosophy*, chap. 13.
18. Fraenkel, p. 153.

lished by Leibniz,[19] was restored to its rights. Not every combination of characteristics that can be expressed in words suffices to determine a mathematical object and guarantee its possibility. In every case, rather, this possibility can only be guaranteed if meaning is substituted for words and the decision is made through the criteria of this meaning.[20] In particular, we cannot operate with infinite totalities, without previously inquiring how and by what means such totalities can be "given" to thought. The paradoxical sets show clearly that this giving is never a merely collective act, that it can never occur through the throwing together of random elements that are determined only by some common attribute. For in the first place the demand that everything which shares in this attribute should be grouped together is a mere postulate; we have no guarantee of any sort that it can be fulfilled. Basically such a guarantee can be supplied by no mere collective unity, but only by the constitutive unity of a law which determines the construction of the set. For the law not only embraces an infinite number of possible applications but produces them out of itself. With this insight modern mathematics essentially returns, over new paths that are entirely its own, to the point from which Leibniz as a mathematical methodologist took his departure. Once again the connection between "real definition" and "genetic definition" is recognized. In this sense, Weyl also stresses that in order to arrive at a truly secure and tenable foundation for analysis, one must start from the process of "iteration." The pure theory of numeration becomes again the center of mathematics, so that the category of natural number together with the original

19. See above, pp. 357–60.

20. As far as I can see, certain paradoxes in the theory of sets are nipped in the bud by insistence on such a substitution of meaning. Let us, for example, consider Richard's well-known paradox. This paradox starts with natural numbers which meet this condition: they must be "definable" in a minimum number of syllables, i.e. at most 30 syllables in the German language. Then it is shown that a concept such as the "concept of the smallest natural number which cannot be defined in thirty syllables or less" contains a contradiction—since this same combination of words has defined the number in less than thirty syllables (cf. Fraenkel, pp. 22 ff.). Against this antinomy—which its author, Richard, set up solely as a reductio ad absurdum of certain mathematical concept formations and not as a serious difficulty—one might argue that it can contain no actual "contradiction," if only because it does not move in the sphere of "possible" mathematical meaning. For obviously a mathematical object can be meaningfully defined in words only if for the mere words we substitute their significative intention and define the object thereby —and not by counting the words or syllables out of which the definition, as a purely linguistic structure, is composed.

relation it embodies, whereby the notion of immediate inference is expressed in the order of numbers, determines the absolute operational field of mathematics. From the process of iteration, of possible serial progression into the infinite, we can derive the fundamental insights regarding natural numbers on which all pure mathematics is logically built.[21]

What is essential and crucial in this principle from an epistemological point of view is that with it the primacy of the functional concept over the thing concept is for the first time recognized in its full scope. If mathematics is led back to the primal intuition of number, this intuition no longer means an intuition of concrete things but is taken as an intuition of a pure process. The starting point is a determinate sphere of operations; and it is these operations which first lead to the individuals that we designate as "numbers." The "existence" of these individuals is demonstrated and demonstrable only through the disclosure of a principle, in accordance with which they can be posited *ad infinitum* in accordance with a predetermined rule. It is this mode of positing alone that makes it possible to master them fully in thought, for here our knowledge of the "law" is in the strict sense prior to our knowledge of what is posited according to it. It is from the operational sphere of number that the thing-sphere of the countable and the counted first unfolds. Only if it is permeated with this idealistic idea and is understood as an expression of it can modern intuitionism fully develop and maintain its usefulness for the critique of mathematical foundations. The idealism itself, to be sure, must here be understood as a strictly objective idealism: the sphere of mathematical objects must be grounded not in the psychological act of counting but in the pure idea of number.

If I am not mistaken, it is its sharper emphasis on this factor that gives Weyl's formulation of intuitionism its preeminence over that of Brouwer. Even Brouwer's own derivation of analysis starts from the process of iteration. According to Brouwer, analysis begins with the positing of a multiplicity so constituted that it can be fully determined by a single ordering relation.[22] In this case the principle of intuitionistic mathematics is that all objective realms to which it extends must indirectly be referred to this original, fundamental schema and formed on its model. From this it follows that wherever mathematics speaks of "existence" and states any

21. Cf. Weyl, *Das Kontinuum*, secs. 3, 5, 6; pp. 8 ff., 17 ff.
22. Brouwer, "Zur Begründung der intuitionistischen Mathematik, II," *Mathematische Annalen*, 96 (1927), 463. Cf. above, p. 345.

existential theorem, it is not this theorem as such that has value but the construction effected in the proof. In this sense Brouwer says that all mathematics is "far more an action than a theory." But here it must be explained more closely what is meant by action in mathematics. Mathematical action is a purely intellectual action; it does not occur in time but first makes possible a fundamental factor underlying time itself, the factor of ordering. The basic operation in which the realm of numbers is grounded may not therefore not be dissolved into an aggregate of individual actions which stand to one another in a relation of empirical succession, so that they can only gradually build up a totality. Here, rather, the whole is strictly prior to its parts, in the sense that the principle of the operation, the law which produces it, stands at the beginning, and that any individual postulation only takes its meaning from it. The progression from member to member within the series does not create this principle but only explicates it and as it were interprets it. Accordingly, mathematical action is always an absolutely universal action, which in its one fundamental postulation comprises an infinitude of possible partial acts and makes them completely intelligible. The initial ordering relation marks off once and for all a total sphere of possible objects, but to win and secure this sphere it is not necessary to disclose the particular objects in their individuality and to construct them in this sense.

In Brouwer's version of intuitionism these two points of view do not seem to be sharply differentiated. He seems to demand that every mathematical statement in which something is "given" be grounded in an individual act of "giving." But this threatens to blur the boundaries between the purely ideal given and the empirical given. To designate these boundaries we may go back to a distinction made by Leibniz in another connection. In his critique of the Newtonian conceptions of absolute space and time, he starts by saying that objective physical significance must be denied these concepts because they can never be demonstrated in actual observation. A concept that cannot be legitimized in concrete experience, he contends, remains empty—no definite and unambiguous physical object can be correlated with it. To say, for example, that the universe has undergone a change in respect to its "absolute motion," is physically meaningless, since we have no means of establishing the existence or nonexistence of such a change. The limits of observation are accordingly the limits of what we are justified in designating as physical reality. As for the argument that certain occurrences in the universe might be inaccessible to our means of empirical observation, Leibniz counters it by a methodological refinement of his original thesis. The elements from which the reality of nature, the reality of the physical object world, is built up for us need not be such that they can be apprehended singly through immediate perception; but they must nevertheless be susceptible of direct confirmation through some datum of experience. Here the decisive factor is not *observation* but *observability*.[23] In the same sense one might say that the decisive factor for the validity of a mathematical object is not its construction but its "constructability." It is not necessary that the actual construction be carried out, once our thinking, on the basis of a universal law, of an insight into the a priori structure of a certain field, has ascertained the possibility of construction.

In the language of the theory of sets, the basic difference at which we are aiming here can most clearly be designated if we recall the diverse meanings that the concept "definite set" has assumed in the course of the theory's development. At first the concept was taken so broadly that a set was regarded as adequately determined if it could be established with certainty whether or not any random object of thought should be counted among the elements of the set or not. Every totality made up of definite elements in this sense is looked upon as a set. Soon paradoxes made it necessary to drop this unrestricted use of the concept of the set: the definiteness of the elements was now replaced by the definiteness of extension as the crucial requirement. Now not every aggregate defined by reference to an attribute or a law is held to constitute a valid mathematical object; in addition this aggregate must be ideally self-contained; all the elements of the set must be comprised in a circumscribed sphere of things, which may be delimited by a definite constructive principle. Then Brouwer went a step further by admitting only "decisively" definite totalities, so constituted that the question of whether they include elements with a prescribed attribute can always be decided by purely finite processes.[24]

The postulate of "extensive definiteness," but not necessarily that of "decisive definiteness," would correspond to the concept of "constructibility" as we have attempted to formulate it. For "decisive definiteness" re-

23. Leibniz' correspondence with Clarke, fifth letter, p. 72, ed. Gerhardt, 7, 403. Cf. my *Leibniz' System*, pp. 246 ff.

24. On this threefold gradation of the concept of the set cf. Oskar Becker, "Beiträge zur phänomenologischen Begründung der Geometrie und ihrer physikalischen Anwendungen," *Jahrbuch für Philosophie und phänomenologische Forschung*, 6 (1923), 403 ff. See also Fraenkel, pp. 38 ff.

quires that the construction be really carried to its conclusion, while "extensive definiteness" is satisfied with the ideal possibility of construction. "Let us assume that . . . *A* is a meaningful attribute in the realm of natural numbers," writes Weyl in distinguishing his view from Brouwer's,

> and that it is established whether, if *n* is any such number, *A* belongs to the number *n* or not. Brouwer says that the question "Is there a number attribute *A* or not?" should be placed in the same class with the number sequence; and this in spite of the fact that the concept of natural number, in contrast to that of sequence . . . is extensively definite. . . . Brouwer supports this view by saying that we have no ground for believing that every such existential question is susceptible of decision. . . . In considered opposition to this view, I have maintained, in my attempt to provide a foundation for analysis, that the essential is not whether we are able with certain means, for example, the inferences of formal logic, to decide a question, but how the matter intrinsically stands; that the natural numerical sequence and the existential concept relating to it are the foundation of mathematics, in the sense that for a meaningful attribute *A* in the realm of numbers it is always intrinsically established whether or not numbers of the *A* type exist.[25]

We cannot renounce the possibility and justification of such "intrinsically" valid statements without dissolving the objective idea of number in the subjective act of enumeration and hence submerging the principle of idealism in that of psychologism. Weyl himself, it is true, seems to go too far in his underestimation of the general and abstract when he refuses to recognize statements of the general form "There is" as judgments in the strict sense, but at most admits them as "abstracts of judgment." According to him the proposition "Two is an even number" is a real judgment, expressing a state of affairs—whereas the statement "There is an even number" is only an abstract of judgment, derived from this judgment. Such an abstract of judgment, he declares, might be compared to a piece of paper which indicates the presence of a treasure without revealing the place where it is to be found. Actual cognitive value cannot be attributed to such a piece of paper; for only the immediate, the absolutely singular, has real value comparable to that of foodstuffs in economics; the general

25. Hermann Weyl, "Über die neue Grundlagenkrise der Mathematik," *Mathematische Zeitschrift, 10* (1921), 53.

partakes only indirectly of this real value.[26] But the metaphor used here might be carried further and reversed: do "real" economic values include only what is tangibly present in a given moment, only what presents itself as a directly available and directly useful commodity? Must we not, here too, make a distinction between what is in this sense really given and what is realizable under certain conditions? The critique of knowledge cannot attempt to question or shake the credit of the universal but can only inquire how the universal can be properly grounded. It is possible that the general, as understood by Weyl, can be taken not as coin of the realm but only as something that represents it and takes its place, as a mere order of payment, but this detracts in no way from its value, provided there is a guarantee and assurance that it will be "redeemed." Mathematics at least can nowhere dispense with such purely representative values, and it cannot restrict itself to particular statements; it consists of a system of purely functional determinations. For the validity of its general propositions, it never demands that they be filled—but only that they should be susceptible of being filled—with determinate, singular content. And for the truly universal basic judgments of mathematics this is assured: they are concretely universal in the sense that they enable us to embrace a comprehensive rule and at the same time its infinitely diverse applications in one and the same intellectual view. And here the singular application does not ground the rule but merely documents it; in it the rule is represented, but the significance of the rule is not exhausted.

In this sense, general "orders of judgment" relating to existential relationships are not, as Weyl maintains, "an empty invention of the logicians." For if, as he himself admits and stresses, the general "abstracts of judgment" conceal within them an infinite abundance of real judgments, if indeed they "formulate the justification for all the singular judgments in terms of which they are redeemable," this justification cannot originate in a mere nothing but must possess an objective foundation. But modern mathematical intuitionism also seems, not infrequently, to fall into the error that has so often cropped up in the philosophical controversy over the problem of universals. Its well-founded critique of the pseudo-universal, of the universal of the abstract concept, carries over into an attack on the genuine universal, on that of the constructive principle. But the two must be strictly differentiated, particularly if we are to arrive at

26. Ibid., p. 54.

a strict grounding of mathematics and "exact science." Never can such a grounding be successful if we impugn the meaning of the universal, if we dissolve it in the singular. The only thing that we can and must demand is that this meaning should not simply be abstracted, that it should not be made into a separate being for itself, but should be kept in constant contact with the particular and conceived in a thoroughgoing relation to it.

But this form of the concrete universal is equally misunderstood if we regard it as something merely secondary and derived, which must in some way be reduced to the reality of "things." The attempt at such a reduction is characteristic not only of certain empiricist derivations of the numerical concept, but also of a certain trend of pure "logicism." Here empiricism and logicism meet in a common realistic assumption: the belief in both cases is that the validity of number can be secured only if it is grounded in a previously given stratum of real existence. Here empiricism reverts to the existence of concrete, sensuous quantities, seeking to interpret the purely numerical statements in such a way as to turn them into mere statements about immediate data of perception. If we think this view to its end, arithmetic becomes a part of physics. Thus Mill was perfectly consequent in regarding arithmetical truths as dependent on the material and mileu of experience when he concluded that the statement $1 + 1 = 2$ need have no necessary validity for, say, the inhabitants of Sirius, who would live under different empirical conditions.

Today, since Frege's incisive critique, such "grounding" of arithmetic has been generally abandoned. But the structure of the pure theory of numbers, built up by Frege and the logicians who followed in his footsteps, is no less removed—though in an entirely different direction—from the ideal of a truly autonomous arithmetic. For here again the ultimate truth of number rests not in itself but in something else: statements about numbers acquire their objective meaning and validity only by being recognized as statements about classes. The existence of such classes, which now to be sure are taken no longer as sensuous but as purely conceptual manifolds, forms the foundation for all the propositions of the pure theory of numbers. Just as Mill starts from the stratum of empirical things, so Frege starts from definite conceptual things, which he regards as the absolutely necessary substrate of the realm of pure numbers. Without such a substrate, he maintains, number would lose its support in reality and hover utterly in the void.[27] But the purely functional meaning of number is equally missed whether we seek to derive it from the empirical existence of things or from the logical essence of concepts. For in both cases number no longer signifies an original form of positing but calls for something that is pre-given and pre-posited. This realism is characteristic also for Russell's derivation of the numerical concept from the class concept. For him the first thing is not the concept of number but the concept of numerical equivalence, which can be defined only as a property of certain classes, and the nature of this property is that their elements can be unequivocally correlated. Thus, for example, the concept "two" expresses nothing other than a determination which is found immediately in certain groups of things, in the things we ordinarily designate as "pairs," and which can be abstracted from them, while the number "twelve" designates a common property of all "dozens." The meaning of the "twelve" depends on the existence of the "dozens," for the number as such can be thought only as a "class of classes," which are connected with one another by the relation of equivalence. Here again the relation follows "being," however logically formulated and logically purified this being may be—it is not the order and articulation of being that derive from the basic relation.[28]

It is the achievement of intuitionism over against all such theories, to have restored the primacy of the *relation* and to have brought about the recognition of its universal role. Any attempt to deepen the foundations of the pure theory of numbers by conceiving this theory as a mere subdivision of a universal theory of sets and logically deducing the natural numbers from the concept of classes and sets is now consciously abandoned. Such deduction is replaced by complete induction. This name, it is true, may arouse misgivings; it suggests an attempt to assimilate mathematics to empirical science rather than to logic, and to anchor it in one of the basic methods of this science. But the induction here involved differs sharply from the method of empirical generalization that the term usually indicates. It has preserved the original historical meaning of the word:

27. On this purely methodological analogy between Mill's and Frege's derivations of the concept of number cf. the apt remarks of Burkamp, *Begriff und Beziehung*, sec. 77, pp. 208 f.

28. That the "realism" of the class concept forms the actual core and basic presupposition of Russell's theory of number has been pointed out by Léon Brunschvicg in his critique of logicism: *Les Etapes de la philosophie mathématique* (2d ed. Paris, 1922), pp. 394 ff., 413 ff.

the sense of ἐπαγωγή, of "leading to." The "leading" would not be deserving of the name—it would remain a mere groping in the dark—if it did not possess a universal standard. True mathematical induction does not seek the way to the universal, but rather points it out; indeed, it is itself this way. And its actual guide is not that "inductive inference" which progresses from a given multiplicity to a hypothetical assumption or assertion regarding the totality of cases, but the so-called "inference from n to $n + 1$." In this inference, determinations that have been found and proved through singular instances, through particular numbers, are not collected and transferred to other, equally singular cases; rather, there is a kind of return to the absolute principle of number: it is recognized that this fundamental relation which connects one member of the numerical series with its immediate successor continues through the whole of the series and determines it in all its parts. In this sense a genuine a priori synthesis—as Poincaré, in particular, repeatedly stressed—actually underlies the principle of complete induction.[29]

For Weyl, too, this principle is neither needful nor susceptible of further demonstration, because it represents nothing other than the primary mathematical intuition, the intuition that there is always one more.[30] The so-called "recurrent proofs"[31] in mathematics follow no aim other than to carry a given mathematical problem back to its ultimate cognitive source, to the point where it can be resolved with certainty. No relations between things, but only pure relations of postulation—relations which go back to the functions of unity postulation and the postulation of difference, of sequence and correlation—can provide a foundation for the apriority of mathematical judgments and the specific evidence that is peculiar to them. In their attempts to derive the concept of number from the concept of sets, the logicians have always argued most emphatically against any imputation of a *petitio principii;* they have pointed out that the sense in which logic speaks of "identity" and "difference" does not include the numerical one and the numerical many, and that it is conse-

29. Henri Poincaré, *La Science et l'hypothèse* (Paris, 1902), and *Science et méthode* (Paris, 1909). German eds. by F. and L. Lindemann, *Wissenschaft und Hypothese* (Leipzig, 1906) and *Wissenschaft und Methode* (Leipzig, 1914). Eng. trans. by George Bruce Halsted, *Science and Hypothesis* (New York, 1905), and Francis Maitland, *Science and Method* (New York, 1952).

30. Cf. Weyl, in *Mathematische Zeitschrift, 10,* 58.

31. On the methodological character of the "recurrent proofs" cf. Hölder, *Die mathematische Methode,* pp. 298, 304.

quently a decided advance in knowledge if we can reduce the numerical sense to a purely logical sense.[32] But regardless of the formal justification of this imputation of a *petitio principii,* one thing can scarcely be denied, namely that the deduction of the numerical concept from the class concept contains a ὕστερον πρότερον in the epistemological, strictly transcendental sense. For in order to fill the class concept with a definite meaning, one must always invest it with the thought functions of postulation, of identity and difference—the very same relations that are prerequisite to the constitution of the numerical concept and out of which the numerical concept can be derived directly, without detour through the class.[33]

3. The Position of the Sign in the Theory of Mathematics

If we now look back once again at the various attempts made in modern mathematics to arrive at the foundation of number, their most striking feature is that they all seem ultimately to lead to a point beyond the competence of pure mathematics. Ultimately the mathematical problem leads to a context of an entirely different meaning and origin. The decision seems to be taken out of the hands of pure mathematics and left to the "weltanschauung" of the individual mathematician. Paul du Bois-Reymond had already drawn this paradoxical inference in his work on the universal theory of functions, declaring that the controversy between the idealist and the empiricist could not be decided according to strictly objective universally valid criteria, but that here a territory had been reached where the philosophical credo of the individual entered into its rights. And indeed, Brouwer's theory has sometimes been designated as "idealism thought to its end in mathematics"—while the theories of Frege and Russell reveal an unmistakable kinship with certain trends in scholastic realism. In medieval universalism, we recall, the problem entered into a new phase with the emergence of Occam's new doctrine of terminism. And an analogous development seems to be taking place today in pure mathematics. In the battle for the objectivity of mathematics a change of front seems to occur as soon as mathematical objects give way to mathematical signs as the object of inquiry. A formalism standing outside both idealism and realism now arises as an independent power. And for the

---

32. Cf. Louis Couturat, *Die philosophischen Prinzipien der Mathematik* (German ed. Leipzig, 1908), chap. 2; Russell, *Principles of Mathematics,* pp. 132 ff.

33. Cf. Burkamp, "Klasse und Zahl in der Begriffslogik," *Begriff und Beziehung,* pp. 182 ff.

first time the danger that mathematics will overstep its bounds, the danger of a methodological μετάβασις εἰς ἄλλο γένος seems definitely overcome. Now it seems that mathematics can retrieve its threatened autonomy only by becoming a pure theory of signs. Among present-day mathematicians it is Hilbert who has drawn this conclusion most decisively. In direct opposition to intuitionism he strives to rehabilitate the classical form of analysis and theory of sets. However, his own theory itself grew out of an extreme critical caution respecting the free formation of sets and distrust of the transfinite modes of inference in the theory of sets. Hence he rejects not only intuitionism but also the extreme conceptual realism that he finds embodied in Frege's theory. And although Dedekind's idea of grounding the finite number in the infinite, in the "system of all things," strikes him as brilliant and seductive, he stresses that this road is proved untenable by the paradoxes of the theory of sets.[34]

Nevertheless, one would be misconstruing the peculiar nature of Hilbert's theory were one to regard it solely as a compromise and middle road between two extremes of thought. What it aspires to provide is, rather, a new general intellectual orientation. Over and over again, Hilbert points out, the abstract operation with universal conceptual quantities and contents has led mathematics astray: the essential, then, is to break resolutely with this method and find a way by which thought can not only progress according to a definite, prescribed plan but also submit to verification at every step. It is a critical authority of this sort that Hilbert strives to create in his theory of proof. Here the fundamental idea of Leibniz' "universal characteristic" is resumed and given pregnant and acute expression. The process of verification is shifted from the sphere of content to that of symbolic thinking. As precondition for the use of logical inferences and for the practice of logical operations, certain sensuous and intuitive characters must always be given to us. It is in them that our thinking first gains a sure guiding thread, which it must follow if it wishes to remain free from error. "In diametrical opposition to Frege and Dedekind," writes Hilbert in summing up his fundamental point of view, "I find the objects of the theory of numbers in the signs themselves, whose form we can recognize universally and surely, independently of place and time and of the special conditions attending the production of the signs as well as of insignificant differences in their elaboration. Here lies the firm phil-

34. D. Hilbert, *Neubegründung der Mathematik,* Abhandlungen aus dem mathematischen Seminar der Hamburgischen Universität, 1 (1922), 157 ff., 162.

osophical orientation which I regard as requisite to the grounding of pure mathematics, as to all scientific thinking, understanding, and communication. 'In the beginning,' we may say here, 'was the *sign*.' " [35]

If we take this position seriously, all pure mathematics seems to dissolve into a mere game. For if the signs do not merely play a mediating role, representing determinate ideal relations—if, instead, they themselves and the manner of their combination, the manner in which they unite into intuitive groups and formulas, become the object of mathematical inquiry —then this inquiry must henceforth remain entangled in itself. It moves with perfect certainty within its sphere, but this movement has no further goal by which to orient itself. In support of this view Hilbert invokes no less an authority than Kant himself. He finds the meaning of the "transcendental aesthetic" to be precisely this: mere logic can never produce mathematics, but the support of intuition is indispensable. But he does not take intuition in the sense of Kant's "pure intuition"—he takes it not as a priori form but as a totality of concrete sensuous data. "If logical inference is to be certain, it must be possible to survey the objects fully in all their parts, and their presence, their differentiation, their succession or juxtaposition are at the same time immediately and intuitively given with the objects, as something that cannot be further reduced to something else and requires no such reduction. . . . In mathematics the objects of our contemplation are the concrete signs themselves, whose form, in our view, is immediately distinct and recognizable." [36]

On the strength of these sentences Hilbert has occasionally been branded as a kind of intuitionist, but this seeming analogy disappears as soon as we look more closely into the presuppositions of Hilbert's system. For here the position and function of intuition are entirely different than in the intuitionistic foundation of mathematics. Its role is not active, as in intuitionism, but passive—it is a kind of datum, not a mode of giving. For the intuitionist the primary intuition of the whole number signifies a constructive principle, whose continued application produces an infinite manifold of numerical individuals; for Hilbert the function of intuition consists wholly in providing us with certain extra-logical discrete objects which we have simply to accept as immediate experience preceding all thought.[37] Of course the signs in Hilbert's symbolic mathematics cannot

35. Ibid., p. 162.
36. D. Hilbert, "Über das Unendliche," *Mathematische Annalen*, 95 (1926), 170 ff.
37. Cf. Hilbert, *Neubegründung der Mathematik*, p. 162.

be understood simply as singular things, demonstrable by a simple act of indication, as a "this" and "that"—a τόδε τι. For they may vary greatly in certain determinations (for example, the material they are made of, their color, size, etc.) without ceasing to be the same signs. Inherently different sensuous contents can thus function as the same sign: though they may differ in subordinate particulars, they are still recognized. Nevertheless, Hilbert adheres strictly to the principle that mathematical thinking need not substitute any abstract meaning for the signs but holds fast to them as concrete intuitive forms and orients itself by these forms. According to Hilbert, the formalization of the processes of mathematical inference must be carried through to the point where every contradiction in thinking will be directly revealed in the appearance of certain constellations of signs.

Once the universal theory of proof has advanced to this point, thought is relieved of the need of considering content. Possible contradictions in which it may have become entangled now need no longer be discovered through a difficult discursive process, but are immediately apparent. Wherever formulas of a kind prohibited by the general theory appear in a demonstration, the presence of a contradiction may be established through them; but if, on the other hand, it turns out that however far a chain of inferences is carried, no such "forbidden" formulae occur in it, we know this chain to be free from contradiction. Here, then, modern mathematical terminism seems to be driven in the very direction that was crucial for the development of the logical terminism of the Middle Ages. Just as medieval terminism looked on the words of language as mere sounds, *flatus vocis,* so our mathematical terminism looks on signs as mere intuitive figures without independent meaning. The opponents of Hilbert's theory have repeatedly attacked it at this point. Even if the *truth* of mathematics is secured by Hilbert's theory of proof—they argue —it is at the same time transformed into a monstrous tautology; for the validity that is now allowed it is no longer the validity of objective knowledge but only that of a conventional rule, quite comparable to the rules governing the game of chess. For the intuitionist an essential tendency and character of the human intellect is expressed in mathematical symbols; for the formalist they are nothing more than signs on paper.[38]

But Weyl, who raises this objection, gets into difficulties himself as soon

38. Cf. Weyl, "Philosophie der Mathematik," pp. 44 ff., and Weyl's article "Die heutige Erkenntnislage in der Mathematik" in *Symposion, 1,* 24 ff.

as he seeks to overcome the negative thesis of conventionalism and replace it by a positive statement. He seeks to secure the objective significance of mathematical symbols in two different ways: on the one hand he considers them in respect to their physical applications, and on the other he regards them in the light of metaphysics. If mathematics is to remain "a serious cultural activity," he argues, it must be possible to attach some *meaning* to Hilbert's play of formulas. But where then is the other world, toward which the symbols of mathematics are directed? "I do not find it unless I let mathematics fuse entirely with physics and assume that the mathematical concepts of number, function etc. (or Hilbert's symbols) fundamentally partake in the theoretical construction of the real world, in the same way as do the concepts of energy, gravitation, the electron, etc." But this is not enough: for an independent meaning must also be imputed to the transfinite components of mathematics, which go far beyond the requirements of physics. We cannot renounce the idea of such a meaning, but, Weyl goes on, we must not close our eyes to the fact that this takes us into a territory which can no longer be seen but only believed in.

> In theory, consciousness succeeds in "jumping over its own shadow," in leaving given matter behind it and in representing the transcendent; but it goes without saying that this can be accomplished only in the symbol. Theoretical formation is something other than intuitive insight; its aim is no less problematic than that of artistic formation. Over the idealism that is destined to destroy epistemologically absolutized naive realism, there rises a third realm. . . . If I designate phenomenal insight as knowledge, then theoretical insight rests on faith—faith in the reality of one's own ego and that of others, or in the reality of the outside world or of God.[39]

Here we have before us in its acutest form the opposition that dominates the methodological controversy within modern mathematics. Either the mathematical signs may be regarded as an end in themselves, as the actual objects of mathematical knowledge, or else some sort of intellectual life must be breathed into them; and it seems that this can be done only if we refer them to something other, something outside themselves, and understand them as symbolic representations of this other. But once this road has been taken, once a transient meaning is

39. Cf. Weyl, "Philosophie der Mathematik," pp. 53 ff.; *Symposion, 1,* 30 ff.

imputed to the figures of mathematics, no further limit seems to be imposed on thought: from transient meaning it is driven inexorably to transcendent meaning.

But at this point in our investigation of the present situation of knowledge in mathematics, let us pause to consider our own fundamental problem. What the study of this problem has taught us is precisely that the disjunction we confront here is not unequivocal or complete. Over and over again, in the course of our inquiry, we have seen that the true and genuine concept of the symbolic does not fit into the traditional metaphysical classifications and dualisms but goes beyond them. The symbolic never belongs to the sphere of immanence or of transcendence; its value, rather, consists precisely in the fact that it overcomes this opposition which arises from a metaphysical theory of two worlds. It is not the one or the other but represents the "one in the other," and the "other in the one." Thus language, myth, and art each constitutes an independent and characteristic structure, which does not achieve its value from an outward, transcendent existence that is somehow "mirrored" in it. What gives each of these forms its meaning is that it builds up a peculiar and independent, self-contained world of meaning according to an inherent formative law of its own. Thus in all of them, as we have seen, a principle of objective formation is at work. They are modes of "growing into being," of γένεσις εἰς οὐσίαν, as Plato called it.

If we now apply this universal insight to the world of mathematics, we find ourselves, here too, raised above the alternative of dissolving the symbols of mathematics into mere signs, into intuitive figures without significance, or of endowing them with a transcendent significance which only metaphysical or religious faith can reach. For in either case we should be missing their proper meaning. This meaning does not consist in what they "are" in themselves, nor in something that they copy, but in a specific trend of ideal formation—not in an outward object toward which they aim, but in a determinate mode of objectivization. The world of mathematical forms is a world of ordinative forms, not of thing forms. Consequently, we cannot determine its truth by divesting the signs in which it represents itself of their significative meaning and leaving nothing but their real, physical content,[40] nor can we do it by disclosing

---

40. Cf. for example, Hilbert, *Neubegründung der Mathematik*, p. 163: "The science of the theory of numbers must come into being on this purely intuitive basis. These numerical signs, which are numbers and which fully constitute numbers, are themselves an object of our contemplation, but otherwise have no meaning of any kind."

any existing individual objects to which the numbers immediately correspond. Rather, we can recognize the specific value of the mathematical, we can disclose its *quid juris,* only by assigning to it its position in the whole objectivization process of knowledge. It is a necessary factor in this process, not a part and image of a transcendent reality, whether this be viewed as physical or metaphysical. If we hold fast to this point of view, which is imposed upon us by the whole of our investigation, the difficulties which, as we have seen, surround the relation of the mathematical to logical and of the mathematical to intuitive reality are clarified. The differences that here prevail stand out in true sharpness only if we understand and evaluate them not as differences between things but as functional differences. The logical world, the mathematical world, and the world of empirical objects: all have a common foundation insofar as they are all rooted in one and the same primal stratum of pure relational forms. Without these forms, without categorial determinations such as unity and otherness, identity and difference, it would be equally impossible to conceive of a totality of logical objects, an aggregate of mathematical objects, or an order of empirical objects. But there is a definite gradation from the logical to the empirical, from the pure form of thought to the object of experience, and here the mathematical appears as an indispensable transition. In contrast to the logical object, the mathematical object discloses an abundance of new, concrete determinations; for to the universal form of postulation, of differentiation, of relation it adds a definite mode of postulation, the specific mode of postulation and ordering that is represented in the system of numbers and in the natural numerical series. But on the other hand, this new mode proves to be the indispensable preparation and presupposition for the achievement of an order in the world of perception and hence of that object which we call the object of "nature."

But here again the objective meaning of the mathematical is not that it possesses any immediate correlates in nature, in the physical world, but that it builds up this world according to its structure and so teaches us to understand it through the laws that prevail in it. In this sense the logical object points to the mathematical, and the mathematical to the empirical, physical object—not because one might in any comprehensible sense be regarded as a copy of the other, but because each of them represents a definite stage in the positing of the object, and because the principle of the unity of knowledge contains within it the demand that we conceive all these stages in relation to one another rather than separately.

Only if we set out from this fundamental insight can we gain a really satisfactory answer to the question of the truth value of mathematical symbols. For now we need not measure the mathematical concepts directly by the absolute reality of things; instead, we compare the mathematical form of knowledge with the logical and physical forms. And such a comparison leads us to conclude that none of these forms builds up objective being and the sphere of objective, theoretical validity for itself alone, but that all of them build it together in their mutual interconnections; that consequently an absolutely *isolated* truth and validity may be attributed to none of them, and that they possess such truth and validity only within the whole, as parts of the hierarchy and system of knowledge. Thus we cannot, with Weyl, draw a sharp line between the realm of intuitive insight and that of theoretical formation, assigning the one to knowledge and the other to faith. For us there are no detached, self-subsistent intuitive experiences which are not already permeated with theoretical significative functions of some sort and formed accordingly; and on the other hand, there is no such thing as a sheer signification that must not somehow find its fulfillment in the intuitive. We can grasp "meaning" only by referring it back to "intuition," just as intuition can never be given to us otherwise than in regard to meaning. If we hold fast to this insight, the symbolic factor in our knowledge will no longer be in danger of splitting into an immanent and a transcendent component. The symbolic is immanence and transcendence in one, for in it a fundamentally supra-intuitive meaning is expressed in intuitive form.

Now the formalistic structure of mathematics also appears in a new light, and its value can scarcely be overestimated; indeed it would scarcely be too much to assert that mathematics can only justify and preserve its old rank as an exact science if the task of its formalization, as understood by Hilbert, can really be carried to its end. For this would once again produce the logical miracle that is grounded in the very essence of the mathematical: the question of the infinite would be made accessible to finite resolution, to resolution through finite processes. In the opinion of Hilbert himself the principle merit of his theory is that through it the idea of the infinite is methodologically grounded and secured by means of the finite.[41]

But however much the perfection of mathematics in its own sphere calls for the carrying through, pure and unhampered, of the strictly formalistic viewpoint, this technical concern is not tantamount to the preoccupation

41. Cf. "Über das Unendliche," *Mathematische Annalen*, 95 (1926).

of pure epistemology. The critique of knowledge must ultimately call for a unification of the two basic factors which mathematical abstraction rightly distinguishes. Actually, formalism and intuitionism are by no means mutually exclusive from an epistemological point of view, and they are not disparate. For the meaning that must be fixated and preserved by the process of formalization must be incorporated into thought as an always available possession. This was already apparent to Leibniz, one of the most consistent proponents of the strictly formalist standpoint, who made no separation between intuitive and symbolic knowledge but linked the two indissolubly. Intuitive knowledge, he held, creates the foundations of mathematics—symbolic knowledge guarantees that we may progress, through unbroken chains of proof, from these foundations to the conclusions.

In this process thought does not require an uninterrupted view of the ideal relationships themselves: it can, for long reaches, content itself with substituting an operation with signs for an operation with ideas. But ultimately it must come to a point where it inquires after the meaning of the signs, where it demands an intuitive interpretation of what is expressed and represented in them. Thus Leibniz compares mathematical symbolism to the telescope or microscope. However much these two may enhance human vision, they cannot replace it. Mathematical knowledge, as a form of intellectual vision, rests on a primary and independent function of reason, which uses the symbolic characters only as an instrument. Even Hilbert's vastly broadened and deepened mathematical formalism never compels us, as far as I can see, to reverse this fundamental distinction. For Hilbert would not have been able to build up and enlarge his system of signs if he had not based it on the primordial concepts of order and sequence. Even when they are taken as mere signs, Hilbert's numbers are always positional signs: they are provided with a definite "index" which makes intelligible the mode of their sequence. Even if we regard the individual signs as nothing more than intuitively given, extra-logical discrete objects, these objects in their totality never stand simply side by side as independent elements, but possess a determinate articulation. If we start from O as the initial sign, we arrive by a definite progression at a "next" sign O' and thence at O'', etc. Ultimately this means only that if the individual numbers are to be securely differentiated, they must be kept apart in a definite order, and this keeping apart is in itself fundamentally an enumeration, a term used in the sense of "content." The strokes that we use to separate O from O', O' from O'' etc. function already as numbers in the sense of a purely ordinal derivation of the numerical concept. On the whole we may say that intuitive thinking provides the foundation of the mathematical edifice, while symbolic thinking builds it up.

From an epistemological standpoint, the two tasks, may be said to belong to different levels. For Hilbert the proposition "In the beginning was number," is valid because he sees the essential task of his theory to be that of avoiding error, of safeguarding mathematical theory against contradiction. But what serves to ward off error is not necessarily the full and adequate ground of truth. Ultimately this ground can be discovered only in definite syntheses of thought, which enable us to build up a determinate objective world and to understand it through universal laws. Along with an analytical logic which provides a complete unbroken survey of the "found" and its systematic relationships, Leibniz called for a *logica inventionis*, a logic of discovery. In line with this distinction one might say that formalism is an indispensable instrument for the logic of what has already been found out, but that it does not disclose the principle of mathematical discovery. Hilbert has said that his theory aims to safeguard the state power of mathematics for all time from all "rebellions," such as those that have been attempted against classical analysis.[42] But even if his theory of proof should fully achieve this aim, the logician and epistemologist may be permitted to ask whether the forces here enlisted for the protection of the mathematical state power are the same as those which have established and never ceased to extend the preeminent position of mathematics in the realm of the intellect. Formalism is an incomparable instrument for the discipline of mathematical reason, but in itself it cannot explain the content of mathematics, or justify it in a transcendental sense.

On the other hand, it is one of the essential achievements of formalism to have taken up once again a problem with which the philosophy of mathematics has persistently struggled since its revival by Descartes, and to have taken long strides toward a final solution of this problem. Descartes distinguishes two fundamental sources of mathematical certainty: intuition and deduction. The former provides the principles which are neither needful nor susceptible of any further derivation, since they are made immediately evident by the light of reason. This light

42. Cf. *Neubegründung der Mathematik*, p. 160.

admits of no diminution or darkening: what it apprehends at all it apprehends whole and undivided, with absolute clarity and certainty. But it is very different with those propositions which are not self-evident but are derived by a mediated process of proof from the self-evident axioms. For here thought is required to proceed discursively; it does not survey at one glance the ideas which it connects with one another, but connects them by a greater or lesser number of middle links which it places between them. Since these middle links never present themselves to the mind all at once, in true unity, since the intellect can only progress successively from one to the other, it is subject in this successive process to the uncertainty which attaches to all change. In progressing from one link in the proof to the next, the intellect must not lose sight of the preceding links, but must reproduce them—and on the other hand it can never be fully certain of the exactitude of its reproduction. Now it can rely no longer on the certainty of intuition but is dependent on the certainty and fidelity of the memory, a cognitive function which, as a matter of principle, is open to every doubt. For Descartes' methodological doubt culminates in the rule that one must not trust a faculty of the intellect if we have even once observed that it can lead us into fallacies and false inferences. And what faculty is more likely to yield false inferences than the merely reproductive memory?

Thus deduction, and with it the core of the method of mathematical demonstration, is menaced by skepticism. This is the occasion for the Cartesian fiction of the "evil demon" who can deceive us and lead us astray even in the seemingly most certain deductions. For even where all the rules of thought are applied with formal correctness, there always remains a possibility that the contents of thought, instead of being repeated in identical distinctness, may change unbeknown to us. As we know, Descartes saw no epistemological but only a metaphysical way out of this labyrinth: his invocation of "God's veracity" does not appease or resolve the doubt but simply strangles it. Yet here precisely lies the point of departure for Leibniz' development of the technique and methodology of mathematical proof. It can be shown historically that Descartes' skepticism about the certainty of the deductive method was the force that impelled Leibniz to his theory of proof. If a mathematical proof is to be truly stringent, if it is to embody real force of conviction, it must be detached from the sphere of mere mnemic certainty and raised above it. The succession of the steps of thought must be replaced by a pure simultaneity of synopsis. This only *symbolic* thinking can achieve. For by its very nature it does not operate with the thought contents themselves, but correlates a definite sign with each content of thought and through this correlation achieves a condensation which makes it possible to concentrate all the links of a complex chain of proof in a single formula, and embrace them in one glance as an articulated whole. It is this basic idea of the Leibnizian characteristic which has been revived in Hilbert's "formalization" of the processes of logical and mathematical reasoning, and which, now that the field of mathematics has been so vastly broadened and its conceptual instruments so amazingly refined and deepened, seems at last to have become ripe for actual fulfillment. Now we understand why Hilbert stresses that the objects to which mathematical inferences refer must be so constituted that they can be fully surveyed in all their parts and can be universally and certainly recognized. It is not things but signs alone which make such a "recognition" possible, and which thus emancipated thought from the dangers and ambiguities of mere reproduction.

4. The "Ideal Elements" and Their Meaning for the Structure of Mathematics

If we now turn back from the theory of mathematical proof to the sphere of mathematical objects and inquire into the intellectual factors that have played a part in building it up, our attention is particularly drawn to the concept of the limit and to the theory of ideal elements. As for the limit, it is one of those fundamental concepts which before finding access to the world of science were discovered and defined in philosophical thought. Number and limit appear as reciprocal concepts in the philosophy of the Pythagoreans. Insofar as one may speak of an "earlier" or "later," the limit must here be accorded logical and metaphysical primacy over the number. What gives number its decisive position and importance in the Pythagorean system is that it alone represents the "fulfillability" of the postulate that is expressed in the concept of the limit. "Limited" and "Unlimited," πέρας and ἄπειρον, are the two poles of being and of knowledge as well. Number has power over being because it strikes a bridge between these poles. In entering into the order of number, the indeterminate and infinite become subject to the power of form. The whole harmony of the universe resides in this synthesis. For the Pythagoreans the certainty of this harmony is unassailable by any doubt; it is the original fact, underlying all philosophical and mathematical knowledge.

But in the long run philosophical thought—and this is inherent in its very nature—could not build on this fact without transforming it into a problem. This took place with Plato. His whole thinking revolves around the concepts of the limit and the unlimited, and in the works of his old age πέρας and ἄπειρον are actually called the source of all logic, the eternal and immortal "pathos of the concept" itself; but the tension between the two poles has now become appreciably sharper. For the opposition between "determination" and "undetermined" now embraces that other opposition which according to Plato's basic theory subsists between the world of ideas and the world of phenomena. Between these two worlds a true harmony in the strict sense of the word is never possible, for it is implicit in the meaning of the idea that no phenomenon can be given that is truly congruent with it. Thus the relation between the two always involves the necessary distance between them, their fundamental "otherness." And no participation of the phenomenon in the idea can bridge this gulf, can efface the factor of ἑτερότης. For Plato it is out of this original opposition that the opposition between the world of knowledge and the world of empirical existence arises over and over again. In its form and essence all knowledge is directed toward determination, while all existence as such is delivered over to indeterminacy: in the Idea thought comes to rest in a fixed and definite being, whereas existence is filled with the flux of becoming, which can never be halted nor contained in sharp limits.[43]

It is noteworthy from both a historical and a systematic point of view that for many centuries this Platonic decision not only dominated metaphysical thinking but exerted a pronounced influence on scientific mathematics. As late as the nineteenth century Paul du Bois-Reymond, in his work on the universal theory of functions, remained very close to Plato in his conception of the truth of mathematical objects. However, he no longer ventured a definitive and unequivocal answer to the question, but left open the choice between two opposing points of view, between idealism and empiricism. According to him, the former goes the way of transcendence, the latter that of immanence. The empiricist sees number as a means of determination; but he carries the determination no farther than the nature of experience permits. It is subject to the limitations of all

43. Cf. in particular Plato, *Philebus*, 15B ff.

practical concrete measurement. The process of measurement can always be sharpened and refined, but it cannot, without losing its comprehensible meaning, be carried beyond the limits of intuitive distinction. The idealist, on the other hand, starts by defining mathematical meaning as essentially free from all conditions of empirical verification. He holds, for example, that an infinite, nonperiodic decimal fraction is not only determined to the degree in which its value has actually been computed—over and above this he endows it with a full objective determinacy, a being in itself. According to Du Bois-Reymond, this opposition cannot be resolved by purely mathematical means, if at all; it belongs to a sphere in which not mathematical knowledge but philosophical faith has the last word.[44]

Strange and paradoxical as this judgment may appear at first sight, it seems to have been very largely confirmed by the development of mathematical theory in the last decades. For in regard to the truth and validity of the ideal elements mathematicians still seem to be divided into two camps, one nominalistic, the other realistic, and so far there has been no suggestion of a decision based on purely mathematical criteria. Some outstanding mathematicians speak as though an answer could be supplied not by the logical conscience of mathematics but only by the ethical conscience and *Weltanschauung* of the mathematician. But from an epistemological point of view, the increased importance assumed by the ideal elements in modern mathematics makes this shifting of the question of mathematical truth seem highly questionable. Of course there have been numerous attempts to restrict the ideal elements or to suppress them entirely. Kronecker's remark that the whole number was made by God and that everything else is the mere work of man is well known. Yet if we follow the development of mathematical thinking from antiquity to the present, it seems to owe its supreme triumphs precisely to this work of man. The unquestionable fruitfulness of the ideal elements has repeatedly inspired attempts to secure their logical foundation and to anchor them in the ultimate grounds of mathematical thinking.

Hilbert has recently reiterated his view that the theory of mathematics can never be truly worked out unless we decide to adjoin the ideal assertions of mathematics to its finite assertions. The right to do so is ade-

44. For the theory of Du Bois-Reymond and an epistemological critique of this theory, see my *Substanzbegriff und Functionsbegriff*, pp. 162 ff.

quately secured if the mathematician can show on the one hand that the new objects which he adopts obey the same formal laws of combination that had been established for the old ones, and if he can furthermore prove that the addition of the new, ideal elements can never give rise to contradictions in the old, restricted sphere—that the relations prevailing among the old elements when the ideal elements are eliminated are still valid.[45] But here the philosophical critique of knowledge must raise still another and sharper demand. For it is not enough that the new elements should prove equally justified with the old, in the sense that the two can enter into a connection that is free from contradiction—it is not enough that the new should take their place beside the old and assert themselves in this juxtaposition. This merely formal combinability would not in itself provide a guarantee for a true inner conjunction, for a homogeneous logical structure of mathematics. Such a structure is secured only if we show that the new elements are not simply adjoined to the old ones as elements of a different kind and origin, but the new are a systematically necessary unfolding of the old. And this requires that we demonstrate a primary logical kinship between the two. Then the new elements will bring nothing to the old, other than what was implicit in their original meaning. If this is so, we may expect that the new elements, instead of fundamentally changing this meaning and replacing it by another, will first bring it to its full development and clarification. And when we survey the history of the ideal elements in mathematics, this expectation is never disappointed. Every step that has enlarged the scope of mathematics and its objects has brought with it a profounder knowledge of its foundations. It is because the two trends support one another that the inner cohesion of mathematics is not endangered by the continuous growth of its elements, but is always more clearly and strictly confirmed. For every new extension amounts to a logical intensification. Meaning, once secured, does not merely spread out on the surface; rather, the total meaning, mathematical truth as such, is increasingly secured and more radically grounded in each new sphere of objects. It is from this point of view that we must understand and justify the decisive achievement of the ideal elements.

But this brings with it an important reversal of our epistemological problem. For now, if we consider the matter closely, our problem will no longer consist of reducing the new elements to the old and in ex-

45. Cf. Hilbert, "Über das Unendliche," pp. 174 ff., 179.

plaining the new through the old; rather, we shall have to use the new as an intellectual medium by which to apprehend the true meaning of the old, by which to know it with universality and depth never before achieved. In this sense we may say that the logical road of mathematics is not directed toward winning an independent justification and field for the ideal elements beside the others; rather, we should say that in the ideal elements mathematical thinking first achieves the actual goal of its concept formation and comes to a critical understanding of what this concept formation is and of what it can do. Even if we assume that the *ratio essendi* of the ideal elements lies in the realm of the old ones, still the *ratio cognoscendi* of these must be sought in the ideal factors. For in these ideal elements a primary stratum of mathematical thinking is disclosed, a stratum in which not only this or that individual sphere of mathematical objects but the intellectual process of mathematical objectivization itself is rooted. In positing the ideal elements, mathematical thinking does not take an absolutely new road, but only frees itself from certain accidental restrictions which had hampered it at first, thus gaining awareness of its full power and scope.

In all the fields where the introduction of ideal elements has proved their importance, this characteristic process of detachment, of logical emancipation may be followed. Here thought could not shun the path through the seemingly impossible, for only by taking this path could it arrive at a truly free and universal survey of its own possibilities, which had hitherto been closed up within it. The discovery of the "imaginary" in mathematics and the various attempts that have been made to justify it logically represent a classical example of this basic trend in mathematical thinking. Where it first appears in the history of mathematics, the imaginary seems very much of a stranger and intruder; but this stranger gradually achieves full rights, and moreover leads the way to a far profounder knowledge of mathematical principles. Thus Hermann Grassmann, by his use of arbitrarily chosen (hypercomplex) numbers, created a new concept of geometry as a truly universal theory of extension. The introduction of imaginary magnitudes also led to a true systematization of algebra, making possible a rigorous proof of its fundamental theorem. In all these cases, logical justification of the new elements is to be found not in the fact that the new dimension in which we are beginning to envisage things somehow displaces the relations that were valid within the former dimension, but rather in the fact that it sharpens our eye for them as they are. The look backward from the newly opened field to the old one first opens up the old field in its entirety to our thinking and gives us an understanding of its finer structural forms. It was the concept of the complex number that enabled us to discover an abundance of hitherto unknown relations between "real" magnitudes, and to demonstrate them with true universality. Thus this concept opened up a new field of mathematical objects and also provided a new intellectual perspective, which made the lawfulness of real numbers far more evident and comprehensible than ever before. Here mathematics confirmed Goethe's dictum that every new object, properly seen, opens up a new organ of sight.

In like fashion Kummer's discovery of ideal numbers had the same effect within the theory of numbers. Algebraic integers now revealed astonishingly simple laws of divisibility, by means of which it was possible to unite numbers which at first sight disclosed no inner relationship, into ideal totalities, into determinate numerical bodies. And it further developed that the theory of the divisibility of whole numbers here established did not apply only to this original field but could be transferred almost in its entirety to another field, the theory of rational functions. Thus when we look back over the history of mathematics the introduction of ideal elements proves everywhere to be justified by the fact. Yet of course the critique of knowledge cannot stop with this mere fact but must inquire concerning its possibility. For the relation here revealed between the various spheres of mathematical objects is no simple one that can be understood at a glance. The new objects in mathematics do not simply take their place beside the old ones, but inwardly change and transform their aspect, lending them a new cognitive form, and this is a peculiar intellectual phenomenon which we can explain and interpret only if we go back to the original motif of all mathematical object formation.

Indeed, the key to a true understanding of the so-called "ideal" elements must be sought in the fact that the ideality by no means begins with them, though it is in them that it first stands out in pregnant sharpness. For there is no single truly mathematical concept which refers simply to given and present objects; in order to find its place in the sphere of the mathematical each object must contain within it a principle of "synthetic production." Here it is always the positing of a universal relation that comes first—and it is only from its thorough application on all sides that the particular sphere of objects develops, in the sense of the genetic definition. Thus, essentially, the introduction of ideal elements, however complex, only continues a process that was already begun and anticipated in the first elements of mathematics. Hilbert, too, points out that the method to which the ideal elements owe their origin can be followed back to elementary geometry.[46] For in both cases the same fundamentally identical logical act of thought is required. The essence of this act is that many possible relations are concentrated into one object and represented by means of this object. Without such ideal representation no single mathematical object, however simple, is possible. Although the specifically ideal elements may be designated as objects of a higher order, there is no radical cleavage between them and the elementary objects. The same process is at work in both; the difference is merely that in the ideal elements the process stands out, one might say, in its pure quintessence. For even in the simplest conceivable object of pure mathematics, in the natural number series, the ordering relation proves to be the first, while what is ordered in it and through it proves to be secondary and derived.

Once we have perceived this, nothing prevents us from extending the ordering relation beyond the field where it was first active. Now it becomes evident that its significance and its creative energy is not exhausted in this work and does not cease with it. The process in which number *formation* is ultimately grounded is not exhausted in the simple form of the whole numbers, although even this itself presents an infinite and infinitely varied structure. Rather, each new system of relations found within this structure—that is to say, derived from the original productive relation—can itself become a point of departure for new postulations and groups of postulations. Here the object is subject to no other conditions than those of mathematical synthesis itself: it is and subsists insofar as the mathematical synthesis is valid. And with regard to this validity the decision resides in no outside, transcendent reality of things but solely in the immanent logic of the mathematical relations themselves. With this we have grasped the simple principle to which the validity and truth of the ideal elements can ultimately be traced. If even the elementary forms of mathematics, the simple arithmetical numbers, the points and straight lines of geometry are understood not as individual things, but only as links in a system of relations, then the ideal elements may be

46. Hilbert, "Über das Unendliche," p. 166.

said to constitute "systems of systems." They are composed of no different logical stuff than these elementary objects, but differ from them only in the mode of their interconnection, in the increased refinement of their conceptual complexion. Accordingly, the judgments we frame concerning the ideal elements can always be formulated in a way that permits them to be transformed back into judgments concerning the first class of objects, except that now it is not individual objects, but groups and totalities that function as the subjects of these judgments.

Thus, for example, instead of taking an irrational number as a simple mathematical "thing," existing in itself and determined for itself, one can define it as a "cut" in the sense of Dedekind's well-known derivation, as a complete class in the system of rational numbers, which is here taken as a whole and enters as a whole into the explanation of the irrational number. Accordingly, when the original realm of numbers is enlarged, we do not mean that new and different individuals are added to the old ones but rather that instead of reckoning with these individuals we reckon with infinite manifolds, with numerical segments, 'and that these segments constitute the new concept of the real number.[47] In general we find that every new mode of number which mathematical thinking is impelled to form, can always by defined in terms of a numerical system of an earlier kind and replaced in its application by this system.[48] This is apparent even in the introduction of fractions, for the fraction—as J. Tannery has stressed—cannot be explained as a union of equal parts of the unit, since the numerical unit as such admits of no division and fragmentation; it must rather be taken as an aggregate (*ensemble*) of two whole numbers which stand in a determinate relation to each other. Such aggregates then form a new kind of mathematical object, for which equality, the greater or lesser, and the various arithmetical operations of addition, subtraction, etc. can de defined.[49]

The introduction of the ideal elements in geometry also rests on the same principle. In Staudt's "geometry of position" the unreal elements are introduced as follows: in a group of parallel straight lines a factor is singled out, in reference to which all the lines belonging to the group agree, and this factor is fixated as their common direction. In this same

47. On the definition of the "real number" as a numerical segment cf. Russell, *Principles of Mathematics*, pp. 270 ff.; and his *Introduction to Mathematical Philosophy*, pp. 72 ff.

48. Cf. Hölder, *Die mathematische Methode*, p. 209.

49. Jules Tannery, *Introduction à la théorie des fonctions d'une variable* (Paris, 1886), p. viii. Cf. Voss, *Über das Wesen der Mathematik*, p. 36 n.

way an identical attribute, a common position, is imputed to all super-imposed parallel planes. Now a straight line is regarded as fully de-termined not only by two points, but equally well by one point and one direction, a plane not only by three points, but also by two points and one direction, by one point and two directions, or finally by one point and one position. In this way Staudt is led to the logical equivalence of a direction with a point, of a position with a straight line.[50]

Here again it is unnecessary to introduce the unreal elements as indi-viduals leading some sort of mysterious existence side by side with the real points; the only logically and mathematically meaningful statement that can be made about them refers to the existence of the relations that are embodied and expressed in them. But of course the *symbolic* thinking of mathematics does not content itself simply with apprehending these relations *in abstracto;* it demands and creates a special sign for the logical and mathematical relationship that is present in them and ultimately treats the sign itself as a fully valid, legitimate, mathematical object. This transposition is unquestionably justified, if only we remember that from the very outset the objects of mathematics are not an expres-sion of any substantially existing things, but that they are intended to be, and can be, nothing other than expressions of function, "ordinal signs." Thus fundamentally every advance to new, more complex ordinal re-lations creates a new genus of mathematical objects, which are not con-nected with the old ones by any kind of intuitive "similarity"—not be-cause they possess any common characteristic that can be indicated in isolation but because they are logically related and homogeneous, because they are formed and built according to an essentially identical logical principle. A deeper similarity, a stricter homogeneity, than is here guaranteed can neither be demanded nor expected, for the mode of the mathematical object is not established prior to the principle of its pro-duction but is first determined by the productive relation on which it rests.

However, such a concentration of a whole system of mathematical statements into a single point should be possible—this is one of the most fruitful, one of the most truly decisive factors in all mathematical concept formation and theory. For it is this that first enables mathematical method to master the abundance of forms produced from its foundations, to deal with their ever increasing diversity and richness. Mathematical

50. Karl G. C. von Staudt, *Geometrie der Lage* (Nurenberg, 1847).

method need no longer evaporate this abundance in a vague generic universality but can now take it in its concrete totality and determinacy, fully certain that it can master and prevail over this concretion. A science that does not synthetically and constructively produce its objects but finds them somehow empirically "present" can gather the manifold of its objects into a methodological focus in no other way than by examining them, as it were, step by step. Such a science must apprehend this manifold as it presents itself immediately to empirical knowledge, adding perception to perception, observation to observation. A uniting of all these particulars into a systematic whole will always be *demanded,* of course, but the demand itself will remain a mere presumption of thought, a kind of *petitio principii.* Each new aspect of empirical investigation opens up a new aspect of the object. Here, too, a direction toward the whole must be preserved, insofar as empirical thinking is understood not as a mere groping but as *thinking,* a function that seeks and posits unity: ultimately the various parts complete one another to form some general picture, but here this completion always retains a presumptive character. Here the datum never becomes anything more than a fragment among fragments, for thought does not start from the immediate apprehension of a whole and go on to develop its individual determinations but attempts to build up a whole, bit by bit, by clinging to the separate empirical data. Mathematics, too, would not be a synthetically progressive science if its total field lay before it from the very start, complete and surveyable at a glance. Its intellectual progress also consists in an unremitting advance into new, previously unknown and inaccessible realms. Every new instrument of thought which it makes for itself opens up new determinations of its sphere of objects. Thus the work of mathematics never consists in a mere dissection, an analytical unrolling of the already known, but in genuine discovery. Yet on the other hand this discovery presents a peculiar methodological trait. The road does not lead simply from determinate beginnings, established once and for all, to ever more richly diversified conclusions: rather, each new territory that we open up and conquer through these beginnings casts a new light on the beginnings themselves. Here the progress of thought always contains its own reversal: it is at the same time a return to its foundations. For the meaning, the intellectual content, of the mathematical principles first stands out fully in their achievement, so that every enrichment of this achievement always discloses a new depth in the principles themselves.

Thus we may say that the whole development of the concept of number in the history of mathematical thinking, the progress from the whole number to the fraction, from the rational to the irrational number, from the real to the imaginary number, is not based on a merely arbitrary generalization, but that in it the essence of number explicates itself and is apprehended more and more deeply in its objective universality.[51] As Heraclitus said that in the *physis,* in active nature, the "way up" is the same as the "way down," so in the ideal concept world of mathematics, the way leads at the same time to the periphery and to the center. Here there is no rivalry or conflict between a centripetal and a centrifugal tendency of thought; rather, the two require and promote each other. And in this intellectual union of polar oppositions lies the true, the epistemologically significant achievement of the ideal elements of mathematics. They are not so much new elements as new syntheses. The pendulum of mathematical thinking swings, as it were, with a twofold movement: toward the relation and toward the object. This thinking continuously dissolves all being into pure relations; but on the other hand it always keeps uniting a totality of relations into the concept of *one* being.

This is true not only for the classes of objects with which mathematics deals; it is also true for its particular disciplines. For it always transpires that the introduction of a new, genuinely fruitful ideal element in mathematics results in a new relationship among these disciplines and a closer and profounder union among them. Their rigid separateness, their differentiation according to objects that are relatively alien to one another, proves now to be an illusion: the idea of the *mathesis universalis* triumphs over all attempts to split this whole into mere departments. Thus, to cite an outstanding example, our profound knowledge of imaginary numbers not only has proved fruitful for specialized mathematical inquiry, but also has done away with one of the partitions which had obstructed insight into the systematic connections between the various fields. For the concept of the imaginary halted at none of these special fields, but permeated them all with the new intellectual form that they contained within themselves. In its first historical application it seemed to be limited to arithmetic and algebra, particularly to the theory of equations; since Cauchy it has been included in the logical inventory of algebraic analysis. But it did not stop here. With Poncelet's development of projective geometry, the concept of the imaginary captured the theory of

51. For further details see *Substanzbegriff und Funktionsbegriff,* chap. 2.

space, producing an entirely new form of geometry. And here it no longer appeared incidental or extrinsic, but consciously moved into the center of geometrical concept formation; for Poncelet bases his use of imaginary numbers on a thoroughly universal principle, the principle of the permanence of mathematical relations.[52] But the supreme triumph of the concept of the imaginary is to be found in its irresistible incursion into physics, into the theory of the knowledge of reality: here, too, the use of the functions of complex variables proves to be an indispensable aid of mathematical determination. Now an entirely new bond is woven between the diverse contents and provinces of mathematical knowledge: their more or less arbitrary separateness is replaced by a relation of mutual illumination that not only places the disciplines themselves in a different light but makes possible a deeper and stricter understanding of the absolute nature of the mathematical as such, which precedes and underlies all its special spheres.

If we adhere to this insight, all fictionalism in the judgment and evaluation of the ideal elements is nipped in the bud. The core of their objectivity can be sought no longer in given particular contents but only in a purely *systematic* context: in the truth and validity of a definite complex of relations. Once this truth is established, the only possible objective foundation for it is disclosed, and it is meaningless to look for another. The meaning of the ideal elements can never be disclosed in particular representations directed toward a concrete, intuitively tangible object, but only in a complex network of judgments. The form of mathematical objectivization implies, to be sure, that this network is itself made into an object and treated as such; however, the strict division between it and empirical things is not thereby annulled, but remains in force. This partition is not situated within the field of mathematics, separating a sphere of unreal formations from the real ones—rather, it separates the mathematical world as a whole from the world of empirical things. Thus we must either decide to brand all mathematics as a fiction, or we must, in principle, endow the whole of it, up to its highest and abstractest postulations, with the same character of truth and validity. The division into authentic and inauthentic, into allegedly real and allegedly fictive elements, always remains a half measure which, if taken seriously, would

52. Jean Victor Poncelet, *Traité des propriétés projectives des figures* (Paris, 1822). Cf. also D. Gawronsky, "Das Kontinuitätsprinzip bei Poncelet," *Festschrift zu H. Cohen's 70. Geburtstag* (Berlin, 1912), pp. 65 ff.

have to destroy the methodological unity of mathematics. And on the other hand, this methodological unity is always attested and guaranteed anew by the postulation of the ideal elements and the position which they acquire in mathematics as a whole. This we have seen above, in connection with imaginary magnitudes; but they represent only a paradigm, an example for a far more universal state of affairs. For wherever mathematical thinking—usually after long preparations and uncertain gropings—decides to gather a rich field of relations, which it had previously considered and investigated separately, into one intellectual focus and designate them with a symbol, then, by virtue of this basic intellectual and symbolic act, factors which had previously been far removed from one another and seemingly without relation join to form a totality. Usually this totality constitutes at first nothing more than a whole new *problem,* but as such it holds within it the pledge of a future solution.

It was from a logical process of this sort that the analysis of the infinite grew. Neither Newton's discovery of fluxional calculus nor Leibniz' discovery of infinitesimal calculus contributed an entirely new content to the mathematics of their time. The crucial concept of fluxion, of the differential, and of differential quotients had been anticipated in every detail by preceding developments. It had been at work in the most various fields—in the dynamics of Galileo, in Fermat's theory of maxima and minima, in the theory of infinite series, in the so-called "inverse tangents problem," etc., before it was universally recognized and fixated. At first Newton's sign x and Leibniz's sign $\frac{dy}{dx}$ accomplish nothing more than to effect this fixation: they designate a common point of orientation for investigations which hitherto had moved in different directions. Once this point of orientation had been determined and fixed in a symbol, a kind of crystallization of problems followed: they poured from all sides into a single logical-mathematical form. Once more the symbol demonstrated a power which we can find in it always and everywhere, in the most diverse provinces, from myth to language and theoretical knowledge: the power of condensation. The creation of a new symbol seems to transmute an immense intellectual energy from a relatively diffuse form into a concentrated form. The mutual tension between the problems and concepts of algebraic analysis, geometry, and the general theory of motion had long been present, but only through the creation of the algorithm of Newton's fluxional calculus and Leibniz' differential calculus was this tension discharged; only then did the spark bridge the gap. Then the road was opened and marked out for future development: what was indicated and implicitly posited in the new symbols had only to be raised to full explicit knowledge.

It was here that the Leibnizian form of analysis ultimately proved its preeminence over the Newtonian form. Newton in his fluxional calculus also strives for a free survey of all the problems involved, for a truly universal formulation of the concepts of magnitude and continuous change. But from the very outset certain limits were imposed on this effort. For Newton's thought derived from mechanics and in the last analysis he always had mechanics as his objective. The consequence of this was that even where his thinking seems to move in wholly abstract channels, it always clings to mechanical analogies. Thus his general concept of change is wholly oriented toward the phenomenon of motion. The concept of fluxion underlying Newton's analysis is modeled on Galileo's concept of velocity and retains certain of its characteristic traits. Leibniz' method seems by comparison formal and abstract. Though it, too, derives from dynamics, he regards dynamics only as a preliminary stage and gateway to a new metaphysics. Thus he is compelled from the start to take it in full universality and to exclude from his basic concept of force all intuitive, secondary notions derived from physical motion. Consequently his concept of change, on which he builds his analysis, is not filled with a determinate, concrete-intuitive content but rests on the "principle of universal order" (principe de l'ordre général), which he defines as the "principle of continuity." Thus the basic problems of analysis are not translated into the form of the problem of motion; rather, the theory of motion is from the start regarded merely as a special case which—like the theory of series or the geometrical problems of the quadratures of curves—is subordinated to a universal logical rule.

In this sense arithmetic, algebra, geometry, and dynamics ceased for Leibniz to be independent sciences and became mere samples (échantillons) of the universal characteristic.[53] From the standpoint of this characteristic, which aspires to be the universal language of mathematics, what were formerly regarded as special fields are merely different idioms. The logic of the sciences can and must transcend this mere idiomatics, for it has the power to penetrate to the ultimate and fundamental relations of thought, which are contained implicitly in all connections between particulars and which provide the justification for these connections.

53. Cf. Brunschvicg, Les Etapes de la philosophie des mathématiques, p. 199.

Thus the true universality of thought issues from the universality of the sign. In justifying his introduction of infinitesimal magnitudes, Leibniz often cited the example of imaginary numbers, and it is only in the context of our central problem that we can understand the logical foundation of this analogy. The common, connecting factor lies in the theory of the symbol which Leibniz as an idealist logician created and which he presupposes throughout the structure of mathematics. This is the ultimate junction of all the threads which connect his theory of the individual sciences with his general scientific theory, and this in turn with his universal system of philosophy.

Looking back once again over mathematical concept formation as a whole, we find that its entire development has followed the path which Plato, at the very beginnings of scientific mathematics, pointed out with truly prophetic clarity. The goal which it has steadily approached is that of definition—the overcoming of the ἄπειρον by the πέρας. The beginning of all mathematical concept formation is that thought, while not absolutely detaching itself from the intuitively given and intuitively representable, strives to liberate itself from the fluid, indeterminate aspect of intuition. It replaces the shifting coloration, the imperceptible involution and transition, of sensory, intuitive data with sharp and clear divisions. As long as we remain within the sphere of mere perception or intuition, such divisions are nowhere given. There are no points, no lines, or surfaces, in the sense which mathematics associates with these concepts. It is the axiomatic thinking of mathematics that first posits the possible subjects for all genuinely mathematical statement. In this sense Felix Klein has gone so far as to define the axioms as the requirements by means of which we rise above the imprecision of intuition, or above its limited precision, to unlimited precision.[54] Similarly Weyl points out, in his distinction between the intuitive and the mathematical continuum, that the latter can be achieved only if thought injects exact elements into the flow of intuition, if it injects the rigorous concept of the "real number" into the indeterminate multiplicity of the intuitive world. And this, as he expressly stresses, is not a "schematizing violence," or a simple operation of the practical economy of thought, but an act of reason which reaches through the given and beyond it.[55]

The actual intellectual miracle of mathematics is that this process of

54. Felix Klein, *Vorlesungen über nicht-Euklidische Geometrie* (Göttingen, 1892; Berlin, 1928), p. 355.

55. Cf. Weyl, *Das Kontinuum*, esp. pp. 37 ff., 65 ff.

reaching through, which already determines its beginning, never finds an end but is repeated over and over, always at a higher level. It is this alone that prevents mathematics from freezing into an aggregate of mere analytical propositions and degenerating into an empty tautology. The basis of the self-contained unity of the mathematical method is that the original creative function to which it owes its beginning never comes to rest but continues to operate in ever new forms, and in this operation proves itself to be one and the same, an indestructible totality.[56]

56. This chapter on mathematical concept formation was already completed in the autumn of 1927 when Oskar Becker's "Mathematische Existenz" appeared in *Jahrbuch für philosophische und phänomenologische Forschung, 8* (1927), 441–809. It would not be doing justice to the significance of this work if I were to attempt, in a brief postscript and in passing, to make a criticism of it, for such a criticism could be provided only on another basis than that of our own systematic problem. I should like to make only a few remarks: I thoroughly grant Becker the starting point of his investigation, the principle which he calls the "principle of phenomenological approach." "To all objectivity"—he formulates—"there is (in principle, i.e. technical difficulties aside) an approach. It is this that first characterizes all objectivity as a phenomenon and satisfies the absolutely universal claim of transcendental phenomenology (for which all being is synonymous with being constituted)" (p. 502 n.). I also agree fully with the consequence that Becker draws from this principle, namely his assertion of the primacy of the concept of number over the concept of quantity (cf. pp. 559 ff.). But what strikes me as not demonstrated by Becker's argumentation, and moreover seems to me indemonstrable in the present state of mathematics, is the necessity and the justification for linking the universal "serial principle" underlying number with the phenomenon of *time*, as Becker does throughout his work. Even if we recognize "the decisive role of temporality for the character of mathematical objects," this temporality is nothing other than the universal schema of "order in progression" (to use W. Hamilton's term). This "objective" time of mathematics must not be confused with "historical" time, or with the "experiential" time of the mathematician (cf. Becker, pp. 657 ff.). As far as I can see, mathematics today offers no more justification than ever before for an attempt to anthropologize transcendental idealism. The "subject" to which the pure constructive principles of mathematics and hence the realm of mathematical objectivity must be referred, remains the "I think" of Kant's "transcendental apperception," hence the "pure ego," the "I-pole," which is also Husserl's original starting point. Becker, however, seeks rather to refer the content and meaning of mathematics to a definite mode and trend of "factual life phenomena": he sees mathematical "existence" as ultimately grounded in certain "modes of factual life" (pp. 621 ff.). Mathematics, I believe, will always have to resist any such grounding in a mere facticity, because of the fundamental postulate of "objectivity" that is inherent in it. In a recent work, "Über den sogenannten Anthropologismus in der Philosophie der Mathematik," *Philosophischer Anzeiger, 3* (1929), 369 ff., which became accessible to me only while I was correcting the present volume, Becker says that the Marburg Neo-Kantians had rightly attempted to approach the problem of the philosophical foundations of mathematics from an "idealistic" point of view but goes on to say that they failed, because "they formulated the idea of the subject of knowledge too indeterminately, or rather, they did not even bring the already achieved determinacy of subjectivity to bear in their formulation of the problem" (p. 381). If this

reproach of "indeterminacy" means merely that logical idealism rejects a mixture of *pure* subjectivity with determinations of *man's* subjectivity, I believe that it is based on a *petitio principii*. Logical idealism starts from an analysis of mathematical "objects," and seeks to apprehend the peculiar determinacy of these objects by explaining them through the peculiarity of the mathematical "method," the mathematical concept formation and formulation of its problem. As to what this method itself "is"—this the logical idealists derive solely from its immanent achievement. And in this achievement subjectivity, insofar as it is understood as the concrete subjectivity of the mathematician, is not present; as a constitutive factor, rather, this subjectivity is consciously eliminated. When Becker attempts to deny this state of affairs—when he puts forward the thesis that the mere *definition* of mathematics (as the science which strives to master the infinite with finite means) points immediately and necessarily to the mathematician himself (p. 379), such a conclusion, it seems to me, is nowhere justified by the "content" of mathematical knowledge, but can stem only from an artificial interpretation of it. For even in the cited definition of mathematics the emphasis is not on the fact that mathematics uses "finite means," but on the fact that through these finite means it masters the infinite. If we start from the problem of this mastery and go on to ask how it is "possible," we are led to an entirely different "time form" than that in which the "existence of man," as a necessarily finite existence, moves. As far as I can see, no path leads either from the object of mathematics nor from its method to the "very definite and concrete structures" (death, historicity, "freedom," "guilt") which Becker's analyses seek to disclose: it seems to me that the "essential and evident relation between the structure of mathematical meaning" as such and the "existential meaning of the finite being, man" (cf. p. 383), can be found no more in the present stage of mathematics than in any previous stage.

Chapter 5

The Foundations of Scientific Knowledge

1. Empirical and Constructive Manifolds

THE REALM OF NUMBERS shows us, in typical purity and perfection, the example of a sphere of objects which takes form from an underlying original relation, and which may be wholly surveyed and determined through this relation. Thought starts from a pure relation, which at first seems to be of the simplest conceivable form—which comprises nothing other than an ordering of intellectual elements through a law of sequence that is imposed on them. But from this elementary law flow ever broader and more complex determinations, which in turn are interwoven in a strictly lawful way, until the totality of these connections gives rise to the aggregate of the "real numbers," in which the wonderful edifice of analysis is grounded. Here there is never any danger of reaching absolute bounds or internal contradictions as long as mathematical knowledge remains true to its own constructive principle—as long as it admits of no other objects than those which it can gain and derive directly from this principle. It is the fundamental form of the relation itself which posits and marks off a determinate sphere of objects, and which in this determination makes them into a totality which knowledge can master in theory.

But this kind of intellectual mastery seems to stop as soon as we pass beyond the sphere of the mathematical—as soon as we take the step from the ideal to the real. For here begins the realm of matter as opposed to that of pure form. In place of an original unity, which lawfully unfolds and explicates itself into a multiplicity, we now have a manifold which lies before us purely as such, an existing multiplicity. This manifold—at least in its immediate presentation—is not "constructible": we must accept it as simply given. Precisely this givenness seems to be the specific characteristic which distinguishes the physical from the purely mathematical. Here it is not an objective world that is built up for us with inner consequence and consistency but, rather, an outward existence that is given to us through the intermediary of sensations and sensory intuition. And this form of "giving" can only be fragmentary. We must move—not according to a predetermined plan but according to the dictates of planless, accidental observation—from one point in this existence to another. And we may be well pleased if, at the end of our road, we can connect all these points into a line whose form can be described and expressed in general terms. At every moment we must be prepared to replace this form by another whenever there is a change in the data on which our intellectual synthesis is based.

In the face of such empirical constraint, theoretical thinking seems powerless. *Natura non vincitur nisi parendo;* it is not by forcing its universal form on nature that thought can gain access to the physical world, but only by immersing itself in its particular structures and seeking to copy them trait for trait. Our horizon is no longer sharply delimited, marked off from the start; on the contrary, every extension of the contents seems to compel a change in the modality of our view, a shift in our line of sight. What we call "nature," what we call the "existence of things," confronts us at first as a mere rhapsody of perceptions. It may be possible to line up these perceptions as on a string and describe them in their co-existence and succession; but this mode of listing remains radically different from the fundamental form of series that we found expressed in the progression of the whole numbers. For here when one member follows another, this does not mean that it follows from that other, that the second can be derived from the first in accordance with a universal rule that can be determined for the whole of the series. The development, the progression, the method has become a mere empirical succession. But this implies a fundamental change in the relation between individuality and universality. Each single number is also an individual concept, an object with determinations and characteristics pertaining to it alone. This individuality does not belong to it as such, but only in the system of numbers. Here, then, the individual is conceived as a pure positional value.

But the individual perception aspires to be something more than a mere position in a series. It stands, one might say, for itself and on itself, and its meaning resides precisely in this particularity. Of course it, too, is articulated with the totality which we designate as space and time. But it fills this totality, it fills the particular point of space and moment of time in which it is situated with a unique content, which cannot be reduced to a mere determination of "where" and "when." And herein lies the character of the mere "datum." Each perception is given only to one observer, under his special spatio-temporal conditions. It is by no means self-evident—indeed it is incomprehensible at first sight—how the perception can emerge from this isolation, how it can be connected with other perceptions. For such a connection seems to demand a grouping together of elements which must be regarded not only as accidental but as fundamentally dissimilar. Without its inherent heterogeneity, perception would not seem to be perception, for then it would lose the qualitative particularity pertaining to its very essence; and with this heterogeneity it seems to defy the form of the system, which is an indispensable condition for all knowledge and theoretical understanding.

This antinomy contains the dialectical germ of all scientific concept formation. For when thought passes from the sphere of mathematical objects to that of physical objects, it does not, of course, cast off its own form and its own presuppositions; on the contrary, it seeks confirmation of these presuppositions in the resistance presented by the datum. And through this resistance thought discovers in itself a new power which had hitherto seemed locked within it. It now aspires to perform the impossible: to treat and regard the given as though it were not alien to thought, as though it were posited by thought itself and produced by its constructive conditions. The form of the merely factual manifold, in which perception first presents itself, must now be transposed into the form of a conceptual manifold. Concrete physical thinking, as it operates in the history of natural science, does not inquire whether such a transposition is possible but directly turns the problem into a postulate. It translates the conceptual aporia into an act. All scientific concept formation begins with such an intellectual act. Thought preserves its discursive nature not by contenting itself with the order of the given but by striving actually to "run through" this series. And this it can do only by seeking a rule of transition that will lead from one link to another. This rule, which is not immediately given but is solely postulated and sought, remains the characteristic by which the peculiar "facticity" of scientific thinking differs from every other form of mere factual knowledge. Even the *vérités de fait* that are disclosed and established in physical thinking are determined by the special character of the physical ratio and are impregnated with it.

This becomes strikingly evident as soon as we compare the facts of physics with those of another field, such as history for example. Here we find immediate confirmation of Goethe's saying: "the highest thing would be . . . to recognize that everything factual is itself theoretical." There is no such thing as a sheer facticity, as an eternal and immutable datum: on the contrary, what we call a fact must always be theoretically oriented in some way, must be seen in reference to a definite conceptual system, which implicitly determines it. The theoretical means of determination are not subsequently added to the sheer fact but enter into the definition of the fact itself. Thus the facts of physics are distinguished at the very outset from those of history by their specific intellectual perspective. "Carlyle says somewhere," remarks Henri Poincaré in *La Science et l'hypothèse*, "that the fact alone is decisive. John Lackland has passed by here; that is noteworthy, that is a reality for which I would give all the theories in the world. That is the language of the historian. The physicist would say on the contrary: John Lackland has passed by here; that is a matter of indifference to me, because he will not pass by again."[1] This pregnant formulation shows us the fundamental contrast between the two basic meanings of facticity. Even where the physicist describes a single event, confined to a definite situation in space and moment in time, he is not concerned with the particular as such, but considers it under the aspect of its repeatability. What he wants to establish is not that something has happened here and now; rather, he is interested in the conditions of the occurrence. His question is whether, under these same conditions, the same occurrence will be observed at other places and times, or how it will change under determinate variations of these conditions. Even where a single fact is investigated and confirmed, the inquiry aims not at this fact alone but at the rule according to which it is conceived as recurring. At the start the form of this rule is still an open question, and we must take care not to make any definite statement about it prematurely.

There was a period in physics when it looked as though this form had been definitively established. In his epoch-making article "On the Conservation of Energy" (1847) Helmholtz set forth the universal theory of causality as this original form of physical thinking. For him it is the *conditio sine qua non* for the formulation of the scientific problem, the condition for the "comprehensibility of nature." In the present state of physical knowledge, epistemology must judge more cautiously. The ques-

1. Poincaré, *La Science et l'hypothèse*, p. 168.

tion of whether all explanation of nature must necessarily lead to causal laws of a definite type, or whether it must content itself with mere laws of probability cannot, however it may be decided, be resolved by a simple edict of thought. Here only immersion in the conceptual order of physics itself can bring a decision, can teach us how, within scientific thinking, the realm of the purely dynamic laws can be marked off from that of mere statistical laws.[2] But even where physical thinking does not lay claim to understanding a process in a strictly causal sense but contents itself with establishing statistical rules, its essential goal is not the occurrence itself but its regularity. And the judgment which establishes this regularity can never be dissolved into a mere sum, an aggregate of statements about particular instances.

Of course, in accordance with its basic trend, strict empiricism must attempt such a dissolution. Mach, for example, seems to regard the law of gravity as nothing more than the summation of a large number of concrete observations which undergo no change in the summation except that they are given a common linguistic expression. Here Galileo's law is regarded solely as an abbreviated expression of a table in which certain individual values of t are correlated with certain individual values of d. The only reason why we choose a general formula instead of applying this table explicitly to all hitherto observed cases must be sought in the economy of thought, which demands that we make the most sparing use of signs. But our formula takes on meaning only if we replace the indeterminate variables with definite numerical values.

If this view held good, the world of physical facts would be reduced to a mere historical facticity: the difference between the two would reside not in the facts themselves but solely in the signs we employ to represent them. But even if we follow radical empiricism in that view, a new question arises at this point within the frame of our universal problem. The philosophy of symbolic forms has shown us everywhere that the "sign" is never a merely accidental and outward garment for the thought, but that the use of the sign represents a basic tendency and form of thought itself. We must ask, then: what tendency in physical thought is it that compels us to single out a determinate sign language, the sign language of the mathematical formula, and favor it over all others? In view of all the

2. Cf. esp. M. K. E. L. Planck, *Dynamische und statistische Gesetzmässigkeit* (Berlin, 1914); reprinted in *Physikalische Rundblicke, Gesammelte Reden und Aufsätze* (Leipzig 1923), pp. 82 ff.

insight we have gained in regard to language and its spiritual constitution, we can no longer suppose that mere grounds of convenience prevail here; we cannot but suppose a deeper and more intimate relation between the form of thought and the form of language. Whether this presumption or, if you prefer, this systematic "prejudice," is confirmed can be shown, of course, only by a penetrating analysis of concept formation and signification in physics. Here again the way leads from an understanding of the signs to an understanding of the things, of what is designated; an investigation and analysis of the symbols in which physical judgments are expressed and in which they first take on their appropriate form, will, it is to be hoped, make intelligible the modality and character of physical objectivity.

It was the merit of Pierre Duhem that he first took this road, in his book on physical theory. With extraordinary sharpness this work discloses all the ideal mediations through which we must pass if we are to gain physical theorems and judgments from a mere observation of individual phenomena. Duhem shows that it is the construction of a determinate world of symbols that first opens up access to the world of physical reality. And each of the symbols here created presupposes the original symbol of "real number" as its actual foundation.[3] What appears at first sight as a purely factual manifold and as a factual diversity of sense impressions takes on physical meaning and value only when we reproduce it in the realm of number. Of course we shall not do justice to this reproduction and the highly complex formal law under which it stands if we take it in a purely material sense, if we start from the assumption that to enter into the world of physics, it suffices to substitute contents of a different mode and imprint for the contents given in perception. With each perceptual class we should then merely have to correlate a particular substrate, which would be the complete expression of its genuine, its truly physical reality. What presents itself to the senses as a feeling of warmth would then be recognized in its physical truth as molecular motion; what is given to the eye as color would be defined as vibration of the ether. But this mode of transference, in which the content of immediate perception is transformed, piece by piece as it were, into another, mediated content, is far from exhausting the meaning of physical method. Physical method is concerned, far more, with relating sensory phenomena—colors, tones, tactile sensa-

3. In regard to Duhem's theory of physical objectivity see above, pp. 21–2; also *Substanzbegriff und Funktionsbegriff*, 2d ed., pp. 189 ff.

tions, etc.—as a whole, to another, intellectual standard and thereby elevating them to a new dimension. In principle we can never compare the particular sensation with its determinate objective-physical substrate; what can be compared is, rather, on the one hand the totality of the phenomena of observation, and on the other hand the total system of concepts and judgments in which physics expresses the order and lawfulness of nature; and here we can measure the one by the other. There was a period in the history of physics, when it was believed that we could overcome scientific materialism by replacing the notion of a unitary, fundamental substance with another conception that was also taken substantially. Substantial matter was replaced by substantial energy or substantial ether. But no really new deepening of the critique of knowledge was ever achieved in this way.

A new perspective opened only when the concept of the physical copy was analyzed more closely as to its meaning and achievement. For now it became evident that the copy never leapt immediately from an element in the perceptive series to an element in the series of physical concepts, so that the two could be examined for direct similarity or correspondence. Rather, such a correspondence may be sought only between the totality of the data of empirical observation and the totality of the theoretical concepts, physical laws and hypotheses. It is through an increasing awareness of this relationship and its logical consequences that modern physics has overcome materialism, not only in an ontological sense but in a more comprehensive methodological sense. More and more it abandoned the explanation of natural phenomena, which consisted solely in replacing certain groups of concrete sensuous phenomena by their abstract geometrical representatives or mechanical models. The turn away from this form of explanation seemed to mean only a step toward the positivism which regards physical laws as nothing more than a description of the natural process, but this was not so. The difference became evident as soon as physicists, instead of stressing only the negative factors, turned toward positive determination and reflected on the specific character of their means of description. These means are far removed from the mode of facticity which positivism regards as the sole criterion of reality: they belong to the same sphere as the structures of pure mathematical thinking.

The recognition of this original duality is the necessary condition for an understanding of the harmony which the scientific concept demands and institutes. This harmony signifies something fundamentally different from mere agreement: it is a genuinely synthetic act, which links opposites together. Such a synthesis of opposites is included in every genuine physical concept and in every genuine physical judgment. For physical concepts and judgments are always concerned with relating two forms of manifold and, one might say, permeating them with each other. The starting point is a merely empirical, given manifold: but the aim of theoretical concept formation is to transform such a manifold into a rationally surveyable, "constructive" multiplicity. This transformation is never concluded—it is always begun anew, with increasingly complex means. The basic epistemological question concerning the possibility of applying mathematical concepts to nature goes back ultimately to this relationship and the problem it comprises. The difficulty is that such a transference seems possible only on the basis of a conscious μετάβασις εἰς ἄλλο γένος, that it may be said to force the phenomena into an order other than that to which they originally belong.

Yet if we take the standpoint not of a realistic metaphysics but of the philosophy of symbolic forms, this transformation loses a large part of its paradoxical character. For we have shown from the most diverse angles that all intellectual life and development operate through transformations and metamorphoses of this kind. The very beginning and possibility of language were conditioned by such a metamorphosis, for language cannot simply designate given impressions or representations: the sheer act of naming always comprises a change of form, an intellectual transposition. We have seen that this transposition becomes more and more pronounced as language progresses, as it comes into its own. Gradually language breaks away from its confinement to the given, its similarity to the given: from the phase of mimetic and analogical expression it progresses to purely symbolic formation. Scientific knowledge repeats the same process in a different dimension. It, too, gains approximation to nature only by learning to renounce it, by moving the given into an ideal distance. Accordingly, the problem here does not lie in this removal, in this intellectual positing of distance; our problem is, rather, to determine the special direction in which the work of physical thinking progresses, and to distinguish it sharply from other fundamental trends of formation. And we shall gain an insight into this difference not only by considering the universal goal toward which physical thinking strives but, in addition, by breaking down the road that leads to it, into its separate stages. We shall have to retrace this road step by step, for only in this way shall we be able to describe it. In speaking of the portrayal of great men Goethe once said that the source can only be described as it flows. The same is true of any living movement of the human spirit. The nature of its progress cannot be described solely in abstract formulas, but must be grasped in its actuality, in the energy of the movement itself. The methodological law of development cannot be explained except through the concrete process, its beginning and subsequent development, its intellectual crises and vicissitudes.

Dogmatic empiricism and dogmatic rationalism both end in failure, because they cannot do justice to this actuality, this pure process-character of knowledge. They negate the process by denying polarity, which is the true driving force of knowledge, the very principle of its movement. This polarity is destroyed if, instead of relating the opposing factors to one another and connecting them intellectually, we seek to reduce the one to the other. Empiricism does this by dissolving the constructive concepts in the given; rationalism, conversely, does it by reducing every datum to the form of its conceptual determination. But in both cases we have a leveling of the fundamental oppositions whose clash truly builds up the objective world of physical knowledge. Fruitful correlativity is replaced by naked coincidence. This is to neglect the creative factor in the concept and in experience as well, for concept and experience develop the forces inherent in them only by measuring themselves one against the other. The succession of perceptions, the empirical series of coexistence and succession, present the question that is to be solved by means of the conceptual, constructive series. Experience sets up a coexistence and succession that are to be transposed progressively into a unity. A totality of members $a, b, c, d \ldots$ which are at first given solely in their "thatness," in the actuality of their spatio-temporal togetherness, are to be recognized as belonging together, are to be linked by a rule on the basis of which the production of the one from the other can be determined and foreseen. This law of production is never immediately given in the same way as perceptions: it must be injected into them in a purely intellectual, hypothetical way. We attempt to order the elements $a, b, c, d \ldots$ in such a way that they can be thought of as members in a series $x_1\, x_2\, x_3\, x_4 \ldots$ which is characterized by a determinate "universal member." When particular magnitudes are appointed for this universal member, the individual case "results" in the strictest sense.

But this result never exists absolutely: it must always be gained and ascertained anew through increasingly refined methods of series formation. The relating of the empirical series form to the mathematical, ideal form is a process that never ceases. But on the other hand, the one never passes wholly into the other: each retains its distinct structure. In this connection we again perceive how the mathematical-physical concept begins with experience but does not arise from it. Experience comes first, in the sense that it formulates the problem. But we cannot expect it to solve the problem; the solution must follow from the basic trend of mathematical-constructive thinking. Platonically speaking, perception is and remains the paraclete of physical thought, but it does not produce the powers that it awakens. The objective world of physics arises and is affirmed through such an interplay of forces. Time and time again the contact with empirical intuition and its immediate reality has led the mathematical-physical concept to its own development, compelling it to yield up its own latent possibilities. Yet in this process of self-unfolding the concept is soon carried beyond the limits of the initial question. It not only provides a framework for present empirical problems; it also reaches out into the future; it prepares the intellectual instruments for possible experience and points the way by which this purely theoretical possibility can be translated into actuality.

This twofold movement is already evident in the realm of numbers, which we have considered as the prototype of a purely constructive order. The realm of real numbers could not have been constituted in the form it has taken in modern analysis if the whole number, conceived by the Pythagoreans as the primary principle of thought and being, had not pressed continuously beyond its own confines, if it had not been progressively amplified. The need for such an extension of the original numerical concept arose when this concept confronted questions that had not arisen within its own sphere but were propounded by the intuitive world, the world of magnitudes. It was primarily the problems connected with the measurement of distances that compelled number to burst its original limits and led to the discovery of the irrational. The irrational, as the term itself suggests, was at first regarded as something alien to number and to its inherent logos: as an ἄλογον and ἄρρητον. Yet it was through this opposition that number discovered its own intellectual power and inner wealth. The subsequent development consisted not merely in juxtaposing the world of magnitudes to the world of numbers as a new and different world but in transforming the step provoked by an outward impetus into an inwardly necessary, conceptual progress.

Modern analysis stands at the end of this logical process. As the foundation of his whole theory of irrational numbers, Dedekind states the proposition that it is possible, without any notion of measurable magnitudes, to create the pure, continuous realm of number by a finite system of simple logical operations—and that it is this intellectual instrument which first makes possible an intelligible notion of continuous space.[4] And this view also constitutes the principle and driving force of Cantor's theory of the continuum.[5] Thus it is characteristic of the numerical concept in the form which it takes in modern analysis that it preserves its absolute autonomy over against the spheres of concrete-intuitive being, with which number would seem to have been inwardly interwoven throughout its history. Henceforth, so far as its *foundation* is concerned, number ought to stand entirely by itself. And this same relationship prevails between constructive and empirical concept formation, between experience and mathematical-physical theory. Over and over again empirical intuition has proved to be the element that fertilizes the theory—but on the other hand the process of fertilization requires a vigorous germ in the theory itself. Contact with the world of intuition does not drive thought outside of itself but leads it deeper within itself, into its own "ground." Out of this ground it develops the new forms that can do justice to the complex structure of intuitive being. The history of exact science teaches us over and over that only such concepts as have thus grown out of the very source of thought have ultimately proved equal to experience. We may say, with an image borrowed from the language of chemistry, that sensory intuition acts as a catalyst for the development of scientific theory. It is indispensable for the process of exact concept formation—but it is no longer discoverable as an independent component in the product of this process or, one might say, in the logical substance of the exact concept. The farther this concept progresses, the more the sensuous-intuitive determinations from which it started, though not forgotten or annihilated, seem to be taken up into a new mode of formation. This change of form is not merely an outward relation between the otherwise unchanged elements of sensuous intuition; rather, it seizes the elements themselves at their root; it gives them a new meaning and in this meaning a new being.

This method of intellectual and symbolic formation may be illustrated

4. Richard Dedekind, *Stetigkeit und irrationale Zahlen* (2d ed. Braunschweig, 1892). Eng. trans. by Wooster Woodruff Beman, *Essays on the Theory of Numbers* (Chicago, 1909). Cf. the preface to Dedekind's *Was sind und was sollen die Zahlen?* p. xiii.

5. See Georg Cantor, *Grundlagen einer allgemeinen Mannigfaltigkeitslehre* (Leipzig, 1883), p. 29.

by an example in which the general trend is almost self-evident. Physics cannot build up its peculiar object world without the help of another constitutive concept beside that of number, namely the concept of space. These two elements can only be effective in their mutual permeation; and so close is their involvement that it even dominates the original discovery of the scientific concept of number. For the Pythagoreans the factor of number is still inseparable from that of space: the relations between numbers can be developed and described only if they are demonstrated to be spatial relations, relations between points. But significant and fruitful as this synthesis of space and number has proved for the history of mathematical and scientific thinking, it contains within it, from a purely logical point of view, the germ of a problem and dialectic which had burst forth as early as the paradoxes of Zeno.[6] For even if we assume that space, the form of outward intuition, inclines to the domination of the logos, the logos of space is still necessarily different from that of number. The two are very distinct in their logical structure. The manifold of spatial points and positions does not confront consciousness as a freely produced, synthetically constructed manifold. Here we cannot, as with number, start from the determination of a universal order, the order of sequence, and from it derive the whole wealth of special relations, in a strict and unbroken series of logical operations. Compared with this kind of derivation, space always seems to retain a character of the alogical: it cannot be exhausted through the pure activity of ordering, differentiating and relating. There remains an indissoluble residue: the specific form of space cannot be produced constructively, but can only be accepted as a mode of the given.

Here, then, we have a barrier which no "rationalization," however far it is carried, can surmount, but which thought must recognize at some point in its development. And the trend toward a thoroughgoing logicalization of mathematics, which dominates the modern development of analysis, seems not to have eliminated this barrier but to have brought it out all the more clearly. For Russell, who admits of no dividing line between the realm of numbers and that of purely logical form, whose whole effort is directed toward proving that the concept of number can be built up from purely logical constants, the problem of space creates a kind of

6. For the connection between Zeno's paradoxes and the problems of Pythagorean mathematics the reader is referred to my "Geschichte der antiken philosophie" in Dessoir's *Lehrbuch der Philosophie.*

logical hiatus. Russell, to be sure, also regards abstract geometry as a purely mathematical and hence strictly logical structure: its object differs from that of the pure theory of numbers only insofar as it investigates more complex forms of series, series of two or more dimensions. But this purely conceptual, hypothetical-deductive system of geometry contains no determination with regard to real, "actual space." This determination can be taken only from experience, so that the study of actual space becomes a branch of physics, of empirical science.[7] But precisely where the two spheres part, where pure thought seems to have come to the end of its resources, its meaning and goal are manifested in a new direction. For now the same fundamental relation as we have generally found to prevail between constructive and empirical manifolds, is confirmed in respect to the problem of space. The law of an empirical manifold cannot be established, it cannot be "found" by experience, except insofar as it has already been sought and in a certain sense anticipated theoretically. Without such an ideal anticipation the manifold of an empirical perception would never concentrate into a spatial form. The experience of the spatial is only possible if we ground this special experience in certain universal systems of order and measurement. We possess such systems of order and measurement, of diverse intellectual types, in the various kinds of projective, descriptive, and metric geometry. These systems contain essentially no statement of any kind about real things or facts; they state nothing but pure possibilities, an ideal readiness for the order of the factual. Experience as such contains no principle for the production of its possibilities; its role is limited to effecting a choice between them for application to each concrete individual case. Its actual achievement lies not in constitution, but in determination. The larger the sphere of possibilities, which thought has built up independently and spontaneously—the less thought is immured in itself—the more it stands open to experience and its determining function. Thus the hypothetical-deductive systems of geometry as such stand on the same logical plane as the pure numerical concepts. Experience as a constitutive factor enters into its foundations, its axioms, no more than it does, for example, into the realm of complex numbers.[8]

7. Cf. Russell, *Principles of Mathematics,* esp. pp. 372 ff.

8. In this conception of the relation between "geometry" and "experience," I stand, as far as I can see, closest to Max von Laue, among modern physicists. Cf. Vol. 2 of his *Die Relativitätstheorie* (Braunschweig, 1921), p. 29: "In 1864 Riemann took the step

If these systems independent of experience are to be made fruitful for experience; if a relation is to be created between the conceptual elements of geometry and the data provided by experience, a definite intellectual mediation is first of all required. For one series cannot be compared with the other or examined for similarity. Between empirical and ideal elements—as the discoverer of the ideal, Plato, clearly stated—there is no possible relation of similarity, of total or partial coincidence. Whatever community, whatever κοινωνία or παρουσία can be promoted between them, does not negate the fundamental character of "otherness," of ἑτερότης between them. Here similarity or congruence is replaced by the specific and new factor of "participation." This participation of the physical in the arithmetical and geometrical can be achieved and grounded in only one way: with certain physical "things" or "processes" we correlate certain mathematical concepts, but this correlation does not imply a relation of identity between them. Once the basic concepts and axioms of certain geometries are established, we may ask whether there are any elements of physical experience that are in agreement with these concepts and axioms. Thus, for example, a certain phenomenon, the phenomenon of the propagation of light, is used to provide a physical analogue to what is defined as a straight line in a certain hypothetical-deductive system of pure geometry. It is through such analogical relations that the concept of measurability first achieves an almost unrestricted meaning: it is through them that a determinate order of measure first follows from the ideal arithmetical order of number and the universal geometrical order of space. This order of measurement arises at exactly the point where, through the linking of geometrical concepts to physical experience, these concepts depart from the stage of abstract detachment and enter into a definite bond with the real, with the existence of physical phenomena. But this bond has no bearing on the validity of the con-

---

which later assumed fundamental importance for the universal theory of relativity: he established (in place of the simple Euclidean formula for distance $ds = \sqrt{dx_1^2 + dx_2^2 + dx_3^2}$) a homogeneous quadratic function of dx^i with any desired functions of x^i as coefficients $ds^2 = \sum_{i,k} \gamma_{ik} dx^i dx^k$, as the square of the linear elements. This step may be called the universalized Pythagorean theorem. Every choice of the function γ_{ik} determines a particular kind of geometry. . . . At this point we should like only to state that nothing physical ever entered into this whole development of geometry from Euclid to Riemann. Deductions were drawn solely from certain axioms. These axioms themselves, to be sure, are not the only possible ones; the human mind can create others. But in establishing them it need borrow from experience no more than in creating the concept of complex number: geometries are therefore all a priori."

cepts and axioms as such; it applies only to the use we make of them in the determination of the elements of experience. We do not base the presuppositions and principles of Euclidean geometry on our experience of rigid bodies—rather, we make use of this experience in order to gain physical "correspondences" for the ideal statements of this geometry. According to the mode of these correspondences, according to our decision as to which bodies we wish to regard as rigid and which motions as rectilinear, our basic determination of measure changes, and with it the form of our geometry. In this sense—but only in this sense—every concrete geometry, every geometry that is characterized by a fixed determination of measurement, comprises certain physical presuppositions and postulates: but the fact that it can only be filled with empirical content through such postulates does not mean that it is logically grounded in this content. There must first be a universal order of number and a universal geometry, a science of possible spatial forms, before a determinate physical order of measurement can be constituted. It was in this sense that Leibniz characterized the methodological relation between the abstract and the concrete. Arguing against Locke, he wrote:

> Quoiqu'il soit vrai qu'en concevant le corps, on conçoit quelque chose de plus que l'espace, il ne s'en suit point qu'il y a deux étendues, celles de l'espace et celle du corps; car c'est comme lorsqu'en concevant plusieurs choses à la fois, on conçoit quelque chose de plus que le nombre, savoir *res numeratas*, et cependant il n'y a pas deux multitudes, l'une abstraite, savoir celle du nombre, l'autre concrète, savoir celle des choses nombrées. On peut dire de même qu'il ne faut point s'imaginer deux étendues, l'une abstraite de l'espace, l'autre concrète du corps; le concret n'étant tel que par l'abstrait.[9]

Here the strict idealist inference is drawn: the realm of the "idea" is recognized in its independence and original significance, but this meaning does not imply that pure space leads a separate existence side by side with the empirical, corporeal world.

Here again we have confirmation of the fact that the relation between the world of pure forms and the world of things never consists in correspondences between single forms and single things, but rather that only the two structures can be related to each other and measured by each

9. Leibniz, *Nouveaux essais sur l'entendement humain*, II, 4; *Philosophische Schriften*, 5, 115.

other as totalities. This, it is true, seems to make for an almost arbitrary freedom in the determination of the particular. Whether in order to give definite physical content to the concept of the "rectilinear" we connect it with the phenomenon of the propagation of light or whether we select a different analogy seems at first sight to be purely a question of choice, of free convention. But even this convention must be grounded in some way: it must, to speak in scholastic terms, have a *fundamentum in re.* However, the foundation cannot be disclosed in any particular thing, in an individual "this" and "that," but follows only from a synthesis of experience as a whole. We select those assumptions on the basis of which we can formulate a simple and systematically complete explanation of the natural phenomena. And since both the simplicity and the systematic completeness are always relative, there is always a possibility that we may arrive at another and more satisfactory result through a suitable variation of the original assumption. But this renunciation of absolute validity deprives the symbols of mathematics and exact science of none of their objective meaning. For they derive this meaning not from transcendent objects which stand behind them and which they copy, but from their achievement, their function of objectivization.

Even though this function may never achieve its end, may never arrive at a *non plus ultra,* its direction is established. The endlessness of the road does not negate the determinacy of the direction: for it is precisely through their relation to "infinitely distant" points that directions are defined. Here we see once more how all our knowledge of nature—insofar as it is knowledge—that is, an ideal goal and an ideal task—rests ultimately on an act of freedom, on a standpoint that reason appoints itself. Yet true freedom is not the opposite of obligation, but is its beginning and source. The first act: the choice of certain empirical elements which we take as correspondences to certain constructive forms, is free—but in the second and all subsequent acts we are bondsmen, unless thought, by a new act, suspends the whole fabric of inferences and begins with a new assumption. For of course it lies in the nature of the empirical manifold itself that it can never, in a strict sense, dissolve into a pure constructive manifold. It is never "constructed" to the end—but must always be conceived as indefinitely "constructible." Thus in its relation to the empirical datum the thread of thought never breaks off; but neither can it be spun to its end: such a conclusion would not mean the completion of the fabric, but its veritable destruction, because it would run counter to the meaning of experience as a progressive *process* of determination.[10]

The dimension of thought in which we are moving here may be elucidated and distinguished from other dimensions in reference to the natural space, the space of objective physical measurement. Space as such, conceived as a mere possibility of coexistence, has no definite and unambiguous form but stands equally open to the most diverse modes of formation. In his natural philosophy Plato called space the πρῶτον δεκτικόν; for him space is absolutely receptive and plastic, the raw material of all determination, which receives form and determinacy only through the legislation of the "idea." The philosophy of symbolic forms has given us a still broader notion of this inner plasticity that inheres in space, not limiting the sphere of the ideal to the realm of theoretical knowledge, but tracing the power and efficacy of the ideal back into other, deeper strata, particularly those of linguistic and mythological thinking, and finding that a peculiar mode of "spatiality" corresponds to each of these fields. The form of coexistence is always subject to a definite formative law, without which it could not be constituted, but in each instance the process of formation varies. At the present juncture we are concerned with understanding the transition leading from the empirical space of intuition to the conceptual space of theoretical physics. We recall that this empirical space of intuition proved to be shot through with symbolic elements, and that linguistic thinking in particular played an essential part in its whole formation and structure. With empirical space we have left the sphere of the mere datum far behind us; once language has coined its first indicative adverbs for the "here" and the "there," the near and the far, the process of construction has already begun. But in the progress to the space of abstract geometry and objective natural science, the formation assumes a wholly different character. Here, too, we start from certain elementary distinctions, which characterize space as a system of purely "topological" determinations. We apprehend relations of proximity between points of "apartness," the bisection of lines, the incidence of surfaces or segments of space. But from this manifold and complex fabric thought gradually detaches definite threads. It brings its own presuppositions and postulates to intuition, and so creates a new system of orientation. According to the modality of these presuppositions, a "projective" or a "metric" space develops from the original topological space. The form of metric space is contingent on an order of measurement which

10. For more detailed treatment, cf. my *Substanzbegriff und Funktionsbegriff*, pp. 410 ff.

appears freely chosen in the sense discussed above. We determine a body considered rigid, as being invariable in its measurements; we attribute the character of "straightness" to an empirically existing line. Through such postulations of measurement and straightness different "spaces" arise, each distinguished by a different structure.

Even the purely topological view comprises a theory of the combinations of spatial forms; here, too, a simply connected surface is distinguished from a multiple connected surface and very definite mathematical criteria are given for this difference. But our attention dwells exclusively on the relations of contiguity or of unbroken connection between the spatial forms, without forming a definite concept of their magnitude or shape. Size and shape become determinable only with the appearance of new postulations, new "hypotheses," whose special character determines each particular form of geometry.[11] If we now look back once again over the whole development of the motif of space, we perceive the whole extent of the oppositions that must be traversed. There is no single basic tendency or power of the human spirit that has not in some way participated in this vast process of formation and dominated it in certain phases. Sensation and intuition, feeling and fantasy, productive imagination and constructive conceptual thought are all equally at work—and in each instance the manner in which they interlock and condition one another creates a different form of space. But at the same time we find that with all its inner multiformity this process always preserves an identical direction and that in the process the sundering of the I and the world becomes increasingly clearer and more vivid in consciousness. The mythical consciousness of space still remains wholly interwoven with the sphere of subjective feeling. And yet even here the elementary contrasts in the primary life feeling give rise to definite oppositions in being, to a clash and separation of cosmic powers. Language carries this differentiation farther and gives it new depth: through its mediation mythical "expressive space" is transformed into "representative space." But

11. The most succinct and at the same time the most acute epistemological analysis of this relationship has, I believe, been given by Rudolf Carnap, *Der Raum. Ein Beitrag zur Wissenschaftslehre*, in *Kant-Studien, Ergänzungshefte* 56 (Berlin, 1922). Carnap distinguishes sharply between "formal" space (which is a pure structure of relation and order), "intuitive" space, and "physical" space. And he goes on to show how within each of these three spaces a definite distinction must be made between "topological," "projective," and "metric" space. Here I shall not enter into these distinctions—since in the framework of our problem we are concerned only with the principle of differentiation as such, and not with the concrete differences themselves—but refer the reader to Carnap's penetrating exposition.

only conceptual, geometrical, and physical thinking effects the last, decisive step. Here all the purely anthropomorphic components are suppressed more and more resolutely and replaced by strictly objective determinations which result from a universal method of counting and measuring. All elements arising from the sphere of feeling and even the images, the pure schemata of intuition, are progressively excluded. The step is taken from "expressive space" and "representative space" to a pure "significative space." [12] But this transition requires a number of other intermediary processes. The history of mathematics and the mathematical sciences shows that this process of transformation, though consistent, has been very gradual. Here we shall not follow the historical development but shall attempt, through the system of knowledge represented in modern physics, to single out the factors which throw light on the goal toward which this process tends and the methods it employs.

2. Principle and Method of Physical Series Formation

Physical concept formation does not begin with a wholly amorphous material, with a sheer "manifold," given to it only as such, without any kind of order. As long as we remain within the sphere of phenomena, we never encounter any such wholly structureless manifold. Even the most elementary sensuous stratum to which we can go back offers us a multiplicity determined by some sort of serial principle. The physical concept would possess no point of attack for the work it has to perform if it could not start from this series in the sensuous phenomena themselves. True, it does not stop at the form of series that it finds here; it does not content itself with a descriptive fixation of this series but transforms it. Yet this would not be possible if perception did not already contain certain structural elements within itself. It breaks down into definite spheres, within which there is no mere coexistence but a fundamental "relatedness" of the particular determinations. Relations of similarity or dissimilarity, of affinity or contrast, of gradation and articulation crystallize out. Thus the sensuous manifold is not given as a mere aggregate of different elements; its very existence expresses a definite type of manifold. The world of colors, for example, proves to be articulated in three respects, since tone, brightness, and saturation may be

---

12. Cf. the more detailed treatment in my "Das Symbolproblem und seine Stellung im System der Philosophie," *Zeitschrift für Ästhetik und allgemeine Kunstwissenschaft,* 21 (1927), 295 ff.

distinguished in every color. The sum of the relations that can exist between colors on the basis of these original factors of reference, can, as we know, be represented by certain geometrical schemata, for example by the color octahedron. The significance of these schemata does not lie in a reduction of the color manifold to something different and wholly outside its sphere, to a system of geometrical forms: such schemata give us, rather, a purely symbolic representation of relations that are peculiar to color as such, that are implicit in its basic nature, in its sensuous-intuitive facticity. For us there is no single sensuous datum which does not, though in varying degrees of clarity, stand in such involvements with others, and which is not thereby articulated with a universal, though for the present sensuous-intuitive order. In this sense it is a prejudice—from which the traditional theory of rationalism suffers no less than sensationalism—to suppose that the sphere of "universality" begins with the concept, which is here taken as the logical generic concept. For even within the concrete particularity of sensuous phenomena, definite threads of combination run back and forth from one particular to another, and through these threads the particulars are woven into a whole. Even strict sensationalism, whose basic epistemological intention is to break down the world of sensation and intuition into its separate elements, into the atoms of sensation, was unable to disregard this original totality.

In his very first statement of his epistemological leitmotiv that there can be no "idea" that is not grounded in an original "impression," Hume found himself compelled to recognize a circumstance that provides a scarcely controvertible argument against this basic principle of all sensationalist psychology. If the sensationalist thesis were wholly valid, consciousness would be reduced to mere reproduction; all power of construction would be denied it once and for all. And yet this radical inference does not seem to be confirmed by experience, even if we remain within the sphere of the merely sensory consciousness. For we can disclose sensuous "representations" which are not simply copies and reprints of previous sensations but which comprise a "production," however modest, of new impressions. If two color tints are set before us and we are asked to imagine a third that lies between them, we are able to project an image of this intermediary color quality, even if we have never before experienced it as an immediate sense impression. This makes it evident that the manifold of impressions itself comprises a kind of inner form—a rule of combination which permits us within this manifold not only to line up one real thing, one actual sensation beside another, but also to reach out from the real to the possible. By a pure activity of the imagination we can also inject a definite content into parts of a sensuous totality that have been left empty by direct experience. Hume himself, it is true, merely brings up this problem in order to thrust it aside; the single exception which forces itself on his attention, and which he admits, cannot, in his opinion, controvert the general principle that representations are nothing other than copies of impressions.[13] But the historical continuation of the psychology of elements, which ultimately caused it to be superseded, began at precisely this point. This was the starting point of the theory of "indirect perception," developed by the school of Brentano—and here, too, lie the germs of a new and deeper "psychology of relations," which apprehends the basic forms of relation in their independent significance, and recognizes them as "objects of a higher order."[14] Psychology attained to a true clarification of the fundamental meaning of relations only as it achieved the insight that pure relations represent a problem *sui generis:* that they embody formal factors which can never be reduced to mere contents but which form the constitutive presuppositions through which alone a determinate content can be "given" to us.[15]

It is with the simple basic relations of "similarity" and "dissimilarity," of "nearness" and "farness," as they can be disclosed in the sensuous phenomena, that the formation of linguistic concepts begins. But we have seen in the course of our investigation that with these concepts a general change of attitude sets in. For the act of appellation signifies a new articulation of phenomena: linguistic designation goes hand in hand with an inner transformation of the perceptual world. Now one definite, concrete "impression" does not simply stand beside another; rather, the flowing, always identical series is articulated in a characteristic way. Definite centers crystallize out, to which the manifold is referred and around which it is grouped. The name "red" or "blue" functions as

13. Cf. Hume, *A Treatise of Human Nature*, Pt. I, sec. 1.

14. Cf. esp. A. Meinong "Hume-Studien," *Sitzungsbericht der Wiener Akademie der Wissenschaften, philosophisch-historische Klasse* (1877), and his articles "Zur Psychologie der Komplexionen und Relationen" and "Über Gegenstände höherer Ordnung und deren Verhältniss zur inneren Wahrnehmung," *Zeitschrift für Psychologie*, 2 (1891), 245–65; and 21 (1899), 182–272.

15. For more detailed treatment see the last chapter of my *Substanzbegriff und Funktionsbegriff*, pp. 433 ff.

a name only by indicating such a center—it does not mean this or that particular shading of red or blue but expresses a specific way in which an indeterminate multiplicity of such shadings is seen and thought as one. The red and the blue are no longer names for individual color experiences; rather, they are designations for definite color categories.

As we have seen, the distance between this "categorial" view and formation and immediate sensory experiences of coherence becomes particularly evident when we consider the changes brought about in the structure of the perceptual world by pathological speech disturbances.[16] And yet, fundamentally, language as such does not reach beyond the sphere of intuition. It singles out and fixates certain basic factors in intuition, but it does not transcend them. To be sure, "red" or "blue" no longer possesses any correlate directly corresponding to it in the world of sensory impressions; nevertheless, there are an infinite number of color impressions which concretely fulfill the meaning of red or blue, which can be disclosed as special "cases" of what the universal name signifies. Yet even this bond between the "universal" and the "particular" dissolves as soon as we enter into the sphere of mathematical-physical concepts. The very beginning of these concepts places us in another sphere. Here the given is not only divided in a determinate way and gathered around fixed centers but is recast in a form that is directly opposed to its original mode of givenness. For nowhere in the sensuous phenomena as such can we arrive at truly exact determinations: rather, a certain vagueness lies in the very nature of these phenomena. When we differentiate them, every distinction we make has a threshold—a limit beyond which it cannot be carried without becoming unrecognizable and meaningless. The mathematical-physical concept begins by eliminating this fact of the threshold. It posits and demands sharp boundaries, where perception discloses only fluid transitions. The new ordinal form which thus arises is by no means a copy of the former but belongs to an entirely different general type. This divergence is manifested in peculiar paradoxes, which appear as soon as we attempt to translate the relations prevailing in a sensuous manifold directly into the language of mathematical-physical concepts.

If, for example, we designate those elements as equal which are not distinguishable in a sensuous manifold, this determination of equality is far removed from the ideal meaning of equality in mathematics. The

16. Cf. above, Pt. II, Chap. 6.

"equality" that can be stated concerning sensuous contents fails to fulfill the decisive condition for mathematical equality, through which it is first truly constituted. A perceived content a may be indistinguishable from another content b, and the latter in turn from a content c; a and b and c would then have to be designated as "equal" in the above-mentioned sense, and yet we should not be able to infer that a and c are indistinguishable. Here the equations $a = b$ and $b = c$ do not imply that $a = c$: the equality is not, as in the realm of numbers and of exact thought in general, a transitive relation. From this one example we may see that in passing from mere perception to mathematical determination we do not merely replace differences in the "given" by intellectual differences, but that the general conception, the point of view as such, undergoes a change. Wherein consists this change and through what phases does it pass?

The first step was already designated when we spoke of the aim and trend of purely mathematical concept formation. We have seen it to be characteristic of this concept formation that even where it relates to intuition it does not stop at intuition. Here lies the core of the axiomatic method whose specific meaning and central importance have been increasingly recognized in the modern development of mathematics. Axioms do not apply to given intuitive elements: rather, in accordance with the above-mentioned formulations of Felix Klein, they are "postulates by means of which we raise ourselves above the imprecision or the limited precision of intuition to an unlimited precision." This character of postulates is not borrowed from intuition; rather, it forms an original determination of thought, which is held up to intuition as a norm. The validity of an axiom is not based on a pre-given property of elements; rather, it is in accordance with the axioms that the elements are posited and defined in their nature and essence. Thus in Hilbert's axiomatics, for example, there are no longer any independent contents which we determine as points or straight lines and which later turn out to apply to definite geometrical relations: instead, the sheer whatness of a point or a straight line is first established through these relations. The finished meaning of the elements does not enter into the axiom but is first constituted by the axiom. Thus in establishing an axiom or a system of axioms, we do not merely designate the "how" of the connection between previously known and in some way intuitively "given" contents; rather, it is through the axioms that we gain and logically ascertain the actual "whatness" of the elements to be connected. The logical postulate inherent in the axiom cannot be directly fulfilled in any sensuously or intuitively existing content; but the deficiency is compensated for by the fact that this same postulate determines and literally defines a content appropriate to it.

But, though such implicit definition may suffice for pure mathematics, this does not answer the question of how it can be made fruitful for physics. Mathematics may content itself with the separation, the χωρισμός, of the purely intellectual from the intuitive: but physics demands a relation of "participation," of μέθεξις, between the two. Such participation is possible only if we can see the "given" itself in the light of what is postulated. True, there can never be a simple relation of congruence between them: but it must be possible to draw up certain series in the "given," which when continued will lead to those factors that thought, by its purely constructive effort, has established as the foundations of all determination. Such a relation becomes possible when for the "serial values" that we can establish by observation or empirical measurement, we substitute the value-limits toward which the series as a whole converges. No physical "law" can be stated and strictly grounded without such a method of substitution. The "classical" theories of science offer instances of this process of transition to the limit at every step. As examples we need only mention such concepts as those of the "rigid body," the "ideal gas," the "incompressible liquid," the "perfect circular process," etc.[17] It is only through the intellectual metamorphosis which they undergo in this method that the contents of immediate observation first become possible subjects for physical judgments. In respect to space, the space of mere perception or representation—in which there are still no clearly delimited "elements," no "points," "lines," or "surfaces"—must first of all be grounded in and replaced by a freely produced schema. The geometrical logos reaches through and beyond the given.[18]

It is this logical act which also conditions and makes possible the concept of the "physical" body and the "physical" event—insofar as these concepts are taken not in their substantial but in their functional sense—that is, not primarily as an expression of a simple existence or occurrence

17. Concerning "idealizations in physics," cf., for example, Hölder, *Die mathematische Methode*, pp. 398 ff.

18. Cf. the words of H. Weyl in *Das Kontinuum*, quoted above, p. 403.

but as an expression of a determinate order, a specific mode of contemplation. Thus, for example, classical mechanics cannot arrive at strict laws of motion except by creating the limiting concept of the "material point." The rules it sets up are' no longer concerned with the real movements of given bodies, but relate to this limiting idea, and only through it to a concrete empirical content. And what is true of mechanics obtains no less for all other branches of theoretical physics. Newton's law of the attraction of masses finds a rough correspondence in Coulomb's law, according to which electrical or magnetic masses, conceived as points, act upon each other in direct proportion to their mass and in inverse proportion to the square of the distance between them. It is obvious that a statement of this sort cannot be "experienced" in the strict sense, that it cannot be verified by immediate observation.[19] It is transpositions of this sort that enable us to replace the pseudocontinuum, given to us in sense perceptions, by a genuine continuum. And it is through the relation to such a genuine continuum—ultimately to the fundamental series which analysis defines as the "continuum of all real numbers"—that perception is made ripe for mathematical-physical treatment and determination. Rich and many-sided, complex and intricate as physical method may seem, it is always determined by this essential aim. From this standpoint, the abrupt antithesis between induction and deduction, put forward in the controversies between epistemological schools, loses its force. Instead, induction and deduction, experience and thought, experiment and computation appear as different but equally indispensable factors in physical concept formation—factors which ultimately meet and combine in the solution of a single problem: in the transposition of the given into the form of the pure numerical manifold.

The necessary preparation for this universal intellectual process requires first of all that we differentiate the particular spheres of perception presented by empirical intuition, but also that we replace the fluid transitions within each of these spheres by exact determination which can be strictly fixed in number. The world of the physicist also takes its first articulation from the differences directly supplied by sensation. At the outset the physicist preserves the differences he finds here, and builds up an architectonic schema of scientific knowledge in accordance with them. Optics is the theoretical authority correlated with sensations of light

19. Cf. the apt remarks of H. Bouasse, "Physique générale," in *De la méthode dans les sciences* (Paris, 1909), pp. 73 ff.

and color, thermodynamics with sensations of heat, acoustics with sensations of tone. But here again, before the sensory contents can enter into the newly created schema they must undergo a thorough transformation. The indefinite "more" or "less," "nearer" or "farther," "stronger" or "weaker" that we can immediately apprehend in the sensations themselves must be replaced by a strict gradation. Sensation as such is not capable of any such strict division into "degrees" but must first undergo an intellectual transposition. It is through such a transposition, for example, that the concept of temperature takes form from the mere sensation of heat, the concept of pressure from mere tactile and muscular sensation. The vast intellectual effort contained in such transformations is unmistakable—and it cannot be overlooked even by a strictly empiricist theory of knowledge. The example of such a work as Ernst Mach's *Principles of Thermodynamics* shows clearly how wide a difference there is between the simple sensation of heat and the strict concept of temperature developed by modern thermodynamics.

Complex as this achievement and the intellectual processes it requires may be, however, theoretical physics does not stop here. Its central and most difficult task does not consist exclusively in raising sensuous "qualities" to mathematical, exactly definable magnitudes. Actually it is only after this preparatory work has been done that its central question arises: the question of the connection and functional combination of the various spheres of qualities. They must not be apprehended in their mere apartness or juxtaposition but must be conceived as a totality that can be determined and dominated by law. In his lecture on the "unity of the physical world view," Planck followed the historical course by which physics has progressively approached this goal, and showed how this decisive methodological advance could be achieved only insofar as theoretical thought tore down the barriers created by its original bond with the immediate content of sensation and the articulation prevailing in this sphere. Only by casting off these accidental bonds was theory able to progress to its true form. "The signature of the whole development of theoretical physics up to now," so Planck summed up his conclusions, "is a unification of its system, which has been achieved through a certain emancipation from anthropomorphic elements. If we consider, on the other hand, that sensations, as has been generally recognized, form the starting point of all physical investigation, this conscious turn away from the basic presuppositions must seem astonishing and even paradoxical. And yet in the whole history of physics there is no more evident fact. Beyond a doubt there must be inestimable advantages to compensate for so fundamental a self-alienation." [20]

Yet this paradox seems less glaring if we consider that it does not attach to physical concept formation alone but discloses an essential trait of the logos as such. In order to come to itself, the logos must always go through such a seeming process of self-alienation. The development of language shows us how speech can penetrate to its own essential form, the form of symbolic representation, only by turning away from the sensuous image. [21] And it is only through this turning away from sensation that physics arrives at its specific concept of the object. Here lies the dividing line between the "object" in the physical sense and the mere "thing" of sense perception. Indeed, even the object of perception as such is sharply divided from the mere content of perception: it is itself never perceived, but comprises an act of purely intellectual synthesis. However, the synthesis that holds its different determinations together is of a different and, one might say, less stringent kind than the unification which is effected in the physical concept of the object. In the "thing" of naive intuition the particular elements or "properties" are indeed related to one another, but they still form a relatively loose fabric. One attribute stands beside another, they are related by no other bond than that of accidental empirical coexistence, particularly coexistence at a determinate point in space. Hegel, in his *Phänomenologie des Geistes,* regards this outwardness and looseness of attributes as the essential characteristic of the empirical-phenomenal thing.

This block of salt is simply here, and at the same time it is manifold; it is white as well as sharp, and cubical in form; it is also of a definite weight, etc. All these many properties are in a simple "here," in which they permeate each other; none has a different "here" from the other; rather, each is always in the same "here" as the other, and yet, though they are not divided by different "heres," they do not affect each other in this permeation—the white does not affect or change the cubical, neither of these affects the sharp, etc.; rather, since each is itself a simple relatedness to itself, it leaves the others in peace and is related to them only by the indifferent "also." This "also" is then the

20. Max K. E. L. Planck, "Die Einheit des physikalischen Weltbildes," in *Physikalische Rundblicke* (Leipzig, 1922), p. 6.

21. Cf. above, *1*, 188 ff.

pure universal itself or the medium, the thingness that gathers them together.[22]

Strict empiricism has always attempted to hold the thing concept at its first stage. Just as it regards the ego as a "bundle of perceptions," it regards the thing as a mere bundle of separate and dissimilar properties. And the empiricists also stress that the object concepts of strict science do not negate this state of affairs, that they can never surpass the barrier that is here erected. Locke finds herein the fundamental and irreducible difference between the world of purely mathematical objects and the world of physical objects. Mathematics, he holds, is governed by the principle of necessary connection: here the simple ideas from which a complex structure is built up do not merely stand side by side; we understand with intuitive certainty how the one issues from the other and is grounded in the other. But Locke holds that such grounding and intelligible connection are denied us when it comes to determining an empirical object. Though we may amplify and refine our intellectual instruments and advance from immediate sense perception to universal concepts and theories, we can never establish anything more than coexistences, which we must simply accept as such. The substance we are accustomed to call by the name "gold" has, along with its yellow color, a definite degree of hardness, a definite specific weight, etc.; it reacts in a certain way to other substances, being, for example, soluble in aqua regia—we must take all this simply from experience, and there is no way of understanding the ground for such a combination of properties. Says Locke:

> I deny not but a man, accustomed to rational and regular experiments, shall be able to see farther into the nature of bodies, and guess righter at their yet unknown properties, than one that is a stranger to them: but yet, as I have said, this is but judgment and opinion, not knowledge and certainty. This way of getting and improving our knowledge in substances only by experience and history, which is all that the weakness of our faculties in this state of mediocrity we are in in this world can attain to, makes me suspect that natural philosophy is not capable of being made a science. We are able, I imagine, to reach very little general knowledge concerning the species of bodies, and their several properties. Experiments and historical observations we may have, from which we draw advantages of ease and health, and

22. Hegel, *Phänomenologie des Geistes*, in *Sämtliche Werke*, 2, 84.

thereby increase our stock of conveniencies for this life; but beyond this, I fear, our talents reach not, nor are our faculties, as I guess, able to advance.[23]

When we inquire to what extent this prediction of Locke has been confirmed in modern theoretical physics, we see once again how far removed the statements of the empiricists are from the facts of concrete empirical science. True, they agree on one purely negative point, the rejection of a certain metaphysical ideal of knowledge. Modern physics, like empiricism, has given up the hope of penetrating the "inwardness of nature," if by "inwardness" we mean the ultimate substantial source from which empirical phenomena are derived. It has no higher aspiration than to "spell out phenomena in order to read them as experience." But on the other hand it draws a far sharper dividing line between sensory "appearance" and scientific "experience" than do the systems of dogmatic empiricism—whether we have in mind Locke and Hume, or Mill and Mach. In the pure actuality, the "matter of fact," described by these systems, there is no discernible methodological difference between the "fact" of theoretical science and the "fact" of history. In the passage we have just quoted from Locke, the two determinations mingle and merge. But this leveling cuts at the root of the true problem of physical "actuality." The facts of physics are not on the same footing with the facts of history—because they rest on entirely different presuppositions and intellectual procedures. If we set aside the gamut of these procedures, we do not disclose the pure core of physical actuality, but destroy it by taking away its specific meaning. Here we find a peculiar dialectic in the development of empiricism itself. For the blow that the empiricists thought they were striking against the "rational" falls back on themselves. The empiricists believed that there was no better way to establish the right of experience as the actual foundation of all knowledge than to ground it purely in itself. Experience—Locke once declared—must no longer rest on borrowed or begged foundations, but must be recognized as a fully independent and autonomous source of knowledge.

But this declaration which was intended to liberate the sphere of the a posteriori sharply and clearly from that of the a priori strikes not only at the a priori factors but also at the form of empirical concept formation itself. In view of the thoroughgoing correlation between the "particular"

23. Locke, *An Essay Concerning Human Understanding*, Bk. IV, chap. 12, sec. 10.

and the "universal," the "factual" and the "rational," any attempt to separate one of these factors from the intellectual totality in which it stands is equivalent to destroying its positive meaning. For the factual never subsists in itself as a pre-given, undifferentiated material of knowledge, but enters as a categorial factor into the process of knowledge. And this factor first takes on its meaning through the other pole to which it refers—through the structural form at which it aims and which it plays a part in building. It is from this point of view that the whole wealth of determinations and differentiations comprised in the concept of the "factual" first stands out clearly. According to the form with which it is articulated, the fundamental meaning of pure actuality itself changes. The rational is not the logical antithesis to the factual but one of its essential determinants—the factual itself takes on different intellectual significance according to the transformations of this determinant. It becomes a fact of physics, a fact of descriptive natural science, a fact of history, according to the theoretical question that is asked of it and according to the special presuppositions which enter into each of these characteristic forms of question.

If we restrict ourselves here to the problem of physics, it becomes immediately evident that the "given" of sense perception undergoes a thoroughgoing transformation through the original and basic trend of physics. For the data of physics are no longer simple sensations as such, any more than the objects it deals with and whose existence it asserts can be dissolved into mere groups of sensuous qualities. As long as we stand on the ground of the mere perceptive consciousness there seems to be no serious objection to the thesis *esse = percipi*. Within this sphere the "object" itself, though it can never be disclosed in the form of a single perception, nevertheless appears to be definable as a mere aggregate of simple ideas. Accordingly the unity of the object appears here to be no more than a nominal unity. Says Berkeley:

> By sight I have the ideas of light and colours with their several degrees and variations. By touch I perceive hard and soft, heat and cold, motion and resistance, and of all these more and less either as to quantity or degree. Smelling furnishes me with odours; the palate with tastes, and hearing conveys sounds to the mind in all their variety of tone and composition. And as several of these are observ'd to accompany each other, they come to be marked by one name, and so to be

reputed as one thing. Thus, for example, a certain colour, taste, smell, figure and consistence having been observ'd to go together, are accounted one distinct thing, signified by the name *apple*. Other collections of ideas constitute a stone, a tree, a book and the like sensible things . . .[24]

But however we may judge this nominalistic dissolution of the object of perception, it does not affect the object of physics, because in it something entirely different from a simple aggregate of sensory ideas is intended and posited. It, too, forms a complex whole; yet this is not a totality of impressions but an aggregate of determinations of number and measure. Every component of this object must, before it can be used for its construction, undergo a kind of transsubstantiation: it must be transformed from a mere sense impression into a pure magnitude of measure. Here it is not tastes or smells, auditory or visual sensations that form the components of the object; such sensations have been replaced by elements of an entirely different kind. The individual thing has ceased to be a concrete coexistence of sensuous properties: it has become a totality of "constants," each of which characterizes it within a determinate system of magnitudes. It no longer "consists" in smell or taste, in color or tone; instead, its existence and individual difference from other things are grounded in such pure magnitude. The nature of a body, in the physical sense of the word, is determined not by the manner of its sensory manifestation but by its atomic weight, its specific heat, its exponents of refraction, its index of absorption, its electrical conductivity, its magnetic susceptibility, etc.

To be sure, this transformation in the predicates of the thing seems at first sight to have no bearing on the subject to which all these determinations are conceived as adhering. For the mode of connection between the particular physical and chemical constants would appear to be no more firmly grounded than the connection among sensuous properties. Here, again, it would seem that we must content ourselves with the simple acceptance of a coexistence and juxtaposition, without being able to look any more deeply into the "why" of it. Yet, on the other hand, the entire development of physics and chemistry, particularly in the last few decades, shows that they have not given up inquiring into this "why." They have not contented themselves with empirically determining the

24. George Berkeley, *The Principles of Human Knowledge* (London and New York, T. Nelson and Sons, 1945), Pt. I, sec. 1.

coexistence of constants but have gone on to establish universal systematic relationships, through which to explain various complexes. This explaining, to be sure, does not mean to derive "accidents" and "modes" from the essence of the substance. It means a search for certain universal laws governing the relationships between different kinds of constants. On the basis of such laws, fields which had previously been regarded as utterly dissimilar were now seen from a single point of view—problems that seemed utterly heterogeneous were recognized to be not only analogous but actually identical. Hesitant at first, this tendency in modern physics soon advanced more and more resolutely from isolated problems to universal contexts. First a rapprochement was made between constants describing the physical and chemical behavior of the various substances: firm relationships were formed between different groups of these constants. As early as 1819 Dulong and Petit found a very definite relation between the atomic weight of an element and its specific heat: the specific heat of an element is inversely proportional to its atomic weight. This relation found its theoretical confirmation and explanation when Richards succeeded in deriving it from the kinetic theory of heat. Yet there still seemed to remain a tension between theory and experience when it was discovered that certain solids of low atomic weight show a deviation in the product of their atomic weight and specific heat, which according to the law of Petit and Dulong should have been identical for all elements. These deviations became comprehensible only when Einstein introduced them into a new theoretical context, applying the principles of the quantum theory to the thermics of solid bodies. Through this way of conceiving the matter, a new relationship was disclosed between the specific heat of solids and absolute temperature as formulated in Debye's theorem.

An analogous rapprochement between constants occurred when Maxwell determined the relation between the constants determining the optical behavior of certain substances and those governing their electrical behavior. On the basis of the electromagnetic theory of light the dielectric constant of a medium was found to be equal to the square of its exponent of refraction. But at first this relation, too, had only a limited empirical validity: exact empirical confirmation was attainable only for gases, and not for such substances as alcohol or water. Yet here again the exceptions that experience seemed to offer could not invalidate the rule established on the strength of general theoretical considerations, but actually pro-

moted a more exact determination of the rule itself. The seeming deviations were explained when the concept of the dielectricity constant was
more sharply defined through the electron theory of dispersion.[25] Another
illuminating example of the progress achieved by the identification of
constants that had previously been regarded as disparate is to be found in
the connection which Einstein's theory of gravitation established between
the weight and inertia of masses. The purely empirical connection had
long been recognized and confirmed by the experiments of Eötvös and
Zeemann with the torsion balance. The decisive factor in Einstein's theory
was that it brought an entirely new interpretation to the equivalence of
weight and inertia, which had hitherto been regarded as an unexplained
fact, a kind of curiosity. The equivalence of weight and inertia, which
in the old theory appeared to be a mere accident, was raised by Einstein
to the level of a strict principle, and through this principle he arrived at
a fundamental law which embraces the phenomena both of inertia and of
gravitation.[26]

In all these relations and connections the intervention of the universal
schematism of the numerical concept is decisive. Number, one might say,
functions as the abstract medium in which the various sensory spheres
meet, and in respect to which they cast off their specific dissimilarity.
Thus, for example, the phenomenon of light is identified with electrical
phenomena in Maxwell's theory, because the same relation is manifested
in both phenomena once we attempt to express them and exactly formulate them in numbers. The apparent gap between optical phenomena
and electrical phenomena as such closes as soon as we recognize that a
definite constant c, which appears in Maxwell's equations, is exactly
identical to the measure of the velocity of light in a vacuum. It is through
this purely numerical relation that the heterogeneity of sensuous properties is bridged and a homogeneity of physical "essence" established.
"True," Planck remarked in this connection,

> the nature of electromagnetic processes is no whit more comprehensi-
> ble to us than that of optical phenomena. But anyone who counts it

25. On the facts in this connection, cf. Arthur E. Haas, *Das Naturbild der neuen Physik*
(2d ed. Berlin and Leipzig, 1924), first, third, and fourth lectures.

26. For details see the well known expositions of the general theory of relativity. Cf.,
for example, von Laue, *Die Relativitätstheorie*, 2, 2 ff., 18 ff.; Erwin Freundlich, *Die
Grundlagen der Einsteinschen Gravitationstheorie* (Berlin, 1920), pp. 35 ff. of 3d ed. Eng.
trans. by Henry L. Brose, *Einstein's Theory of Gravitation* (Cambridge, 1920).

as a disadvantage of the electromagnetic theory of light that it replaces one riddle by another fails to understand the significance of this theory. For its achievement consists precisely in uniting two fields of physics which had previously been treated separately, so that now all statements which are valid for the one field are directly applicable to the other—an advance which the mechanical theory of light did not and could not accomplish.

The identity toward which theoretical physics aims is not an identity in the substantial source of phenomena, but an identity in their mathematical —that is, symbolic—representation. Thus the more it perfects its system of signs, the more completely it succeeds in encompassing the totality of phenomena in this system and assigning to each phenomenon a definite place in it, the farther theoretical physics has progressed in its own characteristic process of explanation. Today this progress in explanation, consisting essentially in strict serial combination and representation, is demonstrated by the fact that there really seems to be a fundamental series encompassing the whole of what may be designated as the physical process. The modern theory of radiation has enabled us to group together fields and processes which were previously far apart. First of all it was recognized that all the laws which apply to light rays—the laws of reflection and refraction, interference and polarization, emission and absorption—are applicable in the exact same way to heat rays. This promoted an intellectual union between the two sets of radiations, and through it the qualitative difference in the phenomena manifested to us as heat and light was surmounted. Since then the two have been distinguished—in the objective sense of the physical judgment—by nothing other than a pure numerical and positional value, by a definite index which designates the "wave length" of the two kinds of rays. This union between light rays and heat rays was then augmented, at the other end of the spectrum, by the chemically effective ultraviolet rays; and finally, through the discovery of Hertz waves at the one end and of X rays and gamma rays at the other, the field of radiation underwent a new broadening, which brought with it a deeper and more meaningful unification.[27] It then developed that the totality of radiation processes can be represented in a strictly unitary form; that all cases of radiation repre-

27. See the succinct survey of the general development given by Max Planck in *Das Wesen des Lichts* (1919), rep. in *Physikalische Rundblicke* (Leipzig, 1922), pp. 129 ff.

sent electromagnetic waves which differ from one another only in their magnitudes or periods. The sphere that is attested by sense perception and accessible to it appears as a mere segment within this total system, and a very small segment relative to the whole. The visible spectrum which embraces the colors of the rainbow from red to violet occupies the space of a single octave within the total spectrum, whereas the sphere of the X rays begins only eight to sixteen octaves beyond the violet, while the sphere of radio waves begins only some thirty octaves beyond the red.[28] It is the consequent working out of the specifically physical form of thought and of the symbolism which this form has created as its appropriate language that have made possible this broadening, have enabled us to recognize the limits of sensation as merely accidental anthropomorphic limits, and to eliminate them as such.

The independent part played by symbolism in this whole development, the significance of a scientific language of formulas for the establishment of a universal system of natural objects and natural processes, can also be shown from another angle. What has made chemistry an exact science is not only the steady refinement of its methods but above all its sharpening of this intellectual instrument, its progress from the simple chemical formula to the structural formula. Generally speaking, the scientific value of a formula consists not only in its summing up of given empirical facts but in its power, one might say, to call forth new facts. The formula states relationships, connections, series which far outdistance direct observation. It becomes one of the most outstanding instruments of what Leibniz called the "logic of discovery," the *logica inventionis*. Even the simple chemical formula which merely indicates the type and number of atoms contained in a certain molecule seems to be filled with fruitful methodological indications. In the language of this formula, for example, certain known combinations of chlorine, hydrogen, and oxygen were designated as $ClOH$, ClO_3H, ClO_4H. This mere compilation raised the question of the missing link in the chain, of a combination ClO_2H, and the empirical discovery of this combination became possible only after its position, as it were, had been determined in advance. Here we have proof of the cognitive value which inheres in every methodically constructed scientific language as such. It is never a mere designation for the given and present, but also points the way to a new, hitherto unex-

28. Cf. Haas, pp. 15 ff.; and Bernhard Bavink, *Ergebnisse und Probleme der Naturwissenschaft* (2d ed. Leipzig, 1921), pp. 98 ff.

plored field: it leads to a process of interpolation and extrapolation. "From this we see," writes A. Job, from whom I have taken the above example,

> how at every step the language of chemical formulas creates a closer accord between symbols and reality, and how a language which was originally intended to describe only the composition of substances in accordance with their weight relations now describes, and urges us to an insight into, the manner of their production. We no longer have before us a process of designation; we have a guide to discovery and a method of synthesis. . . . Our classification takes on a new face: it no longer signifies an order which we accept just as it is presented by nature or the accident of observation but becomes an order created by ourselves, a deductive order. And this contributes to giving chemistry its peculiar character.[29]

This character becomes still clearer when we consider the chemical formula at the stage of its development when it becomes an actual "constitutive formula." A constitutive formula, such as that given by Baeyer for indigo, replaces mere empirical description by a genuinely genetic construction: it becomes a statement not of the "what" but of the "how," for it may be said to build up the substance in question before our inner eye.

This turn toward genesis is not merely an isolated motif that appears sporadically in particular fields of science; it must rather be regarded as a fundamental trait in physical and chemical concept formation. This becomes clear as soon as we consider the greatest systematic achievements of this concept formation in the course of the last century. The "natural system of elements" attempted in 1870 by Lothar Meyer and Mendelejeff, marks an important turning point. For here it was stated more sharply than ever before that we must not simply accept the manifold of elements and the diversity expressed in their physical and chemical properties; we must find a point of view from which this manifold can be surveyed and ordered according to a fixed principle. First, atomic weight was chosen as such an ordering principle. If we list all the known elements according to increasing atomic weight, each element in this series is assigned to a certain position which is designated by its characteristic number, its "ordinal number." When the elements are thus arranged, a characteris-

29. A. Job, "Chimie," in *De la méthode dans les sciences,* pp. 126 f.

tic periodicity is disclosed in the most important elements. They are not scattered promiscuously over the whole field, but follow a fixed rule of recurrence. The well-known curve of atomic volumes set up by Lothar Meyer shows the existence and the mode of this rule with graphic clarity. The elements which occupy analogous positions on this curve—on its rising or descending arc, at its maxima or minima—also prove to be analogous in their most important chemical and physical properties, in their valence, volatility, ductility, electrical and thermic conductivity, etc. From the very first the discoverers of the periodic system were convinced that there must be a profound reason for this dependence of the properties on the ordinal number, that it must in some way be grounded in the nature of the atom itself. This presupposition may be said to have been their heuristic maxim.

Yet at first this maxim was far from having a "constitutive" significance, for the connection between the atomic weight or atomic volume of an element and its chemicophysical behavior had been established merely as a fact, for which no satisfactory theoretical explanation had been arrived at. In the tabular representations of the natural system the ordinal numbers functioned simply as conventional marks, which within certain limits indicated the properties of the elements, but conveyed no definite physical *meaning*. However, as the theory developed, this meaning was increasingly recognized and worked out; the conventional order became a systematic order. The first step in this direction was the acquisition of a more accurate ordering principle, which was provided by roentgen spectroscopy. When the various elements were arranged in a series according to their characteristic roentgen spectra, the shift of lines from one element to another in the direction toward an increasing index of vibration disclosed a regularity far surpassing that of the classification by atomic weight. According to the law formulated by Moseley in 1913, the square of the vibration number of a characteristic roentgen line is almost exactly proportional to the ordinal number of the chemical element. This fact immediately led physicists to attribute a profound physical meaning to the ordinal number: for according to modern theory the roentgen spectrum originates in the nucleus of the atom, whereas the optical spectra and chemical properties spring from more "external," peripheral zones of the atom.[30]

30. For all particulars of this development, which we need not follow in detail here, I refer the reader to Arnold Sommerfeld, *Atombau und Spektrallinien*, 1919; (4th ed. Braun-

Soon the appearance of new empirical facts, particularly the discovery of the so-called isotopes and the development of the isotope theory, drove the concept of atomic weight, which had served as the starting point for the development of the natural system, from its dominant position in chemistry, which now passed to another concept, that of "nuclear charge." Moseley had already built his system around it: he had interpreted the ordinal number simply as the index of the positive charge of the atom nucleus, which now became the accepted serial principle. The number of an element in the periodic system, its ordinal number, was now replaced by the number of its nuclear charge—and this in turn was indicated by the number of electrons surrounding the nucleus (van den Brock 1913). The physical *meaning* of the ordinal number was now found in the assumption underlying Bohr's atomic theory, namely that the positive electrical charge of the atomic nucleus increases by one unit from element to element. "The atomic structure is electrically regulated, entirely from the inside outward to the periphery of the atom, by the magnitude of the nuclear charge." [31] In his work *Atombau und Spektrallinien* Sommerfeld sums up the intellectual significance of this development: "We have reached a goal which ten years ago still seemed nebulous and remote: a theory of the periodic system." [32]

If we consider the purely logical character of this theory, we see that though its achievement holds strictly to the sphere of what can be observed and empirically established, it nevertheless goes far beyond the resigned "empiricism" put forward by Locke in his theory of substances. [33] It does not define the substance as a mere aggregate of properties without inner bond; yet on the other hand it does not take this bond in the sense of the *vinculum substantiale* of dogmatic metaphysics but inquires solely into the necessity—that is the thoroughgoing universality and lawfulness —of the combination. This lawfulness can never be arrived at by observation of isolated facts, however far such observation is carried; it can be found only through clearly defined constructive presuppositions and principles. These principles cannot be imposed on the empirical material, though on the other hand they cannot be directly derived from it. Accordingly, the concept formation of physics and chemistry proves to be just as

schweig, 1924), chap. 3; and Fritz Paneth, "Das natürliche System der chemischen Elemente" in *Handbuch der Physik*, 22, ed. Geiger and Scheel (Berlin, 1926), 520 ff.

31. Cf. Paneth, pp. 551 ff.; Sommerfeld, pp. 73 ff., 168 ff.

32. Sommerfeld, p. 179.

33. See above, p. 434.

genuinely genetic as that of pure mathematics. But this genesis may be said to be of a hypothetical rather than categorical character. We do not start with a universal serial law and produce the manifold of the elements from it; we content ourselves with experimentally introducing an ordering principle into the given manifold in various intellectual operations, and thus, step by step, transform the mere empirical multiplicity into a "rational" multiplicity.[34] This principle itself is never simply "given" but represents a perpetual problem, and one of the essential achievements of all natural science is to be sought in a steady advance toward a more complete solution of this problem.

The historical development of modern physical theory throws a clear light on the progress from "individual constants" to "universal constants," as one of the most important and fruitful factors in the whole process of scientific cognition. Thus, for example, the beginning of modern spectroscopy is marked by the law which Balmer established in 1885 for the hydrogen spectrum. Balmer's law states that the wave lengths of the lines in this spectrum can be expressed in the formula

$$\frac{1}{\lambda n} = R \left(\frac{1}{4} - \frac{1}{n^2} \right),$$

in which R signifies a constant and n a whole number. Balmer himself still regarded the magnitude R that appears in this formula as a basic number peculiar to hydrogen, and he believed that future investigation would find analogous numbers for other elements. But subsequent research showed that the same basic number that had here been established for hydrogen recurs in the spectra of all other elements. Balmer's formula now appeared as a mere special case of a universal law which, in the form given it by Rydberg and Ritz, became the foundation of all spectroscopy. In Rydberg's formula

$$\frac{1}{\lambda n} = A - \frac{R}{(n+a)^2}$$

or in the more general formula of Ritz:

$$\frac{1}{\lambda} = R \left(\frac{1}{n_1^2} - \frac{1}{n_2^2} \right),$$

34. Modern theoreticians are well aware of this character of physical method and concept formation. Sommerfeld writes, for example: "We need scarcely stress that with this speculation [on the new theoretical perspectives opened up by the theories of radioactive displacement and the isotope theory] we depart at first from the field of facts. . . . Nevertheless such speculation is indispensable today. The demonstration of the isotopes in non-

the number R means a universal constant, which applies to the spectra of all elements. Thus this Rydberg-Ritz number no longer designates any particularity of hydrogen but points to a very general relationship.

The nature of this relationship could be disclosed, however, only by a further broadening of the whole context. When Niels Bohr, in "Über das Wasserstoffspektrum" (1913),[35] proceeded to investigate the laws of the spectrum not only in themselves but above all in connection with other properties of the elements, he was led to a conception of atomic structure which linked the observations gained by the study of heat radiations, and by the study of radioactive phenomena, with the data of spectroscopy, and which enabled him to interpret all these observations from a single fundamental viewpoint. This for the first time provided a strict theory of Balmer's series, which could not only derive Balmer's formula itself but could exactly compute the universal constant R.[36] With this computation the universal constant lost its seemingly accidental character: from then on it was recognized as necessary—within the hypothetical assumptions on which Bohr's theory is based. And by necessary we mean that from now on it does not stand for itself and on itself but is carried back to other numerical magnitudes of universal significance. Balmer's number as well as the Rydberg-Ritz number became, strictly speaking, "comprehensible" only when they were fitted into the general intellectual framework of the quantum theory and linked with the magnitude h of the so-called Planck energy quantum.

Contrary to this, a dogmatic empiricism will perhaps argue that next to nothing has been gained by this whole development; that Planck's quantum itself is a mere fact—a fact which we can only accept and cannot in any profound sense understand. But apart from the fact that such an objection would prejudge the future development of physical theory and set an arbitrary limit to it, this argument completely misconstrues the characteristic logical bent of physical theory. For although physical theory cannot surpass the factual as such, it teaches us to know and finely distinguish varying degrees and levels in facticity itself, and precisely therein reside its meaning and value. Theory loses all its gains when we

radioactive substances challenges us to look for genetic connections in the periodic system and to extend the theories of displacement to the whole system and makes it seem highly probable that the nuclei too are composed and constructible. With this a new field of investigation opens up to us . . . nuclear physics."

35. Rep. in *Drei Aufsätze über Spektrum und Atombau* (2d ed. Braunschweig, 1924).

36. For details of Bohr's theory cf. esp. Sommerfeld, chap. 2, sec. 4.

allow all these distinctions to flow together.[37] Theoretical thinking assigns the various phenomena to different levels and through these differences in level enables us to order and articulate them. Factors which lie close together in the synthesis effected by the popular thing concept are clearly and sharply differentiated in the object concepts of theoretical science, which are based on exact concepts of law. This increasing differentiation is everywhere the essential outcome of the seemingly opposite process of progressive generalization. When asked wherein the strictly objective factor in nature consists, the modern physicist can only point to the universal constants arrived at by investigation and, on the other hand, trace the road leading from these universal constants down to the individual constants, the particular thing-constants. At the summit of his system stand certain invariable magnitudes, such as the velocity of light in a vacuum, the elementary quantum of energy, etc., which are free from any merely subjective contingency, since they prove to be independent of the standpoint of the individual observer.[38] The process of physical objectivization is an ascent from mere material constants, from the particularity of thing-unities to universal unities of law.

The quantum theory is eminently characteristic of this trend. Planck himself, in a general survey, "Of the Origin and Development of the Quantum Theory," [39] tells us that his first ideas and experiments related to Gustav Kirchhoff's law of heat radiation. This law established that in a vacuum bounded by emissive and absorptive bodies at a constant temperature, heat radiation is unaffected by the special properties of these bodies, and so disclosed the existence of a universal function depending only on temperature and wave length and not on the specific properties of any substance. The further investigation of the problem involved two other important constants. According to the law of Stefan and Boltzmann, the emissive power of a body is proportional to the fourth power of its absolute temperature, so that the ratio between these two values is identical for all bodies. This ratio was designated as Stefan's constant, and the law of displacement, formulated by Wien in 1893, disclosed a new

37. Cf. above, pp. 408–10.

38. For particulars see Planck, "Die Stellung der neueren Physik zur mechanischen Naturanschauung," *Königsberger Naturforscher-Versammlung* (1910), rep. in *Physikalische Rundblicke* (Leipzig, 1922), pp. 38 ff.

39. Planck, "Über die Entstehung und bisherige Entwicklung der Quantentheorie," a Nobel Prize lecture rep. in *Physikalische Rundblicke*, pp. 148 ff.

constant, defined as the product of wave length and absolute temperature.

All these questions, which had thus far been taken up separately, were joined together and given a surprising solution through the fundamental conception of the quantum theory as developed by Planck in 1900. The general theory of radiation which Planck developed on the basis of his fundamental theory provided two equations which linked the empirically determined constants of Stefan and Wien with two fundamental magnitudes: the elementary energy quantum and the mass of the hydrogen atom.[40] A number of special fields and problems had thus been interpreted on the basis of a theoretical idea. It is only if we understand the central physical concepts as expressions not of mere "facts," but of such ideas that we can appreciate them in an epistemological sense, and in particular that we can recognize the superiority of these concepts over the thing concepts of the "naive" world view. The thing concepts can at most connect, but the physical concepts combine—the thing concepts create a coexistence of properties as mere particulars, but the concepts of physics go on to posit truly universal unities. It is this synthesis, this new ordinal form, that first opens up to us the world that we call the world of physical bodies and physical events, and indicates the vantage point from which we can survey them as a whole, as a self-contained structure.

3. Symbol and Schema in the System of Modern Physics

Now let us pause in our analysis of scientific concept formation, and consider its findings in the light of our general problem. We have seen that the form of physical series formation and the new order it creates establish the foundation for a new relation to the object. The basic physical concepts are genuinely synthetic concepts in the sense defined by Kant: they are "concepts of combination and thereby of the object itself."[41] And while epistemology can content itself with disclosing the reciprocal relation between concept form and object form, between the formal and the material significance of nature, the philosophy of symbolic forms must, from the very start, envisage this problem in a far broader context. When we inquire into the possibility of mathematical science, we look upon this science only as a special case of objectivization in general.

40. For particulars see Fritz Reiche, *Die Quantentheorie, ihr Ursprung und ihre Entwicklung* (Berlin, 1921). Eng. trans. by H. S. Hatfield, *The Quantum Theory* (2d ed. New York, 1930). See also Haas, *Das Naturbild der neuen Physik*, fourth lecture.

41. Cf. Kant, *Prolegomena*, sec. 39.

We consider the world of exact science not as the beginning but as the end of a process of objectivization, whose roots reach down into other and earlier strata of formation. Thus it becomes incumbent on us to compare the ideal content of the physical world with that of those earlier strata—to inquire into their connections and divergencies, their community and the specific difference between them. Is there any common prime factor in the structure of the three form worlds that we have examined up to now, and what are the intellectual transformations, the characteristic metamorphoses that this factor undergoes in the transition from mythical concepts to linguistic concepts and from these in turn to the concepts of physical law?

In all spiritual growth we can discern a twofold trend. It is related to natural, purely organic growth insofar as both are subject to the law of continuity. The later phase is not absolutely alien to the earlier one but is only the fulfillment of what was intimated in the preceding phase. On the other hand this interlocking of phases does not exclude a sharp opposition between them. For each new phase raises its own pregnant demand and sets up a new norm and "idea" of the spiritual. Continuous as the progress may be, the accents of meaning are forever shifting within it—and each of these shifts gives rise to a new total meaning of reality. We may succinctly characterize this shift of accent in the process of symbolic formation by distinguishing three steps, or one might say dimensions, within it.[42] We have already distinguished the sphere of expression from that of representation. Now a third sphere comes into being; for just as the world of representation disengaged itself from that of mere expression and set up a new principle in opposition to it, so ultimately a world of pure meaning grows out of the world of representation. It is through this transition, as we shall now attempt to show, that the form of scientific knowledge is first truly constituted, that its concept of truth and reality definitively breaks away from that of the naive world view. But here again—as in the progress from expression to representation—the breach does not occur all at once. Rather, thought clings desperately to the sphere of representation, even though driven beyond it by the inner law and necessary trend of its own unfolding. It is in this conflict of two movements, in this dialectic, that the world of the scientific concept is

42. On the following see the detailed exposition in my "Das Symbolproblem und seine Stellung im System der Philosophie," *Zeitschrift für Ästhetik und allgemeine Kunstwissenschaft*, 21, 191 ff.; several passages from it have been incorporated into the following.

built up. The scientific concept does not immediately break away from intuition and linguistic representation, but as it becomes permeated with its own form imprints a new character upon the representative world. If we wish to understand the nature of this transformation, we must not content ourselves with considering its product; we must investigate from within the mode and direction of its production. The differentiation becomes truly visible and comprehensible only when we look beyond all the mixed transitional forms presented by the finished *work* and consider the *workings* of the formative powers themselves—if we direct our question not toward the mere *ergon* but rather toward the energies upon which the new mode of formation rests.

The first form in which a sensing and feeling subject has an environment consists in the possession of this world as a manifold of expressive experiences. The surrounding world was ordered in this way long before it was given to the subject as a complex of "things" with objective characteristics, with fixed qualities and attributes.[43] Whatever we call existence or reality, is given to us at the outset in definite forms of pure expression. Thus even here we are beyond the abstraction of sheer sensation, which dogmatic sensationalism takes as its starting point. For the content which the subject experiences as confronting him is no merely outward one, resembling Spinoza's "mute picture on a slate." It has a kind of transparency; an inner life shines through its very existence and facticity. The formation effected in language, art, and myth starts from this original phenomenon of expression; indeed, both art and myth remain so close to it that one might be tempted to restrict them wholly to this sphere. High as myth and art may rise, they remain on the soil of primary, "primitive" expressive experiences. Language, it is true, discloses the new turn, the transition to a new dimension, more clearly than the other two; we cannot doubt its connection with the world of expression. There is always a certain expressive value, a certain "physiognomic" character in words, even in those of highly developed language.[44] But this is only a single factor, and language must reach out beyond it to constitute itself as a lasting intellectual form. For not the word but the

43. Cf. above, pp. 60–2.

44. Cf. esp. Heinz Werner, "Über allgemeine und vergleichende Sprachphysiognomik," *Kongressbericht des 10. Kongresses der Gesellschaft für experimentelle Psychologie* (Jena, 1928); and "Über die Sprachphysiognomik als einer neuen Methode der vergleichenden Sprachbetrachtung," *Zeitschrift für Psychologie und Physiologie der Sinnesorgane, 109* (1929), 337–63.

sentence is the basic structure of language, in which the form of linguistic statement is fulfilled. And every purely expressive sentence includes within it a certain postulation: it aims at a certain objective relationship which it strives to describe and arrest. The "is" of the copula is the purest and most pregnant manifestation of the new dimension of language, of its pure representative function.

Yet with all its intellectual value it, too, retains an attachment to bodies. All linguistic representation clings to the world of intuition and returns to it again and again. The distinguishing marks that the process of linguistic denomination singles out and holds fast are of an intuitive kind. Even where language progresses to its highest, specifically intellectual achievements—even where, instead of naming things or attributes, occurrences or actions, it designates pure relations—this purely significative act does not, by and large, surpass certain limits of concrete, intuitive representation. Over and over again an intuitive image or schema injects itself into the logical determination. Even the terms by which language expresses the "is" of the predicative statement usually preserve a secondary intuitive significance—the logical relation is replaced by a spatial one, a "being-here" or "being-there," a statement of existence.[45] Thus all logical determination belonging to language is originally contained in its power of demonstration. The linguistic process of objectivization begins with the demonstrative pronouns, the designation of a definite place, of a "here" or a "there." The object toward which it aims is a τόδε τι in the Aristotelian sense: a something which stands in the presence of the speaker and can be pointed out with the finger. At this stage even substantivization, the positing of things, makes use of linguistic forms—such as the definite articles—which are merely a continuation of the demonstrative pronouns.[46] Language may be said to gain its first foothold in the sphere of space, whence it progressively extends its sway over the whole of intuitive reality.

In this progress we have distinguished three stages. In the first stage language holds fast to the intuitive world, filling itself directly with intuitive content, which, one might say, simply flows into it. Sometimes it attempts to recall a certain objective happening in onomatopoeic formations; at other times it holds fast to certain physiognomic characters in the outside world and makes them known by means of elementary phonetic distinctions, the higher or lower intonation of the vowel. And even where

45. Cf. above, *1*, 313 ff., and the present volume, pp. 74–5.
46. Ibid., *1*, 200 ff.

language renounces such direct proximity to sensuous impression and feeling, even where it treats the phonetic world as a world in its own right, it often discloses a tendency to express relations between outward objects by relations between sounds. Mimetic expression passes into analogical expression. But ultimately language leads beyond this phase as well and becomes purely symbolic expression. Here even the appearance of any direct or indirect similarity between it and the world of immediate perception has vanished. Only with this detachment, this distance from the world of perception has language truly come into its own; only now can it take its place in full self-consciousness as an autonomous formation of the human spirit.[47]

If to this development of linguistic form we now compare the development of the concept form in scientific thinking, we find ourselves from the outset on a different level. The most essential difference is that scientific concept formation, even in its earliest stage, has surpassed the world of expression. Even when approached by the most rudimentary methods, the mere problem of a natural science implies a conscious detachment from the world of expression. Nature, as an object of knowledge, of thought and inquiry, is given to man only when he has learned to draw a dividing line between it and his own world of subjective feeling. Nature is enduring and uniform recurrence, detached from the stream of experience and set over against it as a content in itself. But at first the departure from the sphere of subjective affectivity leaves the sphere of immediate sensation intact. The subject seems unable to break away from the sphere of sensation without losing all contact with reality. Once the distance between the "I" and the "world" has been posited, once it has been recognized as such, there seems to remain no other way of surpassing it than the way shown by sense perception. What characterizes "perception" is that in it we see not only our own nature but the objective form, the being of the object itself. Thus in its beginnings the theoretical concept clings to perception as though to exhaust it, as though to gain possession of all the reality it contains.

But the progress toward this goal leads to the peculiar *peripeteia* which Plato experienced and which he described as the necessary fate of all theoretical knowledge. The movement toward the things, toward the πράγματα, is replaced by a return to the ideas, to the λόγοι.[48] Again the chasm opens: the bond between concept and reality is consciously severed.

47. Ibid., *1*, 186 ff.
48. Plato, *Phaedo*, 99D ff.; cf. above, p. 331.

Over reality as a reality of appearance a new realm rises: the realm of pure meaning; and henceforth it is in this realm that all the certainty and definitive truth of knowledge are grounded. But though the world of ideas, of meanings, relinquishes all similarity to the empirical, sensuous world, it cannot dispense with all *relation* to it. The modern founders of exact science, the modern Platonists like Galileo and Kepler, not only insist on this relation but institute it in a new way. They start from certain basic concepts, from presuppositions and hypotheses, which as such possess no immediate correspondence with sensuous reality but which nevertheless claim to disclose the "structure," the thoroughgoing order of this reality. This achievement falls not to the single concept and presupposition but to the system of these presuppositions. Here again we find that modern science becomes truly systematic only by resolving to become symbolic in the strict sense. The more it seems to lose sight of similarity with things, the more clearly aware it becomes of the lawfulness of being and events.

But even the founders of classical mechanics, Galileo and Kepler, Huyghens and Newton, stand only at the beginning not at the end of this development. Their achievement consists essentially in taking the step from empirical intuition to pure intuition: in taking the world not as a manifold of perceptions but as a manifold of forms, figures, and magnitudes. But this figurative synthesis still preserves a certain limitation: it is restricted to the datum of pure space. It is pure space that serves as model and schema for the building of all the geometrical and mechanical models to which classical physics reduces the multiplicity of empirical phenomena and in which it sees the prototype of all scientific explanation of nature. But the advance from the mechanical view of nature to the modern electrodynamic view of the world takes us one step further. It creates a type of natural science from which the special data of the senses are excluded, and which moreover has given up all dependency on the world of intuition in its earlier form. Now the supreme universal concepts of nature are so constituted as to evade all possibility of direct intuition. The function they fulfill, their specific meaning, resides in universal principles of correlation, which are not susceptible of any immediate representation in intuition. Thus if we apply to the development of the scientific concept the categories to which our investigation of language has led us— though of course this can be done only with a certain methodological reservation—we find at the beginning a kind of mimetic phase, which is followed by a transition through an analogical phase, until at length the truly symbolic mode of concept formation is achieved.

So far, to be sure, we have gained nothing but an abstract schema which stands in need of confirmation and concrete fulfillment. Here we shall not seek to give it body by following the historical course of natural science,[49] but only by considering its reflection in the philosophical systems. We may sum up the progress of scientific theory and its logical form by referring to three great names: Aristotle, Descartes, and Leibniz. Aristotelian physics is the first example of a natural science in the strict sense. This distinction might be claimed, instead, for' the atomists. But although, with their concepts of the atom and of "empty space" they created a fundamental conception and a methodological frame for all future explanations of nature, they were not destined to fill in this frame. For in its ancient form the atomic theory could not master the central and fundamental problem of nature, the problem of change. It solved the problem of the body by reducing all sensuous attributes to purely geometrical determinations, to the form, position, and arrangement of atoms. But it possessed no universal instrument for the representation of change —no principle by which the reciprocal action of the atoms could be made intelligible and lawfully determined.[50]

Aristotle, for whom nature, φύσις, was distinguished from the mere product of art by its possession of an inherent principle of motion, was the first to advance to a true analysis of the phenomenon of motion. But from a purely methodological point of view, this analysis bears a twofold and peculiarly contradictory character. Its orientation is wholly logical: it explains change by reducing it to the ultimate and universal concepts of Aristotle's metaphysics, to substance and form. But at the same time, in order to make these supreme categories applicable to the concrete natural phenomena and fruitful for their explanation, it must everywhere connect them with observations that are taken simply from the sensory sphere. Essentially the Aristotelian theory of elements does not go beyond this sphere. It orders and classifies the sensuous data, it collects them into groups, but it undertakes no true intellectual transformation of them. In this respect the fundamental concepts of Aristo-

49. For the actual history of the modern concept of nature, into which we cannot enter here in detail, the reader is referred to my *Erkenntnisproblem*.

50. How this deficiency impeded the scientific development of the atomic theory for centuries may be seen from the excellent exposition of Kurd Lasswitz, *Geschichte der Atomistik vom Mittelalter bis Newton* (2 vols. Hamburg and Leipzig, 1890).

telian physics scarcely go further in their function and achievement than the attributive concepts of language. Language already divides the manifold of sensuous phenomena according to definite properties: it creates pairs of contrasting characters: "heavy" and "light," "cold" and "warm," "moist" and "dry," etc.

Aristotelian physics starts from these same antinomies. It regards them as ultimate determinations, neither needful nor susceptible of any further analysis, and on them it builds up a theory of basic elements, the στοιχεῖα. The combination of the qualities of warm and dry produces fire, that of warm and moist produces air; while the combination of cold and moist results in water, and that of cold and dry in earth. And to each of these elements corresponds a definite type of motion, which is not merely accidental to it but arises from its inner essence, its substantial form. Fire, as the absolutely light element, tends upward by nature; earth, as the absolutely heavy element, downward, while to the ethereal substance from which the unchanging and imperishable heavenly bodies are formed Aristotle attributes an eternal circular motion, without beginning and without end. In this physics, as we see, sensuous experience taken from direct observation, logical determinations, and teleological principles and norms still form a relatively undifferentiated unity. Perhaps it was this indifference, this immediate concretion of the empirical and the purely intellectual, which for centuries assured Aristotle's system of nature its leading position and its centuries-long supremacy. It represented something other and more significant than any specialized accomplishment— in it a definite mode of thought, through which scientific concept formation had to pass, achieved its typical, truly classical imprint.

Modern philosophy begins by dissolving this form of thought, by questioning not its results but its presuppositions. The new criterion of truth on which the philosophy of Descartes is built destroys the domination of substantial forms. Truth, genuine cognitive value, can be claimed only by what can be known clearly and distinctly, but clear and distinct insight can never be gained into the sensuous as such. Thus sensuous content can no longer enter into the formation of genuine natural concepts. It must be eradicated down to the last trace and replaced by purely mathematical determinations, determinations of number and magnitude. The way in which Descartes set out to accomplish this is well known. All qualities of sensation are banished from the objective view of nature: they express solely the nature of the perceiving subject, not that of the object.

Not only are smell and taste, color and tone thus eliminated as objective characteristics, but also such properties as hardness or heaviness have ceased to be necessary and constitutive attributes of the natural body. What we designate by such names stands on one and the same line as all the other sensuous qualities that we ascribe to the natural body on the direct testimony of perception. If we exclude tactile and muscular sensation, we must also exclude heaviness and hardness as objective traits. In a world where all bodies we attempted to touch ceded from us with the same velocity at which our hands approached them, we could gain no idea of hardness or resistance. And yet, even in this world, the objective definition of a body would be the same as in ours: for this definition includes only the purely geometrical determinations of length, breadth, and depth.[51] Thus the pure being of what we habitually call matter is reduced to space, to extension. And with this a new norm has been established for all exact knowledge of nature. We can speak of an understanding of nature, of a true insight into its being and lawfulness, only if we are able to represent its material fullness and diversity by a diversity of form, a geometrical schematism. All elements of sensation are replaced in this schematism by elements of pure intuition. In his first work, which laid down his fundamental method, in the *Regulae ad directionem ingenii,* Descartes called for this replacement of sensation by purely intuitive schemata.[52] And his whole physics—from *Le Monde* to the *Principia philosophiae*—may be said to be nothing other than a consequent development of this one fundamental idea. The road to a rational analysis of natural phenomena leads through spatial intuition. Where spatial intuition forsakes us, where phenomena cannot be constructed geometrically, our insight into them ceases.

It is precisely at this point that Leibniz attacks the Cartesian physics.

51. Cf. Descartes, *Principia Philosophiae*, *1*, 53; 2, 4 ff.

52. Cf. *Regula*, xiv: "Ex quibus facile concluditur non parum profuturum, si transferamus illa, quae de magnitudinibus in genere dici intelligemus, ad illam magnitudinis speciem, quae omnium facillime et distinctissime in imaginatione nostra pingetur. Hanc vero esse extensionem realem corporis abstractam ab omni alio, quam quod sit figurata . . . per se . . . est evidens, cum in nullo alio subjecto distinctius omnes proportionum differentiae exhibeantur . . . Maneat ergo ratum et fixum quaestiones perfecte determinatas . . . facile posse et debere ab omni alio subjecto separari ac deinde transferri ad extensionem et figuras. . . . (Nam) certum est omnes proportionum differentias quaecumque in aliis subjectis existunt, etiam inter duas vel plures extensiones inveniri." For more detailed treatment of this concept of geometrical "reproduction" and its significance for the Cartesian system of physics, see my *Erkenntnisproblem*, 2, 457 ff.

For Leibniz came not from geometry but from arithmetic, and he regarded arithmetic itself as only a special branch of "combinatorics." From this standpoint the concept of form assumed a new and universal meaning for him. It is by no means essential to form, he held, that it be manifested as spatial form; rather, it is fundamentally and primarily logical form. A strict law of form, which may serve as a basis for exact understanding, exists wherever a manifold is governed and determined by an ordering relation of any kind. To establish the totality of these relations with systematic completeness and to determine the structure, the general logical "type" of each one of them, becomes the task of Leibniz' scientific theory. This places the whole problem of the natural object and of natural science in a far broader intellectual framework. The reality of the phenomenon, its objective nature, no longer rests on merely geometrical determinations, but is achieved by a far more complex mode of determination. "In the phenomena we neither possess nor are justified in demanding any other criterion of reality than that they should accord with one another and with the eternal truths . . . We shall seek in vain for another truth or reality than that which is thus provided: the sceptics can demand nothing more and the dogmatic philosophers can promise nothing more." [53]

Among these "eternal truths" the axioms of geometry form only a special branch, which we are not justified in making into a general touchstone or norm of scientific knowledge. From this newly gained standpoint, Leibniz subjects the foundations of the Cartesian system of nature to a critique no less sharp than that to which Descartes subjected Aristotelian physics. Whereas Descartes had criticized the Aristotelian explanation of nature for failing to recognize the limitations of sensation as such and to transcend them in principle, Leibniz attacks the Cartesian definition of substance for remaining wholly within the boundaries of that which can be represented intuitively; for this made the imagination into a judge over the understanding. A true theory of nature, Leibniz held, could be achieved only if we learned to disregard both barriers, the sensuous as well as the intuitive. From mechanics we must progress to dynamics, from mere intuition to the concept of force, which defies any immediate representation in terms either of sensation or of intuition.

53. Leibniz, *Philosophische Schriften*, ed. Gerhard, 2, 282 f.; 4, 356 ff.

Let no one suppose that he has correctly apprehended the nature of a body until he has understood that the crude, purely imaginative concept of corporeal substance, according to which it consists in mere extension, is incomplete, not to say false. . . . For in addition to size and impenetrability, we must assume the existence of something in the body, upon which the conception of forces is based. . . . Thus aside from the purely mathematical foundations accessible to intuition, we must also recognize other, metaphysical foundations, which can be apprehended only through the pure understanding, and to the material mass we must add a higher, one might say a formal, principle. For the totality of truths about corporeal things cannot be derived from merely arithmetical and geometrical principles, from the axioms of the whole and the parts, of big and little, of shape and position; in addition we need other theorems about cause and effect, action and reaction.[54]

Here, as we see, Leibniz finds that the Cartesian theory is still confined to bodies, to the image of extensive mass. In his own physics he aspired to take the last decisive step: to free thought from the structures of sense perception, and also from its confinement to the image. It would, for the first time, open up the road to a universal knowledge of nature. And it would once again confirm Leibniz's epistemological principle that "Nihil est in intellectu, quod non antea fuerit in sensu, nisi intellectus ipse": the ultimate statements about the essence of reality would be grounded in purely intelligible truths.

But for the time being the philosophical demand here stated had no profound consequences for the history of physics. Leibniz' contribution to empirical physics was essentially limited to his formulation of the theory of the "conservation of active force," which prepared the way for the discovery of the principle of the conservation of energy.[55] As for Leibniz himself, his concept of force led him in a different direction: it brought him not to the problems of matter and of the physical body but to the problem of the monad. This metaphysical turn could have no immediate influence on the progress of scientific thought, which for the time being followed the stricter methodology of induction, taught by

54. Leibniz, "Specimen dynamicum," Pt. I of *Mathematische Schriften*, ed. C. I. Gerhardt (Halle, 1849–63), 6, 235, 240.

55. For particulars see my *Leibniz' System*, pp. 302 ff.

Newton in his mathematical principles of natural philosophy. And the next great philosopher of science invoked Newton and not Leibniz. At first this meant a peculiar reversal in the progress of philosophical principles: the Leibnizian tendency toward intellectualization was followed by Kant's concept of pure intuition. Here the absolute rule of geometrical construction, combated by Leibniz, seems to be rehabilitated. For no concept of the understanding can lay claim to empirical truth, to objective validity, unless it is schematized in intuition. And this schema of realization is at the same time restrictive: it confines the concept within the limits of spatial representability. Thence follows the reciprocal relation between the transcendental aesthetic and the transcendental logic, which determined the whole structure of the critique of reason.

On the other hand, Kant, as a logician, as an analyst of the pure understanding, could not fail to define the function of the concepts of the pure understanding in such a way as to give them a broader and more universal meaning. Thus they are limited to intuition only in their use, but not in their meaning. The concept of substance, for example, comprises only the form of an intellectual synthesis which as such is nonintuitive. It is supreme among the concepts of pure relation, which constitute the object of experience; it belongs to the "analogies of experience," through which alone the totality of sensory phenomena can be joined into a unitary structure, a context. But in order to perform this work, a connection with certain spatiotemporal schemata is required. Thus permanence—in the form of spatial constancy and thing constancy— becomes the necessary condition under which alone phenomena can be determined as objects in a possible experience. "A philosopher was asked: 'What is the weight of smoke?' He answered: 'Subtract from the weight of the burnt wood the weight of the remaining ashes, and you will have the weight of the smoke.' Thus he presumed it to be incontrovertible that even in fire the matter (substance) does not perish, but that only the form of it undergoes a change." [56]

But this equation of the systematic principle of substantiality with the assumption of matter as a permanent something, which through all its temporal transformations can be recognized as the same, as identical with itself, represents one of the internal difficulties of the critical system. For the principle on which Kant bases his "transcendental deduction of the categories" does not in itself suffice to ground this equation. According

56. Kant, *Kritik der reinen Vernunft*, 2d ed. p. 228. Eng. ed. (Meiklejohn), p. 145.

to him, phenomenal nature consists entirely of relationships: but "among these there are permanent and lasting relations, through which an object is given to us." In itself this kind of constancy demands nothing more than the possibility of singling out certain constant relations in the flow of change, of fixating certain universal "invariants." And this demand is by no means synonymous with the postulation of a material substrate which we must regard as the foundation for all changes: the representation of something permanent in existence, as Kant occasionally said, is not identical with the permanent representation.[57] If nevertheless Kant was able without difficulty to transpose the *formal* principle of substance into the concept of matter, into the assumption of something spatially invariable, it was in large part because of his historical relation to the Newtonian theory. Wholly in line with this theory, he declared material substance to be that substance in space which can be moved independently —that is, separately from everything else which exists in space.[58] The axiom that space itself and what fills it, what is substantial and real in it, are separate, that they may be split conceptually into two sharply divided modes of being, is taken from the system of classical mechanics. But with this of course Kant's theory of pure intuition and the whole relation he sets up between the transcendental analytic and the transcendental aesthetic, runs into a difficulty which was bound to become apparent as soon as this axiom itself began to be questioned—as soon as the theory of classical mechanics gave way to the general theory of relativity.

Up until now we have contented ourselves with an indirect approach to our methodological problem. We have attempted to grasp its reflection in the philosophical systems. But when we follow the problem into the nineteenth century, this guiding thread forsakes us. For in the nineteenth century there is no longer any great representative philosophical system in which we can discern the status of scientific theory and methodology. Philosophical synthesis has now been replaced by numerous separate movements which at first sight discloses no direction toward a common goal. It was theoretical physics itself, in its own immanent progress, which gained as it were a new line of sight, which worked out gradually and more and more clearly a new norm for a universal view of the

57. Cf. ibid., preface to the 2d ed., p. xli.
58. Cf. Kant, "Metaphysische Anfangsgründe der Naturwissenschaft: Dynamik," in *Werke,* ed. Cassirer (2d ed. Berlin, 1922), *4,* 407.

world over and above the fragmentary special view. This norm is characterized primarily by a new relation between "concept" and "intuition" and a move away from the ideal of scientific knowledge established by classical mechanics. At the beginnings of the new development the intuitive retained its dominant position. The understanding of a natural phenomenon was equated with its representation in an intuitive model. And physicists seemed far more concerned with constructing numerous special models than with relating them to one another in a system. Not infrequently a thinker, in attempting to explain the same phenomena or closely related phenomena, simply set totally different intuitive representations side by side. Even so significant a work as Maxwell's *Electricity and Magnetism* does not shun such a listing of inherently heterogeneous images, which pass before our eyes in an almost kaleidoscopic array.[59] Here Maxwell continues to follow a tradition which his own work was highly instrumental in overcoming. This is the traditional view once formulated by William Thomson. The true meaning of the question, "Do we understand a process in nature or do we not understand it," he wrote, "seems to me to be tantamount to the other question of whether we can build a mechanical model which will render this process in all its parts." [60] And yet there were trends in nineteenth-century physics which worked against this view from the very start. In its general structure nineteenth-century physics might be characterized as a physics not of images and models but of principles. The true and essentially methodological issue was not one of images but of principles, an endeavor to comprehend the different forms of natural law in one supreme, all-embracing rule. In this respect a definite and unmistakable line runs from the principle of the conservation of energy to the general principle of relativity.

But a principle has from the very start an entirely different status than a mere concept of nature, as far as the possibility of its purely intuitive grounding and interpretation is concerned. One can always attempt to interpret such a concept as a mere abstraction from immediately given sensuous-intuitive data and thus, in accordance with the prevailing view of such abstractions, to dissolve it into a mere sum of such data. But a

59. Cf. the exposition and critique of Pierre M. M. Duhem in *Les Théories électriques de J. Clark Maxwell. Etude historique et critique* (Paris, 1902).

60. W. Thomson, *Molecular Dynamics and the Wave-Theory of Light* (Baltimore, 1884), p. 131; quoted from Duhem, *La Théorie physique*, p. 112.

scientific principle, regardless of its particular character, belongs, if only because of its universal logical dimension, to a different sphere of validity. It expresses itself not in a concept but in a judgment; it is fully expressed only in a universal proposition. And every such proposition comprises a specific mode of postulation. Its relation to the world of intuitive phenomena is mediated throughout—that is, it passes through the medium of signification. The meaning of a principle must ultimately be fulfilled empirically, hence intuitively; but this fulfillment is never possible directly; it can only occur when other propositions are derived by a hypothetical deduction from the assumption of the principle's validity. None of these propositions, none of these particular stages in a logical process, need be susceptible of direct intuitive interpretation. Only as a logical totality can the series of inferences be related to intuition, and confirmed and justified by intuition.

Thus to return to our comparison between physical and linguistic thinking, we might say that the progress from "model" to "principle" comprises an intellectual achievement similar to that of language when it advances from the word to the sentence: it is with the recognition of the preeminence of the principle over the model that physics begins, as it were, to speak in sentences rather than words. Nineteenth-century physics discloses several concrete examples of this competition between the two tendencies; perhaps the most illuminating is provided by the different interpretations of the principle of energy. In Helmholtz the principle of the conservation of energy appears as a simple inference from the fundamental presuppositions of the mechanical world view, which is recognized a priori as a "condition of the comprehensibility of nature." The task of physical science, in this view, is to reduce natural phenomena to invariable attractive and repellent forces, whose intensity depends on the distance between masses. If we start from this postulate and from Newton's general laws of motion, the principle of the conservation of energy seems essentially to reduce itself to the mechanical principle of the conservation of active forces.[61]

Such a reduction is not the goal which Robert Mayer sets himself in his exposition and proof of the law of the conservation of energy. For him this law signifies nothing other than a universal relation which links

61. Cf. Hermann L. F. von Helmholtz, *Über die Erhaltung der Kraft*, 1847; in *Ostwalds Klassiker der exakten Wissenschaft*, *1* (Leipzig, 1889), 6 ff. Eng. trans. *On the Conservation of Force* (New York, 1917).

together the diverse spheres of physical phenomena, which makes them quantitatively comparable and commensurable. The validity and truth of this relation does not depend on a reduction of all particular phenomena to mechanical processes. The principle states the fixed numerical relations according to which heat is transformed into motion and motion into heat, but it does not assert that heat in its physical nature is nothing other than motion. The value of the theory of the conservation of energy is rather, according to Mayer, that it enables us to draw an exact comparison between different things, without sacrificing their differentness. Motion is transposed into gravitational force and gravitational force into motion, but we cannot infer that the two are identical; and the same is true for all spheres of phenomena which the law of the conservation of energy teaches us to connect by fixed numerical measurements, by definite equivalences.[62]

As we know, nineteenth-century energetics started from this observation of the first discoverer of the principle of energy and went on to unleash what might be called an iconoclastic controversy in the field of physics. But such criticism as that leveled for example by W. Ostwald against the kinetic theory of heat [63] misses the epistemological essence of the question, quite aside from the physical significance of the theory. For this question relates not so much to the content of natural theory as to its form, its logical structure. There can be no question of excluding mechanical hypotheses or denying their fruitfulness in certain special cases; the question is, rather, what position we should accord these hypotheses in the general system of physics and what logical rank we should ascribe to them. Are they necessary conditions of physical concept formation and necessary premises of all physical theorizing whatsoever, or are there still higher principles by which they must be measured? Today the long controversy over this question can generally speaking be regarded as settled. Perhaps the change of view that has been gradually and steadily effected can best be illustrated by the example of Planck. In his first work on the principle of the conservation of energy (1887), Planck remained wholly within the "mechanical world view," which he still regarded as the regulative principle of all physical investigation. Yet even here Planck

62. Cf. R. Mayer, "Bemerkungen über die Kräfte der unbelebten Natur," 1842; in *Die Mechanik der Wärme* (3d ed. Stuttgart, 1893), p. 28; and Mayer's letters to Griesinger of December 5, 1842, and July 20, 1844, in *Kleinere Schriften und Briefe*, ed. Weyrauch (Stuttgart, 1893), pp. 187, 225.

63. Cf. Wilhelm Ostwald, *Vorlesungen über Naturphilosophie* (Leipzig, 1902), pp. 210 ff.

renounced any actual mechanical derivation of the principle of energy. When it came to establishing the hierarchy of principles, their position in the progress of his deduction, he decided for the preeminence of the principle of conservation in its most universal form, a form unrestricted by any special interpretation. "When we consider," he writes,

> that the mechanical view of nature played a significant role long before the discovery of the principle of energy . . . when we further consider how very plainly the concept of energy can be defined and the principle formulated and proved from the mechanical standpoint, it is quite understandable that this proof should have gained preeminence among the deductive methods. . . . And nevertheless it seems to me that we should be more justified in making the principle of the conservation of energy the basis for the mechanical view of nature, than conversely in making the latter the foundation for the deduction of the principle of energy, since after all this principle is far more securely grounded than the assumption, however plausible, that all change in nature can be reduced to motion.[64]

A quarter of a century later Planck defined the relationship far more sharply. In his lecture on the relation of modern physics to the mechanistic view of nature (1910), the decisive methodological conclusion is drawn and the primacy of principles over models is recognized and carried out in every particular. The true standard for the evaluation of a physical hypothesis—it is now expressly emphasized—can never be sought in its intuitive reference but only in its efficacy. It is not the simplicity of the image that is decisive, but the unity of the explanation, the subsumption of the totality of natural phenomena under supreme comprehensive rules. This consideration then leads to a physical theory far more universal than the postulates on which the mechanical view is grounded, even more universal than the principle of the conservation of energy.

The first step toward such a theory was implied by the principle of relativity, according to which the four dimensions of the physical world are fundamentally equivalent and interchangeable. The supreme physical law, the crown of the whole natural system, then proves to be the principle of least action, which contains the four cosmic coordinates in a perfectly symmetrical arrangement. "From this central principle four fully equivalent principles radiate in four directions, corresponding to the four dimen-

64. Max K. E. L. Planck, *Das Prinzip der Erhaltung der Energie* (Leipzig, 1887), p. 136.

sions of the cosmos: to the spatial dimensions corresponds the (threefold) principle of dynamic magnitude; to the temporal dimension corresponds the principle of energy. Never before was it possible to trace the underlying meaning and common source of these principles so far back toward their roots." And indeed the "principle of least action" does present a new and comprehensive aspect of nature, since the principle of the conservation of energy may be inferred from it, whereas conversely the principle of least action cannot conversely be derived from the principle of the conservation of energy. And both in meaning and application it proves wholly independent of the mechanical world view. It has been particularly fruitful in its application to "extramechanical physics"; Larmor and Schwarzschild, for example, were able to derive the basic equations of electrodynamics and electronics from the law of least action.[65] The physics of the nineteenth century and the early twentieth century could not have achieved this advance to principles of ever increasing breadth and universality, could not have attained its present intellectual heights, if it had not steadily freed itself from the barriers not only of sensation but also of intuition and geometrical-mechanical "representation." It is self-evident that this did not mean turning its back upon the world of intuition, for of course it is in intuition that all physical theory must seek its ultimate confirmation. But physical theory can arrive at this confirmation, this enrichment and fertilization of intuition, only because it does not confine itself a priori to intuition but learns to know and assert its own peculiar autarchy with ever increasing depth and purity.

Perhaps the history of modern physics offers no clearer example of this relationship than the development of the theory of the ether. Almost every step in this development represents a characteristic stage in a universal methodological process. Newton's emission theory explains the phenomenon of light propagation by directly relating it and reducing it to the phenomenon of material motion. Light consists of infinitesimal material particles, which are emitted by the source in all directions with set velocities that are different for each color. New observations showed this form of explanation to be untenable: the phenomena of interference necessitated a reversion from the emission theory to the undulation

---

65. For particulars see Planck, "Die Stellung der neueren Physik zur mechanischen Naturanschauung," *Königsberger Naturforscher-Versammlung* (1910); and his "Das Prinzip der kleinsten Wirkung," in *Kultur der Gegenwart* (1915), rep. in *Physikalische Rundblicke* (Leipzig, 1922), pp. 38 ff., 103 ff.

theory that had already been formulated by Christian Huyghens. But the tendency persisted to employ empirically known, intuitively tangible processes as a basis for explaining the unknown that was manifested in the phenomenon of light. All sorts of analogies were brought to bear at this point. It seemed possible to conceive the motion of light only by comparing it with the spreading of a wave on the surface of the water or the vibrations of an elastic string. But the more these analogies were spun out, the greater difficulties they encountered. The more refined became the intuitive description of the light ether, the more paradoxical it seemed. In time it became a veritable "wooden iron," a substance that was expected to combine properties which conflicted with each other in all ordinary observation. Every attempt to eliminate these contradictions with the help of new *ad hoc* hypotheses, only led deeper into the labyrinth: the ether became the "woe-begotten child of mechanical physics."

Yet, essentially, the Ariadne's thread that was to lead out of the labyrinth was found, once Maxwell had defined light as an electrodynamic process. For now the most important step had been taken: the step from the physics of matter to pure "field physics." The reality that we designate as a "field" is no longer a complex of physical things, but an expression for an aggregate of physical relations. When from these relations we single out certain elements, when we consider certain of its positions by themselves, it never means that we can actually separate them in intuition and disclose them as isolated intuitive structures. Each of these elements is conditioned by the whole to which it belongs; in fact it is first defined through this whole. It is no longer possible to separate an individual part, a substantial particle, from the field and follow the movement of these parts for a certain time.

Here, then, the method of defining a physical "object" by a mode of "indication," a τόδε τι, however subtle, is precluded from the very first. This form of demonstration fails, and must be replaced by a far more complex form of physical deduction. In the ether of modern physics—as Eddington declared on occasion—we can no longer set our finger on a definite place and maintain that this or that one of its parts was in this place a few seconds ago.[66] Here, accordingly, the numerical identity which we otherwise regard as one of the essential determinations of "things"—including the things of immediate experience and mechanical

66. Cf. Sir Arthur Stanley Eddington, *Space, Time, and Gravitation* (Cambridge, 1923), p. 40.

masses as the substantial vehicles of motion—can no longer be maintained. On the other hand the objective validity and meaning of the physical concepts is in no way jeopardized by this abandonment of the thing-form. True, the single position in the ether can no longer be designated and distinguished from others by any sort of concrete characteristics. Rather, each of these positions is defined abstractly by two coordinates, by the magnitude and direction of the electrical and magnetic vector. And the essence of light no longer consists of something comparable to an undulation or a vibration in the intuitive sense of the word, but in the periodic changes of a vector, whose direction is always to be conceived as perpendicular to the direction of propagation. It was this formalistic theory of light that first succeeded in eliminating the contradictions that inevitably clung to every intuitive image of the ether.[67] It was only when physics abandoned in principle its notion of the ether as a kind of "elastic solid"[68] that the way lay open for a new approach that was soon to bring about a fundamental change in the concept of matter.

And this transformation again shows an inner consequence, a strict methodological continuity. It seemed at first as though physics could content itself with simply setting the newly acquired concept of ether side by side with the concept of matter. There arose a dualism between "matter" and "field"; ether and matter form two different and separate entities, which, however, are linked together by a continuous interaction. But this dualism was overcome by the theory of relativity. Now matter no longer appears as a physical entity side by side with the field, but is reduced to the field: it became a "product of the field."[69] Faraday prepared the way for this turn; for him the "reality" of matter ultimately dissolves into lines of force. In Mie's theory of matter the opposition of "body" and "field" is eliminated altogether: the body itself is built up purely of electricity.[70] But if matter is, as it were, a product of the ether, it would obviously be a ὕστερον πρότερον to attribute any properties analogous to those of matter to the ether itself. We must think of it, relative to

67. On the development of the formalistic theory of light cf. Bavink's exposition in *Ergebnisse und Probleme der Naturwissenschaft*, 2d ed., pp. 89 ff.

68. On the development that finally led physics to abandon this view, cf. Max Born, *Die Relativitätstheorie Einsteins und ihre physikalischen Grundlagen* (Berlin, 1921), pp. 78 ff., 158 ff.

69. For particulars cf. Weyl, *Raum, Zeit, Materie*, 4th ed., pp. 181 ff.

70. For particulars of Mie's theory of matter, see ibid., sec. 26, and Laue, *Die Relativitätstheorie*, 2, sec. 8.

matter, as "without properties," in order to arrive at a strict derivation of the properties of matter.[71] If we still wish to speak of a particular object, this object must be conceived not as a substantial background for relations but solely as their expression and aggregate.

In his Leyden lecture "Ether and the Theory of Relativity" Einstein declared that even the general theory of relativity did not have to abandon the concept of ether: but it must cease to attribute any definite state of motion to the ether, since the ether may be said to be at rest in any system, however moved. But an ether which may be said neither to be at rest nor to move with a determinate velocity is obviously no longer a particular "thing" that can in any way be realized in the imagination and endowed with definite intuitive characteristics and properties. The ether in this sense has no other determinations than those belonging to the field itself, and thus differs from the field only in name. But with this a peculiar dialectical process in physics has reached its conclusion: the consistent development of the notion of ether has led to the negation of this very notion. And thus physics has definitively left the realm of representation and of representability in general for a more abstract realm. The schematism of images has given way to the symbolism of principles. Of course the empirical source of modern physical theory has not been affected in the least by this insight. But physics no longer deals directly with the existent as the materially real; it deals with its structure, its formal context. The tendency toward unification has triumphed over the tendency toward representation: the synthesis guided by the pure concepts of law has shown itself superior to summation in thing-concepts. Ordering has thus become the actual and absolute foundation of physics: the world itself is represented no longer as a coexistence of thing unities but as an order of "events."[72] "Intuitive space and time," writes Weyl, "may not serve as the medium in which the physics of the external world is constructed, but are replaced by a four-dimensional continuum in the

71. Cf. the remarks of Eddington in *Space, Time, and Gravitation*, p. 39: "Mathematicians of the nineteenth century devoted much time to theories of elastic, solid and other material aethers. Waves of light were supposed to be actual oscillations of this substance; it was thought to have the familiar properties of rigidity and density. . . . The real death-blow to this materialistic conception of the aether was given when attempts were made to explain matter as some state in the aether. For if matter is vortex-motion or beknottedness in aether, the aether cannot be matter—some state in itself. . . . If physics evolves a theory of matter which explains some property, it stultifies itself when it postulates that the same property exists unexplained in the primitive basis of matter."

72. Cf. ibid., pp. 12 ff., 184 ff.

abstract arithmetical sense. Whereas for Huyghens the colors were 'really' vibrations of the ether, now they appear only as mathematical, functional processes of a periodic character: and in these functions four independent variables appear as representatives of the spatiotemporal medium related to coordinates. Thus what remains is ultimately a symbolic construction in the exact sense as that carried out by Hilbert in mathematics." [73]

And in another respect as well the name of Huyghens may provide a deeper insight into the mode and trend of the development leading from classical mechanics to the world view of modern relativistic physics. Huyghens represents a definite methodological summit within the classical theory: he was the physical thinker who first carried through a purely kinetic interpretation of the world process with true universality and scientific rigor. All the phenomena of nature were subjected to this viewpoint. For Huyghens there was no opposition between the realm of active forces and of forces in tension, between kinetic and potential energy. For him all natural process resolves into the actual motion of infinitesimal material particles, which themselves are regarded as invariable substantial things. The physics of the ether which he projected and the physics of "ponderable" masses were identical in this respect. According to Huyghens, we can explain light and gravitation only by reducing them to motions, to spatial translations of the smallest independently existing particles of ether. And he regarded the law of the conservation of active force as the fundamental principle determining and regulating the interaction between moving particles. All action in nature consists of a change in the spatial distribution of kinetic energy, whose sum remains invariable. In order to gain a complete picture of the world process, intuitable in all its parts, we must, as it were, follow this translation of energy from place to place. Where direct observation shows us—as in phenomena of unelastic collision—a loss of kinetic energy, we are compelled, in order to obtain a satisfactory systematic explanation, to regard this loss as illusory. The energy that is lost in perceptible bodies is transformed into another form, into the motion of the ether atoms, whence under certain conditions it is transferred back to corporeal masses. The supply of kinetic energy that has gathered in the ether as in a great reservoir flows back from it into the atoms of bodies. Thus it is in the

73. Weyl, "Philosophie der Mathematik und Naturwissenschaft," *Handbuch der Philosophie,* p. 80.

law of collision that Huyghens finds the model and prototype of all natural laws. Collision itself is not regarded merely as a sensory phenomenon but is carried back to purely rational, mathematically formulable general principles. Such principles, along with the hypothesis that the atoms are the ultimate parts of matter, which must be invariable and absolutely solid, form the necessary condition in which alone a science of nature can be grounded.

In his history of atomic theory Lasswitz gives an excellent exposition of this doctrine of Huyghens and also attempts a critical justification, or "transcendental deduction" of it. According to him the kinetic theory of atoms does not represent a special physical view, beside which we may set other equally justified views; rather, it is the norm and prototype of all exact natural science. Here for the first time the various intellectual instruments that are indispensable for detaching a permanent physical being, an objective nature, from the flux of our conscious experiences are placed in a perfect ideal balance. The first of these intellectual instruments is the category of substantiality. It expresses the first fundamental relation of unity, namely the adherence of determining predicates to a subject, making it into a perceptible individual thing, endowed with properties. The scientific expression for this individual-thingness is the concept of the atom as the fixed, indestructible vehicle of all changes. But so far the changes themselves are not yet posited and determined. Change in its true sense is not so much grounded as negated by the concept of substance. Here, then, another principle is required before changes of determination can be objectified. Just as substance relates to form, so this new principle relates to time. It establishes a lawfulness which links the various successive states of one and the same substance. We require a means by which to think the given as becoming.

Science discovered this new intellectual instrument, "variability," only when it learned, through the analysis of the infinite, to define the concept of variable magnitude and to give exact mathematical expression to the relation between different variable magnitudes. "Here we are dealing with that unitary relation of consciousness which links the sensuous datum in this way: the datum does not, as in the substance, obtain identity with itself through its predicate, while remaining detached from any relationship with other data; rather, it is apprehended as a fulfillment of time. Though it is a unitary element marking a continuum, it is not separate from that continuum but is a position which independently contains within it a law of change, of continuation, and guarantees the further lawful fulfillment of time." It is through this intellectual instrument that a relation is set up between substances, that a causality between them becomes definable. And Huyghens' theoretical development of kinetic atomics strikes Lasswitz as one of the high points of modern scientific thinking, because here the two basic postulates of this thinking, which are separated in epistemological analysis, work together in an exemplary way. In his principles of mechanics Huyghens objectifies the sensuous fact of the change of bodies as a continuous and reciprocal relation of causality. The invariable vehicle of motion is provided by the concept of the rigid atom, and the reciprocal relation between the various elements of the physical world is supplied by the law of the conservation of the algebraic sum of kinetic magnitudes, and the law of the conservation of energy. Here there is no longer any trace of the sensuous representation which had accompanied atomic theory throughout its history, the representation of atoms as small, hard bodies.

Huyghens made the corpuscular theory into a science by this advance, by overcoming this sensuous image and replacing it with rational, mathematically formulated concepts. The absolute atom and the totality of moving atoms are conceptual entities; their meeting in space no longer signifies the anthropomorphism of a collision, but the geometrical determination of a position at a given time; and their behavior after the so-called collision is not derived according to the analogy of the bouncing back of sensuous bodies, but determined by the mathematical formula which regulates the distribution of velocities.[74]

The critical deduction here given for a system of physics is a hypothetical deduction: it relates to a definite historical stage, which it treats as an underlying fact of science. Lasswitz himself, as a strictly critical thinker, is far from regarding this fact as immutable and definitive. "Never," he stresses,

may critical philosophy presume to define the conditions of experience and the principles of physics a priori; it can do so only through the historical process; and just as physical knowledge changes, so, too, will the theory of the transcendental conditions of experience change

74. Lasswitz, *Geschichte der Atomistik*, 2, 374 f.; cf. 1, 43 ff., 269 ff.; and 2, 341 ff.

in the course of history. The essential difference between the transcendental principles and the changing theories lies not in how the principles of scientific knowledge are formulated in the consciousness of the mankind of a given epoch but in the fact that they must be formulated, that there is an eternal determination for the direction of consciousness, a supreme law of objectivization. What intellectual instruments will be newly discovered, which ones will vanish from the consciousness of man, is an insoluble problem. It suffices if each cultural epoch becomes conscious of its own intellectual instruments as the synthetic unities which guarantee the possibility of scientific experience amid the vacillations and gropings of the special investigations and hypotheses, by showing the shifting theoretical content to be dependent not only on empirical accident but also on an enduring trend of consciousness.[75]

If we approach modern relativistic with the general philosophical attitude expressed in these lines and compare it with Lasswitz's picture of kinetic atomics, the salient features of the theoretical change undergone by physics in the last decades stand out in a peculiarly incisive and instructive manner. Modern physics cannot dispense with Lasswitz' two basic intellectual instruments, "substantiality" and "variability." But in making use of these instruments, it moves them into a new systematic relationship. It can no longer separate them by relating substance essentially and primarily to space and change essentially to time. For this separation would imply that space and time themselves can be sharply differentiated in the construction of physics, that they confront each other as independent forms. It is the very questioning of this assumption that forms the beginning of relativistic physics. Here, according to Minkowski's well-known formulation, space for itself and time for itself sink into shadows, and there remains only a kind of union of the two. What is given by phenomena is only the four-dimensional world in space and time, a world in which the projection in space and time can still be undertaken with a certain freedom.[76]

From this it follows that we may not, as Huyghens does in his deriva-

75. Ibid., 2, 393.

76. Cf. Hermann Minkowski, *Raum und Zeit* (Leipzig, 1909), rep. in H. A. Lorentz, A. Einstein, H. Minkowski, and H. Weyl, *Des Relativitätsprinzip, eine Sammlung von Abhandlungen* (Leipzig, 1920), pp. 54 ff. Eng. trans. of 4th ed. (1922) by W. Perrett and G. B. Jeffery, *The Principle of Relativity* (London, 1923).

tion of kinetic atomics, simply take the factors of permanence and change as contrary factors, which can indeed complement one another but must remain sharply separate in their fundamental meaning. Here rather there is *one* principle that determines both permanence and change and links the two together in thoroughgoing correlation. The world is no longer taken as a world of constant "things" whose attributes change in time; it has become a self-contained system of "events," each of which is determined by four equivalent coordinates.[77] And now there is no longer an independent physical content, which is simply taken into the finished forms of space and time; rather, space, time, and matter are indissolubly linked and are definable only in respect to one another. As real in the physical sense we may now regard only the synthesis, the reciprocal relation between space, time, and matter, whereas each taken for itself has ceased to be anything more than a mere abstraction. Spatiality, temporality, and materiality are still factors in physical reality; but these factors can no longer be treated, as in the older view, like pieces from which reality is composed. Now there is no longer, as in the Newtonian theory, an empty space into which the substantially real moves as into a ready-made apartment house. The "metric field" provides a unitary and supreme concept which links together the special viewpoints of space, time, and matter in an entirely new way. The world is defined with systematic unity as a $(3 + 1)$ dimensional metric manifold; all physical field phenomena are expressions of world metrics.[78]

Energy, too, is no longer the indestructible object which Robert Mayer, for example, saw in it, and which formed a kind of counterpart to a likewise indestructible mass. The dualism between mass and energy is negated by Einstein's principle of the "inertia of energy." The principles of the conservation of mass and the conservation of energy are united into a single principle by the theory of relativity.[79] The principle of the conservation of energy is indissolubly linked to the principle of the conservation of impulse: it is only the time component of a law which is invariant with respect to Lorentz transformations, and whose spatial components

77. Here the reader is particularly referred to Alfred North Whitehead, *An Enquiry Concerning the Principles of Natural Knowledge* (Cambridge, 1925), in which this character of the relativistic "world of events" is clearly worked out.

78. On the concept of the metric field cf. Weyl, *Raum, Zeit, Materie*, secs. 12, 35.

79. Cf. Einstein, "Ist die Trägheit deines Körpers von seinem Energieinhalt abhängig?" *Annalen der Physik*, 4th ser. *18* (1905), 639–41, for further particulars see Haas, *Naturbild der neuen Physik*, Lecture 6.

state the conservation of impulse. This formulation of the law of conservation discloses a "substance" of an entirely new order. And this perhaps is the supreme triumph of the pure *idea* of substance over the mere *representation* of substance. What we define as the ultimate physical reality has cast off all appearance of thingness: there is no longer any meaning in speaking of one and the same matter at different times.[80] And yet here again the abandonment of thingness does not impair the objectivity of physics but grounds it in a new and deeper sense. For this objectivity is no problem of representation; it is a pure problem of meaning. What we call the object is no longer a schematizable, intuitively realizable "something" with definite spatial and temporal predicates; it is a point of unity to be apprehended in a purely intellectual way. The object as such can never be "represented": in accordance with the definition which Kant worked out clearly in principle, it is a mere X "in relation to which representations have synthetic unity."

In an earlier investigation I have attempted to show that this progress from thing concepts to concepts of relation, from the positing of constant thing unities to that of pure lawful constancy is characteristic of the whole scientific view of the world in modern times, beginning with Galileo and Kepler, and that this universal logical tendency was clearly at work in the system of classical mechanics. The last phase of physics, which was ushered in by Einstein's special theory of relativity, was not included in this investigation. Today we may say that it was this phase which drew the ultimate consequences from the preceding development, which in a purely methodological sense may be said to form its conclusion. Here the substantial is completely transposed into the functional: true and definitive permanence is no longer imputed to an existence propagated in space and time but rather to those magnitudes and relations between magnitudes which provide the universal constants for all description of physical process. It is the invariance of such relations and not the existence of any particular entities which forms the ultimate stratum of objectivity.[81]

There remains only one field of modern physics which at first sight

80. Cf. Weyl, *Raum, Zeit, Materie,* secs. 20, 24 f., and *passim.*
81. Cf. my *Substanzbegriff und Funktionsbegriff;* for the general epistemological foundations of the above exposition I refer the reader esp. to chaps. 4, 7. Here I have not wished to repeat what was there set forth but have contented myself with applying the basic thesis of this work to the present situation of theoretical physics and its development in the last decades, and with bringing out certain details more sharply.

seems to stand opposed to this fundamental view and the inner law of its progress. Although atomics has been abandoned in the form given it by the classical system—although the purely kinetic world view of nature developed by Huyghens has been given up—the concept of the atom as such has experienced a brilliant resurrection. The theory of the atomic structure of matter has been confirmed on all sides and is among the most certain conclusions of modern physics. Since spectroscopy made possible an insight into the heart of the atom, since Laue, for example, using crystals as a "point lattice," obtained his well-known "diffraction patterns," [82] there has been an increasingly firm impression that the world of the atom has been unlocked and made accessible to direct intuition. Even the extraordinary fruitfulness of Bohr's atomic theory seemed to be due to the fact that it gathered a vast wealth of empirical facts into one view and represented them by a simple model of supreme intuitive clarity. Nevertheless, it is precisely in the difference between Bohr's atomic model and the manner of representing it that prevailed in the classical form of atomics, that one can appreciate the change in general methodological approach. For as Bavink has pointed out, the atom has become a "thoroughly extensible relative concept." "The old concept of a rigid little ball with a very definite mass and invariable properties has totally disappeared. Instead we have a highly complicated system of electrical charges and fields in continuous motion and change." This is a completely dynamic world view; matter has become a process: what we habitually call its fixed "properties" are a function of processes. Even the most fundamental properties of all matter, such as inertia and weight, are regarded and derived as pure field phenomena.[83] While for the older theory the atom was absolutely indivisible, a *non plus ultra* of analysis, it has now become a system comparable in its inner diversity and complexity to the great cosmic systems. The atom is a planetary system, the planets are electrons which circle around the nucleus as a center. Thus the electron becomes the actual element of physical reality, though it cannot, like the absolutely hard atom of the older theory, arm itself in rigidity. For even conceived as an individual, it is bound to the field and cannot be detached from it as an independent substance.

82. Cf. Max T. F. von Laue, "Zur Theorie der Kontinuierlichen Spektra," *Jahrbuch für Radioaktivität und Elektronik*, *1* (1904), 400–13; and Sommerfeld, *Atombau und Spektrallinien*, chap. 4, sec. 1.

83. Cf. Bavink, *Ergebnisse und Probleme der Naturwissenschaft*, pp. 120, 150, and *passim*.

Essentially the electron appears to be nothing other than a point distinguished in a field, a position into which electrical force lines flow from all sides.[84] For atomics in its original form, the dualism between matter and the space in which it is situated and moves, is irreducible and necessary. Democritus himself differentiated the παμπλῆρες ὄν of the atom from "empty" space and contrasted the two as irreducible modes of being. Even where atomics passes from its mechanical to its dynamic form, this opposition was generally retained. Even Boscovich's "simple" atom remains a kind of self-enclosed being for itself. It is and exists in its simplicity, and only afterward enters into relation with other equally independent physical individuals, with other simple points of force. Such a conception does not apply to the electron as defined by modern physical theory: the electron does not precede the field but is first constituted by its relation to the field. Accordingly, even mechanics must depart from its strictly kinetic form. The development of quantum mechanics discloses a tendency toward increasing abstraction: in its most recent form it seems to renounce all "representation" of the processes within the atom, and all spatial images in general. But this must not be regarded as a purely negative achievement; it is rather the beginning, the first necessary step toward a new mode of formation and conceptual unity.[85]

Of course it is implicit in the character of this unity formation that the objectivity toward which it progresses and aims can never be conclusively determined. Whereas the "thing" of naive intuition may appear as a fixed sum of definite properties, the physical object by its very nature can be conceived only in the form of an "idea of limit." [86] For here it is not a

84. Cf. Sommerfeld, *Atombau und Spektrallinien*, p. 8.

85. For the fundamental concept of the quantum theory, the concept of the "elementary action quantum," Planck himself, in an article written in 1915, stresses that the meaning of the elementary action quantum, the central concept of his theory, "has thus far almost entirely defied representation." "Nevertheless," he continues, "there can be no doubt that a time will come when, like the atomic weights of chemistry, the elementary action quantum, under some name or form, will constitute an integral part of general dynamics. For physical research cannot rest until the theory of static and radiant heat has been welded into a unitary theory with mechanics and electrodynamics" (Verhältnis der Theorien zueinander," in *Kultur der Gegenwart*, 1915; *Physikalische Rundblicke*, p. 128). Even Niels Bohr stresses, in "Atomtheorie und Mechanik," *Die Naturwissenschaften, 14* (1926), that the general problem of the quantum theory involves a "profound failure of the spatiotemporal images" by means of which one had previously sought to describe natural phenomena.

86. Cf. Weyl's remarks in the introduction to his *Raum, Zeit, Materie:* "It lies in the essence of a real thing to be something inexhaustible in content, which we can approach

matter of disclosing the ultimate, absolute elements of reality, in the contemplation of which thought may rest as it were, but of a never-ending process through which the relatively necessary takes the place of the relatively accidental and the relatively invariable that of the relatively variable. We can never claim that this process has attained to the ultimate invariants of experience, which would then replace the immutable facticity of "things"; we can never claim to grasp these invariants with our hands so to speak. Rather, the possibility must always be held open that a new synthesis will instate itself and that the universal constants, in terms of which we have signalized the "nature" of certain large realms of physical objects, will come closer together and prove themselves to be special cases of an overarching lawfulness. It is this new law that will then form the true nucleus of objectivity; but it, too, must expect to be recognized in its merely contingent universality and replaced by a still broader universal relation. "The One reality," as I have formulated this fundamental relationship in another context,

can only be disclosed and defined as the ideal limit of the diversely changing theories; but the setting of this limit itself is not arbitrary; it is inescapable, since the continuity of experience is established only thereby. No particular astronomical system, the Copernican no more than the Ptolemaic . . . may be taken as an expression of the "true" cosmic order, but only the whole of these systems as they continuously unfold in accordance with a certain context. . . . . Physical concepts are valid not insofar as they reproduce a given rigid being but insofar as they comprise a project for possible postulations of unity, which project must progressively be confirmed in practice, in application to the empirical material. But the instrument itself which leads to the unity and hence the truth of what is thought, must itself be firm and secure. If it did not possess a certain stability in itself, no sure and enduring application of it would be possible; it would crumble at the first attempt and dissolve into nothingness. We do not need the objectivity of absolute things, but we do require the objective determinacy of the way of experience itself.[87]

---

only through ever new, partly contradictory observations, whose interplay is unlimited. In this sense the real thing is a limit-idea. Thereupon rests the empirical character of all knowledge of reality." Precisely this inconclusive character of empirical-physical object formation was sharply stressed by Galileo. For particulars see my *Erkenntnisproblem*, 3d ed., 2, 402 ff.

87. *Substanzbegriff und Funktionsbegriff*, pp. 427 f.

It is precisely this basic character of theoretical physics that demonstrates how requisite, how inwardly necessary to such thinking is its tie with determinate symbols. And it may similarly be seen how the symbols permeate one another and build upon one another, how they disclose the objective structure of the physical world as a structure of pure order. The most striking example of this relationship is at present to be found in the general theory of relativity.[88] Here physical thinking has risen step by step to ever higher areas; yet in so doing it has not loosened, but rather tightened, its tie with physical reality. Every new view so achieved proves, of course, to be dependent on the specific viewpoint, the intellectual perspective from which it has been seen. However, the different modes of this view follow one another not accidentally but according to an immanent lawfulness: they are conditioned and ordered not only by the empirical material that flows in from outside but also by the development of the physical form of thought itself.[89] Each higher stage of objectivization sets a limit to the preceding stage; but in this limitation it does not destroy the earlier phase; rather it embraces it in its own perspective. The aim here followed consists precisely in increasingly disregarding the particularity of the perspective, in progressively excluding everything that belongs not so much to the object itself as to the accidental standpoint from which it is regarded. In this light the world view of the older physics shows itself to be not absolutely valid but conceived from a particular standpoint, the standpoint of observers who are relatively at rest in relation to one another.

If instead of this standpoint we introduce systems of reference that are in motion relative to one another, all the fixed "attribute concepts" that were valid for the classical view must undergo a shift, a variation. It is not only the so-called sensuous qualities that show this kind of dependency on the state of the perceiving subject; according to the special theory of relativity, the magnitude, form, mass, and energy content of the thing also change with the observer's state of motion. This process of relativization draws in broader and broader spheres; and over and over again the center of the physical concept of reality is shifted to a different position. The ancient physicists regarded the position of a thing as a physical attribute: certain physical positions produced definite effects which be-

88. How the structure of the theory of relativity may serve to confirm and illustrate the epistemological view here put forward has been excellently shown by Karl Bollert in *Einsteins Relativitätstheorie und ihre Stellung im System der Gesamterfahrung* (Dresden and Leipzig, 1921).

89. I have tried to demonstrate this in detail in my *Zur Einsteinschen Relativitätstheorie*.

longed to no other position. The center of the cosmos, where the earth rests, sent out forces which drew heavy bodies to this point as to their natural position. This view was overcome by Copernicus, who stated the principle of the relativity of position. The relativity principle of classical mechanics drew the same inference for velocities, and finally the general theory of relativity went still further, relativizing motion as such and showing that one can always "transform any point in a mass to a state of rest." [90] Thus we see time and time again that certain determinations which we attribute to the object as its properties are definable only if we add a certain index, if we indicate the system of reference according to which they are thought to be valid. Now "motion" and "force," "mass" and "energy," "length" and "permanence" no longer *are* "in themselves," but only *signify* something; and in general they mean different things for observers who are in motion relative to one another. But this would seem inevitably to give rise to a new question: is it possible to eradicate this last remnant of contingency, of subjectivity, from the description of the natural process? Is there not some world concept which is free from all particularities, which will describe the world as it is, not from the standpoint of this man or that man, but from the standpoint of no one? [91] But insofar as this question is admissible to begin with, it is in any case directed toward an infinitely distant point that is attainable at no given stage of science. Here we are dealing with a genuine transcendental idea in the Kantian sense, and no definite individual experience can accord with it. But to this idea we shall also have to impute an "admirable and necessary regulative use," namely "as regulative ideas, directing the understanding to a certain aim, the guiding lines towards which all its laws follow, and in which they all meet in one point. This point—though a mere idea (*focus imaginarius*), that is, not a point from which the conceptions of the understanding do really proceed, for it lies beyond the sphere of possible experience—serves notwithstanding to give to these conceptions the greatest possible unity combined with the greatest possible extension." [92] Physics gains this unity and extension by advancing toward ever more universal symbols. But in this process it cannot jump over its own shadow. It can and must strive to replace particular concepts and

90. Cf. Laue, *Die Relativitätstheorie*, 2, 18 ff.

91. Eddington, for example, frames the logical problem of the theory of relativity in this way. According to him, the aim of the theory is "to obtain a conception of the world from the point of view of no one in particular." Cf. *Space, Time, and Gravitation*, pp. 30 ff.

92. *Kritik der reinen Vernunft*, 2d ed., p. 672. Eng. ed. (Meiklejohn), p. 374.

signs with absolutely universal ones. But it can never dispense with the function of concepts and signs as such: this would demand an intellectual representation of the world without the basic instruments of representation. The physical concept of reality should ultimately be so formulated as to unite the totality of aspects resulting for different observers, so as to explain them and make them understandable; but in precisely this totality the particularity of the viewpoint is not extinguished but preserved and transcended. In this whole movement scientific knowledge confirms and fulfills, in its own sphere, a universal structural law of the human spirit. The more it concentrates in itself, the more clearly it grasps its own nature and strivings, the more evident becomes the factor in which it differs from all other forms of world understanding, and the meaning which links it with them all.

Index

Composed by Alfred Stiernotte

481

DATE DUE
